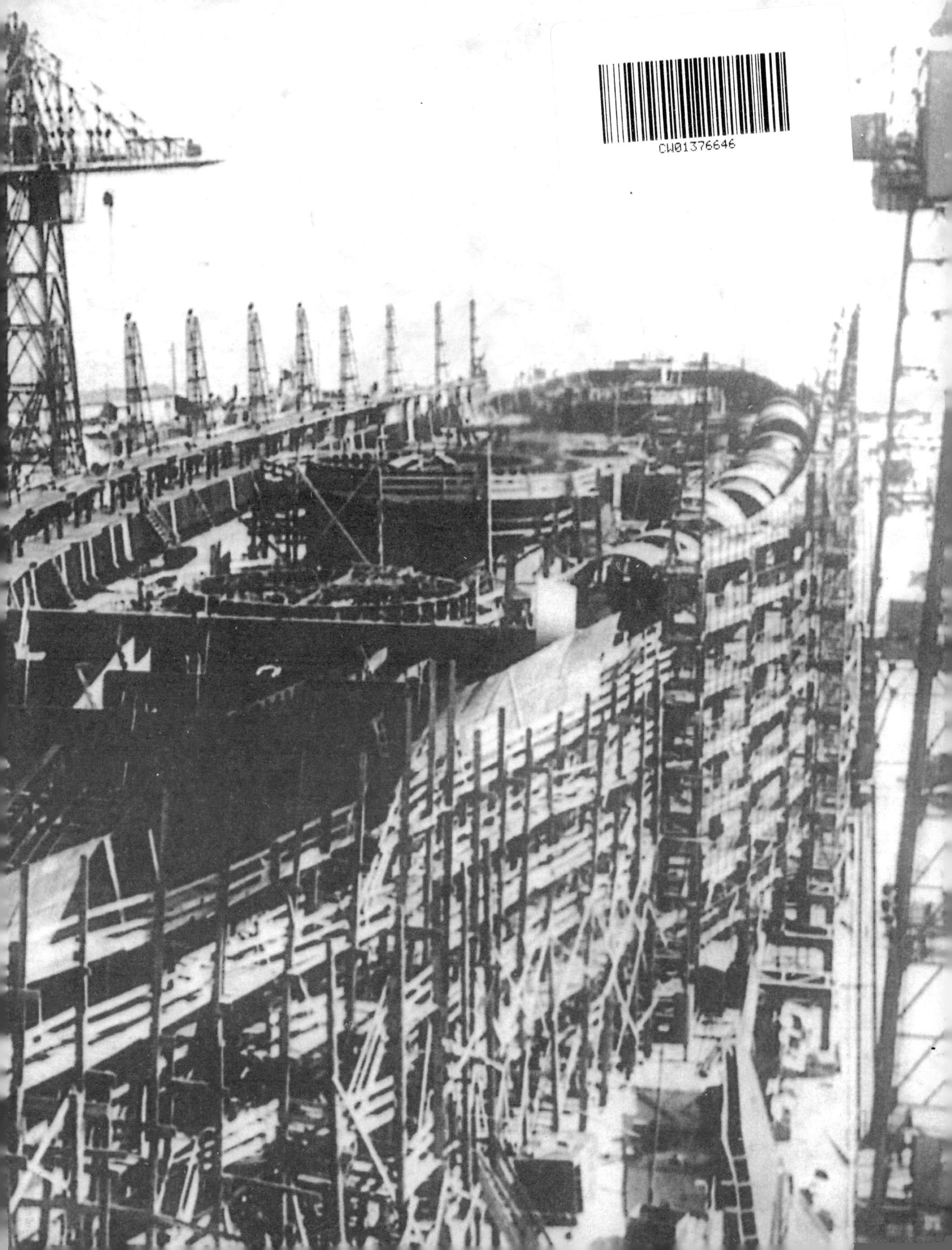

Nicholas Hodgson
Exeter, July 2006

Stalin's Ocean-Going Fleet

CASS SERIES: NAVAL POLICY AND HISTORY
ISSN 1366-9478

Series Editor: Holger Herwig

The series consists primarily of manuscripts by research scholars in the general area of naval policy and history, without national or chronological limitations. It will from time to time also include collections of important articles as well as reprints of classic works.

1. *Austro-Hungarian Naval Policy, 1904–1914*
   Milan N. Vego

2. *Far Flung Lines: Studies in Imperial Defence in Honour of Donald Mackenzie Schurman*
   Edited by Keith Neilson and Greg Kennedy

3. *Maritime Strategy and Continental Wars*
   Rear Admiral Raja Menon

4. *The Royal Navy and German Naval Disarmament 1942–1947*
   Chris Madsen

5. *Naval Strategy and Operations in Narrow Seas*
   Milan N. Vego

6. *The Pen and Ink Sailor: Charles Middleton and the King's Navy, 1778–1813*
   John E. Talbott

7. *The Italian Navy and Fascist Expansionism, 1935–1940*
   Robert Mallett

8. *The Merchant Marine in International Affairs, 1850–1950*
   Edited by Greg Kennedy

9. *Naval Strategy in Northeast Asia: Geo-strategic Goals, Policies and Prospects*
   Duk-Ki Kim

10. *Naval Policy and Strategy in the Mediterranean: Past, Present and Future*
    Edited by John B. Hattendorf

11. *Stalin's Ocean-going Fleet: Soviet Naval Strategy and Shipbuilding Programmes, 1935–1953*
    Jürgen Rohwer and Mikhail S. Monakov

12. *Imperial Defence, 1868–1887*
    Donald Mackenzie Schurman; edited by John Beeler

13. *Technology and Naval Combat in the Twentieth Century and Beyond*
    Edited by Phillips O'Brien

14. *The Royal Navy and Nuclear Weapons*
    Richard Moore

15. *The Royal Navy and the Capital Ship in the Interwar Period: An Operational Perspective*
    Joseph Moretz

STALIN'S OCEAN-GOING FLEET

Soviet Naval Strategy and Shipbuilding Programmes 1935–1953

Jürgen Rohwer
HONORARY PROFESSOR
UNIVERSITY OF STUTTGART

and

Mikhail S. Monakov
CHIEF OF THE HISTORY BRANCH
MAIN STAFF, THE RUSSIAN NAVY

FRANK CASS
LONDON • PORTLAND, OR

First published in 2001 in Great Britain by
FRANK CASS PUBLISHERS
Crown House, 47 Chase Side
Southgate, London N14 5BP

and in the United States of America by
FRANK CASS PUBLISHERS
c/o ISBS, 5824 N.E. Hassalo Street
Portland, Oregon 97213-3644

Website: www.frankcass.com

Copyright © 2001 J. Rohwer and M.S. Monakov

British Library Cataloguing in Publication Data

Rohwer, Jurgen
 Stalin's ocean-going fleet: Soviet naval strategy and
shipbuilding programmes, 1935–1953. – (Cass series. Naval
policy and history; 11)
 1. Sea power – Soviet Union 2. Shipbuilding – Government
policy – Soviet Union 3. Naval strategy 4. Soviet Union –
History, Naval 5. Soviet Union – Military policy
 I. Title
 359' .03'0947'09041

ISBN 0-7146-4895-7 (cloth)
ISSN 1366-9478

Library of Congress Cataloging-in-Publication Data

Rohwer, Jurgen.
 Stalin's ocean-going fleet: Soviet naval strategy and shipbuilding
programmes, 1935–1953 / Jurgen Rohwer and Mikhail S. Monakov.
   p. cm. – (Cass series–naval policy and history, ISSN 1366-9478;
 11)
 Includes bibliographical references and index.
 ISBN 0-7146-4895-7 (cloth)
 1. Soviet Union. Voenno-Morskoi Flot–History. 2. Soviet
Union–Military policy. 3. Soviet Union–History–1935–1953. 4. Naval
strategy–Soviet Union.   I. Monakov, Mikhail S. II. Title. III.
Series.
 VA573 .R54 2001
 359' .00947'09041–dc21
                                                                    2001017494

All rights reserved. No part of this publication may be reproduced, stored in or introduced into a retrieval system
or transmitted in any form or by any means, electronic, mechanical, photocopying, recording or otherwise,
without the prior written permission of the publisher of this book.

Design and production by Mike Moran

Typeset in 11/12 Baskerville by Vitaset, Paddock Wood, Kent
Printed in Great Britain by Bookcraft (Bath) Ltd, Midsomer Norton, Somerset

Contents

List of Plates	ix
List of Drawings	x
Foreword by David M. Glantz	xi
Series Editor's Preface	xiii
List of Abbreviations	xv
1. **Introduction**	1
2. **Historiography on the Soviet Navy**	4
3. **The Reconstitution Phase, 1920–25**	6
Condition of the Soviet Navy after the Civil War	6
Personnel	7
First Plans for a Reconstitution of the Navy	8
The *RKKF* and International and National Politics	9
Changes in the Personnel Situation	11
Strategic Considerations	12
Manoeuvres	13
The Restoration of Ships	14
4. **The Consolidation Phase, 1925–32**	19
Stalin on his Way to Dictatorship	19
New Discussions about Strategy	20
The Start of the First Shipbuilding Programme	24
Tanks or Battleships? What Fleet Do We Need?	24
The First Five-Year Plan (1928–32)	27
The 'Small War at Sea' Theory	29
First Repressions of Leaders and Engineers Accused of Sabotage	30
Foreign Aid from Germany	32
Foreign Aid from Italy	34
Shipbuilding in the First Five-Year Plan	35
5. **The Second Five-Year Plan, 1933–37**	41
International Politics and Strategy	41
Shipbuilding and the Forced Industrialization Programme	42
Strategy and Shipbuilding Plans	43
Foreign Aid during the Second Five-Year Plan	45

Submarine Building in the Second Five-Year Plan	46
Medium Submarines	46
Small Submarines	48
Big Submarines	48
Surface Ships in the Second Five-Year Plan	49
Cruisers	49
Destroyer Leaders and Destroyers	51
Minesweepers	53
Motor Torpedo Boats and Other Small Vessels	53
Reasons for Delays during the Second Five-Year Plan	54

6. The Change to the Big High Seas and Ocean-Going Fleet — 58

Stalin's Role	58
International Situation	59
Domestic Policy and the Start of the Purges	60
A New International Naval Arms Race	60
First Soviet Battleship Plans	62
The Spanish Civil War	64

7. The Third Five-Year Plan — 69

The Great Purges against the Army and Navy	69
The Strategic Considerations in 1935–36	70
The Pacific Fleet	72
The Baltic Fleet	72
The Black Sea Fleet	73
The Northern Fleet	73
The Battleship Building Plans of 1936–37	74
Changes in Strategic Planning and New Purges	77
New Leaders and a New Strategy in 1939	79
The Pacific Fleet	80
The Baltic Fleet	81
The Black Sea Fleet	83
The Northern Fleet	84
The River Flotillas	85
The Shipbuilding Organization in the Third Five-Year Plan	85
Foreign Aid in Shipbuilding in the Third Five-Year Plan	88
The State of the Soviet Fleets and the Shipbuilding Programme in the Summer of 1939	90
Old Ships and Submarines	90
New Surface Ships	90
Submarines	92
New Battleships and Battlecruisers	94
Aircraft Carriers	97
Light Cruisers	98
Destroyer Leaders and Destroyers	99
Smaller Surface Combatants	100
Operations and Tactics Reconsidered	102

8.	**The Second World War: The First Two Years**	110
	Soviet Foreign Policy in Spring and Summer 1939	110
	The First Period of Soviet–German Co-operation 1939–40	111
	Changes in the Strategic Situation, Autumn 1939–Summer 1940	114
	Change from Co-operation to Confrontation, Autumn 1940	116
	New Changes in the Soviet Naval Strategy in 1940	117
	New Changes in the Shipbuilding Programme	119
	Conferences on Operations and Tactics in October and December 1940	121
	Hitler and the German *Wehrmacht* Prepare for 'Barbarossa'	127
	The Debate about a Preventive or a Pre-emptive Attack in the Historiography	130
	Soviet Preparations for War	131
	The Soviet Navy at the Start of the Great Patriotic War	135
9.	**The Great Patriotic War, 1941–45**	144
	The German Attack	144
	Consequences for the Soviet Navy of the German Attack up to mid-1942	145
	Planning and Design Processes during the War: Surface Ships and Vessels	148
	Battleships and Battlecruisers	150
	Heavy and Light Cruisers	151
	Aircraft Carriers	152
	Destroyer Leaders and Destroyers	153
	Patrol Ships and Minesweepers	154
	Small Surface Combatants	156
	Building and Planning the Submarines	158
	Big Submarines	158
	Medium Submarines	159
	Small Submarines	160
	Special and Midget Submarines	161
	Lend-Lease Deliveries of Naval Vessels	162
	Lend-Lease Ships for the Northern Fleet	163
	Lend-Lease Ships for the Pacific Fleet	165
	War Booty Ships up to the End of the War	167
	Operations and Losses from mid-1942 to the End of the War	168
	Baltic Fleet	168
	Black Sea Fleet	168
	Northern Fleet	169
	Pacific Fleet	170
	The Soviet Fleets at the End of the War, September 1945	170
	Baltic Fleet	170
	Black Sea Fleet	171
	Northern Fleet	172
	Pacific Fleet	172
10.	**From 1945 to the End of Stalin's Regime**	178
	First Plans for the New Navy	178
	The Soviet Diplomatic Offensive, 1944–45	179
	Ships as Reparation	179
	Return of the Lend-Lease Ships	184

	The Ten-Year Programme of 1945 (1946–55)	185
	Experiences, Strategies and Industrial Capacities	188
	Reorganization of the High Command and Purges	190
	New Discussions about Strategy	191
	Completion of Ships from Pre-war Designs	192
	New Surface Ships	193
	Battleships	194
	Battlecruisers and Heavy Cruisers	195
	Light Cruisers	197
	Aircraft Carriers	199
	Destroyers	201
	Patrol Ships	202
	Minesweepers	203
	Small Combatants	204
	Submarines	204
	Big Submarines	205
	Medium Submarines	205
	Small Submarines	206
	New Technologies and Changes in the Programme	209
	Nuclear Power and Nuclear Weapons	210
	Cruise Missiles and Rockets	210
	Politics and Strategy, 1951–56	215
11.	**Why Did Stalin Build his Big Ocean-Going Fleet?**	221

Appendices: 225

1. Warships and submarines of the former Imperial Navy, serving in the *RKKF/VMF*   226
2. Warships of the *RKKF/VMF*, laid down or ordered, 1926–45   229
3. Submarines of the *RKKF/VMF*, laid down or ordered, 1926–45   243
4. Lend-Lease vessels in the *VMF*, 1941–53   257
5. Soviet warships and submarines lost, 1939–45   260
6. Warships and submarines, taken as war booty into the *VMF*, 1944–53   268
7. Warships of the *VMF*, laid down or ordered, 1945–53   276
8. Submarines of the *VMF*, laid down or ordered, 1945–53   283

Note on Soviet and Russian Sources   293

Bibliography   299

Index: 315
    Names   315
    Ships   319
    Projects   331

List of Plates

Between pages 48 and 49

1. Submarine *D-6/Spartakovets*.
2. Three patrol ships of *projekt 2*, *Uragan*-class.
3. Destroyer leader *Leningrad* of *projekt 1*.
4. Big submarine *P-1/Pravda*.
5. Small submarine of series VI.
6. Medium submarine *S-56*.
7. Destoyer leader *Tashkent*, of *projekt 20-I*.
8. Big submarine *K-21* of series XIV.
9. Cruiser *Kirov* of *projekt 26*.
10. Destroyer *Gordyi* of *projekt 7*.
11. Destroyer *Soobrzitel'nyi* of *projekt 7-U*.
12. Minesweeper *Iskatel'* of *projekt 53*.
13. Battleship *Sovetskaya Ukraina* of *projekt 23*.
14. Battleship *Sevastopol'*.
15. Medium submarine *S-125* of series V-bis 2.
16. Destroyer *Ognevoi* of *projekt 30*.
17. Heavy cruiser *L*.

Between pages 144 and 145

18. Battleship *Arkhangel'sk*.
19. Light cruiser *Admiral Makarov*.
20. Cruiser *Frunze* of *projekt 68K*.
21. Cruiser *Sverdlov* of *projekt 68-bis*.
22. Destroyer *Smetlivyi* of *projekt 30-bis*.
23. Destroyer *Besslednyi* of *projekt 56*.
24. Patrol ship of *projekt 29*.
25. Destroyer *Neustrashimyi* of *projekt 41*.
26. Patrol ship of *projekt 42*.
27. Patrol ship of *projekt 50*.
28. Big submarine of *projekt 611*.
29. Medium submarine of *projekt 613* in the original version.
30. Small submarine of *projekt A615*.
31. Nuclear submarine of *projekt 627*.
32. Missile destroyer *Prozorlivyi* of *projekt 56M*.

List of Drawings

1.	Aircraft carrier project *Komsomolets*	21
2.	Fast battleship project *Frunze*, design variant A	27
3.	Battleship *projekt 21*	62
4.	Battleship *projekt UP-41* from Ansaldo, Genova	63
5.	Battleship *projekt 25*	74
6.	Battleship *projekt 23*	76
7.	Battlecruiser *projekt 69*	77
8.	Battleship design of Gibbs & Cox, variant *B*	89
9.	Heavy cruiser *projekt X*	96
10.	Aircraft carrier *projekt 71A*	97
11.	Destroyer leader, *projekt 48*	99
12.	Light cruiser *projekt MK*	152
13.	Experimental submarine *R-1*	161
14.	Experimental submarine *M-401*	162
15.	Transport submarine *projekt 607*	163
16.	Battleship *projekt 24*	194
17.	Battlecruiser *Stalingrad* of *projekt 82*	196
18.	Aircraft carrier *projekt 85/VI*	200
19.	Medium submarine *S-99* of *projekt 617*	207
20.	Fore part of test missile cruiser *Admiral Nakhimov*	212
21.	Missile battlecruiser *projekt* variant *F-25A*	212
22.	Light cruiser *projekt 64*	213
23.	Missile submarine *B-62* of *projekt 611AV*	213
24.	Missile submarine *K-96*, ex *B-92*, of *projekt 629*	213
25.	Missile submarine *projekt P-2*	214
26.	Nuclear missile cruiser, *projekt 63*	215

Foreword

Legions of historians, Western and Russian alike, have written literally thousands of volumes about the formation, evolution, and performance of the Red Army in peace and war. These works range from the heavily censored tomes of the Stalin era, through the slightly more candid revelations of Brezhnev's time and the remarkable products of Khrushchev's de-Stalinization and Gorbachev's *glasnost'* programmes, to the superb works prepared by such Western historians as Malcolm MacIntosh and John Erickson. More recently, a veritable flood of Soviet archival releases, though selective, has added flesh to or corrected much of what has been previously written. Sadly, however, virtually all of this literature has focused on the Red Army alone, relegating the Red Navy and its history to a state of benign neglect. In large measure, Jürgen Rohwer and Mikhail Monakov have corrected this grievous omission.

This imposing volume fills a yawning gap in the historiography of the Soviet Armed Forces by providing a uniquely complete account of the creation and evolution of the Soviet Navy in peacetime as well as during war. Exploiting a wealth of hitherto-inaccessible archival materials, the authors, both of whom are authorities without peer in their field, present a coherent narrative, organized chronologically, that traces the institutional and physical development of the Soviet Navy within the essential context of evolving naval strategies.

The book is replete with unprecedented detail regarding a wide range of topics. Most important for those interested in military history, it surveys the Soviet Navy's record in war, ranging from its reformation during the Civil War years through its emergence as an ocean-going force during the early Cold War years. The work provides unique insights into Soviet naval developments, strategic, operational, institutional, and intellectual, during the turbulent crises and conflicts of the late 1930s, including the Spanish Civil War, the Russo-Finnish War, and the conflicts with Japan in the Far East. Above all, it details the Navy's contributions to Soviet victory in the 'Great Patriotic War' with Nazi Germany, including a wealth of detail on the naval dimension of that titanic conflict.

Above and beyond the Navy's wartime experiences, this book spells out the actual composition of the Soviet Navy throughout each period of its development, painstakingly revealing the processes of ship development and design within the context of evolving naval doctrine and naval operational and tactical techniques. While doing so, it examines such controversial but hitherto-forbidden topics as the effects of the Great Purges on naval command personnel and force effectiveness, and the scope, intent, and consequences of Soviet–German naval co-operation prior to the outbreak of the Second World War.

Readers will be fascinated by the authors' extensive, authoritative, and detailed appendices – almost 100 pages in length, which read like a 'Who's Who' for actual naval hardware (ships). In addition, the author's historiographical survey and extensive bibliography, which contains a host of primary archival source materials, stand as stark evidence to the book's vast scope and unique authenticity. *Stalin's Ocean-Going Fleet* will be the standard work in its field and will likely retain that august status for many years to come. It will, undoubtedly, become a fixture in the library of all interested in the subject.

DAVID M. GLANTZ
Carlisle, PA
January 2001

Series Editor's Preface

This is truly an important book. Jürgen Rohwer, for many years editor of the German naval journal *Marine-Rundschau* as well as head of the Library for Contemporary History at Stuttgart, and Mikhail Monakov, Soviet naval officer and now Chief of the Historical Branch in the Main Staff of the Russian Navy, have provided the first analysis of Soviet naval shipbuilding policies between 1935 and 1953. Using formerly closed Soviet naval records, Rohwer and Monakov revise many standard interpretations of the Red Navy and offer bold, challenging new concepts and ideas. The very idea that Josef Stalin was a champion of a Mahanian blue-water battle fleet will come as a surprise to many. And that Zhukov was contemplating a 'pre-emptive counterattack' against Nazi Germany early in 1941 will no doubt stimulate debate on this topic as well.

The authors use the first five chapters to bridge the period from the Imperial Navy of 1918 to 1937 – a time when the Soviet Navy still consisted primarily of modernized ships of the Tsarist fleet. There existed no coherent naval strategy, just endless debates among the adherents of cruiser warfare ('small war at sea') and those of a blue-water battle fleet ('old school'). The fleet was dispersed among four theatres: the Baltic Sea, the Black Sea, the North, and the Far East. Stalin's purges of alleged 'enemies of Soviet ideals' and 'saboteurs' (30,514 military and naval personnel were shot) were important for naval policy insofar as the dictator now came round to the notion that the USSR needed an ocean-going fleet. This became official defence policy in December 1935, and the 'Big Navy Programme' of May 1936 included 24 battleships of 43,000 to 75,000 tons each to be built by 1947. In part, the breakdown of the naval accords of the Washington conference of 1922 and the London conference of 1930 had urged action upon Stalin. Furthermore, Germany had launched its first *Deutschland*-class 'pocket battleships' and France the *Dunkerque* and the *Richelieu*; thereafter came the *Bismarck*, *King George V*, *North Carolina*, *Littorio*, and finally the *Yamato*. Obviously, the Soviets could not afford to fall behind and still hope to be a global naval power.

Rohwer and Monakov reject the standard argument that no operational concept accompanied this massive naval buildup. They argue, rather, that there *was* a unified operational concept: the fleet would attain 'mastery of the sea' in the Sea of Japan, in the Gulf of Finland, and in the Black Sea; in addition, it would repel any invasions from the sea in the Baltic Sea and the Northern Sea. In 1939 Stalin entrusted the 'big ocean-going fleet' to a protégé, the 36-year-old N.G. Kuznetsov. When war came in 1941, the fleet was obviously still very much on the drawing board. But the authors reject another standard interpretation, namely, that Stalin now shifted resources and emphasis exclusively on to the land forces. They argue, using Soviet naval records, that fleet-building remained a top priority, yet one that Stalin refused to share with Kuznetsov! With their naval bases in the Baltic Sea and in the Black Sea quickly threatened with German occupation, the Soviets had no choice but to pursue a 'small war at sea'. Construction of heavy units was cancelled from 1942 to 1944.

Admiral Kuznetsov emerged with detailed plans for a blue-water fleet as early as August 1944. Stalin remained keen as ever on naval expansion, and in November 1945 approved a ten-year naval expansion act that called for a Red Navy of no fewer than 5,800 warships. By February 1950, Stalin, no doubt fearing the power accumulated by the Red Army's marshals through their success in the Great Patriotic War, created an independent Naval Ministry. The 'big ocean-going navy' was on the books again. And despite a veritable revolution in military affairs – jet and rocket propulsion, nuclear weapons, electronic sensors – Stalin remained wedded until the end to the concept of a Mahanian battleship fleet. Whether this fleet was designed to thwart perceived naval threats or whether it was the first step on the road to Soviet global naval power, as these authors assert, awaits further research. For Stalin, as earlier for Hitler, the 'big ships' were visible manifestations of power; generally speaking, Stalin's naval policy exhibited 'an offensive tendency'. Scrapped by N.S. Krushchev and Z.G. Zhukov after the dictator's death in 1953, the 'big ocean-going navy' was resurrected by S.G. Gorshkov, only to end in failure and defeat in the Cold War.

Overall, this is an impressive and original work of solid research in Soviet naval archives that were closed until recently. The book revises many of our standard concepts of Stalin and the sea, and it makes a major contribution to the historiography of Soviet naval policy, defence policy, and strategic studies. The authors' meticulous analysis of the purges is an added bonus to what is already a superb piece of scholarship.

Holger H. Herwig

List of Abbreviations

A/A weapons	anti-aircraft weapons
A/Cs	aircraft
APSS	code name for midget submarine
BUMS	combat regulations for Naval Forces
ChF	*Chernomorskii Flot* (Black Sea Fleet)
D/Cs	depth charges
FYP	Five-Year Plan
GAVA	*Gosudarstvennyi Arkhiv Voennyi Armiya* (State Archive of the Army)
GKO	*Gosudarstvennyi Komitet Oborony* (State Committee for Defence)
GRT	gross registered tons
GRU	*Glavnoe razvedyvatel'noe upravlenie* (Main Intelligence Directorate)
KB	*Konstruktorshoie Byuro* (Design Bureau)
KBF/Kfl	*Krasnoznamennyi Baltijskii Flot* (Red Banner Baltic Fleet)
KVF	*Kaspijskoe Voennaya Flotiliya* (Caspian Naval Flotilla)
MGs	machine guns
MGSh	*Morskoe Genralyi Shtab* (Ministry of Naval Forces and the Naval General Staff)
MTBs	motor torpedo boats
Narkom	*Narodnyi Kommissar* (People's Commissar)
NF	Northern Fleet
NKVD	*Narodnyi Komissariat Vnutrennykh Del* (People's Commissariat of Internal Affairs)
NTK	*Nauchno-Tekhnicheskii Komitet* (Scientific-Technical Committee)
OGPU	*Ob'edinennoe Gosudarstvennoe Politicheskoe Upravlenie* (United State Political Administration)
OTZ	*Operativnoe Tekhnicheskoe Zadanie* (Operational Technical Requirements)
REDO	*Regenerativnyi edinyi dvigatel' osobyi* (closed cycle drive for submarines)
RGA	*Rossijskii Gosudarstvennyi Arkhiv* (Russian State Archive)
RGA VMF	*Rossijskii Gosudarstvennyi Arkhiv Voenno-Morskogo Flota* (Russian State Archive for the Navy)
RGVA	*Rossijskii Gosudarstvennyi Voennyi Arkhiv* (Russian State War Archive)
RKKA	*Raboche-krest'yanskaya Armiya* (Red Workers and Peasants Army)
RKKF	*Raboche-krest'yanskii krasnyi Flota* (Workers-Peasants Red Fleet)
RVS	*Revvoensovet* (Revolutionary War Council)
SF	*Severnyi Flot* (Northern Fleet)
SKR	*Storozhevye korabli* (patrol boat)
SNK	*Sovet Narodnykh Komissarov SSSR* (Council of People's Commissars))
STO	*Sovet Truda I Oborony* (Council of Labour and Defence)

t		metric tons, used for submarine displacements
t stdd.		standard tons, used since 1922 Washington Conference for displacements of warships
TOF		*Tikhookeanski Flot* (Pacific Fleet)
TsGA		*Tsentral'nyi Gosudarstvennyi Arkhiv* (Central State Archive)
TsK VKP(b)		*Tsentral'nyi Komitet VKP (b)* (Bolshevik Party's Central Committee)
TsKB		*Tsentral'noe Konstruktorshoe Byuro* (Central Design Bureau)
TTZ		*Taktico-Tekhnicheskoe-Zadanie* (tactical-technical requirement)
VMF		*Voenno-Morskoi Flot* (Naval Fleet)
VMS		*Voenno-morskie sily* (Naval Forces of the USSR)

EQUIVALENT MILITARY AND NAVAL RANKS

Soviet military rank (1935–39)	(after 1939)	*Anglo-American rank*
	Marshal SSSR	General of the Army
Komandarm	*General Armiya*	General
Komkor	*General Polkovnik*	Lieutenant-General
Komdiv	*General Leitenant*	Major-General
Kombrig	*General Mayor*	Brigadier-General
	Polkovnik	Colonel
	Podpolkovnik	Lieutenant-Colonel
	Mayor	Major

Soviet naval rank (1935–39)	(after 1939)	
	Admiral Flota SSSR	Fleet Admiral
Flagman Flota 1 Ranga	*Admiral Flota*	Admiral
Flagman Flota 2 Ranga	*Admiral*	Vice Admiral
Flagman 1 Ranga	*Vitse Admiral*	Rear Admiral
Flagman 2 Ranga	*Kontr Admiral*	Commodore
	Kapitan 1 Ranga	Captain
	Kapitan 2 Ranga	Commander
	Kapitan 3 Ranga	Lieutenant Commander

1

Introduction

Planning for this book started in earnest when the authors first met during 'Kieler Woche' (Kiel Week) in June 1993 aboard the newest destroyer of the Russian Baltic Fleet, the *Nastoichivyi*. But this meeting had a long pre-history. Both of us had worked for a long time on the history of the Russian and Soviet Navy.

Jürgen Rohwer was for 30 years editor-in-chief of the German naval journal *Marine-Rundschau*, which since the early 1960s had published several articles by competent authors, such as *Kapitan 1 Ranga* V.I. Achkasov, Admiral V.F. Tributs, Admiral N.N. Amel'ko, and even Admiral of the Fleet of the Soviet Union S.G. Gorshkov.[1] Jürgen Rohwer had also published many articles in German-language and foreign journals[2] and edited Soviet publications in translation.[3]

As an officer in the Soviet and Russian Navy, Mikhail Monakov took a course at the Higher Naval College in 1971 and a Higher Naval Officer's Course in 1976, before becoming Chief of the Historical Branch in the Main Staff of the Russian Navy. He started publishing, together with several colleagues, a Naval Dictionary[4] and articles in the journal *Morskoi sbornik*, of which he became a co-editor. Most important was his series of articles about the 'Doctrines and Fates' in the journal from 1990–94.[5]

We were both for many years hampered to different degrees by the inaccessibility of the relevant archives in the Soviet Union. Up to about 1990 we were only able to count on the more or less official publications by Soviet authors, who used materials provided to them by the officials responsible, or on intelligence sources in Western archives and publications in Western countries. Even though Rohwer had had contact since 1975 with the then Director of the Institute of Military History of the Soviet Army, Lt-Gen. Prof. P.A. Zhilin, during the annual meetings of the International Commission of Military History (ICHM), there was no real exchange of materials possible during this period of 'stagnation'. This began to change when in 1988 *General Polkovnik* Prof. D. Volkogonov and his assistant, *Kapitan 1 Ranga* I.A. Amosov, became the Soviet representatives at the ICHM. During the International Congress of Historical Sciences held in Madrid in 1990 they arranged a meeting with the then head of the archives of the Soviet General Staff, *Polkovnik*

I. Venkov, and his assistant, then Major O. Starkov. With their unconventional assistance Rohwer was allowed access for the first time to important documents on the shipbuilding plans of the Soviet Navy from 1926 to 1941. These became the source for several articles in Western journals and publications.[6] They were also the basis for the presentation of a joint paper by Rohwer and Amosov at the Naval History Symposium of the US Naval Academy at Annapolis in 1993 on parallels between Stalin's and Hitler's naval programmes, published in a slightly different version in Germany.[7]

This was also the starting point for our meeting aboard the *Nastoichivyi* in preparation for our first joint article on our topic.[8] Of great importance for our work was the close co-operation with *Kapitan 2 Ranga* S. Berezhnoi, an expert on the building dates of Russian and Soviet warships and submarines, who had already published some books with detailed documentation on the fate of all ships from 1917 to the present and who provided us with the dates for the appendices in this book.[9] Sadly, Capt. Berezhnoi died in November 2000.

NOTES

1. V.F. Tributs, 'Die U-Bootoffensive der Baltischen Rotbannerflotte in der Ostsee 1942', *Marine-Rundschau*, 60 (1963), pp. 80–107. V.I. Achkasov, 'Die sowjetische Kriegsflotte im Verlauf des "Großen Vaterländischen Krieges"', *Marine-Rundschau*, 62 (1965), pp. 268–77. V.I. Achkasov, 'Die Durchbruchs-Operation der Baltischen Rotbanner-Flotte von Reval auf Kronstadt', *Marine-Rundschau*, 64 (1967), pp. 26–44. V.F. Tributs, 'Die Räumung der Garnison von Hangö', *Marine-Rundschau*, 64 (1967), pp. 103–10, 158–74. N.N. Amel'ko, 'Der sowjetische Weg zur Sicherheit', *Marine-Rundschau*, 79 (1982), pp. 458–9. S.G. Gorshkov, 'Die Stärke der Seestreitkräfte des Sowjetstaates – ein wichtiger Faktor der Sicherheit der UdSSR', *Marine-Rundschau*, 80 (1983), pp. 5–7.
2. Jürgen Rohwer, 'Die sowjetische U-Bootwaffe in der Ostsee 1939–1945', *Wehrwissenschaftliche Rundschau*, 6 (1956), pp. 547–68. Jürgen Rohwer, 'Die sowjetische Flotte im Zweiten Weltkrieg', *Jahresbibliographie 1959 der Bibliothek für Zeitgeschichte*, 32 (1960), pp. 383–410. Jürgen Rohwer, 'Esperienze tecniche e tattiche dell'arma subaquea Sovietica nel secondo conflitto mondiale', *Rivista Marittima*, 7–8 (1967), pp. 39–83. Claude Huan, and Jürgen Rohwer, 'La Marine Soviétique', in *Notes et Études Documentaires No. 4479–4480*, Paris, 1978. Jürgen Rohwer, 'Admiral Gorshkov and the Influence of History upon Seapower', *US Naval Institute Proceedings*, May (1981), pp. 150–74. Jürgen Rohwer, 'Das Ende der Ara Gorschkow', *Marine-Rundschau*, 83 (1986), pp. 88–97. Jürgen Rohwer, 'Alternating Russian and Soviet Naval Strategies', in P. Gillette and W.C. Franks (eds), *Sources of Soviet Naval Conduct*, Lexington, MA, Lexington Books, 1990, pp. 90–120.
3. N.A. Piterskij, *Die Sowjetflotte im Zweiten Weltkrieg*, trans. Erich Pruck, ed. Jürgen Rohwer, Oldenburg, Stalling, 1966.
4. *Voenno-morskoi slovar*, ed. V.N. Chernavin, Moscow, Voenizdat, 1990.
5. Mikhail Monakov, 'Sud'by doktrin i teorii', *Morskoi sbornik*, 11, 12 (1990), 3,4 (1991), 3 (1992), 3,5 (1994). Mikhail Monakov, 'Strategicheskiye zadachi VMF v posledniye 100 let', *Morskoi sbornik*, 10 (1996). Mikhail Monakov, 'Dolgoye echo voyny', *Morskoi sbornik*, 8 (1997).
6. Jürgen Rohwer, 'Les stratégies navales soviétiques et les programmes de construction navale (1921–1941)', in *Dossier 47. L'évolution de la pensée navale III*, Paris, 1993, pp. 171–208. Jürgen Rohwer, 'Soviet Naval Strategies and Building Programs, 1922–1941', *Acta No. 19*, XIXth International Colloquium of Military History, Ankara, 1994, pp. 421–50. Jürgen Rohwer, 'Il programma navale di Stalin', *Storia Militare*, No. 20: III (May 1995), pp. 4–13. Jürgen Rohwer, 'Stalin's Battleships and Battlecruisers', *The Northern Mariner*, VII, No. 3 (July 1997), pp. 1–11.
7. Jürgen Rohwer, 'Weltmacht als Ziel? Parallelen in Stalins and Hitlers Flottenbau-

Programmen', in *Politischer Wandel, organisierte Gewalt und nationale Sicherheit*, Munich, Oldenbourg, 1995, pp. 161–80.
8. Jürgen Rohwer and Mikhail Monakov, 'The Soviet Union's Ocean-Going Fleet 1935–1953', *The International History Review*, 18, IV (1996), pp. 837–68.
9. Sergei S. Berezhnoi (ed.), *Korabli i vspomogatel'nye suda Sovetskogo Voenno-morskogo flota (1917–1927)*, Moscow, Voenizdat, 1981. Sergei S. Berezhnoi, *Korabli i suda VMF SSSR 1928–1945*, Moscow, Voenizdat, 1988. Sergei S. Berezhnoi, 'Sovetskii VMF 1945–1995. Kreisera, bol'sh'ie protivlodochnie korabli, esmintsy', *Modelist-Konstruktor*, No. 1 (1995), pp. 1–32.

2

Historiography on the Soviet Navy

For a long time the history of strategic thinking and planning in the Soviet Navy between 1922 and the reconstruction of the government following the death of Joseph Stalin in 1953 has been obscured. Since the Second World War many publications have appeared in the Soviet Union about the history of the Soviet Navy since the revolution.[1] These gave many details about general developments and the various conferences held but always followed the pre-set party line. Details of the internal discussions on strategies and shipbuilding programmes were seldom revealed. The information on persons involved was mainly restricted to those not prosecuted during the time of Stalin, and the accounts on shipbuilding were restricted to some unrelated details on several ship-types and summaries of the ships built or laid down during the first three Five-Year Plans. Yet no information on building dates was given. Western experts took great pains to sift out from the sketchy materials the truth about the shipbuilding programmes.[2]

With the onset of *Perestroika* and *Glasnost* in the 1980s many and far more detailed publications appeared in Russia,[3] and since 1990 more details have been released from what had been up to then secret archives. Combining the earlier publications and the new materials, it is now possible to present a more accurate description of the development of naval thought in the Soviet naval, military and Party circles as well as an accurate tabulation of the reconstruction and building programmes of the years 1922–41 and some hints about the planning for the Fourth Five-Year Plan.[4]

Besides the books mentioned there are many articles in Russian journals and periodicals such as *Morskoi sbornik, Sudostroenie, Gangut* and others about the different ship and submarine types, not only the built and finished ones but also the uncompleted projects. Such articles will be mentioned when relevant developments are being described. We are very grateful for the assistance received from some of the authors of these books and other Russian colleagues, such as *Kapitan 1 Ranga* Igor A. Amosov, *Polkovnik* Igor Venkov, *Podpolkovnik* Oleg Starkov, *Kapitan 2 Ranga* Sergei Zonin, K.B. Strel'bitskii, and the late Col.-General Dmitrii Volkogonov. Western experts on the Soviet Navy also gave us much very interesting and helpful advice, such as Siegfried Breyer (Hanau, Germany), Rolf Erikson (Phoenix, USA), Professor Willard

C. Frank Jr (Norfolk, USA), Dipl.-Ing. René Greger (Prague, Czech Republic), *Capitaine de vaisseau* Claude Huan (Paris, France), and Jürg Meister (Canowindra, Australia).

NOTES

1. Some of the more recent Soviet publications in this field are: *Boevoi put' Sovetskogo voenno-morskogo flota*, ed. N.A. Piterskii, Moscow, Voenizdat, 1964; 3rd edn, ed. V.I. Achkasov *et al.*, Moscow, Voenizdat, 1974. *Istoriya voenno-morskogo iskusstva*, ed. S.E. Zakharov, Moscow, Voenizdat, 1969. Sergej G. Gorshkov, *Morskaya moshch' gosudarstva*, Moscow, Voenizdat, 1970, 2nd edn, 1976.
2. The following are some of the many Western publications on the subject: *Das deutsche Bild der russischen und sowjetischen Marine*, Supplement 7/8 of *Marine-Rundschau*, September 1962; David Woodward, *The Russians at Sea*, London, Kimber, 1965; Robert W. Herrick, *Soviet Naval Strategy: Fifty Years of Theory and Practice*, Annapolis, MD, US Naval Institute, 1969; Donald W. Mitchell, *A History of Russian and Soviet Sea Power*, London, Deutsch, 1974; Harald Fock, *Vom Zarenadler zum Roten Stern*, Herford, Mittler, 1985; *The Sources of Soviet Naval Conduct*, ed. Philip S. Gillette and Willard C. Frank Jr, Lexington, MA, Lexington Books, 1990. For documentary works about shipbuilding: Jürg Meister, *Soviet Warships of the Second World War*, London, Macdonald and Jane's, 1977; Marek Twardowski and Boris Lemachko, 'Soviet Union', *Conway's all the World's Fighting Ships, 1922–1946*, London, Conway's, 1980, pp. 318–46; Siegfried Breyer, *Enzyklopädie des sowjetischen Kriegsschiffbaus*: Vol. I: *Oktoberrevolution und maritimes Erbe*. Vol. II: *Konsolidierung und erste Neubauten*. Vol. III: *Flottenbau und Plansoll*, Herford, Koehler, 1987, 1989, 1991.
3. Aleksei V. Basov, 'Der Bau der Seekriegsflotte der UdSSR vor dem Zweiten Weltkrieg – 1921–1941', in *The Naval Arms Race 1930–1941*, ed. Jürgen Rohwer, *Revue Internationale d'Histoire Militaire, No. 73*, Bonn, Bernard & Graefe, 1991, pp. 119–35. Sergei S. Berezhnoi, *Korabli i suda VMF SSSR 1928–1945*, Moscow, Voenizdat, 1988. Vladimir I. Dmitriev, *Sovetskoe podvodnoe korable-stroenie*, Moscow, Voenizdat, 1990. E.A. Shitikov, V.N. Krasnov and V.V. Balabin, *Korable-stroenie v SSSR v gody Velikoi Otechestvennoi vojny*, Moscow, Nauka, 1995.
4. V.N. Burov, *Otechestvennoe voennoe korablestroenie v trete'em stoletii svoej istorii*, St Petersburg, Sudostroenie, 1995. V.P. Kuzin and V.I. Nikol'skii, *Voenno-morskoj flot SSSR 1945–1991*, St Petersburg, Istoricheskoe Morskoe Obshchestvo, 1996. A.S. Pavlov, *Voennye korabli SSSR i Rossii 1945–1995*, Yakutsk, 1994. English-language edition: *Warships of the USSR and Russia 1945–1995*, Annapolis, MD, US Naval Institute Press, 1997. A.V. Platonov, *Sovetskie boevye korabli 1941–1945*, St Petersburg, 1996. Vol. III: *Podvodnye lodki. Istoriya Otechestvennogo sudostroeniya*, ed. I. Spasskii *et al.* Vol. IV: *Sudostroenie v period pervykh pyatiletok i Velikoi Otechestvennoie vojny 1925–1945gg*. Vol. V: *Sudostroenie v poslevoennyi period 1946–1991 gg.*, St Petersburg, 1996.

3

The Reconstitution Phase, 1920–25

CONDITION OF THE SOVIET NAVY* AFTER THE CIVIL WAR

At the beginning of this period the principles of the Soviet State's military policy were determined by the fact that the Civil War of 1918–20 had ended in decisive victory for the Red Army. It seemed that the system of political and strategic leadership of the Soviet Armed forces, formed during the Civil War, had proved its efficiency, but at the same time it became quite clear that numerous formations of the Red Army were not able to match this because of the poor financial and material resources which the Soviet state could allocate to satisfy defence needs. The massive reduction in the size of the Army and Navy during the first months after the Civil War was not accompanied by measures for the preservation of their combat readiness. This resulted in a serious loss of combat capacity, a decrease in discipline and in some cases loss of command and control.

In February 1921, the incompetence and arbitrariness of party and state officials caused mass disobedience among the Baltic Fleet personnel. On 1 March 1921 a rebellion in the Kronshtadt fortress garrison broke out. It had to be violently suppressed by Red Army troops under the command of M.N. Tukhachevskii.[1] The problems of feeding the urban population and events such as Kronshtadt made the problem of transition to the 'new economic policy' (NEP) all the more acute,[2] and forced the leadership of the country to accept urgent measures for strengthening the ideological and administrative control over the armed forces, to search for ways of tightening up the discipline and political reliability of Army and Navy personnel in order to restore the combat capacity of the troops and forces.

The People's Commissar for the Army and Navy, Leon Trotskii, had in 1919 proposed a defensive strategy in the Baltic and Black Seas, but an offensive strategy in the Caspian Sea. Two years later, at the end of 1921, a special commission, echoing his ideas, directed him to strengthen the Caspian

---

* The Soviet Navy's official name until 1926 was the *Raboche-krest'yanskii Krasnyi Flot* or *RKKF* (Workers-Peasants Red Fleet); for the convenience of the readers the authors will use the terms 'Red Fleet' or 'Navy'.

Flotilla as a vehicle by means of which to export the Bolshevik revolution to the East.[3]

But at that time external and internal conditions were not suitable for the development of an adequate military doctrine and, consequently, prospective plans for military reconstruction. An analysis of the Bolshevik Party's resolutions and the Party's Central Committee decisions on military questions reveals that the measures which were carried out by the Soviet leadership were of a short-term character. Those measures corresponded to the main purposes of:

- strengthening the leading role of the Party in the Army and Navy
- reducing the size of the Armed Forces to the smallest possible level
- liquidating extraordinary and excessive supply agencies and introducing a system of scheduled state deliveries
- improving the social structure of personnel and its political reliability.

The obvious insufficiency of these measures could be concluded from an objective analysis of actual conditions in the Red Navy in 1921. The most exact characteristic of this state was given in the mid-1920s by the People's Commissar for the Army and Navy and the Chairman of the Revolutionary War Council (equivalent to Minister of Defence) M.V. Frunze. He said:

> We have lost the greater and better part of the Navy's strength and a great majority of experienced and competent commanders, which were more important for the Navy's activities than commanders in other services; we have lost several naval bases and imported a number of non-commissioned naval personnel. It meant, we had no Navy.[4]

Personnel

The upheavals during the Civil War and the purges following the mutiny at Kronshtadt led to many changes in the high command and to the promotion of former ordinary seamen, such as M.F. Izmailov, K.I. Dushenov and G.I. Levchenko, who graduated from the Naval War College of the Red Navy in 1922, of non-commissioned officers, such as I.K. Kozhanov and M.V. Viktorov, and even party functionaries, such as V.I. Zof, I.M. Ludri and A.P. Aleksandrov. But the deficiencies of the new commanders forced Trotskii to retain some of the former Imperial Navy officers, such as E.A. Berens, A.V. Nemits, A.P. Zelenoi, A.S. Maksimov, B.B. Zherve, M.A. Petrov, A.V. Dombrovskii and L.M. Galler among the higher ranks, and younger officers such as F.K. Raskol'nikov, V.A. Kukel', I.S. Isakov and E.S. Pantserzhanskii as *specialists* to support them.[5]

When the Naval Academy reopened after the end of the Civil War, B.B. Zherve and M.A. Petrov took over the courses taught by Major-General N.L. Klado, often called the Russian Mahan, who had died in 1919. And owing to the lack of matériel, funds, and also personnel, even Trotskii was at first opposed to any reinterpretation of the established principles of military and naval strategy. Notwithstanding the gap between theory and the ships available, instruction at the Naval Academy and the Naval War College continued until 1925–27 along the lines set by the 'classical school' of naval strategy in which battleships played the decisive role.[6] To fill the gaps in personnel eligible for future promotion to the higher ranks, officer candidates were recruited from the Party and the Komsomol' youth organization and pushed through the first courses at the Naval College. Some of them, such as N.G. Kuznetsov, V.A. Alafuzov, and V.F. Tributs, would hold the most important posts in the Navy during the Second World War.[7]

First Plans for a Reconstitution of the Navy

According to the complement tables of the fleets in 1921 the *RKKF* had on the active list 223 combat ships, including one battleship, 24 destroyers and torpedo-boat destroyers, 13 submarines, 6 mine- and net-layers, 101 minesweepers, 11 gunboats, 16 patrol ships, 51 combat motorboats, and also 152 auxiliaries.[8]

In comparison, at the beginning of the revolution in 1917 the Imperial Russian Fleet had on active service 18 battleships, 14 cruisers, 84 destroyers and torpedo-boat destroyers, 22 torpedo boats, 41 submarines, 45 mine- and net-layers, 160 minesweepers, 11 gunboats, 110 patrol ships, and 42 combat motorboats.[9]

The overall displacement of the *RKKF*'s main combatants was only 16.2 per cent from the overall displacement of the Russian Imperial Fleet, because 77 per cent of the largest combatants such as battleships, cruisers and *Novik*-class destroyers had been lost or put out of action. Sixty-one per cent of the most modern ships, built between 1910 and 1917 had been lost.[10] The continued fighting in the Far East had no effect on the Navy, because no ships were left there.

In the Baltic the Russian Fleet was reduced to one serviceable battleship, one old cruiser, 9 *Novik* destroyers, 4 smaller torpedo-boat destroyers, 11 submarines, and many damaged vessels or remnants of obsolete classes of ships. These could not be repaired or modernized, nor could the unfinished new vessels be finished, owing to lack of funds. Up until 1925 most of them had to be sold for scrap, even three of the launched but laid-up hulls of new big battlecruisers. The *Borodino*, *Navarin*, and *Kinburn*, together with some other vessels such as the old armoured cruisers *Gromoboi*, *Admiral Makarov* and *Bayan*, had to be sold to Germany in 1922/23 for scrap in order to obtain some foreign currency.[11] The new-found independence of Finland and the Baltic states in the meantime bottled up the few seaworthy ships in the innermost waters of the Gulf of Finland.

In the Black Sea, the last operational vessels, especially the modern battleship *General Alekseev*, had sailed with the remnants of the Vrangel Army to Istanbul and then to Bizerte. Only unserviceable wrecks, one cruiser and one submarine in a damaged state, and some unfinished vessels remained behind.[12] Similarly, only one obsolete small destroyer and one submarine were left in the Arctic with the evacuation of the Allied intervention troops. They had taken off some of the vessels there, like the old battleship *Chesme*, and the cruisers *Varyag* and *Askold*. In the Caspian Sea there were ten smaller torpedo-boat destroyers, four submarines and four gunboats.[13]

These facts resulted in a serious reduction of the combat potential of the *RKKF*. In 1917 the summary weight of main calibre (8–12in) guns pro salvo was 44,720kg or 60 per cent of the summary weight of the main calibre gun salvo of the German 'High Seas Fleet' in 1916. There were only twelve 12in guns aboard the sole operational *RKKF* battleship *Marat* (ex-*Petropavlovsk*) in 1921. Practically all combat ships needed repairs of some kind or another, and the largest surface ships were in need of capital repair and modernization.

There were 441 coastal guns in 1917, including 262 in the Baltic, 158 in the Black Sea, and 21 in the Arctic. By the end of the Civil War and the foreign intervention in Russia (1918–20) the overall number of coastal guns was only 154, including 88 in the Baltic and 66 in the Black Sea. The Arctic coastal artillery was completely lost. The state of the guns and equipment of the coastal artillery was evaluated as unsatisfactory. The most essential of the losses in the Baltic was a sharp reduction in the 'sea defence depth'. The distance from Petrograd to the front line of the 'Main Defence Position', preventing an enemy invasion from the sea, was shortened from 280 nautical miles (500km) to 50 nautical miles (90km).

Naval Aviation was deleted from the *RKKF*. Its small formations in the Baltic and the Black Sea remained only in operative subordination to the naval commanders. By 1921 the total number of naval planes in Russia was 36 old ones.

The distressing state of the Red Navy was caused by the deep crisis which had spread over the whole country. The economy was disrupted by 'war communism'[14] and economic experiments by the Bolshevik Party. It was impossible to keep the Red Fleet ships in technical and combat readiness, when the Russian industry was in ruins. In 1921 Soviet shipbuilding yards produced only 8 per cent of the 1913 level.

The elaboration of long-term plans for the Navy's restoration and development were at first prevented also by the military-political situation which had formed in the world at the beginning of the 1920s. The so-called 'Versailles' system was clearly unstable. At the start of its creation the Soviet State was completely excluded from the process of discussing and elaborating the most important decisions on problems of international security, including negotiations on naval arms limitation.

The RKKF *and International and National Politics*

During the 1920s the Soviet leadership was seeking ways to compensate for the deterioration in its strategic situation on the seas, at first by trying to get a favourable international legal regime for its own littorals, and also to participate on equal rights in negotiations on naval armament limitations. However, these attempts were doomed to failure, because the Soviet government had then no diplomatic relations with the Allied powers, and the Soviet state was too weak to be recognized as important by the Great Powers. In 1921–22 Soviet Russia was not invited to the conference at Washington on naval arms reduction, which brought the ratio for battleships and aircraft carriers for Great Britain, the United States, Japan, France and Italy to 5:5:3:1.75:1.75. Germany and Soviet Russia remained excluded, but they had concluded a treaty on 16 April 1922 at Rapallo which restored diplomatic relations and provided a structure on which to reconstruct economic relations.[15] Again at the Lausanne conference in 1922–23 the Soviet delegation was not able to insist that combat ships be prohibited from passing Black Sea exits, despite the fact that such a decision would be of vital importance for the interests of the Soviet Union. But the Great Powers did not find it necessary or possible to consider those interests at this time.

Besides that, the Soviet Navy's development was influenced by subjective reasons:

- The lack of unity in the opinions of the Soviet highest political and military leadership about the main political aims, and the strategic and operational character of a future war
- The utopian character of the Bolshevik Party's doctrine, based on the theory of 'World Revolution' and the concept of an 'armed people', which diverted thinking away from the search for adequate forms and methods to defend the national interests
- The uncompleted analytical work and theoretical research on the experience of sea warfare during 1914–18
- The absence of significant navies in the neighbouring states and, as a consequence, the feeling that there was no direct threat from the sea
- The low level of theoretical and practical education of the high-level military leaders promoted during the October Revolution and the Civil War
- A lack of understanding about the nature of naval activities and its importance for the development of the Soviet state by its leaders
- The lack of trust in the loyalty of the commanders' corps of the Navy, in which, at the beginning of the 1920s, 80 per cent were former Imperial Russian naval officers.[16]

In 1922–23 the Soviet government undertook measures which resulted in important qualitative changes in the priorities of military construction. These had immediate effects on the status, combat efficiency and also personnel strength of the Navy.

The measures were:

- A significant reduction in Navy personnel from 86,560 men in March 1921 to 36,929 by December 1921
- A curtailment of the Navy's share in general military expenditure to 8.7–9.7 per cent, and a sharp reduction in appropriations for shipbuilding and repairs from 26.1 to 8 million rubles (70 per cent)
- The elimination of the post of Commander-in-Chief of the Republic's Naval Forces, and the abolition of the Naval General Staff
- A 'filtration' (political purge) of naval personnel, which resulted in the illegal repression of more than 400 former Imperial officers

- The initiation of three mobilizations, during which 1,900 Party members and 4,600 members of the *Komsomol'* (the Communist Young League) were called up into the Navy.

Objective analysis shows that those measures were contradictory in character, and their long-term consequences exercised both positive and negative influences on subsequent developments in the Navy. But first of all it should be noted that the results expected by the Party and the Soviet state leadership were basically achieved. The Soviet leaders prevented the complete loss of combat ships, auxiliaries, and naval bases. The descent into moral corruption of the Red Fleet personnel was stopped.

In 1921–23 the shipbuilding yards completed one destroyer, two submarines, and finished the restoration of one battleship, four destroyers, one submarine, five gunboats, seven minesweepers, and two combat motorboats. At least 171 combat units and 172 auxiliaries underwent repairs.[17] The system of educating and training personnel was fully restored. From 1922 normal training processes and naval activities were renewed. By the end of 1923 the Baltic Fleet had twice conducted naval manoeuvres, and the Black Sea Fleet once. During this period Soviet ships made 40 cruises, including three cruises in the high seas.

The minesweeping formations of the Navy completed minesweeping operations in the Soviet littorals, covering 1,422.9sq. nautical miles and swept 345 mines.

All this testified that as a result of the measures undertaken conditions in the Navy were starting to normalize. But some negative trends did continue – in particular the reduction in the number of ships. In 1922–24, 180 units were struck from the active list and sent to the scrapyard.[18] As mentioned, there were even some new and unfinished ships sent to be scrapped in Germany, like the three launched but laid-up battlecruisers. Twenty-nine units were transferred to the Sea Border Guard.

Changes in the Personnel Situation

Filtration, purges and the desire to increase the proportion of 'working-class' representatives among the higher and senior naval commanders resulted in significant changes in the 'social origin' of the command personnel. The number of 'old' officers was quickly and steadily reduced. In 1922 the share of commanding personnel from 'workers' was 8.4 per cent, from 'peasants' 20.4 per cent, and 'others' 71.2 per cent. By 1926 the figures had changed to 'workers' 15.7 per cent, 'peasants' 35.9 per cent, and 'others' 48.4 per cent. But these changes caused problems of another sort. In 1924 the shortage in the commanding corps was about 24 per cent, and remained so over the following years. There was a steady drop in the general level of education and professional abilities of the commanding officers, including the superior commanders. For example, V.I. Zof, the Chief of the Soviet Navy from 1924 to 1926, and his successor R.A. Muklevich were both Party functionaries, who had not even received primary naval education. Trying to minimize the negative consequences of such a policy, Soviet leaders decided to step up the naval school system and the number of naval students in order to raise the educational level of the commanding personnel. In the spring of 1922 the Naval Academy renewed its work. By a decision of the Party's Central Committee (TsK) a special preparatory course was introduced for Red Navy commanders who had participated in the Civil War from 1918 to 1920. But only 9.6 per cent of students from the first set had received higher education and about 19 per cent had not even graduated from high school.

Strategic Considerations

In consequence of this lack of adequate education and experience, the Soviet Naval authorities could not formulate a real plan for the development of the Navy, without using the expertise of the remaining 'old' officers. The first drafts of the strategic missions of the Soviet Navy were presented in the explanatory notes for the restoration programmes elaborated at the beginning of the 1920s. At first the prospective strategic missions were formulated in February 1921 by the authors of the draft called 'The Decree for the Re-establishment of the Sea Power of the Republic'.[19] In accordance with this decree the Red Fleet should have been able to carry out:

- Operations to defend the sea borders of the Soviet state
- Operations to defend sea communications
- Operations to support Red Army troops.

The main sea theatre was considered to be the Baltic, where the Red Fleet should be able to achieve 'mastery of the sea'. The authors of the draft thought that it was possible, because the Imperial German Fleet had been annihilated and the navies of the other Baltic powers were not comparable with the Soviet Baltic Fleet. It was assumed to be enough to create a number of mine-artillery positions on the eastern approaches of the Baltic Strait zone to prevent the main sea powers from interfering in the struggle between the Red Fleet and the navies of the Baltic states.

A similar plan was worked out for the Black Sea Fleet. The achievement of 'mastery of the sea' and a blockade of the Bosporus were considered the main strategic aims there. These were believed to be achievable in the future.

The Soviet High Command stated that the Arctic and Pacific Oceans would be very important in the future, but in the mid-1920s it was thought possible to abstain from the deployment of naval formations in the Arctic and the Far East until the restoration of Soviet industry. They believed that a temporary loss of those areas would not pose a mortal threat to the Bolshevik government.

In August 1921 the members of the Navy Reorganization Committee, including Trotskii, Kamenev, Nemits, Gusev and Zof, affirmed the main strategic missions of the Soviet Navy.[20]

In the Baltic:

- the support of the *Karelskii Front* operations
- the education of personnel for the future Navy.

In the Black Sea:
- to maintain a strong coastal defence.

In the Caspian Sea:
- to maintain 'mastery of the sea'.

In the Arctic:
- to defend the fishery
- to defend the two main areas in the mouth of the Northern Dvina and the Kola Peninsula.

For the first time, the basic idea of the Soviet Navy's application was outlined in autumn 1921 by Nemits, the Commander-in-Chief of the Red Fleet and Chairman of the Naval Branch of the 'Military Industry Re-creation Committee'. Nemits suggested that the rest of the old fleet be deployed to defend the coastal flanks of the Red Army and to create powerful defence positions in front of Kronshtadt. It should, he said, be possible to equip the defence positions with 465mm coastal guns, new mines, powerful formations of modern submarines, seaplane units and only small surface-ship formations.

Manoeuvres

The plans were tested during the first naval training operations. The first manoeuvres of the Baltic Fleet took place in the autumn of 1922. The sole battleship, eight destroyers, four submarines, eleven minesweepers, eleven airplanes, the Kronshtadt fortress garrison, and Sea-Guard formations (one destroyer, seven patrol ships, a minesweeper, a motorboat and several coastal guard posts) had

- to weaken the enemy fleet before it approached the forward defence position
- to fight against the enemy squadron in the forward defensive position as far as possible, but if the enemy should penetrate the forward defensive position not to allow the enemy fleet to approach Kronshtadt
- not to allow an enemy landing at any point situated east of the Krasnoflotskii Fort.

In September 1923 the Navy's readiness was tested with regard to carrying out landing operations supporting the Red Army formations which were in action at the seashore. At the same time the Red Navy had to prevent an enemy penetration into the eastern part of the Gulf of Finland.

The possibilities of repulsing an enemy amphibious operation against the Crimea were tested during manoeuvres of the Black Sea Fleet in November 1923. At the same time the Caspian Flotilla carried out some training for landing operations in support of the Army from the coastline.

But the high-ranking Soviet commanding officers could not give assurances that the Red Navy was able to carry out its main strategic missions. In their opinion, the Navy needed well-trained and experienced personnel, new surface combat ships and submarines, a modern coastal defence and a naval aviation. At the same time they believed that the leaders of the state and the Bolshevik Party just after the restoration of the Soviet economy would allocate more funds to the development of the Navy. On 8 November 1923 the Revolutionary War Council (*RVS*) approved the establishment of a Scientific-Technical Committee (*NTK*) to solve the problems of the administration and the pre-projects for new shipbuilding. As chairman of the former, *Kontr Admiral* P.N. Leskov was nominated. The Committee had several sections for artillery, shipbuilding, mine warfare, one mechanical-electrical section and one for submerged operations, one for communications and one physico-chemical section. Until 1925–27 the principles of Soviet naval strategy corresponded with the 'classical school' and there was a gap between the theory and the ships available. The most prominent theorists of the Red Fleet, such as the author of the Naval Tactical Manual and the first draft of the Naval Battle Instructions, M.A. Petrov, and the professor of the Naval Academy, B.B. Zherve, asserted that battleships would play the decisive role in future sea warfare.

The Restoration of Ships

Apart from the efforts to solve the personnel problems and to develop a strategic concept, the main emphasis was put on rebuilding ships for active service. The 'Decree of the Re-establishment of the Sea Power of the Republic', presented by some of the *spetsialists* as early as February 1921, proposed rebuilding the four existing battleships of the *Gangut*-class, which were in great need of repair, finishing the last battlecruiser *Izmail'*, as well as four unfinished light cruisers of the *Svetlana*-class and five 1,300-ton destroyers of the *Novik*-type, and keeping in active service one pre-*Dreadnought*-battleship *Andrej Pervozvannyi*, the old cruiser *Avrora*, nine destroyers of the *Novik*-type and 16 600-ton destroyers built between 1906 and 1909, for the Naval Forces of the Baltic Sea.

In the Black Sea the situation was worse, because the last serviceable ships had left in late 1920 with the Vrangel squadron – of one battleship, one cruiser and five destroyers – for Bizerte, where they were interned in December 1920. Only the old cruiser *Pamyat merkuriya* could be re-commissioned in 1922 as *Komintern*. Besides the wrecks of old battleships and smaller vessels there were some unfinished ships, one battleship, four cruisers and eight unfinished or scuttled modern destroyers available, which could be finished, salvaged or repaired.

However, the plan had to be reduced in scale, owing to the situation in the shipbuilding yards and the lack of financial funds. Most of the unfinished ships had to be sold – as previously mentioned – for scrap in Germany in order to obtain some foreign currency or be scrapped in Russia. The following example illustrates the reluctance of the government. On 29 October 1924 the Chief of the Naval Forces (*Voenno-morskie sily* – *VMS*) of the Red Workers and Peasants Army (*Raboche-krest'yanskaya Armiya* – *RKKA*), E.S. Pantserzhankii, obtained the approval of the Council of Labour and Defence (*Sovet Truda i Oborony* – *STO*) for the general repair and completion of two cruisers and five destroyers from the pre-war programmes. Up to 1925 only three battleships, two cruisers, and 14 destroyers in the Baltic could be restored to active service, some of which had to undergo general repairs for some years. The old small destroyers had to be scrapped. In the Black Sea only two of the cruisers and five of the destroyers were finally commissioned, the last cruiser not until 1931.[21]

But other plans were prepared. One proposed the rebuilding of two of the damaged or unfinished battleships, converting the unfinished battlecruiser into an aircraft carrier, finishing four of the unfinished cruisers and five destroyers, and bringing home the ships of the Vrangel squadron. In December 1924 a commission with the shipbuilding engineer A.N. Krylov and the former Chief of the Naval Forces E.A. Berens was sent to Bizerte to ascertain the state of the ships before entering into negotiations for their restitution. However, they found the ships in poor condition, and so nothing came of this expedition. The ships were finally scrapped in France.[22]

Another plan envisaged the building of eight new battleships, 16 cruisers and more than 40 destroyers. And during the conference at Rome in February 1924 of the sea powers not represented at the Washington Naval Conference in 1921–22, the Soviet delegate, E.A. Berens, proposed a battleship tonnage of 491,000 tons, almost as much as the 525,000 tons allowed to Great Britain and the United States.[23] Some *spetsialists* in the Soviet Navy were planning an ocean-going homogeneous fleet with all types of warships, able to compete with the fleets of the other sea powers.

The first real planning for new naval shipbuilding began after Pantserzhanskii was replaced by Zof as Chief of the *VMS RKKA* in December 1924. A leading role during the development of the programmes was played by some former officers of the Imperial Fleet, such as S.P. Blinov, the Chief of Staff of the *VMS*, and A.A. Toshakov, Head of the Operational Department of the Staff. A five-year project for the strengthening of the *VMS* was prepared under Toshakov and presented in March 1925. It was based on the experiences of the Great War and took industrial capacity into consideration. For the active defence of the coasts of the USSR in the Baltic and the Black Sea strong homogeneous fleets were needed. In the Baltic it was proposed to have six battleships, including four new ones, four monitors, eight cruisers, two aircraft carriers, 28 destroyers, 17 submarines, 36 motor torpedo boats and 36 patrol cutters as well as three minelayers. For the Black Sea the proposal contained four battleships (two new ones), four cruisers, one aircraft carrier, 12 destroyers, 17 submarines, 24 motor torpedo boats, 36 patrol cutters, and two minelayers. The authors of the project proposed dispensing with a fleet in the Far East for the time being, but strengthening the Amur Flotilla somewhat by eight gunboats or river monitors, six armoured cutters and two minelayers. For the Caspian Flotilla it was considered enough to have the two existing destroyers and two gunboats.[24]

Such numbers were the first and maximum variant of the plan. The second variant, co-ordinated with the industry, was cut down to solve only the minimum needs for the actual tasks for the fleets. This variant had 165 combat ships and cutters to be built from scratch or reconstructed. By 1931 the fleet should then have four battleships, four cruisers, one aircraft carrier, and 162 smaller vessels as well as 40 submarines. On 31 March 1925 Zof and

Blinov presented the variants to the chairman of the *RVS* and the *Narkom* for the Army and Navy M.V. Frunze for their approval. It would include the restoration of the battleship *Frunze* (ex-*Poltava*), badly damaged by a fire in November 1919, and the completion of the battlecruiser *Izmail'*. Besides capital ships they wanted about 100 ocean-going ships for the Red Navy at the beginning of the 1930s. The leaders of the fleet argued that the proposals rather than the postponed measures to replace the ships and submarines up to 1930 should be condemned. In an appendix they also presented the tactical elements of the ships, worked out by the Chief of the Operational Department A.A. Toshakov. But this plan was rejected. Frunze declared: 'We have turned down an aggressive naval policy, so we shall construct only a defensive navy, consisting of small vessels.'[25]

On 6 April 1925, Zof also sent a plan for the finishing, ordnance and modernization of ships of the *VMS RKKA* and for the supplying of the ships with fuel and other items to the same people. It envisaged the repair and modernization of three battleships, 12 destroyers and 14 submarines, as well as the completion of two cruisers and other ships. On 4 June 1925 Zof's deputy assistant, V.I. Bzhezinskij, presented to the *STO* a new plan for a naval programme covering the years 1925–26 to 1930–31, containing for the Baltic Fleet ten new 4,000t destroyers, 10 1,300t submarines, two minelaying submarines, four small monitors, 36 motor torpedo boats, 18 patrol vessels and 14 minesweepers. For the Black Sea he proposed 11 1,300t submarines, two minelaying submarines, 24 motor torpedo boats, 18 patrol vessels and 14 minesweepers. Finally he requested the completion of the battlecruiser *Izmail'* and the battleship *Frunze* as aircraft carriers, and the cruisers *Admiral Butakov* and *Admiral Lazarev* as minelaying cruisers.[26]

Both projects were discussed for some time, despite the fact that the government, the Chairman of the *STO* and the Council of the People's Commissars (*Sovet Narodnykh Komissarov SSSR – SNK SSSR*) A.I. Rykov and the *Narkom* for the Army and Navy Frunze accepted in principle the important political and military role of a strong fleet and therefore supported plans for its reinforcement. So on 6 July 1925 Rykov approved the rebuilding of an aircraft carrier, the completion of two cruisers, the repair and modernization of two battleships and of the Amur gunboats.[27]

But the proposals of the naval leaders to start the building of new ships in early 1926 were strongly opposed by the *RKKA* staff, who proposed retention of the existing ships and the limitation of new building to MTBs and patrol cutters, thus giving priority to the strengthening of the Army.

NOTES

1. N. Vasetskii, 'Kronshtadt skimyatazh vzglyad skvoz' gody', *Morskoi sbornik*, No. 3 (1991), pp. 79–86.
2. Manfred Hildermeier, *Geschichte der Sowjetunion 1917–1991*, Munich, Beck, 1998, pp. 157–232.
3. Dmitrii Volkogonov, *Lev Trotskii. Politicheskii portret*, Moscow, 1992, pp. 9–11.
4. *Krasnyi Flot*, No. 8 (1925), p. 5.
5. V.D. Dotsenko, *Morskoi biograficheskij slovar'*, St Petersburg, Logos, 1995. *Voenno-morskoi slovar*,

ed. V.N. Chernavin, Moscow, Voenizdat, 1990, pp. 218, 303. B. Evgrafov, 'Dvaventsa a admirala Levchenko', *Morskoi sbornik*, No. 11 (1990), pp. 82–97. D. Volkogonov, *Lev Trotskii*, op. cit., pp. 229–72. Letter of S. Zonin to J. Rohwer. Changes between 1920 and 1926 in the position of the Commanding Chief of the Naval Forces of the Republic: E.A. Berens (05.19–02.20), A.V. Nemits (02.20–12.21), E.S. Pantserzhanskii (12.21–12.24), V.I. Zof (12.24–08.26). For the Commander of the Naval Forces in the Baltic Sea they were: A.P. Zelenoi (01.19–06.20), F.F. Raskol'nikov (07.20–01.21), V.A. Kukel' (01.21–3.21), I.K. Kozhanov (03.21–05.21), M.V. Viktorov (05.21–06.24), A.K. Vekman (06.24–26). For the Commander of the Naval Forces of the Black Sea and the Azov Sea they were: M.F. Izmailov (03.20–05.20), A.V. Dombrovskii (04.20–12.20), E.S. Pantserzhanskii (12.20–12.21), A.S. Maksimov (12.21–08.22), A.K. Vekman (08.22–06.24), M.V. Viktorov (06.–12.24), E.S. Pantserzhanskii (01.25–10.26). For the Commander of the Naval Forces of the Caspian Sea they were: E.S. Pantserzhanskii (11.20–12.20), S.A. Kvitskii (12.20–12.21), I.M. Ludri (08.21–07.23), P.M. Mikhailov (07.23–05.26).

6. B.B. Zherve, 'Flot segodnyashnego dnia. Boevye sredstva', *Krasnyi Flot*, Feb. 1922. M.A. Petrov, 'Zametki o taktike malogo flota', *Morskoi sbornik*, No. 9 (1925), pp. 45–61. Robert W. Herrick, op. cit., pp. 9–18. M.S. Monakov, 'Sud'by doktrin i teorii', op. cit., pt 2, pp. 17–23.
7. *Boevoy put' Sovetskogo Voenno-morskogo flota*, 3rd edn, ed. Vasilii Achkasov and Aleksei Basov *et al.*, Moscow, Voenizdat, 1974, pp. 128–30.
8. Rossijskii Gosudarstvennyi Arkhiv Voenno-Morskogo Flota (RGA VMF), formerly Tsentral'nyj Gosudarstvennyj Arkhiv Voenno-Morskogo Flota (TsGA VMF). St Petersburg, F. r-1, op.1, d.669; II 1, 156, 162–3, 239–41; f. r-5, op.4, d.1, II, 50–53, f. r-307, op.2, d.14, II, 14–17, 19–22, 27–9, 33–4. Siegfried Breyer, op. cit., vol. I, *Oktoberrevolution und maritimes Erbe*, Herford, Mittler, 1987.
9. Ministerstvo Oborony SSSR. Voenno-morskoi flot, *Korabli i Vspomogatelnye Suda Sovetskogo Voenno-Morskogo, Flota (1917–1927). Spravochnik*, ed. S.S. Berezhnoi, Moscow, Voenizdat, 1981.
10. Igor Amosov and Jürgen Rohwer, 'Strange Parallels in Stalin's and Hitler's Naval Programmes', paper written for a presentation at the Naval History Symposium at the US naval Academy, Annapolis, MD, Oct. 1993.
11. Siegfried Breyer, op. cit., Vol. I.
12. Ibid.
13. Ibid.
14. Manfred Hildermeier, op. cit., pp. 134–56.
15. Tobias R. Philbin, *The Lure of Neptune: German–Soviet Naval Collaboration and Ambitions, 1919–1941*, Columbia, SC, University of South Carolina Press, 1994, pp. 6–7. Olaf Groehler, *Selbstmörderische Allianz. Deutsch–russische Militärbeziehungen 1920–1941*, Berlin, Vision, 1992, pp. 34–5.
16. *Rossijskii Gosudarstvennyi Arkhiv Voenno-Morskogo Flota* (RGA VMF), f. r-1483, op.1, d.65, l.5 – N.Yu. Berezovskii, S.S. Berezhnoi and Z.V. Nikolaeva, *Boevaya Letopis Voenno-Morskogo Flota 1917–1941*, Moscow, Voenizdat, 1992, pp. 473, 474, 498, 501–2, 514, 517.
17. S.S. Berezhnoi, op. cit.
18. Included in the Baltic were the pre-dreadnought-battleships *Respublika* (ex-*Imperator Pavel I*), *Andrej Pervosvannyi*, *Grazhdanin* (ex-*Tsesarevich*), *Zarja Svobody* (ex-*Imperator Aleksandr II*), the armoured cruisers *Rjurik*, *Bayan*, *Admiral Makarov*, *Gromoboi*, *Rossiya*, and the protected cruisers *Diana* and *Bogatyr*, as well as the older destroyers and torpedo boats. In the Black Sea most of the older ships were damaged during the occupation of Sevastopol by the Allies and also scrapped the pre-dreadnought battleships *Revolutsiya* (ex-*Svjatoi Evstafi*), *Ioann Slatoust*, *Tri Svjatitel'ya*, *Boretsza Svobodu* (ex-*Pantelejmon*), *Rostislav*, and *Sinop*, as well as the smaller destroyers, torpedo boats and so on. See S.S. Berezhnoi (ed.), *Korabli i Vspomogatel'nye Suda Sovetskogo Voenno-morskogo (1917–1927gg)*, Moscow, Voenizdat, 1981 – Siegfried Breyer, op. cit.
19. *Rossijskii Gosudarstvennyi Voennyi Arkhiv* (RG VA), f.33988, op.1, d.436, l.50-51 – *Istoriya Otechestvennogo Sudostroeniya. Vol. IV: Sudostroenie v period pervykh pjatiletok i Velikoi Otechestvennoi vojny 1925–1945 gg*, ed. I.D. Spasskii, St Petersburg, Sudostroenie, 1996, p. 14.
20. RG VA, f.33988, op.2, d.314, l.19-33.

21. Sergei S. Berezhnoi (ed.), *Korabli i vspomogatel'nye suda Sovetskogo Voenno-morskogo flota (1917–1927), Spravochnik*, Moscow, Voenizdat, 1981, pp. 14–32, 170–9. Sergei S. Berezhnoi, *Korabli i suda VMF SSSR 1928–1945, Spravochnik*, Moscow, Voenizdat, 1988, pp. 16–39. *Istoriya Otechestvennogo Sudostroeniya*, ed. Igor Spasskii, Vol. III: *Sudostroenie v nachale XX vv.*, St Petersburg, Sudostroenie, 1995, pp. 487, 492, 497, 503, 507–9.18. Op. cit., vol. IV: *Sudostroenie v period Pervikh Pyatiletki i Velikoi Otechestvennoit voyny 1925–1945gg.*, St Petersburg, Sudostroenie, 1996, pp. 142–3.
22. Siegfried Breyer, op. cit., vol. 1.
23. League of Nations, Official Journal, 21 February 1924, pp. 708–10.
24. *Istoriya Otechestvennogo Sudostroeniya*, op. cit., vol. IV, p. 15.
25. RG VA, f.4, op.2, d.98, l.265-77.
26. J.N. Westwood, *Russian Naval Construction, 1905–1941*, London, Macmillan, 1994, pp. 138–9.
27. *Istoriya Otechestvennogo Sudostroeniya*, op. cit., vol. IV, p. 16.

4

The Consolidation Phase, 1925–32

STALIN ON HIS WAY TO DICTATORSHIP

Since Lenin's illness, it was obvious that a power struggle in the leadership had started. After Lenin's death on 24 January 1924, during the XIIIth Party Congress a new Politburo was elected: L.B. Kamenev became the chairman, his deputy was G.E. Zinov'ev, A.I. Rykov became chairman of the *SNK SSSR*, other important leaders were members such as Trotskii as *Narkom* for the Army and Navy, Bukharin and Tomskii, chief of the labour organization. Stalin as Secretary General of the *KP(b)* was also a member, but not in the first place. Yet he had the organizational centre of the Party at his disposal. Step by step he eliminated his rivals for leadership from their positions of power. First he joined with Kamenev and Zinov'ev against his most potent competitor Trotskii, who was forced to retire from his position as *Narkom* for the Army and Navy on 17 January 1925, to be replaced – as mentioned – by Frunze.

At the XIVth Party Conference in March/April 1925 Stalin defended the theory of 'Socialism in one country' against Trotskii's theory of permanent revolution. At the XIVth Party Congress in December 1925 Stalin initiated a major campaign for the industrialization of the country and attacked the 'left opposition' around Zinov'ev and Kamenev, who now tried to join up with Trotskii. But in October 1926 Stalin managed to eject Trotskii from the Politburo, and one year later he and Zinov'ev were ejected from the *Tsentral'nyi Komitet (TsK,* Central Committee*)*, while during the XVth Party Congress in December 1927 they were expelled from the Party. Trotskii was exiled to Alma Ata. Zinov'ev and Kamenev submitted themselves to Stalin, but he was only waiting to finish with them. At the same congress the 'Socialist Build-Up' was decided, translating itself into forced industrialization and the forced collectivization of agriculture which led to organized purges of the *kulaks*, the peasant farmers. The resistance, especially in the Don and Kuban districts in 1928/29, was broken up by the deportation of the *kulaks*, many of whom had to go to the new industrial areas in the Urals or Siberia, such as the big metallurgic centre of Magnitogorsk. But the repression of the *kulaks* led to a grave famine with a very great number of victims.

Next Stalin started to subdue the 'deviation to the right' by Bukharin and Rykov, who were heavily reprimanded at the XVIth Party Congress in April

1929. From this time on Stalin was the absolute dictator, against whom nobody dared stand in opposition.[1]

NEW DISCUSSIONS ABOUT STRATEGY

In spite of the stabilization of the Soviet regime the discussions about military and naval strategy continued and did not become any clearer. In early 1924 the outstanding Chief of Staff of the *RKKA* M.N. Tukhachevskii declared: 'Tsarist Russia followed Germany. Imperialistic dreams caused the excessive development of the Navy. The involvement in the naval armament race was a fatal error for Germany, Austria and Russia.'[2] He and his Chief of the Operations Department, V.K. Triandafillov, proposed as a defence in case of an attack by the 'bourgeois' powers mass counterattacks by mobile forces striking deep into enemy territory to crush the enemy's forces beyond the borders of Russia.[3] Their suggestions were to cut down on naval expenditures and allocate funds only to the build-up of the Army and the Air Forces. Some of the Soviet functionaries accepted these proposals with great enthusiasm, because there were reasons to choose such a course of military policy.

In this period the international situation around the USSR was gradually improving. But the contradictions inherent in the post-war world order, and the ideological incompatibility of the two social systems caused dangerous crises, ending in explosions of hostility on both sides. The situation on the borders with Poland, Romania, Afghanistan and China remained tense. Anti-Soviet organizations operated in those countries. There were military camps and logistic bases of terrorist formations, which from time to time penetrated into the border areas of the Soviet Union. The threat of incursions forced the Soviet leaders to maintain the *RKKA* troops. The tenfold reduction in the strength of the Army after the Civil War and the low combat readiness were evaluated as the principal threats to the regime's stability and the security of the state. Separate measures for partial improvements in the work of the military establishment and in the defence structure of the country did not produce the necessary effect. The situation demanded decisive measures for a complete reorganization.

In January 1924 by a decision of the Bolshevik Party's Central Committee (*Tsentral'nyi Komitet VKP (b) – TsK VKP (b)*) – a special commission inspected the Red Army. The verdict of the commission members was that: 'In the present state the Red Army is not combat ready'.[4]

In May 1924 the XIIIth Party Congress confirmed the general directives for carrying out radical military reforms. On 26 January 1925 the People's Commissar for the Army and Navy, L.D. Trotskii was replaced by the prominent Soviet military leader M.V. Frunze, who had distinguished himself during the Civil War of 1918–20. Whereas Trotskii never gave up his cherished dream of a continuous revolution in Europe, or even world-wide, which would be supported by the Red Army acting as a workers' militia, Frunze looked to conventional military power. He saw a standing army as the only means of waging some kind of limited war. He attempted to develop a unified military and naval doctrine, called the 'proletarian military doctrine'.[5]

In the course of this reform the Soviet armed forces adopted new principles of recruitment and maintenance, based on a combination of regular and so-called 'territorial militia formations'. The Red Army rules of conduct were generally reorganized. At the same time the organizational structures and formations, units and logistic services were radically changed. A firm order for supplying the troops and forces was established. During those years the system of military education was further developed, an annual call-up for military service was introduced, and the system of personal combat and political education was firmly established. On 18 September 1925 a law on obligatory military service was voted in. The troops received new regulations and manuals. The new plan for the development of the Army and Navy was confirmed.

But Frunze did not accept Tukhachevskii's proposals concerning the Red Navy, saying: 'We could not stop our naval development.'[6] So new plans were required to match the development of new strategic concepts for the Navy. B.B. Zherve was one of the first men to see the need for the systematic re-examination of the use of Soviet naval forces. Similarly, in an address to the Naval College in 1925, the Chief of the Naval Forces, V.I. Zof, who had replaced E.S. Pantserzhanskii on 9 December 1924, reminded the audience of the impossibility of satisfying the demands of those who championed the classical theories of sea power, some of whom had even asked for aircraft carriers, using designs based on the hulls of the unfinished battlecruiser *Izmail*' or on a reconstruction of the training ship *Komsomolets*.[7]

In June 1925 manoeuvres of the Baltic Fleet took place. The exercises were observed by the *Narkom* for Military and Naval Affairs and the Chairman of the *STO*, M.V. Frunze. From 20 to 24 September 1925 the Baltic Fleet's readiness to solve the operational tasks 'according to the fourth version of the campaign plan' was examined. The Baltic Fleet carried out training operations

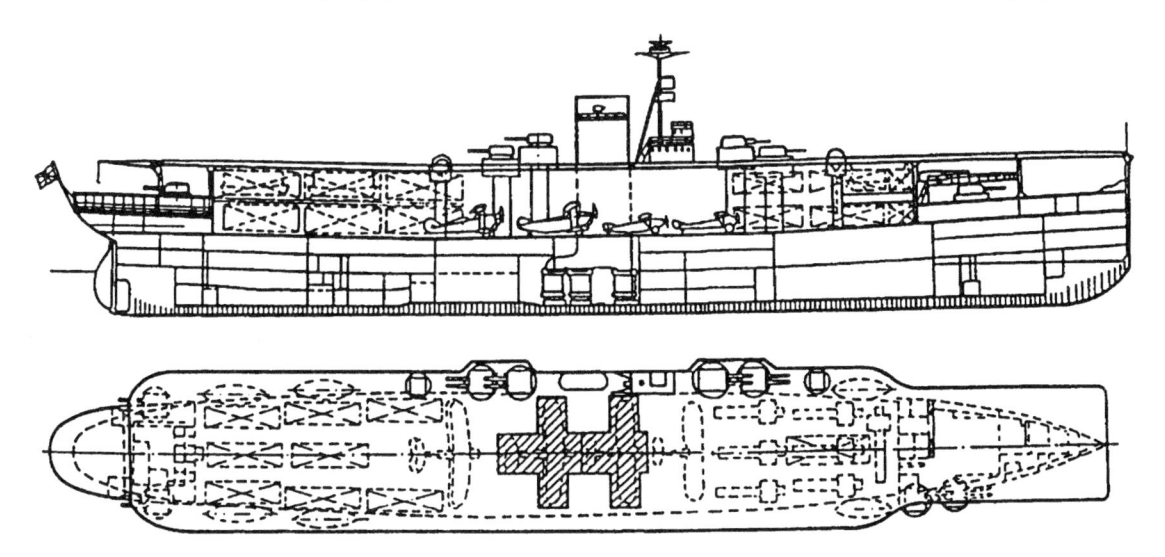

Fig. 1. Aircraft carrier project *Komsomolets*, 1927, displ. 12,000t stdd., length 143.2m, max. speed 15kt, 42 planes, 16 10.2cm, 10 4cm. Former training ship, only planned, never realized. Credit: Sudostroenie

against the 'Polish Navy', not supported by the navies of the 'Great Entente' states. Then the Baltic Fleet units conducted a training sea battle with forces of the 'British and French Navies'.

In the Black Sea the manoeuvres were conducted from 25 to 29 August 1925. In the first phase of the manoeuvres the Black Sea Fleet was examined on its readiness to conduct active operations off the Romanian shore and in the second phase on the plan for the defence of the main base jointly with the garrison of the Sevastopol fortress. The Caspian Flotilla had to master the conducting of amphibious operations again.

The manoeuvres of the Navy in 1925 in comparison with some of the exercises in previous years were much more complex. In particular, the September manoeuvres in the Baltic saw the participation of the battleship brigade (two ships), the destroyer division (four ships), the submarine brigade (seven units), the gunboat squadron (two units), the minelayer and minesweeper brigade (two minelayers and four minesweepers), a naval aviation group, observation posts, the garrison of the Kronshtadt Fortress and main base formations on the 'Red Side'. The 'enemy forces' consisted of a cruiser, two destroyers, four minesweepers, two submarines, a training ship and a hydroplane flight.

All units of the Black Sea Fleet were supporting amphibious forces (two naval infantry battalions of the 51st Infantry Division), two artillery platoons and also one platoon of horse-scouts as well as one communications platoon).

The results of the manoeuvres were studied and the conclusions became the basis for the essential definition of the Navy's application plan and the shipbuilding programme. It was especially determined that the Baltic Fleet needed more battleships than it had. It was also found that the Baltic Fleet could not resolve its operational tasks because of the absence of new light cruisers and destroyers, naval aviation and aircraft carriers 'which allowed the use of modern means of sea warfare'.[8] It was also noted that the naval aviation in the Baltic was unfit for action because of a shortage of land-based airplanes. In the opinion of the Soviet Naval Staff officers the Baltic Fleet formations could not conduct a successful defensive combat, notwithstanding the mine covering and the support by the coastal artillery of the Kronshtadt Fortress. The same results were analysed after the manoeuvres in the Black Sea.

The conclusion of the naval experts was that the state of the Red Navy was not satisfactory.[9] The Red Army experts came to the same conclusion. The Chief of the Naval Forces Zof proposed to the Soviet leadership that urgent measures for a strengthening of the Navy be undertaken. They were presented to the new *Narkom* for Military and Naval Affairs and Chairman of the *Revvoensovet (RVS)*, K.E. Voroshilov, who had succeeded Frunze after his sudden death in the autumn of 1925.[10]

But the Chief of Staff of the *RKKA*, Tukhachevskii, had an alternative opinion. He declared that the Soviet Navy had no exclusive strategic missions, but only had to solve limited operational tasks in order to support the Red Army. His conclusion was: 'The Red Fleet does not need urgent reinforcements, because the Soviet State could not create a Navy comparable with its strongest competitors.'[11] At the same time he attempted to assure the Soviet military leadership, that the Red Army troops supported by the Air Force could repulse an enemy invasion of any size from the sea. In accordance with the land strategy of the USSR, Soviet leaders in the mid-1920s paid more attention to the Army. Therefore the Navy's requests were rejected time and again.

An analysis of the concluding documents about the Navy's training operations in 1925–28 shows that the general plan of the Soviet Navy's operational tasks had not changed in comparison with the period of 1921–25. However, after considering the results, the Soviet Navy's authorities became more realistic about the possibilities of counter-mine support for the Baltic Fleet operations. In connection with the reform of the military, the operational tasks for the Navy were in 1925 defined according to the specified war plans. They envisaged also the conducting of offensive operations.

At this time the Soviet leadership, being convinced by Tukhachevskii, decided to establish a 'strategic unity' for the Armed Forces. The Headquarters of the Red Fleet was abolished. On 22 July 1926 the Navy was reorganized as the *Voenno-morskie sily (VMS)*, the Naval Forces of the *RKKA SSSR*. Zof could not agree with such reorganization of the Naval High Command and was therefore replaced on 23 August by the prominent Bolshevik functionary R.A. Muklevich.[12]

He was tasked with protecting the Soviet Union from the threat of 'counter-revolutionary' or 'interventionary' landings, especially by the British Navy, of which the officers who fought in the Civil War had become so fearful. The Red Fleet had to plan an active coastal defence compatible with small ships and simple weapons built cheaply and without the need for advanced industrial technology. Men such as K.I. Dushenov, I.K. Kozhanov, I.M. Ludri and A.P. Aleksandrov quickly became the most prominent proponents of a line of thinking called in 1927 by Dushenov the *jeune école* after the French *jeune école* before the First World War.[13]

Although the *jeune école* predominated in the fleet, within the high command and the academies, the battleships retained powerful advocates, among them A.M. Petrov, now Chief of the Training and Exercise Administration of the *VMS RKKA* (a position equivalent to the chief of the navy staff). He and Zherve had developed the idea of a 'small war at sea', a war fought primarily by small vessels, and submarines, but using battleships as the backbone of Soviet defence. They were opposed not only by the *jeune école* but also by the theorists of the Red Army, especially Triandafillov. He and Tukhachevskii planned to use the available resources to develop the artillery, tanks, and air and parachute forces they needed to implement their concept of mobile warfare. Stalin – since April 1922 Secretary-General of the Communist Party – although showing little interest in the navy at the time, agreed with them, and cut the fleet's budget by almost 60 per cent from the sum requested by the *VMS* high command.[14]

When the *classical school* drew up a plan in November 1926 to bring the strength of the fleet to four battleships, one aircraft carrier, four cruisers, 26 destroyers and 40 submarines, besides many other small vessels, the *jeune école* countered with one to employ large numbers of mines, submarines, MTBs, and aircraft.

The first new building programme, the compromise 'Plan of the Soviet Naval Leadership', of 27 November 1926, approved by the *STO*, integrated ideas from both groups. It provided in the years 1926–27 to 1929–30 for not only six new submarines, eight patrol ships (*storozhevye korabli*, *SKR*) to be used as fleet escorts, and six MTBs, but also for the completion of the cruisers *Krasnyj Kavkaz* (ex-*Admiral Lazarev*) and *Voroshilov* (ex-*Pravda*, ex-*Admiral Butakov*), and three destroyers; during a second term, from 1928–29 to 1931–32, one monitor, six submarines, ten patrol ships, and 30 MTBs were to be built, and the damaged battleship *Frunze* (ex-*Poltava*) and two additional destroyers were to be modernized.[15]

In addition to the ships, eight 12in guns, 12 8in guns and 48 anti-aircraft batteries were planned.[16] However, the naval coastal artillery belonged until the end of the 1920s to the Red Army, and the naval air forces remained a branch of the *RKKA* Air Force until the mid-1930s.

THE START OF THE FIRST SHIPBUILDING PROGRAMME

At first, work was done on restoring and repairing the ships and submarines from the Imperial Fleet. In the Baltic the battleships, the *Marat* (ex-*Petropavlovsk*) and the *Parizhskaya kommuna* (ex-*Sevastopol'*), were repaired, and the *Oktyabrskaya revolyutsiya* (ex-*Gangut*) was repaired and commissioned in 1926. And besides the nine destroyers of the *Novik*-class, which were renamed on 31 December 1922 after Bolshevik functionaries, three more unfinished vessels were commissioned in 1925/26. Of the submarines of the *Bars*-class nine were still in service and had new Bolshevik names. In the Black Sea the old cruiser *Komintern* (ex-*Pamyat merkuriya*) was repaired and up to 1926 five destroyers came into service as well as one *Bars*- and four 'Holland'-type submarines. Other ships remained in the yards for completion.

In accordance with the first shipbuilding programme, approved by the *STO*, the first ships and submarines were laid down – on 5 March 1927 the first three submarines of the *Dekabrist*-class (*Series I*) at Leningrad and three more on 14 April 1927 in Nikolaev. On 13 August 1927 an order for six patrol ships was placed in the Baltic, and on 4 September 1928 the first ship *Uragan* was laid down. Two vessels followed for the Black Sea and the building of the MTBs was started.

But the discussions about the 'small war at sea', which had started in November 1927, did not end and provoked a crisis in Soviet naval thinking. Debates in the second half of the 1920s on military-theoretical problems carried on into 1929, but did not produce positive results in the way of naval thinking. Furthermore, A.P. Aleksandrov, K.I. Dushenov, A.M. Yakimychev and others, who had achieved popularity as the theorists of the *jeune école*, acted in a united front with M.N. Tukhachevskii. Articles by prominent members of the naval leadership, like R.A. Muklevich and Ivan Ludri, in *Morskoi sbornik* documented the disagreements.[17]

TANKS OR BATTLESHIPS? WHAT FLEET DO WE NEED?

On 8 May 1928, the *STO*, presided over by the *Narkom* for Military and Naval Affairs, K.E. Voroshilov, formally discussed 'The Role and Tasks of the Naval Forces on the System of Armed Forces of the Country'.[18] Participating besides others were the Deputy *Narkoms* of the Army and the Navy, J.S. Unshlikht and R.A. Muklevich, the Chief of Staff of the Army, M.N. Tukhachevskii, and his Deputy S.A. Pugashev, Commanders of the Military Districts and other high-ranking army commanders like S.M. Budyennyi, A.I. Yegorov, B.M. Shaposhnikov, P. Ye. Dybenko, A.I. Kork, I.E. Yakir, V.K. Triandafillov, the artillery expert G.N. Pell', and the Deputy Chief of the Air Force, S.A. Mezheninov from the Army, and M.A. Petrov, Chief of the Training and Exercise Department of the *VMS*, M.V. Viktorov, Chief of the Naval Forces of the Baltic Sea, his Chief of Staff, A.A. Toshakov, and his Chief of the Political Administration G.P. Kire'ev, N.I. Vlas'ev, Chief of the Technical Department, and N.I. Ignat'ev, Chief of the Artillery Department.

Voroshilov first asked Tukhachevskii to present his opinion. He criticized the different proposals of the Navy about the battleships. Were they to be put out of service after 10 years, were they to be repaired one after the other or were new battleships to be built? He said that the fleet had only to give support for the operations of the Army which could together with the Air Force secure the defence of the Soviet Union. In the past Russia, like Germany and Austria, had built battlefleets which were not used decisively in the Great War and had to be surrendered at the end. So it made no sense to put considerable financial and industrial resources into building big battleships. Resources had to be used for the decisive fields of defence, the mobile Army and the Air Force. The tasks of the heavy artillery of the battleships could also be fulfilled by heavy mobile coastal batteries or by heavy bombers, which were a great threat to the big ships. A battlefleet would be too strong against the small border states but not strong enough against the big sea powers.

In response to this presentation M.A. Petrov dismissed the first argument by arguing that the history of Russia showed that the country could not achieve its war aims without a strong navy, such as in the 1877 war against Turkey, when Russia had had to retreat from the Bosporus in the face of the combined British–French fleet at Constantinople. The typical tasks of the fleet were coastal defence, combat against enemy fleets, cruiser warfare, amphibious operations, and so on. There was a need for mine barrages, small attack vessels, landing forces, a coastal defence and strong reconnaissance. Battleships were needed to support 'small war operations'. They were mobile and could be used against any hostile landing, while heavy coastal artillery in most cases could not be moved to such places. This was only possible in narrows like the Dardanelles, but not in larger coastal areas. It was not possible to count only on coastal batteries or the air force, which were not available at that time. It was necessary to have a well-composed fleet of both large and small ships.

A.I. Kork then took the floor, and reminded the audience that the most important area at the time was the defence of Leningrad, the Gulf of Finland, and the Baltic. The Arctic and the White Sea, as well as the Far East, and also to some extent the Black Sea could not be covered with the industrial resources available, and since there was no possibility of investing large sums of money, it might not be a good idea to decommission the battleships, which could be of help in securing the main area.

The Air Force delegate S.A. Mezheninov emphasized the ability of the Air

Force to defend the Black Sea coasts against any enemy. Without a strong bomber fleet no offensive operations at sea were possible, so it made no sense to build expensive battleships: for just one battleship a strong bomber fleet is possible. Against this argument the naval artillery expert G.N. Pell' emphasized the experience of the Great War, when only a few aircraft could break through against an air defence, while heavy artillery shells were far more effective than bombs.

The Chief of the Moscow Military District, B.M. Shaposhnikov, was of the opinion that the existing Baltic Fleet was too weak for an effective coastal defence, and felt that a strengthening of the 'moskito-fleet' was necessary. If battleships were needed, it was a question of whether they would be expected to execute offensive operations or only support the 'moskito fleet'. For the last option battleships rather than fast battlecruisers might be necessary. The role of the Air Force was not to be overrated. First, it was most important to have small cruisers and submarines, and, second, aircraft for supporting the coastal defence. Finally, the battleships should be held in their present condition, because they were necessary in the actual situation.

M.V. Viktorov, the Chief of the Baltic Fleet, felt that it was not possible to defend the Baltic area only with coastal artillery batteries, which might not fire any shot if the enemy did not come into range. Battleships are mobile and can go to the area to be defended. R.A. Muklevich said that a fleet could not be substituted by an air fleet or by tanks, which were not yet available. There were also no light cruisers at that moment but the battleships were there, and their guns were far more cost-effective than heavy coastal batteries. And the battleships had the effect of deterring the Germans and any other Baltic states with their weaker ships from attacking the Finnish Gulf and Leningrad.

I.A. Yakir, the Commander of the Kiev Military District, warned against using the restricted resources for secondary tasks like a supporting role of the Navy as long as the needs of the Army were not fulfilled. Against this and Tukhachevskii's idea of cancelling the big fleet programme, G.P. Kire'ev, Chief of the Political Department of the Baltic Fleet, wanted to know if the battleships would be liquidated and only a small flotilla on the Baltic organized. Then the Chief of the Technical Department of the Navy, N.I. Vlas'ev, stood up and attacked Tukhachevskii's presentation in strong words. His statistics were not correct. With his idealized view of the British Navy he had overlooked the fact that it was impossible to move the heavy coastal artillery to the threatened areas where the bridges were not strong enough. Of the 50 battleships existing in the world, 35 were inferior to Soviet ships, and only 15 were stronger. This was the actual situation without modernization. But over the next ten years modernization and construction of new ships could change things. And A.A. Toshakov, Chief of Staff of the Baltic Fleet, said he had been confronted over the last two years with such proposals from the Army leadership. He argued that Great Britain had to use its battleships mainly in the Mediterranean and at Singapore. And how could an army advancing along the coast be supported by coastal batteries far behind the front? Three battleships or four were necessary.

After Voroshilov finally asked for a decision on the battleships, Tukhachevskii spoke up again and said that there was no question of scrapping the available battleships, but that it was not wise to invest large amounts of money in a new fleet.

But not only did the confrontation between the Army and the Navy intensify with this meeting the arguments also continued within the Navy about the type of fleet it needed. The ideas of the *jeune école* carried the most weight. Its most outspoken propagandist was A.P. Aleksandrov, who tried to silence his opponents with an article, 'A Critical Analysis of the Theory of Naval Supremacy',[19] which closed with the exclamation: 'Down with the idea of naval supremacy!' Aleksandrov and the *jeune école* theorists argued that, because of the development of submarines, light craft, and aircraft – now the main strike element of the fleet – the battleship had lost its function, and naval supremacy based on the battleship no longer made sense. The conclusion was that the Soviet Navy should operate only in the littoral areas. Operations of light naval forces were to be the backbone of Soviet naval strategy. Furthermore, A.P. Aleksandrov, K.I. Dushenov, A.M. Yakimyshev and others acted in a united front with Tukhachevskii against Petrov and Zherve. As a result both were purged in 1930 and eliminated from active scientific work, as were Vlas'ev and Ignat'ev, Chief of the Artillery Department. They were forced to retire or were at least downgraded on trumped-up charges and were for some time imprisoned. Zherve and Ignat'ev were pardoned after a while, Zherve becoming a professor at the Military Political Academy and head of a department at the Military Engineering Academy until his death in 1934. But Petrov and Vlas'ev became victims of the 1937 purges.[20]

THE FIRST FIVE-YEAR PLAN (1928–32)

After a month's intense struggle to enlarge his building programme, Muklevich partly had his way. He had to forgo the repair and completion of the battleship

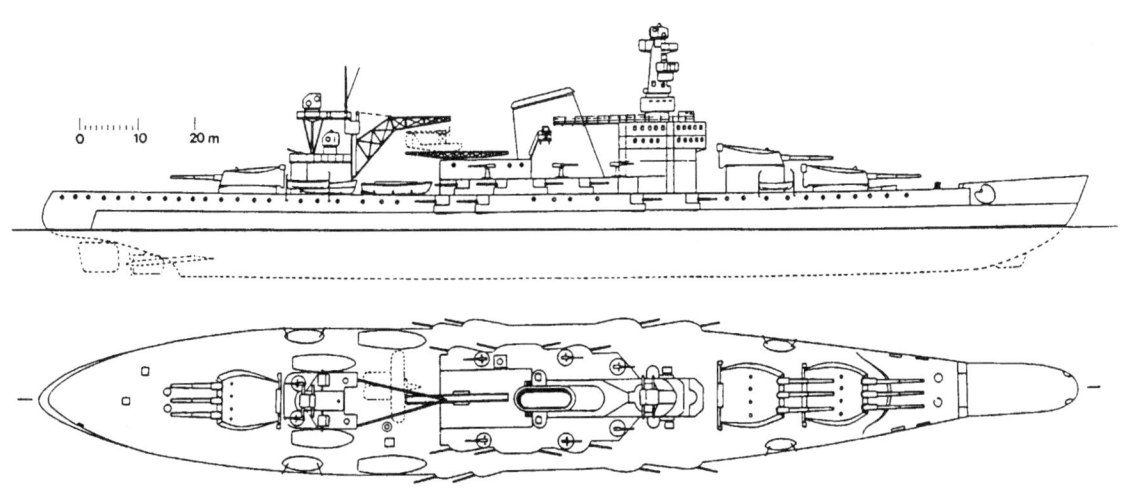

Fig. 2. Design variant A to rebuild the damaged battleship *Frunze*, 1933, displ. 27,000t stdd., length 185m, max. speed 27kt, 9 30.5cm, 16 13cm, 8 10cm. Catapult, 3 planes. Credit: Breyer, Sudostroenie

Frunze and the cruiser *Voroshilov* in favour of new designs, but was allowed to have work carried out on some other vessels. The *STO* decided on 4 February 1929 to embark on a revised shipbuilding programme in accordance with the first Five-Year Plan, which defined as the primary goal the restoration of the merchant fleet, since its remaining part of only about 15 per cent of pre-revolutionary numbers was evidently insufficient for foreign trade. Of the ships planned for the programme of 27 November 1926 the monitor was postponed, but the 12 submarines, 18 patrol ships and 36 MTBs were to go ahead, and, in addition, three destroyer leaders, three big, three medium and four small submarines, and 16 MTBs were authorized. The three battleships would be modernized.[21]

But in July 1929 Stalin ordered that naval expenditure be cut by about 40 per cent because there was a shortage of resources to build tanks. The Chief of the *VMS RKKA*, Muklevich did not agree with this reduction in naval expenditure. In December 1929 he presented Stalin with a Memorandum from the Naval Staff. Muklevich stated that a delay in the construction of new ships would cause a loss of operational ability in the Navy. In April 1930 the *STO* approved the resolution to increase naval expenditure. But the urgent measures taken did not prevent the failure of the five-year shipbuilding plan.

Most ships were late in completion – these included three rebuilt cruisers of the *Svetlana*-class, the *Chervona Ukraina* (1927, ex-*Admiral Nakhimov*), the *Profintern* (1929, ex-*Svetlana*) as light cruisers with 130mm guns, and the *Krasnyj Kavkaz* (1932, ex-*Admiral Lazarev*) with the new 180mm guns. But of the other ships only 8 patrol ships of the *Uragan*-class, 6 submarines of the *Dekabrist*-class (series I) and 59 MTBs were commissioned up to the end of 1932.[22]

The *Dekabrist* submarines were comparable with the best foreign vessels of the time. The experience gained during their development laid the foundation for the further designing of Soviet submarines. The *Sh-4*-class motor torpedo boats were also a novelty in Soviet shipbuilding and became the prototypes for future boats.

An analysis of the development of the Soviet Navy from 1924 to 1932 shows that its basic results were determined by the role and place allocated to the Navy in the Soviet Union's defence planning: It only ranked in third place after the Army and Air Force. The results were:

- A certain harmonization of views on the main strategic missions and structure of the Naval Forces was achieved in the decision of the Revolutionary Military Council of 8 May 1928.
- There was a stabilization of ship and personnel complements with a total of 98 combatant ships and 28,000 men in the Navy by the end of 1928.
- The operational independence of the Red Navy was abolished.
- The share of the Navy in the total military expenditure increased somewhat (from 8.7 to 11–13 per cent).
- The first shipbuilding plan was adopted.

From the 12–19 September 1928 the Black Sea Fleet held manoeuvres in order to master the methods of 'small fleet tactics'. The details of the Soviet view on the 'small war at sea' were the following: the heterogeneous light naval forces should include formations of submarines, light cruisers, destroyers, MTBs and naval aviation. They would fight against the enemy who would possess 'mastery of the sea'. The Soviet Navy would conduct its operations along the USSR littorals backed up by strong sea defensive positions covered by coastal artillery and minefields. It was the job of the Soviet Navy to weaken a hostile fleet 'step by step' by conducting a number of sudden joint attacks from several directions.

THE 'SMALL WAR AT SEA' THEORY

The basic idea of the 'small war at sea' was the 'combined or concentrated blow theory' influencing the operational planning of the Soviet Navy until the end of the 1930s. The 'small war at sea' conception was finally adopted as the official doctrine of the Soviet Navy. The 'Battle Instructions of the *VMS RKKA*' ('*BU-30*') issued in 1930 seemed to represent the triumph of the *jeune école* and became the theoretical basis of all naval operations. They laid down that 'the naval forces of the *RKKA*, as an indivisible part of the Red Army, responsible with it for defending the interests of the working people, have to be ready for a brave and decisive fight against the enemy, directed at the defence of the coasts of the USSR, and to support the operations of the land forces of the Red Army by covering it from the sea, on rivers, and on interior seas'.[23]

From 7–12 August 1929 the Baltic Fleet, along with troops of the Leningrad Military District, exercised the conduct of landing operations. According to the opinion of experts, such actions failed because of the absence of special landing craft, poor interaction and a lack of joint previous planning.

In 1930 the readiness of the Caspian Flotilla to conduct landing operations was examined, the results of such training operations being considered as satisfactory.

From 1930 onwards it seemed that the operational plans of all Soviet fleets were mastered over several training operations. For example, the Black Sea Fleet jointly with the Army mastered the defence of the Ochakovskii Section of the Western Fortified Area, the counter-landing operations in order to prevent an enemy invasion into the Crimea, and the coastal defence of the Northern Caucasus Area.

But it was concluded through analysis of such training operations that only two strategic missions of the Soviet Navy were really mastered between 1921 and 1931:

- Combat against enemy naval forces
- Giving assistance to the Army along the littoral zones.

The operational goals of the Soviet Navy were above all to defeat a hostile fleet breaking through the Sea Defence Position into the eastern part of the Gulf of Finland and to defend the main Soviet ports on the Black Sea coastline.

By 1931 the operational plan of the Soviet Navy was defined more exactly.

It was planned to defeat the enemy 'step by step'. The naval formations, trying to solve operational tasks, should combine offensive and defensive forms of sea warfare. All branches of the 'light naval forces', covered by minefields and coastal artillery, had to play a decisive role in the struggle against a strong enemy. The basic method of the Navy's application was finally defined. It was called the 'small war at sea'. The concept of a combined or concentrated blow became the backbone of this.

But while the *jeune école* won the argument inside the Navy, a demand for new heavy ships began in 1929 in circles outside the Navy. The shipbuilding industry articulated its fears about losing the technological capability to design and build bigger warships, and outstanding diplomats such as L.M. Karakhan, Deputy *Narkom* for Foreign Relations, declared in 1930 that the USSR, apart from the Sea Border Guard units, needed fast ships with good endurance and strong gunnery to defend Soviet interests in the Pacific. The support of a powerful and visible symbol such as a heavy warship might be necessary.[24] This was caused to some extent by the Soviet–Chinese conflict of 1929 which followed the crisis with the Chinese Eastern Railway, administered by Russian experts.

When the Soviets learned, in 1929, that Turkey was strengthening its fleet by modernizing the battlecruiser *Yavuz* (ex-German *Goeben*) with French help and by ordering four modern destroyers and two submarines to be built in Italy, they decided to transfer the battleship *Parizhskaya kommuna* and the cruiser *Profintern* under the command of L.M. Galler from the Baltic to the Black Sea over Christmas and New Year 1929/30. The ships would reinforce the one sister cruiser *Chervona Ukraina* stationed there and so once again achieve parity with the Turkish naval forces.[25]

FIRST REPRESSIONS OF LEADERS AND ENGINEERS ACCUSED OF SABOTAGE

Because the process of forced industrialization of the USSR met with many delays and problems, resulting from the inexperience of many of the leading functionaries and the insufficient training of new workers, this was to be compensated for by looking for 'saboteurs' and 'enemies of the socialist buildup'. Purges started in the spring of 1928 with the Shakhty trial against 'bourgeois specialists' – mine engineers – including five German engineers of the *AEG*. Hard sentences were given for in most cases fictitious accusations.[26]

In 1929 Stalin started his attack against 'right-wing deviations' of N.I. Bukharin, A.I. Rykov and M.P. Tomskii, who lost all their Party functions.[27] But such repression was not limited to the Party or to some industrial complexes, but led also to the first purges in the Navy. In autumn 1930 some of the *spetsialists* of the Imperial Navy, such as the Chief of the Training Administration, M.A. Petrov, and the Naval Academy Professor Zherve, but also officers like the Chief of the Operational Department, A.A. Toshakov, the Chief of the Scientific-Technical Committee, N.I. Ignat'ev, and Petrov's deputy, V.P. Rimskii-Korsakov, went to jail. This was in part a consequence of the accusations of young officers of the *jeune école* during the controversial discussions about the strategy of the 'small war at sea'. And it was not limited to the top positions in the Naval Staff, many of the engineers also went into *Ob'edinennoe Gosudarstvennoe Politicheskoe Upravlenie (OGPU)* detention camps, where they had to work under close observation, like the well-known aircraft and motor torpedo boat designer A.N. Tupolev, and the submarine engineers B.M. Malinin, E.E. Kryuger, and S.A. Bazilevskii.[28] They were accused of 'pernicious work' and were released only some time later. This had detrimental effects on the tests of their first built submarine *Dekabrist*, since there were many defects which were difficult to correct during their absence.

So the commissioning of the first six submarines of the *Dekabrist*-class and the first eight patrol ships of the *Uragan*-class, laid down in 1927, was delayed until the end of 1930 for the first vessels and until 1931 and 1932 for the others.[29] N.I. Vlas'ev, head of the Technical Administration, was arrested by the *OGPU* in April 1930 with a faked accusation of having messed up the tasks for the patrol ships.

On 10 January 1931 the Chief of the *VMS RKKA*, Muklevich said that it would be wrong to avoid the construction of battleships, because the neighbours of the USSR in the West and the Far East were building coastal defence ships – for example, Finland's *Ilmarinen*-class, light and heavy cruisers and even battleships like the German *Deutschland*-class pocket battleships or the French fast battleships of the *Dunkerque*-class. But Muklevich suffered for his requests: he was forced in July 1931 to relinquish his post to become an inspector of the *VMS RKKA*, and in 1934, Chief of the Main Administration for Warship Building. V.M. Orlov, the Commander of the Black Sea Fleet, became the new Chief of the *VMS RKKA*.

But requests for new big ships continued. In November 1931 a group of Baltic shipbuilding engineers suggested that construction of capital ships be renewed as soon as possible. In their opinion, the lack of new battleships and cruisers became a threat to the security of the USSR. The background to this was the worsening situation in the Far East, where the Japanese invasion of Manchuria and the establishment of a puppet state there, gave rise to fears about the dangers of Japanese expansion. So on 21 April 1932 the 'Naval Forces of the Far East' were established. Because neither warships nor shipyards were available in the Sea of Japan, orders were placed with shipyards in Leningrad and Nishni Novgorod/Gorkii for 12 medium and 24 small submarines, which would be transported in parts by the Trans-Siberian railway to Khabarovsk and Vladivostok for assembling and commissioning.[30]

The opening of the Northern Sea Route allowed summer shipping to sail between the north-western and the Far Eastern seaports of the USSR. The growth in importance of the Polar region of the Soviet Union's provinces demanded the strengthening of their sea and coastal defences. So, on 1 June 1933 a 'Northern Flotilla' was established. In two operations led by I.S. Isakov, three *Novik*-destroyers, three patrol ships of the *Uragan*-class and the three submarines of the *Dekabrist*-class were transferred between May and September 1933 from the Baltic through the newly completed Baltic–White Sea Canal to Sorokskaya Bay, the terminal of the Baltic–White Sea Canal, where Stalin himself greeted them together with K.E. Voroshilov and the Party Secretary of Leningrad, S.M. Kirov, before they went on to Ekaterinskaya Gavan renamed Polyarny from 1939.[31] Then the leaders of the USSR went on to the Kola Gulf to inspect the bays where the future bases of a Northern Fleet were to be built.

FOREIGN AID FROM GERMANY

The Red Army had already tried in 1921–22 to arrange an exchange of information with the German *Reichswehr*, which was looking for a way to develop the weapons technology forbidden by the Treaty of Versailles. So the *Narkom* for Foreign Trade, L.B. Krasin, during a visit to the German Foreign Ministry on 2 March 1921, proposed that Germany should build combat airplanes, forbidden by the Versailles Treaty, in the Soviet Union. In 1921 several German experts visited Russia together with the authorized representative of the Soviet Government in Germany, V.L. Kopp and the designated ambassador N.N. Krestinskii who met with officers of the *Reichswehrministerium*, such as the then Major K. von Schleicher, and the new *Chef der Heeresleitung*, General H. von Seeckt and the head of the aircraft firm Junkers, Professor H. Junkers. In February 1922 Seeckt also met with an official from the *Komintern*, K.B. Radek. In November/December 1922 an agreement was signed between Junkers and the Soviet government to produce 100 combat aircraft at the *Fili zavod* near Moscow. The first contacts of the German Navy with the Soviet Commissariat for the Army and Navy were established in December 1921 by Captain W. Lohmann who visited Moscow and Petrograd in May/June 1922 to arrange the return of 'embargo-ships' interned in Petrograd.[32]

On 16 April 1922 during the first international conference with Soviet participation in Genoa, the *Narkom* for Foreign Relations, G.V. Chicherin, concluded with the German delegation the Treaty of Rapallo, which led to the establishment of diplomatic relations, some economic agreements and exchanges of visits by high-ranking officials and experts on both sides. Some military agreements followed, such as the opening of a training school in April 1925 for pilots at Lipetsk. Exchanges of visits to manoeuvres were also arranged, and in July/August 1925 Tukhachevskii visited Germany for the first time.[33] During a visit of the Deputy *Narkom* for the Army and the Navy, I.S. Unshlikht, to Berlin the establishment of a tank school and a school for gas warfare were discussed. The gas warfare school started its operation in 1928 at Tomka near Saratov; the tank school in 1929 at Kazan. In addition the enrolment of officers on to the General Staff courses of the other side was arranged.[34]

The naval contacts intensified after a visit of the former *Chef der Marineleitung*, Admiral P. Behncke, in Moscow in February 1924, when he was travelling to the Far East. He conferred with the *Narkom* for Foreign Relations, Chicherin, and with Litvinov, who became his successor in 1930. the contacts increased in 1926. In March during the visit of Unshlikht to Berlin the Chief of the Naval Scientific-Technical Committee, P.Yu. Oras, and one other officer represented the Soviet Navy. On 26 March he conferred with officers of the German *Marineleitung* – for example, with the U-boat expert, Rear Admiral A. Spindler, and the Head of the Fleet Department, Captain W. von Loewenfeld, and others. The Soviet delegation wanted to establish Soviet–German collaboration in naval affairs. They were eager to obtain access to German shipbuilding experience, especially in the field of submarine construction, and proposed that an agreement be signed on joint submarine design that would be based on previous German plans, and joint construction projects in Soviet shipbuilding yards. Besides submarine construction the draft on Soviet–German naval co-operation included suggestions on the joint construction of patrol ships and MTBs, German technical assistance in the development of the Soviet Navy, and in the participation of Soviet naval personnel in German naval activities.[35]

But the German *Reichsmarine* was reluctant, and most of the suggestions were turned down. It was proposed that Oras go to The Hague and ask the secret German U-Boat construction bureau, the *Ingenieurskantoor voor Scheepsbouw (IvS)*, for plans. On 2 April Oras arrived and ordered a plan for a 600-ton submarine. A week later he was back and went to see the new light cruiser *Emden* which was being fitted out at Wilhelmshaven, and the old battleship *Elsaß*.[36] From 2–18 June 1926 Spindler was sent to Moscow and Leningrad/Kronstadt to learn more about the actual situation of the Soviet Navy. He had discussions in Moscow with Unshlikht and the Chief of the *VMS RKKA*, Zof. Zof criticized the *IvS*-plan for the 600-ton submarine and said that the Italian offers were much more detailed. From Germany he wanted to see the plans of the *IvS*-submarines for Turkey, the last U-Boat construction plans at the end of the First World War, an analysis of the submarines needed for the Soviet Navy, and support for the delivery of equipment for the new Soviet submarines, like diesel motors, and a delegation of German U-Boat officers to instruct Soviet submariners.[37] After some visits to schools Spindler was able at Kronstadt to visit the submarine *Batrak*, the destroyer *Engels*, and the battleship *Marat*. But Spindler's recommendations were accepted only with reluctance in Berlin.[38]

On 29 July 1926 four plans of German U-Boats drawn up in the last stages of the First World War were sent to Moscow. But then the new Chief of the *VMS RKKA*, Muklevich, who had participated in the Unshlikht mission, still as deputy Chief of the Air Force *RKKA*, discussed several plans and agreements with the head of the German military bureau *Zentrale Moskau*, Lt-Colonel H. von der Lieth-Thomsen on 2 December 1926. He said that he was not interested in outdated plans from the war, but in new ones, and offered to set up a submarine school at a Black Sea port along the lines of the army schools. The *Chef der Marineleitung*, Admiral A. Zenker, turned down the proposal: the German Navy, with the memories of the mutinies of 1917–18 in mind, was very wary of the Soviets out of fear of Bolshevik infiltration.[39]

The contacts with the German Navy bore no real fruit at this time, but there were some contacts with German industrial companies which were more successful. In 1929 the Heinkel aircraft factory delivered two catapults for the equipment of the reconstructed battleship *Oktyabrskaya revolyutsiya* and the newly completed cruiser *Krasnyi Kavkaz*. And in 1930 successful negotiations took place with the German firms *Atlas* (navigational systems), *MAN* (diesel-motors), *Siemens-Schuckert* (electro-motors), *Anschütz* (compass equipment), and the Swiss firm *Brown-Boveri* (turbines). Apart from this the Soviet Navy wanted submarine storage batteries and ship radio sets, but in this they failed.

FOREIGN AID FROM ITALY

For shipbuilding the Soviets had to turn elsewhere. The first contacts with the Italian Navy were established when the *Gruppo Autonomo Exploratori Leggeri*, led by Captain D. Cavagnari (later Commander-in-Chief of the Italian Navy) visited in summer 1925 with the new big destroyers *Pantera*, *Leone*, and *Tigre* and came to Leningrad/Kronshtadt.[40] Then the Italian *Cantiere dell'Adriatico* shipyard delivered plans for a submarine which was to become the basis for the first Soviet submarines of the *Dekabrist*-class.[41] Some additional contacts were established by visits of Soviet ships to Italian ports and vice versa. In October 1925 the Black Sea destroyers *Nezamozhnik* and *Petrovskii* came to Italy, and in September 1929 the destroyers *Nezamozhnik* and *Frunze* visited Naples. During their transfer to the Black Sea the battleship *Parizhskaya kommuna* and the cruiser *Profintern* came in January 1930 to Cagliari and Naples, and a delegation of sailors visited the writer Maksim Gorkii who was living at the time in Sorrento. Official visits were exchanged during these stays. On 16 May 1930 in Rome the Italian Minister of the Navy, Admiral G. Sirianni, received a visit from the Deputy *Narkom* for Trade, P. Lubimov. Sirianni proposed to sell to the Soviet Navy modern Italian submarine and naval gunnery technologies. The Soviets accepted such proposals with great satisfaction.[42]

On 28 August 1930 the Chief of the *VMS RKKA*, Muklevich, presented to the Deputy *Narkom* of Defence, I.P. Uborevich, a list of officers to be sent to Italy. The Soviet delegation visited Italy in autumn 1930, headed by A.K. Sivkov, Chief of the Technical Department of the Navy. He was ordered to obtain information about the 450mm and 533mm torpedoes, anti-aircraft guns, mines, and plans for modern submarines, destroyers, and cruisers. In addition Sivkov was to learn the opinions of the Italian theorists on subjects like coastal defence, battleships, and submarine operations, and about the combat activity of large and small destroyers and motor torpedo boats. The Soviet naval delegation were also expected to acquire information about the operational activities of surface ships and submarines jointly with naval aviation and coastal defence and about anti-aircraft warfare.

On 9 September 1930 the first negotiation between Sirianni and Sivkov took place, but the Soviets did not achieve the expected results. In November 1930 Sivkov reported that the Italians could not sell cruisers and submarines, because deals of this kind were prohibited by the Washington Treaty. Nevertheless Muklevich proposed to buy a 5,200t *Condottieri*-class cruiser and a 900t *Manara*-class submarine. On 31 March 1931 Muklevich reported to Stalin that the Navy needed modern cruisers and again suggested buying Italian ships.

In March 1932 a new Soviet delegation visited Italy, this time headed by the Chief of Staff of the Black Sea Fleet, K.I. Dushenov. The Soviets now wanted plans of submarines and surface ships, three completed submarines, which were built in Italy for the Argentine Navy, designs of cruisers and destroyers, and a complete set of torpedo plant equipment. But again the Soviet's attempts were not entirely successful. They visited the Naval Academy at Livorno, where they met with the commanding officer (later an admiral), D. Cavagnari, and visited the destroyer *Francesco Nullo* and the heavy cruiser

Trento during exercises. Finally, several groups from the Soviet delegation were able to visit ten cities and bases and 13 ships as well as the submarines *Balilla*, *Manara*, *Narvalo*, *Des Geneys* and *Settembrini*, and some ships being built at the yards in Naples, Monfalcone, La Spezia and Taranto, including the heavy cruiser *Fiume*. From this time on several more visits of Soviet officials to Italy were recorded.[43] So P.Yu. Oras was taken to the submarine *Bandiera*, and together with the radio and artillery expert Professor A.I. Berg saw many installations at yards and technical departments. In autumn 1933 new ship visits were exchanged. The Italian submarines *Tricheco* and *Delfino* visited Batumi, and a force of the Naval Forces of the Black Sea under Yu. F. Rall' with the new cruiser *Krasnyi Kavkaz* and the destroyers *Petrovskii* and *Shaumyan* again went to Naples.

SHIPBUILDING IN THE FIRST FIVE-YEAR PLAN

During the time of the First Five-Year Plan, the completion of the unfinished ships of the Imperial Navy, and the repair and modernization of the battleship *Marat* and the cruisers and destroyers were all finished. But the realization of many projects developed in the preceding years, such as the rebuilding of the damaged battleship *Frunze* (ex-*Poltava*) into a fast battlecruiser, the transforming of the unfinished battlecruiser *Izmail'* and the training ship *Komsomolets* into aircraft carriers for 50 and 42 airplanes respectively, the building of big monitors of 11,000t with a 356mm triple gun turret, the cruiser *Voroshilov* (ex-*Admiral Butakov*) into a modern fast cruiser, or the building of projected cruiser-, or fleet- or minelaying-submarines, was put aside.[44] The lessons learned from rebuilding the raised British submarine *L-55*, sunk on 4 June 1918 by the Russian destroyer *Azard* in the Gulf of Finland, were applied to the next six series II/*L*-class submarines.[45]

The designs for the new ships of the First Five-Year Plan were developed in the *Tsentral'noe Konstruktorskoe Byuro (TsKBS)*, which in 1933 was divided into one section for surface ships (*TsKB-1*) and one for submarines (*TsKB-2*). These were respectively headed by V.I. Bzhezinskii and B.M. Malinin. First the *Nauchno-Tekhnicheskii Komitet (NTK)* had to develop the conceptual pre-sketch, to be checked by the *Taktio-Technicheskoe-Zadanie (TTZ)*, then given to the construction bureaus. In most cases several variants of a design were produced. The different projects were given numbers, so *projekt 1* became the destroyer leaders of the *Leningrad*-class, *projekt 2* the *Storozhevye korabli (SKR)* or patrol ships of the *Uragan*-class, while the submarine types got numbers like *Series I* for the *Dekabrist*-class etc.

The first ships to be laid down were the patrol ships of the *Uragan*-class of 580t stdd., after other projects like the *NTK* variant 9 of 300t were discarded. Eight *SKR*s of the first planned 18 units were laid down in 1927 and completed between 3 July 1932 and 5 March 1933, six of *projekt 2* for the Baltic Fleet, and two of a slightly different *projekt 4* for the Black Sea Fleet.[46] The other vessels were postponed.

But most important of all was the start of the building of the fast motor torpedo boats (MTB). In 1927 a test vessel *Pervenets*, designed by A.N. Tupolev, was tested in the Black Sea, then a series of 59 very fast MTBs of 10t with a designed maximum speed of more than 50kt was built, the first commissioned in 1928, with 11 more in 1929, 11 in 1930, 10 in 1931, and 26 in 1932.[47]

Submarine building was started and remained in the forefront in the next Five-Year Plan. After discussions about several project-variants in 1925/26, the design of B.M. Malinin was finally selected. He had included in his design the information he had obtained during his visit to Italy in 1925 about the Italian submarines *Balilla* (1,427t) and *Giovanni Bausan* (866t). In March 1927 three submarines of *series I*, the later *D*-class, of 934t for the Baltic, and in April 1927 three more for the Black Sea were laid down. After some troubles during the test phase the first boat *Dekabrist* was commissioned in November 1930, followed by the other five vessels in 1931.[48]

The other vessels and submarines agreed for the First Five-Year Plan were much delayed and only completed in most cases during the Second Five-Year Plan.

Following many discussions after 1925 about big destroyers of up to 4,000t, in 1929 three destroyer leaders of *projekt 1/Leningrad*-class were selected. The sketch project was, from May 1929 to February 1930, designed by the *NTK* under Yu. A. Shimanskii, but the detailed construction was made by the *TsKBS-1* under V.A. Nikitin. Because he was often absent, much of the work was done by P.O. Trakhtenberg. The vessels were designed at 2,050ts stdd. and were expected to achieve with 67,250 HP a maximum speed of 43kt. They received an armament of five 130mm guns, two 76mm A/A and two 45mm A/A guns as well as two quadruple 533mm torpedo tube sets with eight reserve torpedoes. The first keels were laid down in October/November 1932, two at the *Zavod A. Marti* at Nikolaev for the Black Sea Fleet, while the lead ship *Leningrad* was laid down in the presence of the Party chief of Leningrad, S.M. Kirov, at the *Severnaya verf'* at Leningrad. Because important components were often delivered late or were faulty, the building after the launching was greatly delayed, and the *Leningrad* was commissioned only in December 1936, and its sisters in the Black Sea finally in August and November 1938.[49]

The ten postponed *SKR*s of the *Uragan*-class were built in three batches from late 1931 to 1938. Four vessels of *projekt 2* (580t stdd.) and two of *projekt 4* (487t stdd.) for the Far East were prepared at the *Severnaya verf'* in Leningrad and the *Marti zavod* at Nikolaev, and transported in parts by rail to the *Dalzavod* yard in Vladivostok for assembling and completing, commissioned there from November 1934 to November 1936. Two more of *projekt 2* for the Baltic Fleet were built from 1934 to 1936, while two more improved *projekt 39* vessels followed in Leningrad from 1935 to 1938.[50]

The main emphasis was laid on submarine building, but there continued to be long delays. Since 1925 there had been several projects for minelaying submarines, one of 1,200–1,300t for 60 or even 100 mines, and one of 1,034t for 40 mines. Finally the design of B.M. Malinin was selected. He proposed construction of a submarine of 1,025t with two long horizontal mine tubes at the stern for 20 mines, and six 533mm torpedo tubes at the bow. The surface speed was planned as 14.2kt, submerged as 8.5kt. The first three vessels for the Baltic Fleet were laid down on 6 October 1929 at the *Baltijskii zavod* at Leningrad, followed by three more in March/April 1930 at the *Marti zavod* at

Nikolaev. On the basis of experiences with the raised and rebuilt former British submarine *L-55*, the lead submarine *Leninets* and the others had to incorporate some amendments, which led to delay, so that the vessels were not commissioned until October 1933, the last in the Black Sea not being until May 1934.[51]

The third type of submarine in planning was a medium-sized vessel, intended for mass production to reach the given target number of 200 units. The *series III/Shch*-class was developed from a sketch project of the *NTK* with the assistance of B.M. Malinin. With 578t the first series of these medium boats had four 533mm bow and two stern torpedo tubes and could load 10 torpedoes. The surface speed was relatively low at 11.6kt, submerged 8.5kt. The first three units were laid down on 5 February 1930 at the *Baltijskii zavod* at Leningrad, and one more, funded by donations from the *Komsomol'* youth organization, was given to the new, greatly enlarged river yard *Krasnoe Sormovo* at Gorkii on the Volga. This yard was planned to become one of the most productive submarine builders. The submarines had to be transported over inland waterways to the fleets. These four vessels were also commissioned from August to November 1933.[52]

Even more delays were experienced with the next *series IV/P*-class. In May 1930 the Staff of the *VMS RKKA* gave a *TTZ* for a fast *eskadrennoi*- or fleet submarine for the Baltic and Black Seas to the designers. With 1,200–1,300t the vessel should achieve a speed of 22–23kt and have 10 torpedo tubes as well as a 102mm gun. The design of A.N. Asafov, working in an *OGPU* camp, was selected. It had some unconventional details. He used outside framing for his pressure hull to save weight. So the vessel had a surface displacement of only 955t, but submerged 1,690t. Heated discussions erupted over this design, and while the first vessel *Pravda* was laid down in May 1931, followed by two sisters in October, the construction was halted in mid-1932 by the new chief of the *VMS*, V.M. Orlov. After criticisms by a commission under Yu. A. Shimanskii, head of the *NTK* group, and other engineers such as P.F. Papkovich, B.M. Malinin, and E.E. Kryuger who had been released from their *OGPU* camp, the design was amended, but the vessels were only finished in 1936 to become training submarines owing to their many faults in construction.[53]

The establishment of the Naval Forces of the Far East made it necessary to build up a strong submarine force there. Because the yards in the Far East were not ready to build ships or submarines from the keel-laying on to completion, it was necessary to select types which could be pre-produced in the West and then transported by rail to the Far East. In 1932 the preparations were finished and in March 1932 the first 12 medium submarines of an improved *Shchuka*-type, the *series V* of 592t were laid down in Leningrad, six at the *Baltijskii zavod*, two at the *Marti zavod*, and four at the *Severnaya verf'*. They were sent in sections by rail to the Far East, eight for assembly and completion at *Dalzavod* in Vladivostok, four to the *Sudomekhanicheskii zavod* at Khabarovsk. They were completed from November 1932 to October 1934 and had improved diesel-engines for a top surface speed of 12.3kt.[54]

To boost production and speed up the process, the 30 small submarines, ordered on 2 April 1932, were also built under pressure. After 19 special railway cars were readied for taking the entire small submarine hull, the first *series VI/M*-class of 161t with two 533mm torpedo tubes at the bow, one diesel-

and one electro-motor for speeds of 13.2kt on the surface, and 7.2kt submerged, also designed by A.N. Asafov, were started at the *Marti zavod* and the *No. 61 Kommunar zavod* at Nikolaev, and transported to the *Dalzavod* in Vladivostok for completion. The first vessels were laid down in October 1932, and transport to the Far East began in December 1933. Twenty-seven boats were completed there up to the end of 1934, but one boat was destroyed by fire, and so the 28th boat had to be laid down separately and was only completed on 28 July 1935. The two other boats remained in the Black Sea and were ready in September 1934.[55]

NOTES

1. Manfred Hildermeier, op. cit., ch. 4.
2. M.N. Tukhachevskii, *Izbrannye proizvedeniaya*, Vol. 1, 2 (1919–37), Moscow, Voenizdat, 1964.
3. V.K. Triandafillov, *The Nature of the Operations of Modern Armies*, ed. J. Kipp, London, Frank Cass, 1994. John Erickson, *The Soviet High Command: A Military-Political History, 1918–1941*, London, Macmillan, 1962; Dmitrii Volkogonov, *Lev Trotskii. Politicheskii portret*, Moscow, 1992, pp. 229–72.
4. RGA VMF, f. r-1, op.3, d.2651, l.272-6; RG VA, f.4, op.2, d.102, l.31-2; M.N. Tukhachevskii, *Strategiya organizatsii*, 1924; *Izbrannie proizvedeniya, T.1*, Moscow, 1964, pp. 180–4.
5. John Erickson, op. cit.; D. Volkogonov, op. cit.
6. *Krasnyi Flot* (Red Fleet), No. 8 (1925), p. 5.
7. Robert W. Herrick, *Soviet Naval Strategy: Fifty Years of Theory and Practice*, Annapolis, US Naval Institute, 1968, pp. 19–27; Sergei Gorshkov, *Die Rolle der Flotten in Krieg und Frieden*, Munich Olzog, 1973, pp. 75–105; Mikhail S. Monakov, 'Sud'by doktrin i teorii', *Morskoi sbornik*, 1 (1994), pp. 22–3; N.N. Afonin, 'Uchebnoe sudno Komsomolets', *Sudostroenie*, No. 10 (1988), pp. 42–3; Siegfried Breyer, op. cit., vol. I.
8. RGA VMF, f. r-1483, op.1, d.65, l.5.
9. RG VA, f.33988, op.1, d.436, l.50-1. F.4, op.1, d.63, l.106-107.
10. N.Yu. Berezovskii, S.S Berezhnoi and Z.V. Nikolaeva *Boevaya Letopis Voenno-Morskogo Flota 1917–1941*, Moscow, Voenizdat, 1992, pp. 398, 473, 501–2, 514, 517.
11. M.N. Tukhachevskii, *Izbrannye proizvedeniya*, Vol. 1 (1919–27), Vol. 2 (1928–37), Moscow, Voenizdat, 1964.
12. *Boevoj put' Sovetskogo Voenno-morskogo flota*, 3rd edn, ed. Aleksei Basov *et al.*, Moscow, Voenizdat, 1974, p. 529.
13. Op. cit., pp. 136–7; V.M. Orlov, 'Na strazhe morskikh granits SSSR', *Morskoi sbornik*, No. 3 (1937).
14. E. Shitikov, 'Stalin i voennoe korabl'stroenie', *Morskoi sbornik*, No. 12 (1993), pp. 58ff.
15. Postanovlenie soveta truda i oborony 26.XI.1926, O programme stroitel'stva morskikh sil RKKA. Pr. STO No. 295, RGA VMF f.r-360, op.2, d.78, ll.192–9.
16. RGA VMF, f.r-1843, op.1, d.80, l.103.
17. R.A. Muklevich, 'Desiatiletie oktyabrskoi revolutsii i morskoi flot', *Morskoi sbornik*, No. 10 (1927); I. Ludri, 'Desiat' let bor'by i stroitel'stvo', *Morskoi sbornik*, No. 2 (1928).
18. Stenogramma zasedeniya RVS SSSR s Komandoyushchimi vojskami MVO, UVO i BVO i nachal'kami morskikh sil Baltijskogo i Chernogo morej ot 8-go Maya 1928 goda. Ts(entral'nii G(osudarstvennyi) A(rkhiv) S(ovetskii) A(rmii), Moscow, f.4, op.1, d.752, l.213ff.
19. A.P. Aleksandrov, 'A Critical Analysis of the Theory of Naval Supremacy', *Morskoi sbornik*, No. 10 (1929).
20. V.D. Dotsenko, *Morskoi Biograficheskii Slovar*, St Petersburg, Logos, 1995, pp. 99–100, 164–5, 180, 323–4.
21. Postanovlenie soveta truda i oborony 26.XI: O programme stroitel'stva morskikh sil RKKA, 1 Pr.STO, no. 295. M.S. Monakov, 'Sud'by doktrin i teorii', pt. 4, in *Morskoi sbornik*,

No. 4 (1991), pp. 24–31. S. Breyer, op. cit., vol. II: *Konsolidierung und erste Neubauten*, Herford 1989.
22. S.S. Berezhnoi, op. cit., pp. 31–2, 42–3, 197–9, 130ff.
23. Boevoi ustav VMS RKKA 1930, Moscow, 1931, p. 9.
24. L.M. Karakhan, see RGA VMF, f.r-1483, op.1, d.80, l.04-94ob.
25. *Boevoj put' Sovetskogo Voenno-morskogo flota*, 3rd edn by V.I. Achkasov and A.V. Basov et al., Moscow, Voenizdat, 1974, pp. 137–9. A.A. Zonin, *Admiral L.M. Galler: Zhizn' i flotovodcheskaya deyatel'nost*, Moscow, Voenizdat, 1991, pp. 236–50.
26. Manfred Hildermeier, op. cit., pp. 219, 362, 409–11, 476, 575.
27. Dmitrii Volkogonov, *Stalin, Triumph und Tragödie*, Düsseldorf, Claassen, 1989, pp. 258–67.
28. *Istoriya Otechestvennoi suostroenie*, op. cit., vol. 4, pp. 18–20. J.N. Westwood, *Russian Naval Construction 1905–1945*, University of Birmingham, 1994, pp. 157–8.
29. Sergei S. Berezhnoi, op. cit., pp. 42–3, 297–9.
30. Morskoi general'nii shtab, Sbornik materialov po poitu boevoi deyatel'nosti voenno-morskikh sil SSSR, No. 39, Opyt perevozok podvodnykh lodok i malykh korablei po zheleznym dorogam v Velikuyu Otechestvennuyu vojnu, Moscow, Voenizdat, 1951. V. Aleksandr Basov, 'Der Bau der Seekriegsflotte der UdSSR vor dem Zweiten Weltkrieg', *Revue Internationale d'Histoire Militaire*, XXIII (1991), p. 121. S.E. Zakharov, et al., *Krasnoznamenny Tikhookeanskii flot*, 2nd edn, Moscow, Voenizdat, 1993 – building dates and dates for the transfer of the submarines: A.V. Platonov, *Sovetskie Boevye korabli 1941–1945 gg, III. Podvodnye lodki*, St Petersburg, Al'manakh Tsitadel', 1996, pp. 41–2, 90–94.
31. I.A. Kozlov and V.S. Shlomin, *Severnyi flot*, Moscow, Voenizdat, 1966, pp. 79–81.
32. Jürg Meister 'Det tysk-sovietiska marina samarbetet aren 1920–1941', *Tidskrift i Sjöväsendet*, September 1955, pp. 491–513. Olaf Groehler, *Selbstmöderische Allianz. Deutsch-Russische Militärbeziehungen 1920–1941*, Berlin, Vision, 1992. Tobias R. Philbin, *The Lure of Neptune. German–Soviet Naval Collaboration and Ambitions, 1919–1941*, Columbia, University of South Carolina Press, 1994. Manfred Zeidler, *Reichswehr und Rote Armee 1920–1933. Wege und Stationen einer ungewöhnlichen Zusammenarbeit*, Munich, Oldenburg, 1993.
33. Manfred Zeidler, op. cit., p. 334.
34. Ibid., pp. 135–54.
35. Ibid., pp. 237–8. Tobias Philbin, op. cit., pp. 11–17.
36. Tobias Philbin, op. cit., p. 14.
37. Manfred Zeidler, op. cit., p. 238.
38. Tobias Philbin, op. cit., pp. 14–15.
39. Jürgen Rohwer and Mikhail Monakov, 'The Soviet Union's Ocean-Going Fleet', *The International History Review*, XI (1996), p. 845.
40. Franco Bargoni, *Esploratori Fregate Corvette ed Avvisi Italiani 1861–1968*, Rome, Ufficio Storico della Marina Militare, 1969, pp. 320–21.
41. V.I. Dmitriev, *Sovetskoe podvodnoe korabli/stroenie*, Moscow, Voenizdat, 1990, pp. 32–63. V.N. Burov, *Otechestvennoe voennoe korabl'stroenie v tret'em stoleti svoei istorii*, St Petersburg, Sudostroenie, 1995, pp. 73–9.
42. Luciano Zani, 'La Marina Italiana e l'Unione Sovietica tra le due guerre'. Parte prima, 1929–1933, *Bolletino d'Archivo dell'Ufficio Storico della Marina Militare*, Anno VIII, June 1994, pp. 99–151.
43. Ibid., pp. 108–16. On pp. 131, 151 many documents about the visits with itineraries of the Soviet officials in Italy and their requests and the Italian answers are recorded.
44. Jürg Meister, *Soviet Warships of the Second World War*, London, Macdonald, 1977, pp. 46–8. V.N. Burov, op. cit., pp. 97–101. S. Breyer, op. cit., vol. 3, pp. 14–15. *Istoriya Otechestvennoi sudostroenie*, op. cit., vol. IV, pp. 100–4, 155–62.
45. *Istoriya ...*, op. cit., vol. IV, pp. 189–95.
46. *Istoriya ...*, op. cit., vol. IV, pp. 189–96.
47. S.S. Berezhnoi, op. cit., pp. 184–91.
48. V.I. Dmitriev, op. cit., pp. 32–66. *Istoriya ...*, op. cit., vol. IV, pp. 102–11. J.N. Westwood, op. cit., pp. 153–9.
49. *Istoriya ...*, op. cit., vol. IV, pp. 173–82, 324. N.N. Afonin, 'Lideri eskadrennykh minonostsev tipo "Leningrad"', *Sudostroenie*, 37/1985, pp. 66–9. S. Breyer, op. cit., pp. 46–51.
50. *Istoriya ...*, op. cit., vol. IV, pp. 190–6. S. Breyer, op. cit., vol. 2, pp. 46–51.

51. *Istoriya* ..., op. cit., vol. IV, pp. 113–19. B. Tyurin and V. Balabin, 'Podvodnyi minnyi zagraditel "Leninets"', *Morskoi sbornik*, pp. 71–3. V.I. Dmitriev, op. cit., pp. 75–90. S. Breyer, op. cit., vol. 2, pp. 52–4. A.V. Platonov, *Sovetskie boevye korabli 1941–1945. Vol. III, Podvodnye lodki*, St Petersburg, 1996, pp. 122–9. J.N. Westwood, op. cit., pp. 159–64.
52. *Istoriya* ..., op. cit., vol. IV, pp. 119–22. V.I. Dmitriev, op. cit., pp. 93–100. S. Breyer, op. cit., vol. 2, pp. 66–8. A.V. Platonov, op. cit., vol. III, pp. 36–40.
53. *Istoriya* ..., op. cit., vol. IV, pp. 127–33. V.Yu. Gribovskii, 'Podvodnye lodki tipa "Pravda"', *Sudostroenie*, 7 (1989), pp. 54–6. V.I. Dmitriev, op. cit., pp. 110–17. S. Breyer, op. cit., vol. 2, pp. 63–6. A.V. Platonov, op. cit., vol. III, pp. 24–7.
54. *Istoriya* ..., op. cit., vol. IV, pp. 123–5. V.I. Dmitriev, op. cit., pp. 100–10. S. Breyer, op. cit., vol. 2, pp. 70–75. A.V. Platonov, op. cit., vol. III, pp. 41–2.
55. *Istoriya* ..., op. cit., vol. IV, pp. 133–7. V.N. Maslennikov, 'Podvodnye lodki tipa "Malyutka"', *Sudostroenie*, 5 (1989), pp. 62–4. V.I. Dmitriev, op. cit., pp. 117–28. S. Breyer, op. cit., vol. 2, pp. 68–9. A.V. Platonov, op. cit., vol. III, pp. 87–92.

5

The Second Five-Year Plan, 1933–37

INTERNATIONAL POLITICS AND STRATEGY

While the Western democracies at the start of the 1930s were struggling to overcome the Great Depression, the Soviet Union tried to use its own planned economy as a propaganda weapon against the 'catastrophic economic situation' in the bourgeois democracies. This was having some success in Western intellectual circles, where people joined the communist parties of their own countries and saw the Soviet Union as an example worth emulating. In several countries elections led to a strengthening of rightist parties but left-wing parties were also establishing 'people's front' governments.

During the first half of the 1930s the international situation worsened from the Soviet point of view. The Japanese invasion of Manchuria in 1931 and the rise to power of Adolf Hitler in Germany led to fears which seemed to make a change in Soviet foreign policy necessary. While Stalin was strengthening the internal regime by making 'Soviet patriotism' a top priority in educational efforts, and put his close follower V.M. Molotov into the chair of the *Sovet Narodnykh Komissarov SSSR (SNK SSSR)*, the *Narkom* for Foreign Relations, M.M. Litvinov, was engaged in establishing improved relations with foreign countries by signing a series of treaties and agreements. On 3 September 1932 a pact of non-aggression and friendship was concluded with Italy. On 12 December 1932 an agreement with China followed. In 1933 a new German–Soviet economic treaty was signed on 29 May, and diplomatic relations were taken up with Spain on 28 July, the United States on 16 November, and with Romania and Czechoslovakia on 9 June 1934. Finally on 18 September 1934 Litvinov secured the entry of the Soviet Union into the League of Nations. On 2 and 16 May 1935 pacts of mutual assistance were concluded with France and Czechoslovakia. Besides such efforts to participate in a policy of 'collective security', on 25 July 1935 the VIIth Congress of the *Komintern* decided to support a tactic of 'people's fronts'.[1]

The main strategic aim in this situation was to establish 'a reliable active defence of the USSR's land and sea borders'. For the Navy this meant being able to conduct a series of co-ordinated blows by the various classes of naval forces – submarines, MTBs, and naval air forces, backed up by a pattern of minefields and a strong coastal artillery, to defeat an enemy's attack from the sea, and to support the operations of the Army.

SHIPBUILDING AND THE FORCED INDUSTRIALIZATION PROGRAMME

Stalin on 4 February 1931 had ordered an intensification of industrialization. The Second Five-Year Plan, developed in 1932 and finally approved on 11 July 1933, attempted to align the available and the planned resources with the principal tasks in a more reasonable manner. The directives for economic development, adopted by the XVIIth Bolshevik Party Congress on 16 March 1934, put forward the task of creating new industrial centres in the eastern part of the country. The growth in the importance of this area resulted in a considerable build-up of industrial centres in the Ural and Siberian areas. But the attempt to feed the growing population of the new industrial centres by forcing the delivery of food supplies by coercive measures led to the catastrophic famine of 1933/34 in the Ukraine and other agrarian regions. Notwithstanding this, the big metallurgical centres in the east, such as at Magnitogorsk, began to produce steel, tractors, and so on, and the new plants of the armament industry were delivering the first new tanks and aircraft, and new shipbuilding yards were being built not only at seaports but also close to inland waterways.

In autumn 1933 L. Ivanov and P. Smirnov published their joint book on the subject of naval competition between Great Britain and the United States since the Washington Conference of 1922.[2] They asserted that battleships were the backbone of the naval strategy of all participating naval powers. The Chief of the *VMS RKKA*, V.M. Orlov, did not agree with the authors' conclusion. He claimed it was a 'false book, because it blew up the principles of the Soviet naval strategy adopted by the Party'.[3] But Stalin had read the book before Orlov and accepted it with great satisfaction. By the beginning of the 1930s he had become a supporter of the Navy.

Deploying two new fleets, the Naval Forces of the Far East on 21 April 1932 and the Northern Naval Flotilla on 1 June 1933, made it necessary to get a number of combat ships and auxiliaries for the new fleets. Owing to the lack of new ships the first units of the re-established Pacific Fleet were converted merchant vessels. But it was quite clear that the new Pacific Fleet would suffer from a shortage of combat ships for a long time without shipbuilding yards in the Far East. Therefore urgent measures were undertaken in order to increase the maritime repair plants at Vladivostok and Khabarovsk.

In addition, the Soviet authorities decided to build a huge modern shipbuilding yard and to establish a new industrial centre on the Amur at Komsomol'sk. As already mentioned, it was decided in December 1931 to build small and medium-sized submarines in Leningrad and Nikolaev, to be transported in sections or with the whole pressure hull by rail on the *Transsib* to the assembly yards at Khabarovsk and Vladivostok.[4] And at the same time it was planned to construct combat vessels at river yards, like the new submarine yard at Gorkii on the Volga.[5]

On 25 July 1932 the Soviet Government decided to start building a gigantic yard at Molotovsk near Arkhangel'sk, capable of constructing the biggest ships in roof-covered dry docks. But it was expected that new ships would be completed at this yard only later, and that the new Northern Fleet had at first to be sent from the Baltic by the completed Baltic–White Sea ('Stalin') Canal, a feat which was first accomplished in the summer of 1933.

In January 1934 K.E. Voroshilov in a speech at the XVIIth Party Congress noted that Stalin would now manage the build-up of the Navy himself. But in actual fact a new stage of the Soviet Navy's pre-war development began only two years later.

STRATEGY AND SHIPBUILDING PLANS

The proposals for the development of the *VMS RKKA* during the Second Five-Year Plan were based on the operational tasks of the naval forces on the now four main theatres, the Baltic, the Black Sea, the North, and the Far East, as well as at the closed area of the Caspian Sea and the Amur river. The main tasks were the effective defence of the coastal areas and the prevention of amphibious landings by the enemy. At the beginning of 1933 it was planned to conduct defensive actions of a tactical scale at the approaches to Vladivostok and the Tartar Strait, as well as at the approaches of the Kola Gulf and the White Sea. An entrance of enemy forces into either the Black or Caspian Seas had to be prevented. In the Baltic the fleet had to support the *RKKA* and to hinder enemy landings in Finland, Estland or on the islands of the Finnish Gulf. And raid operations were included in the operational plan of the Black Sea Fleet. Beside the tasks of the sea forces, the tasks of the Dnepr Flotilla to destroy in case of war the Polish river flotilla and to support the Army's operations, and the securing of the Amur river by the Amur Flotilla were mentioned.[6]

For the tasks mentioned the development of the necessary forces were planned as follows:[7]

- Fundamental for the development of the *VMS* was the strengthening of the mobile forces, especially the submarines and the attack air forces.

- Basic to the programme of the submarine force were the medium-sized vessels of 600–750t. At the same time it was necessary to build some big submarines of 900–1000t for operations with surface forces and for operations at greater distances from the coast, and for operations against the sea communications of the enemy. In connection with the defence of the bases the small submarines of 150t would be restricted to the accepted number of 30 units.

- For the support of submarine operations and the stability of the sea defence of the USSR as well as for the successful fight against the anti-submarine forces of the enemy the close co-operation of the submarine forces with the surface forces was necessary, and therefore destroyers and cruisers were necessary. This was especially important in the Far East and the Black Sea. The availability of some cruisers offered the additional possibilities of using other naval weapons like torpedoes, mines, and gunfire.

- Important was the development of support forces for the fleet, like minesweepers, submarine chasers, depot ships, training vessels, and so on. They were necessary for the conduct of operations and combat training.
- The development of the merchant fleet was to be organized according to the use of the merchant ships in times of war.
- For the effective defence of the sea borders of the USSR close co-operation between the fleet, the air force and the coastal defence was necessary, and the decisive role for the Navy was to be placed on the operations of the submarines and the attack air forces.

It was concluded from the estimates that the big and medium submarines had to be available for all four fleets, the small ones only for the Far East. For the Black Sea as for other areas new cruisers (four), destroyer leaders and destroyers were necessary, for the Baltic and Far East two new cruisers each, destroyer leaders and destroyers, for the North only submarines and the transfer of the modernized old *Novik*-class destroyers was envisaged.

The Second Five-Year Plan for 1933–37 was developed in 1932 and decided by the *STO* on 11 July 1933. In the following months several corrections were made. The plan placed the primary emphasis on the armaments and shipbuilding industry. But the principles of Soviet naval strategy had not yet been revised, therefore the second shipbuilding programme was directed above all to the construction of submarines.

The first version of the plan called for 281 submarines, 123 for the Far East, 79 for the Black Sea, 32 for the Baltic, and 47 for the Northern Flotilla. There were plans to deploy nine ocean-going submarines in the Pacific in wartime, 30 in the Korean Strait, 18 in the Laperouse and Tsugaru Straits, and 18 in the Sea of Japan against the sea communications of the expected enemy, Japan. Nine big and 18 medium submarines would be deployed in the Black Sea near the Bosporus, to close the Straits to any enemy; six big and 24 medium submarines in the Central and Eastern Baltic, and nine ocean-going submarines of the Northern Flotilla against Britain's oceanic sea communications. The Navy's share of the Soviet defence budget was increased by 1933 from 4.7 per cent to 8.9 per cent.[8]

The version of 11 July 1933 increased the number of submarines, including the number of 74 submarines from earlier orders, to 369: 69 big, 200 medium, and 100 small. In addition there were eight cruisers with 180mm guns and torpedo armament, called 'cruisers for the concentrated blow', 22 destroyer leaders (including three ordered earlier), 40 destroyers, 28 patrol vessels, 267 MTBs, 60 submarine chasers, 27 sea-going minesweepers, 15 base minesweepers, 12 river monitors, 8 river gun boats, and 28 armoured cutters. And the modernization of the battleships *Oktyabrskaya revolyutsiya* and *Parizhskaya kommuna*, the completion of the cruiser *Voroshilov* as a training cruiser, the mine cruiser *Marti* and the training vessel *Polyarnaya zvezda* were included. In addition it was planned to build or to get 143 auxiliaries and 26 vessels for the fleet of the *OGPU* (Sea Border Guard), including two big patrol ships and four medium patrol ships, developed from the fast minesweeper type.[9]

In November 1933 some changes were made, correcting the number of submarines to 321, the cruisers to four, the destroyer leaders to eight, and the destroyers to 22, to be commissioned at the end of 1937.[10]

During the discussions with the industry the *Glavnoe Upravlenie Morskogo Sudostroeniya (Glavmorprom* – Main Administration for Marine Shipbuilding) proposed to reduce the submarines to 246 and to postpone the laying down of the river monitors and the armoured cutters. But it was decided to use the yards of the *Glavnoe Upravlenie Rechnogo Sudostroeniya (Glavrechprom* – Main Administration for River Shipbuilding), the *Krasnoe Sormovo* yard at Gorkii and the *Kolomenskii zavod*, so that 33 medium submarines could be built there; the river monitors and the armoured cutters were given to the yards *Leninskaya kuznitsa* at Kiev and *A.M. Gorkii* at Zelenodol'sk.

Glavmorprom was able to limit the reduction of ships of some types, but proposed building 450 MTBs in five years. For 1934 *Glavmorprom* planned to lay down 243 units, including 137 submarines, and to deliver from 1933 to 1935 some 269 surface ships and cutters. But these production quotas were not in fact achieved.

FOREIGN AID DURING THE SECOND FIVE-YEAR PLAN

To complete this big programme by the end of 1937 in a period of rapid industrialization presupposed an immense expansion of the shipbuilding yards. Equipment and weapons, however, would have to be made in the interior and transported along the rivers and canals.[11] And because of the inexperience of Soviet engineers, and the detention of some of the more experienced, foreign aid had to be sought again.

The French were reluctant during 1934–35 to deliver plans for cruisers, big destroyers of the *L'Audacieux*-class, or submarines, or to help with the development of torpedoes.[12] But from the German-owned construction bureau *IvS* at Den Haag the plans for the submarine *Gür*, built in Spain to a German design *E-1*, and sold to Turkey, were purchased and became the model for the Soviet *series IX/N*, later *S*-class, which was built at Leningrad with the support of some engineers from the German yard *Deschimag* at Bremen. The design was also the basis for the later first new German U-Boats of *Type I/U 25*.[13]

But most of the assistance during this period was coming from Italy. The *Ansaldo* shipyard at Genoa in 1934 built two patrol ships *Kirov* and *Dzerzhinskii* of 810ts stdd. with *Fiat*-diesel motors for the Far East *OGPU*.[14] But more important was assistance in the construction of cruisers and destroyers. From April to June 1932 E.S. Pantserzhanskii, I.M. Ludri and V.M. Orlov had been discussing a new cruiser of 6500ts stdd with 180mm guns like those of the *Krasnyi Kavkaz*. The shipbuilding engineers V.L. Bzhezinskii and V.A. Nikitin had designed a cruiser of 10,000ts stdd. But after several visits of Soviet experts to Italy on 28 August 1933 the Chief of the *VMS RKKA*, V.M. Orlov, proposed buying the plans of the modern Italian cruiser *Raimondo Montecuccoli*, which since 1931 had been under construction at the *Ansaldo* yard at Genoa, including the machinery set, and if possible a real cruiser. On 19 December 1934 the Technical Director of the *Ansaldo* yard, Mr Enrico, with the head of the engine design bureau of the company, Mr Cortese, visited Moscow. The Fascist regime had agreed to deliver the plan of the cruiser *Raimondo Montecuccoli*, and the two men had to negotiate the delivery of the machinery set for the first new Soviet cruiser *Kirov* and the plans to build the sets for its sisters under licence.[15]

A special case was the invitation in early 1935 to three Italian yards to build a special high-speed destroyer leader. Of the offers from the yards *Cantiere dell'Adriatico* at Monfalcone, *Ansaldo* at Genoa, and *Odero-Terni-Orlando* at Livorno this last was selected, and in September 1935 the contract to build the first ship and to assist in the building of replicas in the USSR was signed. The *projekt 20* vessel of 2,830ts stdd., got the name *Tashkent* and was laid down on 11 January 1937, and achieved during the trials in the Mediterranean, still without weapons, a speed of 43.5kt. She was handed over to the Soviet commission on 6 May 1939 and went to the Black Sea, after the planned assignment to the Baltic Fleet was changed because of the difficult situation. In the Black Sea it was not until 1941 that she got the final armament of three 130mm twin turrets and three 533mm triple torpedo tube sets. Of the two replicas planned for the Baltic, and one for the Black Sea, only the first got a name, *Baku*, but the ships were never laid down and finally cancelled because of difficulties with the adaptation of the Italian design to Soviet practices.[16]

But of the greatest importance was the support of the Italians for the Soviet destroyer building. Already the commission under K.I. Dushenov in 1932 had visited the new Italian destroyers *Dardo* and *Baleno* of 1480 and 1465ts stdd, respectively, which influenced the design of the *projekt 7/Gnevnyi*-class destroyers, planned for a designed stdd. displacement of 1425t, a speed of 38kt, and an armament of four 130mm guns, and two triple 533mm torpedo-tube sets. The fate of this class is described in a later chapter.[17]

SUBMARINE BUILDING IN THE SECOND FIVE-YEAR PLAN

The submarine building programme was at the centre of Soviet efforts in the Second Five-Year Plan. Several improved or new types were designed and laid down. Table 5.1 gives the planning and commissioning details for 1933 to 1938.[18]

Medium Submarines

But such high target dates could not be met, as will be seen. The main effort was with the medium submarines. Two batches of *series V* of about the same size but with increased diesel output to attain a slightly higher surface speed were laid down. Of 13 *series V-bis* boats 12 were laid down at the *Marti* and *Ordzhonikidze* (the former *Baltiiskii zavod*) yards at Leningrad and one with the *Krasnoe Sormovo* yard at Gorkii. Of those boats eight were sent in sections by rail to the Far East, where six were completed at *Dalzavod* in Vladivostok, and two at Khabarovsk, three were sent for completion to the *No. 61 Kommunar* yard

THE SECOND FIVE-YEAR PLAN

Table 5.1: Planning and commissioning details for 1933–38

Class of submarines	1933 plan to lay down	1933 commiss.	1934 plan to lay down	1934 commiss.	1935 plan to lay down	1935 commiss.	1936 plan to lay down	1936 commiss.	1937 plan to lay down	1937 commiss.	1938 plan to commission	Total commission
Big	–	6	8	1	15	5	26	15	13	18	24	69
Medium	23	13	33	30	43	35	55	43	24	55	24	200
Small	–	30	20	20	20	20	30	30	–	10	–	110
Total	23	40	61	51	78	60	111	88	37	83	48	369

at Nikolaev for the Black Sea, and two remained with the Baltic Fleet. Of the 14 units of the *series V-bis2*, eight were laid down at the two yards in Leningrad, five of which went to Vladivostok, one to Nikolaev and two remained with the Baltic Fleet. Three were built by the *No. 61 Kommunar* yard at Nikolaev for the Black Sea, and three at Gorkii for the Baltic Fleet. The vessels were laid down between October 1932 and November 1933, and completed between January 1935 and December 1936.[19]

In 1934 a new version of these medium *series X* submarines followed. These had slightly lower displacement but a higher surface speed of 14.1kt against the 12.3kt of the earlier boats. Thirty-two of this series were laid down from May 1934 to January 1936. Nine boats were built at the two yards in Leningrad for the Far East, of which eight were assembled and commissioned at Vladivostok, and one at Khabarovsk. Eight units for the Black Sea were built at the *No. 61 Kommunar* yard in Nikolaev, nine were built at the two yards in Leningrad and six at Gorkii for the Baltic Fleet. Of these four were transferred in 1937 by the Baltic–White Sea Canal route to the Northern Fleet. It is of interest that the periscopes of these boats were from the Italian firm *Galileo*.[20]

For the medium submarines there was some foreign assistance, as previously mentioned, from the German firm IvS in Den Haag which had provided on 12 August 1933 the plans for its design *E-2*, and a team under Z.A. Deribin together with engineers from the German yard *Deschimag* developed the final plan, to be accepted by the members of the *Politburo*, Voroshilov and Ordzhonikidze on 4 August 1934. The *series IX*-class first had *N*-numbers for *Nemetskii* (German), later S-numbers for *srednie* (medium). These submarines had a displacement of 840t, a speed of 19.5kt on the surface and 9kt submerged, and four bow- and two stern 533mm torpedo tubes with six reserve torpedoes. One 100mm gun and one 45mm gun were added. Three submarines of this type were started from December 1934 to April 1935 at the *Baltiiskii zavod* at Leningrad and completed with the assistance of some engineers from the *Deschimag* yard in October 1937 (two) and July 1938 (one).

This type was improved upon to some extent by the *series IX-bis*, with minimal changes in the mentioned data, and this would became the most successful type built during the next Five-Year Plan and up to the end of the Second World War. The first three vessels were built at the *Baltiiskii zavod* (soon to be renamed the *Ordzhonikidze zavod*) in Leningrad from December 1935 to November 1939. Before the end of the Second Five-Year Plan period from November 1936 the *Marti zavod* at Leningrad began to build three units, followed in April 1937 by two more at the *Ordzhonikidze zavod*, to be sent by rail in sections to the *Dalzavod* at Vladivostok for assembly and commissioning between January 1941 and June 1943. For the Black Sea the *Marti* yard at Nikolaev started construction in October and November 1937 on two vessels each, to be completed between June 1940 and April 1941. And from December 1936 the *Krasnoe Sormovo* yard at Gorkii was included in the production line, laying down up to the end of 1937 six vessels for the Baltic Fleet and two more for the Northern Fleet, which were completed in 1940 and 1941 just at the beginning of the war.[21]

Small Submarines

In order to build up speedily a submarine force for the defence of the Far East coastal areas A.N. Asafov designed a small submarine of only 157t, which could be constructed both rapidly and cheaply, and could be transported, without division into sections in 19 special railway transport carriages, built also at Nikolaev, from the building yards at Nikolaev to Vladivostok for completion. Asafov had requested a welded construction, but the hulls had to be riveted. During the first test in spring of 1933 the vessel achieved only 5kt submerged, needed 80 seconds to dive, and was difficult to handle after firing its torpedoes when it broke the surface. Corrections had to be made. As mentioned, the series of 30 boats was ready in December 1934, but a replacement for one boat damaged beyond repair by fire, did not come until June 1935.[22]

After the first tests V.M. Orlov organized a commission to isolate any defects with Yu.A. Shimanskii, E.P. Papkovich, and Asafov so as to develop an improved design, which was then ordered with the support of the then Deputy *Narkom* for Defence Tukhachevskii, and the deputy to Orlov, I.M. Ludri, a submarine enthusiast. The *series VI-bis* was a little larger than its predecessor with 161t, but of welded construction with a much improved hull surface enabling it to attain a higher speed of 13.2kt (against 11.1kt) on the surface, and 7.2kt submerged (against 6.4kt); other faults were also corrected. Building started between February 1934 and March 1935. Twelve vessels were laid down at the *Marti* yard and three at the *No. 61 Kommunar* yard at Nikolaev, and five at the *Sudomekh* yard in Leningrad. But of the *Marti* vessels only the leading unit remained in the Black Sea, while the others were transferred to the Baltic Fleet.[23]

But more improvements were needed for this type of small submarine. So in 1936 a new *series XII* of 206t was started, designed by P.I. Seldyuk and B.M. Malinin, with stronger diesel- and electric motors for a speed of 14.4/7.8 kt. The first four boats were laid down in June and September 1936 at the *Sudomekh* yard in Leningrad for the Baltic Fleet, of which two were completed before the end of the year. In 1937 construction was started at the *Krasnoe Sormovo* yard in Gorkii with six boats, four for the Black Sea and two for the Baltic, and three more from the *Sudomekh* yard also for the Baltic. The construction of this series was continued into the first years of the war.[24]

Big Submarines

After the relative success of the *series II* minelaying submarines, a new improved *series XI* was decided upon for the Far East on 13 August 1933. At 1040t the vessel was slightly faster (14.5/8.0kt) and could load 16 instead of

1. Submarine *D-6/Spartakovets*. Of this series I, six vessels were built from 1927 to 1931, three each for the Naval Forces of the Baltic and Black Sea.
(*Source:* Library of Contemporary History)

2. Three patrol ships of *projekt 2*, the *Uragan*-class, during an exercise in the Baltic during the 1930s. Twelve vessels were built during 1927–36; two more of the similar *projekt 4* were built for the Naval Forces of the Black Sea and the Pacific. Up to 1938 two more of the similar *projekt 39* were completed for the Baltic Fleet. Of *projekt 2* four were transferred to the Pacific and three to the Northern Flotilla.
(*Source:* Library of Contemporary History)

3. Destroyer leader *Leningrad* of *projekt 1*. Three vessels were built from 1932 to 1938, one for the Baltic Fleet, two for the Black Sea Fleet. From 1934 to 1940 there followed three of the improved *projekt 38*, one for the Baltic and two for the Pacific, of which one was transferred on the Northern Seaway to the Northern Fleet in 1942. (*Source:* US National Archives/Library of Contemporary History)

4. Big submarine *P-1/Pravda*. Of this series IV, only three vessels were built from 1931 to 1936 for the Baltic Fleet. They developed many problems and were used mostly for training. (*Source:* Library of Contemporary History)

5. Small submarine of the series VI, of which 30 were built at Nikolaev from 1932 to 1934; 28 were sent by rail on the 'Transsib' to the Naval Forces of the Pacific, and two remained in the Black Sea. From 1934 to 1936 there followed 20 units of the improved series VI-bis, 16 for the Baltic Fleet and four for the Black Sea Fleet. Four of the Baltic and two of the Black Sea boats were transferred by rail on the 'Transsib' to the Pacific. (*Source:* Library of Contemporary History)

6. Medium submarine *S-56* of the series IX-bis. First, from 1934 to 1937 there were three units built for the Baltic Fleet from German plans as series IX. In 1936 building then started of the Soviet adapted series IX-bis, of which by 22 June 1941 14 had been completed, nine for the Baltic, four for the Black Sea and one for the Pacific; 31 more were in different stages of construction, as was *S-56*, commissioned in October 1941 and shown here during her transfer from the Pacific Fleet to the Northern Fleet on the Panama Canal in 1942.
(*Source:* US Navy/Library of Contemporary History)

7. Destroyer leader *Tashkent*, *projekt 20-I*, built between 1936 and 1939 in Italy, and transferred to the Black Sea Fleet, where the ship got final armaments. A plan to build three replicas in the USSR was cancelled.
(*Source:* Library of Contemporary History)

8. Big submarine *K-21* of series XIV. Twelve of these cruiser submarines were laid down from 1936 to 1938; six were completed before June 1941 and transferred by inland waterways to the Northern Fleet, five more completed during the war for the Baltic Fleet, the sixth damaged beyond repair by air attack and cancelled.
(*Source:* Library of Contemporary History)

9. Cruiser *Kirov* of *projekt 26*. Two ships were built from 1935 to 1940, one each for the Baltic and Black Sea Fleets. Two more followed of the improved *projekt 26-bis*, as well as one each for the Baltic and Black Sea Fleets. And from 1938 to 1944 two more of the further improved *projekt 26-bis2* were built at Komsomol'sk for the Pacific Fleet.
(*Source:* Library of Contemporary History)

10. Destroyer *Gordyi* of *projekt 7*. Fifty-three vessels were laid down in 1935 and 1936. Up to 1939 ten were completed for the Baltic Fleet, of which five were transferred to the Northern Fleet, and six built for the Black Sea Fleet. Up to 1942 the Pacific Fleet got 12, built from materials prepared in Nikoalev, with one more being lost before commissioning. Of the remaining ships, 18 were stopped on the slips and re-laid down as *projekt 7-U*, and six were cancelled.
(*Source:* Library of Contemporary History)

11. Destroyer *Soobrazitel'nyi* of *projekt 7-U*. Eighteen vessels of *projekt 7* were halted before launching, reconstructed and re-laid down in 1938/39 as *projekt 7-U*. Eight were completed before 22 June 1941, the rest in the second half-year 1941 and in early 1942; 13 vessels served in the Baltic Fleet, and 5 in the Black Sea Fleet.
(*Source:* Library of Contemporary History)

12. Minesweeper *Iskatel'* of *projekt 53*. Of the similar *projekt 3* eight vessels were built from 1933 to 1938, four each for the Baltic and the Black Sea Fleets. Of *projekt 53* ten vessels were built from 1935 to 1938, four for the Black Sea and six for the Pacific Fleets. Of the improved *projekt 53-U* 17 were laid down from 1937 to 1941, of which 13 were completed between 1939 and June 1941, two more later in 1941 and 1944, and two only in 1946. They served in the Baltic Fleet. Of the similar *projekt 58* seven were laid down from 1937 to 1939, of which two were commissioned for the Pacific Fleet in 1938/39, and five from 1939 to 1941 for the Black Sea Fleet. Two more were laid down but not completed. 
(*Source:* Private Collection of Igor Amosov/ Library of Contemporary History)

13. Battleship *Sovetskaya Ukraina* of *projekt* 23 being built at Nikolaev from 1938 to 1941. Captured in August 1941 on the slip by the Germans and partially broken down to take the materials for other uses. (*Source*: Bundesarchiv Koblenz)

14. Battleship *Sevastopol'*, ex *Parizhskaya Kommuna*, after the last reconstruction in 1938 with additional anti-aircraft armaments and added torpedo bulges. Photo taken after the reversion on 31 May 1943 to the old name of *Sevastopol'*.
(*Source:* Library of Contemporary History)

15. Medium submarine *S-125*, ex *Shch-125*, ex *Muksun*, of series V-bis2. Of this series 14 were built from 1933 to 1936. The five vessels for the Pacific Fleet were built from materials prepared at Leningrad and sent by rail to Vladivostok, like *S-125*, of which this photo was taken after the war, when all the medium submarines became numbers with *S-*. Of the five vessels for the Baltic Fleet three were built at the big inland submarine yard at Gorkii and transferred on inland waterways. Of the four Black Sea boats one was started in Leningrad and transferred to Nikolaev for completion. The earlier series V (12 vessels) and V-bis (13) and the later series X (32) and X-bis (9 vessels in 1941 and two in 1945/46 completed) were similar.
(*Source:* US Navy/Library of Contemporary History)

16. Destroyer *Ognevoi* of *projekt 30*. Of the 26 vessels laid down from 1939 to 22 June 1941, only the *Ognevoi* was completed to the original design in 1945 for the Black Sea Fleet. She was towed away after launch in August 1941 from Nikolaev to Caucasian ports and first laid up but later completed just before the end of the war. The other vessels were also laid up. From 1947 to 1950 ten other vessels were completed to the improved design *projekt 30-K*, four for the Baltic Fleet, one more for the Black Sea Fleet, two to the Northern Fleet, and three for the Pacific Fleet.
(*Source:* Library of Contemporary History)

17. Heavy cruiser *L*, ex German *Lützow*, sold in February 1940 to the USSR, on tow in April 1940 to Leningrad to become the heavy cruiser *Petropavlovsk* as *projekt 83-I*, to be completed in 1942. Damaged during the siege of Leningrad in September 1941 by German gunfire and sank to the harbour bottom; later raised and used as accommodation hulk *Tallinn*. (*Source:* Library of Contemporary History)

12 torpedoes. The mine-capacity was the same with 20 mines in two horizontal mine tubes at the stern. Three boats each were started from April to June 1934 at the *Ordzhonikidze* yard in Leningrad and the *Marti* yard in Nikolaev for transportation in parts by rail to the Far East, four to Vladivostok, and two to the new yard at Komsomol'sk. The Leningrad boats were completed in November/December 1936, and of the Nikolaev boats one was finished in December 1937 and the others at the end of 1938.[25]

This was followed immediately by a new improved *series XIII* minelayer of 1120t, with a higher speed (15/9kt) and two additional 533mm torpedo tubes but the same mine load. Designed by a team under B.M. Malinin, between April 1935 and January 1936 four were laid down at the *Ordzhonikidze* yard in Leningrad, and three at the *Marti* yard in Nikolaev, and transported in sections by rail to be completed at the *Dalzavod* in Vladivostok during the next plan period between October 1938 and November 1939.[26]

From 1930 to 1932 there were discussions about a big submarine of 1000 to 1200t with two 102mm guns, ten 533mm torpedo tubes with 24 torpedoes, mines, and a speed of 21–22 kt, a range of 15,000 miles and a 50-day endurance. This led to the project of a cruiser submarine, which was developed by M.A. Rudnitskii and presented on 15 April 1935 by the *STO* to the Politburo. The idea was to build 20 submarines of this *KE-series XIV* of 1,480t up to 1942, and later on 42 of a successor type. The first three vessels were laid down in December 1936 at the *Marti* yard in Leningrad, to be followed by two more in April and October 1937 at the *Ordzhonikidze* yard, and one in December 1937 at the *Sudomekh* yard also in Leningrad. Five more followed in 1938, but then the programme was interrupted, and of the 12 vessels started only six were ready at the end of 1940.[27]

Finally, there were some special test midget submarines. First in 1935 two very small submarines of the *APSS*-type of 7.2t with one 450mm torpedo were built at the *Sudomekh* yard, and in 1936 the head of the Ostekhbyuro, V.I. Bekauri, designed a midget of 18.6t, named *Pigmei*, carrying two 450mm torpedoes, built in Leningrad to be tested in the Black Sea. The tests were promising but when Bekauri was arrested in 1937 further tests were abandoned for the time being.[28]

SURFACE SHIPS IN THE SECOND FIVE-YEAR PLAN

Cruisers

The biggest ships of the Second Five-Year Plan were the 'cruisers for the concentrated blow'. As mentioned, the Italians had ceded the design plans of the cruiser *Raimondo Montecuccoli*. The first operational tactical request (*OTZ*) of 13 March 1932 was for a 6,000t cruiser with a speed of 37–38kt and two twin turrets of 180mm guns. The technical request (*TZ*) of 19 March 1932 raised the displacement to 6,500t and asked for three twin turrets of 180mm. Then the final tactical-technical request (*TTZ*) of 29 December 1934 was for a cruiser of 7,120–7,170ts stdd., 37k, and three triple turrets of 180mm guns. The project was given to the Central Construction Bureau (*TsKBS-1*) under

Table 5.2: Submarine building in the Second Five-Year Plan, 1933–37[29]

Series	to 1932 ld.d.	to 1932 comm.	1933 ld.d.	1933 comm.	1934 ld.d.	1934 comm.	1935 ld.d.	1935 comm.	1936 ld.d.	1936 comm.	1937 ld.d.	1937 comm.	Total ld.d.	Total comm.
I/D	6	6	–	–	–	–	–	–	–	–	–	–	6	6
II/L	6	–	–	5	–	1	–	–	–	–	–	–	6	6
III/Shch	4	–	–	4	–	–	–	–	–	–	–	–	4	4
IV/P	3	–	–	–	–	–	–	–	–	3	–	–	3	3
V/Shch	12	–	–	8	–	4	–	–	–	–	–	–	12	12
Vbis/Shch	7	–	6	–	–	6	–	1	–	–	–	–	13	13
Vbis2 Shch	–	–	11	–	3	–	–	8	–	6	–	–	14	14
VI/M	4	–	26	–	–	29	–	1	–	–	–	–	30	30
VIbis/M	–	–	–	–	18	–	2	12	–	8	–	–	20	20
IX/N-S	–	–	–	–	2	–	1	–	–	2	–	–	3	2
IXbis/S	–	–	–	–	–	–	1	–	7	–	10	–	18	–
X/Shch	–	–	–	–	29	–	3	–	–	23	–	4	32	27
XI/L	–	–	–	–	–	–	6	–	–	3	–	1	6	4
XII/M	–	–	–	–	–	–	–	–	4	–	9	2	13	2
XIII/L	–	–	–	–	–	–	6	–	1	–	–	–	7	–
XIV/K	–	–	–	–	–	–	–	–	3	–	4	–	7	–
Total	42	6	43	17	52	40	19	22	15	45	23	7	194	143

Table 5.3: Distribution to the fleets at the end of 1937

Fleet	I	II	III	IV	V	Vbis	Vbis2	VI	VIbis	IX	X	XI	XII	total
TOF					12	8	5	28			9	4		66
KBF *		3	4	3		2	5		16	2	11		2	48
ChF	3	3				3	4	2	4		3			22
NF	3										4			7
Total	6	6	4	3	12	13	14	30	20	2	27	4	2	143

* TOF = Pacific Fleet, KBF = Krasnoznamennyi (Red Banner) Baltic Fleet, ChF = Black Sea Fleet, NF = Northern Fleet

A.I. Maslov. Problems arose when the machinery set acquired in Italy to the plans of the new cruiser *Eugenio di Savoia* did not fit exactly into the hull of the new *projekt 26* cruiser *Kirov*, and made some redesigning necessary, so that the ship was not laid down until October 1935 at the *Ordzhonikidze* yard in Leningrad, as was the sister *Voroshilov* at the *Marti* yard in Nikolaev. In August 1937 the lead ship was ready for the first tests, but it developed many faults which led to prolonged additional tests, especially for the machinery and the armament. The ship was 800t heavier than planned, and the turbines could not reach the planned 126,600 HP but only 113,000 HP, so that the speed was 1kt lower than the expected. When all main guns were fired, the deck suffered a deformation, and during torpedo tests one errant torpedo hit the cruiser's propeller, leading to the arrest of the chief of the Navy's acceptance commission, A.K. Vekman. So the *Kirov* was not finally accepted until September 1938, while its sister ship *Voroshilov* for the Black Sea followed in June 1940 because of problems with the production of the home-made machinery.[30]

The design was improved for the next pair of cruisers. The side armour was strengthened and the four-leg control tower was replaced by a turret construction similar to that in the Italian cruisers. The anti-aircraft guns were augmented. The lead vessel *Maksim Gorkii* was laid down in December 1936 at the *Ordzhonikidze* yard in Leningrad and the sister ship *Molotov* at the *Marti* yard in Nikolaev. The completion of the ships was also delayed, because there were problems with the turbines. To some extent this was caused by the redirection of the delivered pipes for the turbines of the *Maksim Gorkii* to the new big icebreaker *Iosif Stalin*, which, being so named, was given priority. Thus the two ships were not commissioned until October 1940 and not long before the outbreak of war in June 1941. Two additional ships for the Far East were begun only in 1938.[31]

Destroyer Leaders and Destroyers

Following the *projekt 1 / Leningrad*-class leaders an improved version, correcting some faults found during the construction of the *Leningrad*, was started in 1934 as *projekt 38*, designed under the leadership of V.A. Nikitin. The lead ship *Minsk* was laid down in October 1934 at the *Severnaya verf* (soon to be renamed *Zhdanov zavod*) in Leningrad. The plan was first to build two more there, and three more at the *Marti* yard in Leningrad and two at the *Marti* yard in Nikolaev. But only the two latter vessels were really laid down in January 1935, to be transported and assembled at Komsomol'sk and Vladivostok. The *Minsk* was ready in February 1939 and achieved 40.5kt at the trials. The first Far East vessel was renamed several times, first its planned name was *Kiev*, to be changed at the launching in July 1938 to *Ordzhonikidze*, adding at the commissioning in December 1939 the first name *Sergo*, but when this name was reused for a new cruiser in September 1940 the ship was renamed *Baku*. The second Far East vessel, the *Tbilisi*, was not commissioned until December 1940.[32] Instead of the cancelled vessels it was planned in January 1935 to build replicas of the Italian-built *Tashkent* but this was also changed – as was mentioned earlier.

The replacement of the *Novik*-destroyers led to several ideas, in 1930–31 concentrating on a vessel of 1,300–1,400t with a speed of 40kt. One experimental design was developed by the head of the *TsKBS-1* design bureau, V.L. Bzhezinskii, using the direct-flow boilers designed by Professor L.K. Ramzin, in part modelled after the German Wagner-Benson high-pressure and high-temperature boilers. The plan was to achieve a speed of 42kt by saving weight with a welded construction for a displacement of 1,570t. This *projekt 45* vessel, also first named *Sergo Ordzhonikidze*, was laid down in June 1935 and launched in December of the same year. The gun armament was light with only three 130mm guns, but she got two quadruple 533mm torpedo-tube sets and 16 torpedoes. Because Bzhezinskii was arrested in 1937 as many other engineers and sent to a guarded *OGPU*-construction bureau, the outfitting and tests were hampered by many delays and the vessel, renamed *Opytnyi* in September 1940, was only preliminary commissioned in September 1941.[33]

The most important type was the new series destroyer of *projekt 7*, planned – as mentioned – with 53 units. The design was modelled after the Italian destroyer *Alfredo Oriani* of 1685ts stdd., and built in 1935 at the *Odero-Terni-*

Orlando-yard at Livorno, where the *Tashkent* also was to be built. The design was developed by the *TsKB-1* under A.V. Nikitin, where P.O. Trakhtenberg became responsible for the design. The Italian plans were altered to the Soviet *TTZ*, but models were tested at test tanks in Rome. The final design was approved and the building started in November/December 1935. The plan was to have 21 units in the Baltic, 10 at the Black Sea, and 22 in the Pacific, while the old *Noviks* were to be transferred to the Northern Fleet. But this had to be changed afterwards. All 53 vessels were laid down at four yards between November 1935 and December 1936, 17 at the *Zhdanov zavod*, and 8 at the *Ordzhonikidze* yard at Leningrad, and 16 at the *Marti*-yard and 12 at the *No 61 Kommunar*-yard at Nikolaev. Of the *Marti* vessels seven were transported in parts by rail to Komsomol'sk and five to Vladivostok to be relaid down and completed there. Because one of these ships, the *Reshitel'nyi*, was stranded during a storm on 8 November 1938 during the transfer from the Amur to Vladivostok and became a total loss, one other vessel from Nikolaev was transferred to the Far East as a replacement.

Some of the ships had developed problems during the construction and tests; the machinery and the turbines especially gave some trouble and delayed the commissioning of some vessels such as the lead ship *Gnevnyi*. But before the tests were finally run another problem came up. During the Spanish Civil War in the spring of 1937 the British destroyer *Hunter* hit a mine and was heavily damaged, its forward boiler room becoming a mass of wreckage, and the ship was laid up for quite a while in Malta.[34] This came up in discussions of the *STO*, chaired by Stalin himself, and when it was mentioned that the en-echelon arrangement of the boilers and the machinery might be an advantage at least in big ships, Stalin intervened and decided that destroyers were also valuable ships and should have this arrangement. So the *STO* decided in August 1937 to interrupt the building of the later ships of *projekt 7*, and a new design had to be developed by the bureau of the *Zhdanov* yard under O.F. Yakob, with the en-echelon arrangement of the boilers and turbines as *projekt 7U*.

So ten of the *Zhdanov*-, three of the *Ordzhonikidze*-, and five of the *No. 61 Kommunar*-boats were broken down and relaid to the new design with two funnels, but with the same armament. Two *Ordzhonikidze*- and four *No. 61 Kommunar*-vessels were completely broken down and cancelled. So finally ten *projekt 7* vessels were completed from August 1938 to December 1939 for the Baltic Fleet, of which five were transferred in 1939/40 to the Northern Fleet. From November 1938 to October 1939 six vessels were commissioned for the Black Sea Fleet. And the Pacific Fleet got its 12 vessels between August 1939 and November 1942.

The lead ship of *projekt 7U*, the *Storozhevoi*, was ready in October 1940, to be followed by 11 other vessels up to September 1941 for the Baltic Fleet, and five vessels for the Black Sea Fleet up to January 1942. The destroyers of *projekt 7* had a displacement of 1,885ts stdd. and the *7U*'s finally 1990ts stdd. – all were armed with four 130mm guns, two with 76mm A/A guns, and two with 533mm triple torpedo tube sets. They were equipped with minelaying reels for 56 or 60 mines.[35]

Minesweepers

The remaining minesweepers in the Baltic were of First World War vintage and in addition there were some acquired former fishing vessels in the Baltic and Black Seas so there was a great need for modern replacements. It seemed attractive to use diesel-motors for the propulsive power as the French had in their 315t *Diligente*-class of 1917. In 1930 a first *OTZ* was formulated along those lines. On 25 April 1931 the bureau of Yu.A. Shimanskii presented a design of a 360t vessel to the *STO*. After some discussions this design became in 1932 a 383t vessel and would get besides the diesel-motors a towed *Schultz*-minesweeping gear. The first vessels of a *projekt 3* were laid down in 1933/34, four each at the *Zhdanov* yard at Leningrad for the Baltic Fleet, and at the *Sevmorzavod* at Sevastopol for the Black Sea Fleet. When the first vessel *Fugas* was completed in December 1936, the ships had a displacement of 428t; some problems arose with the diesel-motors built at the *Kolomenskii* works, and with the minesweeping gear which had to be corrected. So the remaining ships did not come into the fleets until 1937/38. The design needed to be improved and the next series became the *projekt 53* of 417t, four of which were laid down in 1935 at the *Zhdanov* yard but then transferred for completion in 1938 to the *Sudomekh* yard in Leningrad after which they were sent by the way of the Panama Canal to the Far East. Six vessels were laid down in 1936 at the *Sevmorzavod* at Sevastopol and completed in 1938. Two of them went by the way of the Suez Canal to the Far East.[36] Based on this design, other series were built in the Third Five-Year Plan, to be described in a later chapter.

Minelayers and other support vessels were taken from the merchant marine and rebuilt for their new tasks, especially in the Far East. One special case is the complete rebuilding of the former imperial yacht *Shtandart* of 1893–96 into the modern minelaying cruiser *Marti*. Rebuilt from 1932 to 1936 at the *Marti* yard in Leningrad the vessel finally had a displacement of 5,665ts stdd., could load 545 mines and was equipped with four 130mm and seven 76mm A/A guns. But she could only reach 14kt, and was too slow for offensive minelaying.[37]

Motor Torpedo Boats and Other Small Vessels

Of special importance to the proponents of the 'small war at sea' concept were the small and fast MTBs, which they wanted in great numbers. Because the first series of the *Sh-4*-class was too small and vulnerable at sea, the aircraft designer A.N. Tupolev helped develop the new series *G-5* with aluminium hulls from an Italian prototype, and the first 1,000 HP motors of Italian design came into being. But then a *Tupolev AM-34* aero-motor was modified in such a way (becoming *GAM-34*) that it could be used in the *G-5* boats, some of which reached 65kt in unloaded condition, and 58kt loaded. Because aluminium was scarce at the time, wooden hulls were constructed and after some trials were used for later boats. They could launch two torpedoes from chutes at the stern. They were built in several series of 14 to 16t displacement. From 1934 to 1936 no less than 152 boats were commissioned, followed by 20 boats in 1937. The building was continued into the Third Five-Year Plan and during the war.

Several other experimental types were not continued and the main line of construction remained the *G-5*. They were built at inland yards.[38]

One other important small type was the small submarine chaser of about 51t displacement, first the *MO-2*, but when this type experienced some petrol explosions in the motors, construction was halted, and after two improved prototypes of the *MO-4* series with three engines were tested in 1936, their mass production started with the Third Five-Year Plan. The improved *MO-4* which could reach 24 and later 26kt, was fitted with two 45mm guns and depth charges. They were also built by inland yards in great numbers up to and during the war.[39]

REASONS FOR DELAYS DURING THE SECOND FIVE-YEAR PLAN

Already in 1932 the authors of the 'Memorandum on the Naval Forces of the RKKA Status' had asserted that the Navy was suffering from a shortage of petrol-engines, diesel-engines, turbines, optical sets, torpedo and gunfire control sets and radio communications sets. There were not enough factories and equipment to produce the number of shells demanded for the existing naval guns.[40] In 1931–34 the Soviet Union had already imported a number of range-finders, anti-aircraft guns, gyro-compasses and acoustic sets.

In June 1933 the *Narkom* for Foreign Relations M.M. Litvinov reported to the participants of the London Economic and Financial Conference that the Soviet Union could allocate $1 billion for the purchase of metal and industrial equipment.[41] And in 1933–34 the USSR bought about 25,000 tons of steel, because the Soviet shipbuilding factories were suffering from shortages.[42]

Such obstacles prevented the Soviets from developing an ocean-going naval capacity at this time and were responsible for many of the delays, which were in addition caused by the inexperience of many young engineers and workers at the yards and the supplying factories. This led to problems when the lead vessels of new types of ships were tested. In addition changes in the organization of warship design and construction played a role. While the attacks of the representatives of the *jeune école*, especially I.M. Ludri, A.P. Aleksandrov, K.I. Dushenov and A.M. Yakymichev, against the 'old school', and the tracking down of 'enemies of Soviet ideals' and 'saboteurs' had led – as mentioned – to the elimination of many older, experienced officers, like M.A. Petrov, B.B. Zherve. N.I. Vlas'ev, and some chiefs of departments, like G.N. Pell' of the artillery section, Yu.Yu. Kimbar of the mine section, and A.N. Garsoev of the submarine section, the inexperienced 'young men' rose to top positions.[43]

So up to the end of the Second Five-Year Plan, at 31 December 1937, of the surface ships planned and laid down, only the first destroyer leader *Leningrad*, 16 of the 18 patrol ships, six of the 27 minesweepers, but also no fewer than 262 MTBs and submarine chasers, had been finished and commissioned.[44]

At the end of 1937, then, the surface fleets still had to rely mainly on the rebuilt and modernized vessels of the Imperial Navy. The biggest fleet was that on the Baltic, based at Leningrad and Kronshtadt, with two battleships, one training cruiser, one destroyer leader (new), seven destroyers, five patrol ships (new), and two minesweepers (new) besides some old minesweepers. The Black Sea Fleet, based at Sevastopol, was made up of one battleship, three cruisers, one training cruiser, five destroyers, two patrol ships (new), and four minesweepers (new). The Northern Flotilla, based at Catherine Harbour, comprised three destroyers, and three patrol ships (new). And the Pacific Fleet, based at Vladivostok, had two destroyers, transferred in 1936 by the Arctic sea route, and six patrol ships (new), built in the West and transferred by rail in parts to the Far East.[45]

The submarine building programme was more successful. Even if the numbers stipulated in the plan could not remotely be achieved, at the end of 1937 of the planned 69 big submarines, six *series I/D*-class, six *series II/L*-class, three *series IV/P*-class and four *series XI/L*-class were ready. Of the 200 medium submarines, four *series III/Shch*-class, 39 *series V, Vbis, Vbis2/Shch*-class, and two *series IX/S*-class, and 27 *series X/Shch*-class were commissioned. And from the 100 small submarines 50 *series VI, VI-bis/M*-class and two *series XII/M*-class were in service, altogether 143 submarines, which made the Soviet submarine force the strongest in the world.[46] Its distribution attests to the efforts made to strengthen defences in the Far East. The Pacific Fleet received four big, 34 medium, and 28 small submarines, prefabricated in the West and transported by rail to the Pacific for completion. Six big, 22 medium and 16 small, as well as two old submarines were attached to the Baltic Fleet; six big, ten medium and six small, and five old boats comprised the submarine force in the Black Sea Fleet; and in 1937 the Northern Flotilla received, by way of the Baltic–White Sea Canal, four additional medium submarines to augment the three big ones already there.[47]

Lastly, a fleet air arm was also developed to include – besides the old reconnaissance seaplanes – modern fighter, bomber, and mine-torpedo squadrons, mostly using planes developed for the Army, such as the *I-153* and *I-16* fighters, and the *DB-3* bomber.[48]

NOTES

1. *Der große Ploetz. Auszug aus der Geschichte*, Karl-Julius Ploetz et al. (eds), Würzburg, Ploetz, 1980, pp. 968–70.
2. L. Ivanov and P. Smirnov, *Anglo-amerikanskoe morskoe sopernichestvo*, Moscow, Institute of World Economics and Politics, 1933. A.P. Aleksandrov demanded the 'unmasking in the press and its withdrawal from circulation … because it is an attack on the party line in naval construction, which undermines the confidence of the personnel'.
3. V.Yu. Gribovskii, 'Linejniye korabli tipa "Sovetskii Soyuz"', *Sudostroenie* 7 (1990), pp. 55–9.
4. S.E. Zakharov, *et al.*, *Krasnoznamennyi Tikhookeanskii flot*, 2nd edn, Moscow, Voenizdat, 1973, pp. 117–25.
5. RGA VMF, r.441, op.9c, d.38, l.55.
6. *Istoriya …*, op. cit., vol. IV, pp. 26–7.
7. Ibid., p. 27.
8. RGA VMF, f. r-1483, op.1, d.201, l.1-3, 4-6, 7-9. *Istoriya …*, op. cit., vol. IV, p. 270.
9. *Istoriya …*, op. cit., vol. IV, pp. 28–9. *Boevaya letopis' Voenno-morskogo flota 1917–1941*, op. cit., p. 591.
10. *Istoriya …*, op. cit., vol. IV, p. 29.
11. M.S. Monakov, 'Sud'by doktrin i teorii', *Morskoi sbornik*, op. cit., pt. 8, p. 36.

12. Direction Centrale des Constructions Navales to Directeur du Cabinet Militaire, No. 11,863, 30 June 1938. Naval Archives, Vincennes.
13. Eberhard Rössler, 'Vom UG-Typ der Kaiserlichen Marine zur russischen S-Klasse', *Die deutschen U-Boote und ihre Werften*, Munich, Bernard & Graefe, 1979, pp. 25–31.
14. *Istoriya* ..., op. cit., vol. IV, pp. 190, 196.
15. Ibid., pp. 162–4. V.V. Yarovoi, 'Kreisera tipa "Kirov" i "Maksim Gorkii"', *Sudostroenie*, No. 7 (1985), pp. 46–8. A.F. Aleksandrovskii, '"Kirov", Pervenets Sovetskogo kreiserostroeniya', *Sudostroenie*, 11 (1986), pp. 31ff. René Greger, 'Anfänge des sowjetischen Kreuzerbaus', *Marine-Rundschau*, 6 (1989), pp. 228ff.
16. N.N. Afonin, 'Lider eskadrennykh minonostsev "Tashkent"', *Sudostroenie* 7/1985, pp. 49–51. Christopher C. Wright, 'The Fate of the "Tashkent"', *Warship International*, No. 4, pp. 349–60. *Istoriya* ..., op. cit., vol. IV, pp. 321–4.
17. A.B. Morin, *Eskadrennyie minonostsy tipa 'Gnevnyi'*, St Petersburg, Biblioteka 'Gangut' No. 2, 1994. S.A. Balabin, 'Gremyashchii i drugie. Eskadrennye minonostsy proekta 7', *Modelist-Konstruktor*, No. 2, 8/1996. *Istoriya* ..., op. cit., vol. IV, pp. 181–9.
18. V.I. Dmitriev, op. cit., p. 129. A.V. Platonov, op. cit., vol. III.
19. V.I. Dmitriev, op. cit., pp. 100–10, 244–6. A.V. Platonov, op. cit., pp. 42–51.
20. A.V., Platonov, op. cit., vol. III, pp. 51–63.
21. V.I. Dmitriev, op. cit., pp. 133–49. *Istoriya* ..., op. cit., vol. IV, pp. 138–42. A.V. Platonov, op. cit., vol. III, pp. 68–84.
22. V.I. Dmitriev, op. cit, pp. 117–26. *Istoriya* ..., op. cit., vol. IV, pp. 133–6. A.V. Platonov, op. cit., vol. III, pp. 87–95. J.N. Westwood, op. cit., pp. 167–9.
23. A.V. Platonov, op. cit., vol. III, pp. 95–9. V.I. Dmitriev, op. cit., pp. 149–62.
24. *Istoriya* ..., op. cit., vol. IV, pp. 353–8. V.I. Dmitriev, op. cit., pp. 149–63.
25. V.I. Dmitriev, op. cit., pp. 89–93.
26. Ibid., pp. 92–3.
27. Ibid., pp. 179–91. V.N. Burov, op. cit., pp. 144–8. *Istoriya* ..., op. cit., vol. IV, pp. 338–44. A.V. Platonov, op. cit., vol. III, pp. 26–35.
28. *Istoriya* ..., op. cit., vol. IV, 141–2. J.N. Westwood, op. cit., pp. 213–14.
29. V.I. Dmitriev, op. cit., pp. 240–64.
30. V.V. Yarovoi, 'Kreisera tipa "Kirov" i "Maksim Gorkii"', *Sudostroenie* No. 7/1985, pp. 46–8. A.F. Aleksandrovskii, '"Kirov" Pervenets Sovetskogo kreiserostroeniya', *Sudostroenie*, No. 11 (1986), pp. 31ff. René Greger, 'Anfänge des sowjetischen Kreuzerbaus', *Marine-Rundschau*, 86 (1989), pp. 228ff. *Istoriya* ..., op. cit., vol. IV, pp, 162–72. J.N. Westwood, op. cit., pp. 179–89.
31. TsGA VMF, f. r-441, op.1, d.1446, 1480, op.16, d.53. V.Yu. Usov: 'Krasnoznamennyi kreiser "Maksim Gorkii"', *Sudostroenie*, No. 12/1990, pp. 59–61. V.N. Burov, op. cit., pp. 169–74. *Istoriya* ..., op. cit., vol. IV, pp. 309–14. J.N. Westwood, op. cit., pp. 187–8.
32. V.N. Burov, op. cit., pp. 97–191. *Istoriya* ..., op. cit., vol. IV, pp. 177–9. J.N. Westwood, op. cit., pp. 152–3.
33. *Istoriya* ..., op. cit., vol. IV, pp. 179–82. J.N. Westwood, op. cit., pp. 198–9.
34. Edgar J. March, *British Destroyers. A History of Development 1892–1953*, London, Seeley, 1966. p. 312. 'Pis'ma tsitadelej po voprosam istorii', *Sudostroenie*, No. 7 (1995), pp. 82–3.
35. A.B. Morin, *Eskadrennyie minonostsy tipa 'Gnevnyi'*, St Petersburg, Izdat Gangut, 1994. 'Gremyashchii i drugie eskadrennye minonostsy proekta 7', St Petersburg, Morskaya Kollektsiya No. 2/1996. *Istoriya* ..., op. cit., vol. IV, pp. 181–9, 326–30. J.N. Westwood, op. cit., pp. 189–97. A.B. Morin, 'Pavel Osipovich Trakhtenberg – glavnyi konstruktor proekta 7', *Sudostroenie*, No. 9 (1997), pp. 85–6.
36. A.B. Morin and N.P. Petrov, 'Bystrokhodnye (Bazovye) Tral'shchiki tipa "Fugas"', *Sudostroenie*, No. 19 (1994), pp. 62–9. *Istoriya* ..., op. cit., vol. IV, pp. 197–8, 366–9.
37. *Istoriya* ..., op. cit., vol. IV, pp. 171–3.
38. Ibid., pp. 208–11, 382–5. *Conway's All The World's Fighting Ships*, Vol. 1922–46, pp. 341–3.
39. *Istoriya* ..., op. cit., Vol. IV, pp. 392–4.
40. RGA VMF, f. r-1483, op.1, d.241, l.153. op.1, d.143, l.101-31. K.K. Stolt, *Stroitel'stvo Sovetskogo VMF vo Vtoroi Pyatiletke*, Leningrad, 1978 (candidate of science thesis).
41. *Istoriya diplomatii*, Vol. III, Moscow, 1965, pp. 594–5.
42. K.K. Stolt, op. cit., p. 33.

43. N.Yu. Beresovskii *et al.*, *Boevaya letopis' Voenno-morskogo flota 1917–1941*, Moscow, Voenizdat, 1992, p. 679.
44. S.S. Berezhnoi, *Korabli i suda VMF SSSR 1928–1945*, Moscow, Voenizdat, 1988.
45. Ibid.
46. V.I. Dmitriev, op. cit., pp. 240–56. V.N. Burov, op. cit., pp. 129–52.
47. S.S. Berezhnoi, op. cit., pp. 42–75.
48. *Boevoi put' Sovetskogo Voenno-morskogo flota*, ed. V.I. Achkasov and A. Basov *et al.*, 3rd edn, Moscow, Voenizdat, 1974, p. 123.

6

The Change to the Big High Seas and Ocean-Going Fleet

Already, before the Second Five-Year Plan had ended, there were signs of a change in naval policy, away from the 'small war theory' to ideas of a big ocean-going navy. On 23 December 1935 the just decorated petty-officers of the Pacific Fleet were assembled at the Kremlin for a meeting with Stalin. The Soviet military leaders, including the *Narkom* for Defence, K.E. Voroshilov, the Chief of the Army General Staff, A.I. Yegorov, and the Chief of the *VMF*, V.M. Orlov, participated in the meeting.[1] When the meeting was over, Stalin must have ordered that a huge shipbuilding programme be developed.[2]

On 24 December 1935 the Chief Editor of the Party's official newspaper *Pravda* published an article concerning the big ocean-going fleet build-up. The author of the article wrote: 'Enemies of the proletarian state believed that after their intervention in the Civil War the Soviet Union would be incapable of becoming one of the great sea powers again for a long time.' He stated that the temporary weakness of the Soviet Navy would very soon be overcome.

On 16 January 1936 Marshal Yegorov wrote to *Flagman Flota 1 Ranga* V.M. Orlov, proposing an additional shipbuilding programme. Orlov, in turn, wrote to Marshal Voroshilov, citing Yegorov's paper, proposing that the Navy's responsibilities should be redefined and that the programme for light surface vessels should be replaced with one for capital ships. In reply, Voroshilov ordered the Naval Staff to draw up a 10-year plan for building up the fleets. Unless the change had been demanded by Stalin himself, it is difficult to account for the sudden change of mind by the top Army officers and the *jeune école* supporters of the small ship navy.[3]

What, then, may have been the reasons for the change of mind of the above-mentioned Army and Navy officers and especially of Stalin?

STALIN'S ROLE

By 1933, Stalin had achieved a dominant position in the Politburo and the Central Committee of the Bolshevik Party, after eliminating most of the leading revolutionaries such as Trotskii, Kamenev and Zinov'ev from influential posts in the hierarchy. He had never supported Trotskii's ideas of a 'world revolution', and now followed a policy of building 'socialism in one country', forcing the pace of industrialization with such reckless methods as the destruction of the 'class' of big and medium landowners, the *kulaks*, and deporting them, with great loss of life, to supply the necessary manpower for the new industrial centres. When some of his earlier followers and close associates such as Bukharin tried to slow down the forced industrialization, even they were arraigned in show trials and in most cases during the purges between 1935 and 1940 liquidated, or, like Kirov, the popular Party chief of Leningrad, murdered – in this case in a most probably *NKVD*-instigated plot on 1 December 1934. While Stalin increasingly became a dictator against whom nobody dared to stand, he himself saw the country and also his own person as surrounded by enemies.[4] He could see those in his close surroundings either as willing friends or enemies.[5] But to some extent this perception derived also from the changes in the international situation, to which Stalin responded mostly pragmatically and even opportunistically.

INTERNATIONAL SITUATION

Developments in the Far East, where Japan had conquered Manchuria and established a satellite state there, thus creating a long direct border with the Soviet Far East provinces, had led to a new perception of Japan as the most dangerous likely enemy in Asia. In Europe, Adolf Hitler's anti-Soviet policy revealed him to be the most likely enemy in the West. The danger was illustrated on 26 January 1934 by the 'Pact of Non-Aggression and Friendship' that Hitler concluded with Poland's Chief of State, Marshal Josef Pilsudski, bringing the former common enemy during the period of Red Army co-operation with the German *Reichswehr*, into the camp of the now most dangerous enemy in Europe. This was followed by the introduction of conscription in Germany on 16 March 1935, and the Anglo-German Naval Treaty of 18 June 1935. And after the conclusion of the 'Anti-Comintern Pact' between Germany and Japan on 25 November 1936, the two likely enemies were linked.[6] Italy then joined the 'aggressor states' by its invasion of Ethiopia in October 1935.

At this time, the Soviet Union tried to obtain support in its efforts to check the perceived threats from the expansionist policies of Japan, Germany and Italy, and to some extent its former enemy Great Britain, which had helped Germany by concluding the naval agreement to drop the Versailles restrictions. So the Soviet Union now participated in the international policy of 'collective security', which was propagated in the Soviet Union by the *Narkom* for Foreign Relations, Litvinov. Thus the Soviet Union tried to enter into closer relations with the Western democracies by establishing diplomatic relations – as previously mentioned – with Spain, the United States, Romania and Czechoslovakia, and by joining the League of Nations. And the *Komintern* (Communist International), as the parent and guiding organization of the Communist parties, decided to join parties in the Western democracies in a tactic of forging 'people's fronts' against Nazi Germany.[7]

DOMESTIC POLICY AND THE START OF THE PURGES

In the interior Stalin had celebrated the XVIIth Party Rally of the Bolshevik Party in January/February 1934 as the 'Party Rally of the Victors', and was able to force many of his critical former associates like Zinov'ev, Kamenev, Pyatakov, Bukharin, Rykov, Tomskii and others to join in fulsome praise of his leadership. But it was the last time that so many people critical of his policies attended such Party rallies. No less than 1,108 of the delegates (that is, 56.4 per cent) were arrested during the next few years under false accusations, mostly for 'counter-revolutionary crimes'. But many of the new young members coming in had their particular favourite, the Party Chief of Leningrad, S.M. Kirov, who became, despite himself, a possible competitor to Stalin in the struggle for power. With his assassination the period of show trials and big purges began. In a 'Three Point Decree' the 'organs' of the *NKVD* were allowed to rush investigations and to execute the condemned defendants immediately.[8] Kirov's successor at Leningrad, A.A. Zhdanov, had already named the first victims in mid-December 1934: Zinov'ev and Kamenev and their associates were arrested and accused of 'high treason' and 'Trotskyism'. Following torture they admitted during their show trial from 19 to 25 August 1935 their 'crimes' and were sentenced to the 'highest penalty' and shot. This was the first of the 'successes' of the chief prosecutor, A. Yu. Vyshinskii, in this and subsequent show trials. And because the Chief of the *NKVD*, G.G. Yagoda, had not been able to 'unmask the Trotskyist–Zinov'evist block' Stalin replaced him with N.I. Yeshov, who ordered the executions in the Stalinist purges – the so-called 'Yeshovshchina' – but in all important cases Stalin was behind such executions.[9]

Stalin was now forcing the idea of 'Soviet Patriotism', and in this connection reintroduced the old military ranks on 22 September 1935, promoting five officers to Marshals: the *Narkom* for Defence, Voroshilov, the Chief of Staff of the *RKKA*, Yegorov, the now Deputy *Narkom* for Defence, Tukhachevskii, the Commander-in-Chief in the Far East, Blyukher, and the legendary cavalry leader, Budennyi. In the Navy four flag ranks were established. On 20 November 1935 the Chief of the *VMS*, Orlov, and the Commander of the Pacific Fleet, Viktorov became *Flagman Flota 1 Ranga*, the Commanders of the Baltic and Black Sea Fleets, Galler and Kozhanov, *Flagman Flota 2 Ranga*.[10]

To bring the centrally planned economy to 'production successes' the title 'Hero of Labour' was established. And when on 30/31 August 1935 the miner A. Stakhanov 'overfulfilled' his planned norm fourteenfold, this feat was used to establish a 'Stakhanov Movement' to force up production in all factories.[11]

During the VIIIth Soviet Congress of the USSR from 25 November to 5 December 1936 Stalin pushed through a new 'democratic' addition to the constitution, which was accepted with acclamation, establishing the leading role of the Bolshevik Party at all levels of the state.[12]

A NEW INTERNATIONAL NAVAL ARMS RACE

The Washington Treaty of 1922 had limited the battleship tonnage of the five remaining great sea powers and interrupted the building of new battleships. The building of aircraft carriers was also restricted, and so shipbuilding competition was shifted to cruisers, which were limited in their tonnage to 10,000t stdd. and would get only 203mm guns. The consequence of this trend was a demand for further treaties to limit naval rearmament. Initial negotiations were held in Geneva, but they failed because Great Britain and the United States could not agree on the size and number of the cruisers to be allowed. Japan pressed for an increase in its quota from 60 to 70 per cent. Neither France nor Italy were satisfied with their equal standing at 35 per cent. France would not agree to a British proposal to ban submarines.[13]

The London Treaty of 22 April 1930, which France and Italy did not sign, restricted the number of battleships to 15 each for Great Britain and the United States, and 9 for Japan, and extended the building moratorium to 1936. A compromise was agreed concerning the cruisers which involved dividing them into heavy and light cruisers with the dividing line set at a gun calibre of 155mm. The USA was allowed 18, Great Britain 15, and Japan 12 heavy cruisers. Compensation was planned for the light cruisers, and limits were laid down for the tonnage and size of the destroyers and submarines, and the building of aircraft carriers of less than 10,000t was forbidden.

An attempt was made to soften the effects of naval armaments limitation by means of a further London Treaty, but it too failed. Signed on 25 March 1936 only by Great Britain, the USA and France, it added qualitative restrictions concerning the size and gun calibre of warship categories already defined, but it did not establish tonnage ratios between the powers. Great Britain strove to include other nations by means of bilateral agreements. A treaty signed with Germany on 18 June 1935 fixed the strength of its fleet at 35 per cent of the British one. A supplementary treaty of 1937 allowed Germany to go up to 100 per cent with submarines. Another treaty was signed with the USSR, to be mentioned later. But without Japan and Italy, and with various loopholes in the treaties, the restrictions on maritime armaments had become a farce. A naval arms race had begun.

The first step in the new arms race was the laying down of the German *Panzerschiff A/Ersatz Preußen* on 19 May 1931, to be launched on 1 April 1933 as *Deutschland*. This vessel did not fit into the categories laid down in the treaties of Washington and London. It was built to the limits of the Versailles Treaty as a replacement for the old pre-*Dreadnought*-battleships with 10,000t displacement and 280mm guns. France and Italy, which were allowed in the treaties to replace some of their old battleships with three smaller or two bigger ones, responded by laying down new ships: France with the fast battleship *Dunkerque* of 26,500t and 330mm guns; Italy with its first new 35,000t battleship *Littorio*.[14]

Germany's rejection of the Versailles limitations, the Japanese and Italian revocation of the Naval Treaties, and the aggressive policy of these nations, forced the USA, Great Britain and France to adopt new fleet-building programmes, each action causing more rigorous reactions.[15] Germany first planned to build eight improved *Panzerschiffe* of 20,000t which were called by the others *pocket battleships*. But when the French plans became known this was changed in late 1934 to fast battleships of nominally 26,000t; however, the *Scharnhorst*-class had finally 31,800ts stdd. France responded to this and the Italian plans with the 35,000t battleship *Richelieu*. And in 1935/36 all the sea powers started to build 35,000t battleships – the Germans the *Bismarck*, the British the *King George V*, and the United States the *North Carolina*. The last to do so was Japan, which started its super-battleships of 62,315ts stdd., the *Yamato*-class, in 1937. The building of new aircraft carriers also started during this period in the United States, Great Britain and Japan, while the cruiser, destroyer and submarine fleets were augmented steadily by all powers.[16]

No wonder that with such goings-on battleship plans in the Soviet Union were also being developed and discussed as is to be mentioned in the next chapter.

FIRST SOVIET BATTLESHIP PLANS

At the beginning of 1935 research work into the possibilities of future Soviet naval construction was launched under the direction of the Chief of the *VMS*, Orlov, and the Chief of the Main Shipbuilding Department (*Glavmorprom*) Muklevich. At various institutions plans for battleships were discussed and developed. At the Naval War College under P.G. Stasevich several operative-tactical arguments and pre-drawings for 'big gun-armed armoured ships' were asked for. Designs of five variants of such ships were prepared under A.P. Shershov, armed with 305mm guns against the 280mm guns of the German 'pocket battleships' and the new *Scharnhorst*-class. The *TsKBS-1* prepared plans for battleship projects between 43,000 and 75,000t with guns of 406 and 450mm calibre, and armoured ships of 23,000 to 30,000t stdd. with 305mm guns. Also aircraft cruisers of 21,000 and 28,500t with 49 and 60 airplanes, respectively, were discussed. On 24 December 1935 the Chief of the *TsKBS-1*, B.L. Bzhezinskii, and his deputy V.P. Rimskii-Korsakov, presented the plans to Orlov and the Chief of *Glavmorprom*, Muklevich. In February 1936 Orlov selected from the proposals of the *TsKBS-1* two types, one of 35,000t with nine 406mm guns and 350mm armour for the Baltic, called *projekt 21*, and one for the Pacific Fleet of 55,000t with nine 406mm guns and 450mm armour. The guns were arranged in three triple turrets on the forecastle, as on the British *Nelson*-class battleships.[17]

At around the same time, in autumn 1935, the Italian yard *Ansaldo* at Genoa was asked for plans of a battleship of 42,000t, which were delivered on 14 July 1936 and designated *UP-41* with two triple turrets of 406mm at the foredeck and one aft, a design which was influenced by the new Italian *Littorio*-class with

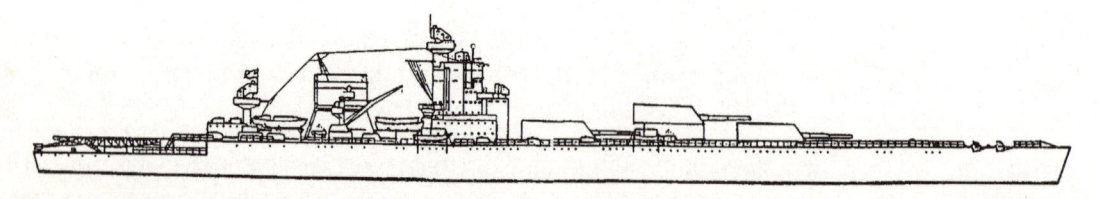

Fig. 3. Battleship of *projekt 21*, no name given, 1935, displ. 35,000t stdd., length 249m, max. speed 30kt, 9 40.6cm, 12 15.2cm, 12 10cm, 36 3.7cm. Only planned, but not laid down. Credit: Sudostroenie

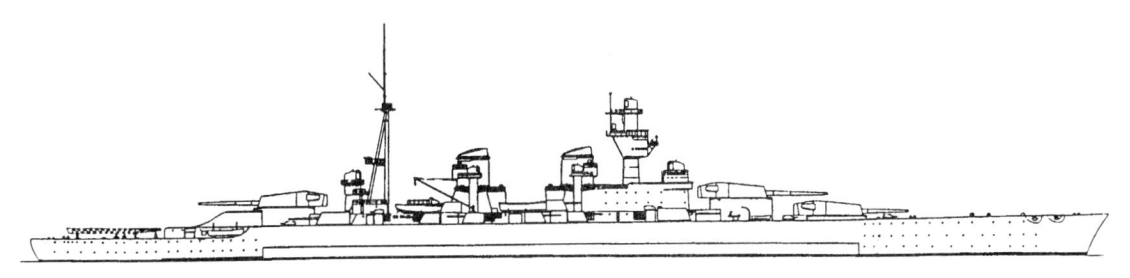

Fig. 4. Battleship, Ansaldo *projekt UP-41*, 1936, displ. 42,000t stdd., length 248.95m, max. speed 32kt, 9 40.6cm, 12 18cm. 24 10cm, 48 5.7cm. Only plans delivered, used for the development of *projekt 23*, not built. Credit: Breyer, *Marine-Rundschau*

its Pugliese shock-absorbing system. This design was a great influence on the final plans of the *projekt 23* battleships.[18]

During the planning for the new light cruiser *Kirov* in 1934/35 the idea of a big cruiser against the 10,000t 'Washington- cruisers with 203mm guns had already come up. On 21 May 1935 Rimskii-Korsakov presented a plan of a cruiser *X* of 15,520t with three triple turrets of 240mm guns and a machinery output of 210,000 HP and a top speed of 38kt, which could also transport two midget submarines of the type *Blokha*. The *TsKBS-1* under V.L. Bzhezinskii and V.A. Nikitin countered this with a design of 19,500t and three 250mm triple turrets and 36kt top speed from 210,000 HP turbines. In addition the *Ansaldo*-yard presented in 1936 a design for a heavy cruiser of 19,000–22,000t with three triple turrets of 250mm guns and a speed of 37kt.[19]

In February 1936 two alternative plans for the creation of the big ocean-going fleet were worked out, one by the *RKKA* General Staff's naval experts, and one by the Staff of the Chief of the *VMS*. Both included proposals on the construction of battleships, aircraft carriers and a great number of cruisers. On 15 April the Navy High Command presented its first draft of the fleet to be build by 1947. No fewer than 15 battleships, 22 heavy cruisers, 31 light cruisers, 162 destroyers and destroyer leaders, 412 submarines, and many smaller vessels and auxiliaries were demanded.[20] Including the smaller vessels and auxiliaries, the fleet would by 1947 contain as much as 1,727,000t. At the same time the proposal of the Chief of the General Staff of the *RKKA*, Marshal Yegorov, advocated even more: 1,868,000t, including six aircraft carriers, two for the Northern Fleet and four for the Pacific Fleet, while Orlov argued that only two carriers of 8,000t for the Pacific Fleet would be sufficient.[21]

The *STO* 'decided' on 27 May 1936 to approve the shape of the 'Big Navy Programme' to be completed by 1947 and assigned 450,000t to the Pacific Fleet, 400,000t to the Baltic Fleet, 300,000t to the Black Sea Fleet, and 150,000t to the Northern Fleet – that is, a total of 1,300,000t.[22] This meant that Stalin's ocean-going fleet would be comparable with the navies of the main sea powers. In May/June 1936 the idea was to build two types of battleship: type *A* of 35,000t with 406mm guns, and type *B* of 26,000t with 305mm guns.

When the plan was presented to the Politburo and the Defence Committee of the *SNK SSSR* on 26 June 1936 no fewer than 24 battleships, 20 cruisers, 182 destroyers and 344 submarines were on the adopted draft list of the planned deliveries of new ships. Four type-*A* battleships, four type-*B* battleships, three 7,500t cruisers of a new type and three *Kirov*-class cruisers would be built for the Baltic Fleet. An equal number of battleships was planned to strengthen the Black Sea Fleet, but only four cruisers of the *Kirov*-class. Six type-*B* battleships and eight *Kirov*-class cruisers were planned to be deployed as battleship and cruiser formations in the Pacific. The Northern Fleet was to be reinforced by two type-*B* battleships and two new 7,500t cruisers.[23]

But there was still some resistance to the big ship programme. In February 1936 the First Deputy of the Chief of the *VMS*, *Flagman 1 Ranga* Ludri, one of the outstanding spokesmen of the *jeune école* faction, wrote a critique on Wilson's book *Battleships in Action*, just translated into Russian. He again asserted that battleships by the end of the First World War were finally being overwhelmed by submarines. On the other side, on 28 November 1936 the earlier supporter of the *jeune école* Orlov made a speech at the VIIIth Extraordinary Soviet Congress. He said: 'Taking into account the situation in the world and tendencies in developments in the capitalist countries we are forced to create a really big fleet and this will be done. Such a fleet should include ships of all types, and keep to the highest technical level.'[24]

Therefore, a decision was needed from Stalin to clear up the differences. At the end of 1936, he convened a conference of senior naval officers, at which the *jeune école* debated priorities and strategy with the 'classical school' for the last time. Everyone agreed that large numbers of submarines should be built as quickly as possible, but they disagreed about the sort of surface vessels they needed. Whereas the Commander of the Black Sea Fleet, *Flagman Flota 2 Ranga* Kozhanov, the leader of the *jeune école* group, advocated the continuation of the existing policy of building light craft, especially MTBs, the Commander of the Pacific Fleet, *Flagman Flota 1 Ranga* Viktorov, spoke up for the 'Mahanian school', on the grounds that small light vessels were of little use in a theatre as huge as the Pacific. When Stalin interjected 'You possibly do not know what you need!', he must have already decided to build the large ocean-going navy.[25]

That the decision was Stalin's own was shown in the behaviour of the senior officers. Not only did the Army Chief of Staff argue for a large ocean-going navy, but also Orlov, when he presented the speech to the VIIIth Extraordinary Soviet Congress on 28 November, which had been called to 'decide' on the new constitution, strongly supported a big-ship navy. The conversion of the most prominent officers, who formerly had supported the *jeune école* ideas, whatever their own views might have been, now tried only to follow or even to anticipate the wishes of Stalin.

THE SPANISH CIVIL WAR

Many historians believe that the change to the 'big ocean-going fleet' in Stalin's mind had its roots in the Spanish Civil War. This cannot be correct, because the Spanish Civil War started with the uprising of the Spanish Nationalist generals Franco and Mola in Morocco and Asturias on 18 July

1936 against the Republican government, while the change in naval planning – as we have seen – had already taken place by the second half of 1935.

The Spanish Civil War became an almost three-years-long trench war with heavy losses on both sides, and led to interventions from many sides. The Nationalists were supported by Italy and Germany, the Republicans by the Soviet Union, with huge deliveries of war materials and supplies as well as military formations for the Nationalists, and on the Republican side volunteers from many nations, wanting to fight against Fascism in the International Brigades. When in late 1936 the Nationalists achieved superiority at sea and ran a blockade of the Republican coasts they intercepted 84 ships, from October 1936 to April 1937, for inspection of 'contraband'.

In February 1937, the Soviet ambassador to London, M.M. Maiskii, reported to Stalin that representatives of the 'great powers' had tried to localize the Civil War in Spain. He stated that deploying a strong naval formation would be the best way of defending the interests of the USSR in the Mediterranean. On 19 April 1937 the Commission on Non-Intervention in London, in which 26 nations participated, decided to set up a sea control over the Spanish coastline. The British took the Republican coastline in the North, the area on both sides of Gibraltar and the Canaries. The French became responsible for the Nationalist north-west coast, Spanish Morocco, and Mallorca, and the Germans and Italians for the Republican coast from Almeria to the French border in the Mediterranean and the two other Balearic islands.[26]

Originally, Soviet naval experts proposed sending to the western Mediterranean two cruisers from the Black Sea Fleet, four submarines and one submarine depot ship. At the same time the Soviet naval attaché in London proposed sending one cruiser, four destroyers, and no less than six patrol ships. These suggestions were rejected by Orlov. He asserted that the squadron, which would be deployed in the Mediterranean, would be weak and vulnerable. Besides, Orlov stated, the Soviet Union would suffer a gap in their own sea defences if these ships were to be sent overseas. Therefore he proposed that involvement of the Soviet Navy in the international naval operations be avoided.[27]

Owing to a lack of ships that were ready to operate in the Spanish littorals, Stalin accepted Orlov's suggestions, but did not forgive him, because without the Mediterranean squadron the Soviet leader could not compete successfully with Hitler and Mussolini. It may be that Orlov's suggestions were evaluated as wrong. In any case, just after the first Soviet merchant vessels were sunk in the approaches to Spain, Orlov was relieved of his command in July 1937, arrested and sentenced to be shot under the false accusation of spying for Great Britain.[28]

During the Civil War of 1936–39 many Soviet naval officers were sent to Spain as 'volunteers'. Junior officers went to surface ships and submarines as 'assistant' commanders. More senior officers like N.G. Kuznetsov,[29] A.G. Golovko, V.P. Drozd, I.S. Yumashev, and other young 'Stalin Admirals' took part as advisors in the higher echelons of the Republican Navy. All of them had graduated from the Naval Academy in the mid-1920s and become students at the Naval College at the beginning of the 1930s, when some of the outspoken leaders of the *jeune école* held important professorships at the schools. For example, A.P. Aleksandrov headed the strategy and operational faculty there. It allows us to draw the conclusion that the officers mentioned were educated and experienced as 'small fleet commanders'. But Stalin, after the violent purges of 1937/38, which are described in the following chapter, ordered them to create 'a big ocean-going fleet'. They were not distinguished theorists, but all of them were prominent commanders and brilliant executors of Stalin's magnificent naval plans.

No wonder that during the 'non-intervention patrols' some incidents occurred that had grave consequences. On 6 March 1937 the British destroyer *Gallant* was just missed by a Nationalist airplane, as was a few days later the German torpedo boat *Albatros* by a Republican plane, while the Italian auxiliary cruiser *Barletta* was also hit by a Republican plane. And on 27 May 1937 the German 'pocket battleship' *Deutschland* was hit close to Ibiza by two bombs from a Republican plane, in which incident 32 sailors were killed and many others wounded. Hitler was outraged and ordered the sister ship *Admiral Scheer* to bombard the Republican port of Almeria on 31 May.[30] But earlier on Italian and German submarines had already made clandestine submerged torpedo attacks against Republican warships. The Italian submarine *Torricelli* hit and damaged the cruiser *Miguel de Cervantes* with two torpedoes off Cartagena on 22 November 1936, and on 12 December 1936 the German U-boat *U34* torpedoed and sank the Republican submarine *C-3* off Malaga. Two days later the Nationalist cruiser *Canarias* intercepted and sank the Soviet freighter *Komsomol'*, a frequent supplies carrier, off Cartagena.[31]

From May to August 1937 the attacks by 'unidentified' submarines against ships with supplies for the Republicans became very frequent. The first of the attacks were made by two submarines the Italians had loaned to the Nationalists. So the *General Sanjurjo* (ex-*Torricelli*) and the *General Mola* (ex-*Archimede*) sank some Republican ships. But now it is known that most of the attacks were made by Italian submarines – from November 1936 to September 1937 52 different boats made no fewer than 65 patrols with 1,183 sea days, which sank 15 ships. Apart from the Spanish vessels, these were two British, two Soviet – for example on 1 September the *Blago'ev* was sunk by the submarine *Ferraris* – and one each from Greece, Panama and the Netherlands. From August also Italian surface ships, and mostly destroyers, took part in such operations and intercepted some ships in the Central Mediterranean, as, for example, the destroyer *Turbine* on 30 August against the Soviet freighter *Timiryazev*.[32] To counter this the British government convened a conference at Myon, at which the Soviet Union, Greece, Egypt, Romania and Bulgaria participated. Italy 'postponed' its participation, while Germany declined. A decision was taken to establish convoys on special routes, and the warships of the participating nations were allowed to attack suspected submarines. So the Italian Navy called the operations off, but ceded to the Spanish Nationalist Navy four destroyers and four submarines.[33]

While the international 'non-intervention' patrols proved to be ineffective, the Soviet Navy was unable to protect its supplies to its own protégés. Yet the described time differences speak for a decision by Stalin to build the 'big ocean-going fleet' independently of the Spanish Civil War. No doubt, the events of this war strengthened Stalin's conviction that a great power needed such a fleet.[34]

NOTES

1. *Morskoi sbornik*, No. 1 (1936), p. 10.
2. RGA VMF, f.2041, op.1, d.72, pp. 1–33.
3. V.N. Krasnov, 'Stalinshina v VMF i korablestroenie', *Sudostroenie* No. 7 (1990), pp. 64–9; M.S. Monakov, op. cit., p. 39; E.A. Shitikov, V.N. Krasnov and V.V. Balabin, *Korablstroenie v SSSR v gody Velikoi Otechestvennoi vojny*, Moscow, Nauka, 1995, pp. 3–4.
4. D. Volkogonov, *Stalin. Triumph und Tragödie*, Düsseldorf, Claassen, 1989; M.S. Monakov, op. cit., part 8, *Morskoi sbornik*, part 8, pp. 36–7, 41–2.
5. Manfred Hildermeier, *Geschichte der Sowjetunion 1917–1991*, Munich, Beck, 1998, pp. 431–4.
6. *Der Große Ploetz. Auszug aus der Geschichte*. 39th edn, Würzburg, Ploetz, 1980, pp. 864–9, 969–71.
7. Alexander Fischer, 'Kollektive Sicherheit und imperialistischer Krieg', *Saeculum*, XXVIII (1977), pp. 432ff; M.S. Monakov, op. cit., p. 36; *Ploetz*, op. cit., pp. 969–70.
8. The methods of gaining the confessions of the defendants is described in an example by the former member of the German Communist Party Arthur Koestler in his novel *Sonnenfinsternis*, written in 1940, and republished by the Büchergilde Gutenberg, Frankfurt/Main, 1999.
9. D. Volkogonov, op. cit., pp. 290ff; M. Hildermeier, op. cit., pp. 444–51.
10. *Boeroj put' Sovetskogo Voenno morskogo flota*, op. cit., pp. 530–1.
11. M. Hildermeier, op. cit., pp. 521–5.
12. Ibid., pp. 436–44.
13. Jürgen Rohwer, *Der Krieg zur See 1939–1945*, Gräfelfing, Urbes, 1992, pp. 8–14.
14. *Rüstungswettlauf zur See 1930–1941: von der Abrüstung zum Wettrüsten*, ed. Jürgen Rohwer with David K. Brown (Great Britain), Dean C. Allard (USA), Saburo Toyama (Japan), Philippe Masson (France), Alberto Santoni (Italy), Jost Dülffer (Germany) and Aleksei V. Basov (Soviet Union), Bonn, Bernard & Graefe, 1991.
15. E.B. Potter, C.W. Nimitz and J. Rohwer, *Seemacht. Von der Antike bis zur Gegenwart*, Herrsching, Pawlak, 1982, pp. 445–85.
16. *Conway's All the World's Fighting Ships 1922–1946*, London, Conway's, 1980.
17. *Istoriya …*, op. cit., vol. IV, pp. 278–81.
18. René Greger, 'Sowjetischer Schlachtschiffbau', *Marine-Rundschau*, 71 (1974), pp. 466ff; Siegfried Breyer, 'Großkampfschiffbau in der Sowjetunion', in S. Breyer, *Großkampfschiffe*, Vol. III, Munich, Bernard & Graefe, 1979, pp. 139–69.
19. *Istoriya …*, op. cit., vol. IV, pp. 296–9.
20. Letters of S. Berezhnoi to J. Rohwer, 1992.
21. M.S. Monakov, op. cit., *Morskoi sbornik*, part 8, p. 39.
22. Tablitsa raspredeleniya po teatram po programme stroitel'stva Voenno-morskogo flota, TsGA VMF, f.1877, op.9, d.56; TsGA VMF, f.1483, op.-1, d.503, l.112–113.
23. V.Yu. Gribovski, *Raboche-Krestiansky Voenno-morskoi flot v predvoyennye gody 1936–1941*, St Petersburg, 1996, p. 9.
24. *Morskoi sbornik*, No.12/1936, pp. 3–26.
25. Nikolai G. Kuznetsov, *Nakanune*, Moscow, Voenizdat, 1966, p. 257; M.S. Monakov, op. cit., p. 39.
26. *Seemacht. Eine Seekriegsgeschichte von der Antike bis zur Gegenwart*, ed. E.B. Potter, Ch.W. Nimitz and J. Rohwer, Herrsching, Pawlak, 1982, pp. 466–8; René Sabatier de Lachadenede, *La Marine française et la Guerre Civile d'Espagne*, Vincennes, Service historique de la Marine, 1993; Willard C. Frank, 'International Efforts at Sea to Contain the Spanish Civil War 1936–1939', in *Maintien de la paix de 1815 à aujourd'hui*, Quebec, CIHM, 1995, pp. 184–97.
27. RGA VMF, f.r-1483, op.3, d.-244, l.1–3, 6, 7-10, 73.
28. 'Vladimir Mitrofanovich Orlov', Galeriya Sovietskikh flotovodtsev, *Morskoi sbornik*, 1998.
29. N.G. Kuznetsov, 'Ispanskii Flot v borbe za respubliku', *Voenno-istoricheskii zhurnal*, IV/1962, No. 3, pp. 53–72.

30. Werner Rahn, 'Ibiza und Almeria, Eine Dokumentation der Ereignisse vom 29. bis 31. Mai 1937', *Marine-Rundschau*, 68, No. 7 (1971), pp. 389–406.
31. Willard C. Frank, 'German Clandestine Submarine Warfare in the Spanish Civil War, 1936', *New Interpretations in Naval History*, IXth Naval History Symposium, Annapolis, 18–20 October 1989, ed. W.M. Roberts and J. Sweetman, Annapolis, MD, US Naval Institute, 1991, pp. 107–23.
32. Franco Bargoni, *L'impegno navale italiana durante la guerra civile spagnola 1936–1939*, Ufficio Storico della Marina Militare, 1992.
33. Willard C. Frank, 'Naval Operations in the Spanish Civil War 1936–1939', *Naval War College Review*, XXXVII (1984), pp. 24–55; Franco Bargoni, op. cit.
34. General literature for the Spanish Civil War: Francisco Moreno *et al.*, *La guerra en mar*, Barcelona, ed. AHR, 1959; Hugh Thomas, *The Spanish Civil War 1936–1939*, London, Eyre & Spottiswoode, 1961; Dante A. Puzzo, *Spain and the Great Powers*, New York, 1962; Gabriel Jackson, *The Spanish Republic and the Civil War 1931–1939*, Princeton University Press, 1965; Willard C. Frank, 'The Spanish Civil War and the Coming of the Second World War', *The International History Review*, IX (1987), pp. 368–409.

7

The Third Five-Year Plan

In January 1937 Stalin began to reorganize both the naval high command and the defence industry. The Commissariat for the Defence Industry under M.M. Kaganovich, brother of the Politburo member L.M. Kaganovich, was transferred from the Commissariat for Heavy Industry and took over responsibility for the Office of Shipbuilding under the Deputy Commissar R.A. Muklevich. At the same time Orlov became a Deputy Commissar for Defence, responsible for naval affairs. The two men met in their new positions for the first time on 28 January 1937 to outline the work to be done and, by April, the new plan for the shipbuilding industry was ready. But before they could present their plan, they fell victim to the 'Yeshovshchina', Stalin's purges against the Army and Navy officer corps.[1]

THE GREAT PURGES AGAINST THE ARMY AND NAVY

Several seemingly independent sources of information had intensified Stalin's habitual mistrust of Red Army leaders, especially of Tukhachevskii. A 'document', forged by the German *Gestapo* about Red Army co-operation with the German *Generalstab*, found its way into the hands of the Czech President Eduard Beneš, who passed it on to Stalin. Stalin was also told about one of Trotskii's publications in which he stated that some senior Red Army officers were critical of Stalin's dictatorial regime. And Tukhachevskii himself had criticized the *Narkom* for Defence, Marshal Voroshilov, for incompetence and resisting reforms. These snippets were said by the head of the *Narodnyi Komissariat Vnutrennykh Del (NKVD)*, N.I. Yeshov, to be 'evidence' of a 'great conspiracy' in the Army. He then forced the imprisoned Deputy Commander of the Leningrad Military District, V.M. Primakov, to confirm the prefabricated accusations against Tukhachevskii and some of his comrades. They were arrested in May and June 1937, and taken before a secret military tribunal headed by V.V. Ul'rikh, head of the Military Board of the Supreme Court, and immediately Tukhachevskii, P.P. Ejdeman (1925–35 Commander of the Frunze Academy), B.M. Fel'dman (1931–37 Chief of the Main Administration of the *RKKA*), I.E. Yakir (1925–37 Commander of the Military District

Kiev), A.I. Kork (1937 Military Attaché in Berlin), V.K. Putna (1934–36 Military Attaché in London), J.P. Uborevich (1937 Commander of the Military District Belorussiya), and Primakov, were accused of being spies, Trotskyists and Zinovevists, condemned to the 'highest sentence' and immediately shot.[2] Notwithstanding the fact that all of them had visited Germany during the period of co-operation with the *Reichswehr* – for example, Uborevich was seconded in 1927–28 for one year to the German *Reichswehrministerium*[3] – there is no doubt that all of these officers were loyal to their government and had no plans for an uprising against Stalin.

The Chief of the Main Political Administration of the *RKKA*, Y.B. Gamarnik, who refused to become a member of the tribunal against Tukhachevskii and his comrades, even after Marshal Blyukher had tried to persuade him to participate, committed suicide, as did the *Narkom* for Heavy Industry G.K. Ordzhonikidze. A year later, in 1938, two of the ablest military leaders, the Chief of the General Staff, Marshal A.I. Yegorov, and the Commander of the Far East, Blyukher, as well as many other officers of all ranks were put to death.[4]

Although one of the secondary accusations against Tukhachevskii was his opposition to the plans for a big-ship Navy, the Navy High Command was hit as hard as the Army by the purges. The Deputy Chief of the *VMF*, L.M. Ludri, was first sent to the Naval Academy, and later dismissed. He was replaced by L.M. Galler, at this time Commander of the Baltic Fleet. His successor became A.K. Sivkov. In July 1937 he was relieved and replaced by I.S. Isakov, who after only a few months was replaced by G.I. Levchenko, and took over at the Commissariat for Heavy Industry the post of Muklevich, who was arrested on 28 May 1937. On 10 July Orlov was arrested and replaced by Viktorov, Commander of the Pacific Fleet, a position his deputy G.P. Kire'ev took over. The Commander of the Black Sea Fleet, I.K. Kozhanov, was replaced in October by P.I. Smirnov-Svetlovskii, the former Inspector of the Navy. On 27 September E.S. Pantserzhanskii, Chief of the Naval Section of the General Staff Academy, was also arrested.[5] Ludri, Muklevich, Orlov, Kozhanov, Zof, and Pantserzhanskii were executed in 1937–38.[6] Some historians had the idea that the liquidation of these officers had something to do with their leaning towards the now outdated *jeune école* school, but this seems not to have been the case, because they were mostly accused of spying for Great Britain or Germany, and at least some of them had loyally changed their opinion to conform with the new Stalin line. And it is of interest to follow the fate of many of the technical experts and leading shipbuilding engineers responsible for the new big ships, many of whom were also arrested and had to work in the *NKVD* camps, as will be described later.

THE STRATEGIC CONSIDERATIONS IN 1935–36

In 1935 the Soviet fleets mastered in accordance with the plans of combat training the following tasks:

- The Baltic Fleet: the defence of the eastern part of the Gulf of Finland.

- The Black Sea Fleet: raid operations.
- The Pacific Fleet: counter-landing operations and the defence of the main base in winter conditions.
- The Northern Fleet: the defence of the Kola Gulf.

Operations to strike at the enemy's sea commerce were not conducted as before. It was not until the beginning of 1936 that the single and group submarine autonomous raid operations were started, but also the submarine commanders had to carry out intelligence-gathering missions during patrol duty.

Some of the outstanding Soviet naval experts spoke about the impracticability of Stalin's naval planning just before 'the big ocean-going fleet build-up' was started. For example in the spring of 1936 the Chief of the Naval Department of the *RKKA* General Staff, *Kapitan 1 Ranga* P.G. Stasevich, presented to K.E. Voroshilov a report about the latest Anglo-Soviet negotiations on the subject of naval armaments. In his conclusion he wrote that in his opinion it would be impossible to increase all the Soviet fleets, as the authors of the 10-year programme had proposed. Therefore Stasevich suggested that treaty limitations concerning tonnage and armament of the battleships and cruisers in the negotiations be turned down. He stated that the Soviet Navy would be in need of 45,000t battleships with guns of 356mm to 457mm calibre, 18,000t heavy cruisers with 254mm and 305mm guns, and light cruisers with 180mm guns, because geographical conditions did not allow the transfer of combat ships as soon as they were needed, and each Soviet fleet would have to fight against its enemies without reinforcement from other fleets.[7]

The Soviet leaders paid great attention to Stasevich's proposals. On 25 March 1937 a British–Soviet treaty was signed in London by the British and Soviet representatives, granting the Soviets a special right. Because of the non-participation of the Japanese in the naval treaties they were allowed to build new ships for the Pacific Fleet outside the treaty limitations.[8]

Between the 1960s and 1980s Soviet naval historians stated that the programme of the 'big fleet build-up' had no operational basis. But this is incorrect. The documents declassified during the last decade allow us to draw the conclusion that in the start phase of the 'big fleet build-up' the members of the Soviet Naval High Command thought that a new shipbuilding programme would outline a great addition to the Second Five-Year Plan programme of 1933–37.[9]

Reporting on the number of ships demanded for the creation of the new naval formations, the leaders of the Soviet Navy took into account their operational capabilities. After the completion of the 1936–47 programme the Soviet Navy would be able to obtain 'mastery of the sea' in the Sea of Japan and in the Gulf of Finland. Besides that the Soviet Navy had to conduct a successful struggle against the German Fleet which would be more powerful than the Baltic Fleet. The Black Sea Fleet had to maintain 'mastery of the sea' and prevent enemy attacks from the sea along the coastline of the Soviet Union. The Northern Fleet should be able to defend the Soviet sea borders and conduct combat activity in order to disrupt eventual enemy communications in the Northern Sea.

It was assumed that 676 combatants including 238 ocean-going surface ships and 348 big and medium submarines, would be enough to achieve these operational aims.[10] The operational basis of the big shipbuilding programme was revised several times in accordance with the Third Five-Year Plan for 1938 to 1942. In September 1937 the new Chief of the Naval Forces, Viktorov, presented an explanatory note about the operational tasks of the Soviet Fleets after the completion of the 'big fleet programme', to the Chief of the General Staff of the *RKKA*, Marshal Yegorov.

The Pacific Fleet

The Pacific Fleet had:

- to prevent the enemy from landing at the most important points situated on the Soviet Far Eastern coastline;
- to break up enemy troop transports through North Korean ports and ports in the Korea Strait;
- to stop supplies for the Japanese troops going through the Yellow Sea ports;
- to destroy the military and economic might of Japan by surface raids against Japanese commerce in the Western Pacific;
- to prevent the penetration of the Tartar Straits by Japanese ships by using submarine operations.

Formulating such operational tasks, the Soviet naval experts believed that the ships of the Pacific Fleet in 1947 would include no fewer than eight battleships, one aircraft carrier, four heavy cruisers, eight light cruisers, 56 destroyers and destroyer leaders, as well as 39 big, 79 medium, and 46 small submarines. At the same time they took into account that 'strong naval aviation' support would be available in order to solve the Pacific Fleet's operational tasks jointly with the surface ships and submarines.[11]

The Baltic Fleet

The Baltic Fleet had:

- to maintain the 'mastery of the sea' in the Gulf of Finland, being ready to support the Red Army offensive operations against Estonia, Latvia and Finland;
- to prevent strong naval formations of eventual enemies from penetrating into the northern Baltic and the Gulf of Riga;
- to disrupt enemy sea communications in the Baltic Sea, and first to break up the transport of strategic materials from northern Sweden to Germany.

It seemed that air warfare and mine warfare in the Baltic Area would be very intensive, especially during the initial stage of warfare. In accordance with the prospective operational tasks the Baltic Fleet's list of combat ships would include eight battleships, two heavy cruisers, six light cruisers, 44 destroyers and destroyer leaders, and 14 big, 46 medium, and 28 small submarines.[12]

Soviet naval experts asserted that the surface ships and the submarines of the Baltic Fleet would be in need of strong air support. Besides that, the fleet's naval bases and the ship formations would be in need of safe anti-aircraft cover, and of a number of minesweepers and special small ships. It was stated that the Baltic Fleet's combatants would correspond to the climatic and geographical conditions of the Baltic theatre of war. Therefore the naval specialists proposed reinforcing the Baltic Fleet, besides capital ships, by a number of 'strongly armoured small ships, equipped with good gunnery'. They wanted ships such as the two Finnish coastal defence monitors (the *Ilmarinen* class), designed to operate in the skerries and archipelagos of Finland.

The Black Sea Fleet

The Black Sea Fleet had:

- to achieve 'mastery of the sea', to defeat hostile fleets and to destroy naval bases of eventual enemies;
- to prevent units of the 'Imperialist Navies' from coming into the Black Sea;

It was presumed that five battleships, one heavy cruiser, seven light cruisers, 32 destroyer leaders and destroyers, 11 big, 31 medium, and 28 small submarines would be enough to solve the operational tasks.[13]

The Northern Fleet

The Northern Fleet had:

- to prevent an enemy occupation of the northern coasts of the Soviet Union, to maintain a strong defence of the Murmansk and White Sea districts;
- to defend the Northern Sea Route;
- to defend Soviet sea communications between the seaports of the USSR and ports of neutral states;
- to break up the sea communication links of eventual enemies, including Germany, Great Britain and Finland;
- to provide the plan of the Northern Fleet's deployment for the creation of probable reinforcements for the Pacific Fleet by units of the Northern Fleet transferred through the Northern Sea Route. After the completion of the 'big shipbuilding programme' the list of combat ships of the Northern Fleet would contain two battleships, one aircraft carrier, three heavy cruisers, four light cruisers, 28 destroyer leaders and destroyers, and 20 big, 28 medium and 12 small submarines.[14]

THE BATTLESHIP BUILDING PLANS OF 1936–37

The design proposal of the *TsKBS-1* under V.L. Bzhezinskii, V.A. Nikitin and A.I. Maslov for a 35,000t battleship, following the model of the British *Nelson*, was dismissed when the *Ansaldo* design *UP-41*, with two triple turrets at the bow and one at the stern, was considered advantageous from a tactical point of view. But it became clear that the tactical and technical requirements could not be achieved with 35,000t.

Of the competitive design proposals of the *TsKBS-1* and the design bureau of the *Ordzhonikidze* yard under S.F. Stepanov it was decided by Orlov and Muklevich on 21 August 1936 to prepare the plans for the battleship *A/projekt 23* with the *Ordzhonikidze* yard and to entrust the management of the project to L.S. Grauerman and B.G. Chilikin, while the battleship *B/projekt 25* was to be developed by the *TsKBS-1* (renamed *TsKB-17*) under N.P. Dubinin, the young successor of Bzhezinskii, and V.A. Nikitin, A.I. Maslov, and V.P. Rimskii-Korsakov. As supervisors of the projects were installed the Chief of the Research Institute for Warship Construction, *Inzhener Flagman 2 Ranga* N.V. Alyakrinskii, and the *Voennyi engineer 2 Ranga* E.P. Libel', and the members of Muklevich's office, B.Ya. Streltsov and A.S. Kassatsier, especially for *projekt 23*.[15]

In November 1936 the draft projects for both types were considered by the Naval administration's Department of Shipbuilding under *Inzhener Flagman 2 Ranga* Alyakrinskii. Now the displacement of *projekt 23* had to be raised to 45,930t, because of a strengthening of the armour deck, and was confirmed by Orlov on 26 November 1936.[16] *Projekt 25* had to be enlarged to 30,900t to

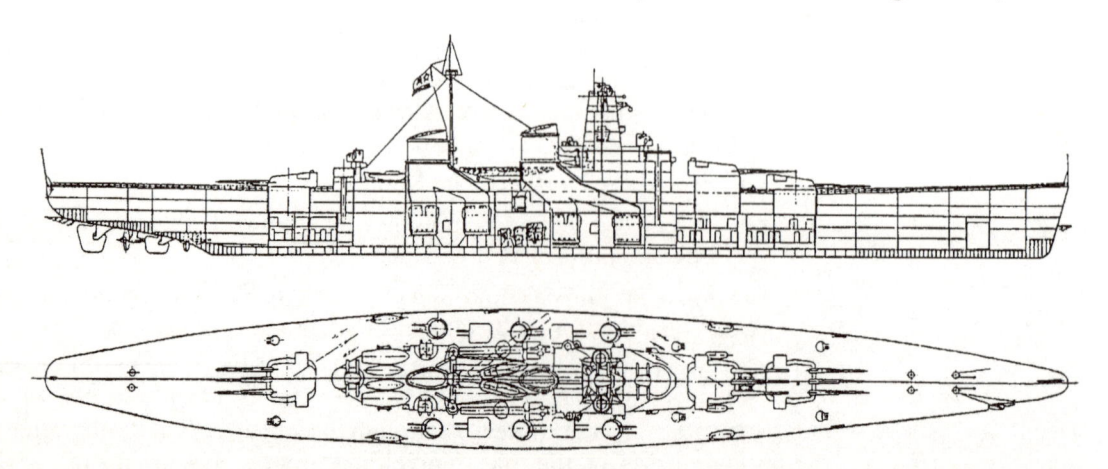

Fig. 5. Battleship of *projekt 25*, no name given, 1936, displ. 30,900t stdd., length 250m, max. speed 35kt, 9 30.5cm, 12 13cm, 8 10cm, 24 3.7cm. Reconstructed to *projekt 64*, but not laid down and cancelled. Credit: Sudostroenie

reach the desired speed of 35kt. Following the decree of the government on 3 December contracts were signed by the Chief of the Shipbuilding Administration to build eight battleships to be completed by 1941: two *projekt 23* and two *projekt 25* at the yards in Leningrad, and four *projekt 25* at Nikolaev, thus supplementing the Second Five-Year Plan.[17]

But there were some changes in 1937. On 23 January the *STO* proposed to the *SNK* the laying down in the last quarter of 1937 of four battleships *type A* and three *type B*, and the fourth *type B* in the first quarter of 1938. The ships would be launched in 1939 and commissioned up to the end of 1941. In a revised plan of 26 May the Committee on Defence proposed to the *SNK* that the planned battleships be divided into eight *type A/projekt 23* units now of 41,500t with nine 406mm guns and 16 *type B/projekt 25* units of 26,400t with nine 305mm guns. Of the planned 20 cruisers 15 were of the 7,500t class and five were of a new type. The 17 destroyer leaders were of 2,030t, and the 182 destroyers of 1,425t. Of the 244 submarines, 90 were big, 62 of them of the new *series XIV/K*-class submarine cruisers, 164 were medium and 90 small.[18]

On 3 July the Committee on Defence made a new plan for the laying down data: in December 1937 and January 1938 two *type B/projekt 25* each, in February 1938 three *type A/projekt 23*, and the fourth one in March 1938.[19]

After Orlov's arrest the new Chief of the *VMS*, *Flagman Flota 1 Ranga* Viktorov, organized in August 1937 a commission under *Flagman 2 Ranga* S.P. Stavitskii to investigate the *type B/projekt 25*. They found this design inadequate against the new German 'battlecruisers' of the *Scharnhorst*-class or the French *Dunkerque*-class, and this led to a completely new design, called *projekt 64*, with a displacement of 48,000t.[20] On 15 August 1937 the Committee on Defence gave the armament data to the *SNK*. For the *type A/projekt 23*: nine 406mm in three triple turrets, 12 152mm in six twin turrets, 12 100mm multi-purpose in twin mounts, 40 37mm A/A in twin mounts, and one catapult and four airplanes. For the *projekt 64* the armament should be nine 356mm in three triple turrets, 12 152mm in six twin turrets, 12 100mm in six twin mounts, 24–37mm in twin mounts and also four airplanes. The speed was planned as 29kt and the range 8,000 miles.[21]

In addition there were ten heavy (anti-'Washington') cruisers of 23,000t with nine 254mm guns in triple turrets, eight 130mm and eight 100mm in twin mounts and 16–37mm as well as two airplanes, following closely the *Ansaldo*-design of 1936 as *projekt 22*. Two aircraft carriers of 10,000–11,000t for between 40–45 planes were added as *projekt 71* with 6–8 130mm and 4–6 100mm guns in twin mounts, and 6–37mm. The hull was based on that of the new cruisers of *projekt 68* of 10,000t with 12 152mm guns in triple turrets and eight 100mm in twin mounts. Twenty-two vessels of this type were planned. Of the 20 destroyer leaders the new ones were of *projekt 48* type and of the 144 destroyers the new ones were of the new *projekt 30* type. The proposed submarines were changed to 84 big, 175 medium, and 116 small units. In addition three types of minelayers and two of minesweepers were proposed. The plan was approved by the *Narkom* for Defence, Marshal Voroshilov, on 16 August and presented to Stalin on 7 September 1937, but no document is available bearing his signature of approval.[22]

Table 7.1: Proposed distribution of the ships in the plan of 15 August 1937

Type	Pacific Fleet	Baltic Fleet	Black Sea Fleet	Northern Fleet	Total
Battleships *pr.23*	4	–	–	2	6
Battleships *pr.64*	4	6	4	–	14
Old Battleships	–	2	1	–	3
Aircraft Carriers *pr.71*	1	–	–	1	2
Heavy Cruisers *pr.22*	4	2	1	3	10
Light Cruisers *pr.68*	6	4	2	4	16
Light Cruisers *pr.26*	2	2	2	–	6
Old Cruisers	–	–	3	–	3
Destroyer Leaders	8	4	4	4	20
Destroyers	48	40	28	28	144
Big Submarines	39	14	11	20	84
Medium Submarines	70	46	31	28	175
Small Submarines	46	28	28	12	114

When, in December 1937, the designs of the battleship were presented to the Shipbuilding Administration, both were considered unsatisfactory. In *projekt 23* some unresolved problems remained, the armour had to be strengthened again and with some other changes the displacement rose to 57,825t. But *projekt 64* was evaluated as completely below the requirements and with its armament and its slow speed could not win tactical superiority over the ships of possible enemies. To fulfil the requirements it would be necessary to go to a ship of almost 50,000t. So there was again great uncertainty, when on 9 January 1938 the draft of the 'Memorandum of the Navy's Development in 1938 to 1942' was outlined. The memorandum should have been presented to the members of the Politburo but its draft had already been rejected by the new Chief of the General Staff of the *RKKA*, *Komandarm* Shaposhnikov who had relieved Marshal Yegorov – a victim of the purges in late autumn 1937 and shot in 1938.

So P.I. Smirnov, whom Stalin had made a separate *Narkom* for the Navy, had a little bit more independence from the Army. He and his Deputy L.M. Galler worked on a new plan. They dropped the unsatisfactory *projekt 64*, and planned only one battleship type, an improved *projekt 23* of now 59,150t with 15 units, and replaced *projekt 22*, with 24,450t, a speed of 33.3kt, and nine 254mm guns,

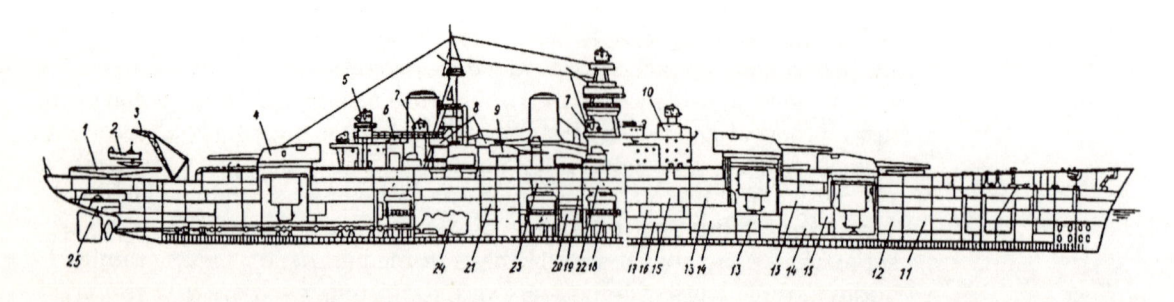

Fig. 6. Battleship *projekt 23*, *Sovetskii Soyuz*, 1938, displ. 59,150t stdd., length 269.4m, max. speed 28kt, 9 40.6cm, 12 15.2cm, 8 10cm, 32 3.7cm. Four ships laid down 1938–40, not completed, broken up on the slips. Credit: Sudostroenie

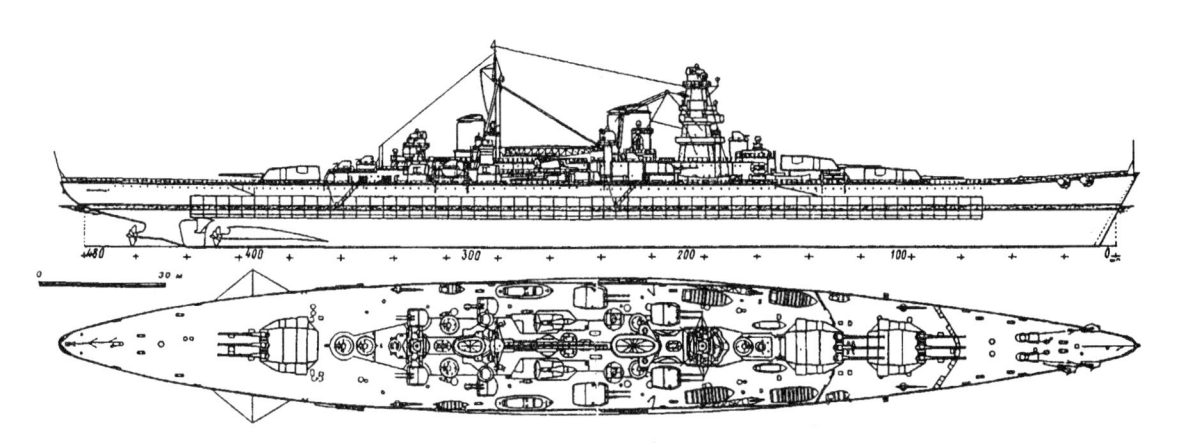

Fig. 7. Battlecruiser *projekt 69*, *Kronshtadt*, April 1940, displ. 35,240t stdd., length 250.5m, max. speed 33kt, 9 30.5cm, 8 15.2cm, 8 10cm, 24 3.7cm. Two ships laid down 1939, not completed, broken down on the slips. Credit: Sudostroenie

and – looking at the German *Scharnhorst*-class – soon to be changed again to a real battlecruiser of 35,420t with three 305mm triple turrets, in order to be stronger than any heavy cruiser or 'pocket battleship' and faster than any enemy battleship, an idea which had also been the principal idea for the German *Panzerschiffe*.[23]

The new plan was presented on 14 February 1938 in a new version to Stalin and Molotov, Chairman of the *SNK SSSR*. At a joint session of both assemblies of the Supreme Council at this time Molotov announced: 'The powerful Soviet State must have a high-seas and ocean fleet according to its interests and as deserved by our great aims.'[24]

CHANGES IN STRATEGIC PLANNING AND NEW PURGES

The prospective operational tasks for the Soviet fleets were corrected and supplemented again. In accordance with those tasks the Pacific Fleet had to support the Red Army offensive in the Posiet and Sakhalin directions, to capture southern Sakhalin and to achieve 'mastery of the sea' in the Laperouse Strait in order to create possibilities for a Soviet naval penetration into the Pacific Ocean, and to defend the eastern exit of the Northern Sea Route. The Baltic Fleet had above all to be ready to support the Red Army's invasion of Estonia, Latvia and Finland. The British Royal Navy was to be excluded from the list of eventual enemies of the Northern Fleet.[25]

Meanwhile, in March 1938 a new, great, but final show trial was held against Bukharin, Rykov and 19 other high-ranking officials, including Deputy *Narkom* for Foreign Relations, N.N. Krestiniskii, three *Narkoms*, and even the former Chief of the *OGPU/NKVD*, G.G. Yagoda. All were forced by torture to admit to being 'members of a block of rightists and Trotskyists', and were sentenced to the 'highest penalty' and shot. M.P. Tomskii, the head of the Labour Union and member of the Politburo, avoided this fate by committing suicide.[26]

The Army was not exempted. Including the already mentioned officers, three of five Marshals, 14 of 15 Army Commanders, 57 of 85 Corps Commanders, 110 of 195 Division Commanders, 220 of 406 Brigade Commanders, all 11 Deputy *Narkoms* for Defence, a great number of Political Commissars, and officers of the Air Force were also victims of the purges. A great number of all these officers were liquidated, others were sent to the *Gulag*, from which some later came back, such as, for example, the later Marshals K.A. Meretskov and K.K. Rokossovskii. But the purges were not limited to the higher ranks; junior officers and soldiers were also arrested. In a report written by V.V. Ul'rikh to the new *Narkom* for State Security and Chief of the *NKVD*, L.P. Beriya, on 15 October 1938 it was stated that between 1 October 1936 and 30 September 1938 30,514 military personnel had been sentenced to be shot, and 5,643 to be imprisoned.[27]

The continuing purges led to quick changes also among the high command and at lower levels in the Navy. The Commanders of the Pacific Fleet, G.I. Kire'ev, who had relieved Viktorov, the Baltic Fleet, A.K. Sivkov, the Black Sea Fleet, P.I. Smirnov-Svetlovskii, the Northern Fleet, K.I. Dushenov, the Caspian Flotilla, Z.A. Zakupnev, and the Amur Flotilla, I.N. Kadatskii-Rudnev, were arrested between January and June 1938, and executed before 1940. Viktorov, who had replaced Orlov as Chief of the *VMF RKKA* in July 1937 was relieved as early as December 1937, arrested on 22 April and sentenced to death on 1 August 1938. On 30 December Stalin appointed *Armejskii Komissar 1 Ranga* P.A.Smirnov as head of a new separate Commissariat for the Navy, only to exchange him for the terrible Chief of the Border Troops and Deputy Head of the *NKVD*, *Komandarm* M.P. Frinovskii, in September 1938. Both proved to be incapable of managing a big naval building programme, and spent most of their time eliminating the 'enemies of the people' and the 'saboteurs' and 'wreckers'. They suffered, however, the same fate as their predecessors and victims, and were shot, as was finally also N.I. Yeshov, the *Narkom* and Chief of the *NKVD*.

Besides these senior commanders, eight leaders of central administrations, five chiefs of staff of fleets and flotillas, 15 other flag officers, 14 chiefs of brigades, 17 commanders of divisions, and chiefs of staff of units, 22 commanding officers, and no less than 3,000 seamen became victims of the purges. Nor did the technicians escape. Several of the experienced engineers fell victim to the repressions and were liquidated, such as N.V. Alyakrinskii, B.P. Rimskii-Korsakov, B.Ya. Streltsov and A.V. Speranski, as well as the chief constructor of the *projekt 7* destroyers, P.O. Trakhtenberg. Others were sent to special *NKVD*-supervised construction bureaus, where they had to work as prisoners, such as V.I. Bzhezinskii, A.S. Kassatsier, A.E. Tsushkevich, and also the aircraft designers A.N. Tupolev and V.M. Petlyakov. In many positions the responsible engineers had to be replaced by very young and inexperienced new men.[28]

The sources now available suggest that the purges should not be attributed to disagreements about the Soviet political, military or naval strategy. Some naval officers purged had formerly been revolutionary Bolsheviks, others formerly commissars, some advocates of the *jeune école*, others of the 'big ship navy'. Despite having tried to anticipate Stalin's ideas, to avoid being tarred with the ideas he thought out of date, and to keep out of the political struggles, they became victims of Stalin's paranoic mistrust, in which he was encouraged by *NKVD* officials and even by such men as Smirnov and Frinovskii. Senior officers like L.M. Galler and I.S. Isakov may have survived, despite being *spetsialists* from the Imperial Navy, because of their connections to A.A. Zhdanov, the Secretary of the Central Committee and First Secretary of the Party in Leningrad, the main base of the Baltic Fleet, which both men had commanded. Stalin might also have valued their long experience.[29]

To establish some closer control over the Navy, Stalin installed in March 1938 a War Council of the Navy, headed by the *Narkom* Smirnov, but controlled by his protégé A.A. Zhdanov, the Party Secretary of Leningrad, and composed of L.M. Galler, I.S. Isakov, and the Commanders of the Pacific Fleet, then N.G. Kuznetsov, and of the Baltic Fleet, G.I. Levchenko.[30]

This 'mopping up' of the Army and Navy brought many young and not so experienced officers into leading positions. On the one side this led to some consolidation, because they were almost all educated in the youth organization of the Party, *Komsomol'*, and willing to follow the Party line. But on the other side they did not dare to oppose their superiors and to develop independent ideas for fear of also becoming victims of repression.

NEW LEADERS AND A NEW STRATEGY IN 1939

On 28 April 1939 Stalin appointed the young new Commander of the Pacific Fleet, N.G. Kuznetsov, as *Narkom* for the *VMF*. He was only 36 years old. In 1934 he had become the commanding officer of the cruiser *Chervona Ukraina* of the Black Sea Fleet, and from 1936 to 1937 was a *Kapitan 1 Ranga* naval attaché and senior adviser to the Spanish Republican Navy, when he was recalled to become the First Deputy and then the Commander of the Pacific Fleet. Notwithstanding the fact that he was the responsible commander of the fleet when the new destroyer *Reshitel'nyi* was wrecked on 5 November 1938 in a storm during the transfer from the Amur yard to Vladivostok for final equipment, he was called to give a speech at the Party Congress in Moscow in early 1939. Stalin seems to have liked this energetic young man and so decided to make him head of the Navy during the difficult time of building the 'big ocean-going fleet'.[31]

He got two *spetsialists* from the Imperial Navy, who were exempted from the purges, as Deputy Commanders *VMF* and his chief advisors: L.M. Galler as Chief of the Main Staff, and I.S. Isakov as Head of the Shipbuilding Department. Galler was 56 years old, had entered the Navy in 1905, commanded several destroyers, and in 1917 became commander of the pre-*Dreadnought* battleship *Andrei Pervozvannyi*. He decided to join the Red Fleet and served mostly with the Baltic Fleet, first as Chief of Staff, and then as Commander.[32] Isakov was 45 years old and had entered the Navy when the First World War began. As a young midshipman (ensign) in 1917 he had taken command of the destroyer *Izyaslav* and transferred this new ship from Tallinn to Petrograd, joining the Red Fleet. He had served in the Caspian Flotilla and the Baltic and Black Sea Fleets, before he became Chief of Staff of the Baltic Fleet from 1930 to 1937.[33]

The fleets also got new commanders. In May 1939 V.F. Tributs took command of the Baltic Fleet, and in August F.S. Oktyabrskii the Black Sea Fleet and I.S. Yumachev the Pacific Fleet. The Northern Fleet had already been taken over by V.P. Drozd, but in July 1940 A.G. Golovko, who transferred from the Caspian Flotilla, took over.[34] In the several river flotillas there were also great changes in the leading positions.

The new leadership of the Navy forced through in mid-1939 a thorough revision of the operational tasks of the future 'big ocean-going fleet', and a correction of the technical tactical data for a number of combat units demanded to solve the main strategic missions. Also a new version of the 'Explanatory Note to the Shipbuilding Programme 1940–1947' was written. Now the main enemy was assumed to be Japan.

The Japanese attack against China in 1937–38, which led to the capture of most harbours on the Chinese coast and the areas along the rivers and railways,[35] and the Japanese attempt to capture some hills at the Khasan Lake in July/August 1938, had augmented Stalin's fears.[36] The Commander-in-Chief in the Far East, the highly decorated Marshal Blyukher, was denounced by the new Chief of the Political Administration (*PURKKA*), L.S. Mekhlis for not having followed orders from Marshal Voroshilov, which aroused Stalin;s suspicions. Blyukher was arrested in October and died after heavy torture during the *NKVD* investigations on 9 November 1938.[37]

The Pacific Fleet

Stalin's fears led to a change in the ranking of the fleets, with the Pacific Fleet becoming the top one, pushing the Baltic Fleet into second place.[38]

The authors of the new 'Explanatory Note' considered that the Japanese would only use 'old ships' at first in a conflict against the Soviet Pacific Fleet because they also had to fear offensive actions from the US Fleet. But it was possible that the Japanese would then use their modern fleet to conduct decisive actions against the Soviets, when the situation with the USA was cleared. The Japanese Navy's offensive actions were expected from the Sea of Japan, the Okhotsk Sea, the North Western Pacific and the Bering Straits. It was considered that the natural conditions of the Pacific theatre were more favourable for the Japanese Navy. They had unlimited capacity for manoeuvre, and could concentrate all their naval forces very rapidly in any operational direction. On the other hand, the Soviet Navy did not have such possibilities. The Soviet Pacific Fleet would have to conduct anti-submarine warfare in this huge theatre of war. The operational efforts of the light forces of the Soviet Fleet had to be very strong. Therefore the Fleet should consist of two main formations. Both should be able to fight against the enemy fleet in separate operational directions, notwithstanding a lack of support from the other formations.

It was estimated that the Japanese would be able to deploy against the Soviet Pacific Fleet eight 'old' battleships, four aircraft carriers, eight heavy cruisers of the 10,000t *Takao* and *Myoko* classes, 12 light cruisers, 32 destroyers, a number of submarines, and many auxiliaries. In the Sea of Okhotsk the Japanese formations were expected to include two 'old' battleships, three aircraft carriers, four cruisers of the *Kinugasa* and *Kako* classes, as well as six light cruisers. It was supposed that both enemy formations could get reinforcements if needed. In addition, the Soviets estimated that the Japanese would be able to confront the Pacific Fleet with 83 ships, including six light cruisers and 60 'old' destroyers. It was expected that the Japanese Navy would conduct landing operations, support Army formations fighting on the land fronts, and the Soviet experts supposed that the Japanese were able to strike at the bases of the Pacific Fleet, and to carry out raids against commerce and the fisheries.

It was estimated that the Pacific Fleet should include no fewer than 15 battleships, 13 heavy, 26 light cruisers, and 130 destroyers to be able to fight successfully against the Japanese Navy. But the Soviet experts realized that it was impossible to get such a number of units into the active list. Therefore in 1947 the Pacific Fleet should include six battleships of *projekt 23*, two battlecruisers of *projekt 69*, 12 cruisers of *projekt 68*, and 36 destroyers of *projekt 30*, and 30 patrol ships. These units would be ordered to conduct counter-offensive operations against the main formation of the Japanese Fleet. In addition, the Pacific Fleet should include 41 big, 118 medium, and 60 small submarines, which could be ordered to raid the enemy communications and to defend the Soviet coastal provinces.

There was no doubt that in 1947 the Soviet Pacific Fleet would be weaker than the Japanese Fleet. To compensate for this weakness, the naval specialists planned to lay mines in the Far Eastern littorals – 17,000 mines at the entrance to Vladivostok, 5,000 close to Kamchatka and the Vladimiro-Olginsky Fortified District. And it was planned to lay 9,000 mines off the approaches to Sovetskaya Gavan, De Kastry, and Nikovaevsk-on-Amur. To fulfil this task the Command asked for 12 minelayers to be put on the active list.

In addition, the Soviet Naval Command suggested building one aircraft carrier for the Pacific Fleet, to be used as cover for the surface ships, but also for strikes against the shore establishments of the Japanese. Finally, they asked for 27 fast ocean-going minesweepers and 36 additional patrol ships, together with 118 big and 49 small submarine chasers, 63 base minesweepers, and nine net-layers. These vessels were needed to conduct anti-submarine operations and to ensure a strong defence of the Pacific naval bases.

The Pacific Fleet had to be able to win a sea battle with the Japanese Fleet, destroy its bases at the Japanese home islands, and the Kuriles, disrupt Japan's sea communications, destroy its fishing grounds, and support Soviet ground forces operating along the coast of the Sea of Japan, and also to defend Soviet sea communications in the Far East.

The Baltic Fleet

The German occupation of Austria in March 1938 (the *Anschluss*), and the Sudeten crisis, which led to the Munich agreement in September/October 1938, followed by the incorporation of the *Memelland*, increased the fears of the Soviet leaders about the German threat. At the same time they were also anxious that the Baltic States, Poland and Finland might become German satellites and thus that the territories of these states could be used for operations by German 'expeditionary forces'. It was assumed that the German Fleet would attempt to blockade the Baltic Fleet in the Gulf of Finland, because the Germans would have to prevent disruption to their vital sea communications to the iron-ore deposits in northern Sweden.

Soviet staff officers stated that the German naval forces, if ordered to blockade the Baltic Fleet, might use several ports in the Åland Islands, and the Moonsund Archipelagos and also the ports of Helsinki and Tallinn. The blockade barrage, as the Soviets expected, would be established between Porkkala-Udd and Nargön/Naisaari. At the same time it was assumed that if a Soviet–German war was to break out, Britain would keep a neutrality more favourable to Germany than to the Soviet Union, and Britain's attitude would allow the Germans to deploy a strong naval force not only in the Baltic, but also in the Arctic.

It was assumed that in 1947 the Germans could concentrate in the Baltic four new battleships of the *Bismarck*-class, two of the *Scharnhorst*-class, two pocket battleships of the *Deutschland*-class, six heavy cruisers of the *Admiral Hipper*-class, and nine light cruisers. In the Arctic it was expected that Germany would keep two battleships of the *Bismarck*-class, one pocket battleship, five heavy cruisers of the *Hipper*-class, and six light cruisers. The Soviet naval experts assumed that no fewer than 37 German heavy ships would be deployed in order to neutralize the Soviet Navy.

The plan for the Baltic Fleet was as follows:

- to conduct naval operations (jointly with Red Army operations) in order to capture the mouth of the Gulf of Finland;
- to achieve 'mastery of the sea' of all littorals belonging to the Baltic States and southern Finland.

Then the Baltic Fleet had:

- to occupy the Åland Islands and the Moonsund Archipelagos and to achieve a 'mastery of the sea' in the Northern Baltic;
- to support an Army invasion into Latvia and Lithuania and defeat the enemy fleet 'step by step'.

Therefore it was assumed that the main operational task of the Baltic Fleet during the initial stage of a future war would be to assist the Red Army's ground troops, which would conduct a strategic offensive along the coast of the Gulf of Finland. At the same time, the Baltic Fleet had to destroy combat ships of the anti-Soviet coalition and to secure the possibility of using its submarines in the whole Baltic Sea. It was presumed that the Baltic Fleet's combat activity in the littorals of southern Finland would be a difficult task. To fight in the Finnish skerries special ships had to be designed. The experts stated that by 1947 the Baltic Fleet would need six special gunboats.

At the same time it was assumed that above all developments of the operational situation in the Baltic, both active navies would look for a 'decisive sea battle'. Therefore the Soviet Naval High Command suggested deploying in the Baltic Sea a force consisting of four battleships of *projekt 23*, two battleships of the *Marat*-class, four battlecruisers of *projekt 69*, five light cruisers of *projekt 68*, two light cruisers of the *Kirov*-class, and 48 destroyer leaders and destroyers. In addition, it was considered that one light cruiser and eight destroyers would be needed to defend the Soviet naval bases and also six 'small cruisers' to lay the minefields in the Southern Baltic Sea. In addition to these units 36 fast minesweepers were planned to conduct anti-mine warfare, and 36 patrol ships to cover the battleships, and also six minelayers to establish the defensive barrages and to lay mines in the Finnish archipelagos.

The submarine operations of the Baltic Fleet would have a great influence on the results of a probable Soviet–German war. In 1939 the Soviet naval staff experts considered that it would be enough to sink about 120,000 GRT of the German merchant tonnage per month to cause a collapse of the German economy. They estimated that such a task could be undertaken by 20 submarines deployed in the Baltic simultaneously. Only small submarines would operate at the approaches to the Soviet naval bases to defend the sea coasts. The number of units of different submarine types asked for the Baltic Fleet in 1939 were 11 big, 48 medium, and 30 small ones.

Additionally, the Soviet naval command requested for the Baltic Fleet a reinforcement of at least 27 base minesweepers, eight patrol ships, 78 patrol motor boats and small submarine chasers, which, as was planned, would defend the Soviet sea coasts, as well as three net-layers to conduct anti-submarine operations against the Finnish Navy.[39]

Finally, the Baltic Fleet had to be able to defeat the German Fleet, as well as the naval forces of Poland, Sweden, Finland and the Baltic States, and support landings by ground forces. The coastal forces had to be able to defend the Soviet coastline in the Gulf of Finland.

The Black Sea Fleet

The situation in the Black Sea was influenced by the aggressive policy of Italy. After the Fascist annexation of Ethiopia in May 1936, its strong support of the Nationalists in the Spanish Civil War, the foundation of the 'Axis' with Germany in October 1936, the announcement of a 'Pact of Steel' with Germany, and the occupation of Albania in April/May 1939 fears arose of Italian participation in a possible war with the Axis powers.

The operational plan of the Black Sea Fleet was worked out in the firm belief that Romania, Bulgaria, Turkey and Italy would all conduct naval operations against the Soviet Navy. Units of the German Navy were expected in the Black Sea too, but that was not considered significant. They also assumed that the Italian Navy would have 'no real enemies in the Mediterranean' should Italy be involved in war against the Soviet Union. But even if France should maintain its neutrality, the Italian naval command would continue to be afraid of a sudden French attack.

The Soviets expected that in 1947 the opposing Allied fleets would include three or four battleships, one battlecruiser, two or three heavy cruisers, five to seven light cruisers, 25 or 26 destroyer leaders and destroyers, nine MTBs, four patrol ships, 38 to 40 submarines, and two or three submarine- and five surface-minelayers.

The Soviet Naval High Command also proposed building, in addition to the old battleship of the *Marat*-class, three battleships of *projekt 23*, five light cruisers of *projekt 68*, two light cruisers of the *Kirov*-class, four destroyer leaders, 28 destroyers, five minelayers, three net-layers, 18 fast and 46 base minesweepers, 30 patrol ships and 60 big submarine chasers.

The submarines of the Black Sea Fleet would be ordered to cover the formations of the main forces which would be under way in the high sea, to raid commerce and to defend Soviet naval bases. As estimated for 1947, the Black Sea Fleet was in need of six big, 31 medium, and 28 small submarines and also eight submarine minelayers.

The Black Sea Fleet would have to be able to defeat the Italian forces coming into the Black Sea, and also the naval forces of Romania, Bulgaria and Turkey.[40]

The Northern Fleet

It was thought that Germany and Finland would become the enemies of the Soviet Union in the Arctic. At the same time Soviet naval experts expected Great Britain and Norway to remain neutral but biased more in Germany's favour.

The Soviet Naval High Command took into account that the German Fleet might conduct a strategic landing operation in order to invade northern Russia. Besides, it was possible that German naval forces would attempt to break up Soviet sea communications in the Arctic.

The Northern Fleet had to cope with German naval support for Finland with two *Bismarck*-class battleships, two pocket battleships, five heavy cruisers, six light cruisers, and destroyers, minesweepers and aircraft.

Therefore the draft plan for strengthening the Northern Fleet was a six-year programme of accelerated warship construction with the German Fleet considered as the competitor. In accordance with this assumption the Northern Fleet had to be raised to a strength of two battleships of *projekt 23*, four battlecruisers of *projekt 69*, four light cruisers of *projekt 68*, and 32 destroyers of *projekt 30*, all intended for a 'decisive battle on the high seas'.

It was calculated that at least two cruisers would be at sail on the high seas simultaneously, defending the sea communications connecting the Soviet Union with Allied and neutral countries. Eight destroyer leaders were asked for to defend the two most important Soviet fisheries in the Arctic, and no fewer than 24 patrol ships, all intended to cover the heavy ships acting on the high seas, to defend the domestic sea communications and to guard the approaches of the Kola Gulf and the White Sea approaches.

Soviet naval experts assumed that the Northern Fleet by 1947 should have a submarine force of 65 units: 25 big, 28 medium, and 12 small submarines. The big and medium submarines should be used to interrupt the enemy's sea communications. The small submarines could be applied to the defence of the Soviet Arctic coastlines.

Nine 'squadron' minesweepers were asked for to maintain a counter-mine defence of the Northern Fleet Squadron. The overall number of base minesweepers would be no less than 36, but only during war-time. The Soviet naval experts firmly believed, that during peace time it would be enough to keep on the active list 18 base minesweepers, because it was planned to compensate for the shortage of such vessels by converting units from merchant and fishing vessels. At the same time they asserted at least three minelayers would be needed to lay the 7,000 mines to create a strong defence of the Northern Fleet.

Besides, it was estimated, the Northern Fleet would be in need of one net-layer and 52 small and big submarine chasers to operate successfully, but the Soviet High Command realized that the shipbuilding industry of the USSR would not be able to satisfy all the Navy's requests. Therefore in 1939 they asked for only 12 submarine chasers, intended for sea guard formations, which would operate in the Kola Gulf, and 14 others to create a strong defence in the White Sea.[41]

The Northern Fleet must finally be able to prevent Germany from landing troops in the Arctic, to defend the Soviet fisheries in the Arctic Ocean and the sea communications with neutral countries, and to disrupt Germany's sea communications in the Atlantic Ocean, the North Sea, the Norwegian Sea and the Greenland Sea.

The River Flotillas

The active list of the Dnepr Flotilla in 1947 should include at least 14 river monitors, 8 river gunboats, 48 armoured cutters and 12 minesweepers.

The Caspian Flotilla had to be strengthened to at least 118 vessels, including 12 gunboats, 74 big submarine chasers, two net-layers, four medium and four small submarines, 18 base minesweepers, and four patrol ships of *projekt 29*.

The Amur Flotilla, as was planned for 1947, should be raised to a strength of 13 river monitors, 72 armoured cutters, 18 fast motor boats, 12 minesweepers, and 10 motor-minesweepers.[42]

The following calculations underpinned these operational assumptions: a *projekt 23* battleship was counted as the equivalent of a new Japanese battleship or a German *Bismarck*-class battleship; 6.8 units of *projekt 23* were counted as the equivalent of 5.2 Italian *Littorio*-class battleships; a *projekt 69* battlecruiser was counted as the equivalent of two *Takao*-class heavy cruisers or one *Scharnhorst*-class fast battleship; and a *Marat*-class battleship was counted as the equivalent of 1.6 *Deutschland*-class pocket battleships, and so on.[43]

Tables 7.2, 7.3 and 7.4 show the strengths of the opposing fleets, as seen by the Soviet Naval High Command in 1938 and as calculated for 1945. These Tables also show a great over-estimation of the building plans of the enemy navies up to 1945. There was obviously no real knowledge of these building plans, as, for example, the German *Z-Plan* or the Japanese *3rd Reinforcement Programme of 1937*.[44]

THE SHIPBUILDING ORGANIZATION IN THE THIRD FIVE-YEAR PLAN

During the late 1930s the expansion of the shipbuilding industry and its supply factories was accelerated. The big old yards at Leningrad and Nikolaev were modernized. In 1939 there were seven shipbuilding yards in Leningrad and

Table 7.2: Comparative strength of navies in the Sea of Japan in 1945 (as foreseen in 1938)

	Soviet Pacific Fleet		Japanese Navy	
Ship types	1938	1945	1938	1945
Battleships	none	8	9	19
Aircraft Carriers	none	1	4	16
Heavy Cruisers	none	4	12	24
Coastal Defence Ships	none	2	–	–
Light Cruisers	none	8	8	74
Destroyers and Torpedo Boats	2	56	112	154
Submarines	66	149	63	137

Table 7.3: Comparative strength of navies in the Baltic in 1945 (as foreseen in 1938)

	Soviet Baltic Fleet		German Navy (Poland, Sweden, Finland, Estonia, Latvia)	
Ship types	1938	1945	1938	1945
Battleships	2	8	5	19
Aircraft Carriers	none	none	none	6
Heavy Cruisers	none	2	none	13
Coastal Defence Ships	none	none	9	12
Light Cruisers	none	6	7	29
Destroyers and Torpedo Boats	8	44	56	138
Submarines	59	80	62	199

Table 7.4: Comparative strength of navies in the Black Sea in 1945 (as foreseen in 1938)

	Soviet Black Sea Fleet		Italian, Turkish, Romanian and Bulgarian navies	
Ship types	1938	1945	1938	1945
Battleships	1	5	6	19
Aircraft Carriers	none	none	none	16
Heavy Cruisers	none	2	7	24
Coastal Defence Ships	none	none	none	none
Light Cruisers	4	7	8	16
Destroyers and Torpedo Boats	5	32	112	186
Submarines	27	60	95	193

two in Nikolaev. The construction of yards, begun in the Second Five-Year Plan, as in Komsomol'sk-on-Amur and Molotovsk (now Severodvinsk) was accelerated, and shipbuilding started before the construction was completely finished. Submarines were also built at Gorkii (now again Nizhnii Novgorod). Combat ships and smaller vessels, especially MTBs and submarine chasers, were built in upgraded repair yards and newly built yards at Sevastopol, Vladivostok, Zelenodol'sk, Kerch, Mariupol', Kiev, Yaroslavl', Rybinsk, Stalingrad, Gorokhovets, and Khabarovsk. The gun factories continued their efforts to produce new heavy and anti-aircraft guns. The machinery industry was put under pressure to construct boilers and turbines, and diesel-motors. Armour production was to some extent transferred from tank production to the Navy. Two hundred factories of different branches co-operated with 21 shipbuilding yards. Notwithstanding the arrest of some older engineers – as mentioned – the young shipbuilders and engineers became more experienced and skilled. It seemed that the Soviet Union was quite ready to participate in a naval arms race. There was also a big programme for recruiting and training crews needed for the new ships.[45]

The development of the Soviet Navy evidently accelerated with the establishment of a separate Commissariat of the Navy and the appointment of N.G. Kuznetsov as *Narkom* of the Navy. He had vision, energy, and the support of the Soviet state and the head of the Bolshevik Party, Stalin. And with L.M. Galler as Chief of the Main Staff and I.S. Isakov as First Deputy *Narkom* he had the two ablest flag-officers at his side.

The positive development in ship designing was caused by the transfer of the design work from the shipyard design divisions to the Central Design Bureaus (*TsKB*) and their departments specialized in particular kinds of ships. There were six such offices when the war began; in addition, several other such departments were engaged in naval weapons and special equipment development. Scientific support for the Navy buildup was provided by research institutes. In addition to the two existing ones two new research institutes for the design of instruments and devices were established. But most important was the establishment of a People's Commissariat for shipbuilding under the prominent Soviet functionary I.T. Tevosyan.

Kuznetsov and Tevosyan both distinguished themselves from 1939 to 1945. They were among the capable young and energetic Soviet statesmen, whom Stalin trusted during this time. Nevertheless they were unable to start building any ship before Stalin gave his approval to a project. And he ordered that all decisions be kept secret, so that subordinates often did not know what was going on.

But there were still some delays, and we must look into the causes. There was probably very strong opposition in Army circles to this big naval build-up, which would have slowed their own build-up. This opposition would not have been expressed openly at this time because of the fear of heavy reprisals against the officers uttering such criticism. The reshuffling of resources must have made planning a very difficult process, as is shown by the many changes in the programme which the Navy put on the desks of Voroshilov and Molotov for Stalin's final decision. This is evident from the ups and downs in the numbers of ships earmarked for each type and the changes in their displacement and their construction details, which came to some extent from Stalin himself. The Soviet leader wanted to attend to the Navy construction programme personally, because, as earlier, Soviet industry was suffering from a shortage of metal, tools, and skilled industrial personnel. Therefore at the end of the 1930s Stalin again had to approve the search for foreign aid to complete his naval programme in time. But it is difficult to find out details of Stalin's decisions and interventions, because he left no notes on this topic, and most of the personnel who carried out his decisions are now dead.

FOREIGN AID IN SHIPBUILDING IN THE THIRD FIVE-YEAR PLAN

To overcome shortcomings in the capabilities of the Soviet shipbuilding and naval armaments and equipment industries additional efforts were made to obtain foreign assistance. Besides the previously mentioned contacts with Italy, negotiations were started with France again but these turned out to be fruitless. Contacts with Czechoslovakia led in August 1938 to an agreement about the establishment of a naval construction bureau at the *Shkoda* works for designing and producing naval guns. But this plan failed after the German occupation of the Czech part of the republic and the establishment of the satellite state Slovakia in March 1939.[46]

In 1937 the Soviets ordered four sets of geared turbines of 70,000 HP each for one of the new battleships, and for getting the licence to build such turbines for the other battleships and battlecruisers from the Swiss firm Brown, Boveri & Cie (BBC) for a price of 17.5 million Swiss francs. It was first planned by the Swiss firm to engage, for financing 50 per cent of this project by credits, the British firm Richardson, Westgarth & Co. but this idea failed, and the Swiss government agreed to a risk guaranty of 60 per cent. It was planned to deliver the first set on 15 April 1940, the second in August 1940, and the other two at intervals of 3.5 months.[47] Engineers of both sides were exchanged. Two of the sets were delivered in 1940, but the other two remained in Switzerland after the German attack against the Soviet Union. In the Soviet Union one set was to be used for the lead battleship *Sovetskii Soyuz*, while the other went to the turbine-generator works *Stalin* at Kharkov for building there the replicas for the three sets to be used for each of the battleships and battlecruisers. But after the German attack this factory was evacuated to Sverdlovsk in the Urals, and because the battleships were never completed, the sets could not be used.[48]

After the negotiations with the Italian shipbuilding industry in 1935, which led – as mentioned – to the delivery of plans for battleships, cruisers, and destroyers, on 25 November 1936 the Soviet government started negotiations with some US shipbuilding companies. The Soviets first asked for plans and material equipment and were quite ready to buy two or three cruisers of the latest classes, which would be built in the United States, and heavy naval guns and armour plates. But the first contacts at this time did not lead to positive results.[49]

In spite of the first negative results the Soviet ambassador in Washington, A.A. Troyanovskii, renewed the requests to the US government, and asked if battleships could be built in the United States for the Soviet Union. He tried to assure the American officials, that all such battleships would only operate in the Pacific, helping the US Navy 'to keep the Japanese within limits'. In August 1937 there was a positive reaction from the US Chief of Naval Operations, Admiral W.D. Leahy, to the State Department for the plan to build a battleship for the Soviet Union in the United States, an idea also supported by President F.D. Roosevelt.[50] On 1 December 1937 permission was given to build three triple 406mm gun turrets. And on 21 December 1937 the Soviet ambassador asked for permission to order from US firms the preparation of battleship plans, which was also granted. Several Soviet commissions were sent to the United States to discuss the plans with the US companies. The firm Gibbs & Cox of New York then prepared three versions of combined battleship-aircraft carriers: *A* with 66,074t stdd., eight 456mm guns and 40 planes; *B* with 71,859t stdd., 12 406mm guns and 40 planes; and *C* with 44,200t stdd., ten 406mm guns, and 28 planes.[51] On 5 June 1938 Stalin himself complained to the US ambassador about the delays, notwithstanding the fact that the Soviet Union was willing to pay immediately US$60–100 million.[52] On 8 June 1938 the Secretary of the Navy informed the President that there were no objections to the delivery of the Gibbs & Cox plans, but that it was not possible to build such ships in the United State, because they were well in excess of the treaty limitations. And the Soviets were also not satisfied with the plans.[53]

Now Gibbs & Cox designed a new plan for a normal battleship of 45,000t stdd., with ten 406mm guns, and a speed of 31kt. To discuss the plans and the required orders, a Soviet delegation, led by the First Deputy *Narkom* of the Navy, I.S. Isakov, visited the United States. He negotiated with the Secretary of the Navy and other high-ranking naval officers for a couple of months, but returned finally to Moscow without any treaty or agreement.[54] The latest efforts to gain US assistance were made just after Isakov's departure by the Soviet ambassador.

The conclusion is that the Soviet leaders were trying to establish Soviet–American military co-operation in the two years before the start of the Second World War. The Soviet government wished quite sincerely to come to an agreement with the United States. So Stalin had an exclusive semi-official meeting with the US ambassador in Moscow. This meeting was organized by V.M. Molotov to promote discussions on the subject of the delivery of US naval technologies.

But developments in Europe overtook these efforts, and after the German–Soviet treaties of August 1939, and the Soviet 'liberation march' to the western Ukraine and western Belorussia (east Poland) in September 1939, the Americans stopped all co-operation on 9 October 1939.[55]

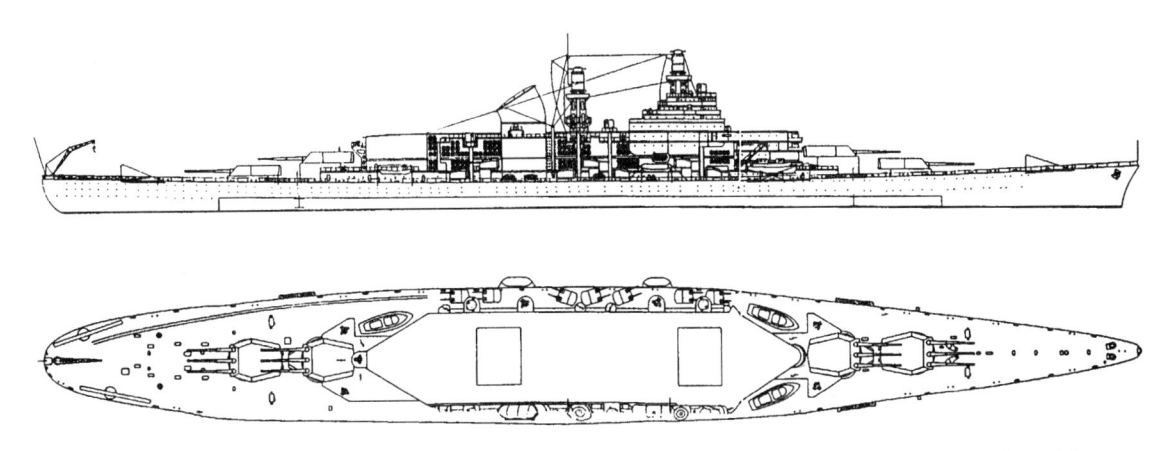

Fig. 8. Battleship design Gibbs & Cox variant *B*, no name given, 1937, displ. 71,850t stdd., length 306.3m, max. speed 34kt, 12 40.6cm, 28 12.7cm, 32 2.8cm, 40 planes. Credit: Breyer, *Marine-Rundschau*

THE STATE OF THE SOVIET FLEETS AND THE SHIPBUILDING PROGRAMME IN THE SUMMER OF 1939

The new leadership started in the summer of 1939 to revise again the shipbuilding plans according to the realities as they saw them. The programme had to be stretched according to the yard capacities. So it was divided into two parts, the first running up to 1 January 1943, and the second to 31 December 1947. On 10 August 1939 Kuznetsov presented the new plan, which contained besides a somewhat reduced number of the bigger ships a great additional number of patrol ships (*SKR*s, but really small destroyers), minesweepers, gunboats, net- and minelayers, MTBs, submarine chasers and armoured cutters with tank guns.

Old Ships and Submarines

But still the real fleets at this time consisted mainly of old surface ships. The completion of many of the ships of the Second Five-Year Plan was delayed. Only the submarines were mostly modern. Table 7.5 gives the number of old ships in commission in August 1939. But of these old ships and submarines not all were operational. The battleships had completed their modernization, the last one being the *Parizhskaya kommuna*, which had got torpedo-bulges and was recommissioned in 1938. Of the cruisers the *Chervona Ukraina* was just undergoing general repair work, to be completed in early 1941. Of the destroyers two in the Baltic and one in the Black Sea were being generally modernized up to 1940–41. And of the old submarines the two in the Baltic could only be used as training vessels or stationary electrical supply stations, while the Black Sea boats were modernized and put to operational use again. Table 7.6 shows the technical data of these ships.[56]

New Surface Ships

With the new surface ships there were great discrepancies between the commissioned ships and the ships in different building stages (in parentheses) in comparison with the plan targets:

Table 7.7 demonstrates the delays in the building of the new ships, of which only a few were commissioned up to August 1939. Of the destroyers of *projekt* 7 in the Baltic Fleet, two started in September their transfer to the Northern

Table 7.5: Old commissioned ships and submarines in the Soviet Fleets in August 1939

Ship types	TOF	KBF	ChF	NF	Total
Old battleships	none	2	1	none	3
Old cruisers	none	none	4	none	4
Old destroyers	2	7	5	3	17
Old submarines	none	2	5	none	7
Total	2	11	15	3	31

Table 7.6: Technical data of the old ships after modernization (up to 1939)

	Battleships			Cruisers		Destroyers
	Marat	*Oktyabrsk. rev.*	*Parizhsk. komm.*	*Krasnyi Kavkaz*	*Krasnyi Krym*	*Novik*
Displacement:	t	t	t	t	t	t
normal	25,000	25,465	30,395	8,295	7,600	1,100–1,350
full load	26,170	26,690	31,275	9,030	8,170	?
Dimensions:	m	m	m	m	m	m
length	184.0	184.9	184.5	169.5	158.4	98–102
breadth	26.9	26.9	32.5	15.7	15.4	9.3–9.5
draught	9.3	9.45	9.63	6.3	6.0	3.0–3.2
HP	61,000	57,500	61,000	55,000	50,000	25,500–40,000
Speed in kt	23.4	22.7	21.5	29.0	29.5	30.0–36.0
Range	2,700/14	2,500/14	2,500/14	3,000/14	3,350/14	?
Armament:	mm	mm	mm	mm	mm	mm
guns	4xIII-305	4xIII-305	4xIII-305	4xI-180	15xI-130	3-5xI/102
	16x120	16x12	16x12	4xII-100	4x102	1-2x40
	6x76	6x76	6x76, 16x37	4x76	6x76	50–80 mines
torpedoes	4x450	4x450	4x533	4xIII-533	3xIII-450	4-5xII-457/
catapults	none	none	none	1	none	or 3-4xIII-457
aircraft	1	1	none	2	2	none
Crew	1,290	1,400	1,545	866	652	150

Table 7.7: Commissioned (and under construction) surface ships in August 1939[57]

Ship types	TOF	KBF	ChF	NF	Total
Battleships *pr.23*	0/(0)	0/(1)	0/(1)	0/(0)	0/(2)
Battlecruisers *pr.69*	0/(0)	0/(0)	0/(0)	0/(0)	0/(0)
Cruisers *pr.68*	0/(0)	0/(0)	0/(2)	0/(0)	0/(2)
Cruisers *pr.26*	0/(2)	1/(1)	0/(2)	0/(0)	1/(5)
Destroyer Leaders *pr.48*	0/(0)	0/(0)	0/(0)	0/(0)	0/(0)
Destroyer Leader *pr.20(I)*	0/(0)	0/(0)	1/(0)	0/(0)	0/(1)
Destroyer Leaders *pr.1, 38*	0/(2)	2/(0)	2/(0)	0/(0)	4/(2)
Destroyers *pr.30*	0/(0)	0/(0)	0/(0)	0/(0)	0/(0)
Destroyers *pr.7U*	0/(0)	0/(11)	0/(5)	0/(0)	0/(16)
Destroyers *pr.7*	1/(11)	5/(2)	4/(2)	3/(0)	13/(15)
Destroyer *pr.45*	0/(0)	0/(1)	0/(0)	0/(0)	0/(1)
Patrol Ships *pr.29*	0/(0)	0/(2)	0/(0)	0/(0)	0/(2)
Patrol Ships *pr.2, 4, 39*	6/(0)	7/(0)	2/(0)	3/(0)	18/(0)
Other Patrol Ships	2/(0)	0/(0)	0/(0)	4/(1)	6/(10)
Minesweepers *pr.59*	0/(0)	0/(4)	0/(2)	0/(0)	0/(6)
Minesweepers *pr.3, 53*	8/(0)	6/(12)	11/(2)	0/(0)	25/(14)

Fleet, while in September and October two additional ships each were commissioned for the Baltic and Black Sea Fleets. Of the patrol ships of *projekt 4* the two Black Sea vessels were in general repair up to 1942, and one of the Baltic Fleet's *projekt 2* started its repair in October. Of the minesweepers of *projekt 3/53* one each of the Baltic and Black Sea Fleets were used for tests.

Table 7.8 gives the technical data for the new ship types commissioned in August 1939:[58]

Table 7.8: Technical data of new ships commissioned (up to August 1939)

	Cruiser	Destroyer Leaders		Destroyers	Patrol Ships		Minesweepers
	Kirov	*Leningrad*	*Minsk*	*Gnevnyi*	*Uragan*	*Kirov*	*Fugas*
Displacement:	t	t	t	t	t	t	t
standard	7,880	2,050	2,280	1,855	412	810	434
full load	9,436	2,675	2,928	2,380	534	1,161	490
Dimensions:	m	m	m	m	m	m	m
length	191.4	127.5	127.5	112.8	71.5	80.0	62.0
breadth	17.7	11.7	11.7	10.2	7.4	8.3	7.62
draught	6.3	3.9	4.1	4.1	2.45	3.75	2.37
HP	113,000	67,250	68,000	48,000	6,850	4,500	2,800
Speed in kt	35.9	43.0	40.5	37.0	25.8	18.5	18.0
Range	4,880/17	2,100/20	2,100/20	?	1,500/16	5,975/	?
Armament:	mm	mm	mm	mm	mm	mm	mm
guns	3xIII-180	5xI-130	5xI-130	4xI-130	2xI-102	3xI-102	1x100
	6xI-100	2xI-76	3xI-76	2xI-76	4xI-45	4xI-45	1x45
	9x45, 4x12.7	2xI-45	6xII-37	2xI-45			
torpedoes	2xIII-533	2xIV-533	2xIV-533	2xIII-533	1xIII-450	none	none
mines		76	76	56	32	24	30
catapults	1	none	none	none	none	none	none
aircraft	2	none	none	none	none	none	none
Crew	734	250	250	246	101	121	52

Submarines

With the submarines (see Table 7.9) the situation was as follows: of the big submarines in the *series I/D*-class, one of the Northern Fleet boats was already in Leningrad for general repair, another followed in September 1939, and of the Black Sea boats one was under repair. Of the *series II/L*-class, two Baltic boats and one Black Sea boat were under repair. Of the *series IV/P*-class all three Baltic boats were under repair. The *series XI/L*-class and the *series XIII/L*-class boats were all actively serving.

With the medium submarines all four *series III/Shch*-class, and *series Vbis* and *Vbis-2*-class boats as well as the *series IX/S*-class boats were serving. Of the *series V/Shch*-class boats in the Far East one, *Shch-103*, was damaged in a collision on 4 November 1935, but salvaged and used as a diving hulk, and another boat was under repair. Of the *series X/Shch*-class, four of the eight boats of the Northern Fleet were on transfer from the Baltic to the Northern Fleet.

Of the small submarines of *series VI/M*-class there are no reports about repairs in 1939, but of the *series VIbis/M*-class, four of the Baltic Fleet boats and two of the Black Sea boats were on transfer to the Far East. And of the *series XII/M*-class, six boats of the Baltic Fleet were being transferred to the Northern Fleet.[59]

Table 7.9 shows the situation with the submarines in August 1939.[60]

Tables 7.10, 7.11 and 7.12 give the technical data of the submarine types which were in commission or being built in August 1939.[61]

Table 7.9: Commissioned (and under construction) submarines in August 1939

Submarine types	TOF	KBF	ChF	NF	Total
Big Submarines, *series I*	0/(0)	0/(0)	3/(0)	3/(0)	6/(0)
Big Submarines, *series II*	0/(0)	3/(0)	3/(0)	0/(0)	6/(0)
Big Submarines, *series IV*	0/(0)	3/(0)	0/(0)	0/(0)	3/(0)
Big Submarines, *series XI*	6/(0)	0/(0)	0/(0)	0/(0)	6/(0)
Big Submarines, *series XIII*	6/(1)	0/(0)	0/(0)	0/(0)	6/(1)
Big Submarines, *series XIIIbis*	0/(0)	0/(3)	0/(3)	0/(0)	0/(6)
Big Submarines, *series XIV*	0/(0)	0/(7)	0/(0)	0/(5)	0/(12)
Total Big Submarines	12/(1)	6/(10)	6/(3)	3/(5)	27/(19)
Medium Submarines, *series III*	0/(0)	4/(0)	0/(0)	0/(0)	4/(0)
Medium Submarines, *series V*	11/(0)	0/(0)	0/(0)	0/(0)	11/(0)
Medium Submarines, *series Vbis*	8/(0)	2/(0)	3/(0)	0/(0)	13/(0)
Medium Submarines, *series Vbis2*	5/(0)	5/(0)	4/(0)	0/(0)	14/(0)
Medium Submarines, *series X*	9/(0)	7/(0)	8/(0)	8/(0)	32/(0)
Medium Submarines, *series Xbis*	0/(4)	0/(4)	0/(1)	0/(0)	0/(9)
Medium Submarines, *series IX*	0/(0)	3/(0)	0/(0)	0/(0)	3/(0)
Medium Submarines, *series IXbis*	0/(6)	0/(15)	0/(4)	0/(4)	0/(29)
Medium Submarines, *series XVI*	0/(0)	0/(0)	0/(0)	0/(0)	0/(0)
Total Medium Submarines	33/(10)	21/(19)	15/(5)	8/(4)	77/(38)
Small Submarines, *series VI*	28/(0)	0/(0)	2/(0)	0/(0)	30/(0)
Small Submarines, *series VIbis*	0/(0)	16/(0)	4/(0)	0/(0)	20/(0)
Small Submarines, *series XII*	0/(1)	7/(6)	2/(10)	0/(0)	9/(17)
Small Submarines, *series XV*	0/(0)	0/(0)	0/(0)	0/(0)	0/(0)
Total Small Submarines	28/(0)	23/(0)	8/(0)	0/(0)	59/(17)

7.10: Technical data of the big submarines

Data	Series I D-class	Series II L-class	Series IV P-class	Series XI D-class	Series XIII D-class	Series XIIIbis D-class	Series XIV K-class
Displacement:	t	t	t	t	t	t	t
surfaced normal	934	1,025	931	1,040	1,120	1,108	1,500
submerged	1,361	1,312	1,685	1,340	1,425	1,400	2,117
Dimensions:	m	m	m	m	m	m	m
length	76.6	78.0	90.0	79.9	85.3	83.3	97.6
breadth	6.4	7.2	8.0	7.0	7.0	7.0	7.4
draught	3.76	3.96	2.83	3.96	4.05	4.05	4.07
HP surface	2x1,100	2x1,100	2x2,700	2x1,100	2x1,100	2x2,000	2x4,200
submerged	2x525	2x600	2x550	2x650	2x650	2x650	2x1,200
Speed in kt	14.6/9.5	14.5/8.3	20.2/10.9	14.5/8.5	15.0/9.0	18.0/9.0	22.6/10.0
Range	8,950/8.9	7,400/9.0	5,535/11.9	7,500/10	10,000/10	10,000/10	16,500/9.0
Armament:	mm	mm	mm	mm	mm	mm	mm
torpedo-tubes	6+2-533	6+0-533	4+2-533	6+0-533	6+2-533	6+2-533	6+4-533
torpedo load	14	12	10	12	18	18	24
mines	none	20	none	20	18	20	20
guns	1x100 1x45	1x100 1x45	2x100 1x45	1x100 1x45	1x100 1x45	1x100 1x45	2x100 2x45
Crew	53	55	56	55	55	56	65

7.11: Technical data of the medium submarines

Data	Series III Shch-class	Series V Shch-class	Series Vbis Shch-class	Series Vbis2 Shch-class	Series IX S-class	Series IXbis S-class	Series X Shch-class	Series Xbis Shch-class
Displacement:	t	t	t	t	t	t	t	t
surfaced normal	572	592	592	593	828	837	584	590
submerged	672	715	716	706	1,068	1,090	708	705
Dimensions:	m	m	m	m	m	m	m	m
length	57.0	58.5	58.7	58.7	77.7	77.7	58.7	58.7
breadth	6.2	6.2	6.2	6.2	6.4	6.4	6.2	6.4
draught	3.76	3.79	3.94	4.0	4.0	4.0	3.96	4.0
HP surface	2x600	2x685	2x685	2x685	2z2,000	2x2,000	2x800	2x800
submerged	2x400	2x400	2x400	2x400	2x550	2x550	2x400	2x400
Speed in kt	11.5/8.5	11.9/8.5	13.5/8.5	12.3/7.8	20.0/9.0	19.4/9.0	14.1/8.6	14.0/8.0
Range	3,130/8.5	3,139/8.5	3,130/8.5	3,130/8.5	9,860/10	9,860/10	?	?
Armament:	mm	mm	mm	mm	mm	mm	mm	mm
torpedo-tubes	4+2-533	4+2-533	4+2-533	4+2-533	4+2-533	4+2-533	4+2-533	4+2-533
torpedo load	10	10	10	10	12	12	10	10
guns	1x45	2x45	2x45	2x45	1x100 1x45	1x100 1x45	2x45	2x45
Crew	40	40	40	40	45	45	40	40

7.12: Technical data of the small submarines

Data	Series VI M-class	Series VIbis M-class	Series XII M-class	Series XV M-class	Test subm. M-401
Displacement:	t	t	t	t	t
surfaced normal	157	161	206	281	102
submerged	197	201	258	351	140
Dimensions:	m	m	m	m	m
length	36.9	37.8	44.5	50.5	37.3
breadth	3.13	3.11	3.3	4.4	3.3
draught	2.58	2.58	2.85	2.81	1.73
HP surface	1x685	1x685	1x800	2x600	
submerged	1x235	1x240	1x400	2x230	1,800
Speed in kt	13.0/7.0	13.2/7.2	14.0/7.8	15.8/7.8	23/14.5
Range	1,065/10	1,065/10	3,330/8.6	4,500/8.0	900/14
Armament:	mm	mm	mm	mm	mm
torpedo-tubes	2+0-533	2+0-533	2+0-533	4+0-533	2+0-533
torpedo load	2	2	2	4	2
guns	1x45	1x45	1x45	1x45	1x45
Crew	19	19	20	32	9

New Battleships and Battlecruisers

During the planning stages of the new ship types there were a great number of changes in the dimensions and the layout of the ships and their armament, their armour and their equipment. This we can observe by comparing the technical data of the ship designs (see Table 7.13).

Table 7.13: Technical data of the new battleships[62]

Year	projekt 21 1935	projekt 23 1936	projekt 23 1939	projekt 25 1936	projekt 64 1937	Ital.UP-41 1936	Gibbs A 1937	Gibbs B 1937	Gibbs C 1937	Gibbs D 1938
Displacement:	t	t	t	t	t	t	t	t	t	t
standard	35,000	45,900	59,150	30,900	48,000	42,000	66,074	71,850	44,200	45,000
full load	41,000	51,000	65,150	37,800	53,000	50,000	?	74,000	55,200	53,680
Dimensions:	m	m	m	m	m	m	m	m	m	m
length	249.0	255.0	269.4	250.0	?	248.95	304.8	306.3	257.5	275.5
breadth	31.8	32.6	38.9	30.6	?	35.5	38.4	39.0	39.5	34.6
draught	8.9	9.5	10.4	7.5	?	9.4	10.5	10.5	10.2	10.2
HP	171,000	200,000	231,000	240,000	200,000	177,538	300,000	300,000	200,000	200,000
Speed in kt	30.0	30.0	29.0	35.0	29.0	32.0	34.0	34.0	31.0	31.0
Range	6,000/14	7,000/14	5,580/14	7,000/?	8,000/?	?	?	?	?	?
Armament:	mm	mm	mm	mm	mm	mm	mm	mm	mm	mm
guns	3xIII-406	3xIII-406	3xIII-406	3xIII-305	3xIII-356	3xIII-406	4xII-457	4xIII-406	2xIII-406	
	6xII-152	6xII-152	6xII-152	6xII-130	6xII-152	4xIII-18	14xII-127	14xII-127	2xII-406	
	6xII-100	6xII-100	4xII-100	4xII-100	4xII-100	12xII-100			10xII-127	
	36x37	40x37	32x37	24x37	32x37	12xIV-57	6xIV-28	8xIV-28	?	
catapults	2	2	1	2	2	1	2+Deck	2+Deck	2+Deck	2
aircraft	4	4	4	4	4	2	36+4	36+4	24+4	4
Crew	1,280	1,360	1,786	1,253	?	?	?	?	?	?

On 5 September 1938 the Soviet government had informed the British, in accordance with the 'Anglo-Soviet Qualitative Naval Agreement' of 1937, about the dates of new ships of 44,190t stdd.[63] Of the 15 battleships of *projekt 23*, planned in the August 1938 programme, the revision of August 1939 now planned to build eight ships in the first part up to 1942, and six in the second part up to 1947. The first two vessels, the *Sovetskii Soyuz* and *Sovetskaya Ukraina* were meantime laid down on 31 July 1938 and 28 November 1938 at the *Ordzhonikidze* yard at Leningrad and the *Marti* yard at Nikolaev respectively. The third and fourth ship, the *Sovetskaya Belorossiya* and the *Sovetskaya Rossiya* were planned to be laid down in autumn 1939 and 1940 at the new yard at Molotovsk.

Even more interesting is the development of the battlecruiser of *projekt 69* from its start as an 'anti-Washington' cruiser, based on some different designs to become the *projekt 22 Tyazhely krejser* and then a replacement for the cancelled battleship *projekts 25* and *64*. As mentioned – there were in 1935–36 several pre-designs of *Bol'shogo krejsera*, first the cruiser *X*, and the design of V.P. Rimskii-Korsakov of *TsKB-1*, and of variants of a *Linejnyi krejser* design by the Italian *Ansaldo* yard, culminating in the *Tyazhely krejser* of *projekt 22*, which was then redesigned into the first version of *projekt 69*, only to be considered inadequate in a session of the *STO* under Stalin's chairmanship against the new German fast battleships of the *Scharnhorst*-class. The designers of the earlier projects, Bzhezinskii and Rimskii-Korsakov, were purged and a commission under *Flagman 2 Ranga* S.P. Stavitskii was installed to consider the situation. Based on Stalin's recommendations the renamed *TsKB-17* under V.A. Nikitin and F.E. Bespolov was ordered to construct in place of the first version

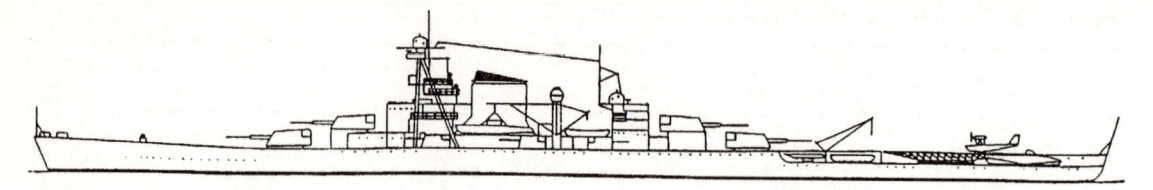

Fig. 9. Heavy cruiser *projekt X*, no name given, 1935, displ. 15,520t stdd., length 236m, max. speed 38kt, 12 24cm, 12 13cm, 6 4.5cm. Only design study, no orders placed. Credit: Sudostroenie

of *projekt 69* and the cancelled *projekts 25/64*, a real battlecruiser superior to the German ships. These were to become Stalin's beloved favourite ships, on which he kept close watch. Table 7.14 gives the dates of the above-mentioned designs.

This intervention by Stalin into the building of battlecruisers, which was not welcomed by the naval experts, had its parallel in Hitler's cancelling of the 12 planned new *Panzerschiffe* of 22,145t stdd. with six 280mm guns of the *Z-Plan* of 1939 for three battlecruisers of 28,900t stdd. with six 380mm guns, as we will see in a later chapter. While it was planned in 1938 to add one unit of *projekt 69* to a class of 16, in August 1939 the revised plan called for five in the first part up to 1942, and six in the second part up to 1947. The first two ships, the *Kronshtadt* and *Sevastopol'*, were laid down in November 1939 before the plan was finally approved at the *Marti* yard at Leningrad and the *No. 61 Kommunar* yard at Nikolaev respectively. A third ship, possibly to be called *Stalingrad*, was never started.[65]

Table 7.14: Technical data of the heavy cruiser designs and the battlecruiser[64]

name	*Krejser X*	*Krejser TsKB-1*	*Krejser Ansaldo*	*projekt 22*	*projekt 69* 1st variant	*projekt 69* Kronshtadt	*projekt 69I* Kronshtadt	*projekt 83* ex-Lützow
year	1935	1935	1936	1936	1938	4/1940	10/1940	1940
Displacement:	t	t	t	t	t	t	t	t
standard	15,520	19,500	22,000	23,000	24,450	35,240	36,420	15,650
full load	20,000	24,000	26,700		?	41,539	42,831	18,400
Dimensions:	m	m	m	m	m	m	m	m
length	236.0	240.0	241.5		232.0	250.5	250.5	212.5
breadth	22.0	24.0	28.0		26.6	31.6	31.6	21.9
draught	6.6	7.45	7.45		7.64	8.9	9.7	7.2
HP	210,000	210,000	240,000		210,000	231,000	231,000	132,000
Speed in kt	38.0	36.0	37.0	34.0	33.3	33.0	33.0	32.7
Range	5,000	5,000	7,000/20		4,500/20	8,300/14.5	8,500/14.5	7,150/14
Armament:	mm	mm	mm	mm	mm	mm	mm	mm
guns	4xIII-240	3xIII-250	3xIII-250	3xIII-254	3xIII-254	3xIII-305	3xII-380	4xII-203
	6xII-130	6xII-130	6xII-130		4xII-130	4xII-152	4xII-152	
			6xII-100		4xII-100	4xII-100	6xII-105	6xII-105
	6x45	12x45	32x45		24x37	24x37	24x37	12x37
torpedo-tubes	2xIII-533	2xIII-533	2xIII-533		none	none	none	4xIII-533
catapults	1	1	2		1	1	1	1
aircraft	11-12	9	4		2	2	2	3
Crew	728	?	?		?	1,037	1,819	830

Aircraft Carriers

After 1935 discussions about aircraft-carrying ships started up again, after the plans to rebuild the unfinished battlecruiser *Izmail'* or the training ship *Komsomolets* had been put aside. First there were some ideas of a combined gun-armed cruiser with a flight deck, and in 1937 the US firm Gibbs & Cox presented – as mentioned – three variants for a combined battleship–aircraft carrier, but they were too fantastic to be realized.

Already by the turn of 1935/36 the then Chief of Staff of the *RKKA*, Marshal A.I. Yegorov, had proposed building four carriers for the Pacific Fleet and two for the Northern Fleet, while the Chief of the *VMF*, M.V. Orlov, was reluctant, and assumed that only two small ones might be enough. So it took almost two years before real planning started. The interest was in a real carrier, mainly as a base for fighter aircraft to protect formations of surface ships against enemy air attacks. In the document 'On Warship Building for the *VMF RKKA*' from 15 August 1937 there was a recommendation to prepare specifications for an aircraft carrier of 10,000–11,000t for 40–50 airplanes, with six to eight 130mm and four to six 100mm guns, and a speed of about 30kt. The then Chief of the *VMF*, M.V. Viktorov, and the Chief of the Main Staff, L.M. Galler, were looking for a ship somewhere between the small Japanese carrier *Ryujo* and the medium US carrier *Ranger*. In 1938/39 the institute *TsNII-45* under I.V. Kharitonov prepared two variants of a *projekt 71*: the *71A* was more to the requested specifications and used the hull of the cruiser *projekt 68*, which seemed to provide a rationalizing effect. The *71B* was for a bigger carrier with two hangar decks and a capacity for 70 planes. Because Stalin was not interested in aircraft carriers, and received some support from ranking naval experts, like I.S. Isakov, the decision was taken to plan for two of the small carriers, to be built after 1941–42, one each for the Pacific and Northern Fleets. It is not quite clear if the orders to the aircraft factory *No. 81* at Tushino near Moscow to develop a carrier-based fighter and a reconnaissance and torpedo bomber bore fruit.[66]

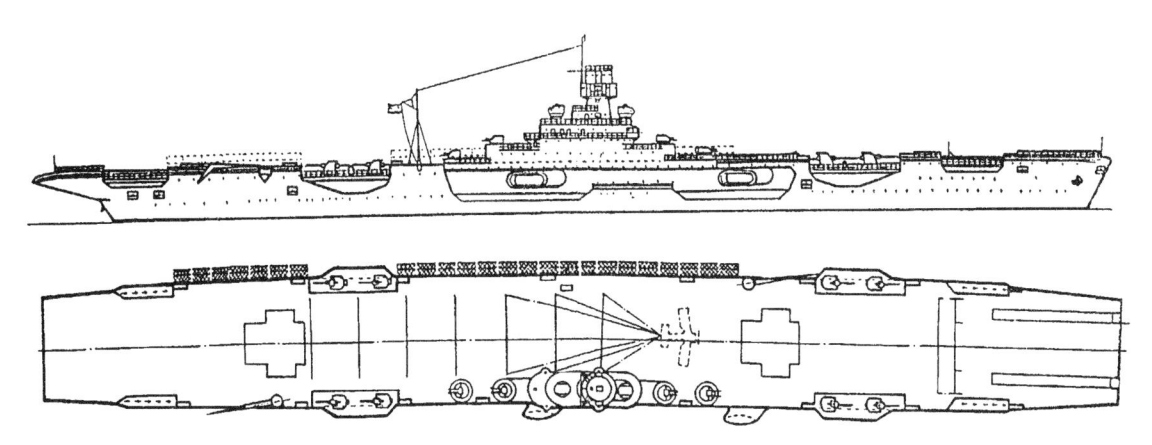

Fig. 10. Aircraft carrier of *projekt 71A*, no name given, displ. 10,600t stdd., length 215m, max. speed 33.75kt, 40–50 planes, 8 10cm, 8 3.7cm. Only planned, not laid down. Credit: Sudostroenie

Table 7.15: Technical data about aircraft carrier projects[67]

Ship type name year	Aircraft carriers Izmail' 1925	Komsomolets 1927	Cruiser Carrier 1935	projekt 71A 1938	projekt 71B 1938
Displacement:	t	t	t	t	t
standard	20–22,000	12,000	27,000	10,600	24,000
full load	?	?	29,800	11,300	?
Dimensions:	m	m	m	m	m
length	223.9	143.2	256.0	215.0	?
breadth			31.0	24.0	?
draught			7.2	5.9	?
HP			210,000	126,500	154,000
Speed in kt	27.0	15.0	36.1	33.75	32.3
Range			5,000	3,800	8,000
Armament:	mm	mm	mm	mm	mm
aircraft	50	42	60	30	70
guns	8xI-183		9xIII-305		
	8xI-102	16xII-102	8xII-130	4xII-100	8xII-130
	4xV-40	2xV-40	9xII-45	4xII-37	16xII-37
Crew					

Light Cruisers

Of the cruisers of *projekt 26*, planned during the Second Five-Year Plan, only the lead ship *Kirov* was commissioned in September 1938 for the Baltic Fleet. While the *Kirov* – as mentioned – got the machinery of the Italian cruiser *Eugenio di Savoia* of 110,000 HP, the sister ship *Voroshilov* had to get home-made boilers and turbines of 122,500 HP, which led to delays and the ship was only commissioned in June 1940 for the Black Sea Fleet, followed already in October by the improved *projekt 26bis Maksim Gorkii* for the Baltic Fleet and the *Molotov* just before the German attack in June 1941 for the Black Sea Fleet. In June and August 1938 the *Ordzhonikidze* yard at Leningrad and the *Marti* yard at Nikolaev had started to prepare the parts of two, somewhat improved *projekt 26bis-2* cruisers *Kalinin* and *Kaganovich* for the Pacific Fleet, to be assembled at Komsomol'sk and finally towed to Vladivostok in order to get their weapons and equipment. The war delayed the completion of these two ships until December 1942 and December 1944.[68]

The follow-on *projekt 68* was really a development of its predecessors, with great similarities, but with a different armament, as Table 7.16 shows. It was first planned to build 22, then 26 ships of this type, but in the naval proposal of August 1939 the number was reduced to 16, ten for the first period up to 1942, six for the second up to 1947. The first two ships *Frunze* and *Kujbyshev* were laid down in August 1939 at the *Marti* and *No. 61 Kommunar* yards at Nikolaev, to be followed in September and October 1939 by three ships for the Baltic Fleet, the *Chapaev* and *Chkalov* at the *Ordzhonikidze*, and the *Zheleznyakov* at the *Marti* yards at Leningrad. More follows about the other ships in a later chapter.

Table 7.16: Technical data of the new cruisers[69]

Ship type name year	projekt 26bis M. Gorkii 1936	projekt 26bis Molotov 1936	projekt 26bis2 Kalinin 1937	projekt 68 Chapaev 1939	projekt 68-I Chkalov 1940	design MK — 1940
Displacement: standard full load	t 8,177 9,792	t 9,760	t 10,040	t 10,624 13,424	t 11,350 14,460	t 6,095 7,745
Dimensions: length breadth draught	m 191.4 17.7 6.3	m 191.2 17.5 6.3	m 191.2 17.7 6.9	m 199.0 18.7 5.9	m 199.0 18.7 7.1	m 183.2 15.6 5.5
HP Speed in kt Range	129,750 36.1 4,880/18	110,000 36.3 3,680/17	109,500 32.2 3,100/16.5	126,500 35.0 5,400/17.5	126,500 34.5 5,000/17	90,000 36.0 7,500/15.7
Armament: guns torpedoes catapults aircraft	mm 3xIII-180 6xI-100 9x45 2xIII-533 1 2	mm 3xIII-180 6xI-100 6x45 2xIII-450? 1 2	mm 3xIII-180 8xI-85 19x37 2xIII-533 none none	mm 4xIII-152 4xII-100 12x37 2xIII-533 1 2	mm 4xIII-150 4xII-105 12x37 2xIII-533 1 2	mm 3xII-152 3xII-100 8x37 2xIII-533 1 2
Crew	734			740		?

Destroyer Leaders and Destroyers

The Italian-built *projekt 20/Tashkent* could not be repeated in the Soviet Union as first planned, but the design was the basis for the development of the new destroyer leaders of *projekt 48*, which were somewhat smaller, but had almost the same lay-out and the same armament, as Table 7.17 shows. The number of ships planned to this design was also several times changed. First, there were 13 units; then it was raised to 30 units, to be reduced in the naval proposal of August 1939 to 15.[70] Eleven were to be built in the first part of the programme, four in the second. In fact, the first vessel, *Kiev*, was laid down in September 1939 at the *Marti* yard at Nikolaev, to be followed in December by

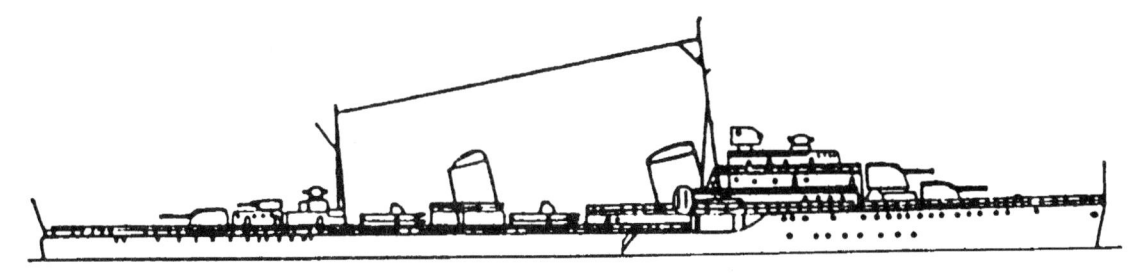

Fig. 11. Destroyer leader, *projekt 48*, *Kiev*, 1939, displ. 2,350t stdd., length 125.1m, max. speed 44kt, 6 13cm, 2 7.6cm, 10 torpedo tubes 53.3cm. Three laid down 1939, two launched 1940/41, but not all completed. Credit: Sudostroenie

Table 7.17: Technical data of the new destroyer leaders and destroyers[71]

Ship type name	Destroyer Leaders		Destroyers		
	projekt 20 Tashkent	projekt 48 Kiev	projekt 7U Storozhevoi	projekt 30 Ognevoi	projekt 35 –
Displacement:	t	t	t	t	t
standard	2,836	2,350	1,834	1,890	2,650
full load	4,157	3,045	2,530	2,628	3,350
Dimensions:	m	m	m	m	m
length	139.7	125.1	112.8	115.5	125.0
breadth	13.7	11.7	10.2	10.7	12.5
draught	4.0	4.2	3.9	3.95	4.2
HP	130,000	90,000	54,000	54,000	84,250
Speed	43.5	44.0	38.2	38.0	40.0
Radius	5,030	4,100	2,700/19	4,080/16	9,000/16
Armament:	mm	mm	mm	mm	mm
guns	3xII-130 6x37	3xII-130 2x76	4xI-130 2x76 3x45	2xII-130 2x76	3xII-130 4x37
torpedoes	3xIII-533	2xV-533	2xIII-533	1xV-533	3xIII-533
Crew	250	269	200	202	?

one each at the same yard and at the *Zhdanov* yard at Leningrad. Only the two vessels were launched at Nikolaev, while the Leningrad vessel was cancelled and broken up.[72]

The *projekt 7U* destroyers were already mentioned in an earlier chapter. Because of the complete reconstruction the 13 Baltic and 5 Black Sea vessels were relaid down in 1938 and launched between October 1938 and April 1940, and commissioning did not start until October 1940. The new *projekt 30* destroyers were planned as a big series; first the number was raised from 99 to 115, but then dropped again to 99, 63 for the first part of the programme, 36 for the second.[73] Building started at the *No. 61 Kommunar* yard at Nikolaev on 20 November 1939 with two ships, and on 2 December 1939 at the *Zhdanov* yard at Leningrad with four ships. More followed in 1940 and 1941, as is to be mentioned later.

Smaller Surface Combatants

The reductions in the bigger ships were made up to some extent by an increase in the smaller combatants. In addition to the 18 completed patrol ships of the *Uragan*-class a new *SKR*, the *projekt 29* was designed as an escort vessel for the big surface ships and for coastal defence purposes. In December 1937 the Naval Command issued a *TTZ* for a vessel of 600–650t with a speed of 34kt. The *TsKB-32* under chief constructor Ya.A. Koperzhinskii could only meet the requests in a vessel slightly over 800t, which was presented on 15 February 1939. In 1938 it was planned to build 96 units, which in 1939 was then raised to 148 units. In August 1939 the Navy proposed 44 units for the first part of the programme. Building started at the *Zhdanov* yard in May 1939 with the lead ship *Yastreb* and a sister, to be followed by one more in October and two

Table 7.18: Technical data of the new patrol ships and minesweepers[74]

Ship type	Patrol ships			Minesweepers			
	projekt 29	projekt 43	projekt 52	projekt 53	projekt 58	projekt 59	projekt 60
name	Yastreb	Zhemchug	Purga	Vepr'	Paravan	V. Polukhin	–
year	1939	1934	1938	1937	1937	1938	1940
Displacement:	t	t	t	t	t	t	t
standard	842	415	3,165	417	406	648	350
full load	995	580	3,819	480	459	840	400
Dimensions:	m	m	m	m	m	m	m
length	85.7	62.0	95.3	62.0	62.0	79.2	52.0
breadth	8.4	7.2	15.2	7.4	7.2	8.1	7.3
draught	2.6	2.6	5.7	2.2	2.2	2.6	2.0
HP	23,000	2,450	12,000	2,900	2,800	8,000	1,000
Speed in kt	34.0	17.2	17.5	13.9	14.7	34.0	14.0
Range	2,700/15	3,500/13	12,588/10	2,800/14	3,300/14	2,700/15	600
Armament:	mm	mm	mm	mm	mm	mm	mm
guns	3xI-100	1x102	4xI-100	1xI-100	1xI-100	2xI-100	1xI-100
		2x45	5xII-37	1x45	1x45	1x45	1x45
torpedoes	1xIII-450	none	none	none	none	none	none
mines	20/40	20/20	30	10/20	10/20	10/20	20
Crew	112	61	219	69	47	84	?

at the Komsomol'sk yard in December, as well as more in 1940 at Sevastopol. Some were earmarked for the use of the *NKVD*.[75] In addition there were two other types of patrol ships, one based on the *Fugas* minesweeper, four of which were completed already in 1936–37, and two big ones with an ice-breaking bow, of which only one was started in December 1938, while the second was cancelled. Both types were for service with the *NKVD* in the Arctic.

There were three types of minesweepers: the diesel-driven *projekt 53/58*, the turbine-driven fleet minesweeper *projekt 59*, and a new base minesweeper *projekt 60*. Of the *projekt 53* ten were laid down in 1935–36 and completed in 1938, six for the Pacific Fleet and four for the Black Sea Fleet. This was followed by the slightly improved *projekt 53U* of which four were laid down in 1937, six in 1938, and two in spring 1939, to be followed up to the war by five more, all for the Baltic Fleet. In August 1939 only two of them were commissioned. Of the *projekt 58* in 1937 five, and in spring 1939, two were laid down in Black Sea yards, of which the first five were commissioned up to March 1939, the first two going to the Pacific Fleet. The last two came only in spring 1941. *Projekt 59* was planned in 1938 with 72 units, increased in summer 1939 to 90 units, but reduced in August 1939 to 46 for the first part of the programme up to 1942. But only the first four for the Baltic Fleet and the first two for the Black Sea Fleet were laid down up to August 1939, while 14 other vessels followed up to the start of the war in 1941 at smaller yards at Leningrad and at Sevastopol. Of the new base minesweeper *projekt 60* no vessel was begun. There was also a plan to build 99, then 120 small steel inshore minesweepers of 180t (*projekt 253*), which was in fact started during the war.

A still prominent role was assigned to the MTBs, of which the plans of 1938 and 1939 foresaw 348 and 359 vessels respectively, mostly of the already mentioned type *G-5*. Of the smaller patrol boats and submarine chasers of the *BO-* and *MO-*types first 115, but then 274 vessels were planned. Of the bigger *BO-*class of 249t ten were laid down up to 1941; of the smaller *MO-IV* class of 57t no fewer than 219 were completed from 1937 to 1945.[76]

In addition there were three types of minelayers of 5,000, 4,000 and 400t, and net-layers of 1,000 and 462t. For the Baltic Fleet there was a plan to build two big monitors of 12,000t and four gunboats of 3,500t, but they were never laid down. For the Amur Flotilla three monitors of *projekt 1190* with 1,704t, three twin turrets of 130mm and two twin 76mm were started in 1936 at Gorkii, but then dismantled and transported to Khabarovsk for assembly and completion, which could only be achieved during the war. Some projects of smaller river monitors could not be realized because of the war. Of great importance for the river war and operations in the littorals were the *Bronekater*, the armoured small river gunboats, produced in great numbers with tank gun turrets up to and during the war.[77]

Table 7.19 shows how the planned size of the combatant ships of the Soviet fleets was raised from 1936 to 1939, which seemed to go far beyond the real capacities of the Soviet shipbuilding industry (standard tonnage in ts).

Table 7.19: Planned Size of Combat Ships in the Soviet Navy

Plan date	Pacific Fleet	Baltic Fleet	Black Sea Fleet	Northern Fleet	Totals
27 May 1936	450,000	400,000	300,000	150,000	1,300,000
7 September 1937	796,000	514,000	342,000	338,000	1,990,000
28 February 1938	910,692	581,787	396,393	343,629	2,232,501
10 August 1939	1,154,078	797,113	558,082	518,628	3,027,901

Reductions were therefore seen as necessary, as we will see later, caused by a more realistic assumption of industrial capacities, but also by re-evaluations, as a result of necessity following Hitler's attack on Poland on 1 September 1939, which started the Second World War.

OPERATIONS AND TACTICS RECONSIDERED

Stalin still needed advocates of a large 'ocean-going fleet', but at first the young naval leaders kept away from discussions concerning naval strategy, after the outstanding spokesmen of the *jeune école*, including A.P. Aleksandrov, K.I. Dushenov, I.K. Kozhanov, I.M. Ludri and others, were 'silenced'. The 'small war at sea' theory was now defined as 'hostile teaching'. But at the same time some prominent 'big ship men', like M.A. Petrov and R.A. Muklevich were liquidated.

Therefore, during the initial stage of the 'Big Fleet' build-up, Stalin appointed the distinguished Soviet economist Leon Ivanov as chief propagandist for battleships and 'mastery of the sea'.[78] Even the then Deputy Chief of the *VMS*, I.M. Ludri, had published a critique on the 'small war at sea' theory. In May 1938 Ludri wrote: 'it would be wrong to state again that just after the appearance of submarines able to hit battleships, the era of battle fleets was over. Submarines and naval aviation could not replace battleships.'[79]

THE THIRD FIVE-YEAR PLAN

Table 7.20: Fleet dispositions as planned in August 1939 for 1947

Ship type	Projekt	Pacific	Baltic	Black Sea	North	Caspian	Dnepr	Amur	Total
Battleships	23	6	4	3	2	none	none	none	5
Battleships	old	none	2	1	none	none	none	none	3
Battlecruisers	69	6	4	2	4	none	none	none	16
Aircraft Carriers	71	1	none	none	1	none	none	none	22
Cruisers	68	10	4	2	6	none	none	none	2
Cruisers	26	2	2	2	none	none	none	none	6
Cruisers	old	none	none	3	none	none	none	none	3
Destroyer Leaders	48	10	4	4	8	none	none	none	26
Destroyer Leaders	20	none	2	2	none	none	none	none	4
Destroyer Leaders	38	2	1	none	none	none	none	none	3
Destroyer Leaders	1	none	1	2	none	none	none	none	3
Destroyers	30	36	30	25	25	none	none	none	116
Destroyers	7U	none	13	5	none	none	none	none	18
Destroyers	7	12	5	6	5	none	none	none	28
Destroyers	43	none	1	none	none	none	none	none	1
Destroyers	old	2	7	5	3	none	none	none	17
Patrol Ships	29	60	37	30	15	4	none	none	146
Patrol Ships	52	none	none	none	2	none	none	none	2
Patrol Ships	45	none	none	none	4	none	none	none	4
Patrol Ships	39	none	2	none	none	none	none	none	2
Patrol Ships	4	2	none	2	none	none	none	none	4
Patrol Ships	2	4	5	none	3	none	none	none	12
Minesweepers	59/60	82	49	39	22	18	12	22	244
Minesweepers	58	2	none	7	none	none	none	none	9
Minesweepers	53/53U	6	19	4	none	none	none	none	29
Minesweepers	3	none	4	4	none	none	none	none	8
Submarine Chasers		118	78	60	21	74	none	none	351
Minelayers		12	6	8	3	none	none	none	29
Net-layers		9	2	4	3	3	none	none	21
Monitors	1,190 etc	none	2	none	none	none	14	20	36
Gunboats		none	4	none	none	none	8	none	12
Motor Torpedo Boats		160	108	72	18	12	none	none	370
Armoured Cutters		none	none	none	none	none	48	109	157
Hyrofoil Boats		none	none	none	none	none	none	18	18
Big Submarines	XIV	28	2	2	22	none	none	none	54
Big Submarines	XIII/bis	7	3	3	none	none	none	none	13
Big Submarines	XI	6	none	none	none	none	none	none	6
Big Submarines	IV	none	3	none	none	none	none	none	3
Big Submarines	II	none	3	3	none	none	none	none	6
Big Submarines	I	none	none	3	3	none	none	none	6
Medium Submarines	XVI	67(?)	1	6	9	none	none	none	83
Medium Submarines	IX	13	21	9	9	4	none	none	56
Medium Submarines	X	13	15	9	10	none	none	none	47
Medium Submarines	V	25	7	7	none	none	none	none	39
Medium Submarines	III	none	4	none	none	none	none	none	4
Small Submarines	XV	21	7	none	none	none	none	none	28
Small Submarines	XII	5	10	14	12	4	none	none	45
Small Submarines	VIbis	6	12	2	none	none	none	none	20
Small Submarines	VI	28	none	2	none	none	none	none	30
Experim. Subm.		none	1	none	none	1	none	none	2

At the beginning of 1936 the teachers of the Naval Academy (P.G. Stasevich, A.P. Aleksandrov, V.E. Egoriev, S.P. Stavitskii) published a common open letter addressed to the *Narkom* for Defence, Voroshilov. They asked the naval scientists to revise Soviet naval thinking in order to adapt it to contemporary views on the Navy's strategic missions.[80]

During 1937 the 'Temporary Naval Forces Combat Regulations (*BUMS-37*)', worked up by S.P. Stavitskii and the 'Temporary Directions on Combat Applications of Naval Aviation (*NBP MA-37*)', were issued. However, both were still elaborated in the spirit of a 'small war at sea'. In accordance with *BUMS-37* only submarines and naval aviation could attack hostile navies on the high seas, 'because they didn't need aircraft cover'. At the same time the Soviet Navy should be able to defeat any strong competitor along the Soviet Union's littorals in the course of a 'deep sea battle'. Fleet commanders, conducting a 'deep sea battle', should form up their forces in accordance with a scheme of organization of temporary naval formations, so-called 'manoeuvre formations', comparable to the later US Navy's 'Task Forces'. A 'manoeuvre formation' should include tactical groups of units of almost all arms of naval forces, except coastal artillery. Battleships would be used jointly with 'light naval forces' to secure the 'combat stability' of the lightweight vessels.

The Soviet Navy should operate rigorously 'in the spirit of offensive action', trying to eliminate the enemy fleet, because its annihilation was defined as the sole purpose of the Navy's combat activity. Thus the Soviet Navy leaders, following the basic principles of offensive military doctrine, proclaimed that the Soviet Navy would be the 'most offensive of the existing navies'. Nevertheless they avoided all terms concerning aircraft carriers and carrier-based aircraft.

In 1939 in addition to *BUMS-37* and the *NBP MA-37* the 'Temporary Directions on Submarine Combat Activity (*NPL-39*)' were issued. The 'Temporary Directions on Torpedo Aircraft (*NBD MTA-40*)' followed in 1940. At the same time the official views on gunnery duty, mine duty, anti-aircraft gunfire and so on were provided by series of official papers on these subjects.

In accordance with the *NPL-39* the Soviet Navy's submarine formations had to carry out:

- reconnaissance operations;
- minelaying operations;
- raid operations (in order to interdict sea lines of communications);
- special operations (securing of ranger raids, transporting of manpower and military cargoes, gunfire against poorly armed enemy vessels and shore objects).

It was stated that there were only two ways of submarine application. These were a period of duty on a fixed sea position (position method) and a patrol at sea (manoeuvre method). Submarines should carry out their operational tasks, cruising alone or in tactical groups, striking the enemy alone or jointly with other arms of the Navy (surface ships, aircraft and coastal defence arms). Thus after the *NPL-39* appeared, the upgraded scheme of submarine application was outlined. In accordance with it the Soviet fleet commanders should organize single or group submarine sorties against the sea lines of communications, or submarine tactical groups, which would be ordered to search for enemy combat ships and merchant vessels, combing the sea by 'submarine screens'. Besides, submarines would strike at the enemy sea commerce carrying out positional duty off hostile ports and naval bases, or attacking the enemy's merchant ships travelling on the sea lines of communications. But the Soviet High Command could not ensure that those recommendations were quite exact.[81]

In May 1939 *BUMS-37* was looked over by the Professor of the Naval Academy S.P. Stavitskii, in order to adapt it to the revised Soviet views on naval tactics, which were shaped above all by the general conclusion of the Spanish Civil War 1936–39. On 14 May 1939 the *Narkom* for the Navy approved the new version of Chapter 1 of *BUMS-37*, entitled 'Basic Principles'. In addition, a new chapter 6a, entitled 'About Sea Battles', was added. In accordance with *BUMS-37* the Soviet Navy was defined as the part of the Soviet Armed Forces that would defend the Soviet Union's sea borders in the course of an offensive action. It was stated that the Soviet Navy consisted of a surface and submarine fleet, naval aviation and coastal defence. The communication and observation service and naval bases were defined as separate branches of the Navy necessary for securing the activity of all naval arms.

The new strategic missions of the Soviet Navy were the following:

- to conduct offensive combat on the high seas and in the air space above the sea, also off the enemy's coasts and naval bases, in order to achieve the operational aims of sea warfare;
- to conduct active defence operations off the Soviet fortified districts and naval bases;
- to support the Army and Air Force formations, operating near the shore;
- to secure the sea lines of communications of the Soviet Union.

Fleet commanders should conduct offensive operations in order to inflict a decisive defeat on the enemy. At the same time it was stated that it would be impossible to deploy strong naval formations everywhere. Therefore they should try to concentrate their forces and means of sea warfare to achieve considerable superiority in the chief operational direction. All the fleet commanders needed to gain the successful co-operation of all naval arms, formations and units ordered to operate jointly.

It was also stated that battleships, cruisers, destroyer leaders and destroyers would be able to carry out all operations tasks with which the Navy would be faced, because they were equipped with strong and effective gunnery and could fight for a long time. But the basic idea of the *jeune école* was expressed in the following terms: 'motor torpedo boats, used massively, would be used to conduct defensive combat along the littorals. They would be able to co-operate with any part of the naval forces, especially with aircraft.'[82]

In accordance with *BUMS-37* submarines were considered as combat units, which would be able to operate for a long time and to use torpedoes and mines effectively, striking the enemy combat ships and merchant vessels in spite of a lack of 'mastery of the sea'. At the same time it was stated that submarines could carry out reconnaissance tasks and all tasks connected with the defence of naval bases, fortified districts and shore areas suitable for an enemy landing. In conclusion, submarines were defined as naval arms, which would play a decisive role operating on the sea lines of communication.

No less attention was paid to naval aviation, which was defined as a naval arm to hit enemy ships, sea lines of communication, naval and air bases in the course of bombing, mining and by torpedo attacks, accomplishing this itself or jointly with other arms of the naval forces and air forces of the Army. Besides, aircraft were considered as the reconnaissance means of the Chief of the Navy.

Coastal defence was defined as the naval arm, consisting of stationary or mobile artillery combined with position means and field troops used to secure the defence of naval bases and the deployment of the Navy.

BUMS-37 obviously did not correspond to the probable strategic missions of the 'Big Navy', which was to be built by the mid-1940s. Therefore it was defined as 'temporary'. Besides, it did not quite correspond to the Soviet theorists' opinion on the achievements of the navies which had operated during the Spanish Civil War 1936–39. When the Soviet volunteers and advisers were returned to the Soviet Union, their reports were studied by the specialists of the Operations Staff and teachers at the Naval Academy. At the beginning of 1939 a general conclusion from the last combat experience was drawn. For example, Soviet naval experts came to the conclusion that the operating navies generally were used to blockade the enemy and to interdict the sea lines of communication. Then it was stated that cruisers and destroyers were used basically to conduct brief sorties to strike against enemy shore objects, including ports, terminals and control positions. Moreover, it was emphasized that one of the most important missions of the Republican Navy was the covering of merchant vessels in the Bay of Biscay and the Mediterranean in the course of convoy operations and control. The most significant of these conclusions were the following:

- that ships anchored in bases became more vulnerable to sudden aircraft attacks;
- that surface ships which were sunk or damaged by aircraft all suffered from a shortage of anti-aircraft guns.

Soviet theorists assumed that aircraft would not hit a ship under way in case she dodged the attack. Therefore Soviet Navy leaders came to the conclusion that the anti-aircraft defence of naval bases should be strengthened with all speed. Urgent administrative measures were undertaken in order to prevent the enemy from carrying out sudden attacks against Soviet naval bases. In consequence the system of the Navy's operational readiness was approved by the *Narkom* for the Navy, N.G. Kuznetsov. During 1938–40 new lectures on naval strategy, and operational art and tactics for students of the Naval Academy and the naval schools were worked on.[83]

NOTES

1. M.S. Monakov, op. cit., part 8, pp. 40–2.
2. D. Volkogonov, *Stalin*, op. cit., pp. 410–34. Steven J. Main, 'The Arrest and "Testimony" of Marshal of the Soviet Union M.N. Tukhachevsky', *Journal of Slavic Military Studies*, vol. 10, No. 1 (1997), pp. 151–95.
3. M. Zeidler, op. cit., pp. 329–40, 355–60.
4. D. Volkogonov, op. cit., pp. 427–32.
5. *Boevoj put' Sovetskogo Voenno-morskogo flota*, op. cit., 521–9. M.S. Monakov, op. cit., part 8, p. 42.
6. V.D. Dotsenko, *Morskoi biograficheskii slovar'*, op. cit., pp. 256, 308–9, 316. 'Gallereya …', op. cit., *Morskoi sbornik*, 1998–99. S.A Zonin, *Admiral L.M. Galler*, Moscow, Voenizdat, 1991, pp. 251ff.
7. RGA VMF, f. r-2041, op.1, d.72, l.37-38.
8. Ibid.
9. RGA VMF, f.2041, op.1, d.72, l.37-38.
10. RGA VMF, f.2941, op.1, d.117, l.22-24.
11. TsVMA, f.2, d.39697, l.16-20.
12. Ibid., l. 1–22.
13. TsGA VMA, f.2, d.30697, l.23-25.
14. Ibid., l.22-23.
15. V.Yu. Gribovskii, 'The "Sovetskii Soyuz" Class Battleship', *Warship International*, No. 2 (1993), pp. 164ff.
16. *Istoriya …*, op. cit., vol. IV, pp. 281–94.
17. V.Yu. Gribovskii, op. cit., p. 164.
18. TsGA VMF, f. r-1483, op.1, d.431, l.9, and d.502, ll.7-8, 110, 133.
19. Op. cit. Letter S. Berezhnoi to J. Rohwer, 15 October 1993.
20. *Istoriya …*, op. cit., vol. IV, pp. 294–5.
21. TsGA VMF, f. r-1483, op.1, d.502, l.224-232.
22. Tablitsa raspredeleniya po teatram po programme stroitel'stva VMF. TsGA VMF, f.1483, op.1, d.502, l.224-232. L.A. Kuznetsov, 'Ne isklyuchalas' i postroika avianostsa', *Gangut*, No. 3 (1992), pp. 63–70. V.N. Burov, op. cit., pp. 158, 174–82. Letter of the *Narkom* for defence, K.E. Voroshilov to I.V. Stalin and V.M. Molotov of 7 September 1937. *Boevoi put' Sovetskogo Voenno-morskogo flot*, op. cit., pp. 521–9.
23. V.Yu. Gribovskii, op. cit., p. 165.
24. M.S. Monakov, op. cit., part 8, p. 41.
25. TsGA VMA, f.2, d.39697, l.36-46.
26. M. Hildermeier, op. cit., pp. 456–63.
27. D. Volkogonov, op. cit., p. 404.
28. *Boevoj put' …*, op. cit., pp. 521–9. D. Volkogonov, *Stalin …*, op. cit. M.S. Monakov, op. cit., pp. 40–2. V. Krasnov, 'Linkori tipa "Sovetskii Soyuz"', *Morskoi sbornik*, No. 6 (1990), p. 60. J.N. Westwood, op. cit., p. 204. S.A. Zonin, *Admiral L.M. Galler*, op. cit., pp. 75–85, and discussion of J. Rohwer with S.A. Zonin in Stuttgart in 1995.
29. Interview of J. Rohwer with S.A. Zonin in Stuttgart on 18 June 1995.
30. *Boevoy put' …*, op. cit., p. 145.
31. N.G. Kuznetsov, *Nahanune*, Moscow, Voenizdat, 1969. V.D. Dotsenko, *Morskoi biograficheskii slovar'*, op. cit., pp. 234–5. 'Galereya Sovetskikh flotovodtsev', *Morskoi sbornik*, No. 1 (1999), pp. 32–3.
32. S.A. Zonin, op. cit. 'Galereya …', op. cit., pp. 32–3. *Boevoi put' …*, op. cit., p. 145.
33. 'Galereya …', op. cit.
34. *Boevoi put' …*, op. cit., pp. 521–7.
35. B.G. Shaposhnikov, *Japono-kitajskaya vojna i kolonial'naya politika Japonia v Kitae 1937–1941*, Moscow, Nauka, 1970. Lincoln Li, *The Japanese Army in North China 1937–1941*, Tokyo, Oxford University Press, 1975.
36. Alwin D. Coox, *Nomonhan. Japan against Russia 1939*, vols 1, 2, Stanford, CA, Stanford University Press, 1985.
37. D. Volkogonov, op. cit., pp. 427–32.

38. TsGA VMF, f.2, d.39524, l.1-4.
39. TsGA VMF, f.2, d.39524, l.5-8.
40. TsGA VMF, f.2, d.39524, l.8-12.
41. TsGA VMF, f.2, d.39524, l.13-16.
42. TsGA VMF, f.2, d.39524, l.17-32.
43. TsGA VMF, f.2, d.39526, l.1-4.
44. *Seemacht* …, ed. E.B. Potter, C.W. Nimitz and J. Rohwer, Herrsching, Pawlak, 1982, pp. 468–83. '*Rüstungswettlauf zur See*, ed. J. Rohwer, Bonn, Bernard & Graefe, 1991.
45. *Istoriya* …, op. cit., vol. IV, pp. 32–52, 260–78.
46. Letters of René Greger (Prague) to J. Rohwer in 1985.
47. Records of sessions of the *Verwaltungsrat* of 7 May 1937, 12 April 1939, and 4 December 1943, provided in copies of J. Meister to J. Rohwer.
48. Letters of Vice Admiral Academician Prof. V. Burov to J. Rohwer of 20 August 1996.
49. Rolf Erikson, 'Soviet Battleships', *Warship International*, No. 2 (1974).
50. Siegfried Breyer, 'Sowjetischer Schlachtschiffbau', *Marine-Rundschau*, No. 72 (1975), pp. 141–63. Harald Fock, *Vom Zarenadler zum Roten Stern*, Herford, Mittler, 1985, pp. 207–9.
51. R. Erikson, op. cit. Breyer, op. cit.
52. René Greger, 'Sowjetischer Schlachtschiffbau', *Marine-Rundschau*, No. 71 (1974), pp. 461–79, especially p. 467.
53. R. Greger, op. cit., p. 467. S. Breyer, op. cit., p. 144.
54. Zapis' razgovora s g-nom Gibbs ot firmy Gibbs i Koks ot 17 Noyabrya 1937g, and other reports on negotiations of the delegation on 22 November 1937 with *General Electric*, on 1 December 1937 with 'Raj't' and 'Vorgan' by D.A. Razov. Report of the Chief of *Amtorg*, A. Kirilyuk to P.A. Smirnov of 27 July 1938. Otchet rabote morskoy komissii v SshA of 20 October 1938. Zapis' peregovorov Zam Narkoma VMF, Flagmana 1 Ranga tov. Isakova s predstavitelem amerikanskoi firmy *Gibbs i Koks* g-nom Dzhois, 13 Noyabra 1938.
55. H. Fock, op. cit., p. 208.
56. *Istoriya* …, op. cit., vol. IV, pp. 150, 161.
57. S.S. Berezhnoi, op. cit. And letters from S.S. Berezhnoi to J. Rohwer in 1997/98.
58. *Istoriya* …, op. cit., vol. IV, pp. 150–90, 196–7, 324.
59. S.S. Berezhnoi, op. cit., pp. 42–70.
60. Ibid. V.I. Dmitriev, op. cit., pp. 240–64.
61. V.I. Dmitriev, op. cit., pp. 265–8.
62. *Istoriya* …, op. cit., vol. IV, pp. 281, 294. René Greger, 'Sowjetischer Schlachtschiffbau', *Marine-Rundschau*, 71 (1974), pp. 461–79. Rolf Erikson, 'Soviet Battleships', *Warship International*, No. 2 (1974). Siegfried Breyer, 'Sowjetischer Schlachtschiffbau', *Marine-Rundschau*, 72 (1975), pp. 141–63.
63. W.G Garzke and R.O. Dulin, *Battleships*. Vol. 2: *Allied Battleships in World War II*, Annapolis, US Naval Institute, 1980, pp. 307–32.
64. *Istoriya* …, op. cit., vol. IV, pp. 298, 302.
65. V. Yu. Usov, 'Tyazhel'ye krejseri tipa "Kronshtadt"', *Sudostroenie*, No. 11 (1989), pp. 57ff. V. Krasnov, 'Krejseri tipa "Kronshtadt"', *Morskoi sbornik*, No. 8 (1990), pp. 53–6. Siegfried Breyer, 'Vor 50 Jahren: Sowjetische Schlachtkreuzer mit Krupp Kanonen', *Marine-Forum*, No. 9 (1991), pp. 301–3.
66. Arkadi Morin and Nikolai Walujew, *Sowjetische Flugzeugträger, Geheim 1910–1995*, Berlin, Brandenburgisches Verlagshaus, 1996, pp. 91–4.
67. *Istoriya* …, op. cit., vol. IV, pp. 153, 305.
68. Siegfried Breyer, *Enzyklopädie des sowjetischen Kriegsschiffbaus*. Vol. III: *Flottenbau und Plansoll*, Herford, Koehler, 1991, pp. 25–31.
69. *Istoriya* …, op. cit., vol. IV, p. 310; S. Breyer, op. cit., p. 29.
70. Postanovlenie Komiteta oborony pri SNK SSSR: Ob utverzhenii pyatiletnego (1938–1942gg) plana sudostroeniya dlya RK VMF i pyatiletnei programme sudostroeniya na 1943–1947gg./s NMA, f.2, d.39526, l.13-33.
71. *Istoriya* …, op. cit., vol. IV, pp. 324–6.
72. Ibid., pp. 324, 327.
73. Komiteta oborony …, op. cit.
74. *Istoriya* …, op. cit., vol. IV, pp. 189–200.

75. *Istoriya …*, op. cit., vol. IV, pp. 360–74.
76. Ibid., pp. 368–74, 382–94.
77. Ibid., pp. 360–1, 395–9.
78. L. Ivanov, 'Morskie vooruzheniya kapitalisticheskikh gosudarstv i ugroza vojny', *Morskoi sbornik*, no. 1 (1937), pp. 109–25.
79. I.M. Ludri, *Morskoi sbornik*, No. 5 (1937), p. 139.
80. *Morskoi sbornik*, No. 1 (1936), pp. 116–17.
81. V.M. Koval'chuk, *Stroitel'stvo VMF SSSR v period mezhdu Grazhdanskoi i Velikoi Otechestvennoi vojnyi. Razvitie operativnikh i takticheskikh vzgliadov v Sovetskom Voenno-morskom flote*, Leningrad, 1958, p. 31.
82. *Vremennyi boevoi Ustav Morskikh Sil RKKA BUMS-37*, 1937, pp. 14–15.
83. V.A. Belli, *Konspekt-tezisy tema: Morskie teatry SSSR v sostave obshchego fronta borby. Zadachi flotov SSSR*, Leningrad, 1938. V.A. Belli, *Konspekt-tezisy tema: Operatsii protiv baz*, Leningrad, 1938. V.A. Belli, *Konspekt-tezisy tema: Operatsii po unichtozheniyu nepriyatel'skogo flota v more*, Leningrad, 1938. V.A. Belli, *Konspekt-tezisy tema: Operativnie rascheti, napriazhenie, normirovanie*, Leningrad, 1938. V.A. Petrovskii, *Vedenie morskikh operatsii*, Leningrad, 1940. A.V. Tomashevich, *Taktika protivolodochnoi borby*, Moscow/Leningrad, Voenmorizdat, 1940.

8

The Second World War: The First Two Years

SOVIET FOREIGN POLICY IN SPRING AND SUMMER 1939

In the spring of 1939 Hilter's expansionist policy forced Stalin, in order to win time to build up the Soviet Army and Navy, to choose between an alliance with the Western democracies or one with Hitler. There is no doubt that to Stalin's mind an agreement with Britain, France and the United States would in the long run be more profitable. In March 1939 Stalin read out a report to the XVIIIth Congress of the Bolshevik Party (10–21 March 1939). He said: 'The aggressive powers unleashed the new imperialist war and destroyed the post-war order … The advocates of non-interference policy would play a dangerous game, which leads to failure.' In conclusion he said that the Soviet government would not allow a situation to develop in which the Soviet Union would have to start a war with Germany on its own.

This alert was sounded in time, because after the destruction of the Czech Republic by Hitler on 15 March, the establishment of the *Reichsprotektorat Böhmen und Mähren*, and the satellite state Slovakia, the leaders of the Western democracies decided to finish with their policy of 'appeasement' towards Germany and to pay more attention to the suggestions of the Soviet Union. When Hitler on 28 April 1939 denounced the 1934 non-aggression pact with Poland and the Anglo-German naval treaties of 1935/37, the danger of war became ever more apparent to Stalin, who wished at all costs to avoid being pushed into a war at this time. In May 1939 negotiations on the military co-operation of the USSR with Great Britain and France started. But these were conducted in an atmosphere of mutual mistrust. Each participant pursued only its own interests. The Soviets wanted to secure their possessions in Eastern Europe but the Western powers were not willing to help the Soviet Union in all cases. They did not want to guarantee the Baltic states' independence and neutrality and rejected the Soviet proposals concerning the Red Army's operations in Poland, although they did not believe that the Polish Army would be able to repulse a German invasion. When Hitler demanded from Poland on 21 March 1939 the return of Danzig to the *Reich* and an extraterritorial railway and road connection with the separated province of East Prussia, which Poland declined, the Western democracies answered with a guarantee declaration for Poland on 31 March. Now they had to agree to the Polish refusal to accept Soviet intervention on Polish territory against Germany.[1]

While Germany forced Lithuania on 23 March 1939 to return the *Memelland* after signing a treaty, on 7 June 1939 Germany signed non-aggression pacts with Latvia and Estonia. The Soviet leaders realized that the strategic situation on the north-western borders of the USSR had changed for the worse. As if in recognition of the dangers to come, Stalin relieved the *Narkom* for Foreign Relations, M.M. Litvinov, of his post and on 3 May 1939 installed V.M. Molotov in this position in addition to his function as Chairman of the *SNK SSSR*. Although many Western historians see this as the date when Stalin moved away from a policy of 'collective security', this view cannot be correct, because the change to an independent security policy would have had to coincide with his change to the massive build-up of the armed forces, especially his big ocean-going navy programme of the mid-1930s, when taking stock of the inadequate defence policies of the Western democracies against the aggressors Hitler and Mussolini.

Moreover, the Soviets had to take into account the Japanese menace. Japan had on 22 December 1938 proclaimed a 'Great East Asia Co-Prosperity Sphere', and the Japanese Kwantung Army in Manchuria attacked on 1 June 1939 across the border of Mongolia near Chalchin Gol and seized some areas there. The *Narkom* for defence, Marshal K.E. Voroshilov, sent *Komkor* G.K. Zhukov to the east to prepare a counter-offensive, which was very successfully fought in the battle of Nomonhan from 20–30 August 1939. The fighting ended with heavy losses for the Japanese 6th Army from Zhukov's mobile tank attacks, with a truce agreement mediated with German assistance.[2]

The Western direction of Soviet foreign policy now had priority because since the early 1920s the Soviet leaders had considered that any foreign troops deployed in the Baltic states or Finland constituted a death threat for the Soviet Union. Therefore Stalin was forced to search for a way to prevent Hitler from a north-eastern expansion. The limitation of such a German expansion became paramount in Stalin's policy. So, when the Western democracies declined to come to an agreement with the Soviet Union, Hitler, already in secret negotiations started in April 1939, offered to divide Poland and not to block Soviet ambitions in the Baltic states. Stalin chose the latter option, improving the defence depth in the west. This led to the conclusion of the Soviet–German non-aggression pact of 23 August 1939, leaving Hitler free to launch his attack against Poland on 1 September, which, with the British and French declaration of war on 3 September, opened the Second World War.

THE FIRST PERIOD OF SOVIET–GERMAN CO-OPERATION, 1939–40

When it became clear that the German Army and Air Force were on the verge of victory, Stalin ordered the Red Army on 17 September 1939 to invade eastern Poland (i.e., the western Ukraine and Belorussia seized by Poland in 1920). A few days later German and Soviet troops met at Brest-Litovsk and held a joint parade. On 28 September a new 'Borders and Friendship Treaty' was signed in Moscow, delineating in a secret protocol the German *Generalgouvernement* in the western part of Poland and the eastern Polish territories incorporated into the Soviet Republics of Belorussia and Ukraine. Germany also declared again its disinterest in the Baltic states and Finland, and on 5 and 10 October the Baltic states Estonia, Latvia and Lithuania were forced to grant the Soviet Union military bases on their territory.[3]

When Finland declined to cede parts of Karelia north-west of Leningrad and to grant base rights to the Soviet Union, the Red Army on 30 November 1939 started an attack against Finland, but was at first repulsed. Only after a regrouping and the concentration of strong additional forces under *Komandarm 1 Ranga* S.K. Timoshenko on 1 February 1940 did a new offensive against the Finnish *Mannerheim*-line take place. After five weeks of heavy fighting a Soviet breakthrough was achieved which forced the Finnish High Command under Marshal C.G. Mannerheim to ask for truce negotiations, which led on 12 March to the Treaty of Moscow. The Finns had to cede the area of Viborg and the Fishermen's Peninsula, as well as some areas in East Karelia to the Soviet Union, which also obtained the leasing of the harbour of Hanko as a naval base.[4]

During the 'Winter War' the Baltic Fleet from the Kronshtadt area supported the sea flanks of the Army with gunfire from destroyers and even the old battleships, while sending submarines, partly from the newly established bases in Estonia, to operate against merchant ships going to Finland. But successes were limited, and one submarine, *S-2*, was destroyed by a Finnish mine in the Åland area. From spring to autumn 1940 the Baltic Fleet accomplished a training programme with the newly commissioned vessels and using the new bases and the experience gained during the short war operations.

During this time the Soviet–German negotiations led to many agreements in the economic field, providing Germany with a great amount of much-needed raw materials. But we will mention here only the results of the negotiations as far as they were of interest in the naval context.

The Soviets allowed the Germans to use a bight in the area of Murmansk as *Basis Nord*, first to give the German merchant ships returning from overseas after breaking the British blockade, such as the big passenger liner *Bremen* and many others, a secure refuge. While this was working well up to the early spring of 1940, the use of the *Basis Nord* for military and naval operations did not bear fruit. Only the whale factoryship *Jan Wellem*, loaded with fuel for the destroyers was sent from there to Narvik before the German attack against Norway started. But with Norway conquered in early June 1940 the Germans did not use the base anymore.[5]

There were also negotiations concerning the use of the Northern Sea Route for merchant traffic between Germany and Japan and for the transfer of raiders. But the route was used only once by the armed merchant raider *Komet* from 14 August to 6 September 1940. The vessel was escorted for parts of the journey by the Soviet icebreakers *Lenin*, *Stalin*, *Malygin* and *Lazar Kaganovich*.[6]

The plans of the German Navy to ask the Soviets to cede submarines to Germany were blocked by Hitler, who did not want to be helped in this way, which would give away some sign of weakness.[7]

Of great importance were the Soviet applications for getting German technological assistance for the big shipbuilding programme. On 27 October 1939 the *Narkom* for Shipbuilding, I.T. Tevosyan, came to Berlin and presented the following requests:

- building plans of the battleship *Bismarck* and the aircraft carrier *Graf Zeppelin*;
- purchase of the heavy cruisers *Prinz Eugen*, *Seydlitz* and *Lützow* including their plans;
- purchase of armour plates, machinery, and equipment for four light cruisers;
- purchase of heavy and secondary gunnery, including 406mm, 380mm, 280mm, and 150mm gun turrets, with fire control instruments, as well as mines, torpedoes, minesweeping gear, submarine periscopes, and submarine batteries;
- building of repair ships, supply ships, and other special vessels.[8]

In exchange, great quantities of oil and grain as well as other resources were offered. Hitler, after discussions with the Commander-in-Chief of the Navy, *Großadmiral* Dr E. Raeder, and the Chief of the *Oberkommando der Wehrmacht (OKW)*, General Wilhelm Keitel, was at first willing to meet many of the wishes if they did not impede the German war effort. But he also wanted the delivery of the plans delayed as much as possible. He declined the transfer of the two first mentioned heavy cruisers, but finally agreed to sell the unfinished *Lützow*.[9] On 11 February 1940 the necessary agreement was signed, and on 15 April 1940 the vessel was towed to Leningrad, where the building of the now renamed *Petropavlovsk* as *projekt 83* continued, assisted by a German commission under Rear Admiral Feige.

Some of the requests were turned down, but the Russians were adamant about getting six 380mm twin gun turrets for two battlecruisers and four 150mm triple turrets for a light cruiser, as well as 280mm turrets, some submarine equipment and some special ships. The firm Krupp was finally allowed to sign a treaty for the six 380mm and the four 150mm turrets, and other firms for two 10m optical rangefinders and six 150mm searchlights.[10]

This led to a curious parallel: in the Soviet Union Stalin had forced the replacement of the 23,000t 'Anti-Washington'-cruisers by the battlecruisers of *projekt 69*. In Germany the *Z-Plan*, ordered by Hitler in early 1939, first envisaged the building of 12 new *Panzerschiffe P1–P12* with 22,145t and two triple turrets 280mm, soon reduced to 8 units. At the same time it was planned to rearm the fast battleships *Scharnhorst* and *Gneisenau* in 1941/42 with three 380mm twin turrets instead of 280mm turrets. But once Hitler planned to start a war he was reluctant to put these two ships out of service for rearmament at this critical time. So he decided to use the 380mm turrets already in production for these two ships, instead of for the newly constructed battlecruisers *O, P, Q* of 28,900t with three twin 380mm turrets, while cancelling the eight *Panzerschiffe*. Thus, he was already able to get in 1943 additional heavy ships for his *Z-Plan* fleet besides the six battleships *H–N* of 52,600t. But when the war started with Hitler's attack against Poland he had to cancel the building of all six and the three big ships to free the slips for U-boat building. So he could now use the 380mm turrets for the deal with the Soviets.

Once the necessary treaties had been ratified, the Soviet designers began to redesign the already started battlecruisers *Kronshtadt* and *Sevastopol* to take the new German 380mm turrets, the range finders and fire-control equipment as well as the searchlights. On 18 October 1940 Admiral Kuznetsov approved the new design *projekt 69I*. The new *projekt 68* cruiser *Chkalov*, under construction at Leningrad, was also reconstructed to get the German 150mm triple turrets as *projekt 68I*.[11]

CHANGES IN THE STRATEGIC SITUATION, AUTUMN 1939–SUMMER 1940

With the Soviet–German Treaties of 23 August and 28 September 1939 the way was open to the Soviet Army and Navy to establish bases on the territory of Latvia and Estonia and to loan the base of Hanko in south-west Finland. It was now considered by the Naval Command, that the Baltic Fleet's presence in the mouth of the Gulf of Finland would help to create a 'deep sea defence' of the Russian second capital Leningrad. But the establishment of the bases and the new situation had a great influence on the buildup of the 'Big Ocean-Going Fleet', generally delaying it.

The start of the Second World War meant that the strategic situation in the Baltic had radically changed. The Baltic exits turned out to be an operational war zone. Since 3 September 1939 the German big-ship building programme had been stopped to build submarines. Now the German Fleet had to fear joint attacks from the British and French Fleets. Therefore the Germans evidently could not order all their capital ships against the Soviet Baltic Fleet. After the agreements 'of mutual help' with the Baltic States were signed, the Baltic Fleet's new bases allowed the Soviet Naval High Command to consider that, although the Baltic exits were closed, the strategic situation in the Baltic Sea had become more favourable.

With the entry of Italy into the war on 10 June 1940 a similar strategic situation developed in the Black Sea. The Black Sea Fleet became a prisoner of Turkey, but the capital ships of the Italian Navy could no longer penetrate into the Black Sea, because the British Navy was operating in the eastern part of the Mediterranean.

All these facts meant that Great Britain did not allow Germany and Italy to conduct a joint attack from the sea against the Soviet Union, even after the French collapse. But at the same time the German successes in the operations against Denmark and Norway, despite the greatly superior British Fleet, and, even more so, the speedy victory against France, raised new fears, even when the official announcements of the Soviet government seemed to welcome the German successes.

The Soviet leaders decided to use the favourable situation presented by the concentration of German forces in western Europe for the occupation of France and invasion preparations of Great Britain to improve and strengthen

Soviet positions in the Baltic countries, against Finland and in the south against Romania.

On 14 and 16 June 1940 an ultimatum was directed against the Baltic countries Lithuania, Latvia and Estonia to allow the entrance of Red Army troops, which was accepted on 14 June by Lithuania and on 17 June by the other two states. The occupation of the three countries started the next day, including a small strip of territory in southern Lithuania which was assigned to Germany in the treaties. On 26 June a similar ultimatum was directed to Romania to cede the former Russian province of Bessarabia and in addition the Northern Bukovina, not included in the Soviet–German treaties. On 27 June Romania agreed and from 28 June to 1 July the occupation took place.[12]

This led King Carol II of Romania to ask Germany on 2 July for a guarantee and the dispatch of a military mission to train the Romanian Army, and to establish on 4 July a new government under Ion Gigurtu. On 10 July Hungary asked for the cession of the northern part of Transylvania and on 27 July Bulgaria followed with a request for the cession of the southern part of the Dobruja. Germany intervened in an effort to avoid a war in the Balkans which might endanger the Romanian oil fields of Ploesti which were so important for the German economy.[13] On 26/27 July Hitler received the Romanian and Bulgarian prime ministers, Gigurtu and Bogdan Filoff, to cool down the situation, but the Romanian–Hungarian negotiations broke down on 23 August. On 26 August Romania asked for German arbitration and on 30 August at Vienna a German/Italian arbitration ceded the disputed territories to Hungary and Bulgaria and at the same time guaranteed the territorial integrity of the remainder of Romania. On 2 September Hitler ordered that a military mission be sent to Romania, and two days later King Carol II appointed General Ion Antonescu as new prime minister and *Conducatorul* and two days later abdicated in favour of his young son Michael.[14]

In the meantime the Soviet Union had forced the three Baltic States to establish Soviet regimes and during 3–6 August the three states became member states of the Soviet Union. Also in August new pressures were applied against Finland, while on 17 August German–Finnish negotiations began concerning the passage of German military transport through Finnish territory to northern Norway, leading on 23 September to an agreement.[15]

All these developments, which were pushed from both sides without consultation, led to a rising mistrust between the Soviet Union and Germany. On the German side Hitler, reluctantly driving ahead the preparations for his operation *Seelöwe*, the invasion of Great Britain, returned to his old aim of winning *Lebensraum* in the East by crushing the Soviet Union in a short *Blitzkrieg*. After some considerations at the end of the war in France and after the rejection of his 'peace proposal' of 19 July by the British Prime Minister Winston Churchill, Hitler on 30 July informed the Commander-in-Chief of the Army, Fieldmarshal W. von Brauchitsch, and his Chief of the *Generalstab*, Colonel General F. Halder, of his decision to crush the Soviet Union in the spring of 1941 in a five-month campaign. On 5 August a first deployment study for such a campaign was presented by Major-General E. Marcks, Chief of Staff of the 18th Army, deployed at the time in the *Generalgouvernement*.[16]

At the same time in July 1940 the new *Narkom* for Defence, Marshal S.K.

Timoshenko, who had relieved K.E. Voroshilov after the Finnish Winter War, and the Chief of Staff, Marshal B.M. Shaposhnikov, presented to Stalin and Molotov their considerations for a strategic deployment of forces in the West and East for 1940 and 1941.[17] In this document it was stated that a 'political situation has developed and now seemed possibly to lead to an armed conflict at our western borders'. Finally it stated that: 'the most important task of our forces is to defeat the German troops in East Prussia and in the area of Warsaw …'. But from the short sentences about the probable operations of the enemy fleets it seems that this document was not discussed with the leaders of the Navy.

CHANGE FROM CO-OPERATION TO CONFRONTATION, AUTUMN 1940

A new edition of this document was prepared by Marshal Timoshenko and the new Chief of Staff, Army General K.A.Meretskov, who had relieved Marshal Shaposhnikov on 1 August, and was sent on 18 September 1940 to the *TsK VKP(b)*, saying 'there is the possibility that the armed clash may be limited only to our western borders, but there is also the possibility of an attack by Japan against our Far East borders'. It contained much more detail about the necessary deployment of the itemized army units for countering such assumed attacks.[18] Despite the short clauses about possible German amphibious landings at the area of Liepaja, and the clause that the Japanese Navy might be active against the Eastern coasts, the tasks of the Navy were again not mentioned.

At this time, in September 1940, Hitler had to 'postpone' the planned invasion of Great Britain, because the *Luftwaffe* could not overwhelm the Royal Air Force and thus gain 'mastery of the air' as a pre-requisite for the planned invasion. To counter the possibility of the entry of the United States into the war in support of the British, Hitler tried to build a large invincible continental block. On 27 September in Berlin the Tripartite Pact with Italy and Japan was concluded, to deter the United States, now threatened also from the Pacific side, from entering the war in the Atlantic. The German ambassador in Moscow, F.W. Graf von der Schulenburg, tried to assure Molotov that this pact was not aimed against the Soviet Union. On 13 October *Reichsaußenminister* J. von Ribbentrop sent Molotov an invitation to come to Berlin to discuss the historical tasks of the four powers, the Soviet Union, Italy, Japan and Germany, in steering the development of their peoples in the right direction.[19] After receiving the letter on 17 October, four days later Stalin had an acceptance for the dates 10–12 November sent to Berlin.

At the same time Hitler tried to include Spain, Vichy-France and Italy in his concept of a continental block by having meetings on 23 October with General Franco at Hendaye, on 24 October with Marshal Pétain at Montoire, and on 28 October with Mussolini at Florence. But he failed in this, because the three powers were not able to agree to Hitler's ideas on how to distribute the colonial empires of Great Britain and France. And when Molotov came to Berlin on 12 and 13 November he countered Hitler's offer to join the

Tri-Partite Pact, to let south-east Europe go to Germany and Italy, and direct its expansion to the south to the Persian Gulf and India, by presenting first some Soviet wishes concerning Finland (to remain in the Soviet sphere of influence), Romania (contrary to the German/Italian guarantee, the occupation of South Bukovina), Bulgaria (to guarantee this as a Soviet ally) and Turkey (to change the Montreux regulations and gain bases at the Narrows), and asked about German intentions in Poland, Hungary and Yugoslavia, the German attitude to Swedish neutrality, and the question of the Baltic exits.[20] During 20–24 November Hungary, Romania, and Slovakia joined the Tri-Partite Pact, and on 25 November a Soviet note arrived delineating the Soviet preconditions for political, economic and military co-operation with the Axis and an entry into the Pact. In particular, the Axis powers should not prevent the Soviet Union from leasing naval bases at the approaches to the Bosporus and the Dardanelles. Hitler did not accept this or the other requests, and did not answer this note, so the negotiations broke down. On 18 December 1940 he issued his *Weisung No. 21/Barbarossa* for his war to crush the Soviet Union.

NEW CHANGES IN SOVIET NAVAL STRATEGY IN 1940

Meanwhile the Soviet naval leaders tried to accomplish their duty as well as possible, but they were not asked to participate in elaborating Soviet military strategy and military conduct. Since the outbreak of the Second World War the USSR had lost both of its most important outlets to the open oceans in the Baltic and the Black Sea. There remained only one free unfrozen exit in the Artic through the Kola Gulf and the Barents Sea, but owing to the climatic conditions and the shortage of well-equipped ports and naval bases it was not really suitable for sea commerce and naval operations. With three uncompleted naval bases the state of the Northern Fleet infrastructure did not allow for the strengthening of its formations with combat surface ships, submarines, auxiliaries and modern aircraft as was needed.

It seemed that all the Soviet statesmen and military leaders who had claimed earlier that a battleship race should be avoided were being proven right. By the beginning of the 1940s, as Soviet naval experts expected, the real operational task of the Soviet active fleets would not demand more capital ships, but rather more light units, which were needed to conduct anti-submarine warfare, counter-mine warfare, and to maintain patrol duties along the Soviet littorals. It wasn't altogether clear that the Soviet Union would need a battle fleet after the Second World War.

In 1943 the American authors E.A. Maurer and M. Reichman, in their book *Global War: An Atlas of World Strategy*, wrote:

> In fact, classifying the Soviets of 1939 as a Two-Ocean Power is a considerable strain on words. Their one real ocean was the selfsame Arctic, most of which is frozen tight for several months a year. Soviet outlets on the Pacific were real enough, except that Vladivostok lies at the end of a long tongue of land stretching right around alien Manchuria, is badly threatened by Japan and closed in winter, while Komsomol'sk is situated

miles up a frigid stream. Petropavlovsk near the southern tip of the Kamchatka peninsula, was out in the fogs nearby a thousand miles from anywhere, in an almost totally uninhabited country and completely inaccessible by land. All of which made it difficult for Russia to develop sea power in the Pacific.[21]

Some historians, taking into account the sharp reduction in the Soviet naval programmes in 1939–40, came to the conclusion that at least the Soviet leadership realized that the USSR could not reach either the Pacific or the Atlantic and chose 'a land strategy', as Hitler did. Today, this opinion must be considered as inaccurate. The latest historical research on the subject of Soviet naval development shows that Stalin did not give up his naval ambitions.

Having reached the peak in 1938, the relative Navy share of funds allocated to the development of the Soviet Armed Forces was 19.5 per cent. In accordance with the plan of 1941 it should have been only 15 per cent. But really the construction and maintenance expenditures for the Navy steadily grew. In 1941 they would exceed by 2.6 times the expenditures foreseen by the military budget in 1938. Still the Soviet government tried to gain more favourable external conditions for future battlefleet deployment, as is to be seen by the demands Molotov uttered during his visit to Berlin and as they were laid down in the note of 25 November 1940, looking for bases at the Turkish Narrows and for an opening of the Baltic exits.

But up to the eve of the Great Patriotic War the chief problem of the Soviet Naval High Command was a lack of understanding of Stalin's naval policy. The Soviet Navy's leaders could therefore not ensure that his orders concerning the 'Big Fleet build-up' would be carried out exactly.

The *Narkom* for the Navy, Admiral Kuznetsov, described the difficulties which he had to overcome in his memoirs:[22]

> Unfortunately the Army leaders did not take into account sea warfare. The classic land-minded doctrine had priority. The General Staff refused all questions concerning the application of the Navy, because the high ranking Army officials didn't consider them as important subjects. The People's Commissariat of Defence and the People's Commissariat of the Navy were both managed on Stalin's orders alone. We had no common point of view on the military doctrine. The doctrine was something intangible. The naval doctrine was only in Stalin's head.

So the Navy had to elaborate the experiences of the Soviet–Finnish Winter War alone, without integration into the general military doctrine. The two operating fleets had maintained 'mastery of the sea' throughout the campaign. More than one hundred combat ships and auxiliaries were ordered against the Finnish Navy in the Baltic, bombarding enemy coastal positions, while submarines tried to interrupt the enemy's seaborne supplies. But ultimately, the capture of the poorly fortified island Suursaari was the only significant achievement of the Baltic Fleet. The Northern Fleet assisted the Army in occupying the port of Petsamo quite successfully. Meanwhile, owing to a lack of good management, thousands of soldiers, staying for a long time on board merchant vessels, which became stuck in the ice in the White Sea, suffered from the cold weather and hunger.

In March 1940 the *Narkom* for the Navy, Admiral Kuznetsov, ordered that a Naval History Commission be established to study the relative experiences of sea warfare. All major fleet commanders were trained in courses to improve steady conduct in the initial stage of a war. On 7 May 1940 Kuznetsov approved the 'Temporary Combat Directions of the Torpedo Aircraft Combat Activity (NBMTA-40)'.[23] In accordance with this, the torpedo aircraft should play a decisive role in sea warfare, resolving its main operational mission by eliminating the enemy's naval forces. On 18 July 1940 the 'Directions of Staff Duty' were adopted. On 16 August 1940 Kuznetsov ordered that combat instructions be worked up and adapted to the operational tasks of each naval formation.[24] But, owing to a shortage of special knowledge and experience, the Soviet fleet commanders could not accomplish such a task. Therefore the Soviet Navy leaders decided to solve it with the assistance of the Naval Academy teachers. The last conference of the naval specialists and theorists took place in Leningrad during 7–14 October 1940, to be described in a later chapter.

NEW CHANGES IN THE SHIPBUILDING PROGRAMME

Developments in the strategic situation on the one hand and the problems of the capacities of the shipbuilding industry on the other led to new reductions in the big ships, but an increase in the smaller vessels. The *Narkoms* of the Navy and of the Shipbuilding Industry, Kuznetsov and Tevosyan, had to work out new target data for shipbuilding in the two next Five-Year Plans for 1938–42 and 1943–47. The possible dangers of a coming war made it necessary to increase the number of small vessels, such as the gunboats, minesweepers, river monitors, armoured cutters and river minesweepers, but also the minelaying submarines in the first part. This and the real capacities made it necessary to reduce the laying down and commissioning of ships up to 1942, as shown in Table 8.1.[25]

For the second part of the programme for 1943–47 there was the problem that most of the bigger ships had to be built at the yards in Leningrad and Nikolaev, as well as the new yard in Molotovsk, while several of the ships were planned to serve in the Pacific. So some reshuffling was planned as follows:

- two of the *projekt 23* battleships being built at Molotovsk were to be sent to the Pacific Fleet to bring the number there to six;
- of the *projekt 69* battlecruisers to be built at Molotovsk one was to be transferred to the Pacific Fleet to bring the number there also to six;
- of the *projekt 71* aircraft carriers to be built at Nikolaev one each had to go to the Pacific and Northern Fleets;
- of the new *projekt 68* light cruisers to be built at Leningrad the Northern Fleet needed to get six and the Pacific Fleet one;

Table 8.1: Changes in the shipbuilding programme

Ship type	Proposal of the VMF to be laid down	Proposal of the VMF to be commissioned	Joint Decision to be laid down	Joint Decision to be commissioned
Battleships *pr.23*	8	–	6	–
Battlecruisers *pr.69*	5	–	4	–
Cruisers *pr.68*	16	–	14	–
Cruisers *pr.26*	–	2 (1941)	–	2 (1942)
Sea-going Gunboats	9	–	2	–
Destroyer Leaders *pr.48*	16	6	11	2
Destroyer *pr.30*	63	20	26	19
Destroyers *pr.7U*	–	18 (1940)	–	9 (1941)
Destroyers *pr.7*	–	5 (1940)	–	4 (1940)
Patrol Ships *pr.29*	44	16	32	13
Minesweepers *pr.59*	46	26	43	25
Minesweepers *pr.53*	41	39	40	38
Amur Monitors	–	1 (1941)	–	1 (1942)
Submarine Hunters	37	25	33	23
Armoured Cutters	8	6	–	–

- of the new *projekt 30* destroyers to be built at Leningrad 12 had to go to the Pacific Fleet;
- of the big and medium submarines built at the Baltic yards 117 had to be commissioned for the Pacific Fleet.

It was also stated that the building times for battleships should be 3.5 years, for battlecruisers 3 years, and for light cruisers 2.5 years. A reduction in the number of battleships from 15 to 10 and of battlecruisers from 16 to 8, an increase in the two types of minesweepers, of submarine hunters and medium submarines, was also envisaged.

The rising fear concerning German intentions, coming from reports of redeployments of German Army formations to the East and reports about German military contacts with Finland and Romania, on the one hand, and the experiences of the 'Winter War' and the perceptions of the roots of the German *Blitzkrieg* successes on the other, led to a reorganization of the Red Army. This made a big reallocation of resources and capacities in the armaments industry to the Army necessary, and as a consequence the Navy had to cut down again its building programme.

On 19 October 1940 the Soviet government decided about the new reduced planning dates, and on 23 October the *Narkom* for the Navy, Admiral Kuznetsov, sent an order with the details to the places concerned.[26] Its contents were as follows:

- Battleships and battlecruisers: no new ships should be laid down. The building of the *Sovetskii Soyuz* at Leningrad and the *Sovetskaya Ukraina* at Nikolaev was to be completed in June 1943. The *Sovetskaya Rossiya* (state 12 per cent) at Molotovsk was to be floated out of the building dock in the third quarter of 1943. The planned laying down of the fourth battleship *Sovetskaya Belorussiya* at Molotovsk for November 1940 was cancelled, and the prepared materials were to be used for the laying down of four additional destroyers of *projekt 30*. The battlecruisers *Kronshtadt* at Leningrad and *Sevastopol* at Nikolaev (state 18 per cent each) were to be launched in the third quarter of 1942.

- Cruisers: the state of the building at Komsomol'sk of the last two *projekts 26-bis2* cruisers was 30 per cent for the *Kalinin*, to be completed in 1942, and 16 per cent for the *Kaganovich*. The state of the cruisers of *projekt 68* was at Leningrad 62 per cent for the *Zheleznyakov*, 52 per cent for the *Chapaev*, and 37 per cent for the *Chkalov*, and at Nikolaev 45 per cent for the *Frunze*, 42.5 per cent for the *Kujbyshev*, 20 per cent for the *Ordzhonikidze*, and 12 per cent for the *Sverdlov*. The *Zheleznyakov, Chapaev, Frunze* and *Kujbyshev* were to be completed in 1942. In 1941 three additional *projekt 68* cruisers were to be laid down at Leningrad and one at Komsomol'sk. In addition the purchased ex-German *Petropavlovsk* (65 per cent) was to be completed in 1942.

- Destroyer Leaders: there were no new ships to be laid down, and the *projekt 48* leader with the building number 542 (*Stalinabad*) at Leningrad was to be cancelled. The *Kiev* and *Erevan* were to be completed.

- Destroyers: of the *projekt 30* in the fourth quarter of 1940 four units were laid down at Nikolaev, in 1941 in addition there were nine to be laid down at Leningrad, eight at Molotovsk (including the four replacing the fourth battleship), two at Komsomol'sk and 14 at Nikolaev after reorganizing the yard there. In 1941 there were four units of *projekt 7* and eight of *projekt 7-U*, in 1942 two of *projekt 7* and ten of *projekt 30* to be completed.

- Patrol Ships: in 1940 there were nine, in 1941 eleven of *projekt 29* to be laid down, and to be completed there were in 1942 eleven, and in 1943 eight.

- Minesweepers: of the fleet minesweepers of *projekt 59* in 1941, 20 units were to be laid down. Of the diesel-minesweepers of *projekt 53* seven were to be launched in 1942. And of the inshore minesweepers in 1941 six, in 1942 twelve, and in 1943 two were to be built.

- Submarines: in 1941 the following were to be completed: four of *series XIV*, six of *series XIII-bis*, four of *series X-bis*, twelve of *series XII-bis* and three of *series XV*. Instead of the patrol icebreakers there were two *IX-bis*, and thirteen *XV* units to be built. And eight orders for *IX-bis* boats were to be changed to the completely welded *series XVI*.

- In addition there were special arrangements for the production of the needed turbines and diesel-motors.

CONFERENCES ON OPERATIONS AND TACTICS IN OCTOBER AND DECEMBER 1940

There were two final conferences of Soviet naval specialists and theory representatives to improve Soviet naval thinking. The first took place from 7–24 October 1940 at Leningrad. During the discussions five basic reports were made by:

- I.S. Isakov, 'Experiences of the Latest Naval Operations'.[27]
- V.I. Rutkovskii, 'Submarine Operations in the War at Sea'.[28]
- V.A. Petrovskii, 'Aircraft Operations in the War at Sea'.[29]
- S.P. Stavitskii, 'Surface Operations'.[30]
- V.A. Belli, 'Amphibious Operations'.[31]

These works presented the essence of Soviet naval operational art at the beginning of the 1940s. In addition, the line of reports demonstrated the Soviet point of view on the relative importance of each naval arm.

Opening the discussion, I.S. Isakov stated: 'Let's keep from talking about the subject of naval strategy. We need only to look over the operational art and tactics.' Then he said that the experience of the latest naval operations made it possible to come to an exact conclusion concerning the influence of aircraft on sea warfare. The essence of it was the following: 'The relative experience of sea warfare refuted a fairy-tale, which defined aircraft as an universal branch of the armed forces.' Nevertheless Isakov criticized theorists and naval experts who didn't take into account the relative results of aircraft combat activities achieved since the start of the European war. At the same time he recommended the achievements of German aviation as a model for the sensible use of aircraft which wasn't limited by 'extreme doctrines'. Isakov's reasoning stated that the Soviet Navy's leaders were deeply impressed by the German Norway operation conducted from April to June 1940. Finally, the Deputy *Narkom* of the Navy ordered a discussion to be broken up on the subject of 'mastery of the sea', just initiated by the official newspaper of the Soviet Navy '*Krasnyi Flot*', because in his mind the Norway operation should be considered as a 'clash of all kinds of naval doctrines'.[32]

Thus, the theoretical foundation of the 'Big Fleet' creation was shaken, and the latest Soviet point of view on the importance of each arm of naval forces was then presented in the reports and speeches made by the participants in the discussion.

Kapitan 2 Ranga V.I. Rutkovskii, reporting on the subject of submarine operations, did not revise previous instructions and recommendations, but emphasized the following:

- Generally, submarines should be used to conduct sea warfare on the sealines of communications, including communications on the high seas. It would be reasonable to deploy submarines on the high seas in advance to organize massed submarine attack raids after the war has started.
- Above all the scale of submarine combat activity would be determined by the state of their logistic system.
- It would be reasonable to deploy a floating logistic system to supply the submarines operating on the high seas.
- It would be inexpedient to use submarines to blockade the enemy's shores.
- Skilful conduct would play a decisive role in future submarine warfare. The best way to control submarine application would be to appoint a

fleet commander's representative to conduct submarine operations in the whole theatre of war. Commanding officers of submarines carrying out a positional duty should be responsible for choosing a way of solving their operational tasks themselves.
- A special system of communications would be needed to conduct submarine operations on the high seas. Such a system should be able to secure reliable and imperceptible combat control.
- Submarine application in the course of positional duty in any case would not be entirely successful. It would be needed to increase their operational positions, and to use them when cruising in a limited sea area. It would probably be necessary to organize tactical submarine groups (submarine screens) or to use submarines in the course of tactical co-operation with other naval arms (surface ships or aircraft).
- It would be reasonable to use for minelaying not only submarine minelayers but all types of submarines, because using a mine as a torpedo then becomes a main weapon of the submarine.

Soviet naval specialists generally agreed with Rutkovskii, but I.S. Isakov did not approve the proposals concerning submarine deployment in tactical groups. He stated that in such cases fleet commanders would be faced with insoluble problems in the field of control of submarine groups. The discussion that followed just after Isakov's remark stated that at the beginning of 1940 Soviet naval theorists had not abandoned the ideas of a 'small war at sea'. As earlier, they suggested using submarines instead of heavyweight surface units. For example, the prominent Soviet submarine tactician, *Kapitan 1 Ranga* A.V. Tomashevich, proposed using submarines in order to defend wide shore sections.[33] In this, he was supported by V.A. Belli.[34]

Kontradmiral Yu.F. Rall' proposed renewing the construction of squadron submarines, in spite of the experience of the combat training of the two units of the *series IV/Pravda*-class, which proved that these vessels were unsuitable and not adapted for squadron service.[35]

V.A. Petrovskii did not only report about aircraft operations. At the same time he described the navy's operations during the initial period of the war. First he emphasized the importance of the anti-aircraft measures to prevent the enemy from sudden aircraft strikes against naval bases and task forces operating at sea.[36] Then he said that aircraft would be able to hit units of all types including battleships.

Petrovskii suggested paying more attention to the aircraft achievements since 1 September 1939. He emphasized that the aircraft share in the overall number of losses inflicted by all kinds of naval weapons was steadily rising and becoming comparable with the share of naval artillery by the end of the First World War. In conclusion Petrovskii said: 'Naval aviation will not operate completely successfully on the high seas if aircraft operations are not secured by an adequate system of bases.'[37] The general conclusions of Petrovskii's report were:
- aircraft should be ready to operate alone or jointly with other arms of the Navy as well as with all kinds of Armed Forces;

- it is necessary to achieve combat superiority to secure all kinds of naval operations;
- aircraft cannot replace land troops as well as surface combat ships and submarines, which should play a decisive role in strategic operations on shore and at sea;
- it is necessary to mass aircraft to achieve combat air superiority particularly in cases when aircraft need to operate alone;
- fleet commanders should not be slow to use aircraft in order to avoid failure.[38]

It was assumed that naval aviation would be used for:

- defeating the enemy naval forces at sea and in naval bases;
- supporting the Army;
- operating on the sea lines of communications;
- securing landing and anti-landing operations.[39]

Major-General of the Air Forces G.M. Stolyarskii emphasized that ship formations would be in need of aircraft cover up to 90–100 miles from the shoreline. Besides, he stated, task forces steaming out to sea would be in need of permanent fighter escort. In conclusion, he said that construction of aircraft carriers accompanied by the development of carrier-borne fighters would be the best way to secure a fleet formation operating on the high seas against enemy aircraft attacks.[40]

Stolyarskii wasn't supported by other participants in the discussion. Moreover, Admiral Isakov said that he had not spoken in favour of aircraft carriers through the period when the latest version of the 'Big Fleet' was under elaboration.[41] This fact showed a lack of understanding of the importance of aircraft carriers. None of the prominent Soviet naval theorists spoke on the subject of squadron service with a fleet of attack aircraft carriers with carrier-based attack bombers and carrier-borne torpedo aircraft. At least all the theorists agreed that surface ships would be the backbone of heterogeneous naval formations (task forces). It was stated that 'heavyweight units would be suitable to defeat an enemy fleet decisively, to support other arms of the Navy, including naval aviation, to allocate command post of fleet commanders, and to conduct submarine operations'.[42]

However, Vice-Admiral S.P. Stavitskii said: 'Light naval forces have an advantage in comparison with other arms of the Navy. They are able to penetrate into the enemy disposition further and to operate there longer'.[43] Stavitskii felt that 'the combined (concentrated) blow' was the best form of heterogeneous naval forces activity. Besides, he stated, 'a manoeuvre formation' should be the basic scheme of a task force creation.[44]

Such facts help us to come to the conclusion that the Soviet naval specialists didn't alter their point of view on the battleship's role in sea warfare, even though Stalin desired 'a Big Fleet'. However, they avoided discussion on the subject of the battleship's combat activity. Only Vice-Admiral A.V. Shtal' remarked that the role of battleships during the German Norway operations was indefinite.[45]

Kontr Admiral V.A. Belli spoke with great admiration about the Norway strategic operation of the German Armed Forces. He especially emphasized the bold German decision to transport the first wave of landing troops on board fast combat ships.[46]

The last pre-war theoretical discussion on the subject of naval operational art took place in Moscow from 2–10 December 1940 during the conference of fleet commanders of the Soviet Navy. At the beginning of this conference the *Narkom* of the Navy, Admiral Kuznetsov, gave a speech. He stated that poor results were achieved by fleets operating during the Soviet–Finnish War 1939–40, which demonstrated a shortage of competence among high-ranking officers. Then Kuznetsov said: 'There wasn't a common point of view on principal subjects concerning the Navy's activity. Exact naval thinking wasn't taught, while fruitless discussions went on far too long. Those discussions didn't bring us anything but harm.'[47]

Nevertheless he could not prevent himself from talking on the subject of the capital ship's role in sea warfare. Kuznetsov, in particular, stated that the experience of the latest war at sea showed that in some cases only capital ships allowed operating fleets to resolve their strategic missions quite successfully. Finally, he declared: 'We are building capital ships'.[48]

Then Admiral Isakov gave a report entitled 'The Essence of Contemporary Sea Warfare'. He emphasized the reasonable course of German naval strategy during the Norway operation, but didn't mention the successful raid against Taranto accomplished by the British Mediterranean Fleet from 10–12 November 1940. Moreover, Isakov ignored the latest decision of the Main Military Council on the subject of the development of naval aviation, although the *Narkom* of the Navy had ordered him to speed up the studying of naval aircraft operations as well as the elaboration of the aircraft carrier plan.[49] Instead he reiterated: 'Stop talking about mastery of the seas.'[50]

The conference ended with the announcement of the *Narkom*'s order which confirmed the 'Temporary Instructions on Naval Operations Conduct' (*NMO-40*).[51] Thus, the initial period of the development of Soviet naval thinking was completed.

In accordance with the *NMO-40*, the Soviet Navy was defined as a component of the Soviet Armed Forces whose duty was to defend the USSR's sea borders and its sea lines of communications. It was stated that the best way of accomplishing their strategic missions would be by the 'annihilation or paralysis of the enemy fleets'.[52]

Surface ships were considered as units, which should be able to accomplish successfully all operational tasks of the Navy. Heavyweight hard-hitting warships (battleships and heavy cruisers) were defined as 'the backbone of naval forces'. At the same time 'the light forces' (cruisers, destroyer leaders and destroyers) were defined as the most universal units of all naval arms.

In comparison with the authors of *BUMS-37*, the creators of the *NMO-40* evaluated submarines more exactly. Submarines were defined as units whose duty, above all, was to interrupt sea lines of communications.

Aircraft were considered as a naval arm ordered to secure all kinds of naval operations and the 'daily combat activity' of the Navy. Coastal defence should be used to cover naval bases and the coastline. Besides, it was defined as the backbone of 'mine-artillery sea defence positions'.[53]

The *NMO-40* provided the official point of view on the operational use of naval arms. The pre-war Soviet opinion on the essence of naval tactics was expressed at the end of 1937 by V. Chernyshev's published article 'Naval Tactics during the Last Two Decades'.[54]

Chernyshev's conclusions were that:

- naval arms diversity and their mass use caused fleet commanders to choose more complicated forms of sea warfare;
- development of aircraft, submarines, and reconnaissance means created considerable trouble for each fleet commander, who tried to secure an imperceptible preparation of units ordered to operate on the sea;
- the threat of sudden simultaneous attacks from the air, from the sea, and from under the sea surface significantly rose. At the same time aircraft and submarines were able to penetrate deeply into the enemy's combat order. A combat ship may become a victim of sudden attack when at anchorage, when at sea or in action;
- advanced combat means of naval forces made sea action brief. Therefore commanding officers should be fast thinking, energetic and well-trained in controlling the manoeuvres of their ships;
- owing to the threat of sudden attacks, combat and marching orders of naval formations should be 'deep';
- combat orders of attacking naval formations should be suitable to encircle the enemy to prevent him from attempting to avoid an attack. Also combat orders should be 'deep' to overwhelm the enemy's 'deep defence';
- 'simple use of naval arms' becomes impossible. Therefore co-operation of all naval arms will be needed to accomplish the operational tasks of the Navy;
- fleet commanders will need to divide their units in order to achieve 'a reasonable co-operation of heterogeneous naval arms'. Attacking tactical groups should be able 'to chain' him. Therefore two kinds of units will be needed to create a task force. These are the units which will be able to annihilate or cripple the enemy's naval formation by mass brief attacks and units which will be able to maintain contact with the enemy for a long time;

The general conclusion of Chernyshev's article was: 'All naval arms as well as ships of all types are needed, but the Soviet Navy will not be in need of aircraft carriers.'[55]

HITLER AND THE GERMAN *WEHRMACHT* PREPARE FOR 'BARBAROSSA'

After Molotov's visit to Berlin Hitler finally realized that his idea of building a big continental block from Spain to Japan, incorporating the Soviet Union into the Tri-Partite Pact, had failed, and with his *Weisung No. 21 Fall Barbarossa* of 18 December 1940 he came back to his general aim of crushing the Bolshevik Soviet Union and winning *Lebensraum* for the German people by subjugating the 'subhuman Slavic peoples' and extinguishing the Jewish population. He wanted to start his ideological and racial campaign in mid-May 1941.[56] To keep the preparations secret, the redeployment of troops to Poland would be made as late as possible, and the Allies were only cautiously introduced. So the Finnish Chief of the General Staff, General Erik Heinrichs, came first on 30 January for a meeting with Colonel General F. Halder, but was not really introduced into the plans until 25 May during a visit to the OKW to prepare the Finnish 'parallel war' to win back the lost territories of the Winter War and to organize command relations in the northern part of Finland. And General Antonescu was not introduced until Hitler was paid a visit on 12 June. Neither of the main German allies, Italy or Japan, were informed until the last minute. When the Japanese Minister for Foreign Affairs, Matsuoka Yosuke, visited Berlin from 27–29 March, the German side tried only to involve the Japanese in an attack against the British position at Singapore, while the Italian leader Benito Mussolini was only informed by letter from Hitler the day before the attack started.[57]

But Mussolini's attack from Albania against Greece on 28 October 1940 and the success of the Greek counterattack, as well as the landing of a British troop contingent to support the Greek Army, led to Hitler's fears that the British might attack the Romanian oil fields at Ploesti from the air. So he tried to strengthen the Axis position in the Balkans by supporting the Italians with an attack against northern Greece from Bulgaria thus pushing the British out of air-range of Ploesti. On 13 December 1940 he issued his *Weisung 20/Marita*.[58] From 13–20 January 1941 he received the visits of King Boris III of Bulgaria, General Antonescu and finally Mussolini to win them over to his plan. On 17 January Molotov received the German ambassador F.W. Graf von der Schulenburg to remind the German government of the Soviet claim that Bulgaria lay in the Soviet zone of interest. But notwithstanding this attempt to block German intentions, on 3 March Bulgaria joined the Tri-Partite Pact and in the following days German troops of the 12th Army and the VIIIth Air Corps became concentrated near the Danube off the Bulgarian border. In addition, Hitler tried to win Yugoslavia for the Tri-Partite Pact in discussions with Prime Minister Svetkovic on 14 February and Prince Regent Paul on 4 March. Yugoslavia joined the Pact on 25 March, but on 27 March a coup d'état overthrew the government of Prince Paul. Hitler reacted that same evening and issued his *Weisung No. 25* to prepare a combined attack against Yugoslavia to be started on 6 April from Austria, Hungary and Bulgaria, and to postpone the *Operation Marita* against Greece from 1 to 6 April. On 3 April he had issued his *Weisung No. 26* on co-operation with the allied countries in the Balkans.[59] The necessary redeployments for these Balkan operations forced a postponement of *Operation Barbarossa* until mid-June.[60]

Meanwhile, military preparations got under way.[61] On 31 January 1941 the *Oberkommando des Heeres (OKH,* the German High Command*)* issued its *Aufmarschanweisung Barbarossa*, to 'make it possible even before the war with Great Britain is decided to crush Soviet Russia in a fast campaign'. The intention was to encircle the bulk of the Russian forces concentrated in western Russia by fast and forceful dashes by armoured mobile groups and to annihilate them by following infantry forces. Strong but secondary pushes were to be made from East Prussia in the direction of Riga and Leningrad, and to the south of the Pripjet swamps in the direction of Kiev and the Dnepr bulge, with the intention also of encircling the Soviet forces massed there. The *Luftwaffe* was to gain air superiority and support the pushes of the Army, while the Navy was to block the Soviet Baltic Fleet by mine barrages, but also to concentrate its efforts against Great Britain's sea lines of communications.[62] The Commander-in-Chief of the Navy, Grand Admiral Raeder, could not win Hitler over to his idea of a Mediterranean strategy.

The German troop deployment into Bulgaria after Molotov's démarche had already strained Soviet–German relations; now the Soviet Union and Yugoslavia concluded a Pact of Friendship on 5/6 April, which strengthened Hitler's antagonism against the Soviets, but did not change his decision to attack Yugoslavia and Greece, starting as planned on 6 April. This led to the capitulation of the Yugoslav Army on 17 April and the Greek Forces on 21 and 23 April. At the end of April the British troops in Greece and remnants of Greek troops were evacuated to Crete. This made a German airborne landing necessary (*Operation Merkur*), which succeeded between 20 May and 1 June against strong resistance from British, New Zealand and Greek troops. Attempts to support the island by the British Mediterranean Fleet were blocked by heavy attacks from the dive bombers of the German *VIIIth Fliegerkorps*.[63]

On 30 April Hitler had finally taken the definitive decision to start the attack against the Soviet Union on 22 June 1941. This was in addition to his general intention made necessary by the re-deployments after the Balkan operations and by reports of the *Abteilung Fremde Heere Ost* of the Army General Staff about the increasing Soviet deployments near their western borders.[64] The German deployments for *Barbarossa* started with the first echelon between the end of December up to 16 March, the second echelon followed up to early April. Then there was an interruption because of the Balkan operations, and the third echelon came with its first part between 8 April and 20 May, the rest and the fourth echelon with most of the armoured formations followed from 23 May up to 23 June, bringing the strength of the Army groups to the following levels:[65]

- *Heeresgruppe Nord:* 20 infantry, 3 armoured, 3 motorized divisions.
- *Heeresgruppe Mitte:* 31 infantry, 9 armoured, 6 motorized, 1 cavalry, 3 security divisions.
- *Heeresgruppe Süd:* 25 infantry, 4 light, 1 mountain, 5 armoured, 3 motor-

ized and 3 security divisions. In addition there were two Romanian Armies and Hungarian and Slovakian units.
- *Finland:* in addition to the Finnish forces 1 infantry, 2 mountain, and 1 motorized divisions.
- *OKH-Reserves:* 24 infantry, 1 mountain, 2 armoured, 1 motorized, 3 security divisions.
- together: 105 infantry, 4 mountain, 9 security, 1 cavalry, 19 armoured, and 14 motorized divisions.

The Air Forces had the following strength:[66]

- *Luftflotte 1 (Nord):* 592 combat and transport aircraft (453 operational), in addition 143 Army planes.
- *Luftflotte 2 (Mitte):* 1,367 combat and transport aircraft (994 operational), in addition 244 Army planes.
- *Luftflotte 4 (Süd):* 887 combat and transport aircraft (694 operational), in addition 239 Army planes.
- *Luftflotte 5 (North Norway):* 108 aircraft (91 operational).
- together: 3,904 airplanes of all types (3,032 operational), of these 2,510 (1,945 operational) were combat aircraft like fighters, heavy fighters, bombers and dive bombers, as well as reconnaissance planes.

The German Navy remained with its main forces concentrated in western Europe against the British Navy. In the eastern Baltic ten minelayers were deployed to lay the mine barrages in and off the Finnish Gulf and in the Baltic between Öland and Latvia to block the movements of Soviet fleet units, and in addition six submarines and three MTB flotillas, three minesweeper flotillas, two motor-minesweeper flotillas, and eight flotillas of submarine hunters, minesweepers and patrol vessels, composed of former fishing vessels.[67]

On 14 June the departure of German merchant vessels for Russian ports was stopped and the German ships in Soviet ports were ordered to leave. On 18 June the minelayers began with the laying of the mine barrages, first in the 'Wartburg' barrage from Öland to Latvia, which was completed on 21 June, and on 21 June the barrages 'Apolda' and 'Corbetha' were laid at the entrance and in the central part of the Finnish Gulf, starting from camouflaged places in the Finnish skerries.[68]

German estimates of Soviet strength were for the Army in the European part of the USSR 154 infantry, 25½ cavalry, 19 armoured divisions and 32 motorized brigades, as well as 7–8 parachute brigades, which was a great underestimation of the armoured forces. In reality, the *North, North-west, West* and *South-west Fronts* had in June 1941 136 infantry, 44 armoured, 23 motorized, and 7 cavalry divisions – altogether 210 divisions. The German Air Force estimated about 7,500 aircraft in the European part of the USSR, of which about 5,700 might be operational combat aircraft. This also was an underestimation. According to new Russian sources there were already in June 1941 in the western part of the Soviet Union 13,300 planes, of which 2,739 were modern combat planes.[69]

The Navy overestimated the strength of the Soviet Baltic Fleet. It was estimated that the Fleet contained two battleships, three cruisers, 41 destroyers, 6 torpedo boats, 110 motor torpedo boats and 96 submarines.[70] In fact, the Baltic Fleet had two battleships, two cruisers, two flotilla leaders, seven old and 12 modern destroyers, seven patrol ships (torpedo boats) and 65 submarines.[71]

The Debate about a Preventive or a Pre-emptive Attack in the Historiography

When the war started on 22 June 1941 the German propaganda tried to justify the attack as a preventive necessity to forestall the attack of the Soviet Army, which was already concentrated with the main elements in the western part of Belorussia and the Ukraine and would soon be ready to strike into the back of Germany, having gained new jump-off areas in 1940 by annexing the Baltic States, eastern Poland (western Belorussia and western Ukraine) and Bessarabia, and demanding bases at the Baltic Approaches and the Turkish Narrows. At the same time the propaganda reverted to its old theme by describing the Bolshevik regime as dominated by 'Jewish' leaders, trying to expand the Soviet 'terror regime' into Central Europe, which had to be driven back by a crusade of the whole of Europe.[72]

On the other hand, the Soviet version during the war and for a long time afterwards postulated that the German attack was completely unprovoked and treacherous, and that it had completely surprised the Soviet leadership and the Army, while the Soviet regime was fulfilling its obligations from the German–Soviet treaties up to the last moment. This thesis was generally upheld until the period of *perestroika* and *glasnost* at the end of the 1980s. And it was also upheld by the historians of the German Democratic Republic until then.[73]

In the German and Western historiographies after the war we can observe very different analyses, some publications following to a great extent the earlier propaganda version of a preventive attack, while in most cases omitting the terminology of the Nazi propaganda machine about the 'Jewish-Bolshevik' leadership, which could not be held up after the revelations about the 'Holocaust' and the subjugation of the peoples of eastern Europe.[74] This was upheld by some authors writing about the military side of the history until recently.[75] Others, and this became the majority, came to the conclusion that Hitler attacked Russia in justification of his prevalent concept to win *Lebensraum* and fight a racial-ideological war to destroy the Soviet Union and eliminate the Jewish population, at least in eastern Europe.[76]

In the Soviet Union the thaw brought about by *glasnost* and *perestroika* and the opening of the archives made it possible for Soviet historians to present a more differentiated picture of the situation and the decision-making processes from autumn 1940 to the spring of 1941. Thus, it became apparent that the Soviet General Staff had been preparing considerations and plans for a possible, and from early 1941 an awaited, war with Germany but could not convince Stalin to agree.[77] Finally, high-ranking General Staff officers tried to follow the offensive Soviet military doctrine. They wanted to launch an offensive operation, shortly after the enemy attack had come to a standstill. Although informed about the size of the German forces deploying along the German borders, they did not realize the essence of plan *Barbarossa*. Therefore, the General Staff decided to make several versions of the Red Army operations schedule, including one for a pre-emptive attack. It is probable that they preferred this type of operation, having been deeply impressed by General Zhukov's successful attack against the Japanese at Khalkhin Gol in 1939.[78]

The plan of mid-May 1941 to counter the shortly awaited German attack by a pre-emptive attack on the German deployments – to prevent under all conditions a German initiative – was never typed up, only drafted by hand by General Vasilevskii, because everyone knew that Stalin was not ready to approve such a suggestion. There was only one copy of this draft made but Stalin became very angry after reading it and criticized Zhukov. Thus, there *was* a memorandum with a plan for a possible Red Army pre-emptive attack on the German forces but it was made by the General Staff only as a draft. Stalin did not order it to be done and refused to agree to it. After the 'Winter War' with Finland, Stalin had given a sober appreciation of the condition of the Red Army and realized that the USSR needed at least two more years to complete the rearming and deployment of the Soviet Armed Forces. Possessed by this idea, Stalin gave a significant speech to Red Army officers graduating from Soviet military academies on 5 May 1941 (see p. 133).[79]

Stalin seems to have believed that Hitler would not start a war before a victory against Great Britain and would not risk a two-front war. So he assumed that the reported German deployments were an attempt to blackmail him into additional concessions and ordered that no measures be taken that might provoke Hitler. Now the revelations about his speech and toast on 5 May 1941 show that he too was of the opinion that the Soviet Army was soon ready to go from a defensive to an offensive strategy, but he wanted to gain more time for the preparations.[80] The development of the Soviet planning process is described in the next chapter.

SOVIET PREPARATIONS FOR WAR

From 23–31 December 1940 the commanders of the military districts, the members of the war councils, the chiefs of staff of the military districts and the armies, the commanders of the military academies with their professors and doctors of military science, the inspectors of the branches of the services, the chiefs of the administration, the leading members of the General Staff and members of the Politburo were summoned to participate in a conference chaired by the *Narkom* for Defence, Marshal S.K. Timoshenko. There were the following reports:[81]

- Army General K.A. Meretskov, Chief of the General Staff, 'The Results of Military Training'.
- Army General G.K. Zhukov, Commander of the Military District Kiev, 'The Character of the Modern Attack Operation'.

- Army General I.V. Tyulenev, Commander of the Military District Moscow, 'The Character of the Modern Defensive Operation'.
- Colonel-General D.G. Pavlov, Commander of the Western Special Military District, 'The Use of Mechanized Formations in Modern Attack Operations and the Introduction of a Mechanized Corps into the Breakthrough'.
- Lieutenant-General P.V. Rychagov, Chief of the Main Administration of the Air Forces, 'The Air Forces in Attack Operations and in the Fight for Air Superiority'.
- Lieutenant-General A.K. Smirnov, Inspector of the Infantry, 'The Combat of the Infantry Division in Attack and Defence'.

In their papers Zhukov and Pavlov emphasized the organization and conduct of attack operations and were supported by Rychagov, while Tyulenev criticized the neglect of defensive operations. Timoshenko summarized the meeting by stating that the massive use of tanks and dive bombers in combination with motorized units and in co-operation with air and naval forces guaranteed the high speed and push of modern attack operations, while defensive operations are important, but only as the preparation for attack operations.[82] There remained between the Soviet military leaders a lack of agreement as to whether the doctrines of a counterattack against aggression or a surprise first strike before the enemy attacked should be chosen.

Then, from 2–6 and 8–11 January 1941, the General Staff organized two war games in which the top military leaders participated. The aim of both games was to investigate the possibilities of strong counterattacks by the 'easterners' into enemy territory after the 'western enemy' had tried to attack; in the first game to the north, in the second to the south of the Pripjet marshes. In the first Zhukov played the western side, Pavlov the eastern side, in the second vice-versa. When Pavlov pushed deep into the area of northern Poland, Zhukov led a strong armoured counterattack from East Prussia, which led to the failure of Pavlov's attack. But in the second direction, which was favoured by Stalin, who thought that Hitler wanted to conquer the rich resources of the Ukraine, Zhukov's counterattack was very successful and reached the area of the Danube near Budapest. On 13 January the results of the games were reported to Stalin, who – looking at the excellent results of Zhukov's operations – named him as the new Chief of the General Staff from 1 February.[83]

Only six weeks later, on 11 March, Timoshenko and Zhukov sent their 'Defined Plan for the Strategic Deployment of the Soviet Forces in the West and East'[84] to Stalin and Molotov for their judgement. In the introduction they said, 'the political situation in Europe has developed and forced us to concentrate our exclusive attention on the defence of our western borders ... but it's not impossible that our Far East borders might be attacked by the Japanese ... A surprise attack from Germany against the USSR might also bring Finland, Romania, Hungary and other allies of Germany into the conflict.' They then analyzed the armed forces of their Axis opponents, listing, including allied forces, 233 infantry, 20 armoured, and 15 motorized divisions with 20,050 guns, 10,810 tanks and 11,000 aircraft in the west, and for Japan 60 divisions with 850 guns, 1,200 tanks and 3,000 aircraft. Looking at the probable strategic plans of the enemies, it was assumed that Germany would put the main effort – as Stalin had surmised – against Kiev and the Ukraine. Secondary attacks might come from East Prussia in the direction of Riga, and from Romania in the south and from Finland on the Karelian Narrows. But as in the earlier plans a main attack north of the Pripjet marshes was not totally excluded. The assumptions about the strength of the German and Axis forces were greatly overestimated, and the Soviet Forces had achieved, in fact, numerical superiority.

Meantime Soviet intelligence received many warnings about German intentions. Even by the end of December 1940 there was certain information about the *Weisung 21/Barbarossa* in the possession of the Main Intelligence Directorate (*GRU*). On 1 March 1941 the Deputy Secretary of State in Washington, Sumner Welles, presented parts of the *Weisung 21* to the Soviet ambassador K.A. Umanskii, and on 20 March the Chief of the *GRU*, General F.I. Golikov, presented a report about probable German intentions to the government, mentioning the probable attack date as 20 May. But Stalin was very reluctant to accept such warnings. He assumed this to be German disinformation because he could not believe that Hitler would attack before he had finished with Great Britain and risk a two-front war. Also other warnings about the German deployments to eastern Poland reached the Soviet General Staff, but nothing could change Stalin's prejudices and his trust in the strength of the Red Army.[85] This might also have had something to do with the differences and divergences of the incoming reports from various sources, and the mistrust Stalin harboured against the Western 'imperialist' democracies.

On 5 May 1941 the graduates of the military academies were assembled at the Kremlin, and Stalin addressed the assembly which also contained high-ranking Soviet military leaders, like Marshals S.K. Timoshenko and S.M. Budennyi, the Head of the Political Administration L.S. Mekhlis and A.Yu. Vyshinskii, now Deputy *Narkom* for Foreign Relations. Stalin mentioned the great changes wrought in the Red Army to enable the forces to wage modern warfare, and said that the most important experiences gained had come from the Finnish War and the observations about the German war in western Europe. The fighting power of the Soviet armoured forces, the artillery and the air forces had been greatly strengthened by the introduction of new weapons. Analysing the roots of the German successes, he said that 'the German forces are not invincible, because arrogance and complacency have spread in their ranks, and their weapons and equipment are no better than ours'. When after Stalin had finished a general made a toast and praised Stalin's peaceful defensive policy, Stalin answered that this 'was correct only as long as the Soviet armed forces were not equipped with the necessary modern weapons, but now this has changed and the defence of our country must now be conducted in an offensive form. The Red Army is now a modern army, but a modern army is an offensive army.'[86]

The Main Administration for Political Propaganda of the *RKKA* received the order to prepare an instruction. 'The Task of Political Propaganda in the Red Army in the Near Future'. The design was presented to Stalin on 20 June. Political propaganda was given the following tasks:[87]

- the members of the Red Army must be prepared for a just and offensive war;
- the members of the Army must learn the roots and the character of the 'second imperialistic war' and the conquest aims of the belligerent nations;
- the roots of the German successes and the defeat of France are to be declared. The perception of many soldiers, commanders and political cadres about the invincibility of the German Army must be destroyed.

But for the General Staff and especially its chief, Army General Zhukov and his assistants, the danger signs were increasing and he was forced to draw up a new operational plan for the deployment and proposed operations of the Red Army in the case of a German attack; this was presented by the *Narkom* for Defence, Marshal Timoshenko, and by Zhukov to Stalin around the 15 May.[88]

Zhukov and Timoshenko now (in mid-May) rated the possible strength of the German Forces for an attack against the Soviet Union to be 137 infantry, 10 armoured, 15 motorized, 4 cavalry and 5 airborne divisions, about 180 divisions in all, of which about two-thirds were then deployed. This was again a great overestimation, because in mid-May only 80 German divisions, including only three armoured divisions were deployed on the Soviet western borders. Both leaders still assumed that the German main effort in the direction of the Ukraine was about 100 divisions, while secondary strikes were conjectured to happen in the direction of Riga, and Minsk. In addition to the German divisions there might be 20 Finnish, 15 Hungarian and 25 Romanian infantry divisions. Counting such massive concentrations Zhukov said that under no circumstances should the Red Army yield the initiative to the Germans. The Red Army must forestall the German deployment and attack when the Germans were still marching up to their attack positions and were not yet ready to attack.

The first strategic aim of the Red Army had to be to annihilate the German forces deployed in the southern direction, by attacking with the main forces from the area of Lvov in the direction of Krakow, and by a secondary strike from the area of Bialystok against Warsaw to encircle the German forces between Brest-Litovsk and Lvov, and in a second phase to attack from the area of Oppeln and Warsaw to the north in the direction of Danzig to cut off the German Forces in the area of East Prussia. In a detailed plan the necessary and available forces were estimated for the western *Fronts* at 163 rifle, 58 armoured, 30 motorized, 7 cavalry divisions – about 269 divisions in total.

The change from a more defensive disposition with the possibility of a strong counterattack to a pre-emptive attack against the German Army marching up for its attack might have been influenced by the reduced danger from Japan after the conclusion of a Japanese–Soviet Neutrality Pact, which the Japanese Foreign Minister Matsuoka Yosuke concluded on 13 April during his return voyage in Moscow. And the fear might have been further reduced by the information that the Japanese did not plan to unleash war on the Soviet Union, because they planned first to conquer new possessions in the Pacific and in the South East Asian area with its rich resources of raw materials. It was good news for Stalin, who wanted to accelerate Red Army deployment along the Soviet–German line of demarcation. For a long time this information was assigned to the reports from the well-known Soviet spy in the German Embassy in Tokyo, Richard Sorge. But from an interview of the American historian David Kahn with the Chief of the Cryptological Service of the Russian Foreign Intelligence Service, General N.N. Andreyev, held on 13 June 1996 in Moscow, we learned that the reports from Sorge were not as important to Soviet intelligence as the success achieved by a Soviet cryptanalist Sergei Tolstoi in breaking the well-known Japanese diplomatic cypher *97-shiki o-burn In-ji-ki* or 'Purple', sometime in 1941.[89]

Stalin did not approve the operational plan, of a pre-emptive counterattack against the German Army. Because of the dangers envisaged in the rising strength of the German forces in Poland, it was important to gain time to complete the deployment of the Red Army, which was somewhat time-consuming because of the insufficient rail and road connections in the newly won areas of the western Ukraine and Belorussia. Stalin wanted to gain time and to avoid rousing German suspicions. So he ordered that the deployments be camouflaged carefully and that reports about German reconnaissance flights over Soviet territory and other signs of German preparations be ignored. He may still have thought that Hitler was trying to blackmail him to get additional concessions. So he ordered that all the economic treaty obligations be honoured until the last minute and ignored all warnings from his military advisors.

THE SOVIET NAVY AT THE START OF THE GREAT PATRIOTIC WAR

The statement of the *Narkom* for the Navy, Admiral Kuznetsov, that the Army leaders did not take into account sea warfare and that in their minds the classic land-based doctrine had priority, can be seen by the omission of any naval aspects in the plans of the General Staff from July 1940 to May 1941, where there are only short sentences about possible amphibious operations of the Germans in the Baltic and of the Japanese in the Far Eastern area, but nothing about possible operations of the Soviet Fleets to support the operations of the Army. The Army leaders didn't consider them as important subjects.

Because of several changes in the strategic concepts and the capacity problems of industry the results of the Soviet Navy's development from 1921 to 1941 were contradictory. Just before the sudden German attack the Soviet Navy had in active service about 930 combatants of all sizes. From 1931 to 1941 the overall number of combat ships and combat boats was increased by almost ninefold but the overall tonnage by only fourfold.

In the middle of the 1930s the share of the Soviet surface ocean-going ships was 8.5 per cent. In 1934 there were only three battleships, four cruisers and 17 destroyers in active service. In addition to those ships at least 29 big and medium submarines might be ordered to operate on the high seas. On 22 June 1941 the share of the ocean-going ships was 7.08 per cent because the Soviets had only 67 surface ships capable of operating on the high seas, and 76 smaller surface ships. Besides the active list the Soviet Navy included at least 129 big and medium submarines with an endurance from 4,000 to 8,000 nautical miles, and 85 smaller ones.

The composition of the sea-going and the smaller surface ships and the submarines of the Soviet Fleets on 21 June 1941 was as follows:[90]

Baltic Fleet

2 Battleships (old): *Marat, Oktyabrskaya revolyutsiya*
2 Cruisers (*projekt 26*): *Kirov, Maksim Gorkii*
1 Training Cruiser (old): *Avrora*
1 Minelayer/Cruiser (old): *Marti*
2 Destroyer-Leaders (*projekt 1, 38*): *Leningrad, Minsk*
7 Destroyers (*projekt 7-U*): *Storozhevoi, Serdityi, Stojkii, Sil'nyi, Surovyi, Slavnyi, Smelyi*
5 Destroyers (*projekt 7*): *Smetlivyi, Gnevnyi, Gordyi, Grozyashchii, Steregushchii*
7 Destroyers (old): *Yakov Sverdlov, Kalinin, Karl Marx, Lenin, Artem, Engels, Volodarskii*
8 Patrol Ships (SKR, *projekt 2, 39*): *Taifun, Vikhr', Tsiklon, V'yuga* (under repair), *Purga, Burya, Sneg, Tucha*
1 Patrol Ship (ex-Estn.): *Ametist* (ex-*Sulev*)
17 Minesweepers (*projekt 3, 53U*): *T-201/Zaryad, T-202/Buj, T-203/Patron, T-204/Fugas, T-205/Gafel', T-206/Verp, T-207/Shpil', T-208/Shkiv, T-209/Knekht, T-210/Gak, T-211/Rym, T-212/Shtag, T-213/Krambol', T-214/Bugel', T-215, T-216, T-218*
2 Minesweepers (old, ex-Latv., ex-Lith.): *Virsaitis, Korall* (ex-*Presidente Smetona*)
Total of 27 sea-going, 28 smaller surface ships.

1 Big Submarine (series I): *D-2*
3 Big Submarines (series II): *L-1, L-2, L-3*
3 Big Submarines (series IV): *P-1, P-2, P-3*
4 Big Submarines (series XIV): *K-3, K-21, K-22, K-23*
4 Medium Submarines (series III): *Shch-301, Shch-302, Shch-303, Shch-304*
2 Medium Submarines (series V-bis): *Shch-305, Shch-308*
5 Medium Submarines (series V-bis2): *Shch-306, Shch-307, Shch-309, Shch-310, Shch-311*
2 Medium Submarines (series IX): *S-1, S-3*
10 Medium Submarines (series IX-bis): *S-4, S-5, S-6, S-7, S-8, S-9, S-10, S-11, S-101, S-102*
7 Medium Submarines (series X): *Shch-317, Shch-318, Shch-319, Shch-320, Shch-322, Shch-323, Shch-324*
2 Medium Submarines (series X-bis): *Shch-405, Shch-406*
2 Medium Submarines (ex-Estn.): *Kalev, Lembit*
2 Medium Submarines (old): *B-2, L-55*
12 Small Submarines (series VI-bis): *M-71, M-72, M-73, M-74, M-75, M-76, M-77, M-78, M-79, M-80, M-81, M-83* (*M-72* to *M-75* laid up at Kronshtadt)
9 Small Submarines (series XII): *M-90, M-94, M-95, M-96, M-97, M-98, M-99, M-102, M-103*

2 Small Submarines (ex-Latv.): *Ronis, Spidola*
Total of 11 big, 36 medium, and 23 small submarines.

Black Sea Fleet

1 Battleship (old): *Parizhskaya kommuna*
2 Cruisers (*projekt 26*): *Voroshilov, Molotov*
4 Cruisers (old): *Krasnyi Kavkaz, Krasnyi Krym, Chervona Ukraina, Komintern*
1 Destroyer Leader (*projekt 20-I*): *Tashkent*
2 Destroyer Leaders (*projekt 1*): *Kharkov, Moskva*
2 Destroyers (*projekt 7-U*): *Smyshlennyi, Soobrazitel'nyi*
6 Destroyers (*projekt 7*): *Bodryi, Bystryi, Bojkii, Besposhchadnyi, Bezuprechnyi, Bditel'nyi*
5 Destroyers (old): *Frunze, Dzerzhinskii, Nezamozhnik, Shaumyan, Zheleznyakov*
2 Patrol Ships (*projekt 2*): *Shtorm, Shkval'*, (both in repair)
13 Minesweepers (*projekt 3, 53U*): *T-401/Tral', T-402/Minrep, T-403/Gruz, T-404/Shchit, T-405/Vzryvatel', T-406/Iskatel', T-407/Mina, T-408/Yakor', T-409/Garpun, T-410/Vzryv, T-411/Zashchitnik, T-412, T-413*
Total of 23 sea-going and 15 smaller surface ships.
3 Big Submarines (series I): *D-4* (in repair), *D-5, D-6*
3 Big Submarines (series II): *L-4, L-5, L-6* (in repair)
4 Medium Submarines (series V-bis): *Shch-201, Shch-202, Shch-203, Shch-204*
3 Medium Submarines (series V-bis2): *Shch-205, Shch-206, Shch-207*
4 Medium Submarines (series IX-bis): *S-31, S-32, S-33, S-34*
8 Medium Submarines (series X): *Shch-208, Shch-209, Shch-210, Shch-211, Shch-212, Shch-213, Shch-214, Shch-215*
2 Small Submarines (series VI): *M-51, M-52*
2 Small Submarines (series Vi-bis): *M-54, M-55*
10 Small Submarines (series XII): *M-31, M-32, M-33, M-34, M-35, M-36, M-58, M-59, M-60, M-62*
5 Small Submarines (old): *A-1, A-2, A-3, A-4, A-5*
Total of 6 big, 19 medium, and 19 small submarines.

Northern Fleet

5 Destroyers (*projekt 7*): *Groznyi, Gromkii, Stremitel'nyi, Gremjashchii, Sokrushitel'nyi*
3 Destroyers (old): *Kujbyshev, Uritskii, Karl Liebknecht* (under repair until November 1944)
3 Patrol Ships (*projekt 2*): *Uragan, Smerch, Groza*
4 Patrol Ships (*projekt 43*, NKVD): *PSK-1/Zhemchug, PSK-2/Rubin, PSK-303/Brilliant, PSK-304/Sapfir*
Total of 8 sea-going and 7 smaller surface ships.

1 Big Submarine (series I): *D-3* (*D-1* lost by accident in November 1940)
2 Big Submarines (series XIV): *K-1, K-2*
6 Medium Submarines (series X): *Shch-401, Shch-402, Shch-403, Shch-404, Shch-421, Shch-422*

6 Small Submarines (series XII): *M-171, M-172, M-173, M-174, M-175, M-176*

Total of 3 big, 6 medium, and 6 small submarines.

Pacific Fleet

2 Destroyer Leaders (*projekt 38*): *Baku, Tbilisi*
5 Destroyers (*projekt 7*): *Ryanyi, Rezvyi, Rastoropnyi, Razyashchii, Rekordnyi*
2 Destroyers (old): *Vojkov, Stalin*
6 Patrol Ships (*projekt 2, 4*): *Metel', V'yuga, Molniya, Zarnitsa, Burun, Grom*
2 Patrol Ships (NKVD): *Kirov, Dzerzhinskii*
8 Minesweepers (*projekt 53U, 58*): *T-1/Strela, T-2/Toros, T-3/Provodnik, T-4/Podsekatel', T-5/Paravan, T-6/Kapsyul', T-7/Vekha, T-8/Cheka*

Total of 9 sea-going and 16 smaller surface ships.

6 Big Submarines (series XI): *L-7, L-8, L-9, L-11, L-12*
7 Big Submarines (series XII): *L-13, L-14, L-15, L-16, L-17, L-18, L-19*
11 Medium Submarines (series V): *Shch-101, Shch-102, Shch-104, Shch-105,* (in repair), *Shch-106, Shch-107, Shch-108* (in repair), *Shch-109, Shch-110, Shch-111, Shch-112*
8 Medium Submarines (series V-bis): *Shch-113, Shch-114, Shch-115, Shch-116, Shch-117, Shch-118, Shch-119, Shch-120*
5 Medium Submarines (series V-bis2): *Shch-121, Shch-122, Shch-123, Shch-124, Shch-125*
1 Medium Submarine (series IX-bis): *S-54*
10 Medium Submarines (series X): *Shch-126, Shch-127, Shch-128, Shch-129, Shch-130, Shch-131, Shch-132, Shch-133, Shch-134, Shch-139*
28 Small Submarines (series VI): *M-1, M-2, M-3, M-4, M-5, M-6, M-7, M-8, M-9, M-10, M-11, M-12, M-13, M-14, M-15, M-16, M-17, M-18, M-19, M-20, M-21, M-22, M-23, M-24, M-25, M-26, M-27, M-28*
6 Small Submarines (series VI-bis): *M-43, M-44, M-45, M-46, M-47, M-48*
3 Small Submarines (series XII): *M-30, M-49, M-63*

Total of 13 big, 35 medium and 37 small submarines.

Of the ships and submarines built in the yards there were already launched and being outfitted: 5 cruisers, 2 destroyer leaders, 18 destroyers, 5 patrol ships, 16 minesweepers, 12 big, 31 medium, 6 small submarines, and one experimental submarine. Laid down and on the slips there were 3 battleships, 2 battlecruisers, 3 cruisers, 24 destroyers, 12 patrol ships, 8 minesweepers, 18 medium and 26 small submarines.

But there was a great discrepancy between the theoretical concepts of the naval strategy and the real possibilities for operational and tactical procedures. The situation in the Baltic had improved by the newly won bases, but they were only partly equipped as necessary for basing the available ships there. So most of the units had to stay at Leningrad/Kronshtadt, which were blocked by ice in the winter months. There were also some problems for the other fleets during the winter. In the Black Sea some harbours in the north-west area froze, in the north the Kola Gulf was ice free, but the White Sea and the area more to the east were also frozen, as were the northern Pacific bases. This badly affected the training exercises of the ships and submarines during parts of the year. In addition, because of the war between Germany and its allies and the Western democracies, the exits of the Baltic and Black Seas were blocked, and in the north they were endangered by the German flanking position in northern Norway, while in the Far East the exits to the open Pacific could quite easily be blocked by the Japanese.

So Stalin's aim of a 'big ocean-going fleet' was still under consideration by the leading naval circles, but they had also to assess the real possibilities of the geographic and strategic situation and the available forces. The great personnel losses not only in the top positions but also among the cadres at the tactical level during the purges had left the young and mostly inexperienced commanders with material conditions far from the 'big fleet strategy'. They had still to follow the regulations of the 1930s, with their emphasis on the defence of the mine barrages supported by the coastal artillery and the use of the ships of the fleet for support of the Army on the sea flanks. But the lack of interest shown by the Army leadership in naval problems, and the lack of risk-taking by the naval leaders hindered bringing the real capabilities and possibilities, and not just wishful hopes for the future, to the attention of the Party and military leaders – all of which had something to do with the fear of being sucked up into the purges. And at the lower levels few took the risk of acting without first looking to the higher authorities and the commissars.

This was the situation when the Germans attacked on the night of 22 June 1941. And when the commanders of the fleets tried to get permission to act in preparation for an imminent German assault they were held back in the last days before the attack by the hesitation of Stalin, who forbade any measure that might provoke the Germans.

NOTES

1. Gerhard Weinberg, *A World at Arms: A Global History of World War II*, New York, Cambridge University Press, 1994; German edition, *Eine Welt in Waffen*, Stuttgart, Deutsche Verlagsanstalt, 1995, pp. 21–64.
2. Alwin D. Coox, *Nomonhan. Japan against Russia 1939*, Vol. 1,2, Stanford, CA, Stanford University Press, 1985. G.K. Zhukov, *Vospominaniya i razmyshleniya, Vol. I*, Moscow, Novosti, 1974. English edition 1985, vol. 1, pp. 177–206.
3. G.I. Antonov, 'The March into Poland', in B. Liddell Hart (ed.), *The Soviet Army*, London, Weidenfeld & Nicolson, 1956, pp. 73–8. Andreas Hillgruber and Gerhard Hümmelchen, *Chronik des Zweiten Weltkrieges*, Düsseldorf, Droste TB, 1978.
4. M.I. Semirjaga, *The Winter War: Looking Back after Fifty Years*, Moscow, Novosti, 1990. Gerd Ueberschär, 'Die "Volksregierung" Kuusinen in der "Demokratischen Republik Finnland" im Kalkül Stalins und Hitlers 1939/1940', *Finnland Studien*, Wiesbaden, Steiner, 1990, pp. 227–47.
5. H. Fock, op. cit., pp. 215–17.
6. Gerhard Hümmelchen, *Handelsstörer. Handelskrieg deutscher Überwasserstreitkräfte im Zweiten Weltkrieg*, 2nd edn, Munich, Lehmanns, 1967, pp. 130–8. V.F. Vorob'ev, 'Krugosvetka rejdera "Komet"', *Gangut*, No. 16 (1998), pp. 82–97.
7. *Lagevorträge der Oberbefehlshaber der Kriegsmarine vor Hitler 1939–1945*, ed. Gerhard Wagner, Munich, Lehmanns, 1972, p. 28.
8. Michael Salewski, *Die deutsche Seekriegsleitung 1935–1945. Vol. I: 1939–1941*, Frankfurt/Main, Bernard & Graefe, 1970, pp. 156–9, 375.

9. Siegfried Breyer, 'Die Kreuzer "K" und "L" der deutschen Kriegsmarine ("Seydlitz" und "Lützow")', *Marine-Rundschau*, 63 (1966), pp. 20–8, 99–100. M.J. Whitley, *The German Cruisers of World War II*, London, Arms and Armour Press, 1985, pp. 48–50. Because Hitler wanted to change the name of the pocket battleship *Deutschland* to avoid the possible loss of a ship with this name, the *Deutschland* was renamed *Lützow*, and the cruiser *Lützow* got back its original designation 'L', to cover the transfer.
10. M. Salewski, op. cit., pp. 156–9.
11. Ibid.
12. O.A. Rzheshevskii, 'Between the Two Fires', paper at the International Conference on Barbarossa at the University of Leeds, 21–23 June 1991.
13. Andreas Hillgruber, 'Stalins Politik der "freien Hand" und der Aufbau einer strategischen Sicherheitszone der UdSSR in Ostmitteleuropa', *Hitlers Strategie. Politik und Kriegführung 1940–1941*, Frankfurt/Main, Bernard & Graefe, 1963, pp. 102–15. A.M. Samsonov, *Krakh fashistskoi agressii*, Moscow, Nauka, 1980, pp. 107–60. Gerhard Weinberg, 'Neue Entscheidungen in Moskau', in *Eine Welt in Waffen*, op. cit., pp. 184–8. Walter Post, 'Das Ende der Kooperation', *Operation Barbarossa. Deutsche und sowjetische Angriffspläne 1940/41*, Hamburg, Mittler, 1995, pp. 146–70.
14. Andreas Hillgruber, *Hitler, König Carol und Marschall Antonescu. Die deutsch–rumänischen Beziehungen 1938–1944*, Wiesbaden, Steiner, 1965. *Das deutsche Reich und der Zweite Weltkrieg. Band 4: Der Mittelmeerraum und Südosteuropa. Von der 'non-belligeranze' Italiens bis zum Kriegseintritt der Vereinigten Staaten*, ed. Gerhard Schreiber *et al.*, Stuttgart, Deutsche Verlagsanstalt, 1984.
15. E. Klink, 'Deutsch–finnische Waffenbrüderschaft 1941–1944', *Wehrwissenschaftliche Rundschau*, 5 (1958), pp. 389–412.
16. General-Major Marcks, 'Operationsentwurf Ost vom 5. August 1940', in W. Post, op. cit., pp. 376–84. Jürgen Förster, 'Die deutsche Kriegspolitik und die Sowjetunion 1940/41', in *Das Deutsche Reich und der Zweite Weltkrieg. Band 4: Der Angriff auf die Sowjetunion*, ed. Horst Boog *et al.*, Stuttgart, Deutsche Verlagsanstalt, 1983.
17. TsGA, f.16, op.2851. d.239, l.14-37, printed in *Voenno-istoricheskii zhurnal* 12/1991, pp. 17–20. German translation in W. Post, op. cit., pp. 397–400.
18. TsGA, f.16, op.2951, d.239, l.197-216, 244, printed in *Voennyi istoricheskii zhurnal* 1/1992, pp. 24–9. German translation in W. Post, op. cit., pp. 401–7.
19. *Akten zur deutschen auswärtigen Politik*, Reihe D, Band XI, Dok.176, pp. 291ff.
20. *Staatsmänner und Diplomaten bei Hitler. Vertrauliche Aufzeichnungen über Unterredungen mit Vertretern des Auslandes 1939–1941*, ed. Andreas Hillgruber, Frankfurt/Main, Bernard & Graefe, 1967, pp. 294–319.
21. E.A. Maurer and M. Reichman, *Global War: an Atlas of World Strategy*, New York, William Morrow, 1943, p. 14.
22. N.G. Kuznetsov, *Nahanune*, op. cit.
23. *Vremennoye nastavlenie po boevoi deyatel'nosty minno-torpednoy aviatsii (NBMTA 40)*.
24. *RGA VMF*, f. r-961, op.1, d.282, l.46-48.
25. *Ob'yasnitel'naya Zapiska k Programme Sudostroeniya boevogo flota RKVMF 1938/47*.
26. *Prikaz Narodnogo Komissara Voenno-morskogo flota SSSR, No. 00263, 23 October 1940*.
27. RGA VMF, f. r.1678, op.1, d.181, l.1-57.
28. RGA VMF, f. r.1678, op.1, d.182, l.1-10.
29. RGA VMF, f. r.1678, op.1, d.183, l.1-144.
30. RGA VMF, f. r.1678, op.1, d.183, l.1-77.
31. RGA VMF, f. r.1678, op.1, d.183, l.1-84.
32. RGA VMF, f. r.1678, op.1, d.183, l.11, 45-46, 50, 52.
33. Ibid., l. 23.
34. Ibid., l. 64–8.
35. Ibid., l. 76–7.
36. RGA VMF, f. r.1678, op.1, d.183, l.25-35.
37. RGA VMF, f. r.1678, op.1, d.183, l.1-4.
38. RGA VMF, f. r.1678, op.1, d.183, l.4-8.
39. RGA VMF, f. r.1678, op.1, d.183, l.9-10.
40. RGA VMF, f. r.1678, op.1, d.183, l.83.
41. Ibid., l.141.

42. RGA VMF, f. r.1678, op.1, d.184, l.10.
43. Ibid.
44. RGA VMF, f. r.1678, op.1, d.184, l.11-13.
45. Ibid.
46. RGA VMF, f. r.1678, op.1, d.185, l.1-84.
47. RGA VMF, f. r.1678, op.1, d.186, l.1-10.
48. RGA VMF, f. r.1678, op.1, d.186, l.6-7.
49. RGA VMF, f. r.1678, op.1, d.370, l.80.
50. Ibid., l.24-25.
51. Ibid., l.137.
52. Vremennoye po Nastavlenie vedeniyu morskikh operatsii (NMO-40), 1940, pp. 5–6.
53. Ibid., pp. 13–14.
54. V. Chernyshev, 'Morskaya taktika za dva desiatiletia', *Morskoi sbornik*, No. 12 (1937), pp. 17–29.
55. Ibid., pp. 27–9, 108.
56. 'Oberkommando der Wehrmacht (OKW)/Wehrmachtführungsstab (WFSt), Abt. Landesverteidugung I (LI)', Nr. 33408/40 g. K. Chefs, *Hitlers Weisungen für die Kriegführung 1939–1945*, ed. Walther Hubatsch, Frankfurt/Main, Bernard & Graefe, 1962, pp. 84–91.
57. A. Hillguber und G. Hümmelchen, *Chronik des Zweiten Weltkrieges*, Düsseldorf, Droste, 1978, pp. 56–65.
58. OKW/Wfst./Abt.L I, Nr. 33406/40g K. Chefs, *Hitlers Weisungen*, op. cit., pp. 81–3.
59. OKW/WFSt/Abt.L Nr. 44395/41 g. K. Chefs, *Hitlers Weisungen*, op. cit., pp. 108–10.
60. A. Hillgruber and G. Hümmelchen, op. cit., OKW/WFSt/Abt.L (IOp) Nr. 44 379/41/g. K. Chefs, *Hitlers Weisungen*, op. cit., pp. 106–8.
61. *Kriegstagebuch des Oberkommandos der Wehrmacht (Wehrmachtführungsstab). Band I: August 1940–31. Dezember 1941*, ed, Hans-Adolf Jacobsen, Frankfurt/Main, Bernard & Graefe, 1965, pp. 244–375. *Kriegstagebuch der Seekriegsleitung 1939–1945, Part A. Band 17–20, Januar bis April 1941*, ed. Werner Rahn und Gerhard Schreiber unter Mitwirkung von Hansjoseph Maierhöfer, Herford, Mittler, 1990–91. *Lagevorträge der Oberbefehlshabers der Kriegsmarine vor Hitler 1939–1945*, ed. Gerhard Wagner, Munich, Lehmanns, 1972, pp. 179–216.
62. OKH/Genst.d.H./op.Abt.(I) Nr. 650/41 g.K. Post, Walter, *Unternehmen Barbarossa*, op. cit., pp. 393–6.
63. OKW/WFSt./Abt.L (IOp), Nr. 44581/41g Kdos.Chefs, *Weisung 28 (Unternehmen Merkur)*, *Hitlers Weisungen*, op. cit., pp. 115–17. KTB OKWB.I/1 u.2, 6.4.-3.6.41, pp. 375–400.
64. *Generaloberst Halder Kriegstagebuch, Band II: Von der geplanten Landung in England bis zum Beginn des Ostfeldzuges (1.7.1940 - 21.61941)* ed. Hans-Adolf Jacobsen, Stuttgart, Kohlhammer, 1963, pp. 345–436.
65. Walter Post, op. cit., pp. 249–50.
66. Der Rüstungsstand der Wehrmacht, *Das Deutsche Reich und der Zweite Weltkrieg*, op. cit., Vol. V, 1, Stuttgart, Deutsche Verlagsanstalt, 1988, pp. 554ff.
67. Oberkommando der Kriegsmarine (OKM)/Kriegswissenschaftliche Abteilung, *Der Ostseekrieg gegen Rußland im Jahre 1941*, Operationen und Taktik Heft 12, Berlin, Januar 1944, p. 36.
68. Jürgen Rohwer and Gerhard Hümmelchen, *Chronology of the War at Sea 1939–1945*, London, Greenhill, 1992, pp. 69–70.
69. Walter Post, *Unternehmen Barbarossa*, op. cit., pp. 241–4, 414.
70. *Der Ostseekrieg*, op. cit., pp. 2–3. OKM/3.Abt.Skl., *Nachtrag zum Handbuch für Admiralstabsoffiziere, Sowjetrußland, Kriegsschiffsliste (abgeschlossen 31.3.1941)*, Berlin, OKM, 1941, pp. 1–54.
71. Rohwer and Hümmelchen, op. cit., p. 68.
72. Weisung No. 21, 'Fall Barbarossa. Richtlinien auf Sondergebieten zur Weisung No. 21 (Fall Barbarossa)', in *Hitlers Weisungen für die Kriegführung 1939–1945 ... Dokumente des Oberkommandos der Wehrmacht*, ed. Walther Hubatsch, Frankfurt/Main, Bernard & Graefe, 1962, pp. 84–95. *Völkischer Beobachter*, 22–30 June 1941.
73. *Vazhnejshie Operatsii Velikoi Otechestvennoj vojny 1941–1945 gg*, ed. P.A. Zhilin, Voenizdat, 1956, esp pp. 76–130; B.S. Telpuchovskii, *Velikaya Otechestvennaya Vojna Sovetskogo Soyuza 1941–1945*, Moscow, Voenizdat, 1959. German edition, *Die sowjetische Geschichte des Großen Vaterlandischen Krieges 1941–1945*, ed. Andreas Hillgruber and Hans-Adolf Jacobsen,

Frankfurt/Main, Bernard & Greafe, 1961. Lew Bezymenski, *Sonderakte 'Barbarossa'*, Stuttgart, Deutsche Verlagsanstalt, 1968. Gerhard Förster, *Totaler Krieg und Blitzkrieg*, Berlin (Ost), Verlag des Ministeriums für Nationale Verteidigung, 1967. *Istoriya Vtoroj Mirovoj Vojny 1939–1945*, 12 vols, Moscow, Voenizdat, 1973–82, esp vols. 3 and 4. *Sovetskij Soyuz v gody Velikoj Otechestvennoj vojny*, Moscow, Nauka, 1985.

74. Hans-Günther Seraphim, *Die deutsch–russischen Beziehungen 1939–1941*, Hamburg, Nölke, 1949.
75. A. Philippi and F. Heim, *Der Feldzug gegen Sowjetrußland 1941–1945*, Stuttgart, Kohlhammer, 1962. Viktor Suworow (pseud. Resun, B. Vladimir), *Der Eisbrecher. Hitler in Stalins Kalkül*, Stuttgart, 1989. Joachim Hoffmann, Die Angriffsvorbereitungen der Sowjetunion, *Zwei Wege nach Moskau*, ed. Bernd Wegner, Munich, 1991. Joachim Hoffmann, *Stalins Vernichtungskrieg 1941–1945*. 2nd eds, Munich, 1995.
76. This was first made clear by Gerhard L. Weinberg, *Germany and the Soviet Union 1939–1941*, Leiden, Brill, 1954, reprinted 1972, and became the leading opinion in West German historiography with the great volume of Andreas Hillgruber, *Hitlers Strategie. Politik und Kriegführung 1940–1941*, Frankfurt/Main, Bernard & Graefe, 1965, which was becoming the standard work on this question and was reprinted in 1982. See also Eberhard Jäckel, *Hitlers Weltenschauung. Entwurf einer Herrschaft*, Stuttgart, Deutsche Verlagsanstalt, 1981. This line was generally followed by many other historians, especially by Jürgen Förster, 'Die deutsche Kriegspolitik und die Sowjetunion 1940/41', and Das Unternehmen 'Barbarossa' als Eroberungs- und Vernichtungskrieg', in *Das Deutsche Reich und der Zweite Weltkrieg. Vol. 4: Der Angriff auf die Sowjetunion*, ed. Horst Boog, Jürgen Förster, Joachim Hoffmann, Ernst Klink, Rolf-Dieter Müller and Gerd R. Ueberschär, Stuttgart, Deutsche Verlagsanstalt, 1983, pp. 3–37, 413–50; or Klaus Reinhard, *Das Scheitern der Strategie Hitlers im Winter 1941/42*, Stuttgart, Deutsche Verlagsanstalt, 1972, or Jochen Thies, *Architekt der Weltherrschaft. Die 'Endziele' Hitlers*, Düsseldorf, Droste, 1976, or Gerd R. Ueberschär, 'Hitlers Entschluß zum "Lebensraum" – Krieg im Osten. Programmatisches Ziel oder militärstrategisches Kalkül?' *Unternehmen 'Barbarossa'*, ed. Gerd R. Ueberschär and Wolfram Wette, Paderborn, 1984, pp. 83–110. Gerhard Weinberg, *Eine Welt in Waffen*, Stuttgart, Deutsche Verlagsanstalt, 1995, Ch. 5, pp. 294–342.
77. This started with Colonel-General Dmitri Volkogonov's big study, *Stalin, Triumph and Tragedy. A Political Portrait*, Moscow, Novosti, 1989, German edition, *Stalin, Triumph und Tragödie. Ein politisches Porträt*, Dusseldorf, Claassen, 1989, pp. 455–566, to be followed by many other studies by Russian historians. See, for example, the documents of the considerations of the *Narkom* for Defense, Marshal Timoshenko, and the Chief of the General Staff of the Red Army, Marshal Shaposhnikov of July 1940, GAVA, f.16, op.2951, d.239, l.1-14, 37; the considerations of Marshal Timoshenko and the new Chief of the General Staff, Army General Meretskov of 18 September 1940, GAVA, f.16, op.2951, d.239, l.197-216,244; the plan for strategic deployment by Marshal Timoshenko and the new Chief of the General Staff, Army General Zhukov of 11 March 1941, GAVA, f.16. op.2951, d.241, l.1-ff.; and the considerations of Marshal Timoshenko and Army General Zhukov of May 1941, GAVA, f.16, op.2951, d.237, l.1-15,
78. Discussion of M. Monakov with Dr Valery Kulikov, Head of the History Branch of the Russian Academy of Military Sciences, March/April 2000.
79. Testimony of Dr Victor Anfilov, who assisted Zhukov in preparing his book *Reminiscences and Reflections* to Valery Kulikov.
80. About the preparations of the General Staff and Stalin's hesitation, see G.K. Zhukov, *Reminiscences and Reflections*, Vol. 1, Moscow, Progress Publishers, 1985, pp. 227–79. About the meeting of the graduates of the Red Army academies on 5 May 1941 and Stalin's speech and toast there, see Lev Bezymenski, 'Die Rede Stalins am 5. Mai 1941', *Osteuropa*, 42 (1992). See also Walter Post, *Unternehmen Barbarossa. Deutsche und sowjetische Angriffspläne 1940/41*, Hamburg, Mittler & Sohn, 1995, pp. 255–99, about the meetings of 5 May 1941, see pp. 274–8.
81. *Istoriya Vtoroi Mirovoi Vojny*. German edition, *Geschichte des Zweiten Weltkrieges*, Berlin (Ost), Militärverlag, Band 3, pp. 492ff.
82. Speech of Marshal Timoshenko on 31 December 1940, *Voenno-istoricheskii zhurnal*, No. 1 (1992), pp. 16ff.

83. G.K. Zhukov, *Vospominaniya i Rasmyshleniya*, Novosti, 1974. English translation: *Reminiscences and Reflections*, Moscow, Progress Publ., 1985,Vol. I, pp. 226ff.
84. RGA MV, f.16, op.2951, d-241, l.1ff., printed in *Voennyi istoricheskii zhurnal*, No. 2/1992, pp. 18–22. German translation in W. Post, op. cit., pp. 408–12.
85. Yu. Kirshin, *The Soviet Military Doctrine of the Pre-War Years*, Moscow, 1990, pp. 401ff. G.K. Zhukov, op. cit., Vol. I, p. 215.
86. *Pravda*, 5 May 1941. L. Bezymenski, Die Rede Stalins am 5. Mai 1941, *Osteuropa*, 42/1992, pp. 242f.
87. Yu. Kirshin, op. cit., pp. 66ff.
88. GAVA, f.16, op.2951, d.237, l.1-15. Printed in a German translation by V. Danilov, *Österreichische Militärische Zeitschrift*, No. 1 (1993), pp. 49–51, see also Walter Post, op. cit., pp. 413–17.
89. David Kahn, 'Soviet Comint in the Cold War', *Cryptologia*, XXII, No. 1 (1998), pp. 1–24, especially pp. 12–13. It may be of interest that this cipher was not only broken by the Americans, as is known since the Pearl Harbor investigation of the US Congress in 1946, but also by cryptanalysts of the German Foreign Office and the OKW, who also broke many other Japanese ciphers, as one of the translators, Prof. Cort Rave wrote to J. Rohwer on 01.03.96.
90. S.S. Berezhnoi, op. cit., pp. 16–75, 197–9, 203, 300–4.

9

The Great Patriotic War, 1941–45 [1]

It is the intention of this volume to describe the development and discussions about the strategy of the Soviet Navy and her shipbuilding programmes, so no operational history of the 'Great Patriotic War' and especially the naval war in the Baltic, the Black Sea and the Arctic can be given here. There are now many more recent publications in English, German and Russian, which are based on the now accessible sources of both sides, to be consulted for detailed information about the operations at sea.[2] Here the events of the war are only mentioned in connection with the actual strength of the Soviet Fleets at selected dates, the situation of the bases and shipbuilding yards, and decisions about changes in the shipbuilding programmes and the development of the ship and submarine designs and shipbuilding during the war.

THE GERMAN ATTACK

When on 22 June 1941 Hitler started his war to crush the 'Bolshevik Soviet Union' in a new *Blitzkrieg* of about five months, the German Army, effectively supported by the Air Force, achieved just what the plan of Timoshenko and Zhukov of mid-May 1941 had envisaged for the Soviet Army. But why did the Soviet Forces seem to be surprised, in view of the fact that there were many warnings about an imminent German attack? One reason was that Stalin in his deep-rooted mistrust would not believe the warnings from the British and American side. But Stalin was reluctant to act, even after warnings from the high Soviet Military ranks and civilians loyal to him, and he would not approve of a sudden attack against the German forces in Poland and East Prussia. So he forbade that any measures be taken against the German 'provocations' such as the many reported reconnaissance flights or movement of forces near the borders, which might antagonize the Germans.

The Soviet Commanders of the Baltic, Black Sea and Northern Fleets were in a difficult situation, having to obey Stalin's orders, and yet needing to prevent their fleets from being surprised by the impending German attack. When more overflights by German aircraft were reported, on 6 June the *Narkom* for the Navy, Admiral Kuznetsov, ordered on his own initiative that the Danube

18. Battleship *Arkhangel'sk*, ex British *Royal Sovereign*, from 1944 to 1949 lent to the Northern Fleet in exchange for the Soviet part of the Italian Fleet.
(*Source:* Imperial War Museum/Library of Contemporary History)

19. Light cruiser *Admiral Makarov*, ex German *Nürnberg*, Soviet war booty, delivered in 1946 to the Baltic Fleet and used as training ship until 1959.
(*Source:* Library of Contemporary History)

20. Cruiser *Frunze* of *projekt 68K*. Seven ships of *projekt 68* were laid down from 1939 to 1941, three for the Baltic and four for the Black Sea Fleet. Two of the Black Sea ships were captured on the slips by the Germans in August 1941 and partly broken down to use the materials for other purposes. The other five ships were laid up for the time of the war and completed in 1950 to the improved design *68K*.
(*Source:* Library of Contemporary History)

21. Cruiser *Sverdlov* of *projekt 68-bis*. Twenty-one vessels of this, following the war experiences, improved design were laid down from 1949 to 1953, but only 14 were completed, from 1952 to 1955. The others were, after the halt in big ship building after Stalin's death, planned to be completed with missile armaments, but this plan was cancelled and the uncompleted vessels were scrapped.
(*Source:* Wright & Logan/Library of Contemporary History)

22. Destroyer *Smetlivyi* of *projekt 30-bis*. Seventy vessels of this type were built from 1948 to 1952, 16 for the Baltic Fleet and 18 each for the Northern, the Black Sea and the Pacific Fleets. But there were many changes in the assignments, and after 1956 several vessels were sold and transferred to other countries.
(*Source:* Wright & Logan/Library of Contemporary History)

23. Destroyer *Besslednyi* of *projekt 56*. Instead of the 110 big destroyers of *projekt 41*, of which only one was completed, 27 vessels of the less expensive *projekt 56* were built – nine for the Baltic Fleet, of which three were transferred to the Northern Fleet, three for the Northern Fleet, eight for the Black Sea Fleet, of which two were transferred to the Pacific Fleet, such as the *Besslednyi* (here passing through the Suez Canal), and seven directly for the Pacific Fleet. Four more were completed as missile destroyers in *projekt 56M*, and one remained uncompleted.
(*Source:* Library of Contemporary History)

24. Patrol ship of *projekt 29*. Eight vessels were laid down for the Baltic Fleet from 1939 to 22 June 1941, six for the Black Sea Fleet, and two for the Pacific Fleet. The six Black Sea vessels were captured by the Germans in Sevastopol' on the slips and scrapped. In the Baltic only the *Yastreb* was completed to the original design before the end of the war. Of the others, three were completed for the Baltic Fleet and two for the Pacific Fleet from 1946 to 1951 to the improved design *projekt 29-K*.

(*Source:* US Navy/Library of Contemporary History)

25. Destroyer *Neustrashimyi* of *projekt 41*. Of the 110 vessels originally planned for 1950–55, only this vessel was actually built; the series was cancelled in June 1951, as it was too complicated, and the somewhat smaller *projekt 56* introduced. The *Neustrashimyi* served in the Baltic Fleet.

(*Source:* Breyer Collection/Library of Contemporary History)

26. Patrol ship of *projekt 42*. Eight vessels were built from 1950 to 1953. The continuation of the series was then stopped for the less expensive *projekt 50*. All vessels served first in the Northern Fleet, but three were later transferred to the Caspian Flotilla. (*Source:* US Navy/Library of Contemporary History)

27. Patrol ship of *projekt 50*. Sixty-eight vessels of this type were built from 1951 to 1959. Sixteen served first in the Baltic Fleet, 14 in the Northern Fleet, 20 in the Black Sea Fleet and 18 in the Pacific Fleet. From 1956 to 1966 16 vessels were sold or transferred to East Germany, Indonesia, Bulgaria and Finland.
(*Source:* Library of Contemporary History)

28. Big submarine of *projekt 611*, already without gun armaments. Twenty-six submarines of this series were built from 1951 to 1958, three for the Baltic Fleet, of which two were transferred to the Pacific Fleet, 21 for the Northern Fleet, of which three were transferred to the Pacific Fleet and two directly for the Pacific Fleet. Six were rebuilt to carry ballistic missiles.

(*Source:* Library of Contemporary History)

29. Medium submarine of *projekt 613* in the original version. Some 215 boats were completed from 1950 to 1958, built in Leningrad, Nikolaev, Gorkii and Komsomol'sk. For many boats the assignments changed several times. After 1956 many vessels were sold or transferred to other countries. Many boats were also rebuilt to carry missiles or to test other equipment.

(*Source:* Library of Contemporary History)

30. Small submarine of *projekt A615*. There was first one submarine of *projekt 615*, built to test the machinery. Then from 1953 to 1957 30 submarines of *projekt A615* were built, 19 for the Baltic Fleet and 11 for the Black Sea Fleet.
(*Source:* Library of Contemporary History)

31. Nuclear submarine of *projekt 627*. Fourteen submarines of this type were built from 1955 to 1963. The first order went out on 25 November 1952; its design was developed from the preliminary design to the final technical *projekt* from March 1953 to June 1954. First tests with nuclear fuel of the lead vessel began in July 1958. A similar submarine of *projekt 645* with liquid metal reactors was built between 1958 and 1963. There was also a design P627A for a submarine with a Ilyushin P.20 long-range cruise missile, which was not built.
(*Source:* US Navy/Library of Contemporary History)

32. Missile destroyer *Prozorlivyi* of *projekt 56M*. Four of the *projekt 56* destroyers were completed in 1958 and had one SM-59 missile launcher for Kshch-missiles. A fifth ship remained unfinished. (*Source*: US Navy/Library of Contemporary History)

Flotilla be put on to Operative-Readiness Grade No. 2. On 19 June the Commanders of the Black Sea, Baltic and Northern Fleets, Vice Admirals F.S. Oktyabrskii, V.F. Tributs and A.G. Golovko were told to follow the order to the Danube Flotilla. When on the night of 21/22 June the Soviet Naval Attaché in Berlin, *Kapitan 1 Ranga* M.A. Vorontsov, sent a new warning, the *Narkom* for the Navy, Admiral Kuznetsov, asked the *Narkom* for Defence, Marshal Timoshenko, and the Chief of the General Staff, Army General Zhukov, for permission to order Readiness Grade No. 1, which was given at 23.50 hours and transmitted to the fleets.[3]

The Commands of the Army Groups and Armies had greater problems. When during the night of 21/22 June reports came in about German deserters who had reported the impending attack, it was very difficult for the Soviet General Staff, closely controlled by the reluctant Stalin, with the crowded rail and road connections in the newly won areas of the western Ukraine and Belorussia, to change from the ongoing deployment for an offensive attack to a defensive deployment. So the deep German thrusts caused great disorder and many unclear situations, which were made worse by the given and often countermanded orders. It took almost a week before Stalin began to react not only by orders to shoot unlucky commanders, but by supporting the efforts of the General Staff to bring order back again into the leadership. On 30 June the defence of the Soviet Union was put under the new *Gosudarstvennyi Komitet Oborony* (*GKO*), of which Stalin took over the chairmanship on 1 July. It was composed of the Bolshevik functionaries N.A. Bulganin, L.M. Kaganovich, G.M. Malenkov, A.I. Mikoyan, V.M. Molotov, K.E. Voroshilov and N.A. Vosnessenskii. Now the High Command of the Red Army *Stavka* tried to organize a coherent defence and to bring up reserves, but the German Army Groups had already achieved deep penetrations and had encircled strong parts of the West Front, and mauled many other formations heavily.[4]

CONSEQUENCES FOR THE SOVIET NAVY OF THE GERMAN ATTACK UP TO MID-1942

For the Soviet Navy the situation was very difficult. The operational planning for a 'Big Ocean-Going Fleet' was out of date, because there were almost no ships for this programme ready for operations. But the 'Small War at Sea' concept could not be put to work either, because after a short time the deep German thrusts had endangered naval bases. In the Baltic, Liepaja and Riga were lost on 28 June and 1 July. The Finnish declaration of war on 26 June threatened the new base Hangö at the entrance to the Finnish Gulf, and the German thrust in the direction of Leningrad endangered the Estonian base Tallinn. In the Black Sea the German–Romanian attack across the Dnestr threatened the important harbour of Odessa with encirclement. In the North the German attack in the direction of Murmansk was stopped at the Litsa, and the Fishermen's Peninsula was held with the support of the Northern Fleet, thus covering the entrance to the Kola Gulf.

In this situation, it was necessary to readjust the shipbuilding programme. So on 9 and 19 July orders went out from the High Command to continue with the completion only of ships in an advanced state, while the others, especially the big ships, were to be put into conservation for the duration of the war, and the laying down of new ships was stopped. The changes ordered are given in Table 9.1.[5]

The necessary evacuations of harbours and bases led to the first losses of, and heavy damage to, ships, especially in the Baltic. In Liepaja some vessels under repair had to be scuttled.[6] Only a few submarines could be sent for operations, while the other ships had to be sent first to Tallinn, which led to additional losses and damage from German minefields.[7] Other ships were able to lay some planned mine barrages off the Finnish Gulf, in the Irben Strait and off Liepaja. In the Black Sea a first offensive operation, a gunfire attack against Konstanţa, ended in failure.[8] The Northern Fleet was engaged in arming a number of former fishing vessels as patrol ships and minesweepers, while the merchant ships were evacuated from Murmansk to the White Sea.[9]

The following are the changes ordered on 9 and 19 July 1941 for the shipbuilding programme:

Table 9.1: Shipbuilding at the outset of the Great Patriotic War (June 1941)

Ship types	Building on 22.6.41	Of those laid down up to 31.12.40	Laid down 1.1–22.6.41	Put into conservation by GKO	Building to be continued
Battleships (*pr.23*)	3	3	–	3	–
Battlecruisers (*pr.69*)	2	2	–	2	–
Cruiser (*pr.83*)	1	1	–	–	1
Cruisers (*pr.68*)	7	6	1	5	2
Cruisers (*pr.26-bis 2*)	2	2	–	–	2
Destroyer Leaders (*pr.48*)	2	2	–	–	2
Destroyers (*pr.30*)	26	19	7	25	1
Destroyers (*pr.7U*)	9	9	–	–	9
Destroyers (*pr.7*)	7	7	–	–	7
Exper. Destroyer (*pr.45*)	1	1	–	–	1
Patrol Ships (*pr.29*)	16	11	5	14	2
Patrol Ship (*pr.52*)	1	1	–	1	–
Minesweepers (*pr.53U*)	4	1	3	3	1
Minesweepers (*pr.58*)	4	2	2	2	2
Minesweepers (*pr.59*)	20	19	1	18	2
River Monitors	6	6	–	3	3
Net-layers	10	8	2	2	8
Big Sub-Hunters	10	6	4	4	6
Test Vessels	2	2	–	2	–
Surface Vessels	133	108	25	84	49
Submarines (*ser.IX-bis*)	21	18	3	7	14
Submarines (*ser.X-bis*)	17	13	4	10	7
Submarines (*ser.XII-bis*)	19	17	2	2	17
Submarines (*ser.XIII-bis*)	6	6	–	–	6
Submarines (*ser.XIV*)	6	6	–	1	5
Submarines (*ser.XV*)	14	4	10	14	–
Submarines (*ser.XVI*)	8	–	8	8	–
Submarines	91	64	27	42	49

The yards made great efforts to finish the vessels already launched for commissioning. In the Baltic the following were completed in the second half of 1941:

Destroyers (*pr.7U*): *Statnyi*, *Sil'nyi*, *Skoryi*, *Svirepyi*, *Strogii*, *Strojnyi*
Destroyer (*pr.45*): *Opytnyi*
Minesweeper (*pr.53U*): *T-217*
Submarines (*ser.IX-bis*): *S-11*, *S-12*, *S-13*
Submarines (*ser.X-bis*): *Shch-407*, *Shch-408*

In the Black Sea the following were completed:

Destroyers (*pr.7U*): *Sovershennyi*, *Sposobnyi*
Submarine (*pr.X-bis*): *Schch-216*
Submarines (*pr.XII*): *M-111*, *M-112*, *M-113*, *M-117*, *M-118*, *M-120*
Submarine (*pr.XIII-bis*): *L-23*

The following were transferred to the Northern Fleet from the Baltic by the 'Stalin'-Canal:

Submarines (*pr.IX-bis*): *S-101*, *S-102*
Submarines (*pr.XIV*): *K-3*, *K-21*, *K-22*, *K-23*
Submarines (*pr.XIII-bis*): *L-20*, *L-22* (to be operational in 1942)

For the Pacific Fleet the following were completed:

Destroyers (*pr.7*): *Reshitel'nyi (II)*, *Retivyi*, *Razumnyi*, *Raz'yarennyi*, *Revnostnyi*
Submarines (*ser.IX-bis*): *S-55*, *S-56*, *S-51*
Submarines (*ser.X-bis*): *Shch-135*, *Shch-136*, *Shch-137*, *Shch-138*
Submarines (*ser.XII*): *M-114*, *M-115*, *M-116*[10]

But soon the new planning dates of July 1941 had to be corrected again. In the Black Sea, Odessa was encircled and the main yard harbour Nikolaev was in danger of being captured by the Germans. So the vessels already launched had to be towed away to Caucasian ports and the vessels on the slips had to be demolished.[11]

In the Baltic the Soviet forces soon had to retreat from the Bay of Riga and the islands of Oesel and Dagoe, there losing some ships and submarines to mines or air attacks. In late August Tallinn was encircled, and Hangö was under siege and both had at first to be supplied by convoys, which had to pass the dense German–Finnish mine-barrages north of Cape Juminda, which caused additional losses. Finally on 28 August Tallinn had to be evacuated in large convoys, which suffered heavy losses on the mines.[12] In early September the German 17th Army arrived off the southern suburbs of Leningrad and heavy batteries started to fire on the ships of the Baltic Fleet which were also bombed by German dive bombers, again causing heavy losses and heavy damage.[13] Of the submarines sent to operate in the open Baltic some were lost in the Finnish Gulf, others on their return voyage or on supply missions.[14]

Finally in November 1941 the base at Hangö had to be evacuated, causing additional losses.[15] At the end of the year Leningrad was enclosed from the south by the Germans, and in the north by the Finns. Under such conditions all efforts had to be concentrated on the defence of the city, and shipbuilding came to a standstill, but when weather conditions permitted, repair work on the damaged ships was continued.

In the Black Sea in October the main base of the Black Sea Fleet at Sevastopol was cut off from its land connections, and supply requirements made the evacuation of the encircled Odessa necessary; this was successfully accomplished. But the supply operations for the fortress of Sevastopol under siege, the efforts to break off the encirclement by a big amphibious operation in December, and the many bombardment missions to support the defenders added great stress to the ships and submarines of the fleet with new losses up to the early part of July 1942.[16] In addition, the submarines of the Black Sea Fleet had up to the end of June 1942 suffered heavy losses, mainly on the German–Romanian flanking mine-barrages off the coastal sea-routes.[17]

The Submarine Brigade of the Northern Fleet was strengthened by some units transferred from the Baltic Fleet by way of the Baltic–White Sea Canal for its operations against the German supply traffic off the coasts off north Norway, where they were supported for some months by a few British submarines, operating out of the Kola Gulf. The destroyers and patrol ships had to support the Army units at the Litsa Front and to assist in escorting the Allied Murmansk convoys on the last part of their voyages north of the Kola Fjord. To help in minesweeping, the British had some minesweepers and minesweeper-trawlers sent to the Kola Gulf.[18]

While shipbuilding in Komsomol'sk and Vladivostok continued, there were also some losses from accidents, and in summer 1942 some destroyers were sent on the Northern Sea Route to the Northern Fleet, as were six submarines by way of the Panama Canal and Iceland.[19]

At the big submarine yard at Gorkii construction continued. Just before the war started some small submarines destined for the Black Sea had been to the *Marti* yard at Nikolaev and were completed before the Germans occupied the city. Others went by rail to Vladivostok or directly via the inland waterways to the Northern Fleet. The launched medium submarines went south down the Volga to Astrakhan and Baku for completion and training in the Caspian Sea, before being sent by inland waterways mostly to the Northern Fleet.[20]

PLANNING AND DESIGN PROCESSES DURING THE WAR: SURFACE SHIPS AND VESSELS

With Leningrad under siege and the main building yards in the Black Sea lost, building of bigger ships in the western Soviet Union came to a standstill from 1942 to 1944. Only in the Far East did the building of the prefabricated vessels continue. More than 50 per cent of the shipbuilding industry capacities were turned over to the manufacture of other military products, mainly for the Army. But the small inland yards tried with great efforts to produce small surface vessels like MTBs, submarine chasers, minesweepers and small patrol boats.

The Main Staff of the Navy continued to plan for new ships. So on 2 May 1942 a new plan for 1942 was confirmed, containing for completion one cruiser, three destroyers and patrol ships, five minesweepers, two big monitors, 29 big sub-chasers (*BO*-), 26 submarines, 198 MTBs (*TK*), small sub-chasers (*MO*), and armoured cutters (*BKA*), 143 minesweeping cutters, and 721 support and auxiliary vessels, of which really one cruiser (*Kalinin* for the Pacific Fleet), three destroyers and patrol ships (*Redkii* and *Rezkii* for the Pacific Fleet and *Svobodnyi* for the Black Sea Fleet), one minesweeper (*Vladimir Polukhin* for the Baltic Fleet), one monitor (*Khasan* for the Amur Flotilla), three *BO*-sub-chasers (*projekt 122 Torpedist, Zenitchik, Botsman* for the Baltic Fleet, later transferred to the Black Sea), 13 submarines (*K-52, K-56* for the Baltic Fleet, *L-24* for the Black Sea Fleet, *L-20, L-22, M-119, M-121, M-122* for the Northern Fleet, and *S-14, S-103, S-104, S-15* for the Caspian Flotilla, later transferred to the Northern Fleet), and the experimental submarine *M-401* for the Caspian Flotilla, 62 *MO-*, *TK-*, *BKA*-cutters, 80 minesweeping cutters, and 508 other vessels were commissioned.[21]

For 1943 there was a new plan for the completion of the following vessels: one cruiser, five destroyers and patrol vessels, four minesweepers, 20 *BO*-sub-chasers, 16 submarines, two monitors (*projekt 1190*), 335 *MO-*, *TK-*, *BKA*-cutters, 112 minesweeping cutters and 433 other vessels. Of these only two destroyers and patrol vessels (the damaged destroyer *Storozhevoi* and the damaged patrol vessel *Tajfun* for the Baltic Fleet), one minesweeper (the new *Vasilii Gromov* for the Baltic Fleet), one *BO*-sub-chaser (*Marsovoi*, later transferred to the Black Sea Fleet), 13 submarines (*K-51, K-53, L-21* for the Baltic Fleet, *M-104, M-105, M-106, M-107, M-108, M-200, M-201* for the Northern Fleet, *S-16* for the Caspian Flotilla and later transferred to the Northern Fleet, *S-52, S-53* for the Pacific Fleet), one monitor (*Perekop* for the Amur Flotilla), 177 *MO-*, *TK-* and *BKA*-cutters, 93 minesweeping cutters, and 403 other vessels were commissioned.[22]

In 1944 the plan was to complete one cruiser, five destroyers and patrol ships, two minesweepers, 24 *BO*-sub-chasers, 12 submarines, 200 *MO-*, *TK-* and *BKA*-cutters, 145 minesweeping cutters, 2 net-layers, and 346 other small vessels. Really completed and commissioned were one cruiser (*Lazar Kaganovich* for the Pacific Fleet), one patrol ship (*Yastreb*) and one minesweeper (*T-219/ Kontradmiral Choroshkhin*) for the Baltic Fleet, 7 *BO*-sub-chasers (*Dal'nomershchik* for the Baltic Fleet and *Shturman, Rulevoi, Mekhanik, Mashinist, Turbinist* and *Tryumnyi* for the Northern Fleet), five submarines (*K-55* for the Baltic Fleet, *S-19* for the Caspian Flotilla and later transferred to the Northern Fleet, and *M-202* and *M-203* for the Black Sea Fleet), 216 *MO-*, *TK-* and *BKA*-cutters, 123 minesweeping cutters, two net-layers, and 205 other vessels.[23]

Up to the end of the European War in May 1945, there had been one destroyer (*Ognevoi* for the Black Sea Fleet), two *BO*-sub-chasers (*Prozhektorist* and *Navodchik*) and two submarines (*S-17* and *S-20*) commissioned for the Baltic Fleet.

The dates show that the main efforts were directed to the building of small vessels like the *MO*-cutters, the torpedo cutters and the armoured cutters for river warfare. No less than 920 combat motor boats and 1,375 other floating units were completed.[24]

In addition to the completion of warships, small combat units and submarines it was of the greatest importance to improve the capabilities of sea transport. In all fleet areas the available merchant ships and fishing vessels were 'mobilized' for use as transport vessels or as naval auxiliaries, especially as auxiliary minesweepers or patrol ships. And the war situation made it necessary in some places to build extremely rapidly special vessels, as for example steel barges for supplying the besieged Leningrad over the Ladoga Lake.[25] And great efforts had to be invested into the repair of damaged ships.

All this made it necessary to reorganise the shipbuilding processes. The *GKO* organized a committee with the Deputy *Narkom* for the Navy, Admiral L.M. Galler, the Chief of the Warship-Building Administration, *Inzhener-Vitse-Admiral* N.V. Isachenkov, for the naval vessels, and the Deputy *Narkom* for Merchant Shipbuilding, A.M. Red'kin, and the Chief of the Central Shipbuilding Administration, V.I. Alferov.[26] They had to formulate the requirements which were then sent to the several construction bureaus, divided for their special tasks. But with the Germans at the threshold of the most important building centres, many of the bureaus had to be evacuated to the east. So the Scientific Technical Committee (*NTK VMF*) under its chief A.A. Zhukov at Leningrad had to establish dependencies at Khazan under V.G. Vlasov, at Gorkii under M.A. Rudnitskii and at Moscow under Yu.P. Potapov. And many of the yards at Leningrad and Nikolaev had to transfer members of their personnel to other yards at Molotovsk in the North, Gorkii and Astrakhan on the Volga, to Poti and Batumi on the Caucasian coast, or to Komsomol'sk, Vladivostok and even Sovetskaya Gavan in the Far East.[27]

Of the construction bureaus, the *TsKB-4* (under Ya.M. Matskii) was now responsible for the development of battleship and aircraft carrier designs, *TsKB-17* (under N.P. Dubinin) for the cruisers and destroyers, *TsKB-18* (under P.A. Apukhtin) for the submarines, *TsKB-19* (under V.V. Manukhov) for special vessels, *TsKB-32* (under A.A. Yakovlev) for small surface vessels, *TsKB-51* (under P.A. Sergeev) for river warships, *TsKB-52* for electro equipment, *TsKB-36* for mines and minesweeping gear, *TsKB-39* for torpedoes. All these bureaus continued with their design work, notwithstanding the fact that most of them had to be evacuated from their pre-war sites to places in the east.[28]

Battleships and Battlecruisers

In December 1939 the design of the battleships of *projekt 23* had been changed to improve the anti-aircraft armament and underwater protection. To gain the space for adding two 100mm twin multi-purpose turrets to the planned four turrets, the six 152mm twin turrets had to be changed into four 152mm triple turrets. The planned underwater side protection after the Italian-designed *Pugliese* system was changed to the American system from the Gibbs & Cox designs. By using slender lines it was hoped to raise the top speed to 30kt. The new design *projekt 23-bis* had a standard displacement of 60,800t. But on 3 March 1940 the then Chief of the Main Staff, Admiral Galler, had proposed another change to *projekt 23NU*, which was about the same size, but with a strengthened A/A armament of eight twin 100mm turrets. In September 1940 two competitive designs were presented by the *TsKB-4* and the *NTK* with differing A/A armaments and displacements, to be followed during the following years by several variants.[29]

In May 1941 a preliminary *OTZ* for battleships of the *VMF* was presented to the design bureaus with an armament of three triple 406mm turrets, six twin 152mm turrets, 16 100mm multi-purpose guns, six *KOR-2* aircraft, a speed of 30kt, and an economic range of 10,000 miles. In July 1941 the *TsKB-4* presented a first treatise for a *projekt 24* battleship, followed in March 1942 by a drawing project, and in July 1942 by a construction proposal. This was further developed in 1943 and 1944, when the design process was given to *TsKB-17*, which prepared several variants of the design with different armaments.[30] At the beginning of 1945 a commission under Vice Admiral S.P. Stavitskii checked the variants and chose the proposal with 75,000t, a maximum speed of 30kt, a cruising speed of 24kt and an economical speed of 18kt, a range of 8,000 miles, and an armament of nine 406mm in three triple turrets, 24 130mm in twin dual purpose turrets, 48 45mm and 60 25mm multi-purpose guns. The armour should withstand a 1,000-kilo aircraft bomb dropped from a height of 5,000m. Two catapults and six aircraft were scheduled. The project was proposed for after the war and the fate of the project is related in a later chapter.[31]

For the battlecruisers of *projekt 69* the final draft with the new German armament was not presented for approval to the *Narkom* for the Navy until 16 October 1940, and by May 1941 the *TsKB-17* had finished the technical details. But after the war began the plans had to be changed back to the original ones. A few weeks later the two laid down vessels were put into conservation, and the *Sevastopol'* at Nikolaev was lost with the German occupation.

Heavy and Light Cruisers

In March 1941 the new Chief of the Main Staff, Admiral I.S. Isakov, sent a new requirement for a heavy cruiser to the *TsKB-17*, which in October 1941 had completed a preliminary drawing, called *projekt 82*, but this had to be put aside for two years. In September 1943 the Main Staff of the *VMF* sent a new *OTZ* to the *TsKB-17* for a heavy cruiser, superior to the 203mm armed cruisers of the other sea powers, armed with nine 210 to 230mm guns, 12 130mm, 32 37mm and four aircraft, with armour against 203mm shells and a displacement of 20,000 to 22,000t. Six variants were designed, and in November 1944 the *OTZ* was changed to a ship of 25,000–26,000t, a speed of 33kt, and an armament of nine 220mm guns.[32]

The building of the light cruisers of *projekt 68* was also interrupted by the war. One of the cruisers on the slip at Leningrad, the *Chkalov*, was redesigned to have German 150mm triple turrets as *projekt 68-I*, but the plan, finished in July 1941, could not be realized and the redesigned ship could only be launched after the war. The *Chapaev* and *Zheleznyakov* at Leningrad remained in conservation, and the *Frunze* and *Kujbyshev* which were towed away from Nikolaev, remained at Poti and Batumi, where the aft of the *Frunze* had to be used to repair the damaged *Molotov*. After the end of the war in the Black Sea both vessels were towed back to Nikolaev for completion to a corrected design *projekt 68K*, to be described in another chapter. The *Ordzhonikidze* and *Sverdlov* on the slips at Nikolaev fell to the Germans heavily damaged. The other four cruisers planned to be laid down in the second half year of 1941 as well as the four additional planned vessels had to be cancelled. The small light cruiser

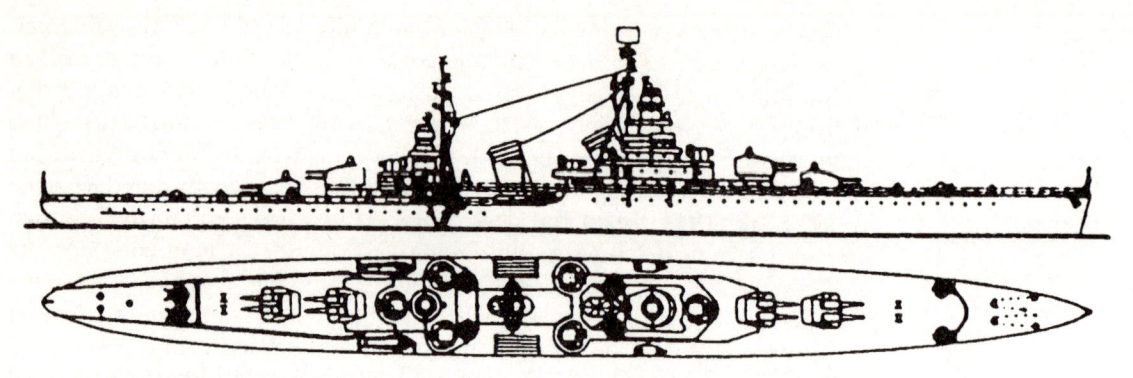

Fig. 12. Light cruiser *projekt MK*, no name given, 1940, displ. 6,095t stdd., length 183.2m, max. speed 36kt, several variants of the design, with 8, 10, 12 13cm, or 8 or 9 15.2cm. This design had 16 13cm in four quadruple turrets with the guns paired and superfiring. Credit: Morskoi sbornik

design *MK* of the *NKVD*-administered construction bureau for the *Sudomekh* yard at Leningrad of 6,100t with six 152mm, six 100mm, eight 37mm and two triple torpedo tube sets of 533mm, a catapult and one aircraft was not continued after March 1940.[33] There were many variants to this design.

Aircraft Carriers

At the start of the war aircraft carriers were not considered as very important, so it was not until the Fourth Five-Year Plan of 1943–47 that two light carriers of *projekt 71* were planned. The director of the construction bureau *TsNII-45*, I.V. Kharitonov, had delivered two variants of this project; the first one to be selected was for a small carrier of 10,600t stdd., based on the hull of the cruiser of *projekt 68*, as described earlier, and a bigger carrier *projekt 71B* of 25,000t stdd., for 70 aircraft in two hangar decks. But this version could not go ahead because the slips had to be used for the battlecruisers. Observation of the first experiences of the war from 1939–40 led to a growing interest in carriers, and so the Chief of Naval Aviation asked the *Narkom* for the Aircraft Industry to develop a fighter and a reconnaissance and torpedo bomber for use from a carrier, which led to an order being placed at *Zavod 81* at Tushino to develop such planes. But in October 1940 the planned carriers were cancelled. One of the leaders opposing the carriers was Admiral Isakov. But the *Narkom* for the Navy, Admiral Kuznetsov, tried to obtain information about the experiences of the other navies, and in late 1942 he ordered the Main Staff to develop carrier designs. *Kontr Admiral* Yu. Panteleev proposed to get designs for carriers with 30, 45 and 60 aircraft. The design of the *TsKB-4* and then *17* under V.V. Ashik led to the carrier of *projekt 72*, a vessel of 23,700t stdd., with a hangar deck for 30 aircraft (a version for 60 aircraft was also designed). For defence only A/A armament was planned: eight 130mm, eight 85mm, 12 37mm and 24 25mm. With 144,000 HP a speed of 30k was envisaged. As aircraft, a Yakovlev fighter *Yak-9K*, and a Tupolev torpedo bomber *PT-M-71* were envisaged. But this project, although discussed from October 1943 to mid-1945, was not realized either. But during the war years there were many variants of aircraft carrier designs prepared, which had no chance of realization, for instance, a big proposal from Kostromitinov of 40,800t for 66 fighters and 40 torpedo bombers, or *variants 2* (escort carrier of 7,920t), *14* (escort carrier of 18,410t), *26* (fleet carrier of 30,560t), *27* (light carrier of 12,706t), *31* ('squadron' carrier of 35,720t), *33* (heavy carrier of 82,370t) or a fleet carrier for the Pacific and Northern Fleets of 30,000t, and a small carrier for the Baltic and Black Sea Fleets of 15,000t.[34]

Destroyer Leaders and Destroyers

The destroyer leaders of *projekt 48* had been cancelled in October 1940, and only the two vessels, launched at Nikolaev and towed to Caucasian ports in August 1941, were put into conservation there. When they were towed back after the end of the war in the Black Sea, the intention to complete the vessels to the improved design *projekt 48K* of 2,810t with a changed armament (six 130mm as before, but 12 37mm A/A and only six 533mm torpedo tubes) was never realized. The design was outstripped by those of the big destroyers of *projekts 35* and *40*, and the two ships were scrapped.[35]

Already on 8 March 1940 Admiral Kuznetsov had issued a *TTZ* for a destroyer of 2,200t with three 130mm twin turrets, a speed of 40kt and a range of 6,000 miles, as *projekt 35*. In April 1941 the *TsKB-32* had presented a drawing project, but it was not taken up when the future armament of the American *Gearing*-class with three 127mm twin-mounts became known. So on 26 August 1942 Kuznetsov asked for a new design, using elements of *projekt 35*, but with a heavier armament, so that the displacement had to be raised to 2,700t. *Projekt 40* was presented in September 1942 by the *TsKB-17* as a drawing project, which was improved up to early 1944 by a team made up of V.A. Nikitin, A.L. Fisher, I.F. Taptygin and others. Then on 10 March 1944 the *VMF* presented a new *TTZ*, raising the displacement to 3,000t to achieve a speed of 30kt. While Nikitin developed a special *projekt 40H* with 130mm turrets, Kuznetsov wanted heavier guns for the heavy destroyers for the Pacific and Northern Fleets. On 6 November 1944 the destroyer had 3,200t, and the armament was raised to two twin mounts of 152mm. The final fate of this project is described in a later chapter.[36]

The building of the destroyers of *projekt 7* continued in Komsomol'sk and Vladivostok until 29 November 1942, when the twelfth and last vessel, the *Redkii*, was commissioned. The last two vessels of *projekt 7U*, were provisionally commissioned on 22 September 1941, but they later got imported *Metro-Vickers* turbines of 24,000 HP to achieve their speed of 36kt. And the damaged lead ship of the type, the *Storozhevoi* was given during the repair a new forecastle with a 130mm twin mount from an uncompleted *projekt 30* destroyer. They also got Radar and Asdic sets.[37]

Projekt 30 suffered the most from the beginning of the war. At Leningrad two vessels of the *Zhdanov* yard were launched and had to be laid up during the war to be completed and updated after the end of the war to the design *30K*. The other six *Zhdanov* and the three *Ordzhonikidze* vessels on the slips had to be put into conservation, but only two of them were completed after the war. Of the Nikolaev ships the *Ognevoi* and *Ozornoi* were in August 1941 towed to Poti and in 1943 the completion was started on again at the *Sevmorzavod* yard, evacuated from Sevastopol to Batumi. But only the *Ognevoi* could be completed before the end of the war in March 1945. The *Ozornoi* returned to Nikolaev and was completed to the design *30K*. The other four vessels on the slips of the *No. 61 Kommunar* yard had to be destroyed before the Germans occupied the city. In the plan of 1942 the continuation of the building at Molotovsk in the North and Komsomol'sk in the Far East was decided. But of the four vessels already laid down at Molotovsk only the first was launched in August 1944 and completed, with the second one after the war to the design *30K*. At Komsomol'sk the building of three vessels was started in October 1940, and two more were laid down in September 1941, but progress there was slow and the first three vessels were completed after the war to the design *30A*, with American Westinghouse turbines, delivered under Lend-Lease. The size of *projekt 30* was increasing over the years: from 1,700t in 1938, to 1,890t in 1939, to 2,016t stdd. for the *Ognevoi* and 2,125t for *projekt 30K*. About *projekt 36*, a special version of this type, not much is known.[38]

In 1942 there was a plan to design a small destroyer for the Baltic and the inner seas of the Pacific. This *projekt 37* was developed from February to November 1944 by the *TsKB-32* under Ya.A. Koperzhinskii up to the technical project as a patrol ship (*Storozhevoi korabl'*) of 1,370t, with three 100mm guns and four 25mm automatic quadruple sets, three 533mm torpedo tubes and two depth-charge throwers, and a range of 3,940 miles.[39]

Patrol Ships and Minesweepers

Of the patrol ships of *projekt 29* on 22 June 1941 there were four already launched at the *Zhdanov* yard in Leningrad, and four more on the slips. Two more were laid down in Komsomol'sk and six in Sevastopol. Of these Leningrad vessels only the *Yastreb*, first put into conservation, was taken up and commissioned in December 1944, the other three were finished in an improved version *29K* with three 85mm guns instead of the 100mm planned, in 1950/51. The Komsomol'sk vessels were taken up again and launched in 1943/44 and commissioned in 1945 and 1947. The six vessels laid down in Sevastopol had to be destroyed before the Germans captured the fortress. The *TsKB-32* developed in 1944 an improved version as *projekt 29-bis* of 1,150t, with a speed of 29kt and three 100mm, four 37mm and a triple set of 533mm torpedoes.[40]

The big icebreaker patrol ship of *projekt 52*, the *Purga*, remained launched in April 1941 in conservation at the *Marti* yard in Leningrad and was not commissioned until 1954. In addition to this a small patrol vessel of 500t as *projekt 39* was designed, but never built.

Of the diesel-minesweepers of *projekt 53U* the last of the 1939 started units, the *T-217*, was commissioned in August 1941, but of the three laid down at the *Ust-Izhora* yard in spring 1941 the first two were taken up again and launched in 1943, but only *T-219*, which was transferred to the *Petrozavod* yard at Leningrad, was commissioned in 1944, the other two vessels only coming into the Baltic Fleet in 1946. Of the two vessels laid down to *projekt 58* for the Black Sea Fleet, the first, *T-414*, was launched at Sevastopol and towed away in January 1942 to Tuapse and in April 1942 to Poti, then brought back to

Nikolaev in April 1945 for completion, but was cancelled. The second had to be destroyed at Sevastopol before the Germans captured the fortress.[41]

The turbine 'squadron'-minesweepers of *projekt 59* were designed by the *TsKB-32* under L.M. Nogid and had originally in 1941 a displacement of 648t stdd., a sweeping speed of 19kt and were armed with two 100mm guns and one 37mm, and equipped with mechanical sweeping gear. Before the war began there were six laid down at the *Petrozavod* yard, and eight at the *Ust-Izhora* yard at Leningrad, and six at the *Sevmorzavod* at Sevastopol. Ten of the Leningrad vessels, and five of the Sevastopol's were launched before 22 June 1941, after which their building was interrupted. Building was started again for *T-250/Vladimir Polukhin* and *T-254/Vasilii Gromov*. These were completed in October 1942 and September 1943 for the Baltic Fleet with a somewhat strengthened A/A-armament of one 45mm, three 37mm, two 20mm and four MGs. Now 690t they achieved a top speed of 22.4kt. The other launched vessels were taken up after the war and completed to an improved design *projekt 59K*, of 725t, with a changed armament of two 85mm A/A and three 37mm A/A guns and six MGs and besides the mechanical sweeping gear also an acoustic gear and an asdic set. Twelve vessels at Leningrad were commissioned from 1947 to 1949. The Sevastopol vessels were towed in January 1942 to Tuapse and later to Poti, but *T-451* was wrecked during a storm at Tuapse on 22 January 1942, and *T-453* was stranded on 19 December 1944 off Sinope during the return towing operation to Sevastopol, where the other three were completed in 1948. The last Sevastopol boat was destroyed on the slips to avoid capture by the Germans.[42]

In August 1941 a new diesel-minesweeper as *projekt 73* was asked for with two diesel motors of 1,600 HP each for a sweeping speed of 14.5kt and a maximum speed of 18.5kt. Two 100mm and one 37mm guns were planned as armament, and it was to have a mechanical sweeping gear. The 1942 plan envisaged a displacement of 665t stdd. During the war there was no real progress with building, but the design was changed in 1945 to *projekt 73K* with General Motors diesel engines of 1,600 HP each, and the sweeping gear was augmented with electromagnetic and acoustic sets as well as an asdic. the displacement was raised to 690t stdd. But no vessel was laid down before the war ended.[43] In July/August 1942 another design for a big minesweeper of 675t was discussed as *projekt 263*, to be built at the *Petrozavod* yard, but nothing came of this idea.[44]

In April 1942 Admiral L.M. Galler issued a *TTZ* for a small inshore minesweeper, first called *projekt 253*, to be developed by the *TsKB-32* and to be built first at the *Ordzhonikidze* yard at Leningrad. The design was improved by the *TsKB-51* under N.G. Loshchinskii in 1943 in two versions, *MT-1* of 126t and *MT-2* of 147t as *projekt 253L*. The Commander of the Baltic Fleet, Admiral V.F. Tributs, and the Commander of the Baltic Fleet Squadron, Vice Admiral Yu.F. Rall', were very eager to get small minesweepers, and on 14 April the War Council of the *Leningrad Front* ordered 12 of these minesweepers, soon augmented to 32 vessels, on which the real building started on 12 June 1943 with the *MT-1* series *T-351–391* at the *Zhdanov* and *Petrozavod* yards. On 31 October 1944 the *MT-2* series was started at the *Ordzhonikidze*, *Petrozavod* and *Ust-Inzhora* yards at Leningrad with *T-222–249* and *T-434, 435,*

439–441, 459–479. Up to the end of 1945 no less than 92 units were commissioned.[45]

In March 1944 the *TsKB-17* presented a drawing project for a minesweeper of 300t, in a new version of 368t as *projekt 254*. No vessel of this type was laid down during the war, and in 1947 and 1950 new variants of this project were presented with 500t displacement.[46]

Small Surface Combatants

The submarine chasers of the bigger *projekt 122* were at first designed by the bureau of the *Marti* yard at Leningrad, and building had already started with recommendations of *TsKB-51* at Zelenodol'sk and Kiev in 1939/40, but the first two vessels *BO-101/Artillerist* and *BO-102/Miner* were transferred to the Caspian Sea and commissioned to an improved *projekt 122a* with 209t and a speed of 23.2kt in November 1941. The following vessels of a second series had 226t, were a little slower at 21.4kt, but had the same armament with one 76mm and three 12.7mm MGs and 16 heavy and 40 light depth charges, and were commissioned from June 1942 (*BO-103/Torpedist*) up to the end of 1945 with 21 additional units. In June 1944 they were transferred to the Black Sea; *BO-108–BO-110* remained on the Caspian Sea, *BO-122* was commissioned for the Pacific Fleet, while *BO-131–BO-142* came from April 1944 to August 1945 to join the Northern Fleet. In 1943 the armament was improved to one 85mm A/A, two 37mm, three MGs and 30 heavy and 20 light D/Cs and two depth-charge throwers. Additional improvements came with the two series of *projekt 122b* of 257t and 284t, developed in 1943 and 1944, but built only after the war. An additional *projekt 152* of 1943 of 273t and with two 85mm but otherwise similar equipment design was not realized.[47]

The small submarine chasers were build in much greater numbers; the biggest series was the *projekt P-10* or *MO-4* of 56.5t after the 1941 version of 26kt, and eight heavy and 24 light D/Cs. Of this type 219 units were commissioned in all. Another version was the *projekt 164/MO-6* of 1941 with 58t, 24.8kt and the same D/Cs, of which four units finally came to the Black Sea. Of the *projekt 194/BMO* of 52.8t in 1942 and 60.5t in 1943, 22kt and 16 D/Cs, 66 units were commissioned between 1943 and 1945 for the Baltic Fleet. Of the *projekt OD-200* of 45t, 28kt and 12 heavy and 24 light D/Cs 88 units were built from 1944 to 1945, and distributed between the Baltic, Black Sea and Pacific Fleets. Of the *projekt PP-19-OK* of 39t 56 units came to the fleets.[48] Some of the units got 20mm Oerlikon guns from Lend-Lease.[49]

The building of MTBs or torpedo cutters (*TK*) remained concentrated on the proved *G-5* type, of 15t, and a maximum speed of 35kt, which was built in several series mostly in inland yards. So the *Zavod 639* at Tyumen produced from 1942 to 1944 63 *TK*s of the *G-5 series XII* and *XIII*. Also the *Zavod No. 341* at Rybinsk was active in building these vessels, as were other metal works near rivers or inland seas. In all, 329 vessels were completed, including the vessels built before the war. They were distributed to all Fleets.[50]

There were some units for experiments with a rocket-gun *M-8-M*, which was also used on other *TK*-types. The leading vessel *AKA-5* or *No. 106* was commissioned at the *Zavod 639* on 5 May 1943.[51]

The second series built in greater numbers was the *projekt P-19/D-3* of 36t, a speed of 32kt, and two 533mm torpedo tubes, of which 59 came to the Baltic Fleet, 13 to the Northern Fleet and one to the Black Sea Fleet.[52]

In 1943 the *TsKB-32* developed a new *TK* as *projekt 123-bis* with 20.5t, and with two Packard diesels of 1,200 HP each with a speed of 51.6kt. It was armed with two 450mm torpedo tubes and four MGs. From this vessel, a development of the *Komsomolets* mentioned earlier, 31 units were built up to the end of 1945, most of them going to the Pacific Fleet.[53]

There were some other somewhat bigger projects, like the *STK-JUL*, *projekt 163* of 50t, or the *TM-200* of 46.9t, but of these types only a few vessels were built and these were mostly used for tests, while the great augmentation of the TKs came from the Lend-Lease deliveries to be mentioned later.

For the campaigns on rivers, on inland seas and along littorals the *Bronekater* (*BKA*), an armoured cutter with one or two 76mm tank guns turrets was developed following a *TTZ* of 1 March 1940 by Admiral Isakov. There were several similar projects with differing numbers like *138, 160, 161, 186, 194, 1124* and *1125* and so on. The bigger types like *161* and *186* had 163 or 164t, a speed of 13–14kt, and were armed with two *T-34* tank 76mm turrets, one 37 A/A gun and 4 MGs, the armour being 20–50mm strong. The crew was made up of 38 to 42 men. The smaller vessels like the *1124* and *1125* had 47 or 29t, a speed of 37 to 38km/h, and were armed with one *T-34* 76mm tank gun, and in some cases with mortars or rocket launchers *M-13-M1* or *M-8-M*. Of the *projekt 161* there were 20 units commissioned, of the *1124* 97 and of the *1125* 151 vessels. Other types were built only in small numbers in most cases for tests. They were used in the Black Sea, in the Baltic and the Pacific and the river flotillas – on the Amur with the bigger *BKAs* with two turrets and on the Dnepr with the smaller ones.[54]

For the river flotillas there were also special river monitors being built when the war started. They were partly based on earlier designs like the *SB-12/Udarnyi* of 367t, which was completed in 1934 and the *SB-30/Aktivnyi*, of which seven vessels came into commission for the Dnepr flotilla in 1936/37. A new, bigger version was the *SB-57* of 720t, the first of three vessels named *Shilka* (later renamed *Vidlitsa*), which were laid down in 1940 at Zaporozhe. They had two twin mounts of 130mm, two 45mm and three 12.7mm multiple A/A guns. But only the second vessel was launched, in September 1941, only to be scuttled at Kiev when the Germans reached the city, while the other two were destroyed on the slips. Two more were planned but not laid down.[55]

For the lower Amur river and the area of the Tartar Sound design work had already started in 1933 on a big river monitor at the *Krasnoe Sormovo* yard at Gorkii. The design was presented at the end of 1935 as *projekt 1190*. They had a displacement of 1703t stdd., with four diesel motors and a speed of about 15kt. Their armament consisted of three 130mm twin turrets, two 76mm A/A twin-mounts and three 45mm A/A twin mounts. In addition they could load 29 mines and 12 depth charges. Three vessels were laid down on 15 July 1936 at Gorkii, and then disassembled and sent in parts by rail to the *S.M. Kirov zavod* at Khabarovsk. They were relaid down from November 1939 to August 1940 and launched from August 1940 to October 1941. Because of great delays in the delivery of weapons and equipment the lead vessel *Khasan* (ex-*Lazo*) was only commissioned in December 1942 with the original armament, while the second, *Perekop* (ex-*Simbirtsev*), was commissioned in February 1944 with a preliminary main armament of three single 130mm guns and did not get its final armament until 1947. The last ship was the *Sivash* (ex-*Seryshev*), which got its final 130mm armoured gun turrets at the commission in October 1946.[56]

BUILDING AND PLANNING THE SUBMARINES

Design work on submarines was carried out at the *TsKB-18* and the designs, after acceptance, sent to the building yards. As mentioned, the war brought great problems to the building yards in the areas threatened by the German advances. Nikolaev was lost in August 1941 and Leningrad was under siege from September 1941, so that building there came to a stop. Only in the Far East could building be continued at a slow pace, while the inland yard *Krasnoe Sormove* at Gorkii continued to produce submarines, but they had in some cases to go south down the Volga river to Astrakhan and the Caspian Sea, and after their shake-down cruises and training to go by inland waterways mostly to the Northern Fleet. From the Black Sea some small submarines were also sent in 1942 to the Caspian Sea for training duty, but returned in 1943–44 to the Black Sea. Of the Far East submarines some of the bigger ones were – as mentioned – sent by way of the Panama Canal to the Northern Fleet, while some small ones in 1944 came by rail transport to the Black Sea, as did some of the small boats of the Northern Fleet.[57]

But, despite the difficulties with the actual building, planning and new design work continued with *TsKB-18*.

Big Submarines

Of the planned 62 big 'cruiser' submarines of the *series XIV/KU/projekt 40* and its successor *KE* only 12 were laid down – as mentioned – and six were commissioned before the war and five during the war, while *K-54*, launched in March 1941, was before completion damaged beyond repair by a German air raid and finally scrapped in 1949. Already by 1939/40 the follow-up *KE* was being designed under the supervision of M.A. Rudnitskii by B.M. Malinin and E.A. Deribin. The design, called *projekt 101*, had 1,550t normal and 2,185t submerged with an increased surface speed of 24kt, but otherwise about the same dates as the *series XIV*. But there was no possibility of building such submarines under wartime conditions when the technical project was ready in April 1942.[58]

The second type of big submarine for which the design had been started before the war was a successor to the minelaying submarines of *series XIII-bis*, at first called *MZ* and later *projekt 99*. Already in 1938 I.S. Isakov had issued a *TTZ* for a minelayer with a greater mine capacity, and the *TsKB-18* and the design bureau of the *Sudomekh* yard developed variants of this type with 1,230t surfaced and 1,580t submerged, a speed of 18kt surfaced and 8kt submerged, and a reduced torpedo armament of only four 533mm tubes with four reserve torpedoes, but 60 mines. One 100mm gun and two MGs were also planned. But this design suffered the same fate as the *KE-projekt*.[59]

In 1943 the project numbers of the submarines were changed from *95–106* to *601*ff. During 1943 the *TsKB-18* produced five variants of a new big submarine, which were presented to Admiral Kutznetsov on 29 January 1944 as the follow-on versions of the *KU/KE*-projects as *projekt 611*. It was planned with 1,100t surfaced and should have had six 533mm torpedo tubes at the bow and four at the stern with 12 and four reserve torpedoes. The surface armament was designed with one 100mm gun and four 45mm automatic A/A guns. The surface speed was planned as 22kt, the submerged speed as 9–10kt. But the building of this type of submarine could also not be started during the war. Its further fate is described in a later chapter.[60]

Medium Submarines

The building of the medium submarines of the *series IX-bis* was continued during the war. Three launched vessels were commissioned in 1941 in Leningrad. The launched submarines at Gorkii were sent to Astrakhan for commissioning and made their training cruises in the Caspian Sea before being transported on the inland waterways to the Northern Fleet, four in 1943 and two in 1944, while three others went in 1945 to the Baltic Fleet. Six launched vessels only were completed from 1946 to 1948, and the other ten just laid down and the ordered units cancelled, as were two others planned at Leningrad. Of the Black Sea vessels, one was towed to Caucasian ports and was not completed until 1948, while three more had to be destroyed at Nikolaev before the Germans occupied the city. Of the Far East vessels five were commissioned during the war, and of these four were transferred to the Northern Fleet.[61]

An improved *series XVI/projekt 97* was designed by the *TsKB-18* and the first 14 orders went to the *Sudomekh* yard at Leningrad (5), the *Marti* yard at Nikolaev (5) and the *Krasnoe Sormove* yard at Gorkii (4). Three each were laid down just before the war started at Leningrad and Nikolaev but had to be cancelled in July 1941 and broken up. But work on the design was corrected up to November 1942 before work was concentrated on the smaller follow-on series for the *series X-bis*.[62]

Of the *series X-bis* – as mentioned – nine submarines were commissioned after the war started in 1941, four for the Pacific, four for the Baltic and one for the Black Sea. Of the four Baltic vessels launched in May and June 1941 the first two were commissioned in 1946, the last two were not taken up again and scrapped after the war.[63] But against the discontinuation of the *series X-bis* planned for improved versions of this size continued during the war. First there was in 1942 a *projekt 106* of 590t, with a speed of 15kt surfaced and 8kt submerged, and six bow and two stern torpedo tubes of 533mm and eight reserve torpedoes. This was continued from August 1942 as *projekt 608*, but on an order of the *Narkom* for the Navy, Admiral Kuznetsov, on 11 September 1943 this project was to be designed as the follow-on medium submarine by the *TsKB-18*. It then had 640t, a surface speed of 18kt, and a submerged speed of 9.5–10kt, and was to have four bow and two stern torpedo tubes of 533mm and only four reserve torpedoes, and for surface engagements one 76mm and one 25mm A/A automatics. For minelaying there were two variants, one for torpedo-mines *PLT-3*, and one for 25–30 mines of type *PLT-N*. In 1944 the design was again improved, with the A/A armament was now to be two 25mm automatics, and the mine capacity of the second variant 40 mines in special tubes. The surfaced displacement rose to 660t. In October 1944 I.G. Malyashkin of the design bureau of the *Marti* yard in Leningrad produced an additional version as *projekt 608-1* of 687t. But after the German U-Boat *U 250*, sunk on 30 July 1944 in the Koivisto Strait by the sub-hunter *MO-103*, was raised on 7 September and put into the dry dock at Kronshtadt on 25 September, Kuznetsov wanted to include the improvements observed from investigations of this boat into the new medium submarine, and in 1945 *projekt 608* was finished and work was concentrated on the new *projekt 613*, described in a later chapter.[64]

Small Submarines

The completion of the *series XII* submarines continued in 1941 with six units for the Black Sea Fleet, three for the Pacific Fleet, built at the *Krasnoe Sormovo* yard at Gorkii and transferred by rail. In 1942 three boats were completed and sent to the Northern Fleet, as were five more in 1943. In 1943 there was one *series VI-bis*, and three *series XII* boats transferred from Poti to Baku and used during the year in the Caspian Sea as training vessels, but brought back at the end of the year and early 1944. The number of submarines in the Black Sea was further augmented in 1944 by the transfer of six *series VI* and four *series XII*-boats from the Pacific Fleet and three *series XII* from the Northern Fleet.[65]

In 1942 the medium *series V-* submarine *Shch-101* was rebuilt at Vladivostok to carry 40 mines in special tubes, after this model the *series XII*-submarine *M-171* was in 1943/44 rebuilt as a minelayer as *projekt 604*, of 234.8t surfaced with mine tubes at the side for 18 mines of the type *PLT*, to be completed in August 1944 for the Northern Fleet and used in October to lay 87 mines.[66]

There was already in 1938 a new *TTZ* for an improved *M*-class submarine of about 250t with four torpedo tubes, and on 23 July 1939 the *TsKB-18* presented the drawing project of a *M-VII*-class submarine, called *series XV*, of 278t, raised to 280t for the finalized technical project, delivered on 8 February 1940. A few weeks later, on 31 March, the first two boats were laid down at the *Sudomekh* yard in Leningrad, followed by five more before the end of the year. In the spring of 1941 there followed eight more at the *Krasnoe Sormovo* yard at Gorkii. The first four Leningrad boats were launched in July 1941 and then transferred on the inland waterways to Astrakhan for completion. The first two were commissioned in 1943 and then transferred to the Northern Fleet, and became operational there in December 1943 and January 1944. The next two vessels were transferred from Baku to Poti and arrived in the Black Sea in June 1944 and January 1945. The last three laid-down boats in Leningrad were not launched until after the war and commissioned in 1947. Of the eight Gorkii, boats six were transferred to Molotovsk, but building did not progress much, and after the war only one was completed there in 1947; the others were transferred to Leningrad for completion, but one was destroyed during transport. The other five were completed in 1947. The two other boats remained in Gorkii and were transferred after the war to Leningrad for completion and commissioned in 1948. The designers of *TsKB-18* under Z.A. Deribin and the chief constructor F.F. Polyushkin were honoured with a 'Stalin' Prize 1st Class.[67]

The design of this small submarine type was continued during the war. First a new *projekt 105* was envisaged in 1942 of 250–300t with a surface speed of 14–16kt, and submerged 8kt, but with four bow and two stern torpedo tubes of 450mm. The *TsKB-18* in addition developed in 1942 a *projekt 602*, and in 1944 a *projekt 612* of 325t, again with four bow and two stern torpedoes but of 533mm, in three variants, of which one finally in 1946 reached 400t. But at the end of the war it was necessary to increase as soon as possible the number of submarines, and so in 1947 a series of 46 *projekt 96-bis* submarines, designed after 1942, was started at the *Sudomekh* yard at Leningrad, and completed between 1948 and 1953.[68]

Special and Midget Submarines

From 1933–36, there was a first experimental design started by S.A. Vasilevskii for a small submarine with diesel exhaust circulation drive, called *Regenerativnyi edinyi dvigatel' osobyi* (*REDO*). On 5 September 1936 a vessel of the *series XII* size was laid down at the *Sudomekh* yard as *S.92* and later *R-1*. It was launched on 4 August 1938, and on 25 November 1938 the tests started. But when the war came it had to be laid up and was never completed. Another design by V.S. Dmitrievskii of such a vessel was built as *projekt 95* at Gorkii with a surface displacement of 102t, submerged 140t. It had a surface speed of 23kt, and submerged 14.5kt. It was armed with two 533mm torpedoes. It was laid down on 28 November 1939 and transferred in May 1941 to the Caspian Sea, where as *M-401* it made several test runs, covering altogether a distance of 2,800 miles, 360 miles of which submerged.[69]

Of the midget submarines there were some designs in the 1930s, as mentioned earlier, for example, the *APSS* of V.I. Bekauri and the *Pigmej* (*APL*) which was sent to the Black Sea but not commissioned. In 1939 there was another *projekt 80* by V.L. Bzhezinskii of a 'submerging torpedo cutter' of 34.3t

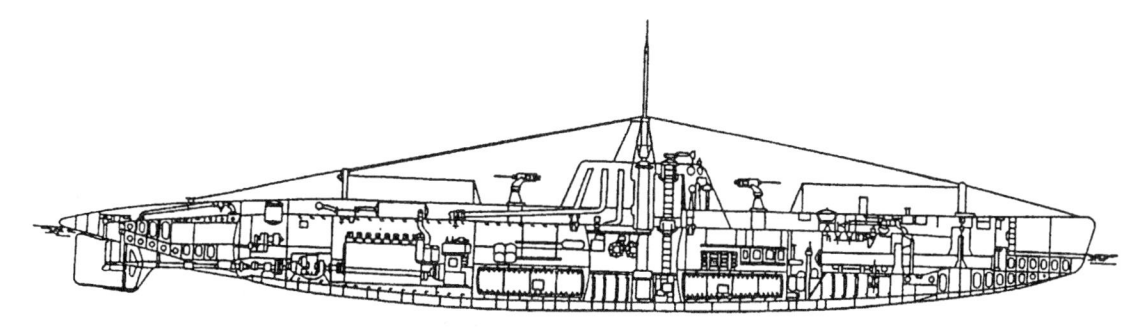

Fig. 13. Experimental submarine REDO, *R-1*, ex-*S.92*, 1938, displ. 203.5/258t normal, length 44.5m, max. speed 13/9.75kt, 2 torpedo tubes 53.3cm, 2 4.5cm. Not completed.
Credit: The Berezhnoi Collection

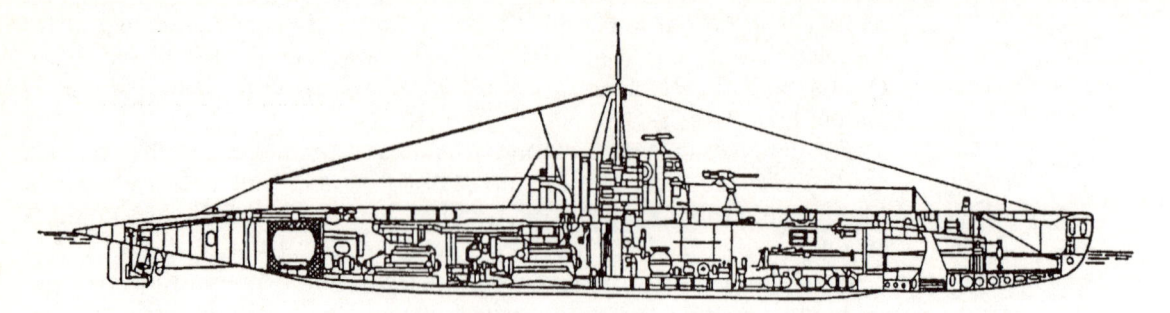

Fig. 14. Experimental submarine *projekt 95*, *M-401*, 1941, displ. 101.8t normal, length 37.3m, max. speed 23/14.5kt, 2 torpedo tubes 53.3cm, 1 4.5cm. Built during 1939–42, tested in the Caspian Sea. Credit: The Berezhnoi Collection

surfaced and 74.0t submerged. It was to have attained a surface speed of 33kt, and 11kt submerged and have two torpedoes of 450mm. The vessel was started in 1939 at Gorkii, but the *M-400* was never completed either. In 1942 the *TsKB-18* prepared a drawing of a *projekt 606* midget of 34t and a speed of 8kt with two torpedoes of 450mm. The vessel was to have been built in *Zavod 345* at Yaroslavl. In 1943 this design was improved to *projekt 606-bis* with 36.5t, a higher speed of 11kt surfaced and 6.5kt submerged, and six instead of four crew members. In August 1943 this design was again improved by the *TsKB-18* to *projekt 610* of 40t and almost the same dates, but despite a conference on 21 August 1943 with Admiral Kuznetsov and the *Narkom* for shipbuilding, I.I. Nosenko, and high-ranking officers, nothing came of the discussions and no vessel was ever completed.[70]

In autumn 1941 the submarines of *series IV* proved during the efforts to supply the besieged fortress of Hangö to be insufficient, so the idea emerged to construct a special transport submarine. But the design *projekt 605* of 250–300t, started on 21 February 1942, was too small, and when in June 1942 the Black Sea submarines were used to transport supplies into the fortress at Sevastopol under siege, a bigger transport submarine was designed by Ya.E. Evgrafov in July 1942 as *projekt 607* of 740t surfaced and 984t submerged, able to load 865t of supplies. This was improved in 1943 and 1944 by the *TsKB-18*, and had then two big loading rooms and was driven by one diesel of 685 HP and one electric motor. But no vessels of this type were really laid down either.[71] After the war even bigger transport and amphibious landing submarines were designed, but never built, as is to be mentioned later.

LEND-LEASE DELIVERIES OF NAVAL VESSELS

Soon after the Lend-Lease conditions were extended to the military and naval assistance for the Soviet Union, the Deputy *Narkom* for the Navy, Admiral L.M. Galler, asked the US officials responsible for American–Soviet military cooperation for delivery of cruisers and destroyers. Although the Americans did not satisfy such large requests, the Soviet Navy leaders tried to seek a way to

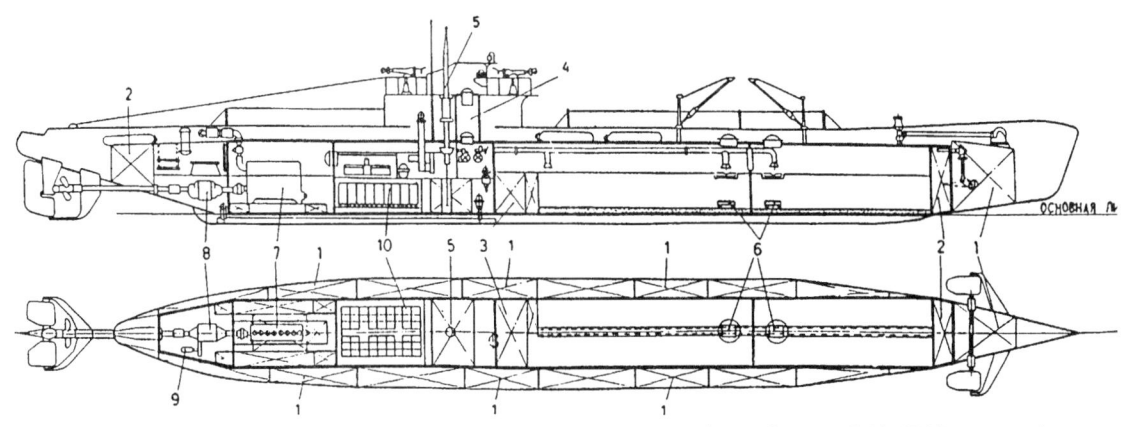

Fig. 15. Transport submarine *projekt 607*, no name or number given, 1943, 740t normal, length 64m, speed 9.5/4.5kt, 2 3.7cm, two freight rooms. Credit: Platonov

reinforce their operating fleets considerably by Lend-Lease deliveries from the USA and Great Britain until 1945.

The first deliveries had already taken place in 1941, first mainly by transports of weapons, equipment and other supplies for the Army and Air Force from American and British ports by strongly escorted merchant convoys to Murmansk and Arkhangel'sk, and by ships sent to the Persian Gulf and to Vladivostok. The first convoy, 'Dervish', with seven ships arrived from Liverpool at Arkhangel'sk on 31 August 1941, covered and escorted by a British carrier task force and a close escort. Up to the end of 1941 seven PQ-convoys sailed for Northern Russia, some of them with British minesweepers as escort, of which 13 remained up to the summer of 1942 at Murmansk and Arkhangel'sk to help the Soviets with minesweeping and escort of the convoys off the Kola Peninsula. In the spring of 1942 there followed the convoys PQ.8 to PQ.16, of which some were attacked by German surface ships, submarines and aircraft, causing some losses. The biggest convoy battle was in early July 1942 against the PQ.17, which lost about two-thirds of its ships. And PQ.18 in September 1942 was the first to be escorted by a British escort carrier and a strong destroyer escort, but also suffered losses from aircraft and submarine attacks. The convoys were continued during the winter each year until the end of the war. The ocean escorting was done by British ships, and was only in the last part assisted by Soviet destroyers and aircraft. The British Home Fleet provided Task Forces with battleships, cruisers and carriers as distant covering groups as long as there was any danger from the heavy German ships in northern Norway.[72]

Lend-Lease Ships for the Northern Fleet

The first deliveries of Lend-Lease ships occurred in February/March 1942, when the British sent with the convoys PQ.11 and PQ.12 nine whalers to northern Russia, of which two were lost on the way, while the others were commissioned as auxiliary minesweepers *T-101–107* between 1 March and

21 May. They were followed in October 1942 by three British motor-minesweepers, commissioned on 10 October as *T-108–110*.[73]

Notwithstanding the fact that President F.D. Roosevelt had declared on 7 November 1941: 'I have today found the defense of the Union of Soviet Socialist Republics is vital for the defense of the United States', and had ordered the Office of Lend-Lease Administration to make every effort to provide military and economic aid to the Soviet Union in its war against Nazi Germany, and had authorized the immediate allocation of $1 billion from funds already appropriated to Lend-Lease, the deliveries were at first concentrated on Army and Air Force needs. The Navy had to wait.[74]

In 1943 the US Navy started to deliver to the Soviet Northern Fleet modern minesweepers and MTBs: from July to November 1943 there arrived ten minesweepers of the *Admirable*-class, 625t stdd., built in 1942–43, which were commissioned as *T-111–120*. These were also to be used as anti-submarine escorts in the Kara Sea where three were lost to German U-boat attacks, while one of them sank a German U-boat. To strengthen the offensive capabilities of the Northern Fleet in spring of 1943 the delivery of American MTBs of three types started. They were transported aboard merchant ships in convoys. But of the first four vessels of the type *Higgins* of 35t, built in 1942, two were lost on 28 February 1943 when the transporting ship *Wade Hampton* was sunk in a convoy battle in the North Atlantic by a German U-boat. The other two were commissioned in May 1943 as *TK-21* and *TK-22* for the Northern Fleet. The next *Higgins/A-2* boats left New York on 9 November 1943. One was again lost on the way, but 12 were commissioned on 14 January 1944 as *TK-202–213*, for the Northern Fleet, while *TK-22* was renamed *TK-214*. *TK-21, 212* and *203* were lost in action in 1943/44. In February and March 1944 six more of this type followed as *TK-215–219* and *222*, of which *TK-217* was lost in action. Two more of a new type *Vosper/A-1* of 33t were also commissioned in March 1944 as *TK-220–221*, but were transferred in May/June 1944 by rail from Arkhangel'sk to Yeisk for the Black Sea Fleet, as were *TK-223–225, 227, 229, 231–236*, while *TK-226, 228, 230, 237–243* remained with the Northern Fleet.[75]

To augment the anti-U-boat capacity of the Northern Fleet off the Kola Peninsula, the US Navy sent in August 1943 12 sub-chasers of the SC-type of 95t to Polyarnoe. Of these *BO-201–212*, six remained with the Northern Fleet, while the other six were transferred to the Black Sea in May/July 1944.[76] New series of anti-submarine vessels came in the spring of 1944. From February to April, 34 small American *PTC*-boats of 27t arrived in northern Russia, but apart from one vessel all were transferred to the Black Sea in May/June 1944 as *MO-435–458*.[77]

The Northern Fleet also needed bigger ships to participate in the escorting of convoys but the Western Allies were not willing to deliver modern ships. After the Italian surrender in September 1943 the Soviet government claimed its share of the Italian surrendered warships. But the Allies were not willing to deliver such ships. As an equivalent to the Italian war booty the Allies delivered some of their older vessels. So in April 1944 the former US cruiser *Milwaukee*, built from 1918 to 1923, arrived at Vaenga, to become on 20 April the Soviet cruiser *Murmansk*. To repatriate the American crew and to transport the crews for the British ships to be transferred with the convoy RA.59 sailing on 28 April, the Americans were distributed aboard escorts, and the 2,300 Soviet sailors on empty merchant ships. The Soviet commander, Vice Admiral G.I. Levchenko, was taken aboard the British escort carrier *Fencer*, and could observe the perfect deck operations of the aircraft in ferocious weather conditions, during which its aircraft sank three German U-boats. The crews arrived in Great Britain on 6 May[78] to take over the following vessels: the battleship *Royal Sovereign*, lead ship of the R-class of 29,150t, and eight destroyers of the former US 'Flush-Deck'-class, built from 1918 to 1919, which were given to Great Britain in 1940 with the Destroyer Naval Base Deal, were included in the convoy JW.59 in August 1944 and arrived in the Kola Gulf on 24 August 1944, to be commissioned as battleship *Arkhangel'sk*, and as destroyers *Derzkii, Deyatel'nyi, Doblestnyi, Dostojnyi, Zharkii, Zhguchii, Zhestkii* and *Zhivuchii*, augmented some time later by a ninth vessel *Druzhnyi*. In addition there were four submarines transferred, one of the S-class, to become *V-1*, sunk in error by a British plane on the transfer route, and three of the smaller U-class, to become *V-2–4*, arriving in early August. While the destroyers were used as escorts off the Kola coast, the submarines could only operate in October 1944,[79] during the Kirkenes operations, but the destroyers and other escorts escorted many local convoys off the Kola Coast.[80]

A new series of anti-U-boat vessels arrived for the Northern Fleet in summer 1944. In July and August 1944 20 *SC*-sub-chasers were transferred to the Soviet Navy and commissioned as *BO-213–232*, of which three were sunk at the turn of 1944/45 by German U-boats. And in September seven *PTC*-boats arrived which became *SK-521–527*.[81]

In January 1945 another batch of 14 *SC*-boats was transferred to the Soviet flag and sent to the Northern Fleet, to become *BO-233-246*.[82]

There were more transfers of minesweepers from the United States and Canada in late 1944 and early 1945, which finally arrived in the Soviet-dominated area at the end of the war in Europe and shortly after its end. So the Americans sent 12 *YMS*-minesweepers of 345t each, six to the Baltic and six to the Black Sea Fleets, which were commissioned as *T-181–186* and *T-187–192*. The Canadians also sent ten MMS-minesweepers of 260t to the Black Sea as *T-193–202*.[83] The delivery of PT-motor torpedo boats also continued: in September 1944 three A-2 boats came, commissioned as *TK-244–246*, to be followed in April 1945 by five more, *TK-247–251*. This was still continued at the end of the war in Europe in June 1945 with *TK-252–259*, in July 1945 with *TK-260–264*, and in December 1945 with *TK-265–272*. Many of these last-mentioned vessels went in May/June 1945 by way of the White Sea–Baltic Canal to the Baltic Fleet.[84]

Lend-Lease Ships for the Pacific Fleet

A few days after Pearl Harbor, on 11 December 1941, the Soviet Ambassador to the USA, M.M. Litvinov, informed the US Secretary of State Cordell Hull that the USSR was in no position to co-operate with the USA against Japan. But in the following years President Roosevelt tried several times to bring this topic up onto the agenda of summit meetings with the Allied leaders. The interest of the US military and naval leaders was at first to find out if there was any possibility of deploying US strategic air forces to Siberia for attacks from there against Japan. So Roosevelt in a letter of 17 June 1942 warned Stalin of the dangers of Japanese attack against the maritime provinces of the USSR, following this with a second letter on 23 June proposing an Alaskan–Siberian ferry route and a survey by American experts of potential airfields. But Stalin refused such proposals, and during a meeting of foreign ministers in Moscow in October 1943 stated 'clearly and unequivocally that when the Allies succeeded in defeating Germany, the Soviet Union would join in defeating Japan'. And this he reaffirmed at the Teheran Conference on 28 November 1943.[85] In October 1944 during the visit of the British Prime Minister Winston S. Churchill to Moscow, Stalin finally agreed to participate in the war against Japan, three months after the future defeat of Germany. In addition, Stalin asked for a build-up of a large reserve of supplies and equipment as well as ships for Soviet forces.

Major-General John R. Deane, head of the US Military Mission to the USSR, took charge of the programme now called *Milepost*. On 5 December 1944, Deane's deputy, Rear Admiral Clarence E. Olsen, met with the Chief of the Main Staff of the Soviet Navy, Admiral V.A. Alafusov, in Moscow to discuss a list of ships and equipment necessary for the Soviet Pacific Fleet, which was finalized on 20 December. This contained two dozen types of ships and aircraft, from escort vessels, minesweepers, and motor torpedo boats, as well as several aircraft types, to port equipment and electronic components. In early January Admiral Kuznetsov proposed getting the envisaged ships at a port of the Aleutians, perhaps Dutch Harbor. But the Chief of Naval Operations, Admiral Ernest J. King, changed this because of logistic problems to Cold Bay, to which the Soviets agreed. On 8 February 1945 both admirals met during the Yalta conference to discuss some details, especially on the transfer of the crews for the ships. In March 1945 it was settled that the Soviet sailors should be sent in merchant ships returning from Soviet harbours after delivering supplies. For the approximately 180 vessels earmarked for the transfer about 15,000 men had to be sent up to 1 November 1945 to man 30 frigates, 24 minesweepers, 36 *YMS*-coastal minesweepers, 56 submarine chasers, 30 large infantry landing craft, and four floating workshops. After the completion of the training programme the vessels would sail in convoys, firstly escorted by US ships to Soviet harbours, passing Petropavlovsk. On the American side Captain William S. Maxwell was ordered to take charge of the programme, and on the Soviet side the operation 'Hula' was supervised by Rear Admiral B.D. Popov.[86]

Meanwhile, the transfer of motor torpedo boats had started in July 1944 by transport as deck load of merchant ships. Up to December 1944 32 PT-boats of the *Vosper*-series/*A-1* class were loaded and arrived up to the end of the year in Soviet harbours to become the *TK-561–566, 578–580, 587–590, 597, 567–570, 547–550, 517, 518, 537–540, 527, 528, 559* and *560*. An additional series of 32 *Higgins/A-2* boats was transferred on 5 July 1945 and arrived until December 1945 to become *TK-851–882*.[87]

The transfers from Cold Bay started with 12 minesweepers of the *Admirable*-class in May 1945, arriving in Petropavlovsk in June to become *T-271–282*, and six *SC*-sub-chasers, becoming *BO-301–306*, and six *YMS*-minesweepers, becoming *T-521–526*. In June the first 15 *LCI*-landing vessels of the 387t full load followed to become *DS-31–45*, and 13 *SC*-sub-chasers to become *BO-307–320*. In July the first ten frigates of the *Tacoma*-class of 1,430t stdd., built at the Kaiser yards to the British *River*-class design, sailed to become *EK-1–10*, six more *Admirable*-class minesweepers to become *T-331–336*, and 12 *YMS*-minesweepers to become *T-588–599*, and 15 more *LCI*-landing vessels to become *DS-2–10, 47–50*. These vessels mostly came in time to participate in the operations against Japan during the landings on the Korean east coast, on South Sakhalin and the Kuriles up to 3 September 1945. Of the vessels transferred in August and September there were 18 frigates of the *Tacoma*-class (*EK-11–30*), six minesweepers of the *Admirable*-class (*T-283–285, 337–339*), 13 *YMS*-minesweepers (*T-527, 600–611*), and 12 *SC*-sub-chasers (*BO-321–329, 331, 332, 335*).[88]

There were some additional transfers after the end of the war, to be described later in connection with the return of the delivered vessels.

WAR BOOTY SHIPS UP TO THE END OF THE WAR

Some of the German allies had already capitulated against the Soviet Union by 1944, and their warships had been confiscated by the Soviet Navy. The first were the Romanian ships and submarines, which were taken in most cases on 29 August 1944, after the turnover of the Romanian government on 24 August and the Soviet occupation of the harbours, especially Konstanţa. There were four destroyers, two First World War vessels, built in Italy for Romania, confiscated in the war by Italy and given back in 1920. They had 1,391t and became the *Legkii* and *Lovkii*. Two were modern destroyers of British design, but also built in Italy in 1928/39, had 1,400t, and became the *Likhoi* and *Letuchii*. Two small torpedo boats of the former Austro-Hungarian Navy of 257 or 262t became the *SKR's Musson* and *Toros*. There were also three submarines, two modern ones of German design, becoming the *TS-1* and *TS-2*, of which the last one was sunk during a torpedo explosion on 20 February 1945, but salvaged and repaired. The third was an older submarine of Italian design, commissioned in 1929 and becoming the *TS-3*. There was also the modern minelayer of 812t, which became the *Don*. Of the river monitors in October 1944 the remaining five vessels were taken over as *Asov*, *Mariupol'*, *Berdyansk*, *Izmail'* and *Kerch*.[89]

At Konstanţa there were also three sunk or damaged German submarines of the *type IIB*, which were salvaged but never full commissioned and later sunk in tests of new weapons. There were also three German KT-ships equipped as A/S vessels which were recommissioned after repairs as *Kuban'*, *Terek* and *Dnestr*. In Konstanţa and Varna in Bulgaria 29 *KFK*-auxiliary minesweepers were found in damaged states and rebuilt. They were taken over in most cases up to January 1945 but some later until June 1945 for the Black Sea Fleet, as *T-651–655, 666–669, 671–680, 685–694*.[90]

OPERATIONS AND LOSSES FROM MID-1942 TO THE END OF THE WAR

As mentioned, we cannot describe the operations in detail here, but only give an outline as a background to the most important losses in the war theatres.

Baltic Fleet

The Baltic Fleet was hampered every year by the icing over of the inner part of the Finnish Gulf. Only from May to early December were operations normally possible. From 1942 to the autumn of 1944 the main bases of Leningrad/Kronshtadt were still under siege, and there was practically no possibility of exercises and training at sea. The coastal forces had to try to keep the route from Kronshtadt to the advanced base of Lavansaari open and to defend them from German/Finnish intrusions. The only possibility for offensive operations was from submarines. In the summer and autumn months of 1942 there were 29 submarines operational and they made 31 patrols, of which 22 penetrated the German/Finnish mine barriers in the Finnish Gulf and reached the open Baltic. But the losses were extremely heavy: *Shch-405*, *M-95*, *Shch-317*, *M-97*, *Shch-320*, *Shch-302*, *Shch-311*, *Shch-308*, *S-7*, *Shch-304*, *Shch-305* and *Shch-306* were lost, in most cases to mines. The losses of surface vessels were relatively light, the patrol ship *Burya*, and the minesweeper *T-204*, besides some smaller and auxiliary vessels. In 1943 the Germans had in addition to the renewed mine barrages laid a net barrier, which prevented the submarines from penetrating the Baltic Sea. During attempts to carry out such operations the following were lost: *Shch-323* (raised), *Shch-408*, *Shch-406*, *S-12* and *S-9*. In 1944 the heavy ships and destroyers were used to assist the Army in breaking out from the besieged Leningrad by their heavy gunfire. Clashes between the German and Finnish light vessels and the Soviet coastal forces and the Soviet Air Forces intensified, but until the Finnish capitulation in September no further offensive operations were possible. With Finnish assistance the submarines could now evade the mines and from October reach the open Baltic. The 19 operational submarines carried out 41 operational patrols, but lost only two during these: *M-96* and *S-4*. The opening of the Finnish Gulf together with the offensives of the Soviet Army made it possible to use the light vessels for amphibious operations against the islands Dagoe and Oesel and to close the Irben Strait to the Germans. During such operations some surface vessels were lost such as the minesweepers *T-210*, *T-353*, *T-379*, *T-387*, *T-377* and *T-76/Korall*, as well as many smaller and auxiliary vessels.[91]

Black Sea Fleet

The Black Sea Fleet had, after the heavy losses of 1941–42 during the defence of Sevastopol, from July to November 1942 to help the Army in the defence of the Caucasian ports by transporting troop and supplies from Poti and Batumi to Tuapse, and to support the defenders of the Mykhako bridgehead, who were blocking the entrance to the harbour of Novorossijsk. At the same time submarines and light vessels were trying to interrupt the German seaborne supply from Romanian harbours to the Crimea and the Kuban peninsula. During such operations they lost the submarines *M-33*, *Shch-208*, *M-60*, *M-118* and *Shch-213*. And the available heavier surface ships were sometimes used to support Army operations with their gunfire. In one such operation the modern cruiser *Molotov* was torpedoed by an Italian MTB, which led to one of the most remarkable repair jobs ever done by Soviet shipbuilders, when they replaced the destroyed stern with the stern of the laid-up cruiser *Frunze*. Of the surface vessels the old cruiser *Komintern* was finally destroyed, and some of the smaller vessels lost. After the victory at Stalingrad the Black Sea Fleet tried to use their heavier surface vessels to interrupt the German sea supply lines more effectively, but, because of the long distances to cover from the Caucasian ports to the West Coast, they were located early on, and the Germans were able to re-route their convoys. And when a group of three destroyers attempted to intercept one of the German convoys bringing back light vessels from the evacuation of the Kuban bridgehead, they were attacked by German dive bombers and all three ships, the leader *Kharkov*, and the destroyers *Besposhchadnyi* and *Sposobnyi*, were sunk. This led to Stalin's order not to use the big ships and destroyers any more in such operations, because they could no longer change the outcome of the war but were instead needed for the training of the crews for the post-war Navy. The tasks at sea could be accomplished by submarines and light vessels and the Air Force.[92] This was true to a great extent, as was shown during the operations to drive the Germans out of the Crimea, when the submarines, the Air Force and MTBs caused some heavy losses in the evacuation transports. Finally, the Navy supported the Army during the recapture of Odessa and the operations against Romania in August 1944, which forced the Germans to retreat from the Balkans. During this time, from late November 1942 to the end of operations in the Black Sea, the following submarines were lost in addition to the three mentioned destroyers: *L-24*, *M-31*, *Shch-212*, *Shch-203*, *M-51*, *A-3*, *D-4*, *M-36*, *L-23*, *Shch-216* and *L-6*. And the surface ships lost the gunboat *Krasnaya Gruziya*, the minelayer *Zarya*, and the minesweepers *T-403*, *T-411* and *T-410*, as well as many smaller vessels, especially during the heavy fights around the Eltigen bridgehead in late autumn 1943.[93]

Northern Fleet

The Northern Fleet had several tasks, an offensive one to interrupt the German supply traffic along the northern Norwegian coast, mainly with submarines, but also with aircraft, MTBs and in some cases destroyers. The next more defensive task was the support of the Allies in bringing in the Murmansk convoys and their return convoys against the German U-boats and aircraft. And the third purely defensive task was the defence of the Northern Sea Route, especially in the Kara Sea, against intrusions of German cruisers and submarines. During the submarine operations from mid-1942 to the end of the war the following submarines were lost, mainly on the German flanking mine barrages: *M-173*, *K-2*, *M-121*, *K-22*, *K-3*, *M-122*, *M-106*, *Shch-422*, *M-172*, *Shch-403*, *M-174*, *S-55*, *M-108*, *S-54* and by errors of British or Soviet aircraft *V-1* and *Shch-402*. And the losses of the MTBs, mainly Lend-Lease vessels, have already been mentioned. Destroyers were mainly used in the escorting of convoys and two of these were lost, the *Sokrushitel'nyi* by heavy damage sustained during a storm, showing the weakness of the *projekt 7* destroyers in heavy weather, and the Lend-Lease *Deyatel'nyi* (ex-*Churchill*) by a U-boat attack, as were some of the *BO*-sub-chasers from the Lend-Lease deliveries, as mentioned. And during the defence of the Northern Sea route the submarine *K-1*, waiting for German intruders, and some auxiliary patrol vessels and four of the Lend-Lease minesweepers, *T-109* (in a storm), *T-118*, *T-114* and *T-120*, became victims of the German U-boats.[94]

Pacific Fleet

The Pacific Fleet served for most of the time as a reservoir for personnel and also for some vessels for the Northern Fleet. So as mentioned, the destroyer leader *Baku* and the destroyers *Razumnyi* and *Raz'yarennyi* were transferred in 1942 via the Northern Sea Route, the latter having been torpedoed in January 1945 by a German submarine but saved. And by way of the Panama Canal and Great Britain the submarines *L-15*, *L-16*, *S-51*, *S-54*, *S-55* and *S-56* made the long journey to Polyarnoe, but *L-16* was sunk by a Japanese submarine off the US West Coast. And the submarine *Shch-138* became a total loss from an accident at sea. And during the short war against Japan in August and September 1945 there were only small losses, mainly from the Lend-Lease vessels: the *YMS*-minesweepers *T-285* and *T-610*, and the *LCI*-landing vessels *DS-5*, *DS-9* and *DS-43*. And the submarine *L-19* did not return from their patrol.[95]

A table of the Soviet Navy's losses during 1941–45 shows the following data for the smaller ships: 11 warship and 25 auxiliary patrol ships, 3 big and 128 small sub-chasers, 139 torpedo cutters, 11 river monitors, 83 armoured cutters, 37 warship and 90 auxiliary minesweepers, 168 minesweeping cutters, 7 landing ships.[96]

THE SOVIET FLEETS AT THE END OF THE WAR, SEPTEMBER 1945

The following lists give the sea-going vessels of the Soviet Fleets that were available on 2 September 1945:

Baltic Fleet

Old battleships: *Oktyabrskaya revolyutsiya*, *Petropavlovsk* (ex-*Marat*, heavily damaged and grounded off Kronshtadt
Cruisers (*projekt 26, 26-bis*): *Kirov*, *Maksim Gorkii*
Destroyer Leaders (*projekt 1, 38*): *Leningrad*, *Minsk*
Destroyers (*projekt 7-U*): *Storozhevoi* (repaired with a changed armament), *Vitse Admiral Drozd* (ex-*Stojkii*), *Sil'nyi*, *Slavnyi*, *Strashnyi*, *Svirepyi*, *Strogyi*, *Strojnyi*
Destroyer (*projekt 45*): *Optynyi*
Destroyers (*projekt 7*): *Grozyashchii*, *Steregushchii*

Patrol Vessel (*projekt 29*): *Yastreb*
Patrol Vessels (*projekt 2, 39*): *Tajfun, Vikhr, Tucha*
Patrol Vessel (ex-*Eston.*): *Ametist*
Minesweepers (*projekt 59*): *T-250/Vladimir Polyukhin, T-254/Vasilii Gromov*
Minesweepers (*projekt 3, 53, 53U*): *T-205/Gafel, T-211/Rym, T-215, T-219/Kontr Admiral Khoroshkin*
Coastal Minesweepers (*projekt 253-L*): *T-351, 352, 354, 355, 356, 357, 358, 359, 360, 361, 362, 363, 364, 365, 366, 367, 368, 369, 370, 371, 372, 373, 374, 375, 376, 378, 380, 381, 382, 383, 384, 385, 386, 388, 389, 390, 391, 440, 441, 459, 460, 461, 462, 463, 464, 222, 223, 224, 225*
Coastal Minesweepers (Lend-Lease YMS): *T-181, T-182, T-183, T-184, T-185, T-186*

Big Submarine (*series I*): *D-2*
Big Submarines (*series II, XIII-bis*): *L-3, L-21*
Big Submarines (*series XIV*): *K-51, K-52, K-53, K-55, K-56*
Medium Submarines (*series III, V, V-bis2*): *Shch-303, Shch-307, Shch-309, Shch-310*
Medium Submarines (*series IX-bis*): *S-13, S-18, S-20*
Medium Submarines (*series X, X-bis*): *Shch-318, Shch-407*
Medium Submarines (ex-*Estonian*): *Lembit*
Small Submarines (*series VI-bis, XII*): *M-77, M-79, M-90, M-102, M-171* (minelayer)
Small submarines (*series XV*): *M-200, M-201*

Black Sea Fleet

Old Battleship: *Sevastopol'* (ex-*Parizhskaya kommuna*)
Cruisers (*projekt 26, 26-bis*): *Voroshilov, Molotov*
Old Cruisers: *Krasnyi Kavkaz, Krasnyi Krym*
Destroyer (*projekt 30*): *Ognevoi*
Destroyer (*projekt 7-U*): *Soobrazitel'nyi*
Destroyers (*projekt 7*): *Bodryi, Bojkii*
Old Destroyers: *Nezamozhnik, Zheleznyakov*
Destroyers (ex-Romanian): *Letuchii* (ex-*Regina Maria*), *Likhoi* (ex-*Regele Ferdinand*)
Destroyers (ex-Romanian): *Legkii* (ex-*Marasesti*), *Lovkii* (ex-*Marasti*)
Patrol Ships (*projekt 4*): *Shtorm, Shkval*
Patrol Ships (ex-Romanian): *Musson* (ex-*Sborul*), *Toros* (ex-*Smeul*)
Minelayer (ex-Romanian): *Don* (ex-*Amiral Murgescu*)
Minesweepers (*projekt 3, 53, 58*): *T-401/Tral, T-404/Shchit, T-406/Iskatel', T-407/Mina, T-408/Yakor', T-409/Garpun, T-412/Arsenii Raskin*
Coastal Minesweepers (Lend-Lease YMS): *T-187, T-188, T-189, T-190, T-191, T-192*

Big Submarines (*series II*): *L-4, L-5*
Medium Submarines (*series V-bis, V-bis2*): *Shch-201, Shch-202, Shch-205, Shch-207*
Medium Submarines (*series IX-bis*): *S-31, S-33*

Medium Submarines (*series X*): *Shch-209*, *Shch-215*
Medium Submarines (ex-Romanian): *TS-1* (ex-*Requinul*), *TS-3* (ex-*Delfinul*)
Small Submarines (*series VI, VI-bis*): *M-23*, *M-24*, *M-25*, *M-26*, *M-27*, *M-28*, *M-51*, *M-52*, *M-54*, *M-55*
Small Submarines (*series XII*): *M-30*, *M-32*, *M-35*, *M-62*, *M-104*, *M-105*, *M-107*, *M-111*, *M-112*, *M-113*, *M-114*, *M-115*, *M-116*, *M-117*, *M-119*, *M-120*
Small Submarines (*series XV*): *M-202*, *M-203*

Northern Fleet

Battleship (ex-British): *Arkhangel'sk* (ex-*Royal Sovereign*)
Cruiser (ex-US): *Murmansk* (ex-*Milwaukee*)
Destroyer Leader (*projekt 38*): *Baku*
Destroyers (*projekt 7*): *Groznyi*, *Gremyashchii* (in repair), *Gromkii*, *Razumnyi*, *Raz'yarennyi* (in repair)
Destroyers (Lend-Lease ex-British), ex-US Flushdeckers): *Derzkii* (ex-*Chelsea*, ex-*Crowninshield*), *Doblestnyi* (ex-*Roxborough*, ex-*Foote*), *Dostojnyi* (ex-*St Albans*, ex-*Thomas*), *Druzhnyi* (ex-*Lincoln*, ex-*Yarnall*), *Zharkii* (ex-*Brighton*, ex-*Cowell*), *Zhguchii* (ex-*Leamington*, ex-*Twiggs*), *Zhestkii* (ex-*Georgetown*, ex-*Maddox*), *Zhivuchii* (ex-*Richmond*, ex-*Fairfax*)
Old Destroyers: *Karl Libknekht*, *Uritskii*, *Valerian Kujbyshev*
Patrol Ships (*projekt 2*): *Uragan*, *Smerch*, *Groza*
Patrol Ships (*projekt 43*): *SKR-28/Rubin*, *SKR-30/Sapfir*
Minesweepers (Lend-Lease, ex-US): *T-111* (ex-*Advocate*), *T-112* (ex-*Agent*), *T-113* (ex-*Alarm*), *T-115* (ex-*Apex*), *T-116* (ex-*Arcade*), *T-117* (ex-*Arch*), *T-119* (ex-*Aspire*)
Minesweepers (ex-British trawlers): *T-101* (ex-*Shika*), *T-102* (ex-*Hav*), *T-103* (ex-*Stefa*), *T-104* (ex-*Vega*), *T-106* (ex-*Sunba*)
Minesweepers (ex-British MMS): *T-108* (ex-*MMS 90*), *T-110* (ex-*MMS 212*), *T-121* (ex-*MMS 1005*), *T-122* (ex-*MMS 1023*)

Big Submarines (*series XIII, XIII-bis*): *L-15*, *L-20*, *L-22*
Big Submarine (*series XIV*): *K-21*
Medium Submarines (*series IX-bis*): *S-14*, *S-15*, *S-16*, *S-17*, *S-19*, *S-51*, *S-56*, *S-101*, *S-102*, *S-103*, *S-104*
Medium Submarine (*series X*): *Shch-404*
Medium Submarines (ex-British U-class): *V-2* (ex-*Unbroken*), *V-3* (ex-*Unison*), *V-4* (ex-*Ursula*)

Pacific Fleet

Cruisers (*projekt 26-bis-2*): *Kalinin*, *Lazar Kaganovich*
Destroyer Leader (*projekt 38*): *Tbilisi*
Destroyers (*projekt 7*): *Ryanyi*, *Rezvyi*, *Razyashchii*, *Rekordnyi*, *Rastoropnyi*, *Reshitel'nyi*, *Retivyi*, *Redkii*, *Revnostnyi*, *Rezkii*
Old Destroyers: *Vojkov*, *Stalin*
Frigates (Lend-Lease ex US): *EK-1* (ex-*Charlottesville*), *EK-2* (ex-*Long Beach*),

EK-3 (ex-*Belfast*), *EK-4* (ex-*Machias*), *EK-5* (ex-*San Pedro*), *EK-6* (ex-*Glendyle*), *EK-7* (ex-*Sandusky*), *EK-8* (ex-*Coronado*), *EK-9* (ex-*Allentown*), *EK-10* (ex-*Ogden*), *EK-11*, *EK 30* (on transfer from Cold Bay to Petropavlovsk, but commissioned only on 05.10.45)

Patrol Ships (*projekt 2, 4*): *Metel', Vyuga, Molniya, Zarnitsa, Burun, Grom*

Patrol Ships (ex-NKVD): *Kirov, Dzerzhinskii*

Patrol Ship (*projekt 29*): *Albatros* (commissioned on 29.09.45)

Minesweepers (*projekt 53, 58*): *T-1/Strela, T-2/Tros, T-3/Provodnik, T-4/Podsekatel', T-5/Paravan, T-6/Kapsyul', T-7/Vekha, T-8/Cheka*

Minesweepers (Lend-Lease ex-US): *T-271* (ex-*Disdain*), *T-272* (ex-*Fancy*), *T-273* (ex-*Indicative*), *T-274* (ex-*Marvel*), *T-275* (ex-*Measure*), *T-276* (ex-*Method*), *T-277* (ex-*Mirth*), *T-278* (ex-*Nucleus*), *T-279* (ex-*Palisade*), *T-280* (ex-*Penetrate*), *T-281* (ex-*Peril*), *T-282* (ex-*Rampart*), *T-283* (ex-*Candid*), *T-284* (ex-*Caution*), *T-285* (ex-*Bond*), *T-331* (ex-*Admirable*), *T-332* (ex-*Adopt*), *T-333* (ex-*Astute*), *T-334* (ex-*Augury*), *T-335* (ex-*Barrier*), *T-336* (ex-*Bombard*), *T-337* (ex-*Caravan*), *T-338* (ex-*Captivate*), *T-339* (ex-*Capable*)

Coastal Minesweepers (Lend-Lease ex-US YMS): *T-521, 522, 523, 524, 525, 526, 527, 588, 589, 590, 591, 592, 593, 594, 595, 596, 597, 598, 599, 600, 601, 602, 603, 604, 605, 606, 607, 608, 609, 610* (lost on 15.10.45), *611* (commissioned on 04.09.45)

Big Submarines (*series XI*): *L-7, L-8, L-9, L-10, L-11, L-12*

Big Submarines (*series XIII*): *L-13, L-14, L-17, L-18*

Medium Submarines (*series V, V-bis, V-is2*): *Shch-101* (minelayer), *Shch-102, Shch-104, Shch-105, Shch-106, Shch-107, Shch-108, Shch-109, Shch-110, Shch-111, Shch-112, Shch-113, Shch-114, Shch-115, Shch-116, Shch-117, Shch-118, Shch-119, Shch-120, Shch-121, Shch-122, Shch-123, Shch-124, Shch-125*

Medium Submarines (*series IX-bis*): *S-52, S-53*

Medium Submarines (*series X, X-bis*): *Shch-126, Shch-127, Shch-128, Shch-129, Shch-130, Shch-131, Shch-132, Shch-133, Shch-134, Shch-135, Shch-136, Shch-137, Shch-139*

Small Submarines (*series VI, VI-bis*): *M-1, M-2, M-3, M-4, M-5, M-6, M-7, M-8, M-9, M-10, M-11, M-12, M-13, M-14, M-15, M-16, M-17, M-18, M-19, M-20, M-21, M-22, M-43, M-44, M-45, M-46, M-47, M-48*

For the dates for the ships of the fleet see n. 97.[97]

NOTES

1. There is a large amount of Russian, German and English language-literature about the Great Patriotic War and the German operation 'Barbarossa'. One of the most recent bibliographic publications is: Rolf-Dieter Müller and Gerhard R. Ueberschär, *Hitler's War in the East 1941–1945: A Critical Assessment*, a publication of the Library of Contemporary History Stuttgart, Providence, Oxford, Berghahn Books, 1997. There are special literature reports and bibliographies of the participating countries in: *Neue Forschungen zum Zweiten Weltkrieg*, ed. Jürgen Rohwer and Hildegard Müller, *Schriften der Bibliothek für Zeitgeschichte*, Band 28, Koblenz, Bernard & Graefe, 1990, with reports by A.G. Khor'kov for the Soviet

Union, Bernd Wegner for Germany (West), Olli Vehviläinen for Finland, Alesandru Dutu for Romania, and Sandor Szakaly for Hungary, etc. Gerda Beitter, *Die Rote Armee im 2. Weltkrieg. Eine Bibliographie*, Schriften der Bibliothek für Zeitgeschichte, Band 24, Koblenz, Bernard & Graefe, 1984.
2. N.A. Piterskij, *Die Sowjet-Flotte im Zweiten Weltkrieg*. German edition of the first edition of *Boevoi put' Sovetskogo Voenno-morskogo flota*, Moscow, Voenizdat, 1964, ed. and augmented with a commentary by Jürgen Rohwer, Oldenburg, Stalling, 1966. *Boevaya letopis' Voenno-morskogo flota 1941–1942*, ed. G.A. Ammon, Moscow, Voenizdat, 1983. There are also volumes about the years 1943–45 in preparation. 'Velikaya Otechestvennaya Denem za Den'. Khronika iyunya 1941 s may 1945.' Monthly in *Morskoi sbornik*, No. 6 (1991) to No. 5 (1995). Jürgen Rohwer and Gerhard Hümmelchen, *Chronology of the War at Sea 1939–1945: The Naval History of World War Two*, London, Greenhill Books and Annapolis, MD, US Naval Institute, 1992.
3. 'Velikaya Otechestvennaya Denem za Den'', op. cit., No. 6 (1991), pp. 18–19.
4. A.G. Khor'kov, *Grozovoi iyun'*, Moscow, Voenizdat, 1991. Dmitrii Volkogonov, 'The German Attack, the Soviet Response', in Erickson and Dilks, *Barbarossa*. Stepan A. Mikoyan, 'Barbarossa and the Soviet Leadership. A Recollection', in *Barbarossa: The Axis and the Allies*, ed. John Erickson and David Dilks, Edinburgh, Edinburgh University Press, 1994, pp. 76–96, 123–33. Some general histories are: A.M. Samsonov, *Krakh fashistskoj agressii 1939–1945. Istoricheskii Ocherk*, Moscow, Nauka, 1980. *Istoriya Vtoroi Mirovoj Vojny 1939–1945gg*. Vols 1–12, Moscow, Voenizdat, 1973–1982 (esp. Vols 3 and 4). Horst Boog et al., *Der Angriff auf die Sowjetunion*. Vol. 4 of *Das Deutsche Reich und der Zweite Weltkrieg*, Stuttgart, Deutsche Verlagsanstalt, 1983. Gerhard Weinberg, 'Die Ostfront und der Wandel des Krieges', in *Eine Welt in Waffen. Die globale Geschichte des Zweiten Weltkrieges*, Stuttgart, Deutsche Verlagsanstalt, 1995, pp. 294–342.
5. TsA VMF, f.1106, op.18448, d.82, l.367. Table printed in A.V. Basov, 'Der Bau der Seekriegsflotte der UdSSR vor dem Zweiten Weltkrieg. 1921–1941', in *Rüstungswettlauf zur See 1930–1941: Von der Abrüstung zum Wettrüsten*, ed. Jürgen Rohwer, Koblenz, Bernard & Graefe, 1991, p. 130. Dates of the shipbuilding also in S.S. Berezhnoi, *Korabli i Suda VMF SSSR, 1928–1945*, Moscow, Voenizdat, 1988.
6. The old destroyer *Lenin* and the submarines *S-1*, *M-71*, *M-80*, *Ronis* and *Spidola*.
7. The destroyer *Gnevnyi*, and the submarines *M-78*, *S-3*, *M-83*, *S-10*, *M-99*, *and M-81*, and the minesweepers *T-206*, *T-299 and T-216*, while the cruiser *Maksim Gorkii* and the destroyers *Smelyi*, *Gordyi*, and *Steregushchii* were damaged by mines and the destroyers *Storozhevoi* and *Strashnyi* by a torpedo and by a bomb hit and mine, respectively.
8. V.V. Kostrichenko states that the destroyer leader *Moskva* was sunk by the Soviet submarine *Shch-206*, which in turn was sunk by the destroyer *Soobrazitel'nyi*, while the cruiser *Voroshilov* and the destroyer leader *Kharkov* were damaged by a mine and an air attack – see 'Nabeg na Konstantsu', *Ocherki Voenno-morskoi istorii*, No. 2, Kharkov, 1998, pp. 46–52. This view should be considered speculative, due to lack of dependable sources. Also the destroyer *Bystryi* became a victim of a German air-laid mine. For detailed data on losses see: Glavnyi Shtab Voenno-morskogo flota, *Poteri boevykh korablei i sudov Voenno-morskogo flota. Transportnykh, Rybolovnykh i drugikh sudov SSSR v Velikoi Otechestvennoi vojny 1941–1945 gg.*, Moscow, Voenizdat, 1959.
9. *Chronology of the War at Sea 1939–1945*, op. cit., pp. 68–73. *Boevaya letopis'* …, op. cit., pp. 15–21.
10. S.S. Berezhnoi, op. cit.
11. From 14–17 August the cruisers *Frunze* and *Kujbyshev*, the destroyer leaders *Kiev* and *Erevan*, the destroyers *Ognevoi* and *Ozornoi*, the submarines *L-23*, *L-24*, *L-25* and *S-35*, and the big icebreaker *Mikoyan* were towed away to Caucasian ports, the almost finished destroyers *Sovershennyi* and *Svobodnyi* going for completion to Sevastopol. The battleship *Sovetskaya Ukraina*, the battlecruiser *Sevastopol'*, the cruisers *Ordzhonikidze* and *Sverdlov*, the destroyers *Otmennyi*, *Obuchennyi*, *Obchayannyi*, *Obshchitel'nyi*, the submarines *S-36*, *S-37*, and *S-38* on the slips of the yards *No. 61 Kommunar* and *Marti* had to be blown up or damaged beyond repair to avoid their use by the Germans.
12. In the fights around the Baltic islands and during the supply operations for Tallinn the following destroyers were lost: *Smelyi*, *Karl Marks*, *Statnyi* and *Engels*, the minesweepers

T-201, T-212, T-213, T-202, T-214, and T-209, and the submarines M-94 and S-11. During the evacuation of Tallinn were lost the destroyers *Yakov Sverdlov*, *Skoryi*, *Kalinin*, *Volodarskii*, and *Artem*, the patrol ships *Sneg* and *Tsiklon*, and the submarines *S-5* and *Shch-301*. Other vessels were heavily damaged. In a later attack L-1 was sunk.
13. The battleship *Marat* was sunk off Kronshtadt, but remained a grounded gun battery renamed in 1943 the *Petropavlovsk*, the building cruiser *Petropavlovsk* (ex-*Lützow*) was sunk at the quay, but also remained as a hulked battery, renamed *Tallinn*. In addition the destroyer leader *Minsk*, the destroyer *Steregushchii*, the patrol ship *Vikhr*, and the submarine M-74 were sunk, but were slavaged later and some of them recommissioned.
14. S-6, M-103, P-1, Shch-319, S-8, Shch-322, L-2, M-98, *Kalev*, and Shch-324.
15. With the Hangö-convoys the destroyers *Smetlivyi*, *Surovyi* and *Gordyi*, and the minesweeper T-206 were lost. Besides the vessels mentioned in the footnotes 12–15 many other auxiliaries and transports were lost.
16. Lost were the cruiser *Chervona Ukraina*, the destroyer leader *Tashkent*, the destroyers *Smyshlennyi*, *Shaumyan*, *Dzerzhinskii*, *Sovershennyi*, *Svobodnyi*, *Bezuprechnyi*, and *Bditel'nyi*, the minesweepers T-405, and T-413, and the submarines Shch-214, S-32. At the evacuation the submarines in repair D-6 and A-1 had to be scuttled, and the patrol ships and minesweepers building at yard 201 had to be blown up.
17. M-58, M-59, M-34, S-34, Shch-211, Shch-204, and Shch-210.
18. In October/November 1941, of the transferred submarines S-102, S-101, K-23, K-22, K-21 and K-3 became operational. The British submarines HMS *Tigris* and HMS *Trident* operated from August to November 1941, followed up to January 1942 by HMS *Sealion* and HMS *Seawolf*. For the successes of the submarines in the Arctic see Jürgen Rohwer, *Allied Submarine Attacks of World War Two: European Theatre of Operations, 1939–1945*, London and Annapolis, Greenhill Books and US Naval Institute, 1997, pp. 15–44. Of the Soviet submarines lost up to July 1942 were: M-175, Shch-421, Shch-401, K-23, D-3 and M-176, of the surface ships the destroyer *Stremitel'nyi*, and patrol vessels *Zhemchug* and *Brilliant* (raised and repaired), 7 auxiliary patrol vessels and 3 auxiliary minesweepers.
19. On 15 July 1942 the destroyer leader *Baku* and the destroyers *Razumnyi*, *Raz'yarennyi*, and *Revnostnyi* left Vladivostok for a transfer on the Northern Sea Route to the Northern Fleet. The *Revnostnyi* had to return after a collision, but the other vessels arrived on 14 October at the Kola Gulf. The submarines L-15, L-16, S-51, S-54, S-55, and S-56 left in September and October 1942 from Vladivostok, and after L-16 was sunk by an erroneous attack of a Japanese submarine off the US West Coast, the other five submarines arrived from January to May 1943 at the Kola Gulf.
20. So M-111, M-112, M-113, M-117, M-118, M-120 joined the Black Sea Fleet, M-114, M-115, M-116 the Pacific Fleet, and M-119, M-121, M-122 in 1942 and M-104, M-105, M106, M-107 and M-108 in 1943 the Northern Fleet. Of the medium submarines S-14, S-103, S-104, S-15, S-16, S-17, S-18 from Gorkii, and from Sudomekh in Leningrad S-19, S-20, and S-21 as well as the small M-200, M-201, M-202, M-203 were sent to the Caspian Sea, to be sent after a year of training to the Northern, Baltic or Black Sea Fleets.
21. TsGA VMF, f.403, d.40304. Printed in E.A. Shitikov, V.N. Krasnov and V.V. Balabin, *Korable-stroenie v SSSR v Gody Velikoi Otechestvennoi vojny*, Moscow, Nauka, 1995, p. 14.
22. E.A. Shitikov, *et al.*, op. cit., p. 16.
23. E.N. Zubov and A.A. Narusbaev, 'Sudostroenie v gody Velikoi Otechestvennoi vojny', *Ekonomika sudostroit, prom-sti*, No. 1 (1969), p. 30, printed in E.A. Shitikov, *et al.*, op. cit., p. 20.
24. I.G. Zakharov, 'Naval Shipbuilding in Russia', *Sudostroenie*, No. 10 (1996), p. 64.
25. *Istoriya ...*, op. cit., vol. IV, pp. 438–9. V.I. Achkasov (ed.), *Krasnoznamennyi Baltijskii flot v Bitve za Leningrad 1941–1944 gg.*, Moscow, Nauka, 1973.
26. Otdel TsG VMA, f.2, op.1, d.39514, l.2-25.
27. *Istoriya ...*, op. cit., vol. IV, p. 450.
28. E.A. Shitikov, *et al.*, op. cit., pp. 24–36.
29. A.M. Vasil'ev, 'Linejnye korabl' VMF SSSR predvoennykh proektov', *Gangut*, No. 16, St Petersburg, 1998, pp. 53–66.
30. There were proposals for 9 or 12 406mm or 9 457mm, 12–24 152mm, or 12 180mm, or 8 220mm guns, 100 or 130mm and 37 76mm A/A guns, a speed between 28 and 33kt, with displacements between 75,000 and 130,000t.

31. A.M. Vasil'ev 'Linejnyi korabl' proekta 24', *Gangut*, No. 15, St Petersburg, 1998, pp. 32–42.
32. V.F. Bil'din, 'Tyazhelye kreisera tipa "Stalingrad"', *Sudostroenie*, No. 7 (1994), pp. 63–7.
33. *Istoriya* ..., op. cit., vol. IV, pp. 310, 319–20.
34. L.A. Kuznetsov, 'Ne isklyuchalas' i postrojka avianostsa ...', *Gangut*, No. 3, St Petersburg, 1992, pp. 63–70. A.V. Platonov, 'Iz letopisi sozdaniya sovetskikh avianostsev', *Sudostroenie*, No. 5 (1992), pp. 42–5. Arkadi Morin and Nikolai Walujew, *Sowjetische Flugzeugträger. Geheim 1910–1995*, Berlin, Brandenburgisches Verlagshaus, 1996, pp. 93–6. TsGA VMF, f. r-441, op.2, l.7-8, 10, 457, r-1483, op.1, d.201, l.1-3, r-1877, op.1, d.435, l.25-33; op.9, d.56, l.34.
35. E.A. Shitikov *et al.*, op. cit., p. 69.
36. Ibid., pp. 33, 35, 64–5. RGFE, f.297, op.2, d.90, l.164. *Istoriya* ..., op. cit., vol. IV, pp. 468–9.
37. *Istoriya* ..., op. cit., vol. IV, p. 466.
38. A.B. Morin, 'Eskadrennye minonostsev "Ognevoi"', *Sudostroenie*, No. 5–6 (1995), pp. 42–52. E.A. Shitikov *et al.*, op. cit., pp. 29, 33, 60–65.
39. E.A. Shitikov *et al.*, op. cit., pp. 35, 66.
40. V.Yu. Gribovskii, 'K istorii sozdaniya storozhevykh korablej tipa "Yastreb"', *Sudostroenie*, No. 4/1997, pp. 97–9. *Istoriya* ..., op. cit., vol. IV, p. 484. E.A. Shitikov, *et al.*, op. cit., pp. 72–3. GRA VMF, f. r-1678, r-1877, r-1483, d.441. RGAE, f-8183.
41. A.B. Morin and N.P. Petrov, 'Bystrokhodnye (Bazovye) Tral'shchiki tipa "Fugas"', *Sudostroenie*, No. 10 (1994), pp. 62–9. *Istoriya* ..., op. cit., vol. IV, pp. 458–9. RGA VMF, f-r-441, op.3, d.188, 205
42. E.A. Shitikov *et al.*, op. cit., pp. 86–8. *Istoriya* ..., op. cit., vol. IV, pp. 487–9.
43. E.A. Shitikov *et al.*, op. cit., pp. 87–9. *Istoriya* ..., op. cit., vol. IV, pp. 488–9.
44. *Istoriya* ..., op. cit., vol. IV, p. 489.
45. E.A. Shitikov *et al.*, op. cit., pp. 29, 92–3. *Istoriya* ..., op. cit., vol. IV, pp. 486, 490–93.
46. E.A. Shitikov *et al.*, op. cit., pp. 35, 92. S.S. Berezhnoi, *Korabli i suda VMF SSSR 1928–1945*, Moscow, Voenizdat, 1988, pp. 320–24.
47. E.A. Shitikov *et al.*, op. cit., pp. 30, 33, 77–81. *Istoriya* ..., op. cit., vol. IV, pp. 367, 485–6.
48. E.A. Shitikov *et al.*, op. cit., pp. 80–6. S.S. Berezhnoi, op. cit., pp. 219–56.
49. E.A. Shitikov *et al.*, op. cit., p. 83.
50. *Istoriya* ..., op. cit., vol. IV, p. 493. S.S. Berezhnoi, op. cit., pp. 153–84.
51. *Istoriya* ..., op. cit., vol. IV, pp. 493–4.
52. S.S. Berezhnoi, op. cit., pp. 13–40. *Istoriya* ..., op. cit., vol. IV, p. 496.
53. *Istoriya* ..., op. cit., vol. IV, p. 497. S.S. Berezhnoi, op. cit., pp. 130–2.
54. *Istoriya* ..., op. cit., vol. IV, pp. 304–509. E.A. Shitikov *et al.*, op. cit., pp. 125–33.
55. *Istoriya* ..., op. cit., vol. IV, pp. 376–8.
56. Boris Lemachko, 'Die "Taschen"-Schlachtschiffe des Amur', *Marine-Rundschau*, 77/1980, No. 6, pp. 356–8. *Istoriya* ..., op. cit., vol. IV, pp. 361, 503–4.
57. For the submarines transferred and the dates of the transfers see S.S. Berezhnoi, op. cit., pp. 42–75.
58. E.A. Shitikov *et al.*, op. cit., pp. 96–100. *Istoriya* ..., op. cit., vol. IV, pp. 338–46.
59. E.A. Shitikov *et al.*, op. cit., pp. 96–100.
60. Ibid., pp. 97–8. *Istoriya* ..., op. cit., vol. IV, p. 473.
61. V.I. Dmitriev, *Sovetskoe podvodnoe korable-stroenie*, Moscow, Voenizdat, 1990, pp. 137–49, 248–9, 259–61, 264. E.A. Shitikov *et al.*, op. cit., pp. 101–2. A.V. Platonov, *Sovietskie boevye korabli 1941–1945. Vol. III: podvodnye lodki*, St Petersburg, Almanakh Tsitadel', 1996, pp. 70–84.
62. E.A. Shitikov *et al.*, op. cit., pp. 101–4.
63. V.I. Dmitriev, op. cit., pp. 258–9.
64. E.A. Shitikov *et al.*, op. cit., pp. 100, 102–3. *Istoriya* ..., op. cit., vol. IV, pp. 473, 276.
65. S.S. Berezhnoi, op. cit., pp. 51, 62–5.
66. E.A. Shitikov *et al.*, op. cit., p. 110. *Istoriya* ..., op. cit., vol. IV, p. 479.
67. V.I. Dmitriev, op. cit., pp. 262–4. E.A. Shitikov *et al.*, op. cit., pp. 105–8. *Istoriya* ..., op. cit., vol. IV, p. 474.
68. E.A. Shitikov *et al.*, op. cit., pp. 30, 34–5, 107.
69. V.I. Dmitriev, op. cit., pp. 255, 264. *Istoriya* ..., op. cit., vol. IV, pp. 358–9.
70. V.I. Dmitriev, op. cit., pp. 255, 264. E.A. Shitikov *et al.*, op. cit., pp. 112–15. *Istoriya* ..., op. cit., vol. IV, p. 359.

71. *Istoriya ...*, op. cit., vol. IV, pp. 477–8. A.V. Platonov, op. cit., pp. 140–2.
72. The details of all the Murmansk/Arkhangel'sk convoys are described in Bob Ruegg and Arnold Hagues, *Convoys to Russia 1941–1945. Allied Convoys and Naval Surface Operations in Arctic Waters 1941–1945*, Kendal (UK), World Ship Society, 1992. See also Michael Howard, 'The Russian Ally', in *History of the Second World War: Grand Strategy*, Vol. IV, London, HMSO, 1970, pp. 31–47.
73. B. Ruegg and A. Hague, op. cit., p. 28. S.S. Berezhnoi, op. cit., pp. 314–16.
74. Richard A. Russell, *Project Hula. Secret Soviet-American Cooperation in the War against Japan*, The US Navy in the Modern World Series, No. 4, Washington, Naval Historical Center, 1997, p. 4.
75. S.S. Berezhnoi, *Flot SSSR Korabli i suda lendliza. Spravochnik*, St Petersburg, Velen, 1994, pp. 20–21, 58–69.
76. S.S. Berezhnoi, op. cit., pp. 120–24.
77. S.S. Berezhnoi, op. cit., pp. 151–70.
78. S.W. Roskill, *The War at Sea 1939–1945*, Vol. III/1, London, HMSO, 1960, pp. 279–81.
80. S.S. Berezhnoi, op. cit., pp. 33–4.
81. S.S. Berezhnoi, op. cit., pp. 125–33, 173–8.
82. S.S. Berezhnoi, op. cit., pp. 133–8.
83. S.S. Berezhnoi, op. cit., pp. 206–11, 224–9.
84. S.S. Berezhnoi, op. cit., pp. 33–42.
85. B. Ruegg and A. Hague, op. cit., pp. 7–8.
86. Richard A. Russell, op. cit., pp. 12–17. Correspondence of J. Rohwer with Mrs Alla Kh. Paperno in 1997/98.
87. S.S. Berezhnoi, op. cit., pp. 43–55, 71–82.
88. Richard A. Russell, op. cit., pp. 30–40.
89. S.S. Berezhnoi, *Trofej i reparatsii VMF SSSR. Spravochnik*, Yakutsk, 1994, pp. 12–14, 33–4, 71–2, 85–7.
90. S.S. Berezhnoi, *Korabli i suda VMF SSSR 1928–1945*, Moscow, Voenizdat, 1988, pp. 324–5.
91. G.F Krivosheev (ed.), *Soviet Casualties and Combat Losses in the Twentieth Century*, London, Greenhill Books, 1997, pp. 265–71.
92. G.F Godlevskii, N.M Grechanyuk and W.M. Kononenko, *Pokhody boevye. Eskadra Chernomorskogo Flota v Velikoi Otechestvennoi vojne*, Moscow, Voenizdat, 1966. Friedrich Forstmeier, 'Die Versenkung des sowjetischen Flottillenführers *Charkov* und der Zerstörer *Sposobnyi* und *Besposhchadnyi* vor der Südküste der Krim am 6 Oktober 1943', *Marine-Rundschau*, 63 (1966), pp. 325–36.
93. G.F. Krivosheev, op. cit., pp. 266–71.
94. Ibid., pp. 266–71.
95. G.M. Gel'fond, *Sovetskii Flot v vojne s Japoni*, Moscow, Voenizdat, 1958. Jürg Meister, 'Der sowjetische–japanische Seekrieg', *Marine-Rundschau*, 57 (1960), pp. 3–18.
96. *Istoriya ...*, op. cit., vol. V, p. 10.
97. S.S. Berezhnoi, *Korabli i suda VMF SSSR 1928–1945*, Moscow, Voenizdat, 1988. For the Lend-Lease vessels from S.S. Berezhnoi, *Flot SSSR Korabli i suda lendliza*, St Petersburg, Velen', 1994.

10

From 1945 to the End of Stalin's Regime

Notwithstanding the fact that against only 75 sea-going surface ships, 57 submarines, 920 combat motor-boats and 1,375 other floating units were completed from 1941 to 1945,[1] showing the high degree of effort put into building light vessels, the Soviet leadership did not abandon pre-war plans for the Soviet Navy's development. In August 1944 the Operations Staff of the Headquarters of the Soviet Navy presented the *Narkom* for the Navy, Admiral Kuznetsov, with a draft plan for the development of the Soviet Navy through the first post-war decade.

FIRST PLANS FOR THE NEW NAVY

A first request of the *VMF* Main Staff contained no fewer than 9 battleships, 12 battlecruisers, 30 heavy cruisers, 60 light cruisers, 9 heavy, 6 light aircraft carriers, 18 heavy monitors, 144 big destroyers, 222 normal destroyers, 42 sea-going gunboats, 546 patrol ships, 327 big sub-chasers, 485 submarines, 644 minesweepers of different types, 564 small sub-chasers, 738 torpedo cutters and 476 landing vessels.[2]

In a reduced draft plan of August 1944 it was stated that the Fleet in the mid-1950s should include at least six battleships, six attack aircraft carriers, six escort aircraft carriers, six heavy cruisers, 24 light cruisers, 156 destroyers, 66 ocean-going minesweepers, 40 big and 88 medium submarines to operate on the high seas. In addition it should include 32 destroyers, 24 small submarines, 143 patrol ships, six minelayers, five net-layers, 112 minesweepers, 162 motor torpedo boats, 72 big and 162 small sub-chasers, 116 motor minesweepers, and 150 landing ships.

On 15 October 1944 Admiral Kuznetsov presented the Central Committee of the Communist Party (B), the first draft plan for the construction of warships for 1945 to 1947. It was envisaged first to complete the ships laid down and launched in accordance with the shipbuilding plans of 1936 to 1940, that is, first, the five light cruisers of *projekt 68*, the ten destroyers of *projekt 30*, and the five patrol ships of *projekt 29*. At the same time Kuznetsov suggested beginning the redesigning and designing of new ships for the post-war Soviet Navy, with the experiences learnt from the war in mind.

THE SOVIET DIPLOMATIC OFFENSIVE, 1944–45

In 1944–45, the Soviet leaders tried to improve the strategic situation along the Soviet littorals by a diplomatic offensive. At first they tried to change the international treaties signed during the period of temporary weakness of the Soviet state. In 1944 V.M. Molotov told the Norwegian Foreign Minister Trygve Lie that Stalin wanted Norway to revise the 1920 Spitzbergen Treaty, to cede Bear Island to Russia, and allow the Red Army to garrison the Svalbard Archipelago. Stalin also sought concessions from the Italian Empire in North Africa, which the Allied powers intended to dismember in order to punish Italy for its role as Germany's major European ally.[3] And at the Yalta Conference in February 1945 Stalin asked the Allies for a new post-war regime of international zones in the sea straits at the exits of the Baltic, the Black Sea and the Pacific. He insisted that South Sakhalin, the Kurile Islands and Port Arthur be ceded as compensation for the Soviet attack against the Japanese troops in north-eastern China and Korea, but first Stalin demanded a revision of the 1936 Montreux Convention, because it 'allowed small Turkey to throttle big Russia'. He said that the anti-Russian Montreux Convention was signed when Soviet–British relations were tense and, now, when the Soviet Union and Great Britain had become Allies, it should be revised.[4] The British premier Winston Churchill did not agree with Stalin's proposals, which could have led to the Soviet domination of the whole Balkan Peninsula. Therefore he did not participate in a prolonged discussion on a new regime for the Black Sea Straits zone at the Yalta Conference. The mutual decision of the Allied powers was as follows:

- to look over the Soviet proposals concerning the 1936 Montreux Convention at the London Conference of Foreign Ministers, which should be conducted some weeks later;
- to inform the Turkish government about the Allied powers' mutual decision in good time.[5]

Soon after the Yalta Conference, the Soviets informed the government of Turkey that the Soviet–Turkish Treaty, signed in 1921, did not correspond with 'the new situation'. In June 1945 they asked Turkey for air and naval bases in the Dardanelles but did not achieve the expected results because the Western powers supported Ankara. And in 1945 the Kremlin demanded naval bases in the Dodecanese, and a role in the occupation of Libya, positions Molotov forcefully advanced again at the London Conference of Foreign Ministers at the end of 1945.[6]

SHIPS AS REPARATION

By April 1945 Admiral Kuznetsov had called Stalin's attention to the problems inherent in distribution of the remains of the German Navy. And on 23 May Stalin informed President Harry S. Truman, the successor to Roosevelt, who had died in April 1945, and the British premier Churchill, of the necessity to divide the ships among the three great powers.[7] At the Potsdam Conference from 17 July to 2 August 1945, it was decided on 19 July to establish a technical commission to solve the details of the distribution of the German ships up to 1 November 1945.[8]

The delegations first met on 31 July; the Soviet Union was represented by Admiral of the Fleet Kuznetsov and the Chief of the Political Department of the Soviet Military Administration in Germany, A. Sobelev, while the American and British delegations were led by Vice Admiral S. Cook and Rear Admiral E. McCarthy respectively. Because of the political difficulties Kuznetsov consulted the then US Chief of Naval Operations, Fleet Admiral Ernest J. King, and the British First Sea Lord, Admiral Andrew Cunningham, so as to come to a diplomatic solution over which ship should go to which of the three Allied powers. Generally it was decided that of the remaining submarines only ten each should be distributed to the three powers – the others had to be sunk by the British Royal Navy in an operation called 'Deadlight', which was accomplished from 27 November 1945 to 12 February 1946 by sinking 115 U-boats in the area north-west of Scotland.[9] In at times difficult proceedings, discussions and final decisions the following distributions were decided upon, divided according to the first proposal of 6 December 1945, with the two final arrangements to be seen in Table 10.1.[10]

Table 10.1: Distribution of the German warships, submarines and merchant vessels

Ship types	6 December 1945 USSR	UK	USA	1st List USSR	UK	USA	2nd Final List USSR	UK	USA
Cruisers	1	–	1	1	–	1	1	–	1
Destroyers and T-boats	10	13	7	10	13	7	10	13	7
U-boats	10	10	10	10	10	10	10	10	10
Minesweepers	44	44	44	44	44	42	44	44	42
Mine counter-measure V	4	4	8	4	4	7	4	4	7
Old T-boats and escorts	6	5	6	6	5	4	6	5	4
M/S boats	51	45	48	50	44	48	51	44	48
MTBs	30	29	30	30	28	28	31	28	28
KFK boats	146	147	148	147	137	101	147	136	101
Trawlers (MS and Patrol)	42	36	40	42	35	45	45	39	48
Landing vessels	136	66	103	136	44	99	135	45	100
Tugs	37	18	26	37	18	25	38	20	27
Depot ships	5	6	3	5	5	3	5	5	3
Tenders	16	9	9	18	8	8	17	8	8
Tankers	7	1	3	7	1	3	7	1	3
Floating cranes	6	6	6	6	6	6	6	6	6
Net-layers	3	4	3	3	4	3	3	4	3
Catapult ships	1	2	1	1	2	1	1	2	1
Diverse vessels	94	98	91	92	98	91	96	99	87
Harbour tugs							26	20	30
Barges							50	45	50
Accommodation vessels							47	45	43
Floating cranes							7	7	5

Source: A. Komarov, op. cit., p. 82.

The German ships were in most cases transferred by German crews to Liepaja, after it was arranged that the German sailors had to be retransported to German ports following the delivery of the ships into Soviet custody. The delivery began in January 1946 and continued for some months. Up to July 1947 790 ships and submarines altogether of all types were delivered.

The Soviet share of German ships was augmented by some wrecks found in the Soviet-occupied area of Germany, but such ships were in most cases in such a heavily damaged state that repair was not meaningful, although some of them were salvaged to be towed to Soviet ports. Such ships were the old battleship *Schleswig-Holstein*, which was sunk on 18 December 1944 by an air attack at Gdynia, salvaged, and on 26 September 1946 towed to Tallin, but because of irreparable damage sunk on 25 June 1947 near the Neugrund Bank in the Finnish Gulf. More important was the aircraft carrier *Graf Zeppelin*, uncompleted lying at Stettin and scuttled there on 25 April 1945. Salvaged by Soviet teams and towed to Kronshtadt in September 1945, to be intensively investigated by the A.N. Krylov Nautical and Scientific Institute, and from 3 February 1947 to 18 August 1947 put under the Soviet flag. For some time it was considered that the ship could be repaired as a carrier, but nothing came from this, and it was sunk on 20 September 1947 in the Central Baltic by bombs and torpedoes from destroyers and *TK*s. Another ship was the heavy cruiser *Seydlitz*, sister of the *Lützow*, bought in 1940 and renamed first *Petropavlovsk*, and then *Tallin*. The *Seydlitz* was never completed as a cruiser, but reconstruction to a light aircraft carrier was under way until January 1943 when this was stopped by Hitler's orders. Damaged by Soviet air attack on 9 April 1945 at the yard at Königsberg and scuttled there, it was salvaged in 1946, and towed to Leningrad, to be put under the Soviet flag on 10 March 1947, but after an unprofitable repair on 9 April 1947 was scrapped. Finally there was the former 'pocket-battleship', now also called a heavy cruiser, *Lützow* (ex-*Deutschland*). This ship was sunk by a heavy Royal Air Force bomb on 16 April 1945 in the 'Kaiserfahrt' south of Swinemünde. It was salvaged by Soviet teams and put under the Soviet flag on 26 September 1946, but as there was no good possibility of repairing it, the ship was sunk on 22 July 1947 in the Central Baltic.[11] The vessels commissioned into the Soviet Navy were (in parentheses German name and time of active service, not as special or experimental vessel):[12]

Light cruiser: *Admiral Makarov* (ex-*Nürnberg*, 13.02.46–20.02.59)
Destroyers: *Prytkii* (ex-*Friedrich Ihn*, 13.02.46–22.03.52), *Pyl'kii* (ex-*Erich Steinbrinck*, 13.02.46–30.04.49), *Prochnyi* (ex-*Karl Galster*, 13.02.46–28.11.54), *Provornyi* (ex-*Z 33*, 13.02.46–22.04.58)
Small destroyer: *Primernyi* (ex-*T-33*, 13.02.46–28.12.54)
Torpedo-boats: *Podvizhnyi* (ex-*T-12*, 13.02.46–30.12.54), *Poryvistyi* (ex-*T-17*, 13.02.46–07.09.49)
Old torpedo boats: *Porayushchii* (ex-*T-107*, 13.02.46–24.12.55), *Prozorlivyi* (ex-*T-158*, 13.02.46–24.12.55), *Pronzitel'nyi* (ex-*T-196*, 13.02.46–30.04.49)
Patrol ships: *Buran* (ex-*F-7*, 25.02.46–08.09.56)

Minesweepers (type 35): *T-912 (ex-M-7, 13.05.46–07.05.57), *T-913 (ex-M-29, 13.05.46–08.09.56), *T-914 (ex-M-30, 13.05.46–22.10.58) (1954–58 Caspian Flotilla), *T-915 (ex-M-151, 13.05.46–08.01.53), *T-916 (ex-M-204, 13.05.46–26.08.52), *T-917 (ex-M-254, 13.05.46–18.12.54), *T-918 (ex-M-3, 13.05.46–17.11.59), *T-919 (ex-M-203, 13.05.46–25.02.53), *T-920 (ex-M-34, 13.05.46–16.03.53), *T-921 (ex-M-17, 13.05.46–01.09.55), *T-922 (ex-M-255, 13.05.46–31.01.58), *T-923 (ex-M-256, 13.05.46–11.03.58), *T-924 (ex-M-155, 13.05.46–29.10.56)

Minesweepers (type 40): T-701 (ex-M-267, 27.12.46–20.10.60), T-702 (ex-M-279, 20.11.45–20.08.65), T-703 (ex-M-324, 27.12.45–24.12.55), T-704 (ex-M-342, 27.12.45–20.01.60), T-705 (ex-M-377, 20.11.45–20.01.60), T-706 (ex-M-401, 27.12.45–10.02.59), T-707 (ex-M-406, 27.12.45–07.04.56), T-708 (ex-M-411, 27.12.45–18.12.54), T-709 (ex-M-423, 27.12.45–24.12.55), T-710 (ex-M-431, 27.12.45–24.12.55), T-711 (ex-M-291, 27.12.45–15.08.51), T-712 (ex-M-330, 27.12.45–24.12.55), T-713 (ex-M-348, 27.12.45–01.09.55), T-714 (ex-M-386, 27.12.45–18.12.54), T-715 (ex-M-405, 27.12.45–18.12.54, 53–54 Northern Fleet), T-716 (ex-M-425, 27.12.45–07.04.56), T-717 (ex-M-446, 27.12.45–24.12.55), T-718 (ex-M-461, 27.12.45–10.02.59), T-719 (ex-M-467, 27.12.45–21.06.51), T-720 (ex-M-470, 27.12.45–04.11.66), T-721 (ex-M-265, 25.02.46–12.11.47), T-722 (ex-M-341, 25.02.46–15.08.51), T-723 (ex-M-369, 25.02.46–15.08.51), T-724 (ex-M-407, 25.02.46–01.09.55), T-725 (ex-M-415, 25.02.46–01.09.55), T-726 (ex-M-437, 25.02.46–24.01.52), T-727 (ex-M-443, 25.02.46–08.01.53), T-729 (ex-M-484, 25.02.46–07.04.56), T-730 (ex-M-496, 25.02.46–01.09.55)

Big submarines (type XXI): B-27 (ex-N-27, ex-U 3515, 13.02.46–19.09.55), B-28 (ex-N-28, ex-U 2529, 13.02.46–29.12.55), B-29 (ex-N-29, ex-U 3035, 13.02.46–18.01.56), B-30 (ex-N-30, ex-U 3041, 13.02.46–29.12.55)

Big submarine (type IXC/40): B-26 (ex-N-26, ex-U 1231, 13.02.46–17.08.53)

Medium submarines (type VIIC): S-81 (ex-N-22, ex-U 1057, 13.02.46–16.10.57), S-82 (ex-N-23, ex-U 1058, 13.02.46–25.03.58), S-83 (ex-N-24, ex-U 1064, 13.02.46–29.12.55), S-84 (ex-N-25, ex-U 1305, 13.02.46–30.12.55). S-81 and S-84 then transferred to Northern Fleet and were used during atomic tests off Novaya Zemlya in September 1957.[13]

Small submarine: M-51 (ex-N-, ex-U 2353, no data known)

In addition the following motor-minesweepers and 'Schnellboote' were delivered to the Soviet Navy, but the new numbers of the R-Boote and times of service have not been made known up to now:[14]

Motor-minesweepers: R 25, R 28, R 53, R 58, R 63, R 65, R 87, R 90, R 103, R 105, R 107, R 113, R 121, R 122, R 124, R 149, R 233, R 237, R 245, R 254, R 257, R 258, R 262, R 265, R 269, R 270, R 288, R 289, R 409, R 410, R 411, R 412, R 413, R 414, R 415, R 416, R 417, R 418, R 419, R 420, R 421, R 422, R 423, R 302, R 303, R 305, R 307, R 308, R 310, R 311, R 312, RA 102, RA 104, RA 111, RA 112, RA 204

*These minesweepers were transferred from 27.04.46 to the Black Sea Fleet.

'Schnellboote': *TK-1002* (ex-*S 11*), *TK-1003* (ex-*S 16*), *TK-1004* (ex-*S 24*), *TK-1005* (ex-*S 50*), *TK-1006* (ex-*S 65*), *TK-1001* (ex-*S 81*), *TK-1008* (ex-*S 82*), *TK-1009* (ex-*S 86*), *TK-1010* (ex-*S 99*), *TK-1011* (ex-*S 101*), *TK-1012* (ex-*S 109*), *TK-1013* (ex-*S 110*), *TK-1014* (ex-*S 113*), *TK-1015* (ex-*S 118*), *TK-1016* (ex-*S 123*), *TK-1017* (ex-*S 132*), *TK-1018* (ex-*S 135*), *TK-1019* (ex-*S 175*), *TK-1020* (ex-*S 204*), *TK-1021* (ex-*S 209*), *TK-1022* (ex-*S 211*), *TK-1023* (ex-*S 214*), *TK-1024* (ex-*S 219*), *TK-1025* (ex-*S 222*), *TK-1026* (ex-*S 227*), *TK-1027* (ex-*S 704*), *TK-1028* (ex-*S 707*), *TK-1029* (ex-*S 708*), *TK-1030* (ex-*S 709*)

Landing vessels: There were also 21 gun-armed landing barges (*AF*) and 78 landing barges (*F*) named *BAD* and *BDB*

There were also some purpose-built auxiliaries and former merchant ships, rebuilt as auxiliaries, taken over by the Soviet Navy: four net-layers (*Akhtuba, Lena, Ponoi, Tyumen-Ula*), four 'Sperrbrecher' (*Vologda*,[15] *Kem', Kuloi, Kushka*), nine minesweeping trawlers (*T-804, 805, 807, 808, 810, 925, 926, 927, 928*), one hydrographic vessel (*Terek*), and the depot ships (*Pechora, Kuban', Tuloma, Donets, Lugan',* and *Desna*), and one staff vessel (*Angara*).

In addition there were ships and submarines in an unfinished state captured in shipbuilding yards in Eastern Germany, for example, especially a number of *type XXI* U-boats, mostly still with some sections put together and other sections waiting for the laying down on the slips of the *Schichau* yard at Danzig (*TS-5–13, 15, TS-17–19, TS-32–38*). There was for some time an intention to complete them as *projekt 614*, as will be mentioned later, but in 1947 they were all scrapped.[16]

There was also one big Finnish ship delivered to the Soviet Navy as reparation, the coastal battleship *Väinämöinen*, which became the *Viborg*, serving from 05.07.47 to 24.12.55 and used until 1966 as a floating base.

The next group of reparation ships came from the remnants of the Japanese navy and were commissioned into the Pacific Fleet:[17]

Destroyers: *Vernyi* (ex-*Hibiki*, 22.07.47–20.02.53), *Vnezapnyi* (ex-*Harutsuki*, 25.09.47–17.06.49)

Escort destroyers: *Vetrepnyi* (ex-*Hatsuzakura*, 22.07.47–17.06.49), *Vozrozhdennyi* (ex-*Kiri*, 22.07.47–17.06.49), *Volevoi* (ex-*Kaya*, 22.07.47–17.06.49), *Vol'nyi* (ex-*Shii*, 22.07.47–17.06.49), *Vnimatel'nyi* (ex-*Kizi*, 21.10.47–17.06.49)

Frigates: *EK-31* (ex-*Shimushu*, 22.07.47–16.05.59), *EK-41* (ex-*Ikino*, 26.08.47–01.06.61), *EK-47* (ex-*Kozu*, 25.09.47–25.01.69)

Corvettes (type D and C): *EK-32* (ex-*No. 34*, 22.07.47–30.11.54), *EK-33* (ex-*No. 196*, 22.07.47–30.11.54), *EK-36* (ex-*No. 52*, 26.08.47–30.11.54), *EK-37* (ex-*No. 78*, 16.08.47–30.11.54), *EK-38* (ex-*No. 142*, 22.07.47–17.11.54), *EK-42* (ex-*No. 48*, 26.08.47–02.06.59), *EK-44* (ex-*No. 76*, 25.09.47–17.11.54), *EK-46* (ex-*No. 102*, 25.09.47–21.01.60), *EK-34* (ex-*No. 105*, 22.07.47–17.06.49), *EK-35* (ex-*No. 227*, 22.07.47–17.06.49), *EK-39* (ex-*No. 79*, 26.08.47–17.06.49), *EK-40* (ex-*No. 221*, 26.08.47–11.03.58), *EK-43* (ex-*No. 71*, 25.09.47–05.07.48), *EK-45* (ex-*No. 77*, 25.09.47–05.07.48)

Minelayers: *Vilyui* (ex-*Katashima Maru*, 15.09.47–11.02.55 delivered to China), *Katun'* (ex-*Kamishima*, 15.09.47–09.11.56)

Minesweeper: *T-25* (ex-*W 23*, 15.09.47–31.10.55)

The last group were the Italian vessels delivered in 1949, when the British ships sent in 1944 were transferred back.[18] They were used in the Black Sea Fleet:

Battleship: *Novorossijsk* (ex-*Giulio Cesare*, 24.02.49–30.10.55 lost by a mine explosion in Sevastopol)
Light Cruiser: *Kerch* (ex-*Emanuele Filiberto Duca d'Aosta*, 30.03.49–11.03.58)
Destroyers: *Legkii* (ex-*Fuciliere*, 13.03.49–21.01.60), *Lovkii* (ex-*Artigliere*, 24.02.49–17.10.55)
Escort destroyers: *Ladnyi* (ex-*Animoso*, 30.03.49–30.11.54), *Letnyi* (ex-*Fortunale*, 30.03.49–30.11.54), *Lyutyi* (ex-*Ardimentoso*, 23.11.49–30.11.54)
Submarines: *S-41* (ex-*N-41*, ex-*Marea*, 24.02.49–17.02.56), *S-42* (ex-*N-42*, ex-*Nichelio*, 24.02.49–17.02.56)

RETURN OF THE LEND-LEASE SHIPS

In spring and summer 1949 the battleship *Arkhangel'sk*, and most of the destroyers with the Northern Fleet were returned to Great Britain, and in most cases soon scrapped there. In early 1950 the destroyer *Zhguchii* and the submarines followed, and in summer 1952 the destroyers *Doblestnyi* and *Druzhnyi*. The cruiser *Murmansk* went back in March 1949 to the USA. The trawler-minesweepers of the Northern Fleet had gone back already in 1948, only *T-105* was under repair and remained up to its scrapping in 1964. The British motor-minesweepers remained also in Russia and were scrapped there. The seven remaining American minesweepers of the *Admirable* class were used up to the mid-1950s by the Soviet Navy in various ways and then scrapped. The remaining sub-chasers of the Black Sea Fleet were given back into US custody at Istanbul in 1954, while the boats with the Northern Fleet were sunk or destroyed under supervision off the Kola Gulf or at a repair yard. The same was the case with the torpedo cutters of the two fleets.[19]

The vessels with the Pacific Fleet, which were at first still augmented by some deliveries after the end of the war, suffered a similar fate. The frigates, of which *EK-11* to *EK-30* arrived only in October 1945, were in most cases in February 1950 transferred to the Japanese port Maizuru and there given back into US custody. Most of them were in 1953 lent to the Japanese Maritime Security Force, and some later to the South Korean Navy, as is mentioned in the appendix. Only *EK-3* remained in Soviet hands and was scrapped in 1960. Of the *Admirable* minesweepers remaining in the Pacific Fleet until the 1950s, some were cast off from 1956 to 1958, most in 1960. Of the *YMS* mine-sweepers, *T-285* was lost after the war in 1945 on a mine and *T-523* had already been scrapped in 1946, the others were destroyed or scrapped under supervision in the mid-1950s. The same was the case with the sub-chasers, of which some had already been stricken under Soviet control, some destroyed under supervision, and two, *BO-303* and *BO-304*, mothballed in 1954. The landing vessels were returned in 1955 and 1956 as far as they could travel, the others being destroyed or scrapped.[20]

THE TEN-YEAR PROGRAMME OF 1945 (1946–55)

On 21 May 1945 Stalin convened a conference of high-ranking officers of the Army and Navy. He made a speech on the subject of the post-war development of the Soviet Armed Forces. He said that only the tank and naval formations would not be reduced.

In midsummer 1945 *Admiral Flota* Kuznetsov had to leave Moscow, because he was appointed a member of the General Headquarters of the Soviet Armed Forces in the Far East. On 25 August 1945 he ordered his deputy, Admiral L.M. Galler, to sign the new version of the post-war shipbuilding programme on his behalf, because it was demanded for urgent presentation to the head of the Soviet government. In accordance with that plan nine battleships, 12 heavy cruisers with 220mm guns, 30 cruisers with 180mm guns and 60 light cruisers with 152mm guns, besides the lighter vessels, were proposed up to the mid-1950s, as Table 10.2 shows.

However some weeks later Kuznetsov wrote: 'No battleships! At least aircraft destroyed the *Tirpitz*. Really she didn't operate, but through her service time she was making obstacles for the German Fleet's combat activity ... Cruisers and destroyers proved their own value. Submarines are combat ships with good prospects, but they will be in need of support by surface ships and aircraft operations. So there should be aircraft carriers!'[21]

The war had badly damaged the industry generally, but especially the shipbuilding capacity, reducing it to 59.2 per cent of the capacity of 1940.

Table 10.2: Shipbuilding plans for the period 1946 to 1955

Ship types	First request VMF	Reduced request VMF	Plan of 27 September	10-year programme	Actually built to 1955
Battleships	9	4	3	0	0
Battlecruisers	12	10	7	4	0
Heavy Cruisers	30	30	10	0	0
Light Cruisers	60	54	30	30	19
Big Carriers	9	6	0	0	0
Light Carriers	6	6	2	0	0
Big Monitors	18	12	–	18	0
Big Destroyers	144	132	0	0	0
Destroyers	222	226	250	188	85
Seagoing Gunboats	42	38	–	36	0
Patrol Ships	546	558	–	177	48
Big Sub-chasers	327	345	–	345	157
Big Submarines	168	168	40	40	6
Medium Submarines	204	204	204	204	151
Small Submarines	117	123	123	123	66
Squadron Minesweepers	110	110	–	30	0
Coastal Minesweepers	237	237	–	400	c.150
Inshore Minesweepers	297	330	–	306	c.100
Small Sub-chasers	564	600	–	600	86
Torpedo Cutters	738	828	–	828	c.730
Landing Vessels	476	135	–	195	1

Source: Dmitrii Litvinenko, 'Plany Vozhdya', *Morskoi sbornik*, No. 2 (1997), p. 102.

The workers in the shipbuilding yards were reduced to 44.9 per cent, and the output was down below the level of 1938. So it was necessary first to reconstruct the yards and to bring the shipbuilding programme into line with such necessities. When the Head of the Operational Administration of the Council of People's Commissars, L.P. Beriya, checked the first requests of the Naval Main Staff, he demanded a reduction in the requested numbers in consideration of the real capacities of the industry. So during September 1945 a Commission with N.G. Kuznetsov, N.V. Isachenkov, I.F. Tevosyan, I.I. Nosenko and other naval commanders and industrial managers discussed the possibilities of the shipbuilding yards and prepared three variants of the demanded ten-year programme.

- The first variant was based on the already existing capacities of the industry, and counted on a minimum financial investment of 730 million rubles. It was proposed to build during the ten years only 15 light cruisers, 48 destroyers, 17 patrol ships and 35 submarines. During this time the shipbuilding yards should enlarge their volume of production by 250 per cent.
- The second variant proposed reconstruction of the destroyed yards and the completion and enlargement of the shipbuilding yards and supply industries with 3.53 billion rubles, and enlargement of capacity by 500 per cent. But this also was not enough to fulfil the requests of the *VMF*.
- The third variant foresaw a development of all production facilities to fulfil the requests of the *VMF*. At least 42 new works had to be built for 42 billion rubles. The production capacity should be 330 per cent bigger than in 1945. Only in this way could the reduced requests of the Navy be fulfilled.[22]

On 5 September 1945 the members of the Politburo of the Communist Party, headed by Stalin, discussed the subject of the ten-year shipbuilding programme. The leaders of the Navy and the *Narkomat* for the Shipbuilding Industry participated in the discussion. The *Narkom* for shipbuilding I.I. Nosenko, rejected the demands of the Naval High Command. He stated, that the Soviet shipbuilding industry could not start construction of newly designed ships. His own proposals were the following:

- to stop new designs;
- to improve the pre-war designs in accordance with Second World War experiences;
- to cut down the number of new ships.

On 27 September 1945 the plan for the Navy's post-war development was again discussed. Stalin had summoned the members of the Politburo L.P. Beriya, G.V. Malenkov, and N.A. Bulganin, the *Narkom* for Shipbuilding, I.I. Nosenko, and his deputy A.M. Red'kin, N.G. Kuznetsov and his deputy L.M. Galler, and the dean of the Naval Academy, S.P. Stavitskii. When Kuznetsov proposed building only four battleships and four battlecruisers, Stalin said that the number of battleships should be cut down, but at the same time he demanded that the number of heavy cruisers be increased, and that they should have not the 220mm guns as proposed by Kuznetsov, but 305mm guns, so that they would be 'rowdy ships', faster than any heavier ship and stronger than any faster one. This meant that they would really be battlecruisers similar to the pre-war *projekt 69*. Kuznetsov tried to convince Stalin that the number of ships of each type should be reasonable to prevent the Soviet Union from creating an unbalanced fleet. Stalin replied:

> We shouldn't follow England. Commanders of our squadrons will need to choose a defensive course of sea warfare through the next ten or twelve or even fifteen years. If you plan to attack America, you need a balanced fleet. We'll not do it. Therefore we'll not exhaust our industry.[23]

In the end it was decided to complete the unfinished battleship *Sovetskaya Rossiya* at Molotovsk to the improved *projekt 23 NU*, and to lay down two new battleships of *projekt 24*, and also seven *projekt 82* battlecruisers, so important to Stalin, who watched closely the progress of their development and the start of construction.

Stalin was very reluctant to build aircraft carriers, and ordered that their number be cut down. He saw no use for them in the Baltic and the Black Sea, whereas in the Far East the airfields on Sakhalin and the Kurile Islands would make them unnecessary. When Kuznetsov offered to reduce the number to four heavy and four light carriers, Stalin agreed to the persisting requests of the Navy and only allowed preparations for two *projekt 72* light carriers, probably with the Northern Fleet in mind.[24]

The 'big fleet' construction demanded not only industrial capacities but also funds. Production capacity allowed only 30 cruisers. Kuznetsov would have preferred ten of the new *projekt 66* heavy cruisers with nine 220mm guns, firing at a greater rate than the 203mm guns of the Western powers, and able to stand up against the newest heavy cruisers of foreign navies, such as the US *Des Moines* class. And there was the request for 30 cruisers with 180mm guns. The Navy would have preferred in addition 54 of the new *projekt 65* light cruisers armed with nine 152mm guns, of which many different versions had been designed.[25] Stalin at first said, that the cruisers with 180mm guns were unnecessary. The heavy cruisers with 220mm guns had already been upgraded to have 305mm guns. So Stalin demanded that 152mm gun cruisers of the improved *projekt 68-bis* design be built.

Stalin disliked the types of the proposed big destroyers of *projekts 35, 40* and the newer *41*. He believed that the variety of ship types hindered the training of the new crews – for example, eight former German reparation destroyers were proving difficult to man. He also disliked the new standard gun that the Navy proposed, in case it should delay the mass production of the destroyers of the improved *projekt 30-bis* of which he demanded 250 units, instead of the 132 heavy and 226 normal destroyers in the Navy's reduced proposal. He criticized Kuznetsov for not allowing for the lack of industrial capacity.[26] He demanded therefore that the heavy destroyers be got rid of and that only the *projekt 30-bis* destroyers with their proven equipment be built.

Stalin, telling Kuznetsov that 'you produce fears for yourself', also questioned the need for so many different types of submarines. He prohibited the planning of more than 40 of the big submarines of *projekt 611*, and preferred the medium submarines of *projekt 613*, and asked that the numbers be made up by building the small submarines of the last pre-war design, now *projekt 96-bis*, to be followed by the more modern *projekt 615*, cancelling all the other projects such as the big minelayer-, or transport-, and landing submarines, as well as the midgets, and especially the completion of the former German *type XXI/projekt 614* vessels captured at Danzig.[27]

The last disagreement came up concerning the coastal defence vessels and the patrol ships. While the Navy wanted ocean-going escort vessels of 1,800t (*projekt 37*), or at least enlarged versions of the last design to be built before the war (*projekt 29-bis*), Stalin demanded ships of not more than 1,000t in much reduced numbers. As a result 177 units instead of the 558 proposed by the Navy appeared in the final programme.[28]

On 27 November 1945 Stalin again convened a commission of the Politburo and experts, consisting of L.P. Beriya, N.A. Vosnesenskii, N.G. Kuznetsov, I.I. Nosenko, A.I. Antonov, I.A. Tevosyan, D.A. Ustinov and A.M. Red'kin, to confirm the final version of the ten-year programme of shipbuilding for the Soviet Navy. It was planned to build 5,850 combatants and auxiliaries between 1946 and 1955, reducing the numbers of 27 September again somewhat for the big ships as is shown in Table 10.2.

EXPERIENCES, STRATEGIES AND INDUSTRIAL CAPACITIES

During the Great Patriotic War the trend in the development of the Soviet Navy was running counter to a 'Big Ocean-Going Navy', demanded to secure Stalin's global policy. The unbalanced character of the Navy was observed during wartime. The obsolete Soviet battleships were generally used only as huge floating batteries. In the Baltic the battleships remained in the area of Leningrad/Kronshtadt, where one was sunk by dive bombers. And since 1941 the cruisers and destroyers had not been used in the open sea. In the North the heavy ships, the battleship *Arkhangel'sk* and the cruiser *Murmansk* that had been delivered in 1944, were only used to augment the anti-aircraft defence of the Murmansk area, while the destroyers participated in the escorting of the Allied convoys. In the Black Sea the only battleship in 1941 and early 1942 supported the defence of Sevastopol, but remained in Caucasian harbours for the rest of the war. The cruisers and destroyers were somewhat more active in the defence of Odessa, Sevastopol and the Caucasian coast, and even tried to attack the German shipborne supply without success, until the *Stavka* forbade their employment in October 1943. And in the Far East the two cruisers as well as the modern destroyers were lying in the harbours camouflaged against potential Japanese air attacks. Owing to the lack of aircraft covering for the ships and of a shortage of mine counter-measures the light ships could not operate entirely successfully, and most losses were inflicted by air attacks and mines. And the results from the combat activity of the numerous Soviet submarines did not correspond to their heavy casualties. Almost three hundred MTBs were generally used instead of small sub-chasers or fast landing vessels for the amphibious operations.

All the units designed in accordance with pre-war Soviet naval thinking had proved themselves inadequate for contemporary sea warfare. The presence in the Baltic or the Black Sea of one new battleship or battlecruiser each could not have had much influence on the outcome of the combat at sea. The Baltic ships would have been enclosed in the besieged fortress area of Leningrad, and the Black Sea vessels were incapable of offensive operations because of the lack of air cover. Only in the North might the availability of a new battleship have had an influence on the improvement of the situation. But the unavailability of an aircraft carrier would have limited the use of this battleship to a zone of land-based air cover. Retrospective evaluation showed that the most important ships in the North and the Black Sea would have been aircraft carriers. In the Black Sea a carrier of *projekt 71* with 20 to 30 fighters might have helped to secure 'mastery of the sea' there. In the North an aircraft carrier was necessary to prevent the heavy German air attacks from Northern Norway. So the start of designing the aircraft carrier of *projekt 72* with variants of 30, 45 and 60 aircraft was a correct step. The experience of the entire Second World War showed clearly that the period of the heavy gun-armed battleship and their gun duels was over, and that they had lost their role as the main element of sea power to the aircraft carriers and submarines. So 47 per cent of the lost battleships, carriers and cruisers of all navies were victims of aircraft, 28 per cent of submarines, 15 per cent of torpedoes of surface ships, and only 8.5 per cent of gunfire. And as was clearly to be seen, anti-aircraft artillery was not able to defend a ship alone against air attacks.

The leaders of the Soviet Navy, headed by *Admiral Flota* Kuznetsov, realized, that the Navy needed a new adequate naval doctrine to renew the construction of a new 'Big Fleet'. But they could not create it, because they were not well-informed about the essence of Stalin's global policy and his opinion on the subject of East–West post-war relations. So the Navy presented at first a programme which on the one hand exceeded by far the real possibilities of the industry, and on the other did not take into consideration the threat estimates of the State and Army leadership. Their hand was to some extent forced by the famous 'Iron Curtain' speech of Winston Churchill in Fulton, Missouri, on 5 March 1946. Looking at the beginning of the Cold War and the necessary demobilization of the Army, they had to take into account the problems of stabilizing their dominant position in the occupied areas of eastern and Central Europe, and to secure the borders of the area under Soviet control, in order to keep the Western former Allies and their superior air power as far away from the centres of the Soviet state as possible. Because of the Allied atomic bomb, this was especially important, as was the fast development of its own nuclear capability, using the research of its own scientists and the important information gained from atomic espionage.[29] And in this context it was of great importance to develop anti-aircraft defence by new jet fighters and to design long-range bombers for delivering its own potential nuclear weapons. The great amphibious capacities of the Western Allies, demonstrated during the invasions of Italy and France, and the many large landing operations in the Pacific had also inspired fear.[30]

The argument over Soviet naval strategy was thus resumed in 1946 in a situation that was far from clear for the Navy. In an article entitled 'About some

Traits of Modern Sea Warfare', published in *Morskoi sbornik*,[31] K. Zotov argued that the naval air forces had become the decisive weapon of the war at sea. High-performance aircraft operating from aircraft carriers would be needed to give the fleet – which must be designed to operate far from home waters for long periods – the necessary air cover against enemy aircraft. He predicted that rockets and nuclear weapons would soon make traditional gunships obsolete, but not aircraft carriers, as submarines alone would not be able to defeat an enemy and maintain naval supremacy. But the representatives of the shipbuilding industry were against aircraft carriers, because they did not have the necessary experience and the industry lacked the necessary capacities for building such ships.

REORGANIZATION OF THE HIGH COMMAND AND NEW PURGES

The efforts of the *Narkom* for the Navy, *Admiral Flota* Kuznetsov, to ask repeatedly for aircraft carriers, must have aroused Stalin's mistrust because he had other problems with setting the priorities for the post-war armed forces. His support of the Navy was interrupted. So on 25 February 1946 he started reorganizing the Armed Forces High Command. The People's Commissariats were abolished and the head of the Defence establishment became the Minister of Defence. Instead of the People's Commissar of the Navy, Kuznetsov became a Deputy Minister of Defence and Commander-in-Chief of the Navy. Ten days earlier Stalin had ordered that the Baltic Fleet be divided into two separate fleets, the 4th Fleet under Admiral G.I. Levchenko and the 8th Fleet under its former C-in-C V.F. Tributs. Kuznetsov was disappointed. And on 17 January 1947 the Pacific Fleet also was divided, into the 5th Fleet under Vice-Admiral A.S. Frolov and the 7th Fleet under Vice-Admiral M.I. Bajkov. Kuznetsov, probably because of his disagreement with Stalin, was replaced as Commander-in-Chief of the Navy and demoted to Vice-Admiral. His successor was Admiral I.S. Yumashev, who had served as the Commander-in-Chief of the Pacific Fleet from 1939 to this time. Owing to a lack of experience in conduct at strategic levels, Yumashev was not very successful as a replacement for Kuznetsov. And in the spring of 1947 Levchenko and Tributs also were relieved and replaced by Vice-Admirals V.A. Andreev and F.V. Zozulya. But this was not all. On 12 January 1948 Stalin ordered a trial against Kuznetsov, his former deputy Admiral L.M. Galler, the Chief of the *Voroshilov* Naval Academy and former Chief of the Main Staff, Admiral V.A. Alafuzov, and Kuznetsov's deputy, Vice-Admiral G.A. Stepanov, based on the accusation that they had given away state secrets to the British, especially concerning the secret equipment and weapons of the German U-boats *U 250*, salvaged and lying in the dry dock at Kronshtadt. The main points were concerned with the German acoustic torpedo *T-5* and the Soviet development *45-36 AVA*, but as Galler's biographer S.A. Zonin said, these must have been only subterfuges to get rid of the four men.[32] Galler died in the Kazan prison in 1950, and Alafuzov and Stepanov were not rehabilitated until 1953 after Stalin's death, while Kuznetsov was appointed on 20 February 1950 as Commander of the 5th Fleet in the Pacific.[33]

NEW DISCUSSIONS ABOUT STRATEGY

No wonder that, with the accusations against Kuznetsov and admirals loyal to him, discussions about necessary strategy and tactics turned to Stalin's preferred course and the Party line. The author of the aforementioned article, Zotov, was followed by *Kontr Admiral* J. Eliseev. Both were challenged by the theorists *Kapitan 2 Ranga* V. Kulakov, *Kontr Admiral* I. Yeliseev, and *Kapitan 2 Ranga* N. Milgram, each of whom dismissed the theory of naval supremacy as politically reactionary.[33] *Kapitan 1 Ranga* D. Rechister, however, supported Zotov, on the grounds that naval supremacy was not a political theory, but a military doctrine.[34] But prominent Soviet naval theorists kept away from that fruitless discussion. Generally they did not agree with Stalin's decision to build out-of-date heavyweight units, but they had no common point of view on the subject of reasonable development for the post-war Navy. Vice-Admiral S.P. Stavitskii, the chief author of the 1937 Naval Forces Combat Regulations (*BUMS-37*), was ordered to make up a new version of it, which would correspond to Second World War experiences. At the end of the war he had accomplished this job, but generally the new version of *BUMS* followed the course of Soviet naval thinking outline during the pre-war period in accordance with the conception of the 'small war at sea'. Admiral I.S. Isakov, who at the beginning of 1946 was again appointed by Stalin as the Chief of the Main Staff of the Navy, usually spoke against aircraft carriers, but demonstrated agreement with Stalin's composition of the fleet. The leading Soviet naval strategist, Professor V.A. Belli, resisted voicing his own opinion on the subject of the principal problems of naval theory in public discussions. The discussion, which failed to penetrate the High Command, came to an end in the late 1950s with a statement by *Kapitan 3 Range* K. Penzin, that 'the Navy is an assistant of the Army'.[35]

By 1950 Stalin had realized that this was counter-productive and decided to re-establish an independent Naval Ministry, because his land-minded marshals were throttling the Navy. On 26 February 1950 the Ministry of Naval Forces and the Naval General Staff (*MGSh*) were established. Admiral I.S. Yumashev was appointed as the head of the Ministry of Naval Forces. And Admiral A.G. Golovko, the former Commander of the Northern Fleet, became the Chief of the *MGSh*. At the same time Kuznetsov was recalled and became Commander of the 5th Southern Pacific Fleet. But the situation changed from bad to worse, because Yumashev and Golovko could not satisfy Stalin's demands, which had changed once again. In addition, they did not organize reasonable co-operation between the Ministry's departments and the *MGSh*, as well as the training of personnel corresponding to the Navy's operational tasks.

In the summer of 1951 the Chief Inspector of the Navy, Admiral G.I. Levchenko, presented Stalin with his memorandum on the state of the Navy's management. He reported to Stalin, that in his opinion the situation of the Naval forces was unsatisfactory. From 13–16 July 1951 in the Kremlin Stalin conducted an extraordinary conference of the Main Military Council of the Navy. The members of the Politburo of the Communist Party, the leaders of the Army and of the Navy including I.S. Yumashev, A.G. Golovko, P.S. Abankin, N.E. Basistyi, G.I. Levchenko, V.I. Platonov, N.M. Kharlamov, S.E. Zakharov, N.G. Kuznetsov, I.I. Bajkov, N.I. Vinogradov, and N.D. Sergeev, participated in this conference. They discussed Levchenko's memorandum. The conference ended with Stalin's conclusion that I.S. Yumashev should not be the Minister of the Naval Forces, although at first he introduced him as 'a brave man and his friend'. Stalin ordered the appointment again of N.G. Kuznetsov as the head of the Ministry. He forgave the admiral for his disagreement over his, Stalin's, decision concerning the Navy's post-war development.

COMPLETION OF SHIPS FROM PRE-WAR DESIGNS

The first step was the completion of the unfinished but in most cases launched ships, lying in conservation at the yards. In the Baltic there were three cruisers of *projekt 68*, which were now taken in hand with some improvements, designed by A.N. Maslov as *projekt 68K* with additional A/A weapons, radar and improved fire control equipment. But they still had riveted hulls. The two launched vessels, the *Zheleznyakov* and *Chapaev*, as well as the redesigned *Chkalov*, launched in 1947, came to the fleet in 1950. In the Black Sea the two sisters, which were towed back from their evacuation ports in the Caucasus to Nikolaev, the *Kujbyshev* and the *Frunze* with her new stern section, were also completed in 1950.[36]

The design *projekt 48K* for the two surviving launched destroyer leaders *Kiev* and *Erevan* was not followed up and the two hulls were scrapped or used for tests. Of the launched destroyers of *projekt 30* two vessels in Leningrad and one each in Nikolaev and Molotovsk came to the fleet in 1947 to 1949 also with improvements as *projekt 30K*, designed by Yu.M. Yunovidov of *TsKB-32*, and equipped now with radar and new fire-control equipment and A/A weapons. And two in Leningrad, one more in Molotovsk and three in Komsomol'sk were launched in 1947/48 and completed from 1947 to 1950. So ten vessels in addition to the lead ship, the *Ognevoi*, commissioned in 1945, came to the fleets: in the Baltic the *Otlichnyi*, *Obraztsovyi*, *Otvazhnyi* and *Odarennyi*; in the Black Sea the *Ozornoi*; in the North the *Osmotritel'nyj* and *Okhotnik* (renamed *Stalin*), and in the Far East the *Vnushitel'nyi*, *Vynoslivyi* and *Vlastnyi* augmented the depleted destroyer flotillas.[37]

Of the patrol ships of *projekt 29* only one was commissioned before the end of the war: *Yastreb*. Of the other three vessels launched before the war around Leningrad two were completed in 1950, the *Zorkii* (ex-*Voron*), and *Orel*, and one in 1951, the *Korshun*, also designed to an improved *projekt 29K* by Ya.A. Kopershinskii of *TsKB-32*. Of the Far East vessels two were launched in 1943 and 1944 and completed, just after the end of the war the *Albatros*, and in 1947 the *Burevestnik* (ex-*Chajka*), also to *projekt 29K*.[38] The only vessel of *projekt 52*, the *Purga*, designed by V.I. Naganov of *TsKB-15*, was laid up until 1951, when construction started up again and was finished in 1954. She had an icebreaker bow and a strengthened hull and was transferred from Leningrad by the Northern Seaway route to the Far East.[39]

Of the minesweepers the last two of *projekt 53U*, the *T-220* and *T-221/ Dmitrii Lysov*, were completed in 1946. The turbine minesweepers of *projekt 59*, designed by K.P. Narykov of *TsKB-32* could not be completed with turbines as the lead ships *T-250/Vladimir Polyukhin*, and *T-254/Vasilii Gromov*, and had to be reconstructed as *projekt 73K* with diesel engines. From 1947 to 1949 at

Leningrad 12 vessels were completed, as were three more of the Sevastopol boats.[40] Of the coastal minesweepers of *projekt 253-LP* and *255K* – a welded construction by S.A. Basilevskii, powered by home-made diesels – many were already built during the war, and the building continued until 1946 at Leningrad and until 1952 at Rybinsk. In all 92 units were commissioned.[41]

Of the big sub-chasers the first 13 vessels of *projekt 122-A* were completed in 1946 and 1947 at the yards *340* at Zelenodol'sk, *402* at Molotovsk, and *199* at Komsomol'sk. An improved design was developed by N.G. Loshchinskii of *TsKB-51* at Gorkii as *projekt 122-B* with 210t and three diesel motors, for the first series of General Motors, for a top speed of 18.7kt, with radar and sonar. The armament was one 85mm gun, two 37mm guns and three twin MGs, two depth-charge throwers and 20 heavy and 16 light D/Cs. They were built from 1948 to 1955 at Zelenodolsk and Molotovsk. One hundred and thirty units were completed. In addition there were small sub-chasers of *projekts OD-220* and *OD-200bis* (63 units), designed by L.L. Yermash, and torpedo cutters, developed from this type as *projekt TD-200* and *TD-200-bis*, of which from 1946 to 1952 167 units had been completed. And there were the torpedo cutters of *projekt 123/Komsomolets*, designed by F.P. Liventsev, of which 31 had already been completed before the new series started in 1946, with 89 units at Tyumen and 255 at Feodosiya up to 1955.[42]

For river warfare the last of the Amur monitors of *projekt 1190*, the *Sivash*, was completed in 1946, as mentioned, and the building of the armoured cutters continued with *projekt 186* with two 85mm turrets (29 units), and *projekt 1125* with one 76mm turret (51 units).[43]

Of the submarines there were relatively few left over from the pre-war programmes; of the medium *series IX-bis*, six of the Gorkii boats, *S-21–S-26* for the Baltic Fleet, and one for the Black Sea Fleet, the *S-35*, that had been towed away in August 1941 from Nikolaev and returned after the war. They came to the fleets from 1946 to 1948. The two last *series X-bis* vessels, *Shch-411* and *Shch-412* came to the Baltic Fleet in 1945 and 1946 with a sail modelled after the *series IX-bis*. The biggest additions were the small submarines of *series XV/projekt 96/96-bis*, designed by F.F. Pol'yushkin, of which the first four boats were commissioned during the war, while the other three launched at the *Sudomekh* yard, *M-204–206*, were completed there in 1947, five vessels from Gorkii were transferred to Molotovsk and taken back after the war to the *Sudomekh* yard for completion in 1947, that is, *M-214–218*, and two more, *M-234* and *M-235*, in 1948. *M-219* was damaged beyond repair as a submarine on the transfer from Molotovsk to Leningrad. To increase as fast as possible the number of new submarines, this type was again taken in hand in 1947/48 at the *Sudomekh* yard. Up to 1952 46 new vessels were commissioned: of types *M-236–253* and *M-270–294*.

NEW SURFACE SHIPS

While the completion of ships of pre-war designs to improved versions continued, the building of new ships started in 1948. They were in most cases updated versions of pre-war designs, whose construction Stalin wanted to accelerate so as to acquire as fast as possible a certain number of combat ships, despite the wishes of the naval leaders who wanted to build new ships, designed according to the experiences of the war.

Battleships

Of the battleships of *projekt 23* at the end of the war only the third ship, the *Sovetskaya Rossiya* at Molotovsk was in conservation in an early stage in the covered dry dock. The remnants of the *Sovetskaya Ukraina* in Nikolaev were destroyed by the Germans when they had to evacuate the city, and the lead ship, the *Sovetskii Soyuz*, on the slip of the *Ordzhonikidze* yard was partly dismantled to get materials to strengthen the defences of the besieged city. So the remnants were launched to clear the slip, and the remnants of the hull were used as a target for weapons tests. The plan of 1945 to renew the building of the *Sovetskaya Rossiya* to an improved design *projekt 23NU*, developed at the *TsKB-4*, was never really started. The dates of the design are given in Table 10.3.[44]

As mentioned, an *OTZ* for an improved and enlarged battleship had already been issued in June 1941 as *projekt 24*. When on 27 November 1945 it was decided to postpone the laying down of such ships until after 1955, *Admiral Flota SSSR* Kuznetsov ordered on 19 December 1945 that a new *OTZ* be prepared for this battleship of 70,000–75,000t, with a speed of 30kt and an improved armament. In 1948 the chief constructor F.E. Bespolov of *TsKB-17* investigated 14 variants, and on 4 March 1950 the selected 13th variant was presented to Stalin. It had a displacement of 72,950t stdd. and a much more modern armament than in the first versions of the project: three triple turrets of 406mm, eight twin mounts of 130mm dual-purpose guns, 12 quadruple mounts each of 45mm and 25mm, but no catapult or aircraft. To attain the requested speed of 30kt it was necessary to install four of the 70,000 HP

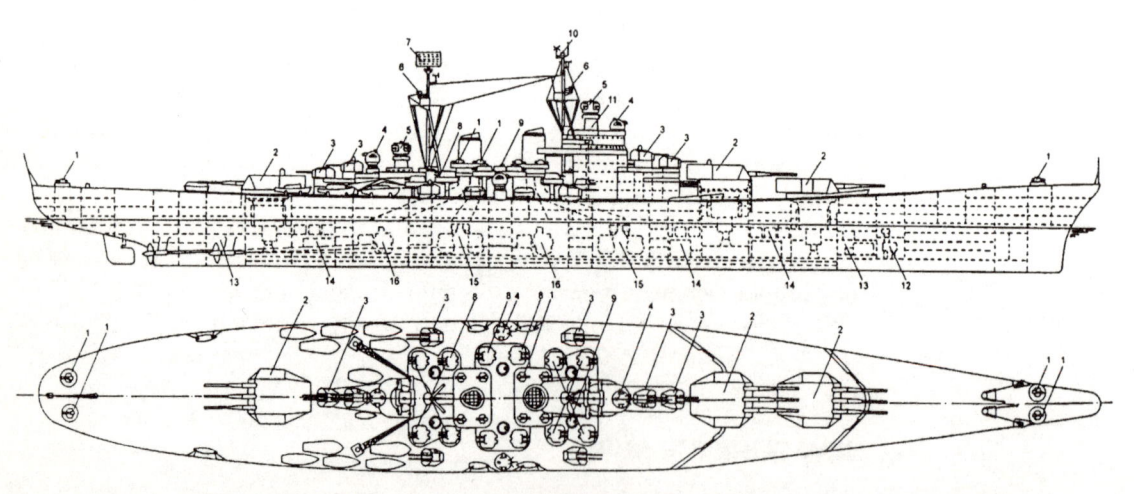

Fig. 16. Battleship *projekt 24*, no name given, 1950, displ. 72,950t stdd., length 282m, max. speed 30kt, 9 40.6cm, 16 13cm, 48 4.5cm. Two ships were planned, but no orders placed and no ships laid down. Credit: Gangut

Table 10.3: Technical data of the battleship projects

Ship type year	projekt 23 1938	projekt 23bis 1939	projekt 23NU 1940	projekt 24 1950	Malyi linkor TsNII-45/1951 III-2p	II+III-3	II-2p
Displacement:	t	t	t	t	t	t	t
standard	59,150	60,800	59,650	72,950	29,700	39,250	31,870
full load	65,150	66,800	70,000	81,150	33,700	44,900	33,870
Dimensions:	m	m	m	m	m	m	m
length	269.4	285.9	269.4	282.0	230.0	260.0	230.0
breadth	38.9	39.9	38.9	40.4	30.0	31.0	30.0
draught	10.1	10.3	10.1	11.5	7.9	9.0	8.3
HP	3x67,000	3x67,000	3x67,000	4x70,000	2x70,000	3x70,000	2x70,000
speed in kt	28.0	30.0	30.0	30.0	30.9	32.7	30.4
range	5,960/	5,770/	5,960/	6,000/19			
Armament:	mm	mm	mm	mm	mm	mm	mm
guns	3xIII-406	3xIII-406	3xIII-406	3xIII-406	1xIII-406 1xIV-180	1xII-406 1xIII-406 1xIV-180	1xII-457 1xIV-220
	6xII-152 4xII-100 8xIV-37	4xIII-152 6xII-100 8xIV-37	6xII-152 8xII-100 11xIV-37	8xII-130 12xIV-45	12xII-57 12xIV-25	12xII-57 12xIV-25	12xII-57 12xIV-25
catapults	1	1	?	–	–	–	–
aircraft	4	3	?	–	–	–	–

Sources: A.M. Vasil'ev, 'Lineynye korabli VMF SSSR predvoennykh proektov', *Gangut*, No. 16 (1998), p. 64. A.M. Vasil'ev, 'Linejnyi korabli proekta 24', *Gangut*, No. 15 (1998), pp. 39, 42.

turbine sets. But because Stalin was more interested in his beloved battlecruisers of *projekt 82*, the project was not pushed ahead, and because of the great investment in one ship some designers of the *TsNII-45* thought it better to propose some variants of smaller battleships of 29,700t to 39,250t with different armaments, as shown in Table 10.3.[45]

Battlecruisers and Heavy Cruisers

The two battlecruisers of *projekt 69* suffered the same fate as the battleships of *projekt 23*. The *Sevastopol'* at Nikolaev was destroyed during the German occupation, and parts of the *Kronshtadt* at Leningrad were also used to strengthen the defences of the city. But after the war some thought was given to rebuilding the hull as an aircraft carrier, but this was not realized and the hull dismantled.

Already in May 1941 there was an *OTZ* for a new heavy cruiser following to some extent the acquired German cruiser *Petropavlovsk* (ex-*Lützow*)/*projekt 83* with eight 203mm guns, but this was not realized. The design changed to a heavy cruiser as *projekt 82*, planned in September 1943 with 20,000–22,000t, a speed of about 36kt, and an armament of nine 210–230mm guns. Because the detailed design was showing that it was not possible to achieve the proposed performances with this displacement, it was in an *OTZ* of 15 November 1944 raised to 25,000–26,000t, and the speed reduced to 33kt, with an armament of nine 220mm guns in triple turrets, and an exchange of 100mm dual-purpose guns following the German design, by six 130mm twin turrets. But this heavy cruiser, which was supported by Kuznetsov, did not meet Stalin's expectations, who wanted a 'rowdy ship' with 305mm guns, a speed of 35kt, and better protection, even if the displacement had to be raised again. So L.V. Dikovich of the *TsKB-17*, then *TsKB-16*, prepared a new design which was presented to Stalin in 1949. Stalin wanted some changes, so that the basic technical details were approved on 25 March 1950 with the dual-purpose 130mm turrets reduced, but put into the centre line to allow better arcs of fire in all directions. Stalin badly wanted these ships and so the preparations had to be accelerated; two ships were to be started in the last quarter of 1951 for completion in 1954–55. The lead vessel, *Stalingrad*, was laid down in December 1951 at yard *No. 444/Nosenko* at Nikolaev, followed by the second ship *Moskva* at the *Ordzhonikidze* yard in Leningrad in September 1951, and the third vessel, named probably *Arkhangel'sk* or *Kronshtadt*, in early 1953 at Molotovsk, probably changed to *projekt 82R* as it was to be armed with cruise missiles as will be mentioned later. But the ships became victims of the changes after Stalin's death, and on 23 April 1953 they were cancelled by order of N.S. Khrushchev. The *Stalingrad*'s hull was launched and used as a target during weapons tests, while the other two were broken down on the slips.[46]

In January 1945 the Central Ordnance *KB* at Moscow had started to work on a new rapid-fire gun of 220mm calibre, to be ready for tests in 1954. In 1946 Kuznetsov ordered the *TsKB-17* to begin new studies for a heavy cruiser for this new weapon, but when Stalin changed the *projekt 82* to the 305mm guns, and Kuznetsov was relieved, the design was put to one side in 1947, because Stalin had no interest in such a ship. He was looking to his favourite ships, the *projekt 82* battlecruisers. When Kuznetsov returned in 1951 he renewed the project now under the designation *projekt 66*, and mentioned to Stalin that the cruisers of *projekt 68-bis*, then on the slips of the yards, could not stand up with their 152mm armament to the latest US cruisers, like the *Des Moines* class of almost 20,000t full load with their quick-firing 203mm guns,

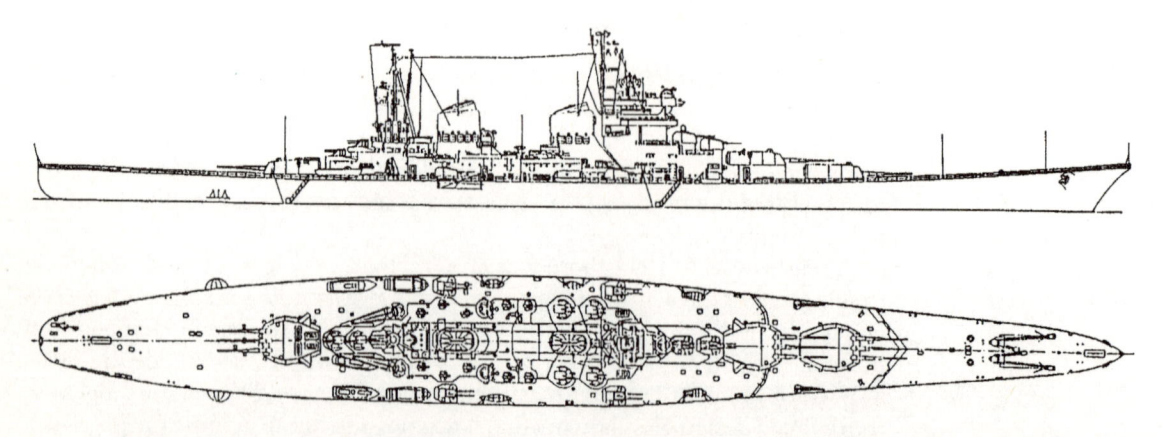

Fig. 17. Battlecruiser of *projekt 82*, *Stalingrad*, 1951, displ. 36,500t stdd., length 273.5m, max. speed 35.2kt, 9 30.5cm, 12 13cm, 24 4.5cm, 40 2.5cm. Building of two ships started 1951/52, cancelled 1953/54 and broken up. Credit: Sudostroenie

Table 10.4: Technical data of heavy cruiser and battlecruiser projects

Ship type year	projekt 83 1941	projekt 82 1943	projekt 82 1944	projekt 82 1951	projekt 66 1953
Displacement: standard full load	t	t 20–22,000	t 25–26,000	t 36,500 42,300	t 26,230 30,750
Dimensions: length breadth draught	m	m	m	m 273.5 32.0 8.7	m 252.5 25.7 8.4
HP				4x70,000	3x70,000
speed in kt range	36.0 10,000	36.0 10,000	33.0 8,000	35.2 5,000/18	34.5 5,000/18
Armament: guns	mm 4xII-203 6xII-100 6xII-37	mm 3xIII-210 6xII-130 8xIV-37	mm 3xIII-220 8xII-130 8xIV-45 5xIV-25	mm 3xIII-305 6xII-130 6xIV-45 10xIV-25	mm 3xIII-220 4xII-130 6xIV-45 6xIV-25
torpedoes catapults aircraft	4xIII-533 1 4	– – –	– – –	– – –	– – –
crew				1,710	1,410

Sources: E.A. Shitikov et al., op. cit., pp. 48–9. *Istoriya* …, op. cit., vol. V, p. 37.

of which three were commissioned in 1948/49. The battlecruisers of *projekt 82* were too expensive for such a task. So he issued a new *OTZ* for a *projekt 66* heavy cruiser, armed with his favourite 220mm guns. In April 1952 N.A. Kiselev of *TsKB-17* presented his sketch project with a displacement of 26,230t stdd., which was finally accepted by Stalin. It was planned to lay down in 1953 the first ship at the *Marti* yard in Leningrad for a planned commissioning in 1957, and to start series building at the yards *No. 444* at Nikolaev, *No. 372* at Sovietski Gavan, and *No. 402* at Molotovsk. The sketch design was reviewed in March 1953 and some revisions were completed in August 1953, and on 23 December the Naval Staff asked the Naval Academy to review it by 1 March 1954. But the ships were considered too large to be worthwhile against the American heavy cruisers, so the plans to build these ships were cancelled, as with the other big surface ships.[47]

Light Cruisers

In the ten-year programme of November 1945 there were besides the five pre-war cruisers of *projekt 68K* 25 new light cruisers planned. They were intended for classic cruiser tasks, defending the fleet against surface and air torpedo attacks, covering convoys, undertaking raiding operations and laying minefields. The Navy had first issued a *TTZ* for a cruiser of 8,000–8,500t stdd., with 152mm guns. But when the *TsKB-17* worked on such a ship it soon became much bigger and reached between 14,500 and 18,000t, and it was suggested that the ships be armed with 180mm guns instead of the 152mm.

In 1947 the *TsKB-17* developed no less than 40 variants of the *projekt 65* cruiser with 12,800–16,850t and three or even four triple turrets of 180mm guns to be superior to the latest US cruisers of this type, the *Worcester*, and the British *Superb*, or to be armed with nine 152mm dual-purpose guns. But Stalin did not like this project, and during a meeting at the Kremlin in 1947 it was cancelled, and Stalin wanted to have the new light cruisers built as improvements of the *projekt 68K*, using the proven systems and some of the German developments in fire control and stabilized 100mm dual-purpose guns.[48]

The design work was done at the *TsKB-17* by A.S. Savichev, and on 27 May 1947 the *projekt 68-bis* was approved for series production, and the first three orders went out on 3 December 1947 to the yards *No. 189* and *No. 194* at Leningrad and *No. 444* at Nikolaev, using the names of the laid-down but not completed ships of the pre-war design *projekt 68*: *Sverdlov*, *Dzerzhinskii* and *Ordzhonikidze*. The *Dzerzhinskii* was the first to be laid down at Nikolaev on 21 December 1948, followed in October 1949 by the other two ships. During 1948–53 18 more orders followed, eight to the *No. 189* yard at Leningrad, five to yard *No. 194* at Leningrad, of which two should be sent to Molotovsk, three to yard *No. 444* at Nikolaev, and two to yard *No. 402* at Molotovsk. One more of each were planned to be ordered in 1954 for each of the four yards. The *Ordzhonikidze* yard *189* built – besides the *Sverdlov*, which was commissioned in May 1952 and surprised the public in the Western countries when it appeared at the coronation parade at Spithead in June 1953 – four more which were commissioned from December 1952 to December 1954: *Zhdanov*, *Admiral Ushakov*, *Aleksandr Suvorov*, and *Admiral Senyavin*. The *Marti* yard *No. 194* at Leningrad completed two more ships in 1952 and 1953: *Aleksandr Nevskii* and *Admiral Lazarev*, the *Marti* yard *No. 444* at Nikolaev in 1953 and 1954 also completed two, the *Admiral Nakhimov* and *Mikhail Kutuzov*, and finally yard *No. 402* at Molotovsk two ships in 1954 and 1955, the *Molotovsk* and *Murmansk* (ex-*Kozma Minin*).

After the completion of the first 14 ships it was planned to complete the other 11 vessels to a changed design as *projekt 68-bis-ZIF* with a changed A/A armament and protection against a radioactive fallout. But after Stalin's death in March 1953 it was decided not to lay down the last four vessels, which were planned to be ordered in 1954 with one unit for the four yards. But in early 1956 the decision was taken to stop the construction of the incomplete vessels, which were in the meantime planned to be rebuilt to *projekt 75*, as is described later. So the *Kronshtadt*, *Tallinn* and *Varyag*, laid down in 1953 and early 1954 at *No. 189*, the *Shcherbakov*, laid down already in 1951 at *No. 194*, the *Admiral Kornilov*, laid down in 1951 at *No. 444*, and the *Arkhangelsk* and *Vladivostok*, laid down in 1954 at *No. 402*, were laid up and from 1959 to 1961 scrapped. The *Kozma Minin* and the *Dmitrii Pozharskii*, laid down in 1952/53 at *No. 194*, were sent in sections to *No. 402* to be used for the *Molotovsk* (renamed *Oktyabrskaya revolyutsiya* in 1957) and the *Murmansk* under construction.

From the mid-1950s there were many plans to rebuild some of the aforementioned cruisers into anti-aircraft vessels armed with rockets and others to be armed with cruise missiles, as is mentioned later. A new *projekt 84* light cruiser, for which an *OTZ* was issued in 1955, was not realized.[49]

Table 10.5: Technical data of the light cruiser designs

Ship type year	projekt 68-K 1950	projekt 68-bis 1947	projekt 68-bis 1952	projekt 68-bis ZIF 1954	projekt 65 1945	projekt 65 1950/51	projekt 84 1955
Displacement: standard full load	t 11,130 14,100	t 13,600 16,640	t 13,230 16,340	t 13,720 16,780	t 8,500	t 13,500	t 14,000 19,400
Dimensions: length breadth draught	m 199.0 18.7 6.9	m 210.0 22.0 7.4	m 210.0 22.0 7.3	m 210.0 22.0 7.4	m	m	m
HP speed in kt range	2x62,300 33.5 6,360/18	2x63,250 32.6 7,400/17	2x60,850 33.0 9,000/17	2x63,250 33.2 7,000/17	4x36,000 35.0 6,000/18	4x36,000 35.0 5,000/18	4x40,000 33.0 5,000/19
Armament: guns	mm 4xIII-152 4xII-100 14xII-37	mm 4xIII-152 6xII-100 16xII-37	mm 4xIII-152 6xII-100 16xII-37	mm 4xIII-152 6xII-100 16xIV-45	mm 3xII-152 6xII-100 4xIV-45 4xIV-25	mm 3xIII-180 6xII-100 6xIV-45 6xIV-25	mm 4xII-180 6xII-100 6xIV-45
torpedoes catapults aircraft	– – –	2xV-533 – –	2xV-533 – –	2xV-533 – –	2xV-533 1 2	2xV-533 – –	– – 2 Heli
crew	1,184	1,270	1,270	1,224			

Sources: A.B. Morin, op. cit., pp. 9, 45. A.M. Vasil'ev, op. cit.

Aircraft Carriers

To Stalin, battleships and especially the battlecruisers and cruisers were the main element of the fleet, while he saw in aircraft carriers only a supporting or covering element. The pre-war designs were obsolete, and with the ex-German *Graf Zeppelin* the problem was that a repair could not be achieved in the time set by the Inter-Allied Commission on the distribution of the German ships; it had to be assigned to 'category C' and be destroyed. So this vessel, whose hull was not much damaged, was towed into the Central Baltic, where a commission under Vice-Admiral Yu. Rall' had to observe the effects of different weapons. On 16 and 17 August 1947 several detonations of depth charges and aircraft bombs damaged the ship, which began to drift. So a motor torpedo boat, *TK-503* and then the destroyer *Slavnyi*, fired torpedoes which sank the ship.[50]

A short while before the end of the war in Europe the Chief of the Shipbuilding Administration, Vice-Admiral N.A. Isachenkov, proposed rebuilding the unfinished battlecruiser *Kronshtadt* into an aircraft carrier, and N. Maltsev prepared a project study for a carrier with 76 aircraft, and a gun armament of 4xII 130mm, 4xIV 45mm and 4xIV 25mm. The HP and the speed would be the same as for the battlecruiser, and the full load displacement would reach 34,000t. There was also a proposal from Vice-Admiral L. Valdimirskii that the possibility of rebuilding cruisers of *projekt 68* and the unfinished German cruisers *Tallinn* (ex-*Lützow*) and *Seydlitz* into light carriers be studied, but the

Table 10.6: Technical data for the aircraft carrier designs

Ship type year	projekt 71A	projekt 71B	projekt 72 II-B	projekt 72 III-M	projekt 85/VI 1954
Displacement:	t	t	t	t	t
standard	10,600	24,050	30,700	23,700	23–24,000
full load	11,300	27,000	34,400	28,800	
Dimensions:	m	m	m	m	m
length	199.0	250.0	273.0	242.0	
flight deck	215x24	250x30	273x33	242x32	250x31.6
breadth	18.7	30.0	33.5	32.5	
draught	6.5	8.0	8.7	7.5	
HP					4x30,000
speed in kt	33.7	31.5	30.0	30.0	32.0
range	3,800	8,000	10,000	10,000	5,000
Armament:	mm	mm	mm	mm	mm
guns	8xI-100	8xI-100	16xI-85	16xI-85	8xII-100
	8xII-37	16xII-37	12xII-37	12xII-37	6xIV-57
					4xIV-45
catapults					2
aircraft	30	70	62	30	40
crew	580	1,600	2,300	2,000	

Sources: A.B. Morin and N. Walujew, op. cit., p. 100. *Istoriya ...*, op. cit., pp. 40–1.

Main Administration for warship-building was against this proposal. And negotiations with the British government to acquire up to five light carriers of the type HMS *Triumph*, which had visited Leningrad, did not lead to any results after the tensions of the Cold War began to be felt. None of these considerations had any good prospects owing to Stalin's aversion to aircraft carriers. The best prospects for realization might have come from the designs of *projekts 71* and *72*. *Admiral Flota SSSR* Kuznetsov signed on 12 December 1945 specifications for such projects, for which the *TsKB-17* prepared some variants for a big and a small carrier. But during Kuznetsov's absence the development was also put aside until he came back in 1951. Because it was obvious that the other great navies looked at aircraft carriers as the main element of sea power, in May 1952 Kuznetsov and his deputy, Admiral A.G. Golovko, tried again to convince Stalin of the need to have aircraft carriers in the Pacific and Northern Fleets, but Stalin again postponed his decision.

Fig. 18. Aircraft carrier *projekt 85/VI*, no name given, 1954, displ. 23–24,000t stdd., length 250m, max. speed 32kt, 40 planes, 16 10cm, 24 5.7cm, 16 4.5cm. No ships ordered or laid down. Credit: Sudostroenie

However, Kuznetsov ordered the Commander of the Naval Air Force, *General Polkovnik* Y. Preobrazhenskii, to prepare a study of the planes necessary for a small 'squadron'-carrier of about 24,000t and a flight deck 240m long and 22.5m wide. This yielded the conclusion that especially fast jet-planes might be necessary, for which the aircraft designers Yakovlev and Tupolev prepared designs for fighters and torpedo-bombers. But Stalin died (in 1953) before a decision was taken and so the *OTZ* for a new carrier of *projekt 85* had to wait, as will be described.[51]

Destroyers

For the ten-year programme the Navy had wanted to get 118 big and 70 normal destroyers, but Stalin had – as mentioned – blocked the building of the big destroyer designs and forced concentration on to the proven *projekt 30*, including easy-to-get improvements for a fast mass series production of about 250 units. This improved design for a *projekt 30-bis* destroyer was started on 8 October 1945. Based on *projekt 30K* the chief constructor of *TsKB-53*, A.L. Fisher, produced a design which was approved on 28 January 1947. The first 20 orders were placed on 3 December 1947, and the building of the lead ship, the *Smelyi*, began on 16 May 1948 at the *Zhdanov* yard/*No. 190* at Leningrad and was completed on 21 December 1949. Up to February 1953 yard *No. 190* built 16 units, the yards *No. 402* at Molotovsk, *No. 445* at Nikolaev, and *No. 199* at Komsomol'sk 18 each, 70 vessels in all, the biggest surface ship series built in the Soviet Union.[52]

A problem was the inclusion of big destroyers, so much asked for by Kuznetsov, into the programme. There were three possible designs, first the upgraded destroyer leaders of *projekt 48K*, of which two uncompleted vessels, the *Kiev* and *Erevan*, were still at Nikolaev. The second possibility was the *projekt 40*, favoured by Kuznetsov for the Pacific, designed in two versions by the *TsKB-17*, one with a forecastle and one with a flush deck, and a *projekt 41*, also a flush decker but with only two twin 130mm dual mounts instead of the three of *projekt 40*, designed by V.A. Nikitin of *TsKB-53*. But *projekt 48K* was cancelled for being out of date, and *projekt 40* as it was too big for mass production. So only *projekt 41* remained, which introduced a great number of innovations for Soviet shipbuilding, such as the pressure-fired steam plant, dual-purpose 130mm main guns and a completely welded hull, and a maximum reduction of structures above the weather deck. The *TTZ* was accepted on 14 June 1947 and the technical design approved on 28 September 1949. The lead ship, the *Neustrashimyi*, was laid down on 5 July 1950 at the *Zhdanov* yard *No. 190*, and launched already on 29 January 1951. But difficulties with the tests, especially the insufficient speed reached, delayed commissioning until 31 January 1955. Despite the fact that in December 1950 four more vessels were laid down at the yards *No. 190* and *No. 402*, the project was cancelled in favour of a smaller *projekt 56* with many of the improvements of *projekt 41* included. Only the *Neustrashimyi* was commissioned, and the others were scrapped on the slips.[53]

When the problems with *projekt 41* became obvious, on 2 June 1951 an order 'to change the military characteristics of *projekt 41*' was issued, and the *TsKB-53* with A.L. Fisher worked out the design for a *projekt 56* series destroyer of

Table 10.7: Technical data for the destroyer projects

Ship type	projekt 30K	projekt 30-bis	projekt 48K	projekt 40 forecastle	projekt 40 flush deck	projekt 41	projekt 56
year	1950	1947	1952	1954	1954	1950/51	1955
Displacement:	t	t	t	t	t	t	t
standard	2,125	2,316	2,740	3,296	3,250	3,010	2,662
full load	2,860	3,066	3,460	4,050	4,000	3,830	3,230
Dimensions:	m	m	m	m	m	m	m
length	117.0	120.5	127.6	135.0	135.0	133.83	126.0
breadth	11.0	12.0	12.2	13.0	13.0	13.57	12.76
draught	4.02	3.9	4.58	4.45	4.42	4.09	4.0
HP	2x27,000	2x30,000	3x27,000	2x38,000	2x38,000	2x32,100	2x36,000
speed in kt	36.5	36.6	37.5	35.8	35.8	33.55	38.0
range	2,950/17	3,660/16		4,150/18	4,150/18	5,210/14	3,850/15
Armament:	mm	mm	mm	mm	mm	mm	mm
guns	2xII-130	2xII-130	3xII-130	3xII-130	3xII-130	2xII-130	2xII-130
	1xII-85	1xII-85	1xII-85	6xII-45	6xII-45	4xII-45	4xIV-45
	6xI-37	7xI-37	3xII-37			2xI-25	
torpedoes	2xIII-533	2xV-533	2xIII-533	2xV-533	2xV-533	2xV-533	2xV-533
A/S weapons	2-BMB-1	2-BMB-1				6-BMB-1	6-BMB-2
crew	301	286				305	284

Sources: Istoriya ..., op. cit., vol. V, p. 46. Conway's ..., op. cit., p. 387.

reduced size, but with most of the armament of *projekt 41* and a speed of 38kt. A production run of 100 vessels was envisaged, and the prefabrication of parts of the first two ships had been started already in February 1952, with the first six ships being laid down at the *Zhdanov* yard *No. 190*, three more at the *Marti* yard *No. 445* at Nikolaev and two at the yard *No. 199* at Komsomol'sk, before the *TTZ* was finally approved on 4 April 1954. In all, 27 vessels were built and completed to the original design, but in October 1955 the building was stopped and the other four ships, for which the material had been prepared, were redesigned as missile ships, to be noted later. It is said that these ships were very well liked in the Soviet Navy.[54]

Patrol Ships

There arose heavy discussions with Stalin on the new patrol ships. While the Navy wanted real sea-going escort vessels, Stalin wanted to limit the displacement to 1,000 or even better 900t stdd., as the *projekt 29K* vessels had been. But even if there were some pre-war vessels completed, this type was outdated and needed improvement, especially in the A/S weapons, but *projekt 29-bis* could not fulfil this requirement and was not built. The previously mentioned *projekt 37* vessel of 1943 was too large. A new requirement was sent on 29 July 1946 for a vessel of 1,800t with a speed of 26–27kt, two twin mounts of 130mm, and two quadruple mounts of 45mm and a triple set of 533mm torpedo tubes, four D/C throwers, two D/C racks and a hedgehog (anti-submarine weapon). The *TsKB-32* and *TsKB-53* made competitive designs

Table 10.8: Technical data of the patrol ships (Storozhevye korabli)

Ship type	projekt 29K	projekt 29-bis	projekt 42 TsKB-32	projekt 42 TsKB-53	projekt 42	projekt 50
year	1944	1945	n.d.	n.d.	1947	1951
Displacement:	t	t	t	t	t	t
standard	906	1,150	1,860	1,930	1,339	1,068
full load	1,059	1,300			1,679	1,200
Dimensions:	m	m	m	m	m	m
length	85.7				96.6	91.6
breadth	8.4				11.0	10.2
draught	3.3				3.13	2.8
HP	2x11,500				2x13,900	2x10,000
speed in kt	33.5	29.0	26.0	26.5	29.6	28–29.0
range	2,200/15	2,300/15	5,000/15	5,120/15	2,810/14	1,000/14.5
Armament:	mm	mm	mm	mm	mm	mm
guns	3xI-100	3xI-100	2xII-130	2xII-130	4xI-100	3xI-100
	4xI-37	6xI-37	2xIV-45	2xIV-45	2xII-37	2xII-37
torpedoes	1xIII-450	1xIII-533	1xIII-533	1xIII-533	1xIII-533	1xII-533
A/S weapons	2xBMB-1	2xBMB-1	4xBMB-2	4xBMB-2	2xBMB-2	2xMBU
crew	127				211	68

Sources: *Istoriya ...*, op. cit., vol. V, p. 53. V.N. Nikol'skii, op. cit.

with diesel and turbine drive, but the designs were again too big, and a new *TTZ* was sent out for a vessel of 1,300t stdd. and a reduced armament. The *TsKB-32* with D.D. Zhukovskii won the competition with a steam design, which became *projekt 42*. But this was still too expensive, and so only eight units were built at the former German *Schichau* yard *No. 820* at Kaliningrad, the former Königsberg. They were built during 1949–53 and sent to the Northern Fleet, where their better sea-keeping qualities were useful.[55]

As *projekt 56* was a simpler follow-on to *projekt 41*, *projekt 42* was also discontinued probably because it was too big, and a new cheaper vessel was needed for the series building. The development of a *TTZ* was ordered on 20 July 1950 and was presented in October 1950 as *projekt 50*, designed by V.I. Neganov of the construction bureau of yard *No. 820*. On 7 December 1951 the first orders went out and already by 20 December 1951 the lead vessel, *Gornostai*, was laid down at yard *No. 445* in Nikolaev. During 1952–58 the yards *Nos. 445*, *820* and *199* completed 68 vessels, of which 15 were sent to the Baltic, 14 to the Northern, 20 to the Black Sea and 19 to the Pacific Fleets.[56]

Minesweepers

The ten-year programme of 1945 envisaged the building of 30 'squadron' minesweepers (*projekt 259*), 400 high-seas minesweepers (*projekts 254* and *264*), and 306 coastal minesweepers (*projekts 255* and *265*), and 50 inshore minesweepers (*projekts 151* and *322*). In 1946 work was started on a new high-seas minesweeper, *projekt 254* of 500t stdd. With super-charged diesels, it was designed by the *TsKB-50* under G.M. Berakso, especially adapted for mass production at the *Izhora* yard in Leningrad and the *Zaliv* yard in Kerch. In all, from 1946–57 no less than 158 units were completed, 60 of the original version, 82 *projekt 254K* and 16 *projekt 254M*, of which some were already somewhat improved versions. In addition 12 were built in Poland, and after 1953 many units were transferred to Allied navies.[57]

As follow-on to the coastal minesweepers of *projekt 253* in 1946 a series of *projekt 255* of 147t was designed by A.G. Sokolov starting at Rybinsk from 1946, and up to 1953 the yards *No. 189* at Leningrad and *No. 341* at Rybinsk produced 125 units of this and the slightly improved *projekt 255K*. Of the inshore minesweepers of *projekt 151* of 46.3t there were about 55 units built in Poland for the Soviet Navy.[58]

Small Combatants

The construction of motor torpedo boats continued in great series. First the building of *projekts 200* and *123* continued, but were soon superseded by *projekt 183*, designed by P.G. Goinkis at the *NKVD TsKB-5*. The lead vessel was started in 1949 at yard *No. 51* in Leningrad, and there, at the yard *Uliss* at Vladivostok and at Sosnovskii the series production was running from 1952 to 1960 with 622 units completed, of which many were transferred to allied navies.[59]

Also from 1946 to 1955 about 195 small landing vessels were built of *projekts 145* and *185*. In 1950 E.S. Tolotskii designed a bigger landing vessel of *projekt 450*, looking like a coastal motor vessel with a landing ramp at the bow, of 660t. Of this type at yard *No. 196* in Leningrad and *No. 369* at Sretensk, 75 units were completed.[60]

SUBMARINES

In the late 1940s and the 1950s, Western navies looked on with some apprehension at submarine building in the Soviet Union, fearing it was an effort to prepare for a new tonnage war against Western sea communications. When the first new submarines appeared they were evaluated as developments of progressive German designs, and at the same time the strength of the Soviet submarine force was mostly overestimated, resulting in great programmes of A/S vessels in the United States, Great Britain and France. But it was overlooked that the main Soviet effort during the first ten years after the Second World War was not concentrated on the big, long-range submarines, necessary to reach the sea lines of communications (SLOCs) in the Atlantic or Pacific, but on medium and even small submarines with too short a range for such tasks. They were built more as a defence against amphibious threat at some distance as far as the medium submarines were concerned and close to the Soviet shores for the small submarines.[61]

In 1949 the submarines were generally renamed: the remaining big submarines of the pre-war programmes, the *D*-, *L*-, *P*-, and *K*-classes, and the big submarines from the reparation deliveries, like the German *type IX-C/40* and *XXI*, became *B* (for *bol'shoi*) numbers, the medium submarines of the *Shch*- and *S*-classes, the *Lembit*, and the former German *type VIIC/41* and the Italian boats got *S-* (for *srednii*) numbers, and the small submarines continued with the *M* (for *malyi*) numbers, as can be seen in the Appendices.

Big Submarines

Preliminary work for a follow-on to the *KE-* and *KU*-submarines of the prewar programmes started in 1943, aiming at a submarine of about 1,100t with six bow and four stern torpedo tubes and 14 reloads, and a speed of 22kt surfaced and 9–10kt submerged, as the *TTZ* of 29 January 1944 required. But with the end of the war this now seemed obsolete and a new *TTZ* was issued on 18 January 1946 for a slightly bigger boat with the same torpedo armament and two 100 and two 37mm twin guns. But the evaluation of the German *type XXI* reparation boats called for some improvements and so in January 1947 a new *TTZ* was issued, and on 28 January 1949 S.A. Yegorov of the *TsKB-18* presented the technical description of a *projekt 611* submarine of 1,831t with the same torpedo armament, but one twin 57mm and one twin 25mm guns, three diesels for a surface speed of 17kt, and electric motors for 9.2kt submerged. As mentioned, the number of big submarines, which the Navy and *Admiral Flota SSSR* Kuznetsov wanted in their programme of 1945 – 68 units – was cut down by Stalin to no more than 40 vessels. The first order for *B-61* went out to the *Sudomekh* yard *No. 196* in Leningrad on 13 November 1950, and the building started on 10 January 1951, to be completed on 31 December 1953. Up to July 1952 eight more orders followed for *B-62–69* to *Sudomekh*, and from December 1954 to January 1957 17 more vessels for *B-70–82* and *B-88–91* to yard *No. 402* at Molotovsk, of which the last one was commissioned on 15 July 1958. Most of the vessels went to the Northern Fleet, six to the Pacific Fleet and only one remained with the Baltic Fleet.[62]

Besides the three reparation *type XXI* German submarines, which were used for tests up to 1958, the Soviet Army captured on 30 March 1945 at the *Schichau* yard in Danzig 20 unfinished boats at different stages of construction. *U 3535–3539* were on the slips almost ready to launch and were taken over as *TS-5–9* on 12 April 1945. They were launched on 15 July 1945, at first with the intention of completing them as *projekt 614*. But this was considered too complicated, because some equipment was lacking, and so the vessels were renamed *R-1–5* and on 7/8 August 1947 scuttled 20 miles north-west of Cape Ristna in deep waters. Also there were on the slips *U 3540–3542* in a less advanced state. They were also taken over as *TS-10–12*, and in 1947 renamed *R-7–R8*, but scrapped in February 1948. Finally there were the sections for *U 3543–3547*, taken over and named *TS-13, TS-15, TS-17–19*, but already broken up by April 1947, as were the incomplete sections for *U 3548–3554* renamed *TS-32–38* but scrapped also in April 1947.[63]

Medium Submarines

The *TsKB-18* had worked from August 1942 to October 1944 on a *projekt 608* for a medium-sized submarine as successor for the *Shch-* and *S*-class submarines. But this was cancelled in favour of a new design, when the details of the salvaged German *U 250* became known. A new *TTZ* was issued in January

Table 10.9: Distribution of *projekt 613* submarines to the yards and their completion

Year	No. 112/*Gorkii*	No. 198/*Nikolaev*	No. 189/*Leningrad*	No. 199/*Komsomol'sk*	No.
1951	S-80	–	–	–	1
1952	S-43–46	S-61–65	–	–	9
1953	S-140–152, 155, 157, 158	S-66–76	S-153, 154, 156	–	30
1954	S-159–186, 192	S-77–79, 86–91, 95–97, S-100, 217	–	S-331	44
1955	S-193–200, 261–289	S-98, 218–234	S-187–191, 355–357	S-332–335	67
1956	S-290–297, 300, 325–329, S-338–349	S-235–246, 250, 374, S-376	S-358–361	S-336, 337, 390, 391	49
1957	–	S-375, 377–384	S-362–364	S-392, 393	14
1958	–	–	S-365	–	1
Total	113	72	19	11	215

1946 for a medium-sized submarine, *projekt 613*, with a diving depth of 200m. The chief designer was at first Ya.E. Yevgrafov and from 1950 Z.A. Deribin of the *TsKB-18*. The technical project was approved on 15 August 1948. The first order for the lead vessel *S-80* went out to the *Krasnoe Sormovo* yard *No. 112* at Gorkii on 8 December 1948, and the yard became the main yard for mass production. Included in the building process were the *Nosenko* yard *No. 198* at Nikolaev, the *Ordzhonikidze* yard *No. 189* at Leningrad and yard *No. 199* at Komsomol'sk. The submarines had four bow and two stern torpedoes with six reserve torpedoes, and they could use the newly developed torpedo-mines of which they could load up to 24. Their A/A armament was at first composed of one twin 57mm and one twin 25mm, which were removed during 1956/57. Their surface speed was 18.2kt, and submerged speed 13kt. No less than 215 vessels in all were completed up to 1958, as Table 10.9 shows.[64] The *projekt 613* series became the largest submarine series ever built in the USSR.

When details about the German *type XXVI* submarine with its *Walter-* hydrogen-peroxide turbine drive and its unconventional torpedo armament with four bow tubes and six side tubes firing aft became known, there was an idea to design such submarines as *projekt 616*, and a special construction bureau was set up in Germany. But this proved to be too difficult, and so the *TsKB-18* started to design a similar vessel using a steam-gas turbine assembled from parts of a German *Walter* turbine and using Soviet technical equipment. The chief designer was A.A. Antipin The only *projekt 617* test vessel *S-99* was laid down at the *Sudomekh* yard *No. 196* at Leningrad on 5 February 1951 and completed in December 1955. During 1956–59 98 test runs in the Baltic, covering 6,800 miles, 315 of them submerged, achieving a speed of more than 20kt. On 17 May 1959 it had an explosion at a depth of 80m, but was able to surface and return to base only to be decommissioned, because now the nuclear drive seemed more attractive.[65]

Small Submarines

As recently mentioned, at first in addition to the last uncompleted submarines of the pre-war programme *series XV*, the same only superficially improved type was built from 1948 to 1953 at the *Sudomekh* yard *No. 196* in Leningrad with

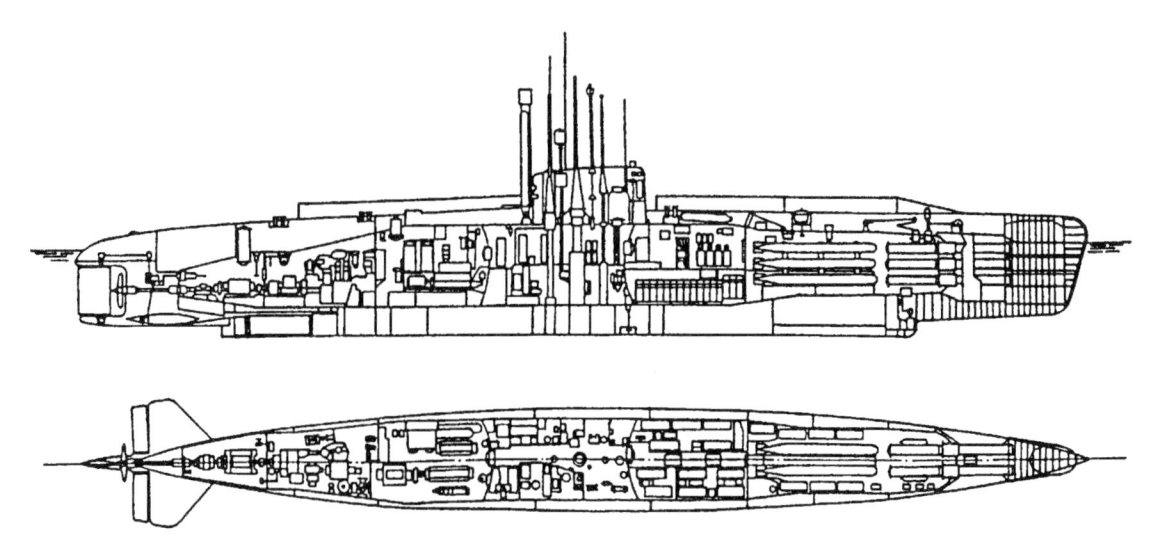

Fig. 19. Submarine *projekt 617*, *S-99*, 1952, displ. 950/1,216t stdd., length 62.2m, max. speed 11/20kt, 6 torpedo tubes 53.3cm, 6 reserve torpedoes. Only one submarine built 1951–55 as test vessel for Walter-turbine drive, tested from 1955–59. Credit: The Berezhnoi Collection

Table 10.10: Technical data of the submarine projects

Submarine type year	*projekt 611* 1949	*projekt 614* 1947	*projekt 613* 1948	*projekt 616* 1947	*projekt 617* 1949	*projekt 96* 1942	*projekt 612* 1946	*projekt A615* 1953
Displacement: surfaced submerged	t 1,831 2,400	t 1,621 1,819	t 1,055 1,346	t 694	t 950 1,500	t 280 353	t 400	t 406 504
Dimensions: length breadth draught	m 90.5 7.5 5.1	m 76.7 6.6 6.3	m 75.9 6.3 4.6	m 56.2 5.4 5.8	m 62.2 6.1 5.1	m 49.5 4.4 2.8	m	m 56.8 4.5 3.6
HP/speed surf. HP/speed subm. range Sea time days	6,000/17 5,400/9.2 22,000/9 75	4,000/15.5 5,000/16.0 11,180/	4,000/18 2,700/13 8,580/10 30	575/ 7,500/24 30	600/ 7,250/20 45	1,200/15.5 436/7.9 4,500/8 15	1,800/15.5 740/8.4 4,000/ 15	/16.1 2,700/15.5 10
Armament: torpedoes bow torpedoes stern reserve torpedoes mines guns	mm 6/533 4/533 12 – 1xII-57 1xII-25	mm 6/533 – 17 (12TMC) 2xII-30 –	mm 4/533 2/533 6 (24AMD) 1xII-57 1xII-25	mm 4/533 side 6/533 – – – –	mm 6/533 – 6 – – –	mm 4/533 – – – 1xI-45 –	mm 4/533 2/533 – – 1xII-25 –	mm 4/533 – 4 – 1xII-25 –
crew	65	57	52	51	51	28		29

Sources: *Istoriya …*, op. cit., vol. V, p. 82. A.S. Pavlov, op. cit., pp. 67–81.

7+46 units as *projekt 96*, to get as fast as possible a number of additional submarines.[66] Improved designs of this size were the *projekts 105* and *612*, but they were not realized. *Projekt 615* was a development of *projekt 612* with a closed cycle drive, based on the earlier experiments with such vessels, the *Redo/ R-1* and *M-401*, as mentioned earlier. The chief designer was A.S. Kassatsier with *TsKB-18*. Based on the experiments with *M-401* a new *TTZ* was issued in July 1946, and the prototype *M-254* was ordered on 26 March 1949, and laid down at the *Sudomekh* yard *No. 196* on 17 March 1950, and completed on 31 July 1953. The submarine had three closed cycle diesels, one *type 32D* for the centre shaft, and two *type M-50* for the wing shafts, and an electric creep motor, whose battery could be charged by the central diesel with a snorkel. To stop the evaporation of the liquid oxygen some changes had to be made for the production *projekt A615*, small batches of which were ordered from 1953 to 1957 for the *Sudomekh No. 196* and *Marti No. 194* yards at Leningrad and yard *No. 444* at Nikolaev. Twenty-nine vessels were completed up to 1958, but they often suffered from fires and explosions, so that the crews called them 'cigarette lighters'; in a few cases these fires led to the loss of boats. The last boat *M-361* was therefore reconstructed to improve the storing of the liquid oxygen and the chemical absorbers, and did not come into service until 1962. But the improvements on its sisters could not prevent the cessation of the development line, and the follow-on *projekt 637* was cancelled, when nuclear power was chosen as a more attractive option.

The completion of the surface ships and submarines of the first post-war programme was as follows:

Table 10.11: Commissioning of surface ships

Ship type/year	45	46	47	48	49	50	51	52	53	54	55	56	57	58	59	Total
Cruisers *68K*	–	–	–	–	–	5	–	–	–	–	–	–	–	–	–	5
Cruisers *68-bis*	–	–	–	–	–	–	–	5	4	4	1	–	–	–	–	14
Destroyers *30K*	–	–	2	4	2	2	–	–	–	–	–	–	–	–	–	10
Destroyers *30bis*	–	–	–	–	8	18	22	18	4	–	–	–	–	–	–	70
Destroyers *41*	–	–	–	–	–	–	–	–	–	–	1	–	–	–	–	1
Destroyers *56*	–	–	–	–	–	–	–	–	–	–	7	12	8	–	–	27
Patrol Ships *29K*	–	1	2	–	–	1	1	–	–	–	–	–	–	–	–	5
Patrol Ships *42*	–	–	–	–	–	–	1	4	3	–	–	–	–	–	–	8
Patrol Ships *50*	–	–	–	–	–	–	–	–	–	26	10	15	9	8	–	68
Total	–	1	4	4	10	26	24	27	11	30	19	27	17	8	–	208

Table 10.12: Distribution of the surface ships to the fleets

Ship type	Baltic Fleet	Northern Fleet	Black Sea Fleet	Pacific Fleet	Total
Cruisers	4	6	5	4	19
Destroyers	27	26	25	30	108
Patrol Ships	18	22	20	21	81
Total	49	54	50	55	208

Source: Data sent by S.S. Berezhnoi to J. Rohwer in 1997.

Table 10.13: Commissioning of submarines 1945–59

Sub. type	Yard	45	46	47	48	49	50	51	52	53	54	55	56	57	58	59	Total
611	196	–	–	–	–	–	–	–	–	2	4	2	1	–	–	–	9
	402	–	–	–	–	–	–	–	–	–	–	–	7	9	1	–	17
IX-bis	112	2	1	2	2	–	–	–	–	–	–	–	–	–	–	–	7
	638	1	1	–	–	–	–	–	–	–	–	–	–	–	–	–	2
	444	–	–	–	1	–	–	–	–	–	–	–	–	–	–	–	1
X-bis	194	1	1	–	–	–	–	–	–	–	–	–	–	–	–	–	2
613	112	–	–	–	–	–	–	1	4	16	29	37	26	–	–	–	113
	444	–	–	–	–	–	–	–	5	11	14	18	15	9	–	–	72
	189	–	–	–	–	–	–	–	–	3	–	8	4	3	1	–	19
	199	–	–	–	–	–	–	–	–	–	1	4	4	2	–	–	11
617	196	–	–	–	–	–	–	–	–	–	–	–	1	–	–	–	1
96	196	–	–	8	5	10	11	8	7	3	–	–	–	–	–	–	52
	402	–	–	–	1	–	–	–	–	–	–	–	–	–	–	–	1
95	196	–	1	–	–	–	–	–	–	–	–	–	–	–	–	–	1
615	196	–	–	–	–	–	–	–	–	1	–	–	–	–	–	–	1
A615	196	–	–	–	–	–	–	–	–	–	–	5	9	6	3	–	23
	194	–	–	–	–	–	–	–	–	–	–	–	4	2	–	–	6
Total		4	4	9	9	11	11	9	18	34	48	74	70	27	5	–	333
Accumulated		4	8	17	26	37	48	57	75	109	157	231	301	328	333		

Source: *Istoriya ...*, op. cit., vol. V, p. 92.

Table 10.14: Distribution of the new submarines to the fleets

Submarine type	Baltic Fleet	Northern Fleet	Black Sea Fleet	Pacific Fleet
Big submarines *pr.611*	1	19	–	6
Medium submarines *pr.613*	43	78	39	54
pr.617	1	–	–	–
Small submarines *pr.96*	15	–	11	26
pr.615/A615	20	–	11	–
Total	80	97	61	86

Source: Data sent by S.S. Berezhnoi and V.P. Semenov to Jürgen Rohwer in 1997.

NEW TECHNOLOGIES AND CHANGES IN THE PROGRAMME

In the early 1950s it became increasingly clear that new technologies, such as jet and rocket propulsion for aircraft, anti-aircraft and ballistic rockets and cruise missiles, nuclear power to drive ships and submarines, nuclear warheads for bombs and missiles, and many electronic sensors and new communication equipment might force a change in the existing programmes of warship building, based mainly on weapons and sensors of the Second World War period. The first steps in the new direction were already being undertaken over the last years of Stalin's regime, and so shall be discussed shortly, even though results of the developments in most cases came only during the time of his successors, who changed the programme of Stalin's time drastically.

Nuclear Power and Nuclear Weapons

Nuclear development was put under the direction of L.P. Beriya and was already being pushed during the last years of the war. A short time after the start of the war the physicist N.G. Flerov had experimented with nuclear fission, and proposed studies to develop an atomic bomb. The *NKVD* made strenuous efforts to get information from its agents in the United States and Great Britain. But it was not until 1946 that I.V. Kurchatov achieved a chain reaction and constructed in 1948 a nuclear reactor, and on 25 August 1949 an atomic bomb was detonated on top of a tower at a test site in the Kazakh desert, causing great surprise in Western countries. This was followed by the results of research undertaken under A.D. Sakharov, who was in charge of the explosion of the first thermo-nuclear device in 1953.[67]

In the area of atomic energy two paths were being taken – one was to build a big icebreaker, called *Lenin*, which was launched on 5 December 1957 and completed on 18 September 1958 with three pressurized water-cooled reactors. The other path was the development of a nuclear drive for submarines. On 9 September 1952 separate design groups were formed to develop a nuclear submarine and a nuclear power plant. At first the *SKB-143/Malakhit* was assigned to the project, which was to produce a submarine able to use a big 1,500mm nuclear-armed torpedo *T015*, with a 3.54t warhead and 20m in length, to be fired from 30–40km distance for strategic attack. Initial research showed that a submarine of at least 2,700t was necessary. The final version of this nuclear-powered strategic attack submarine, the first version of *projekt 627*, was designed by V.N. Peregudov, and had a displacement of 2,896t surfaced. There is rumour that there was also a diesel-driven variant designed. But in 1954 the mission was changed to a normal torpedo attack type *projekt 627*, of which the first vessel, *K-3*, was laid down on 24 September 1955 and completed on 12 March 1959. There was also a variant, *projekt P627A*, with a big container aft of the sail for a 13t *Ilyushin P-20* long-range cruise missile, but this project was stopped in 1958 when it became clear that ballistic missiles might be more worthwhile. Only the normal attack submarine *projekt 627A* was built with 14 units up to 1963. Similar to the US atomic submarine *Seawolf* in 1955 there was an order for Peregudov's design team to develop a submarine following the lay-out of *projekt 627A* with two liquid metal lead-bismuth reactors as *projekt 645*, but only one unit, *K-27*, was completed in 1963, and found no followers as the *Seawolf* had in the USA.[68]

Cruise Missiles and Rockets

Work on cruise missiles had already begun on 13 June 1944, when V.N. Chelomey designed a missile *10-Kh* after the German pulse-jet *V-1*, of which one example was sent in October 1944 by the British. It was to be dropped by a *Tu-2* or *Pe-8* bomber. But the flight tests with the pulse-jet at the Golodnaya Prairie were not very successful. On 13 May 1946 a Special Committee for Rocket Technology was established under the Deputy Chairman of the Council of Ministers, G.M. Malenkov. Three ministries with their Scientific Research Institutes (*NII*) and their construction bureaus (*KB*) participated: the Ministry for Armaments under D.F. Ustinov for liquid-powered rockets, the Ministry for Agricultural Machinery for rockets with a powder charge, and the Ministry for Aircraft Industry for the cruise missiles. The main effort was to be put on the development of a ballistic rocket of the same type as the German *V-2*. On 27 July 1947 the area of Kapustin Yar was selected as a test area, and on 18 October 1947 a *V-2*, captured in Germany, was started up. S.P. Korolev of the *NII-88* constructed the first Soviet ballistic rocket *P-1*, which was successfully launched on 10 October 1948.[69]

In 1948 Chelomey had changed to a liquid-powered rocket *Shchuka*, and a turbo-jet *15-Kh* with two rocket boosters, which was adapted for ship-use by M. Orlov in 1953–55. As a prototype platform one of the unfinished destroyers of *projekt 56*, the *Bedovyi*, was chosen to be finished as *projekt 56E*, and got a start ramp at the stern. In February 1957 the first shipboard tests of this anti-ship missile were made against the laid-up destroyer leader hull of the *Erevan*, repeated in December 1957 also against the hull of the unfinished battlecruiser *Stalingrad*. The *Bedovyi* was followed by three more sister vessels as *projekt 56M*, all of which were commissioned into the fleets in 1958, while one more was cancelled, because a bigger version, the *projekt 57*, had already been ordered by Admiral Kuznetsov on 25 July 1955, with two launching ramps for the missiles.[70]

At the same time, about 1949/50 the *MiG*-bureau developed an air-launched missile *Komet*, based on the fuselage of the jet-fighter *MiG-15*. The developing engineer, A.Ya. Bereznyak, founded a design bureau *Raduga* and developed from the design in 1953 a ship-board missile, the *S-2/Strela*. From April to October 1955 the *projekt 68-bis* cruiser *Admiral Nakhimov* was equipped at the *No. 444* yard in Nikolaev with containers for this missile on both sides of the forward 152mm gun turrets, from which the missiles were transported by rail to the launcher at the bow. From November 1955 to December 1957 firing tests were made, but this design, *projekt 67EP*, was not considered a success, and the cruiser was laid up and scrapped in 1961/62.[71] The *TsKB-17* under the direction of V.V. Ashik, who had designed the *projekt 67EP*, also developed other more advanced projects, such as the *67SI* and *67*, in which the gun turrets were removed and replaced with a big magazine *SM-58* for missiles and on top a container for preparing the missile for launching from a ramp on both ends of the ship. There were also some designs for armoured turrets with one, two and three start ramps for missiles of the type *10KhN* and the improved *16Kh*, and the Ashik bureau even developed sketch designs for rebuilt battlecruisers of *projekt 82*, *projekts F-25*, *F-25A*, and *F-25B*, and other versions of *projekt 68-bis* cruisers, and even for rebuilding the former German cruiser *Tallinn/projekt 83* into a missile ship for the *P-10* missiles designed by G.M. Beriev. The missiles were equipped with a beam-riding guidance, and the horizon-range could be extended by the use of helicopters. And there were

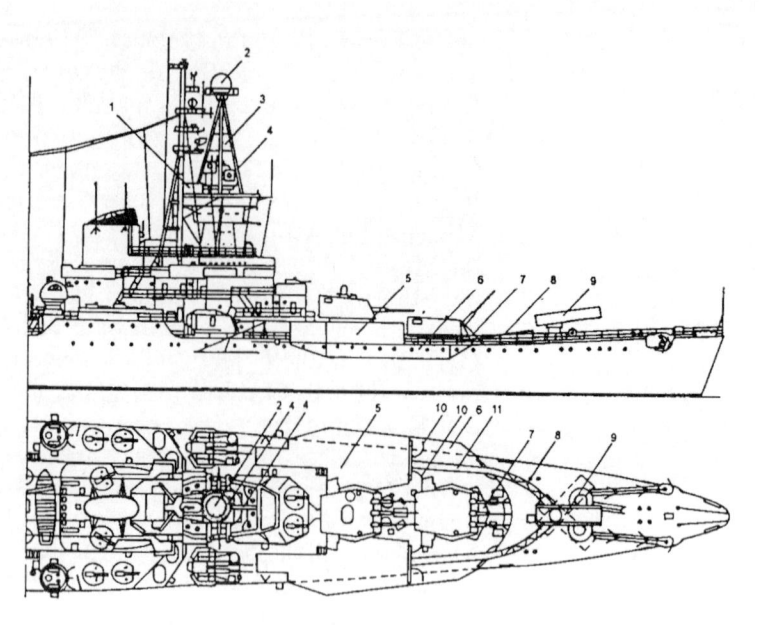

Fig. 20. Light cruiser *projekt 67EP Admiral Nakhimov*, 1955. Rebuilt 1955 from *projekt 68-bis* into a test vessel for 'Strela'-missiles. On the side of the superfiring 15.2cm turret on both sides were two containers each for 'Strela'-missiles added, transported by rails to the launcher on the foredeck. 1955/56 tests, 1961/62 scrapped. Credit: Gangut

in 1948 also designs by F.A. Kaverin of the *TsKB-18* for big submarines with such missiles as *projekt P-2*, with four *R-1* ballistic missiles and 18 cruise missiles *10Kh/Lastochka* as well as three midget submarines and 12 torpedo tubes with 24 reserve torpedoes, and a smaller *projekt 624*, with ten cruise missiles and six torpedo tubes. For these projects one *projekt 611* conventional submarine, the *B-64*, was converted in 1956–57, and used as a test platform. But these projects were rejected in September 1956, and not really started, as occurred with the project of 1959 to equip a *projekt 627A* atomic submarine with a big hangar behind the sail for a long-range *P-20* missile, designed by S.V. Ilyushin. This project was also cancelled, as were the *Regulus* systems in the United States,

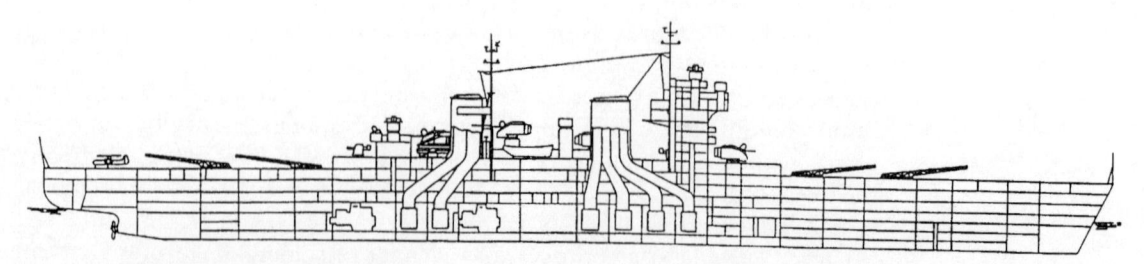

Fig. 21. Missile battlecruiser, variant *F-25A*, no name given, 1949, displ. 21,900t stdd., length 241.7m, max. speed 35kt, 8 missiles 10XH or 16X, 10 10cm. Only plans, no orders placed. Credit: Gangut

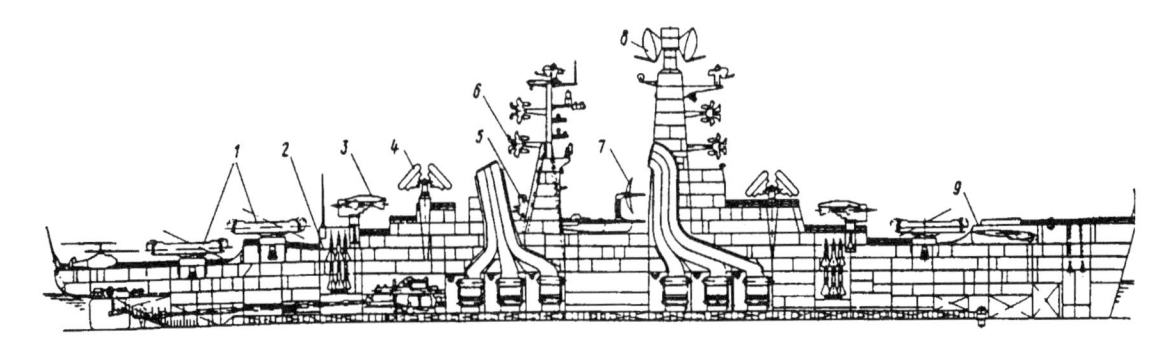

Fig. 22. Light cruiser, *projekt 64*, no name given, 1956, to be rebuilt from a *projekt 68-bis* cruiser. Three launcher *P-6* for cruise missiles, Two twin launcher for A/A missiles M-3, two to four A/A launcher M-1, 8 7.6cm. For 1961/62 start of the rebuilding of six ships planned, but not started. Credit: Sudostroenie

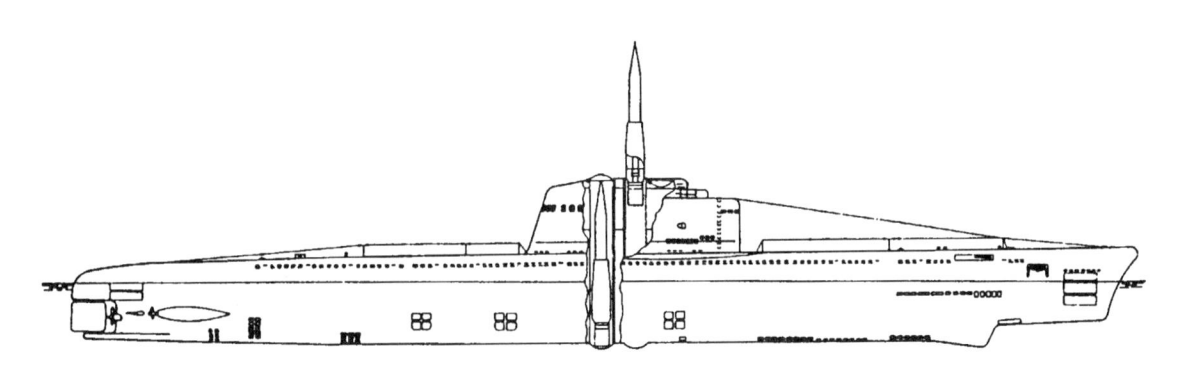

Fig. 23. Missile submarine *projekt 611AV*, *B-62*, 1958, Rebuilt from *projekt 611* to carry two ballistic missiles R-11FM. Torpedo armament remained, guns removed. 6 units rebuilt from 1958–62. Credit: Sudostroenie

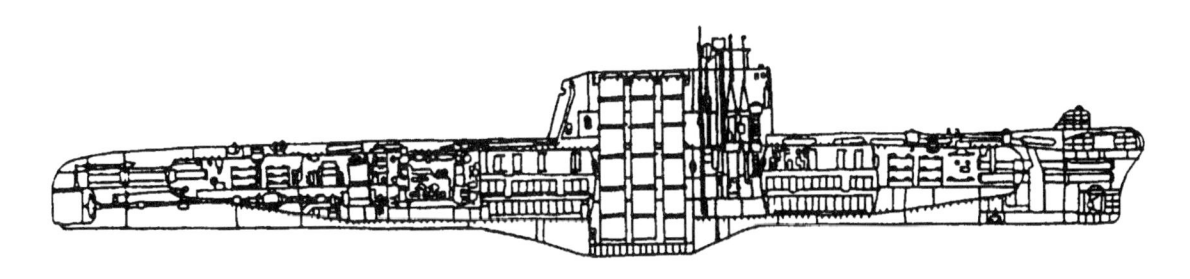

Fig. 24. Missile submarine *projekt 629*, *K-96*, ex-*B-92*, 1955, displ. 2,820/3,553t stdd., length 98.9m, max. speed 15.5/12.5kt, Three tubes SM-60 for ballistic missiles P-13, 6 torpedo tubes 53.3cm. Credit: Pavlov

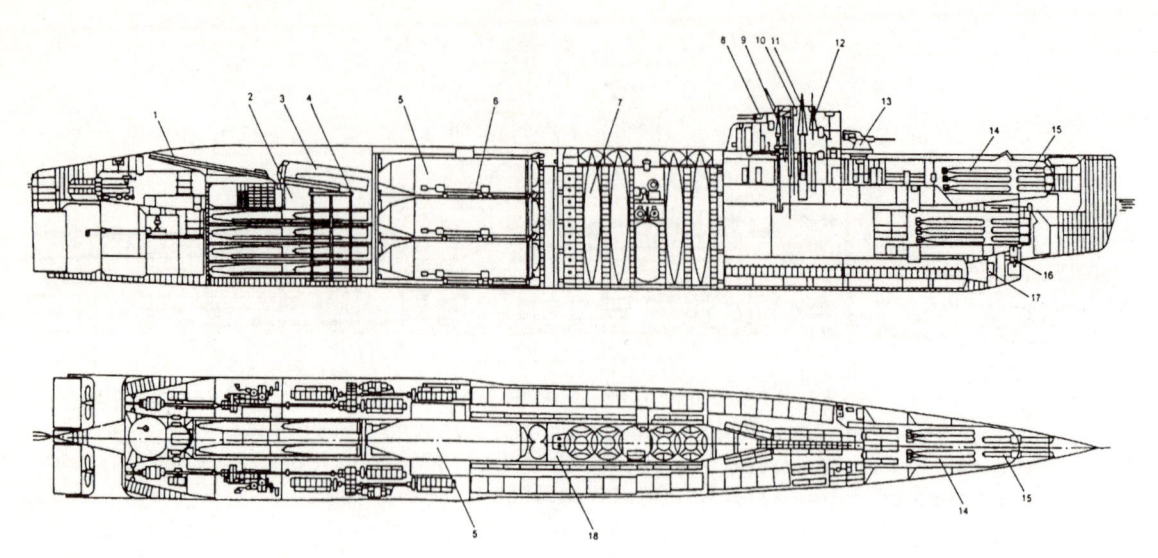

Fig. 25. Big missile submarine *projekt P-2*, no name or number given, 1949. Besides 2 5.7cm and 2 2.5cm and 16 torpedo tubes this vessel had three midget submarines, 4 ballistic rockets R-1 and 16 10XH missiles. No orders placed. Credit: Gangut

when the prospects of ballistic missiles seemed so much more worthwhile.[72] More successful were the turbo-jet *P-5* missiles of V.N. Chelomey, which were used to equip first one *projekt P613 (S-146)* with one and the rebuilt *projekt 644* with two cylinders, and later the *projekt 665*, with four and the atomic submarines *projekt 659*, *projekt 651*, and the conventional *projekt 675*, and the 'rocket'-cruisers of *projekt 58*.[73]

In 1955 A.Ya. Berzhnyak began to develop a rocket-powered short-range anti-ship missile, the *P-15*, tested in October 1957, and used first with the fast attack craft or *projekt 183R* in 1959 and with *projekt 205* in 1960, designed by Ye.I. Yukhnin. It had a range of between 8,000 and 40,000m.[74]

Starting with the German 'Wasserfall', there was a development of several anti-aircraft rockets, on which work began in 1955 with the land-based system, soon adapted for shipboard use as *M-1P/Volna-P*. In 1959 a first version was installed on the rebuilt *projekt 56* destroyer *Bravyi*, and later on most new surface ships. Also a longer range A/A rocket was the *M-2/Volkhov* system, first used on the 1960–62 rebuilt *projekt 68bis* cruiser *Dzerzhinskii* as *projekt 70E*. Also for such anti-aircraft systems there were several other projects, sometimes combined with cruise missiles, such as the *projekts 64* and *81*, for rebuilt cruisers of *projekt 68-bis*, and a new nuclear-powered cruiser of *projekt 63*, but besides the mentioned destroyers and their successors and the *Dzerzhinskii* the other projects were not realized.[75]

Work on strategic ballistic missiles for use in submarines started with an order on January 1954. Chief designer of the rockets was S.P. Korolev. His *R-11FM* rocket was first test-fired from a rebuilt *projekt 611AV* submarine, the *B-67*, in a surfaced position on 16 September 1955. This was necessary because of the liquid fuel used, which could be fuelled into the missile only when surfaced. It was the first live test to fire a ballistic rocket from a submarine.

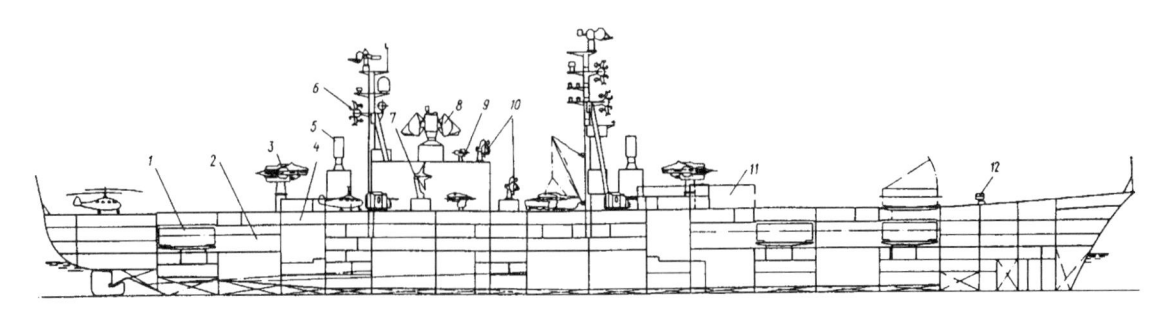

Fig. 26. Nuclear missile cruiser *projekt 63*, no name given, 1958, three launchers for missiles P-40, two twin launchers for A/A missiles M-3, two A/A missile launchers M-2, 8 7.6cm. Credit: Sudostroenie

To the Americans their project with an atomic submarine and a liquid-fuelled *Jupiter* rocket was assessed as too dangerous for a submerged launch, so first a solid-fuel rocket *Polaris* had to be developed, and so the first launch of the American *Polaris A-1* from the submerged nuclear submarine *George Washington* did not take place until 20 July 1960.[76] Then N.N. Isanin of the *TsKB-16* designed the version *projekt 611AV* with two launching tubes for the rocket *R-11FM*, and six *projekt 611* submarines were converted to this version, the first one in 1958 at Vladivostok. To overcome this interim solution N.N. Isanin started in 1955 to redesign the conventional submarine *projekt 641*, which was built in greater numbers as successor to *projekt 611*, to a conventional submarine for three *R-13* ballistic rockets as *projekt 629*, of which 22 units were built from 1959 to 1962. And on 26 August 1956 the Ministry of Defence also ordered the development of a nuclear-powered submarine for three *R-13* rockets. The chief designer of this submarine of *projekt 658* was S.N. Kovalev, and eight vessels were built up to 1964.[77]

As successors to the torpedo submarines of *projekts 611* and *613* in 1952–55, *TTZ* were issued for improved designs, that is, *projekts 641* and *633*, which were built from 1957 and at first planned in large numbers – for example, *projekt 633* was to complete 560 units. But, in fact, from 1957 to 1962 only 22 were completed, before construction was halted. With *projekt 641* 74 units were built, including some export versions which came until 1982 from the yards. And there was a great number of modifications among the submarines built, including the missile and rocket submarines already mentioned; one other interesting version was *projekt 640*, a radar picket version of *projekt 613*, of which five vessels were rebuilt. In addition, there were many other test and special versions, mostly completed after 1960.[78]

POLITICS AND STRATEGY, 1951–56

In 1945, Stalin faced very big problems with the reconstruction of the industry, which in the western parts of the Soviet Union had been destroyed or at least heavily damaged during the German occupation. And there were the priority needs of the Army, as mentioned, and the necessity to build a strong air defence with jet-aircraft and anti-aircraft guns and possibly rockets. And a great amount of effort was being invested in producing a satisfactory nuclear weapon and its delivery systems. The high costs involved in all this prevented Stalin at first from spending funds for the Navy, as their leaders wanted.

In this first phase of the Cold War both sides observed each other with rising mistrust, and most initiatives coming from one side were blocked by the other. The strength of the Soviet Fleet was then overestimated by the West to some extent, and the fears about the big submarine building programme came to the fore, as mentioned. The many harbour visits of the *projekt 68-bis* cruisers and the *projekt 30* destroyers, beginning in June 1953 with the visit of the *Sverdlov* to the coronation parade at Spithead, followed by the visits of such ships to Albania, Yugoslavia, Finland, Sweden, Norway, Denmark, the Netherlands and especially Great Britain, further fuelled the fears of the Western navies.

But Stalin had never given up his idea of building an ocean-going fleet, as was shown by his reinstatement of Admiral Kuznetsov as Minister of the Navy in 1951, after he became convinced that Admiral I.S. Yumashev was not able to manage the first ten-year programme successfully. Stalin demanded his beloved battlecruisers and other sea-going ships and also coastal forces in great numbers. Kuznetsov immediately tried to bring aircraft carriers into the discussion again, and to cancel the gun-armed heavy battleships and battle-cruisers or at least to cut their numbers down, so as to build more cruisers and big destroyers, and submarines with a greater range. As can be seen in Tables 10.11–10.14 the completion of the ships and submarines was speeded up during Kuznetsov's second term in command. But in most cases he was unable to change Stalin's mind, and the dictator became in his last years more and more reluctant to make decisions on shipbuilding and introduce new ship types and new weapons aboard ships.[79] Kuznetsov found fault with the lack of information about Stalin's intentions and on the planning of the land-minded marshals of the Army, which did not take account of the needs of the Navy leaders.

This was already evident during the time of Marshal of the Soviet Union N.A. Bul'ganin as Minister of Defence, who had no interest in the Navy at all and evaded difficult decisions. This became clearer immediately after Stalin's death on 5 March 1953, when Kuznetsov again tried to renew the carrier *projekt 85*, while the battleships of *projekt 24* and the battlecruisers of *projekt 82* were cancelled. His idea to resuscitate the plan for the *projekt 66* heavy cruisers as carrier escorts found no support from the new leaders, especially the new Secretary-General of the Bolshevik Party, N.S. Khrushchev, who supported the decision of the Council of Ministers of 26 January 1954 to plan submarines with cruise and ballistic missiles, while he opposed all efforts to build bigger ships or to reconstruct such ships as missile or rocket ships. In October 1954 Kuznetsov presented Khrushchev with a memorandum for the strengthening of the air defence of the fleet and again asked for a fast decision about the aircraft carriers. This was too much for Khrushchev, who after returning from a visit to China in December 1954 called Kuznetsov to Vladivostok to review the Pacific Fleet with him. There he reprimanded Kuznetsov severely for his requests, all of which were flatly rejected. This and the running disputes with the Army leaders, especially the new Minister of Defence, Marshal of the Soviet Union G.K. Zhukov, might have helped bring on the stroke which hit Kuznetsov in 1955. Khrushchev promoted him again from his demoted rank as Vice Admiral to Admiral of the Fleet of the Soviet Union together with I.S. Isakov. The situation escalated when in September 1955 Zhukov remarked that surface ships had lost their role, and asked Khrushchev to clear the yards of heavy ships, which he said were only good for state visits. When on 30 October 1955 the battleship *Novorossijsk*, the former Italian *Giulio Cesare*, sank after hitting a mine in the harbour of Sevastopol, this was an opportune moment to lay the blame at Kuznetsov's door, notwithstanding the fact that he was already ill when the explosion occurred. On 8 December 1955 he was relieved of his command and demoted again to Vice Admiral because of his 'unsatisfactory handling of his posts as Commander-in-Chief of the Navy and First Deputy Defence Minister'.[80]

NOTES

1. I.G. Zakharov, 'Naval Shipbuilding in Russia', *Sudostroenie*, No. 10 (1996), p. 64.
2. Dmitrii Litvinenko, 'Plany vozhda. Pervaya poslevoennaya programma stroitel'stva flota', *Morskoi sbornik*, No. 2 (1997), pp. 100–4.
3. Robert W. Love, *History of the U.S. Navy. Vol. II, 1942–1991*, Harrisburg, PA, Stackpole Books, 1992, p. 279.
4. Arkhiva Prezidenta Rossijskoi Federatsii, f.no.3, op.63, d.225, l.36, 95.
5. Ibid., l.62, 71.
6. Robert W. Love, op. cit., p. 279.
7. *Perepiska Predsedatelya Soveta Ministrov SSSR a prezidentami SshA i prem'er-ministrami Velikobritannii vo vremya Velikoi Otechestvennoi vojny 1941–1945 gg.*, Moscow, 176, Vol. 1, p. 425, Vol. 2, pp. 254–5.
8. *Berlinskaya (Potsdamskaya) Konferentsiya rukovoditelei trekh soyuznikh derzhav – SSSR, SshA i Velikobritanniya (17 iyulya–2 avgusta 1945 g.), Sbornik Dokumentov*, Moscow, 1984, pp. 300–1.
9. Axel Niestlé, *German U-Boat Losses during World War Two. Details of Destruction*, Annapolis, MD, US Naval Institute, 1998 (lists the fate of all the German U-boats).
10. A. Komarov, 'Konets Krigsmarine. Reshenie voprosa o razdele germanskogo flota', *Morskoi sbornik*, No. 5 (1999), pp. 76–82.
11. S.S. Berezhnoi, *Trofej i reparatsii VMF SSSR*, op. cit., pp. 5–9.
12. Ibid., pp. 14–22, 36–42, 103–21.
13. E.A. Shitikov, 'Ispytaniya korablei na Novoi Zemle', *Morskoi sbornik*, No. 5, 1994, pp. 71–7.
14. Erich Gröner, *Die deutschen Kriegsschiffe 1815–1945. Vol. 2: Torpedoboote, Zerstörer, Schnellboote, Minensuchboote, Minenräumboote*. Fortgeführt von Dieter Jung und Martin Maass, Koblenz, Bernard & Graefe, 1983, pp. 130–9, 192–202.
15. On this ship the author Jürgen Rohwer served in 1944 as a watch officer, see his article, 'Sperrbrecher 104. A Curious Ship of the German Kriegsmarine', *Naval History*, vol. 6, No. 4 (Winter 1992) (Annapolis).
16. S.S. Berezhnoi, op. cit., pp. 34–9.
17. Ibid., pp. 22–4, 74–81, 86–7, 121. The destroyers and escort destroyers were given on 17.06.49 number designations and were used for many years as training and test vessels.
18. Ibid., pp. 6–7, 11, 25–8, 42–3.
19. Ibid.
20. Ibid.
21. B. Rodionov, V. Dotsenko, G. Kostev et al., *Tri veka Rossijskogo flota, Vol. 3*, St Petersburg, 1996, p. 217.
22. D. Litvinenko, 'Plany Vozhdia', op. cit., p. 102.
23. A. Davydov and A. Kilichenkov, *Moskva i sudby Rossijskogo flota*, Moscow, 1996, pp. 319–20.
24. A.M. Vasil'ev, 'Krupnye nadvodnye korabli v programmakh Sovetskogo Voennogo

sudostroeniya (1936–1960gg)', *Sudostroenie*, No. 6 (1997), pp. 82–91.
25. E.A. Shitikov *et al.*, op. cit., pp. 60ff. N.N. Afonin, 'Pis'ma tchitatelei po voprosam istorii', *Sudostroenie*, No. 11–12 (1994), pp. 57–62. B.P. Tyurin, 'Kreiseri tipa 68', *Gangut*, No. 6, 1993, pp. 10–25. A.M. Vasil'ev, op. cit., pp. 84, 86–7. *Istoriya Otechestvennogo Sudostroeniya. Vol. V: Sudostroenie v poslevoennyi period 1946–1991 gg.*, St Petersburg, Sudostroenie, 1996, pp. 23–33.
26. E.A. Shitikov *et al.*, op. cit., pp. 60ff. V.N. Nikol'skii, B. Tyurin and V. Prorozhetskii, 'Eskadrennye minonostsy proekta 30-bis', *Morskoi sbornik*, No. 10 (1992), pp. 51–6. V.N. Burov, *Otechestvennoe Voennoe korablestroenie v tret'em stoletii svoei istorii*, St Petersburg, Sudostroenie, 1995, pp. 277–89. *Istoriya ...*, op. cit., vol. V, pp. 41–51.
27. E.A. Shitikov *et al.*, op. cit., pp. 60ff. V.A. Kueger, Yu.V. Manuilov, V.P. Semenov, 'Podvodnye lodki proekta 613', *Sudostroenie*, No. 5–6 (1994), pp. 61–5. V.N. Burov, op. cit., pp. 256–70. *Istoriya ...*, op. cit., vol. V, pp. 77–94.
28. E.A. Shitikov *et al.*, op. cit., pp. 60ff. V.N. Burov, op. cit., pp. 100–1. *Istoriya ...*, op. cit., vol. V, pp. 50–7.
29. Pawel A. Sudoplatow and Anatolij Sudoplatow, *Der Handlanger der Macht. Enthüllungen eines KGB-Generals*, Düsseldorf, Econ, 1994, pp. 221–52. Norman Polmar and Thomas B. Allen, *Spy Book: The Encyclopedia of Espionage*, London, Greenhill Books, 1997, pp. 34–6.
30. Jürgen Rohwer, *Superpower Confrontation on the Seas*, The Washington Papers No. 26, Beverly Hills, CA, Sage, 1975.
31. *Morskoi sbornik*, No. 1 (1946), pp. 13–30.
32. S.A. Zonin, 'Nepravi sud", *Morskoi sbornik*, No. 2 (1991), pp. 78–84. S.A. Zonin, *Admiral L.M. Galler. Zhizn' i flotovodcheskaya deyatel'nost'*, Moscow, Voenizdat, 1991, 386–407. TsVMA, f.14, op.19, d.1. Interview of J. Rohwer with S.A. Zonin at Stuttgart in 1996.
33. B.D. Dotsenko, *Morskoi biograficheskii slovar*, St Petersburg, Logos, 1995, pp. 30, 111–12, 134–5, 390–91.
34. *Morskoi sbornik*, No. 11 (1947), pp. 36–85; No. 4 (1948), pp. 1–20; No. 9 (1948), pp. 13–20; No. 10 (1948), pp. 31–5; No. 11 (1948), pp. 21–44; No. 12 (1948), pp. 43–7.
35. *Morskoi sbornik*, No. 7 (1950), pp. 91–105; No. 11 (1951), pp. 88–91.
36. V.N. Burov, op. cit., pp. 271–4. *Istoriya ...*, op. cit., vol. V, pp. 26–31. A.S. Pavlov, *Warships of the USSR and Russia 1945–1995*, Annapolis, MD, US Naval Institute Press, 1997, pp. 4–5.
37. V.N. Burov, op. cit., pp. 277–9. *Istoriya ...*, op. cit., vol. V, p. 41. A.S. Pavlov, op. cit., p. 6.
38. V.N. Burov, op. cit., pp. 289–90. *Istoriya ...*, op. cit., vol. V, pp. 50–52. A.S. Pavlov, op. cit., p. 8.
39. *Istoriya ...*, op. cit., vol. V, pp. 56–7. A.S. Pavlov, op. cit., p. 11.
40. V.N. Burov, op. cit., pp. 306–7. *Istoriya ...*, op. cit., vol. V, pp. 67–70. A.S. Pavlov, op. cit., pp. 13, 16.
41. A.S. Pavlov, op. cit., p. 15.
42. V.N. Burov, op. cit., pp. 304–6. *Istoriya ...*, op. cit., vol. V, pp. 57–60. A.S. Pavlov, op. cit., pp. 12, 18.
43. V.N. Burov, op. cit., pp. 294–7. A.S. Pavlov, op. cit., pp. 16–17.
44. A.M. Vasil'ev, 'Linejnye korabl' VMF SSSR predvoennikh proektov', *Gangut*, No. 16, St Petersburg, 1998, pp. 62–6.
45. A.M. Vasil'ev, 'Linejnye korabli proekta 24', *Gangut*, No. 15, St Petersburg, 1998, pp. 32–44.
46. V.N. Burov, op. cit., pp. 276–7. *Istoriya ...*, op. cit., vol. V, pp. 33–9. A.S. Pavlov, op. cit., p. 86. *Conway's All the World's Fighting Ships 1947–1995*, London, Conway Maritime Press, p. 377.
47. E.A. Shitikov *et al.*, op. cit., pp. 46–51. *Istoriya ...*, op. cit., vol. V, pp. 37–9. *Conway's ...*, op. cit., pp. 377–8.
48. *Istoriya ...*, op. cit., vol. V, pp. 30–31. *Conway's ...*, op. cit., p. 377. A.B. Morin, *Legkie krejsera tipa 'Chapaev' i tipa 'Sverdlov'*, St Petersburg, Tsitadel', 1997.
49. A.B. Morin, op. cit. *Istoriya ...*, op. cit., vol. V, pp. 30–33. *Conway's ...*, op. cit., p. 379. A.S. Pavlov, op. cit., pp. 191–4.
50. A. Morin and N. Walujew, *Sowjetische Flugzeugträger. Geheim 1910–1995*, Berlin, Brandenburgisches Verlagshaus, 1996, pp. 98–9.
51. *Istoriya ...*, op. cit., vol. V, pp. 40–1. A. Morin and N. Walujew, op. cit., pp. 102–3.

52. V.I. Nikol'skii and D.Yu. Litinskii, *Eskadrennye minonostsy tipa 'Smelyi', proekt 30-bis*, St Petersburg, Istoricheskoe Morskoe Obshchestvo, 1994. V.N. Burov, op. cit., pp. 279–81. *Istoriya* ..., op. cit., vol. V, pp. 41–3, 46. *Conway's* ..., op. cit., pp. 386–7. A.S. Pavlov, op. cit., pp. 127–30.
53. V.N. Burov, op. cit., pp. 280–85. *Istoriya* ..., op. cit., vol. V, pp. 41–7. *Conway's* ..., op. cit., p. 387. A.S. Pavlov, op. cit., pp. 121–2.
54. V.N. Burov, op. cit., pp. 285–9. *Istoriya* ..., op. cit., vol. V, pp. 45–51. *Conway's* ..., op. cit., pp. 388–9. A.S. Pavlov, op. cit., pp. 123–6.
55. V.N. Burov, op. cit., pp. 289–92. V.Yu. Gribovskii, 'K istorii sozdaniya storozhevykh korablej tipa "Yastreb"', *Sudostroenie*, No. 4 (1997), pp. 87–90. V.N. Nikol'skii, 'Storozhevye korabli proekta 42', *Sudostroenie*, No. 11–12 (1994), pp. 63–6. *Istoriya* ..., op. cit., vol. V, pp. 50–54. *Conway's* ..., op. cit., p. 392. A.S. Pavlov, op. cit., pp. 136–7.
56. V.N. Nikol'skii, 'Storozhevye korabli proekta 50', *Sudostroenie*, No. 1 (1995), pp. 66–9. V.N. Burov, op. cit., pp. 292–4. *Istoriya* ..., op. cit., vol. V, pp. 52–7. *Conway's* ..., op. cit., pp. 392–3. A.S. Pavlov, op. cit., pp. 137–8.
57. V.N. Burov, op. cit., pp. 307–9. *Istoriya* ..., op. cit., vol. V, pp. 67–71. *Conway's* ..., op. cit., p. 421. A.S. Pavlov, op. cit., pp. 193–5.
58. *Istoriya* ..., op. cit., vol. V, pp. 70–72. *Conway's* ..., op. cit., pp. 423–4.
59. A.S. Pavlov, op. cit., p. 184.
60. *Istoriya* ..., op. cit., vol. V, pp. 76–7.
61. Jürgen Rohwer, *Superpower Confrontation on the Seas*, The Washington Papers No. 26, Beverly Hills, CA, Sage, 1975, pp. 19–22. See *Jane's Fighting Ships 1949/50 to 1956/57* and *Les Flottes de Combat 1950 to 1956*.
62. E.A. Shitikov *et al.*, op. cit., pp. 96–100. V.N. Burov, op. cit., pp. 257–9. *Istoriya* ..., op. cit., vol. V, pp. 84–6. *Conway's* ..., op. cit., p. 398. A.S. Pavlov, op. cit., pp. 64–9.
63. S.S. Berezhnoi, *Trofei i reparatsii VMF SSSR*, op. cit., pp. 34–9. Axel Niestlé, *German U-Boat Losses during World War II. Details of Destruction*, Annapolis, MD, US Naval Institute, 1998, pp. 169–71.
64. V.A. Kueger, Yu.V. Manuilov and V.P. Semenov, 'Podvodnye lodki proekta 613', *Sudostroenie*, No. 5–6 (1994), pp. 59–63. B. Tyurin, 'Srednie dela proekta 613', *Morskoi sbornik*, No. (1995), pp. 74–9. V.N. Burov, op. cit., pp. 260–63. *Istoriya* ..., op. cit., vol. V, pp. 79–84. *Conway's* ..., op. cit., pp. 396–7. A.S. Pavlov, op. cit., pp. 71–7.
65. I.D. Spasskii and V.P. Semenov, 'Pervaya Sovetskaya PL s turbinnoi energeticheskoi ustanovkoi (proekt 617)', *Morskoi sbornik*, No. 7 (1994), pp. 65–9. A.M. Antonov, 'Iz istorii sozdaniya podvodnykh lodok s parogazovymi turbinami', *Sudostroenie*, No. 4–5/1994, pp. 64–7. A.S. Pavlov, op. cit., p. 81
66. A.S. Pavlov, op. cit., p. 10.
67. Manfred Hildermeier, *Geschichte der Sowjetunion 1917–1991*, Munich, Beck, 1998, pp. 668–9. Norman Polmar, *Chronology of the Cold War at Sea 1945–1991*, Annapolis, MD, US Naval Institute, 1998, p. 19. V.N. Burov, op. cit., pp. 321–51.
68. A.M. Antonov, 'Atomnye podvodnye lodki pr 627', *Sudostroenie*, No. 7 (1995), pp. 76–81. P. Shmakov (chief constructor of SLMBM 'Malakhit'), 'Pervye sovetskie PLA proekta 627', *Morskoi sbornik*, No. 1 (1995), pp. 53–8. V.N. Burov, op. cit., pp. 356–67. *Istoriya* ..., op. cit., vol. V, pp. 130–36. *Conway's* ..., op. cit., p. 400. A.S. Pavlov, op. cit., pp. 54–5. V. Bil'din, 'Opytnaya torpednaya PLA proekta 645', *Morskoi sbornik*, No. 8 (1993), pp. 59–62.
69. *Conway's* ..., op. cit., pp. 350–2, 355–6. A.V. Karpenko, 'U istokov sozdaniya raketnykh korable', *Gangut*, No. 16, St Petersburg, 1998, pp. 67–82.
70. V.N. Burov, op. cit., pp. 400–4. *Istoriya* ..., op. cit., vol. V, pp. 168–74. *Conway's* ..., op. cit., pp. 389–90. A.S. Pavlov, op. cit., pp. 119–21, 123–6. This missile was called SS-N-1 by NATO.
71. Yu.A. Rabinerzon, 'Perevooruzhenie krejsera "Admiral Nakhimov" udarnym raketnym oruzhiem po proekta 67EP', *Gangut*, No. 15, St Petersburg, 1998, pp. 45–54. The Komet missile was called AS-1/Kennel, the Strela was called SS-C-2/Salish by NATO.
72. A.V. Karpenko, op. cit. A. Antonov, 'Raketnye PLA proektov P-627A, 653 i 639', *Morskoi sbornik*, No. 11 (1986), pp. 72–6. *Istoriya* ..., op. cit., vol. V, pp. 156–68. *Conway's* ..., op. cit., p. 353.

73. *Conway's* ..., op. cit., pp. 352–3, 396–7, 401–2, 380. These missiles were called SS-N-3, the submarines were called Whiskey, Zulu, Echo and Juliett, the cruisers Kynda by NATO.
74. *Istoriya* ..., op. cit., vol. V, pp. 183–90. *Conway's* ..., op. cit., pp. 353, 416–17. These missiles were called SS-N-2, the fast attack crafts Komar and Osa by NATO.
75. *Istoriya* ..., op. cit., vol. V, pp. 160–79. *Conway's* ..., op. cit., pp. 349–50, 379, 388.
76. Jürgen Rohwer, *66 Tage unter Wasser. Atom-U-Schiffe und Raketen*, Oldenburg, Stalling, 1965, p. 60. *Conway's* ..., op. cit., p. 398.
77. G. Kostev, 'Morskie strategicheskie', *Morskoi sbornik*, No. 12 (1999), pp. 6–12. V. Zharkov, 'Raketnye depo na osnove proekta 629', *Morskoi sbornik*, No. 12 (1999), pp. 65–71. *Istoriya* ..., op. cit., vol. V, pp. 141–6. *Conway's* ..., op. cit., p. 401. A.S. Pavlov, op. cit., pp. 34–6. The submarines were called Golf and Hotel by NATO.
78. *Conway's* ..., op. cit., pp. 396–8. A.S. Pavlov, op. cit., pp. 67–77. The submarines were called Foxtrot and Romeo by NATO.
79. A. Morin and N. Walujew, *Sowjetische Flugzeugträger. Geheim 1910–1995*, Berlin, Brandenburgisches Verlagshaus, 1996, pp. 102–3.
80. Ibid., p. 108.

11

Why Did Stalin Build his Big Ocean-Going Fleet?

The decision for the building of the 'Big Ocean-Going Fleet' was taken by Stalin in the last months of 1935. There was during the last part of 1935 a well-considered and exactly planned propaganda campaign to celebrate the successes of the technical reconstruction of the fleet and the progress in the education and combat training of naval personnel. On 23 December 1935 more than 270 naval officers and sailors were decorated with orders and medals for their achievements in spreading the Stakhanov movement in the Navy. And on the same day Stalin, V.M. Molotov, G.K. Ordzhonikidze and K.E. Voroshilov received in the Kremlin a delegation from the Pacific Fleet. After the reception, the High Commands of the Red Army and the Red Navy were ordered to prepare proposals for the development of a great ocean-going Navy and to put them before the Government for acceptance. In the following day's *Pravda* there appeared an article which stated that it was the aim of the Soviet Union to become a great sea power over the next few years.

In February 1936 a first variant for this great fleet project was ready, and on 27 May 1936 the Council of Labour and Defence (*STO*) approved the parameters for the composition of the future fleet and the building programme for 1936–47. It is surprising that only a very short time after the official proclamation of the doctrine of a 'Small War at Sea', which was still supported by the then Deputy Chief of the Naval Forces, *Flagman 1 Ranga* I.M. Ludri, in a review of an American book in the February 1936 issue of the official journal *Morskoi sbornik*, the official doctrine was suddenly changed to one of a 'Big Ocean-Going Navy'. The Chief of the Naval Forces, *Flagman Flota 1 Ranga* V.M. Orlov, who had also been a supporter with the *jeune école* of a small war at sea, now vehemently propagated this viewpoint in his speech to the Extraordinary Congress of the Union's Soviets on 28 November 1936. Nevertheless, the then Chief of the General Staff, Marshal A.I. Yegorov, persisted with his requests that the Navy build heavy ships and even aircraft carriers in greater numbers than the Navy wanted.

Where should we look for the reasons for this sudden change? There can be no doubt that the initiative for this change must have come from the top, from Stalin himself, because at this time his dominant position was so effectively established that nobody dared to criticize his decisions or to present diverging opinions. This is especially obvious here, as the top military and naval leaders, who had before clearly been supporters of the 'Small War at Sea' theory, suddenly switched to the opposite viewpoint. They must have seen or possibly even anticipated the changed aims of the *Vozhd'*, of Stalin. What, then, might have been Stalin's reasons for this change of policy and strategy?

In the mid-1930s Stalin had perceived the 'people's front' concept of co-operation with the Western democracies in a policy of 'collective security', as advocated by the *Narkom* for Foreign Relations, M.M. Litvinov, and promoted by the *Komintern*, to be a failure. Litvinov's influence probably began to diminish much earlier than March 1939, as most Western historians have assumed.[1] Stalin must have already changed to an independent defence policy by the mid-1930s. One obvious reason was the anti-Soviet and anti-communist policy of Germany, and its closer collaboration with the Japanese and Italians, but also with the former common enemy Poland, and Great Britain, as was demonstrated by the German–British Naval Agreement of 1935, which seemed to be a German approach to one of the most important Western democracies to him. No doubt, Stalin felt that the Soviet Union was becoming increasingly surrounded by possible enemy states. This led him to want to build up the military strength of the Soviet Union to a level superior to that of his neighbours, a tendency seen already in the early 1930s, when industrialization was focused on the production of armaments for the Army, to equip their forces according to the doctrine of M.N. Tukhachevskii and V.K. Triandaffilov of countering possible enemy attacks by counterstrokes deep into their territory.

By the mid-1930s it most probably became evident to Stalin that the other great powers had started to build up their navies, and that a real naval arms race had begun. He must have had the intention of acquiring in all fleet areas a strength comparable or even superior to the probable enemy navies, especially the Japanese in the Sea of Japan and the Germans in the Baltic, and to a lesser extent the Germans and their allies in the Arctic, and the Romanians, the Turkish and the Italians in the Black Sea. Because all the possible hostile sea powers started to build new battleships, he also saw a need to have such ships. This was underlined, when in 1936–37 the Soviet Navy was not able to support the Republicans in the Spanish Civil War, despite the fact that Stalin's decision to build the 'Big Ocean-Going Fleet' was taken before the Civil War started, which some historians have erroneously linked with the start of the Soviet naval build-up. One other supporting observation was probably the decision by President Franklin D. Roosevelt, who said at this time, 'It's not possible to believe in treaties, the guarantee lies in a strong fleet. Let's see how the Japanese could endure a naval arms race.' On 21 January 1938 the US Congress accepted a new law for an enlargement of the Navy, and on 17 May a programme of a 'Two-Oceans Navy' was announced. In addition, there might have been information about new building plans for the Japanese Navy. The mentioned strategic aims developed for the August 1939 naval programme show clearly the intention of acquiring naval supremacy in each of the four fleet areas. If we look at the text of the August 1939 documents, the question is, was the aim behind the naval build-up to gain security against naval threats? Or were the battleship fleets perceived to be a necessary step in ensuring that by 1947 the Soviet Union would become one of the world's superpowers? At present, this question cannot definitively be answered, but the wording of the now known documents from 1939 to 1941 shows at the least an offensive tendency in Soviet policy and strategy.

Indeed, was Soviet industry able at this time to fulfil the big programmes? The experiences of the developments that followed are proof that the industrial and technological capacities were at the time insufficient to accomplish the big building programme in the seven to ten years envisaged. The very close dates for the building of the big ships were simply not realistic, as was shown in 1936, when only 53 per cent of the plan dates were achieved, and in 1938 only 60 per cent. Notwithstanding the real difficulties, Stalin pushed the building processes, and many historians have assumed that the purges against the naval leadership in 1937–38 had to do with his wish to get rid of the former supporters of the 'Small War at Sea' theory and the opponents of the 'reactionary theory of sea-power'. But if we look at the victims of the purges, we find not only the most important exponents of these theories, like I.M. Ludri, K.I. Dushenov and I.K. Kozhanov, but also people who changed their mind along the lines given by Stalin, like R.A. Muklevich, V.M. Orlov and finally M.V. Viktorov, and Marshal A.I. Yegorov, who since 1935 had been forcefully asking for an accelerated build-up of the Navy. And we must not forget the imprisonment of many of the engineers who were working on designs for the new big ships; or the men who tried to 'unmask the saboteurs and enemies of the people', who for a short time became the Chiefs of the Navy, like P.A. Smirnov and M.P. Frinovskii, only to become victims of the purges themselves. So this problem must be assigned to Stalin's pathological mistrust and his unreal perception of being surrounded by enemies and traitors, as Dmitrii Volkogonov has so convincingly demonstrated.

So we must assume that in the late 1930s to Stalin – as the American historian Richard Humble has said – a battleship, a dreadnought, was a direct historical predecessor to the atomic bomb, a symbol of the highest grade of power, a most powerful and mobile instrument of power politics, that the world had ever known. A state, which wants to be a fully recognized member in world politics, needs battleships and battlecruisers as symbols of power. This might have been behind Stalin's wish to have a 'Big Ocean-Going Fleet'.

But what was Stalin's intention when the Second World War was over, and a new big naval programme was presented by the naval leaders? The Soviet Union then needed above all to repair the damage done to its industrial base. And the war had itself created much more powerful probable enemies in the United States and its Western allies. The threat perceived lay in the far superior strategic air power of the Western countries, and the capability for amphibious warfare they had demonstrated in Europe and the Pacific from 1943 to 1945. While the high command of the Navy tried to renew the concept of a traditional fleet made up of all types of warships, from battleships and carriers to motor torpedo boats and submarines, Stalin was preoccupied with industrial capacity and the need to counter any threats of aerial bombardment and amphibious landings. Therefore he tried to push the borders of the Soviet-dominated areas as far away as possible from the centres of his Soviet Union, and tried at first to limit the naval programmes to defence against the amphibious threat. Nonetheless, against the wishes of the admirals, he demanded his beloved battlecruisers, the remnants of his great ocean-going fleet, at the expense of aircraft carriers, which shows that he still had the wish to acquire such old symbols of sea power, not understanding the change in naval strategies, with the carriers now as the most important instruments of naval power projection. This became obvious, when he reinstated Kuznetsov, fired in 1947 for his opposition to the cuts in the naval programme and demoted to Vice-Admiral, again as Commander-in-Chief of the Navy in 1951, to manage the delayed naval programme, which was still centred on his outdated battlecruisers. Stalin's reluctance to agree with Kuznetsov's demands for aircraft carriers shows that he was still fixed on the idea that big gun-armed ships were the signs of a naval superpower status.

When, after Stalin's death, Khrushchev and Marshal of the Soviet Union Zhukov took the helm, they looked to the Army and especially to the new strategic rockets as the counter to the perceived dangers from their opponents in the Cold War, which was demonstrated by the first launches of strategic intercontinental rockets and the first satellites into space. But they neglected the Navy. When the Commander-in-Chief of the Navy, Admiral Kuznetsov, opposed this trend and tried to renew the naval programme along the modern lines, he was fired again. His successor Admiral Gorshkov, at first had to follow the wishes of his superiors, especially in the love of modern weapons like rockets and missiles. He was forced at first to cancel the gun-armed ships and to build submarines and ships with anti-ship missiles, before he later also came back to the doctrine of a balanced ocean-going fleet with all the necessary ships from atomic submarines with ballistic rockets, missile-armed cruisers, submarines, and destroyers and escorts, as well as coastal vessels, but finally also to missile-armed battlecruisers and even helicopter and aircraft carriers. It may be that Khrushchev's successors learned from the experience of the Cuban crisis of 1962 about the need to have modern ocean-going surface ships in order to escort seaborne supplies for the support of revolutionary movements in the Third World. So they allowed Gorshkov to follow this new–old line. During his almost 30-year tenure in his capacity as Commander-in-Chief of the Soviet Navy, Gorshkov almost achieved his aims – that is, to establish the Soviet Union not only as an army and strategic rocket forces superpower, but also as a big sea-going superpower. Only a few years after his retirement in 1985, events outside the Navy led to the crumbling of the Soviet Union, in 1991, followed by the deterioration of the Navy, and the rusting away of most of its sea-going ships.

NOTE

1. Alexander Fischer, 'Kollektive Sicherheit und imperialistischer Krieg', *Saeculum*, No. XXVIII (1977), pp. 432ff.

Appendices

Tables A1–8 were prepared by Jürgen Rohwer, based mainly on the publications of S.S. Berezhnoi and corrected by S.S. Berezhnoi. For the full titles see the Bibliography.

Table A1: Warships and submarines of the former Imperial Navy, serving in the *RKKF/VMF*
(*Source*: S.S. Berezhnoi, *Korabli … VMF 1917–27*)

Table A2: Warships of the *RKKF/VMF*, laid down or ordered, 1926–45.
(*Source*: S.S. Berezhnoi, *Korabli i suda VMF 1928–45*)

Table A3: Submarines of the *RKKF/VMF*, laid down or ordered, 1926–45
(*Sources*: S.S. Berezhnoi, *Korabli i suda VMF 1928–45*; V.I. Dmitriev, *Sovetskoe podvodnoe korable-stroenie*; A.V. Platonov., Vol. III, *Podvodnye lodki*)

Table A4: Lend-Lease Vessels in the *VMF*, 1941–53
(*Source*: S.S. Berezhnoi, *Korabli i suda lendlisa*)

Table A5: Soviet warships and submarines lost, 1939–45
(*Source*: Glavnyi Shtab …, *Poteri boevykh korablej i sudov*)

Table A6: Warships and submarines, taken as war booty into the *VMF*, 1944–53
(*Source*: S.S. Berzhnoi, *Trofei i reparatsii VMF*)

Table A7: Warships of the *VMF*, laid down or ordered, 1945–53
(*Sources*: S.S. Berezhnoi, *Sovietskii VMF 1945–95*; A.S. Pavlov, *Voenno-morskoj flot Rossii 1996*; and articles in *Sudostroenie* and *Gangut*)

Table A8: Submarines of the *VMF*, laid down or ordered, 1945–53.
(*Source*: Information from V.P. Semenov from Bureau 'Rubin')

Table A1: Warships and submarines of the former Imperial Navy, serving in the *RKKF/VMF*

No.	Soviet Name	Tsarist name	Original Commission	Soviet Commission	Fleet 22.06.41	Fate	Notes
Battleships							
1	Marat	Petropavlovsk	20.12.14	21.04.21	KBF	23.09.41 Sunk	1
2	Oktyabrskaya Revolyutsiya	Gangut	21.10.14	23.03.26	KBF	17.02.56 Stricken	2
3	Parizhskaya Kommuna	Sevastopol	04.11.14	17.09.25	ChF	17.02.56 Stricken	3
4	Frunze	Poltava	04.12.14	–	–	41	4

[1] 1928–31 main reconstruction, then 25,000t normal; 23.09.41 sunk off Kronshtadt; 31.05.43 renamed again *Petropavlovsk*, used as stationary battery; 1952 broken up. Projekt 26 for a training battleship.
[2] 18.04.25 to 20.07.26 and 12.10.31 to 04.08.34 main reconstructions, then 25,465t normal.
[3] 1922–23, 1924–25, 1928–29 modernization; 22.11.29–18.01.30 transfer to the Black Sea, 1933–38 main reconstruction.
[4] In November 1919 heavily damaged by fire, not reconstructed. Plan for a reconstruction as an aircraft carrier (cancelled, also 1926/27 plan for reconstruction as fast battleship). Hulked at Leningrad.

Battlecruiser

No.	Soviet Name	Tsarist name	Original Commission	Soviet Commission	Fleet 22.06.41	Fate	Notes
1	Izmail	Izmail	–	–	–		1

[1] Launched 27.0.15 but not completed; in 1925/27 planned to be rebuilt as an aircraft carrier, but this was cancelled.

Old Cruisers

No.	Soviet Name	Tsarist name	Original Commission	Soviet Commission	Fleet 22.06.41	Fate	Notes
1	Avrora	Avrora	16.07.03	23.03.23	KBF	17.11.48 Museum	1
2	Komintern	Pamyat Merkurya ex-Kagul	17.05.98	01.05.23	ChF	10.10.42 Stricken	2

[1] Used as training ship, 1948 memorial at Leningrad.
[2] Training ship, on 02.07.42 and 16.07.42 damaged by air attack, irreparable and stricken on 10.10.42.

Cruisers (ex-*Svetlana*-class, 7,600t stdd., *Krasnyj Kavkaz* 8,295t stdd.)

No.	Soviet Name	Tsarist name	Original Commission	Soviet Commission	Fleet 22.06.41	Fate	Notes
1	Krasnyj Krym, ex-Profintern, ex-Klara Zetkin	Svetlana	–	01.07.28	ChF	17.02.56 Stricken	1
2	Chervona Ukraina	Admiral Nakhimov	–	21.03.27	ChF	12.11.41 Sunk	2
3	Krasnyj Kavkaz	Admiral Lazarev	–	25.01.32	ChF	17.02.56 Stricken	3
4	Voroshilov	Admiral Butakov	–	–	–	Cancelled	4

[1] Launched 27.11.15, building resumed 1924. 22.11.29–18.01.30 transfer to the Black Sea. 31.05.49 training vessel; 08.04.53 accommodation vessel.
[2] Launched 06.11.15, building resumed 1923. 12.11.42 sunk by air attack; 03.11.47 raised and 1948 broken up.
[3] Launched 21.06.16, building resumed 1924, 12.05.47 training vessel; 17.02.56 decommissioned but used as target for missile tests.
[4] Launched 05.08.16. Renamed 1926 *Pravda* and then *Voroshilov* to be rebuilt to new plans, but cancelled, in 1940–41. Plans for reconstruction as a modern training cruiser, as *Projekt 78*, not realized and as a minelayer cruiser, 6,189t normal, also not realized.

Mine Cruiser

No.	Soviet Name	Tsarist name	Original Commission	Soviet Commission	Fleet 22.06.41	Fate	Notes
1	Marti	Shtandart	96	25.12.36	KBF	–60 Stricken	1

[1] Former Imperial yacht, 1932–36 rebuilt as a minelayer-cruiser; 1948–49 modernized as training vessel

Table A1 (contd.): Warships and submarines of the former Imperial Navy, serving in the *RKKF/VMF*

No.	Soviet Name	Tsarist name	Original Commission	Soviet Commission	Fleet 22.06.41	Fate	Notes
Destroyers (ex-*Novik*-class, 1,260t normal)							
1	*Yakov Sverdlov*	*Novik*	22.08.13	30.08.29	KBF	28.08.41 Lost	
Destroyers (ex-Pospeshnyi-class, 1,320t normal)							
1	*Frunze*	*Bystryi*	31.05.16	16.12.27	ChF	21.09.41 Lost	
Destroyers (ex-*Novik*-mod-class, 1,260t normal)							
1	*Artem*, ex-*Zinovyev*	*Azard*	10.10.16	21.04.21	KBF	28.08.41 Lost	
2	*Volodarskii*	*Pobyeditel'*	23.10.15	21.04.21	KBF	28.08.41 Lost	
3	*Stalin*	*Samson*	21.11.16	21.04.21	TOF	53 Stricken	1
4	*Uritskii*	*Zabiyaka*	11.11.15	21.04.21	SF	53 Stricken	2
5	*Engel's*	*Desna*	12.08.16	21.04.21	KBF	24.08.41 Lost	
6	*Kalinin*	*Pryamislav*	–	20.07.27	KBF	28.08.41 Lost	
7	*Karl Marks*	*Izyaslav*	16.06.17	21.04.21	KBF	08.08.41 Lost	
8	*Valerian Kujbyshev*	*Kapitan Kern*	–	15.10.27	SF	Stricken	2
9	*Vojkov*, ex *Garibal'di*	*Lejtenant Il'in*	29.11.16	21.04.21	TOF	Stricken	1
10	*Karl Libknekht*	*Kapitan Belli*	–	03.08.28	SF	Stricken	2
11	*Lenin*	*Kapitan Izyl'metev*	11.07.16	21.04.21	KBF	24.06.41 Scuttled	
12	*Dzerzhinskii*	*Kaliakriya*	17	28.08.29	ChF	14.05.42 Lost	
13	*Zheleznyakov*, ex-*Petrovskii*	*Korfu*	–	10.06.25	ChF	49 to Bulgaria	
14	*Nezamozhnik*	*Zante*	–	07.11.23	ChF	Stricken	
15	*Shaumyan*	*Levkas*	–	10.12.25	ChF	03.04.42 Lost	

[1] 1936 transferred from the KBF by the Northern Seaway to Vladivostok for the TOF.
[2] 1933 transferred from the KBF by the Baltic–White Sea Canal to Murmansk for the SF.

Torpedo boats or Small Destroyers (later reclassified as gunboats/*Vsadnik*-class, 759t, normal)

1	*Sladkov*	*Vsadnik*	06.06	31.12.22	KBF	29.07.29 Scrapped	
2	*Zheleznyakov*	*Amurets*	27.09.07	31.12.22	KBF	47 Training V.	
3	*Roshal'*	*Ussuriets*	07	31.12.22	KBF	29.04.27 Stricken	
4	*Konstruktor*	*Sibirskii Strelok*	06	10.12.26	KBF	01.06.57 Stricken	1

[1] 03.08.41 reclassified Patrol Ship (SKR); 04.11.41 damaged; 13.04.43 recomm.; training vessel.

Torpedo boats or Small Destroyers (later reclassified as gunboats/*Turkemeets-Stavropolskii* class, 620t normal)

1	*Sovetskii Daghestan*, ex-*Al'tfater*, *Mariya Kuchuk*	*Turkmenets-Stavropolskii*	05	31.12.22	KBF/Kfl	18.07.49 Dosaaf	
2	*Bakinskii Rabochii*, ex-*Karl Marks*	*Ukraina*	05	10.12.23	KBF/Kfl	18.07.49 Dosaaf	
3	*Markin*, ex-*Fridrikh Engel's*	*Vojskovoi*	06.05	31.02.22	KBF/Kfl	18.07.49 Dosaaf	
4	*Karl Libknekht*	*Finn*	06	13.06.23	KBF/Kfl	01.12.25 Stricken	
5	*Yakov Sverdlov*	*Emir Bukharskii*	05	13.06.23	KBF/Kfl	01.12.25 Stricken	

[2] All vessels transferred from the Baltic by inland waterways to the Caspian Sea. 1929 reclassified gunboats.

Torpedo boats or Small Destroyers (later reclassified as minesweepers/*Vnushitel'nyi*-class, 405t normal)

1	*Martynov*	*Vnushitel'nyi*	06	05.02.25	KBF	12.10.40 Stricken	
2	*Artem'ev*	*Vynoslivyi*	06	05.02.25	KBF	47 Stricken	
3	*Roshal'*	*Inzhener-mekhanik Dmitriev*	06	01.05.22	KBF	18.11.29 Stricken	

Table A1 (contd.): Warships and submarines of the former Imperial Navy, serving in the *RKKF/VMF*

No.	Soviet Name	Tsarist name	Original Commission	Soviet Commission	Fleet 22.06.41	Fate	Notes
Torpedo boats or Small Destroyer (continued)							
4	*Zhemchuzhin*	*Inshener-mekhanik Zverev*	06	01.05.22	KBF	17.01.30 Stricken	
Gunboats (*Khivinets*-class, 1,692t normal)							
1	*Krasnaya Zvezda*	*Khivinets*	06	23.02.22	KBF	28.07.44 Stricken	
Gunboats (*Khrabryi*-class, 1,492t normal)							
1	*Krasnoe Znamya*	*Khrabryi*	97	22	KBF	30.06.60 Stricken	1

[1] 16.11.42 sunk by Finnish MTBs, 1943 salvaged, 1944 rebuilt as modernized gunboat, 1,735t normal

Submarines (*Bars*-class, 650t normal)

No.	Soviet Name	Tsarist name	Original Commission	Soviet Commission	Fleet 22.06.41	Fate	Notes
1	*B-1* ex-*No.1*, ex-*Kommunar*	*Tigr*	08.04.16	22	KBF	10.03.35 Stricken	
2	*B-2*, ex-*No.5*, ex-*Komissar*	*Pantera*	23.07.16	22	KBF	11.05.42 Stricken	
3	*B-3*, ex-*No.7*, ex-*Bol'shevik*	*Rys'*	04.11.16	22	KBF	25.07.35 Sunk	1
4	*B-4*, ex-*No.8*, ex-*Krasnoflotets*	*Yaguar*	12.10.17	22	KBF	43 Stricken	
5	*B-5*, ex-*No.2*, ex-*Batrak*	*Volk*	14.04.16	22	KBF	11.03.35 Stricken	
6	*B-6*, ex-*No.2*, ex-*Proletarii*	*Zmeya*	27.03.17	22	KBF	11.03.35 Stricken	
7	*B-7*, ex-*No.3*, ex-*Krasnoarmeets*	*Leopard*	25.10.16	22	KBF	29.12.40 Stricken	
8	*B-8*, ex-*No.3*, ex-*Tovarishch*	*Tur*	08.08.17	24	KBF	29.12.40 Stricken	
9	*No.9*, ex-*Rabochii*	*Ersh*	15.12.17	22	KBF	22.05.31 Sunk	2

[1] 02.08.35 salvaged, but irreparable and scrapped
[2] 21.07.31 salvaged, but irreparable and scrapped

Submarine (*Burevestnik*-class, 630t normal)

No.	Soviet Name	Tsarist name	Original Commission	Soviet Commission	Fleet 22.06.41	Fate	Notes
1	*Politruk*	*Nerpa*	26.02.15	26.05.22	ChF	03.12.30 Stricken	

Submarines (*Holland*-class, 360t normal)

No.	Soviet Name	Tsarist name	Original Commission	Soviet Commission	Fleet 22.06.41	Fate	Notes
1	*A-1*, ex-*Shakhter*, ex-*Nezamozhnik*	AG-23	21.10.20	31.12.22	ChF	26.06.42 Scuttled	
2	*A-2*, ex-*Kommunist*, ex-*Im.tov. Lunacharskii*	AG-24	22.07.21	23	ChF	45 Stricken	
3	*A-3*, ex-*Marksist*	AG-25	25.05.22	23	ChF	28.10.43 Sunk	
4	*A-4*, ex-*Politrabotnik*	AG-26	–	11.07.23	ChF	Stricken	
5	*A-5*, ex-*Metallist*	AG-21	18	22	ChF	Stricken	

Table A2: Warships of the *RKKF/VMF*, laid down or ordered, 1926–45

No.	Name	Order	Yard	Yard No.	Laid down	Launched	Commiss.	22.06.41	Fleet	Notes

Battleships (*Projekt 21*, 35,000t stdd.)

| – | – | – | – | – | – | – | – | – | – | 1 |

[1] There were only project studies of these ships, planned following the model of the British *Nelson*-class No orders placed

Battleships (*Type 'A'*, later *Projekt 23*, first version of 1936, 45,930t stdd.)

| 1 | – | Nov. 36 | 189? | – | (IV.37) | – | – | – | – | 1 |
| 2 | – | Nov. 36 | 198? | – | (IV.37) | – | – | – | – | 1 |

[1] There were several variants of this project. In May 1937 there was a plan to build 8 ships of this project, 4 to be laid down late 1937, and early 1938, but the plan was cancelled and the project was enlarged to 57,000t standard and then to 59,150t, see below.

Battleships (*Type 'B'*, later *Projekt 25*, 30,900t stdd.)

1	–	Nov. 36	194?	–	(IV.37)	–	–	–	–	1
2	–	Nov. 36	194?	–	(IV.37)	–	–	–	–	1
3	–	Nov. 36	198?	–	(I.38)	–	–	–	–	1
4	–	Nov. 36	198?	–	(I.38)	–	–	–	–	1

[1] There were also several variants of this project, in May 1937 there was a plan to build 16 ships of this project, but in August 1937 the project was cancelled and instead a new *projekt 64* of 48,000t stdd. was started, only to be cancelled in August 1938. In addition there were foreign designs, e.g. the Ansaldo project *UP-42*, asked for in 1935 and delivered in July 1936, and several from the US firm Gibbs & Cox in 1937 and 1939, but they were not considered for real building and no orders were placed.

Battleships (*Projekt 23*, 59,150t stdd.)

1	*Sovetskii Soyuz*	21.01.38	189	299	31.07.38	–	(June 43)	21.19%	KBF	1
2	*Sovetskaya Ukraina*	21.01.38	198	352	28.11.38	–	(June 43)	17.93%	ChF	2
3	*Sovetskaya Belorossiya*	21.01.38	402	101	21.12.39	–	–	2.57%	TOF	3
4	*Sovetskaya Rossiya*	21.01.38	402	102	20.07.40	–	–	4.40%	SF	4
5	–	3 FYP	189	–	(42)	–	–	–	–	5
6	–	3 FYP	198	–	(42)	–	–	–	–	5
7	–	4 FYP	–	–	–	–	–	–	–	5
8	–	4 FYP	–	–	–	–	–	–	–	6
9	–	4 FYP	–	–	–	–	–	–	–	6
10	–	4 FYP	–	–	–	–	–	–	–	6

[1] In July 1939 there was a plan to build 15 ships of this project. In July 1940 this was reduced to 6 vessels in the third and 4 vessels in the fourth Five-Year Plan. On 19 October 1940 it was decided to finish this ship up to June 1943. On 19 July 1941 the ship was put into conservation, but completion was cancelled owing to the war, because materials had to be used for the defence of Leningrad.

[2] On 19 October 1940 it was decided to complete this ship up to June 1943. It was put into conservation on 19 July 1941. The vessel was captured on the stocks by the Germans on 16 August 1941. Materials were used for building some transports for the Germans. The remains were broken up after the war.

[3] This ship was cancelled on 19.10.40 when 2.57% were built in to provide space for 4 new destroyers of *Projekt 30*. Materials were used to accelerate the construction of *Sovetskaya Rossiya*.

[4] In October 1940 it was 0.97% complete, but it was planned to be completed in III quarter 1943 because the turbines should have come from BBC. Work stopped on 19.07.41. Put into conservation. At the end of the war planned to be completed to *Projekt 23.NU*, but cancelled in 1952.

[5] Planned to be laid down in the Third Five-Year Plan, but cancelled on 19 October 1940.

[6] Planned to be laid down in the Fourth Five-Year Plan, but cancelled on 19 October 1940.

Table A2 (contd.): Warships of the *RKKF/VMF*, laid down or ordered, 1926–45

No.	Name	Order	Yard	Yard No.	Laid down	Launched	Commiss.	22.06.41	Fleet	Remarks
Battlecruisers (*Projekt 69*, 35,240t stdd.)										
1	*Kronshtadt*	21.01.38	194	550	30.11.39	–	(autumn 42)	11.65%	KBF	[1]
2	*Sevastopol*	21.01.38	200	1089	05.11.39	–	(autumn 42)	12.10%	ChF	[2]
3	*Stalingrad* (?)	3 FYP	194	–	(42)	–	–	–	–	[3]
4	–	3 FYP	200	–	(42)	–	–	–	–	[3]
5	–	4 FYP	–	–	–	–	–	–	–	[4]
6	–	4 FYP	–	–	–	–	–	–	–	[4]
7	–	4 FYP	–	–	–	–	–	–	–	[4]
8	–	4 FVP	–	–	–	–	–	–	–	[4]

[1] In August 1939 there were plans to build 16 vessels of *projekt 69* instead of the 10 vessels of *projekt 22* (see below). In July 1940 the number was reduced to 8, four each in the Third and Fourth Five-Year Plans. The *Kronstadt* was in Oct.1940 reconstructed to get German 380mm guns and fire control equipment, planned to be completed in autumn 1942. On 19.07.41 put into conservation. After the war there were plans to convert the hull into an aircraft carrier for 72 planes, but plans cancelled in March 1947.
[2] In Oct.1940 reconstructed to get German 380mm guns and fire control equipment, planned to be completed in autumn 1942. On 19.07.41 put into conservation. On 16.08.41 hull captured by the Germans. Materials were used for building some transports, remains were broken up after the war.
[3] Planned to be laid down in the Third Five-Year Plan, cancelled on 19 October 1940.
[4] Planned to be laid down in the Fourth Five-Year Plan, cancelled on 19 October 1940.

Aircraft Carriers (*Projekt 71*, 10,600t stdd.)

1	–	4 FYP	–	–	–	–	–	–	–	[1]
2	–	4 FYP	–	–	–	–	–	–	–	[1]

[1] Planned to be laid down in the Fourth Five Years Plan, cancelled on 19 October 1940.

Heavy Cruisers (*Projekt 22*, 23,000t stdd.)

–	–	–	–	–	–	–	–	–	–	[1]

[1] In 1935 there were several heavy cruiser projects. *Projekt X* with 15,560t stdd. A Baltic Yard project of 19,500t stdd. and a project of the Italian yard Ansaldo of 22,000t stdd. The *projekt 22* was put into the plan in 1937, but in 1939 it was cancelled and as a replacement the *projekt 69* battlecruisers were installed.

Heavy Cruisers (ex German *Lützow* 14,240t stdd., *Projekt 83*)

1	*Petropavlovsk*, ex-*Lützow*	18.07.36DS	189	941 308	02.08.37	01.07.39	(42)	50.10%	KBF	[1]

[1] The German 'L', ex-*Lützow* was purchased in February 1940 and transferred to Leningrad for completion April 1940. In Sept. 1941 damaged by German artillery and partially sunk, later salvaged and used as accommodation hulk *Tallinn*.

Cruisers (*Projekt 26*, 7,880t/7,970t stdd.)

1	*Kirov*	2 FYP	189	269	22.10.35	30.11.36	23.09.38		KBF
2	*Voroshilov*	2 FYP	198	297	15.10.35	28.06.37	20.06.40		ChF

Cruisers (*Projekt 26-bis*, 8,177t stdd.)

1	*Maksim Gorkii*	2 FYP	189	270	20.12.36	30.04.38	25.10.40		KBF
2	*Molotov*	2 FYP	198	329	14.01.37	19.03.39	14.06.41		ChF

Table A2 (contd.): Warships of the *RKKF/VMF*, laid down or ordered, 1926–45

No.	Name	Order	Yard	Yard No.	Laid down	Launched	Commiss.	22.06.41	Fleet	Notes
Cruisers (*Projekt 26-bis2*, 8,400(?)t stdd.)										
1	*Kalinin*	2FYP	189	300						
			199	7	12.06.38	08.05.42	31.12.42	30.00%	TOF	1
2	*Lazar Kaganovich*	2FYP	198	351						
			199	8	28.08.38	07.05.44	06.12.44	16.00%	TOF	2

[1] Materials prepared at Leningrad, transferred for building by rail to Komsomol'sk.
[2] Materials prepared at Nikolaev, transferred for building by rail to Komsomol'sk. Finally commissioned only on 08.12.47.

Cruisers (*Projekt 68*, 10,624t stdd.)

No.	Name	Order	Yard	Yard No.	Laid down	Launched	Commiss.	22.06.41	Fleet	Notes
1	*Chapaev*	25.09.40	189	305	08.10.39	28.04.41	16.05.50	38.36%	KBF	1
2	*Chkalov*	25.09.40	189	306	21.09.39	25.10.47	25.10.50	20.86%	KBF	2
3	*Zheleznyakov*	25.09.40	194	545	31.10.39	25.06.41	19.04.50	24.49%	KBF	3
4	*Frunze*	25.09.40	198	356	29.08.39	30.12.40	19.12.50	33.00%	ChF	4
5	*Kujbyshev*	25.09.40	200	1088	31.08.39	31.01.41	–		ChF	5
			201/198				20.04.50	27.00%		
6	*Ordzhonikidze*	3 FYP	198	364	31.12.40	–	<43>	7.80%	ChF	6
7	*Sverdlov*	3 FYP	200	1090	31.01.41	–	<43>	7.21%	ChF	7
8	*Zhdanov*	3 FYP	189?	308	–	–	<44>	–	KBF	8
9	*Lenin*	3 FYP	189	309	<08.41>	–	<44>	–	KBF	9
10	*Dzerzhinskii*	3 FYP	189	310	<11.41>	–	?	–	KBF	10
11	*Lazo*	3 FYP	199?		<09.41>	–	<44>	–	TOF	11
12	*Avrora*	3 FYP	194	555	<08.41>	–	–	–	KBF	12
13	*Parkhomenko*	4 FYP	200		–	–	–	–	?	13
14	*Shchors*	4 FYP	199		–	–	–	–	?	13
14	*Shcherbakov*	4 FYP	198		–	–	–	–	?	13
15	*Kotovskii*	4 FYP	200		–	–	–	–	?	13

[1] Put into conservation on 19 July 1941. Completed after the war to *Projekt 68K* (11,130t stdd.).
[2] Reconstructed in 1940 to get German 150mm guns in triple turrets. After the war completed to *Projekt* 68K.
[3] Put into conservation on 19 July 1941. Completed after the war to *Projekt 68K*.
[4] Towed incomplete from Nikolaev to Caucasian ports in August 1941 after part of the vessel used to repair the damaged *Molotov*. After the war towed back and completed to *Projekt 68K*.
[5] Towed incomplete from Nikolaev to Caucasian ports in August 1941, 1944 towed back to Sevastopol and Nikolaevsk for completion to *Projekt 68K*.
[6] Put into conservation on 19 July 1941. Captured on 16 August 1941 on the stocks by the Germans.
[7] Put into conservation on 19 July 1941. Captured on 16 August 1941 on the stocks by the Germans. Both ships on the stocks dismantled, materials used partially by the Germans.
[8] Not clear if this ship was really planned, if so cancelled on 19 July 1941.
[9,10,11,12] On 19 October 1940 planned to be laid down in autumn 1941, but cancelled on 19 July 1941.
[13] Planned for the Fourth Five-Year Plan, but cancelled on 19 October 1940.

Light Cruiser (*Projekt 'MK'*, 6,095t stdd.)

–	–	–	–	–	–	–	–	–	–	1

[1] Several versions of this type of light cruiser were designed by the yard 196 in March 1940, but no orders were placed.

Table A2 (contd.): Warships of the *RKKF/VMF*, laid down or ordered, 1926–45

No.	Name	Order	Yard	Yard No.	Laid down	Launched	Commiss.	22.06.41	Fleet	Notes
Destroyer Leaders (*Projekt 1*, 2,030t stdd.)
1	*Leningrad*	1 FYP	190	450	05.11.32	17.11.33	05.12.36	–	KBF	
2	*Kharkov*	1 FYP	198	223	19.10.32	09.09.34	19.11.38	–	ChF	
3	*Moskva*	1 FYP	198	224	29.10.32	30.10.34	10.08.38	–	ChF	
Destroyer Leaders (*Projekt 38*, 2,280t stdd.)
1	*Minsk*	2 FYP	190	471	05.10.34	06.11.35	15.02.39	–	KBF	
2	*Baku* (ex-*Sergo Ordzhonikidze*, ex-*Ordzhonikidze*, ex-*Kiev*)	2 FYP	198 / 199	267	15.01.35 / 10.03.36	25.07.38	27.12.39	–	TOF	1
3	*Tbilisi*, ex-*Tiflis*	2 FYP	198 / 199	268	15.01.35 / 10.08.36	24.07.39	11.12.40	–	TOF	2

[1] Materials prepared and laid down at Nikolaev and transferred by rail for building to Komsomol'sk. 1942 transferred by the Northern Seaway to the Northern Fleet.
[2] Materials prepared and laid down at Nikolaev and transferred for building to Komsomol'sk.

No.	Name	Order	Yard	Yard No.	Laid down	Launched	Commiss.	22.06.41	Fleet	Notes
Destroyer Leaders (*Projekt 20-I*, 2,836t stdd.)
1	*Tashkent*	1934	OTO / 190	– / 528	11.01.37	28.11.37	22.10.39 <41>	–	ChF	1 / 1
2	*Baku*	1936	190	511	–	–	–	–	KBF	2
3	–	1936	190	512	–	–	–	–	KBF	2
4	–	1936	198	–	–	–	–	–	ChF	2

[1] The *Tashkent* was ordered at the Italian yard OTO, Livorno, to be transferred to the KBF for completion. 1940 this was changed to the ChF, to be completed at Nikolaev, first with intermediate armament.
[2] In 1936 it was planned to build two replicas at Leningrad and one at Nikolaev, to be delivered in 1938/39, but after some preparations at Leningrad the ships were cancelled in 1940 to be replaced by *projekt 48*.

No.	Name	Order	Yard	Yard No.	Laid down	Launched	Commiss.	22.06.41	Fleet	Notes
Destroyer Leaders (*Projekt 48*, 2,350t stdd.)
1	*Kiev*	3 FYP	198	357	29.09.39	12.12.40	<42>	48.90%	ChF	1
2	*Erevan*	3 FYP	198	358	30.12.39	29.06.41	<42>	25.40%	ChF	1
3	*Petrozavodsk*	3 FYP	198	359	–	–	–	–	ChF	2
4	*Stalinabad*	3 FYP	190	542	27.12.39	–	–	–	KBF	3
5	–	3 FYP	190	543	–	–	–	–	KBF	4
6	?	3 FYP	190	544	–	–	–	–	KBF	4
7	*Ashkhabad*	3 FYP	190	545	–	–	–	–	KBF	4
8	*Alma Ata*	3 FYP	190	546	–	–	–	–	KBF	4
9	*Perekop*	10.04.41	198	–	–	–	–	–	–	5
10	*Ochakov*	10.04.41	198	–	–	–	–	–	–	5
11	*Murmansk*	10.04.41	402	–	–	<41>	–	–	–	6
12	*Arkhangel'sk*	10.04.41	402	–	–	<41>	–	–	–	6
13	–	4 FYP	?	–	–	–	–	–	–	7
14	–	4 FYP	?	–	–	–	–	–	–	7

[1] *Kiev* and *Erevan* were towed away incomplete from Nikolaev to Caucasian ports in August 1941 to avoid being captured by the Germans. Returned in 1944/45 to be completed as *48K*, but cancelled in 1950.
[2] *Petrozavodsk* planned but not laid down and cancelled on 19 October 1940.
[3] *Stalinabad* was started in Leningrad, but cancelled on 19 October 1940 and broken up.
[4] The planned vessels were not started and cancelled on 19 October 1940.
[5] Two vessels were planned for building at Nikolaev, but they were cancelled on 19 October 1940. Rumours were that the planned names were *Ochakov* and *Perekop*, but this is not proven.
[6] Two vessels were planned to be laid down in 1941 at Molotovsk, but they were cancelled on 19 October 1940. Rumours were that the planned names were *Arkhangel'sk* and *Murmansk*, but this is not proven.
[7] Two additional vessels were planned for the Fourth Five-Year Plan, but they were not started and cancelled on 19 October 1940.

Table A2 (contd.): Warships of the *RKKF/VMF*, laid down or ordered, 1926–45

No.	Name	Order	Yard	Yard No.	Laid down	Launched	Commiss.	22.06.41	Fleet	Notes
Experimental Destroyer (*Projekt 45*, 1,595t stdd.)
1	Opytnyi, ex-*Sergo Ordzhonikidze*	2 FYP	190	500	26.06.35	08.12.36	28.09.41	–	KBF	
Destroyers (*Projekt 7*, 1,885t stdd.)
1	Gnevnyi	2 FYP	190	501	27.11.35	13.07.36	30.10.38	–	KBF	
2	Groznyi	2 FYP	190	502	21.12.35	31.07.36	09.12.38	–	SF	1
3	Gromkii	2 FYP	190	503	29.04.36	06.12.36	31.12.38	–	SF	1
4	Grozyashchii	2 FYP	190	513	18.06.36	05.01.37	–	–		
			189	301			17.09.39	–	KBF	2
5	Gordyi	2 FYP	190	514	25.06.36	10.06.37	23.12.38	–	KBF	
6	Gremyashchii	2 FYP	190	515	23.07.36	12.08.37	28.08.38	–	SF	1
7	Steregushchii	2 FYP	190	516	12.08.36	18.01.38	30.10.39	–	KBF	
8	Stremitel'nyi	2 FYP	189	291	22.08.36	03.02.37	18.11.38	–	SF	1
9	Sokrushitel'nyi	2 FYP	189	292	29.10.36	23.08.37	13.08.39	–	SF	1
10	Smetlivyi	2 FYP	189	294	17.09.36	16.07.37	06.11.38	–	KBF	
11	Lovkii	2 FYP	189	295	17.09.36	–	–	–	KBF	3
12	Legkii	2 FYP	189	296	16.10.36	–	–	–	KBF	3
13	Rezvyi	2 FYP	198	228	05.11.35					
			202		23.08.36	24.09.37	24.01.40	–	TOF	4
14	Reshitel'nyi	2 FYP	198	229	05.11.35					
			199		20.09.36	18.10.37	–	lost	TOF	5
15	Rastoropnyi	2 FYP	198	312	27.02.36					
			199		05.12.36	25.06.38	05.01.40	–	TOF	6
16	Razyashchii	2 FYP	198	313	27.02.36					
			202		15.11.36	24.03.38	20.12.40	–	TOF	4
17	Bodryi	2 FYP	198	314	31.12.35	01.08.36	06.11.38	–	ChF	
18	Ryanyi	2 FYP	198	315	31.12.35					
			202	–	18.09.36	31.05.37	11.08.39	–	TOF	4
19	Rezkii	2 FYP	198	319	05.05.36					
			202	–	20.08.38	29.04.40	31.07.42	–	TOF	4
20	Bystryi	2 FYP	198	320	17.04.36	05.11.36	27.01.39	–	ChF	
21	Bojkii	2 FYP	198	321	31.12.35	29.10.36	09.03.39	–	ChF	
22	Besposhchadnyi	2 FYP	198	322	15.05.36	05.12.36	22.08.39	–	ChF	
23	Retivyi	2 FYP	198	323	23.08.36					
			199	–	29.07.37	27.10.39	10.10.41	–	TOF	7
24	Reshitel'nyi, ex-*Pospeshnyi*	2 FYP	198	324	23.08.36					
			199	–	23.08.37	30.04.39	26.08.41	–	TOF	7
25	Revnost'nyi, ex-*Provornyi*	2 FYP	198	325	23.08.36					
			199	–	17.09.37	22.05.41	28.11.41	–	TOF	7
26	Raz'yarennyi, ex-*Razvitoi*, ex-*Peredovoi*	2 FYP	198	326	15.09.36					
			199		17.09.37	22.05.41	27.11.41	–	TOF	7
27	Rekordnyi, ex-*Prytkyi*	2 FYP	198	327	25.09.36					
			202		07.37	06.04.39	09.01.41	–	TOF	4

[1] Built at Leningrad for the KBF; 1939/40 transferred via the Baltic–White Sea Canal to the SF.
[2] Building started at yard 190, after launch transferred for completion to yard 189.
[3] Building started at Leningrad, but cancelled before launch and broken up at the slips in 1938.
[4] Building started at Nikolaev, but materials transferred by rail to Vladivostok and re-laid down there.
[5] Building started at Nikolaev, but materials transferred by rail to Komsomol'sk. During transfer from the Amur to final commissioning on 08.11.38 lost by accident.
[6] Building started at Nikolaev, materials transferred by rail to Komsomol'sk for completion.
[7] Building started at Nikolaev, transferred to be re-laid down at Komsomol'sk by rail. 1942 transferred to SF. Names were changed on 25.09.40.

Table A2 (contd.): Warships of the *RKKF/VMF*, laid down or ordered, 1926–45

No.	Name	Order	Yard	Yard No.	Laid down	Launched	Commiss.	22.06.41	Fleet	Notes
Destroyers (*Projekt 7*, 1,885t stdd.) *continued*										
28	Redkii,	2 FYP	198	328	28.09.36				TOF	1
	ex-*Pyl'kii*		199		17.11.38	28.09.41	29.11.42	–		
29	Bezuprechnyi	2 FYP	200	1069	28.08.36	23.06.37	02.10.39	–	ChF	
30	Bditel'nyi	2 FYP	200	1070	23.08.36	23.06.37	02.10.39	–	ChF	
31	Burnyi	2 FYP	200	1071	17.08.36	–	–	–	ChF	2
32	Boevoi	2 FYP	200	1072	17.08.36	–	–	–	ChF	2
33	Razumnyi,	2 FYP	200	1075	07.07.36					
	ex-*Proachnyi*		202		15.08.37	30.06.39	20.10.41	–	TOF	3
34	Pronzitel'nyi	2 FYP	200	1079	15.10.36	–	–	–	TOF	2
35	Porayayushchii	2 FYP	200	1080	25.12.36	–	–	–	TOF	2

[1] Building started at Nikolaev, transferred to be re-laid down at Komsomol'sk by rail.

[2] Building started at Nikolaev, but before launch cancelled and broken up on the slips. But there is some information (not yet proven by official Soviet sources) that the *Pronzitel'nyi* materials were transferred to 199, and re-laid down in November 1938, renamed on 25.09.40, possibly to *Rassuditel'nyi*, launched on 28.09.41 but probably wrecked in 1943, refloated and dismantled for spare parts. In addition, there are reports that two of the cancelled vessels were re-laid down as *Projekt 7-u* vessels at 190 in 1938 as *Lesnoi* and *Lepnoi*, transferred incomplete in 1941 to 402; on 25.09.40[?] renamed possibly as *Vernyi* and *Vnimatel'nyi* for the TOF, but remained at Molotovsk. *Vernyi* possibly renamed *Stalin* and completed late 1943, but in early 1944 lost or damaged beyond repair, both then cancelled.

[3] Building started at Nikolaev, transferred to be re-laid down at Vladivostok by rail. 1942 transferred by the Northern Seaway to SF.

Destroyers (*Projekt 7-u*, 1,990t stdd.)

No.	Name	Order	Yard	Yard No.	Laid down	Launched	Commiss.	22.06.41	Fleet	Notes
1	Storozhevoi	2 FYP	190	517	26.08.36					
					31.01.38	02.10.38	06.10.40	–	KBF	1
2	Stoikii	2 FYP	190	518	26.08.36					
					31.03.38	26.12.38	18.10.40	–	KBF	1
3	Strashnyi	2 FYP	190	519	26.08.36					
					31.03.38	08.04.39	22.06.41	–	KBF	1
4	Sil'nyi	2 FYP	190	520	26.10.36					
					31.01.38	01.11.38	31.10.40	–	KBF	1
5	Smelyi	2 FYP	190	521	26.10.36					
					31.03.38	30.04.39	31.05.41	–	KBF	1
6	Strogii	2 FYP	190	523	26.10.36					
					26.10.38	31.12.39	22.09.41	90.00%	KBF	1
7	Skoryi	2 FYP	190	524	29.11.36					
					23.10.38	24.07.39	18.07.41	–	KBF	2
8	Svirepyi	2 FYP	190	525	29.11.36					
					30.12.38	28.08.39	22.06.41	–	KBF	2
9	Statnyi	2 FYP	190	526	29.11.36					
					29.12.38	24.11.39	09.07.41	–	KBF	2
10	Strojnyi	2 FYP	190	527	26.10.36					
					29.12.38	29.04.40	22.09.41	95.00%	KBF	2
11	Slavnyi	2 FYP	189	293	31.08.36					
					31.01.39	19.09.39	31.05.41		KBF	2
12	Surovyi,	2 FYP	189	297	27.10.36					
	ex-*Letuchii*				01.02.39	05.08.39	31.05.41	–	KBF	2
13	Serdity,	2 FYP	189	298	25.10.36					
	ex-*Likhoi*				15.10.38	21.04.39	15.10.40	–	KBF	2
14	Sovershennyi,	2FYP	200	1073	17.09.36					
	ex-*Besstrashnyi*		202	245	38	25.02.39	30.09.41	90.00%	ChF	3
15	Svobodnyi,	2 FYP	200	1074	23.08.36					
	ex-*Besshumnyi*		202	246	38	25.02.39	02.01.42	83.80%	ChF	3

[1] The destroyers were laid down as vessels of *Projekt 7*, but reconstructed to *Projekt 7-u* and re-laid down to a new design.

[2] Building started to *Projekt 7*, building stopped 1938 and re-laid down to *Projekt 7-u*. Names were changed on 25.09.40.

[3] Building started to *Projekt 7*, building stopped 1938 and re-laid down to *Projekt 7-u*. For completion towed to Sevastopol.

Table A2 (contd.): Warships of the *RKKF/VMF*, laid down or ordered, 1926–45

No.	Name	Order	Yard	Yard No.	Laid down	Launched	Commiss.	22.06.41	Fleet	Notes
Destroyers (*Projekt 7-u*, 1,990t stdd.) *continued*										
16	Sposobnyi, ex-*Podvizhnyi*	2 FYP	200	1076	07.07.36 07.03.39	30.09.39	24.06.41	–	ChF	1
17	Smyshlennyi, ex-*Poleznyi*	2 FYP	200	1077	15.10.36 27.06.38	26.08.39	10.11.40	–	ChF	1
18	Soobrazitel'nyi, ex-*Prozorlivyi*	2 FYP	200	1078	15.10.36 03.03.39	26.08.39	07.06.41	–	ChF	1

[1] Building started to *Projekt* 7, building stopped 1938 and re-laid down to *Projekt* 7-u at Nikolaev.

Destroyers (*Projekt 30*, 1,890t stdd. as planned, when completed 2,016t stdd.)

No.	Name	Order	Yard	Yard No.	Laid down	Launched	Commiss.	22.06.41	Fleet	Notes
1	Otlichnyi	27.10.39	190 189	538 307	02.12.39	07.05.41 31.10.48	–	27.30%	KBF	1
2	Obraztsovyi	27.10.39	190 189	539	02.12.39	30.10.41 29.09.49	–	19.10%	KBF	1
3	Otvazhnyi	27.10.39	190	540	30.12.39	02.01.48	02.03.50	–	12.30%	KBF	2
4	Odarennyi	27.10.39	190	541	30.12.39	27.12.48	28.06.50	–	12.30%	KBF	2
5	Organizovannyi	19.10.40	189	311	21.03.41	–	–	3.33%	KBF	3
6	Otbornyi	19.10.40	189	312	21.03.41	–	–	3.33%	KBF	3
7	Otrazhayushchyi	19.10.40	189	313	19.04.41	–	–	3.11%	KBF	3
8	Ognevoi, ex-*Opasnyi*	27.10.39	200	1086	20.11.39	12.11.40	22.03.45	50.82%	ChF	4
9	Ozornoi	27.10.39	200	1087	20.11.39	25.12.40	09.01.49	21.22%	ChF	5
10	Osmotritel'nyi	25.09.40	402	103	05.05.40	24.08.44	29.09.47	2.80%	SF	6
11	Okhotnik	25.09.40	402	104	25.06.40	19.07.47	29.09.48	2.40%	SF	7
12	Vnushitel'nyi	25.09.40	199	3	16.10.40	14.05.47	29.12.47	3.00%	TOF	8
13	Vynoslivyi	25.09.40	199	4	29.10.40	17.11.47	05.12.48	0.80%	TOF	8
14	Vlastnyi	25.09.40	199	5	29.10.40	15.06.48	27.12.48	0.80%	TOF	8
15	Ognennyi	25.09.40	190	547	30.06.40	–	<42>	7.80%	KBF	9
16	Ozhestchennyi	25.09.40	190	548	27.07.40	–	<42>	6,60%	KBF	9
17	Ostryi	25.09.40	190	549	18.12.40	–	<42>	3.90%	KBF	9
18	Oslepitel'nyi	25.09.40	190	550	31.12.40	–	<42>	2.30%	KBF	9
19	Ostorozhnyi	19.10.40	190	557	30.01.41	–	<43>	3.20%	KBF	9
20	Otchetlivyi	19.10.40	190	558	14.02.41	–	<43>	1.70%	KBF	9
21	Otzyvchivyi	19.10.40	190	559	<07.41>	–	<43>	–	KBF	10
22	Otradnyi	19.10.40	190	560	<10.41>	–	<43>	–	KBF	10
23	Ozhivlennyi	19.10.40	190	561	<10.41>	–	<43>	–	KBF	10
24	Otlichitel'nyi	19.10.40	190	562	<10.41>	–	<43>	–	KBF	10

[1] Launched before or during the war; 19 July 1941 put into conservation, completed after the war to *Projekt 30K*, 2,125t.
[2] Put into conservation on 19 July 1941; building resumed after the war to *Projekt 30K*.
[3] Put into conservation on 19 July 1941; materials used for the defence of Leningrad.
[4] In August 1941 towed incomplete from Nikolaev to Caucasian ports, 1944 towed to Sevastopol and completion resumed before the end of the war as *Projekt 30* destroyer.
[5] In August 1941 towed to Caucasian ports; building resumed after the war to *Projekt 30K*.
[6] Put into conservation 19.07.41; building resumed after the war to *Projekt* 30K, 2,135t stdd.
[7] As No.1, after the war renamed *Stalin*.
[8] Put into conservation 1942; building resumed after the war to *Projekt* 30K.
[9] Put into conservation on 19.07.41; materials partly used for the defence of Leningrad, partly to repair damaged vessels, remains broken up on the slips.
[10] Planned to be laid down in autumn 1941, but cancelled on 19.07.41.

Table A2 (contd.): Warships of the *RKKF/VMF*, laid down or ordered, 1926–45

No.	Name	Order	Yard	Yard No.	Laid down	Launched	Commiss.	22.06.41	Fleet	Notes
Destroyers (*Projekt 30*, 1,890t stdd. As planned, when completed 2,016t stdd.) *continued*
25	*Otmennyi*	19.10.40	200	1093	30.10.40	–	<42>	6.79%	ChF	1
26	*Obuchennyi*	19.10.40	200	1094	30.12.40	–	<42>	5.57%	ChF	1
27	*Otchayannyi*	19.10.40	200	1095	30.12.40	–	<43>	3.72%	ChF	1
28	*Obshchitel'nyi*	19.10.40	200	1096	30.12.40	–	<43>	3.75%	ChF	1
29	*Zharkii*	19.10.40	402	120	25.03.41	–	<43>	2.00%	SF	2
30	*Zhivoi*	19.10.40	402	121	25.03.41	–	<43>	1.00%	SF	2
31	*Zhutkii*	19.10.40	402	122	<25.03.41>	–	<43>	–	SF	3
32	*Zhestkii*	19.10.40	402	123	<25.03.41>	–	<43>	–	SF	3
33	*Vedushchii*	19.10.40	199	10	<22.09.41>	–	<43>	–	TOF	4
34	*Vnezapnyi*	19.10.40	199	11	<22.09.41>	–	<43>	–	TOF	4
35	*Zhguchii*	19.10.40	402	130	<10.41>	–	<43>	–	SF	5
36	*Zhestokii*	19.10.40	402	131	<10.41>	–	<43>	–	SF	5
37	*Zorkii*	19.10.40	402	132	<10.41>	–	<43>	–	SF	5
38	*Zvonkii*	19.10.40	402	133	<10.41>	–	<43>	–	SF	5

[1] Destroyed on the slips in Nikolaev in August 1941 to avoid capture by the Germans.
[2] Put into conservation on 19.07.41, building not resumed, broken up on the slips.
[3] Materials prepared for laying down in spring 1941, but not really started and cancelled in 1941.
[4] Building planned to be started in September 1941, but not laid down.
[5] Ordered to replace the cancelled battleship *Sovetskaya Belorossiya*, but never laid down.

Destroyer Projects during the war:
1. There was a *projekt 47*: A big destroyer of ca.4,500t with 15.2cm guns; not ordered and stopped 1941.
2. To replace the destroyer leaders of *projekt 48*, cancelled on 19.10.40, it was planned in 1941 to build a new big destroyer of *projekt 35* with 2,650t and 6–13cm guns in twin turrets, named *Udaloi* and *Udarnyi*, but cancelled before being laid down.
3. In September 1942 the planning of a new destroyer of *projekt 40* was started and continued up to 1944. But no orders placed.

Patrol Ships (Strozhevoj korabl' *Projekt 2*, 580t stdd.)

No.	Name		Yard	Yard No.	Laid down	Launched	Commiss.	22.06.41	Fleet	Notes
1	*Uragan*		190	320	13.08.27	04.09.28	16.12.30	–	SF	1
2	*Tajfun*		190	321	13.08.27	01.06.29	14.09.31	–	KBF	
3	*Smerch*		190	322	13.08.27	22.07.29	13.09.32	–	SF	1
4	*Tsiklon*		190	323	13.08.27	27.11.29	03.07.32	–	KBF	
5	*Groza*		190	324	13.08.27	28.09.30	05.07.32	–	SF	1
6	*Vikhr*		190	325	13.08.27	12.10.30	12.09.32	–	KBF	
7	*Metel'*		190 / 202	423	18.12.31	15.06.34	18.11.34	–	TOF	2
8	*Vyuga*		190 / 202	424	26.12.31	06.07.34	18.11.34	–	TOF	2
9	*Molniya*		190 / 202	478	23.03.34	24.11.34	20.09.36	–	TOF	2
10	*Zarnitsa*		190 / 202	479	21.03.34	06.11.34	06.11.36	–	TOF	2
11	*Purga*		190	480	06.34	11.35	04.09.36	–	KBF	
12	*Burya*		190	481	06.34	11.35	27.10.36	–	KBF	

[1] Transferred in 1933 by way of the Baltic–White Sea Canal to the Northern Fleet.
[2] Materials prepared in Leningrad and transferred by rail to Vladivostok for completion.

Table A2 (contd.): Warships of the *RKKF/VMF*, laid down or ordered, 1926–45

No.	Name	Order	Yard	Yard No.	Laid down	Launched	Commiss.	22.06.41	Fleet	Notes
Patrol Ships (Storozhevoj korabl', *Projekt 4*, 487t stdd.)										
1	Shtorm		200	1019	24.10.27	04.04.30	01.10.32	–	ChF	
2	Shkval		200	1020	24.10.27	30	05.03.33	–	ChF	
3	Burun		198	220	22.04.32					
			202			27.09.34	07.10.35	–	TOF	1
4	Grom		198	221	17.06.32					
			202			22.09.34	22.07.35	–	TOF	1
Patrol Ships (Strozhevoj korabl' *Projekt 39*, 590t)										
1	Sneg		190	495	27.04.35	14.07.36	25.09.38	–	KBF	
2	Tucha		190	496	27.04.35	20.10.36	25.09.38	–	KBF	

[1] Materials prepared in Nikolaev and transferred by rail to Vladivostok for completion.

Patrol Ships (Storozhevoj korabl' for the *NKVD*, Projekt (n.k.), 810t stdd.)

No.	Name	Order	Yard	Yard No.	Laid down	Launched	Commiss.	22.06.41	Fleet	Notes
1	Kirov (PS26, ex-PSK2)	Ans.		298	08.02.33	19.08.34	18.09.35	–	TOF	1
2	Dzerzhinskij (P58, ex-PSK1)	Ans.		299	08.02.33	29.08.34	16.09.35	–	TOF	1

Patrol Ships (Storozhevoj korabl' for the *NKVD*, *Projekt 43*, 580t stdd.)*

No.	Name	Order	Yard	Yard No.	Laid down	Launched	Commiss.	22.06.41	Fleet	Notes
1	Zhemchug, ex-*PSK-301*		190		06.34	11.35	12.37	–	SF	2
2	Rubin, ex-*PSK-302*		190		03.11.34	18.08.35	18.12.36	–	SF	2
3	Brilliant, ex-*PSK-303*		190		10.34	05.11.35	06.06.37	–	SF	2
4	Sapfir, ex-*PSK-304*		190		26.12.34	20.12.35	12.12.37	–	SF	2

[1] Built by Ansaldo, Genoa, for the *NKVD* Far East, and transferred by sea to Vladivostok.
[2] Built in Leningrad and transferred by the Baltic–White Sea Canal to the Northern Area 1938. 05.01.41 to SF.
* There was a plan to build 6 more vessels, but they were cancelled on 05.03.36 before laid down.

Patrol Ships (Strozhevoj korabl', *Projekt 29*, 842t stdd.)

No.	Name	Order	Yard	Yard No.	Laid down	Launched	Commiss.	22.06.41	Fleet	Notes
1	Yastreb	3 FYP	190	533	23.05.39	10.06.40	30.12.44	50.80%	KBF	1
2	Orel	3 FYP	190	534	28.05.39	12.02.41				
			820				21.12.50	24.30%	KBF	2
3	Korshun	3 FYP	190	535	25.10.39	28.05.41				
			820				21.01.51	19.40%	KBF	2
4	Zorkii, ex-*Almaz* ex-*Voron*	3 FYP	190	536	23.05.40	31.10.40				
			820				30.01.50	29.80%	KBF	3
5	Bditel'nyi, ex-Izumrud, ex-*Grif*	3 FYP	190	537	25.05.40	–	–	–	KBF	4
6	Tigr	3 FYP	201	365	40	–	<42>	4.20%	ChF	5
7	Leopard	3 FYP	201	366	40	–	<42>	4.20%	ChF	5
8	Rys'	3 FYP	201	367	41	–	<42>	2.00%	ChF	5
9	Yaguar	3 FYP	201	368	41	–	<42>	2.00%	ChF	5

[1] Laid up on 19.07.41, but continued later and completed to the original project shortly after the end of the war.
[2] Laid up on 19.07.41 and put into conservation, *Korshun* finally completed at 194, both to *projekt 29K*.
[3] Transferred to the *NKVD* under the new name, and completed after the war to *projekt 29K*.
[4] Transferred to the *NKVD* under the new name, but not completed.
[5] Materials for the building were prepared at 198 as yard Nos 1091, 1092, 1097–1100 and then shipped for building to 201. Hulls destroyed to avoid capture by the Germans.

Table A2 (contd.): Warships of the *RKKF/VMF*, laid down or ordered, 1926–45

No.	Name	Order	Yard	Yard No.	Laid down	Launched	Commiss.	22.06.41	Fleet	Notes
Patrol Ships (Storozhevoj korabl', *Projekt 29*, 842t stdd.) *continued*										
10	*Kuguar*	3 FYP	201	369	41	–	<43>	–	ChF	1
11	*Pantera*	3 FYP	201	370	41	–	<43>	–	ChF	1
12	*Burevestnik*	3 FYP	199	1	04.12.39	17.07.43	15.07.47	–	TOF	2
13	*Al'batros*	3 FYP	199	2	04.12.39	02.06.44	29.09.45	–	TOF	2
14	*Berkut*	3 FYP	190	553	08.40	–	–	–	KBF	3
15	*Sokol'*	3 FYP	190	554	10.40	–	–	–	KBF	3
16	*Grif*	3 FYP	190	555	05.41	–	–	–	KBF	3
17	*Voron*	3 FYP	190	556	–	–	–	–	KBF	4
18	*Kondor*	3 FYP	190	563	–	–	–	–	KBF	4
19	*Fregat*	3 FYP	199	6	–	–	–	–	TOF	5
20	*Orlan*	3 FYP	199	9	–	–	–	–	TOF	5

[1] As before, but probably only the first was laid down, because the Germans found only 5 hulls at 201.
[2] Building started at Komsomol'sk but several times interrupted during the war, completed to *projekt 29K*.
[3] Building started in Leningrad, but put into conservation on 19.07.41 and not started again. Broken up on slips.
[4] Building planned in Leningrad, but not started. Cancelled on 19.07.41.
[5] Building planned in Komsomol'sk, but never started.

Patrol Ships (Storozhevoj korabl' *Projekt 52*, 3,165t stdd.)

1	*Purga*	196	116	17.12.38					
		194	630		24.04.41	31.03.54	–	TOF	1
2	(no name)	196	117	–	–	–	–	–	2

[1] Put into conservation on 19.07.41, restarted after the war at 194 and after completion transferred by the Northern Seaway to the Far East.
[2] Planned, but cancelled on 19.10.40, space to be used for two *S*-class submarines.

Patrol Ships (Storozhevoj korabl' for the *NKVD*, projekt 19, 4,680t stdd.)
[1] Four ships were planned for the *NKVD* at the Northern area, but cancelled to use the building space for the Navy

Minesweepers (*Projekt 3*, 428t stdd.)

No.	Name	Yard	Yard No.	Laid down	Launched	Commiss.	22.06.41	Fleet
1	*T-201 Zaryad*	190	459	12.10.33	10.10.34	26.12.36	–	KBF
2	*T-202 Bui*	190	460	12.12.33	05.11.34	11.08.38	–	KBF
3	*T-203 Patron*	190	461	28.12.33	30.09.34	04.07.38	–	KBF
4	*T-204 Fugas*	190	462	05.01.34	25.10.34	10.12.36	–	KBF
5	*T-401 Tral*	201	67	05.11.33	23.08.34	23.12.36	–	ChF
6	*T-402 Minrep*	201	68	34	35	28.01.37	–	ChF
7	*T-403 Gruz*	201	69	34	21.09.35	25.07.37	–	ChF
8	*T-404 Shchit*	201	70	34	14.12.35	30.10.37	–	ChF

Table A2 (contd.): Warships of the *RKKF/VMF*, laid down or ordered, 1926–45

No.	Name	Order	Yard	Yard No.	Laid down	Launched	Commiss.	22.06.41	Fleet	Notes
Minesweepers (*Projekt 53*, 417t stdd.)
1	T-1 *Strela*		190	491	10.05.35	17.05.36				
			196	111			13.08.38	–	TOF	1
2	T-2 *Tros*		190	492	22.05.35	24.06.36				
			196	112			24.09.38	–	TOF	1
3	T-3 *Provodnik*		190	493	30.06.35	30.06.36				
			196	113			04.12.38	–	TOF	1
4	T-4 *Podsekatel'*		190	494	16.04.35	10.12.36				
			196	114			14.11.38	–	TOF	1
5	T-405 *Vzryvatel'*		189		21.07.36	27.04.37				
			201	175			09.05.38	–	ChF	2
6	T-406 *Iskatel'*		189		30.07.36	29.07.37				
			201	176			09.05.38	–	ChF	2
7	T-411 *Zashchitnik*		189		10.08.36	31.07.37				
			201	177			20.08.38	–	ChF	2
8	T-407 *Mina*		189		22.12.36	20.08.37				
			201	178			08.09.38	–	ChF	2
9	T-7 *Vekha*		189		30.12.36	38				
			201	179			16.09.38	–	TOF	3
10	T-8 *Cheka*		189		27.12.36	38				
			201	180			02.11.38	–	TOF	3
Minesweepers (*Project 53U*, 417t stdd.)
1	T-205 *Gafel'*		363	14	12.10.37	29.07.38	21.07.39	–	KBF	
2	T-206 *Verp*		363	15	12.10.37	17.07.38	17.06.39	–	KBF	
3	T-207 *Shpil'*		363	16	17.11.37	18.08.38	23.09.39	–	KBF	
4	T-208 *Shkiv*		363	17	18.11.37	31.10.38				
			196	129			12.10.39	–	KBF	4
5	T-209 *Knekht*		363	18	16.06.38	17.08.39	03.06.40	–	KBF	
6	T-210 *Gak*		363	19	08.08.38	15.04.39	14.11.39	–	KBF	
7	T-211 *Rym*		363	20	21.09.38	05.05.39	25.06.40	–	KBF	
8	T-212 *Shtag*		363	21	06.11.38	02.12.39	26.07.40	–	KBF	
9	T-218		363	22	20.03.39	24.11.39	30.11.40	–	KBF	
10	T-213 *Krambol*		370	92	26.08.38	31.01.39	30.11.39	–	KBF	
11	T-214 *Bugel'*		370	93	26.08.38	31.01.39	29.06.40	–	KBF	
12	T-215		363	24	23.04.39	17.12.39	30.09.40	–	KBF	
13	T-216		363	27	17.09.39	30.04.40	24.12.40	–	KBF	
14	T-217 *Kontradmiral Yurkovskii*		363	28	21.09.39	31.07.40	05.08.41	–	KBF	
15	T-219 *Kontradmiral Khoroshkin*		363	34	27.04.41	24.09.43				
			370				25.09.44	–	KBF	5
16	T-220		363	35	10.04.41	16.11.43				
			370				16.10.46	–	KBF	6
17	T-221 *Dmitrii Lysov*		363	36	27.06.41	06.06.46	05.11.46	–	KBF	7
18	T-222		370	134	–	–	–	–		8
19	T-223		370	135	–	–	–	–		8

[1] Building started at 190, transferred for completion to 196, transferred by Panama Canal to the TOF.
[2] Building started at 198, transferred for completion to 201.
[3] Building started at 198, transferred for completion to 201, transferred by Suez Canal to TOF.
[4] Building started at 363, transferred for completion to 196.
[5] Building started at Izhora, Leningrad, completed at Petrozavodsk.
[6] Building started at Izhora, Leningrad, laid up during the war, completed at Petrozavodsk after the war.
[7] Laid up during the war, completion started after the war.
[8] Ordered, but cancelled before being laid down.

Table A2 (contd.): Warships of the *RKKF/VMF*, laid down or ordered, 1926–45

No.	Name	Order	Yard	Yard No.	Laid down	Launched	Commiss.	22.06.41	Fleet	Notes
Minesweepers (***Project 58***, **406t stdd.**)										
1	T-5 Paravan		189		15.03.37	28.01.38				
			201	187			30.12.38	–	TOF	1
2	T-6 Kapsyul'		189		21.03.37	28.01.38				
			201	188			03.01.39	–	TOF	1
3	T-408 Yakor'		201	189	28.03.37	14.01.38	15.02.39	–	ChF	
4	T-409 Garpun		201	190	37	28.03.38	20.02.39	–	ChF	
5	T-410 Vzryv		201	191	37	38	09.03.39	–	ChF	
6	T-412 Arsenii Rasskin		201	255	13.04.39	05.11.39	03.03.41	–	ChF	
7	T-413		201	256	29.04.39	12.10.40	21.04.41	–	ChF	
8	T-414		201	267	01.41	41	–	–	ChF	2
9	T-415		201	268	03.41	–	–	–	ChF	2

[1] Building started at Nikolaev, transferred for completion to Sevastopol, than transferred by sea to Vladivostok.
[2] *T-414* towed in 01.42 to Tuapse, in 04.42 to Poti, in 04.45 back to Nikolaev for completion, but cancelled. *T-415* destroyed to avoid capture by the Germans.

Turbine Minesweepers (***Project 59***, **648t stdd.**)

No.	Name	Order	Yard	Yard No.	Laid down	Launched	Commiss.	22.06.41	Fleet	Notes
1	T-250 Vladimir Polukhin	3 FYP	370	108	28.05.39	30.03.40	19.10.42	60.00%	KBF	1
2	T-251 Pavel Khokhryakov	3 FYP	370	109	39	40	25.11.49	–	KBF	2
3	T-252 Aleksandr Petrov	3 FYP	370	110	20.04.40	20.11.40	25.11.49	–	KBF	2
4	T-253 Karl Zedin	3 FYP	370	111	20.04.40	30.11.40	10.09.48	–	KBF	2
5	T-254 Vasilii Gromov		363	23	29.05.39	10.40	23.09.43	60.00%	KBF	1
6	T-255 Adrian Zosimov		363	25	10.08.39	09.12.40	29.12.49	–	KBF	2
7	T-256 Vladimir Trefolev		363	26	10.02.40	09.12.40	17.11.47	–	KBF	2
8	T-257 Timofei Ulyantsev		370	124	12.40	29.05.41	10.12.48	–	KBF	2
9	T-258 Mikhail Martynov		370	125	11.40	30.05.41	12.08.48	–	KBF	2
10	T-259 Fedor Mitrofanov		363	29	20.08.40	17.05.41	07.11.47	–	KBF	2
11	T-260 Luka Pankov		363	30	09.40	06.41	31.12.47	–	KBF	2
12	T-261 Pavlin Vinogradov		363	31	10.40	06.41	02.09.49	–	KBF	2
13	T-262 Stepan Gredyushko		363	32	10.40	06.41	24.08.49	–	KBF	2
14	T-263 Semen Paleikhov		363	33	40	06.41	26.08.49	–	KBF	2
15	T-451 Ivan Borisov		201	249	04.04.39	31.12.39	31.08.48	–	ChF	3
16	T-450 Pavel Golovin		201	250	06.08.39	40	–	–	ChF	4

[1] Building interrupted after the start of the war, but resumed and completed during the war.
[2] Building interrupted after the start of the war, resumed only after the war to *projekt 59K*.
[3] Towed away from Sevastopol to avoid capture by the Germans, towed back after the war and completed to *projekt 59K*.
[4] *T-450* wrecked in a storm at Tuapse on 22.01.42.

Table A2 (contd.): Warships of the *RKKF/VMF*, laid down or ordered, 1926–45

No.	Name	Order	Yard	Yard No.	Laid down	Launched	Commiss.	22.06.41	Fleet	Notes
Turbine Minesweepers (*Project 59*, 648t stdd.) *continued*										
17	T-452 *Sergei Shuvalov*		201	251	02.01.40	25.02.41	30.03.48	–	ChF	1
18	T-453 *Semen Roshal'*		201	252	02.40	03.41	–	–	ChF	2
19	T-454 *Ivan Sladkov*		201	253	14.02.40	20.03.41	18.03.48	–	ChF	1
20	T-455 *Nikolai Markin*		201	258	03.41	–	–	–	ChF	3
21	T-456 *Boris Zhemchuzhin*		201	259	–	–	–	–	ChF	4
22	T-457 *Nikolai Pozharov*		201	260	–	–	–	–	ChF	4

[1] Towed away from Sevastopol to avoid capture by the Germans, towed back after the war and completed to *projekt 59K*.
[2] *T-453* stranded on 19.12.44 at Sinope when towed to 201.
[3] Building started at Sevastopol, captured by the Germans and scrapped on the slips.
[4] Cancelled on 19.10.40 when *projekt 59* was limited to 20 units.

Coastal Minesweepers (*Projekt 60*, 350t stdd.)
1 Planned in 1940, but no ship laid down.

Monitors (*Projekt* (n.k.), 11,000t stdd.)
1 Since 1925 there were several projects studied for monitors of different designs. One was in 1925/28/28 of 11,000t, with one triple turret of 14-inch guns. Others were smaller, but no ships were really ordered or laid down.

River Monitor (*Projekt SB-12*, 367t stdd.)

No.	Name	Order	Yard	Yard No.	Laid down	Launched	Commiss.	22.06.41	Fleet	Notes
1	*Udarnyi*		300		21.11.30	17.05.32	01.06.34	–	DVF	

River Monitors (*Projekt SB-30*, 214t stdd.)

No.	Name	Order	Yard	Yard No.	Laid down	Launched	Commiss.	22.06.41	Fleet	Notes
1	*Aktivnyi*		300/368	31		23.08.34	16.10.35	–	AKF	
2	*Zheleznyakov*		300		25.11.34	22.11.35	27.10.36	–	DVF	*Projekt SB-37*
3	*Zhemchuzhin*		300		34	35	27.11.36	–	DF	*SB-37*
4	*Levachev*		300		34	35	27.10.36	–	PVF	*SB-37*
5	*Martynov*		300		34	35	08.12.36	–	DVF	*SB-37*
6	*Rostovtsev*		300		35	36	13.05.37	–	DVF	*SB-37*
7	*Flyagin*		300		34	35	30.12.36	–	PVF	*SB-37*

Monitors (*Projekt 1190*, 1,704t stdd.)

No.	Name	Order	Yard	Yard No.	Laid down	Launched	Commiss.	22.06.41	Fleet	Notes
1	*Khasan*, ex- *Lazo*		112 368	233 9671	15.07.36 04.11.39	30.08.40	01.12.42	–	TOF	1
2	*Perekop*, ex- *Simbirtsev*		112 368	234 9672	15.07.36 09.12.39	14.06.41	07.10.43	–	TOF	1
3	*Sivash*, ex-		112 368	235 9673	15.07.36 20.08.40	01.10.41	31.10.46	–	TOF	2

[1] Building started at Gorkii, materials transferred by rail to Khabarovsk for completion, first only single guns.
[2] Building started at Gorkii, materials transferred by rail to Khabarovsk for completion with double gun turrets.

Table A2 (contd.): Warships of the *RKKF/VMF*, laid down or ordered, 1926–45

No.	Name	Order	Yard	Yard No.	Laid down	Launched	Commiss.	22.06.41	Fleet	Notes
Monitors (*Projekt SB-57*, 720ts stdd.)										
1	Vidlitsa, ex-*Shilka*		300	SB156	40	41	–	–	–	1
2	Kakhovka, ex-*Amgun*		300	SB157	40	18.09.41	–	–	–	2
3	Volochaevka		300	SB158	40	41	–	–	–	3
4	Vidlitsa									
5	Kakhovka									

[1] ½ month from completion in 08.41, ordered to ChF, but scuttled at Zaporozhya on 18.08.41.
[2] Scuttled at Kiev to avoid capture.
[3] ½ month from completion in 08.41, ordered to ChF, but blown up at Zaporozhya on 04.10.41.

Table A3: Submarines of the *RKKF/VMF*, laid down or ordered, 1926–45

No.	Name	Order	Yard	Yard No.	Laid down	Launched	Commiss.	22.06.41	Fleet	Notes
Big Submarines (*Series I*, 934t normal)										
1	D-1 *Dekabrist*		189	177	05.03.27	03.11.28	12.11.30	13.11.40	SF	1
2	D-2 *Narodvolets*		189	178	05.03.27	19.05.29	06.09.31	–	KBF	2
3	D-3 *Krasnogvardeets*		189	179	05.03.27	12.07.29	01.10.31	–	SF	3
4	D-4 *Revolyutsioner*		200	27/192	14.04.27	16.04.29	30.12.30	–	ChF	
5	D-5 *Spartakovets*		200	28/193	14.04.27	28.09.29	05.04.31	–	ChF	
6	D-6 *Yakobinets*		200	29/194	14.04.27	02.05.30	15.06.31	–	ChF	

1–3 All transferred in 1933 by the Baltic–White Sea Canal to the Northern Flotilla

[1] *D-1* sunk during exercises in the Kola estuary.
[2] *D-2* returned from the Northern Fleet for repairs to Leningrad and remained in the Baltic.
[3] *D-3* remained in the Northern Fleet.

No.	Name	Order	Yard	Yard No.	Laid down	Launched	Commiss.	22.06.41	Fleet	Notes
Minelaying Submarines (*Series II*, 1,025t normal)										
1	L-1 *Leninets*		189	195	06.09.29	28.02.31	22.10.33	–	KBF	
2	L-2 *Stalinets*, ex-*Marksist*		189	196	06.09.29	21.05.31	24.10.33	–	KBF	
3	L-3 *Frunzovets*, ex-*Bolshevik*		189	197	06.09.29	08.07.31	05.11.33	–	KBF	
4	L-4 *Garibaldiets*		200	31/201	15.03.30	31.08.31	08.10.33	–	ChF	
5	L-5 *Chartist*		200	32/201	15.03.30	05.06.32	30.10.33	–	ChF	
6	L-6 *Karbonarii*		200	33/203	15.04.33	03.11.32	09.05.35	–	ChF	
Medium Submarines (*Series III*, 572t normal)*										
1	SC-301 *Shchuka*		189	199	05.02.30	01.12.30	11.10.33	–	KBF	
2	SC-302 *Okun*		189	200	05.02.30	06.11.31	11.10.33	–	KBF	
3	SC-303 *Ershch*		189	201	05.02.30	06.11.31	15.11.33	–	KBF	
4	SC-304 *Komsomolets* ex-*Jazh'*		112 189	500/1	23.02.30	02.05.31	15.08.34	–	KBF	1

[1] Built from donations of the Komsomol', laid down and launched at Gorkii, transferred for completion to Leningrad.
* Submarines of *Shch*-class are shown in Table A3, shortened to *SC*.

No.	Name	Order	Yard	Yard No.	Laid down	Launched	Commiss.	22.06.41	Fleet	Notes
Big Submarines (*Series IV*, 931t normal)										
1	P-1 *Pravda*		189	218	21.05.34	03.01.34	09.06.36	–	KBF	
2	P-2 *Zvezda*		189	219	19.12.31	15.02.34	09.07.36	–	KBF	
3	P-3 *Iskra*		189	220	19.12.31	04.12.34	09.07.36	–	KBF	
Medium Submarines (*Series V*, 592t normal) (*SC* = *Shch*)										
1	SC-101, ex-*SC-11*, *Karas'*, ex *Losos*		189 202	229	20.03.32	25.12.32	02.09.33	–	TOF	1
2	SC-104, ex-*SC-14*, *Nalim*		189 202	230	20.03.32	05.33	05.11.33	–	TOF	1
3	SC-112 *Peskar*		189 368	231	20.03.32	04.33	11.09.34	–	TOF	2
4	SC-111 *Karas'*		189 368	232	20.03.32	07.33	12.09.34	–	TOF	2

[1] Material prepared and laid down at Leningrad, transferred by rail to Vladivostok for completion.
[2] Materials prepared and laid down at Leningrad, transferred by rail to Khabarovsk for completion.

Table A3 (contd.): Submarines of the *RKKF/VMF*, laid down or ordered, 1926–45

No.	Name	Order	Yard	Yard No.	Laid down	Launched	Commiss.	22.06.41	Fleet	Notes
Medium Submarines (*Series V*, 592t normal) *continued*										
5	SC-108 Forel'		189	233						
			368		01.04.32	07.33	22.12.33	–	TOF	1
6	SC-105 Keta		189	234						
			368		01.04.32	08.33	05.11.33	–	TOF	1
7	SC-102, ex-SC-12, Leshch		194	159						
			202		20.03.32	19.04.33	22.09.33	–	TOF	2
8	SC-103, ex-SC-13, Karp		194	160						
			202		20.03.32	33	27.10.33	–	TOF	2,3
9	SC-109 Som		190	455						
			202		20.03.32	08.33	18.04.34	–	TOF	2
10	SC-110 Yaz'		190	456						
			202		20.03.32	10.33	18.05.34	–	TOF	2
11	SC-106 Sudak		190	457						
			202		27.03.32	05.33	20.11.33	–	TOF	2
12	SC-107 Sig		190	458						
			202		27.03.32	07.33	27.11.33	–	TOF	2

[1] Material prepared and laid down at Leningrad, transferred by rail to Khabarovsk for completion.
[2] Material prepared and laid down at Leningrad, transferred by rail to Vladivostok for completion.
[3] Sunk on 04.11.35 by a collision, raised and used as diving hulk, later as test vessel for 'Drakon 129' sonar.

Small Submarines (*Series VI*, 157t normal)

No.	Name	Order	Yard	Yard No.	Laid down	Launched	Commiss.	22.06.41	Fleet	Notes
1	M-3		198	236	02.11.32	08.06.33				
			202			01.12.33	22.05.34	–	TOF	1
2	M-1		198	237	03.10.32	08.04.33				
			202			01.12.33	26.03.34	–	TOF	1
3	M-8		198	238	31.10.32	11.08.33				
			202			05.02.34	05.07.34	–	TOF	1
4	M-51		198	239	17.11.32	08.09.33	09.09.34	–	ChF	
5	M-9		198	240		27.09.33				
			202		20.01.33	05.02.34	05.07.34	–	TOF	1
6	M-4		200	241	01.04.33	16.06.33				
			202			18.11.33	02.06.34	–	TOF	1
7	M-7		200	242	19.04.33	05.08.33				
			202			05.02.34	06.07.34	–	TOF	1
8	M-2		200	243	29.06.32	08.04.33				
			202			01.12.33	28.04.34	–	TOF	1
9	M-6		200	244	32	24.04.33				
			202			25.01.34	13.06.34	–	TOF	1
10	M-5		200	245	33	29.10.33				
			202			25.01.34	22.06.34	–	TOF	1
11	M-10		200	246	33	24.08.33				
			202			18.02.34	05.07.34	–	TOF	1
12	M-15		200	247	33	26.12.33				
			202			27.03.34	14.07.34	–	TOF	1
13	M-14		200	248	33	26.12.33				
			202			12.03.34	10.07.34	–	TOF	1

[1] Material prepared and laid down at Nikolaev, transferred by rail to Vladivostok for completion.

Table A3 (contd.): Submarines of the *RKKF/VMF*, laid down or ordered, 1926–45

No.	Name	Order	Yard	Yard No.	Laid down	Launched	Commiss.	22.06.41	Fleet	Notes
Small Submarines (*Series VI*, **157t normal**) *continued*										
14	*M-26*		200	249	33	14.04.34				
			202			15.08.34	18.11.34	–	TOF	1
15	*M-23*		200	250	33	16.05.34				
			202			08.07.34	10.10.34	–	TOF	1
16	*M-25*		198	251	33	16.04.34				
			202			15.08.34	18.11.34	–	TOF	1
17	*M-11*		198	252	16.05.33	29.11.33				
			202			18.02.34	05.07.34	–	TOF	1
18	*M-12*		198	253	26.05.33	02.12.33				
			202			18.02.34	05.07.34	–	TOF	1
19	*M-13*		198	254	07.06.33	03.10.33				
			202			12.03.34	14.07.34	–	TOF	1
20	*M-27*		198	255	14.06.33					
			198			23.07.34				
			202		01.02.34	23.09.34	31.12.34	–	TOF	1
21	*M-28*		198	256	12.07.33	21.06.34				
			202			30.11.34	10.07.35	–	TOF	1
22	*M-17*		198	257	16.07.33	27.12.33				
			202			27.03.34	21.07.34	–	TOF	1
23	*M-19*		198	258	12.07.33	14.05.34				
			202			16.06.34	29.08.34	–	TOF	1
24	*M-18*		198	259	18.07.33	24.12.33				
			202			12.03.34	22.07.34	–	TOF	1
25	*M-16*		198	260	05.08.33	28.12.33				
			202			27.03.34		–	TOF	1
26	*M-52*		198	261	15.08.33	31.12.33	22.07.34	–	ChF	
27	*M-20*		198	262		17.03.34	09.34			
			202		25.08.33	16.06.34	23.09.34	–	TOF	1
28	*M-21*		198	263	27.09.33	11.05.34				
			202			16.06.34	23.09.34	–	TOF	1
29	*M-22*		198	264	06.10.33	15.05.34				
			202			08.07.34	10.10.34	–	TOF	1
30	*M-24*		198	265	21.10.33	01.06.34				
			202			08.07.34	10.10.34	–	TOF	1

[1] Material prepared, laid down and launched, then transferred by rail to Vladivostok for completion.

Medium Submarines (*Series V-bis*, **592t normal**) (*SC = Shch*)

1	*SC-201 Sazan*		194	183	14.08.33					
			200	1026	34	03.04.34	05.08.35	–	ChF	1
2	*SC-202 Sel'd*		194	184	03.09.33					
			200	1027	34	25.05.34	03.09.35	–	ChF	1
3	*SC-120 Navaga*		194	185	02.04.33					
			368			06.34	30.01.35	–	TOF	2
4	*SC-305 Voinst-Vyushchii bezbozhnik*, ex-*Lin'*		194	186	34 11.32	31.12.33	03.12.34	–	KBF	

[1] Building started at Leningrad, transferred in sections to Nikolaev for completion.
[2] Building started at Leningrad, transferred in sections by rail to Khabarovsk for completion.

Table A3 (contd.): Submarines of the *RKKF/VMF*, laid down or ordered, 1926–45

No.	Name	Order	Yard	Yard No.	Laid down	Launched	Commiss.	22.06.41	Fleet	Notes
Medium Submarines (*Series V-bis*, 592t normal) *continued*										
5	SC-113 Sterlyad		194	243	10.10.32					
			202	187	33	12.12.33	11.09.34	–	TOF	1
6	SC-114 Sevryuga		194	244	10.10.32					
			202	188	33	34	11.09.34	–	TOF	1
7	SC-115 Skat		189	225	19.10.32					
			202		33	04.04.34	10.10.34	–	TOF	1
8	SC-117 Makrel'		189	226	09.10.32					
			202		33	15.04.34	18.12.34	–	TOF	1
9	SC-118 Kefal'		189	227	10.10.32					
			202		33	34	18.12.34	–	TOF	1
10	SC-203 Kambala		189	228	10.03.33					
			200	1028	33	29.05.34	04.09.35	–	ChF	2
11	SC-119 Beluga		189	241	12.05.33					
			202		33	07.05.34	02.02.35	–	TOF	1
12	SC-116 Osetr		189	242	12.05.33					
			202		34	34	11.01.35	–	TOF	1
13	SC-308 Semga		112	550/2	10.11.32	28.04.33	20.11.35	–	KBF	3

[1] Building started at Leningrad, transferred by rail to Vladivostok for completion.
[2] Building started at Leningrad, transferred to Nikolaev for completion.
[3] Built at Gorkii for the Baltic Fleet, transferred by inland waterways.

Medium Submarines (*Series V-bis2*, 584t normal) (SC = Shch)

No.	Name	Order	Yard	Yard No.	Laid down	Launched	Commiss.	22.06.41	Fleet	Notes
1	SC-121 Zubatka		194	214	20.12.33					
			202		34	26.08.34	30.04.35	–	TOF	1
2	SC-123 Ugor'		194	215	20.12.33					
			202		34	26.08.34	30.04.35	–	TOF	1
3	SC-204 Minoga		194	216	15.04.34					
			200	1040	34	31.12.34	30.12.35	–	ChF	2
4	SC-125 Muksun		194	217	20.12.33					
			202		34	26.08.34	15.05.36	–	TOF	1
5	SC-307 Treska		189	249	06.11.33	01.08.34	04.08.35	–	KBF	
6	SC-306 Piksha		189	250	06.11.33	01.08.34	04.08.35	–	KBF	1
7	SC-122 Saida		189	251	22.12.33					
			202		34	29.08.34	30.04.35	–	TOF	1
8	SC-124 Paltus		189	252	22.12.33					
			202		34	29.12.34	29.09.35	–	TOF	1
9	SC-205 Nerpa		200	1029	05.01.34	06.11.34	17.11.36	–	ChF	
10	SC-206 Nel'ma		200	1030	05.01.34	06.11.34	14.08.36	–	ChF	
11	SC-207 Kasatka		200	1031	05.01.34	25.03.35	17.11.36	–	ChF	
12	SC-309 Del'fin		112	550/3	06.11.33	10.04.35	14.11.35	–	KBF	3
13	SC-310 Belukha		112	550/4	06.11.33	10.04.35	20.08.36	–	KBF	3
14	SC-311 Kumzha		112	550/5	06.11.33	10.04.35	21.08.36	–	KBF	3

[1] Building started at Leningrad, transferred by rail to Vladivostok for completion.
[2] Building started at Leningrad, transferred by rail to Nikolaev for completion.
[3] Built at Gorkii, transferred by inland waterways to Leningrad.

Table A3 (contd.): Submarines of the *RKKF/VMF*, laid down or ordered, 1926–45

No.	Name	Order	Yard	Yard No.	Laid down	Launched	Commiss.	22.06.41	Fleet	Notes
Small Submarines (*Series VI-bis*, 161t normal)										
1	M-43, ex-M-82	2 FYP	196	58	02.02.34	10.06.35	06.11.35	–	TOF	1
2	M-83	2 FYP	196	59	10.02.34	01.06.35	08.11.35	–	KBF	
3	M-44, ex-M-84	2 FYP	196	60	10.03.34	15.07.35	27.11.35	–	TOF	1
4	M-77	2 FYP	196	61	10.03.34	21.03.36	19.06.36	–	KBF	
5	M-78	2 FYP	196	62	20.03.34	21.03.36	19.06.36	–	KBF	
6	M-47, ex-M-53	2 FYP	198	287	10.02.34	18.10.34	11.06.35	–	TOF	2
7	M-72	2 FYP	198 190	288	10.03.34	23.12.34	24.08.35	–	KBF	3
8	M-71	2 FYP	198 190	289	10.03.34	31.12.34	24.08.35	–	KBF	3
9	M-74	2 FYP	198 190	290	10.03.34	31.12.34	24.08.35	–	KBF	3
10	M-73	2 FYP	198 190	291	10.03.34	05.01.35	24.08.35	–	KBF	3
11	M-75	2 FYP	198 190	292	10.03.34	08.02.35	24.08.35	–	KBF	3
12	M-76	2 FYP	198 190	293	10.03.34	08.02.35	24.08.35	–	KBF	3
13	M-45, ex-M-85, ex-M-77	2 FYP	198	294	29.05.34	15.07.35	04.11.35	–	TOF	4
14	M-46, ex-M-86, ex-M-78	2 FYP	198	301	29.08.34	15.07.35	04.11.35	–	TOF	4
15	M-79	2 FYP	198	302	25.08.34	15.09.35	22.07.36	–	KBF	3
16	M-80	2 FYP	198	303	25.08.34	15.09.35	15.07.36	–	KBF	3
17	M-81	2 FYP	198	304	25.08.34	15.09.35	15.07.36	–	KBF	3
18	M-54	2 FYP	200	1045	20.02.34	15.09.35	14.10.36	–	ChF	
19	M-55	2 FYP	200	1046	25.03.35	20.11.35	21.10.36	–	ChF	
20	M-48, ex-M-56	2 FYP	200	1047	25.03.35	20.11.35	21.10.36	–	TOF	5

[1] Commissioned for the KBF, 31.08.–27.10.39 transferred by rail to Vladivostok
[2] Commissioned for the ChF, 08.–27.10.39 transferred by rail to Vladivostok.
[3] Material prepared at Nikolaev, transferred to Leningrad for completion.
[4] Material prepared at Nikolaev, transferred to Leningrad for completion, commissioned for the KBF, 19.08.–27.10.39 transferred by rail to Vladivostok.
[5] Built at Nikolaev and commissioned for the ChF, 08.–27.10.39 transferred by rail to Vladovostok.

No.	Name	Order	Yard	Yard No.	Laid down	Launched	Commiss.	22.06.41	Fleet	Notes
Medium Submarines (*Series IX*, 840t normal)										
1	S-1, ex-N-1	2 FYP	189	266	25.12.34	08.08.35	11.09.36	–	KBF	
2	S-2, ex-N-2	2 FYP	189	267	31.12.34	21.12.35	11.09.36	03.01.40	KBF	1
3	S-3, ex-N-3	2 FYP	189	268	25.04.35	30.04.36	20.10.37	–	KBF	

[1] Lost during the Soviet–Finnish war on 03.01.40 by a mine.

Table A3 (contd.): Submarines of the *RKKF/VMF*, laid down or ordered, 1926–45

No.	Name	Order	Yard	Yard No.	Laid down	Launched	Commiss.	22.06.41	Fleet	Notes
Medium Submarines (*Series X*, 584t normal) (*SC = Shch*)
1	SC-131	2 FYP	194	292	23.07.34					
			368		35	04.07.35	11.12.36	–	TOF	1
2	SC-134	2 FYP	194	293	23.07.34					
			202		35	04.09.35	27.12.36	–	TOF	2
3	SC-318	2 FYP	194	294	23.07.34	11.08.35	12.08.36	–	KBF	
4	SC-317	2 FYP	194	295	23.07.34	24.09.35	29.09.36	–	KBF	
5	SC-127	2 FYP	194	296	23.07.34					
			202		34	13.06.35	17.10.36	–	TOF	2
6	SC-126	2 FYP	194	297	23.07.34					
					34	20.04.35	03.10.36	–	TOF	2
7	SC-129	2 FYP	194	298	31.12.34					
			202		35	10.10.35	31.10.36	–	TOF	1
8	SC-132	2 FYP	194	299	31.12.34					
			202		35	04.07.35	11.12.36	–	TOF	2
9	SC-319	2 FYP	194	367	31.12.34	15.02.35	29.11.36	–	KBF	
10	SC-320	2 FYP	194	368	31.12.34	15.02.35	29.11.36	–	KBF	
11	SC-401, ex-SC-313	2 FYP	189	253	04.12.34	28.06.35	17.07.36	–	SF	3
12	SC-402, ex-SC-314	2 FYP	189	254	04.12.34	28.06.35	23.09.36	–	SF	3
13	SC-130	2 FYP	189	257	07.08.34					
			202		35	09.06.35	11.12.36	–	TOF	2
14	SC-128	2 FYP	189	258	17.08.34					
			202		35	09.06.35	31.10.36	–	TOF	2
15	SC-133	2 FYP	189	259	07.08.34					
			202		35	04.07.35	09.11.36	–	TOF	2
16	SC-424, ex-SC-321, ex-SC-312	2 FYP	189	260	17.12.34	27.04.35	17.07.36	20.10.39	SF	4
17	SC-403, ex-SC-315	2 FYP	189	261	25.12.34	31.12.35	26.09.36	–	SF	3
18	SC-404, ex-SC-316	2 FYP	189	262	25.12.34	27.12.35	01.10.36	–	SF	3
19	SC-421, ex-SC-313	2 FYP	112	83	20.12.34	12.05.35	05.12.37	–	SF	4
20	SC-422, ex-SC-314	2 FYP	112	84	15.12.34	12.04.35	05.12.37	–	SF	4
21	SC-139, ex-SC-423, ex-SC-315	2 FYP	112	85	17.12.34	27.04.35	05.12.37	–	TOF	5
22	SC-322	2 FYP	112	550/6	31.12.34	10.04.35	03.11.36	–	KBF	
23	SC-323	2 FYP	112	550/7	31.12.34	10.04.35	03.11.36	–	KBF	
24	SC-324	2 FYP	112	550/8	31.12.34	10.04.35	31.10.36	–	KBF	
25	SC-208	2 FYP	200	1032	18.05.34	07.10.35	16.01.37	–	ChF	
26	SC-209	2 FYP	200	1033	25.05.34	02.03.36	31.12.36	–	ChF	
27	SC-210	2 FYP	200	1034	03.06.34	13.03.36	31.12.36	–	ChF	

[1] Material prepared at Leningrad, transferred by rail to Khabarovsk for completion.
[2] Material prepared at Leningrad, transferred by rail to Vladivostok for completion.
[3] Commissioned for the KBF. On 16.05.37 renamed and in May/June transferred by the Baltic–White Sea Canal to the SF.
[4] Commissioned for the KBF. On 19.05.39 renamed and in May/June transferred by the Baltic–White Sea Canal to the SF; SC-424 sunk on 20.10.39 by a collision and lost.
[5] As in note 4 to SF, from 05.08.–17.10.40 transferred by the Northern Sea Route to the TOF.

Table A3 (contd.): Submarines of the *RKKF/VMF*, laid down or ordered, 1926–45

No.	Name	Order	Yard	Yard No.	Laid down	Launched	Commiss.	22.06.41	Fleet	Notes
Medium Submarines (*Series X*, 584t normal) *continued*										
28	SC-211	2 FYP	200	1035	03.09.34	03.09.36	05.05.38	–	ChF	
29	SC-212	2 FYP	200	1036	18.11.34	29.12.36	31.05.38	–	ChF	
30	SC-213	2 FYP	200	1037	04.12.34	13.04.37	31.05.38	–	ChF	
31	SC-214	2 FYP	200	1038	13.07.35	23.04.37	04.03.39	–	ChF	
32	SC-215	2 FYP	200	1039	27.03.35	11.01.37	21.04.39	–	ChF	
Minelaying Submarines (*Series XI*, 1,040t normal)										
1	L-7 *Voroshilovets*	2 FYP	189 202	263	10.04.34	15.05.35	10.12.36	–	TOF	1
2	L-8 *Dzerzhinets*	2 FYP	189 202	264	10.04.34	10.09.35	29.12.36	–	TOF	1
3	L-9 *Kirovets*	2 FYP	189 202	265	02.06.34	25.08.35	29.12.36	–	TOF	1
4	L-10 *Menzhinets*	2 FYP	198 199	284	10.06.34	18.12.36	12.12.38	–	TOF	2
5	L-11	2 FYP	198 202	285	10.06.34	04.12.36	05.11.37	–	TOF	3
6	L-12	2 FYP	198 199	286	10.06.34	07.11.36	10.12.38	–	TOF	2

[1] Material prepared at Leningrad, transferred by rail to Vladivostok for completion.
[2] Material prepared at Nikolaev, transferred by rail to Komsomol'sk for completion.
[3] Material prepared at Nikolaev, transferred by rail to Vladivostok for completion.

Small Submarines (*Series XII*, 206t normal)

No.	Name	Order	Yard	Yard No.	Laid down	Launched	Commiss.	22.06.41	Fleet	Notes
1	M-171, ex-M-87	2 FYP	196	88	10.09.36	10.07.37	11.12.37	–	SF	1
2	M-172, ex-M-88	2 FYP	196	89	16.06.36	12.06.37	11.12.37	–	SF	1
3	M-173, ex-M-89	2 FYP	196	90	27.06.36	09.10.37	22.06.38	–	SF	1
4	M-90	2 FYP	196	91	27.06.36	28.11.37	21.06.38	–	KBF	
5	R-1 REDO, ex-M-92	2 FYP	196	92	05.09.36	04.08.38	–	–	KSF	2

[1] Commissioned for the KBF, from 19.05.39 16.06.39 transferred by the Baltic–White Sea Canal to the SF.
[2] From 25.11.38 rebuilt into a 'Regenerativnyj edincy dvigatel' osobogo naznacheniya'. Transferred by inland waterways to the Kaspian Sea Flotilla, but not commissioned and used only for tests.

Minelaying Submarines (*Series XIII*, 1,120t normal)

No.	Name	Order	Yard	Yard No.	Laid down	Launched	Commiss.	22.06.41	Fleet	Notes
1	L-13	2 FYP	189 202	273	25.04.35	02.08.36	02.10.38	–	TOF	1
2	L-14	2 FYP	189 202	274	25.04.35	20.12.36	10.10.38	–	TOF	1
3	L-18	2 FYP	189 202	275	30.12.35	12.05.38	24.09.39	–	TOF	1
4	L-19	2 FYP	189 202	276	26.12.35	25.05.38	04.11.39	–	TOF	1
5	L-15	2 FYP	198 202	305	05.11.35	26.12.36	06.11.38	–	TOF	2
6	L-16	2 FYP	198 202	306	05.11.35	09.12.37	09.12.38	–	TOF	2
7	L-17	2 FYP	198 202	307	30.11.35	05.11.37	05.06.39	–	TOF	2

[1] Material prepared at Leningrad, transferred in sections by rail to Vladivostok for completion.
[2] Material prepared at Nikolaev, transferred by rail in sections to Vladivostok for completion.

Table A3 (contd.): Submarines of the *RKKF/VMF*, laid down or ordered, 1926–45

No.	Name	Order	Yard	Yard No.	Laid down	Launched	Commiss.	22.06.41	Fleet	Notes
Cruiser Submarines (*Series XIV*, Project KE-9, 1,500t normal)										
1	K-1	2 FYP	194	451	27.12.36	29.04.38	16.12.39	–	SF	1
2	K-2	2 FYP	194	452	27.12.36	29.04.38	16.12.39	–	SF	1
3	K-3	2 FYP	194	453	27.12.36	29.04.38	27.11.40	–	KBF	2
4	K-51	2 FYP	194	454	26.02.38	30.07.39	17.11.43	–	KBF	3
5	K-52	2 FYP	194	455	26.02.38	05.07.39	12.10.42	–	KBF	3
6	K-53	2 FYP	194	456	30.05.38	01.09.39	31.07.43	–	KBF	3
7	K-21	2 FYP	196	108	10.12.37	14.08.39	30.11.40	–	SF	4
8	K-22	2 FYP	196	109	05.01.38	28.04.39	25.09.40	–	SF	4
9	K-23	2 FYP	196	110	05.02.38	28.04.39	25.09.40	–	SF	4
10	K-54	2 FYP	189	288	30.04.37	07.02.41	–	56.00%	KBF	5
11	K-55	2 FYP	189	289	29.04.37	07.02.41	25.12.44	–	KBF	6
12	K-56	2 FYP	189	290	17.10.37	29.12.40	09.10.42	–	KBF	6

[1] Built at Leningrad, transferred from 26.05.–06.08.40 by the Baltic–White Sea Canal to the SF.
[2] Commissioned for the KBF, transferred from 08–09.41 by the Baltic–White Sea Canal to the SF.
[3] Planned for the TOF, but only completed during the war for the KBF.
[4] Commissioned for the KBF, transferred from 07–09.41 by the Baltic–White Sea Canal to the SF.
[5] Planned for the TOF, damaged beyond repair at Leningrad by air attack, not commissioned.
[6] Planned for the TOF, only completed during the war for the KBF.

Medium Submarines (*Series IX-bis*, 836t normal)

No.	Name	Order	Yard	Yard No.	Laid down	Launched	Commiss.	22.06.41	Fleet	Notes
1	S-4, ex-N-4	2 FYP	189	277	03.01.36	17.09.36	30.10.39	–	KBF	
2	S-5, ex-N-5	2 FYP	189	278	28.12.35	16.05.37	30.10.39	–	KBF	
3	S-6, ex-N-6	2 FYP	189	279	28.12.35	31.03.38	30.10.39	–	KBF	
4	S-51	2 FYP	189 / 202	284	29.04.37	30.08.40	30.11.41	–	TOF	1
5	S-52	2 FYP	189 / 202	285	29.04.37	30.08.40	09.06.43	–	TOF	2
6	S-53	2 FYP	189 / 202	286	28.09.38	30.10.41	30.01.43	–	TOF	2
7	S-54	2 FYP	194 / 202	403	24.11.36	05.11.38	31.12.40	–	TOF	3
8	S-55	2 FYP	194 / 202	404	24.11.36	27.11.39	25.07.41	–	TOF	3
9	S-56	2 FYP	194 / 202	405	24.11.36	25.12.39	20.10.41	–	TOF	3
10	S-7, ex-N-7	2 FYP	112	236	14.12.36	05.04.37	30.06.40	–	KBF	
11	S-8, ex-N-8	2 FYP	112	237	14.12.36	05.04.37	30.06.40	–	KBF	
12	S-9, ex-N-9	2 FYP	112	241	20.06.37	20.04.38	31.10.40	–	KBF	
13	S-10, ex-N-10	2 FYP	112	242	10.06.37	20.04.38	25.12.40	–	KBF	
14	S-101	2 FYP	112	243	20.06.37	20.04.38	15.12.40	–	KBF	4
15	S-102	2 FYP	112	244	20.06.37	20.04.38	16.12.40	–	KBF	4
16	S-11	2 FYP	112	245	20.10.37	24.04.37	27.06.41	–	KBF	
17	S-12	2 FYP	112	246	20.10.37	20.04.38	24.07.41	–	KBF	
18	S-31	2 FYP	198	347	05.10.37	22.02.39	19.06.40	–	ChF	
19	S-32	2 FYP	198	348	15.10.37	27.04.39	19.06.40	–	ChF	
20	S-33	2 FYP	198	349	16.11.37	30.05.39	18.11.40	–	ChF	
21	S-34	2 FYP	198	350	29.11.37	02.09.39	29.03.41	–	ChF	

[1] Materials prepared at Leningrad, transferred by rail to Vladivostok, 1942/43 transferred by sea to the SF.
[2] Materials prepared at Leningrad, transferred by rail to Vladivostok, completed only during the war.
[3] Materials prepared at Nikolaev, transferred by rail to Vladivostok for completion. 1942/43 transferred by sea to SF.
[4] Built at Gorkii, transferred by docks on inland waterways to Leningrad, com. for the KBF; transferred in 1941 by inland waterways to SF.

Table A3 (contd.): Submarines of the *RKKF/VMF*, laid down or ordered, 1926–45

No.	Name	Order	Yard	Yard No.	Laid down	Launched	Commiss.	22.06.41	Fleet	Notes
Medium Submarines (*Series IX-bis*, 836t normal) *continued*										
22	S-13	3 FYP	112	263	19.10.38	25.04.39	31.07.41	–	KBF	
23	S-14	3 FYP	112 638	264	29.09.38	25.04.39	21.04.42	–	KSFl	1
24	S-103	3 FYP	112 638	265	13.11.38	25.04.39	09.07.42	–	KSFl	1
25	S-104	3 FYP	112 638	266	13.11.38	25.04.39	15.10.42	–	KSFl	1
26	S-15	3 FYP	112 638	271	10.08.39	24.04.40	20.12.42	–	KSFl	1
27	S-16	3 FYP	112 638	272	10.08.39	24.04.40	10.02.43	–	KSFl	2
28	S-17, Sovetskaya Svanetiya	3 FYP	112 638	273	10.08.39	24.04.40	20.04.45	–	KSFl	3
29	S-18	3 FYP	112 638	274	01.08.40	25.04.40	20.06.45	–	KSFl	3
30	S-19	3 FYP	196 638	132	30.09.39	14.03.41	21.02.44	–	KSFl	2
31	S-20	3 FYP	196 638	133	30.09.39	14.03.41	19.02.45	–	KSFl	4
32	S-21	3 FYP	196 638	134	31.12.39	25.04.41	28.03.46	–	KBF	5
33	S-22	3 FYP	112	295	25.06.40	02.05.41	25.05.46	–	KBF	6
34	S-23	3 FYP	112	296	25.06.40	02.05.41	27.06.47	–	KBF	6
35	S-24	3 FYP	112	297	25.06.40	02.05.41	18.12.47	–	KBF	6
36	S-25	3 FYP	112	298	25.06.40	02.05.41	29.03.48	–	KBF	6
37	S-26	3 FYP	112	299	25.06.40	02.05.41	29.03.48	–	KBF	6
38	S-27	3 FYP	112	300	31.12.40	07.41	–	–	KBF	7
39	S-35	3 FYP	198	360	23.02.40	17.07.41	05.02.48	–	ChF	8
40	S-36	3 FYP	198	361	23.02.40	–	–	–	ChF	9
41	S-37	3 FYP	198	362	28.11.40	–	–	–	ChF	9
42	S-38	3 FYP	198	363	22.02.41	–	–	–	ChF	9
43	S-28	3 FYP	112	312	03.41	–	–	–	KBF	10
44	S-29	3 FYP	112	313	03.41	–	–	–	KBF	10
45	S-30	3 FYP	112	314	03.41	–	–	–	KBF	10
46	S-39	3 FYP	112	315	41	–	–	–	–	11
47	S-40	3 FYP	112	316	41	–	–	–	–	11
48	S-41	3 FYP	112	317	<41>	–	–	–	–	12

[1] Built at Gorkii, transferred by docks on inland waterways to Astrakhan for commissioning. 1943 transferred to SF.
[2] Built at Gorkii, transferred to the Caspian Sea for completion. 1944 transferred to the SF.
[3] Built at Gorkii, transferred by inland waterways to the SF or the KBF.
[4] Building started at Leningrad, transferred by inland waterways to Baku, after completion planned for transfer to the SF, but finally transferred to the KBF.
[5] Building started at Leningrad, transferred by inland waterways to Baku, after completion planned for transfer to the KBF, then transferred to the SF and finally to the TOF.
[6] Building started at Leningrad, after launch transferred by inland waterways, completed only after the war. Planned first for the KBF, but then transferred to the SF and finally to the TOF.
[7] Building interrupted after launching, not completed after the war.
[8] After launch at Nikolaev in August 1941 transferred first to Sevastopol and then to Caucasian ports and laid up there. 1944 towed back to Sevastopol and Nikolaev and completed after the war.
[9] Building started at Nikolaev, but in August 1941 destroyed on the slips to avoid capture by the Germans.
[10] Building started at Gorkii, but in July 1941 work stopped and scrapped on the slips.
[11] Building probably just started at Gorkii, but work stopped in July 1941 and probably scrapped on the slips.
[12] Planned to be started in third quarter of 1941, but never begun. *S-14* and *S-16* additional names *Geroicheskij Sevastopol* and *Geroi Sovetskogo Soyuza Nursentov*.

Table A3 (contd.): Submarines of the *RKKF/VMF*, laid down or ordered, 1926–45

No.	Name	Order	Yard	Yard No.	Laid down	Launched	Commiss.	22.06.41	Fleet	Notes
Medium Submarines (*Series IX-bis*, 836t normal) *continued*
49	S-42	3 FYP	112	318	<41>	–	–	–	–	1
50	S-43	3 FYP	112	319	<41>	–	–	–	–	1
51	S-44	3 FYP	112	321	<41>	–	–	–	–	1
52	S-45	3 FYP	196	145	–	–	–	–	–	2
53	S-46	3 FYP	196	146	–	–	–	–	–	2

[1] Planned to be started in fourth quarter of 1941, but never begun.
[2] Planned to be built at Leningrad, but never begun and cancelled.

Medium Submarines (*Series X-bis*, 590t normal) (*SC = Shch*)

No.	Name	Order	Yard	Yard No.	Laid down	Launched	Commiss.	22.06.41	Fleet	Notes
1	SC-135	3 FYP	194 202	477	06.07.38	21.04.40	01.09.41	–	TOF	1
2	SC-136	3 FYP	194 202	478	06.07.38	27.04.40	05.09.41	–	TOF	1
3	SC-137	3 FYP	194 202	479	31.08.38	30.06.40	18.11.41	–	TOF	1
4	SC-138	3 FYP	194 202	480	28.10.38	22.07.40	30.12.41	–	TOF	2
5	SC-405	3 FYP	194	510	31.12.38	16.12.39	07.06.41	–	KBF	
6	SC-406	3 FYP	194	511	31.12.38	17.12.39	07.06.41	–	KBF	
7	SC-407	3 FYP	194	512	23.04.39	04.06.40	10.09.41	–	KBF	
8	SC-408	3 FYP	194	513	23.04.39	04.06.40	10.09.41	–	KBF	
9	SC-216	3 FYP	200	1085	23.07.39	30.05.40	17.08.41	–	ChF	
10	SC-409	3 FYP			40	–	–	–	SF	3
11	SC-410	3 FYP			40	–	–	–	SF	3
12	SC-411	3 FYP	194	546	31.10.39	31.05.41	21.07.45	–	KBF	4
13	SC-412	3 FYP	194	547	31.10.39	31.05.41	15.08.46	–	KBF	4
14	SC-413	3 FYP	194	552	29.06.40	28.06.41	–	–	KBF	5
15	SC-414	3 FYP	194	553	29.06.40	28.06.41	–	–	KBF	5

[1] Materials prepared at Leningrad, transferred by rail to Vladivostok for completion.
[2] Materials prepared at Leningrad, transferred by rail to Vladivostok for completion. On 18.07.42 destroyed by explosion of own torpedo.
[3] Building started at Murmansk, but cancelled on 19.07.41.
[4] After launch building interrupted and restarted after the war.
[5] After launch building stopped and not resumed after the war.

Minlaying Submarines (*Series XIII-bis*, 1,108t normal)

No.	Name	Order	Yard	Yard No.	Laid down	Launched	Commiss.	22.06.41	Fleet	Notes
1	L-20	3 FYP	189 402	302	10.06.38	14.04.40	28.08.42	–	SF	1
2	L-21	3 FYP	189	303	30.09.38	30.07.40	11.08.43	–	KBF	2
3	L-22	3 FYP	189 402	304	29.09.38	25.09.39	28.08.42	–	SF	1
4	L-23	3 FYP	198	353	23.10.38	29.04.40	31.10.41	86.90%	ChF	3
5	L-24	3 FYP	198	354	23.10.38	17.12.40	29.04.42	75.00%	ChF	2
6	L-25	3 FYP	198	355	23.10.38	26.02.41	–	63.20%	ChF	4

[1] Built at Leningrad, for completion transferred in 08–09.41 by Baltic–White Sea Canal to Molotovsk.
[2] Remained at Leningrad and completed for the KBF.
[3] Launched at Nikolaev, in June 1941 transferred to Sevastopol, in November 1941 to Batumi and Poti for completion.
[4] After launch on 11.08.41 transferred to Sevastopol, then to Tuapse and Poti, laid up in conservation. On the way for completion to Sevastopol sunk on 18.12.44 by a mine.

Table A3 (contd.): Submarines of the *RKKF/VMF*, laid down or ordered, 1926–45

No.	Name	Order	Yard	Yard No.	Laid down	Launched	Commiss.	22.06.41	Fleet	Notes
Small Submarines (*Series XII-bis*, 206t normal)									
1	M-174, ex-M-91	3 FYP	196	105	20.05.37	12.10.37	21.06.38	–	SF	1
2	M-175, ex-M-92	3 FYP	196	106	29.05.37	12.10.37	29.09.38	–	SF	1
3	M-176, ex-M-93	3 FYP	196	107	29.05.37	12.10.37	11.10.38	–	SF	1
4	M-94	3 FYP	196	118	25.12.38	11.09.39	20.11.39	–	KBF	
5	M-95	3 FYP	196	119	25.12.38	11.09.39	20.11.39	–	KBF	
6	M-98	3 FYP	196	120	22.06.39	15.04.40	10.07.40	–	KBF	
7	M-99	3 FYP	196	121	26.06.39	15.04.40	03.07.40	–	KBF	
8	M-102	3 FYP	196	136	31.05.40	12.10.40	05.12.40	–	KBF	
9	M-103	3 FYP	196	137	31.05.40	12.10.40	05.12.40	–	KBF	
10	M-96	3 FYP	112	247	26.07.37	20.09.38	06.10.39	–	KBF	2
11	M-49, ex-M-57	3 FYP	112	248	26.07.37	25.01.39	27.07.39	–	TOF	3
12	M-97	3 FYP	112	249	26.07.37	20.09.39	12.11.39	–	KBF	2
13	M-59	3 FYP	112	250	25.10.37	13.06.39	03.06.40	–	ChF	4
14	M-58	3 FYP	112	251	25.10.37	28.04.39	27.08.39	–	ChF	4
15	M-60	3 FYP	112	252	25.10.37	28.08.39	31.05.40	–	ChF	4
16	M-62	3 FYP	112	253	21.01.38	05.10.39	31.01.40	–	ChF	4
17	M-63	3 FYP	112	254	20.01.38	05.10.39	31.07.40	–	ChF	4
18	M-30	3 FYP	112	255	20.01.38	05.10.39	31.07.40	–	TOF	5
19	M-31	3 FYP	112	258	31.08.38	28.02.40	31.10.40	–	ChF	4
20	M-32	3 FYP	112	259	31.08.38	26.02.40	31.10.40	–	ChF	4
21	M-33	3 FYP	112	260	31.08.38	23.06.40	18.12.40	–	ChF	4
22	M-34	3 FYP	112	268	22.02.39	23.06.40	31.12.40	–	ChF	4
23	M-35	3 FYP	112	269	22.02.39	20.08.40	31.01.41	–	ChF	4
24	M-36	3 FYP	112	270	22.02.39	20.08.40	23.02.41	–	ChF	4
25	M-111	3 FYP	112 / 198	275	25.10.39	31.12.40 / 03.07.41	–	ChF	6
26	M-112	3 FYP	112 / 198	276	25.10.39	31.12.40 / 30.06.41	–	ChF	6
27	M-113	3 FYP	112 / 198	277	25.10.39	31.12.40 / 02.07.41	–	ChF	6
28	M-114	3 FYP	112 / 202	280	27.11.39	31.12.40 / 07.05.41	25.09.41	–	TOF	7
29	M-115	3 FYP	112 / 202	281	27.11.39	31.12.40 / 07.05.41	25.09.41	–	TOF	7
30	M-116	3 FYP	112 / 202	282	27.11.39	31.12.40 / 07.05.41	25.10.41	–	TOF	7
31	M-117	3 FYP	112 / 198	287	29.01.40	12.02.41 / 29.06.41	08.10.41	–	ChF	8
32	M-118	3 FYP	112 / 198	288	29.01.40	12.02.41 / 29.06.41	08.10.41	–	ChF	8
33	M-120	3 FYP	112 / 198	289	29.01.40	12.02.41 / 29.06.41	08.10.41	–	ChF	8

[1] Commissioned for the KBF, from 19.05–16.10.39 transferred by the Baltic–White Sea Canal to the SF.
[2] Transferred from Gorkii for commission with the KBF.
[3] Transferred from Gorkii for commission with the ChF, 1939 transferred by rail to the TOF.
[4] Transferred from Gorkii for commission with the ChF.
[5] Transferred from Gorkii by rail for commission with the TOF.
[6] Built in Gorkii, and transferred to Nikolaev for completion for the ChF.
[7] Built up to launch at Gorkii, transferred by rail to Vladivostok for re-launch and completion for the TOF.
[8] Built at Gorkii up to launch, transferred to Nikolaev for re-launch and completion for the ChF.

Table A3 (contd.): Submarines of the *RKKF/VMF*, laid down or ordered, 1926–45

No.	Name	Order	Yard	Yard No.	Laid down	Launched	Commiss.	22.06.41	Fleet	Notes
Small Submarines (*Series XII-bis*, 206t normal) *continued*										
34	M-119	3 FYP	112	290	28.05.40	26.06.41				
			402				22.10.42	–	SF	1
35	M-121	3 FYP	112	291	28.05.40	19.08.41				
			638				10.04.42	–	KSFl	2
36	M-122	3 FYP	112	292	28.05.40	12.02.41				
			402			01.08.42	31.10.42	–	SF	1
37	M-104 *Yaroslavs-skij Komsomolets*	3 FYP	112	301	30.09.40	10.04.41				
			402			24.09.42	10.02.43	–	SF	3
38	M-105 *Chelyabin-skij Komsomolets*	3 FYP	112	302	30.10.40	10.04.41				
			402			01.10.42	20.02.43	–	SF	3
39	M-106 *Leninskij Komsomolets*	3 FYP	112	303	30.10.40	10.04.41				
			402			09.10.42	13.03.43	–	SF	3
40	M-107 *Novosibir-skij Komsomolets*	3 FYP	112	304	30.10.40	16.04.41				
			402			06.12.42	24.07.43	–	SF	3
41	M-108	3 FYP	112	305	30.10.40	16.04.42				
			402			13.01.43	20.07.43	–	SF	3

[1] Built at Gorkii and transferred to Molotovsk for completion for the SF.
[2] Built at Gorkii and transferred to Baku for completion, commissioned with the KSFl, but 1942 transferred to SF.
[3] Built at Gorkii up to launch, transferred to Molotovsk for re-launch and completion for the SF.

No.	Name	Order	Yard	Yard No.	Laid down	Launched	Commiss.	22.06.41	Fleet	Notes
Small Submarines (*Series XV*, 281t normal; Project 96)										
1	M-200 *Mest*	3 FYP	196	122	31.03.40	17.07.41				
			638				20.03.43	–	SF	1
2	M-201	3 FYP	196	123	31.03.40	17.07.41				
			638				20.03.43	–	SF	1
3	M-202 *Rybnik Donbassa*	3 FYP	196	138	25.05.40	15.07.41				
			638				28.10.44	–	ChF	2
4	M-203 *Irkutskii Rybak*	3 FYP	196	139	31.10.40	07.07.41				
			638				28.10.44	–	ChF	2
5	M-204	3 FYP	196	140	31.10.40	27.08.46	25.06.47	–	ChF	3
6	M-205	3 FYP	196	141	30.12.40	10.11.46	27.07.47	–	KBF	3
7	M-206	3 FYP	196	142	30.12.40	26.04.47	30.09.47	–	KBF	3
8	M-210	3 FYP	196	150	–	–	–	–	–	4
9	M-211	3 FYP	196	151	–	–	–	–	–	4
10	M-212	3 FYP	196	152	–	–	–	–	–	4
11	M-213	3 FYP	196	153	–	–	–	–	–	4
12	M-214	3 FYP	112	306	03.04.41					
			402	113		24.09.46	14.08.47	–	SF	5

[1] Building started at Leningrad, transferred to Astrakhan and Baku for completion, in 04–05.43 to the SF.
[2] Building started at Leningrad, transferred to Astrakhan and Baku for completion, 1944 transferred to the ChF.
[3] Building started at Leningrad, laid up during the war, completed after the war for the ChF and the KBF.
[4] Planned to be built in Leningrad, but never laid down.
[5] Building started at Gorkii, transferred to Molotovsk and completed there after the war. From SF transferred to the KBF.

Table A3 (contd.): Submarines of the *RKKF/VMF*, laid down or ordered, 1926–45

No.	Name	Order	Yard	Yard No.	Laid down	Launched	Commiss.	22.06.41	Fleet	Notes
Small Submarines (*Series XV*, 281t normal; Project 96) *continued*										
13	M-215	3 FYP	112	307	30.04.41					
			402	114						
			196	289		22.07.47	31.10.47	–	KBF	1
14	M-216	3 FYP	112	308	30.04.41					
			402	115						
			196	290		27.07.47	30.09.47	–	KBF	1
15	M-217	3 FYP	112	309	30.04.41					
			402	116						
			196			26.07.47	10.09.47	–	KBF	1
16	M-218	3 FYP	112	310	30.04.41					
			402	117						
			196			10.09.47	10.11.47	–	KBF	1
17	M-219	3 FYP	112	311	30.04.41					
			402	118	–	–	–	–	–	2
18	M-220	3 FYP	112	312	–	–	–	–	–	3
19	M-221	3 FYP	112	313	–	–	–	–	–	3
20	M-222	3 FYP	112	314	–	–	–	–	–	3
21	M-223	3 FYP	Kolom	1	–	–	–	–	–	4
22	M-223	3 FYP	Kolom	2	–	–	–	–	–	4
23	M-225	3 FYP	Kolom	3	–	–	–	–	–	4
24	M-226	3 FYP	Kolom	4	–	–	–	–	–	4
25	M-227	3 FYP	Kolom	5	–	–	–	–	–	4
26	M-228	3 FYP	Kolom	6	–	–	–	–	–	4
27	M-229	3 FYP	Kolom	7	–	–	–	–	–	4
28	M-230	3 FYP	Kolom	8	–	–	–	–	–	4
29	M-231	3 FYP	Kolom	9	–	–	–	–	–	4
30	M-232	3 FYP	Kolom	10	–	–	–	–	–	4
31	M-233	3 FYP	Kolom	11	–	–	–	–	–	4
32	M-234	3 FYP	112	353	20.06.41					
			196			25.04.48	31.07.48	KBF	–	5
33	M-235	3 FYP	112	354	20.06.41					
			196			25.04.48	25.08.48	KBF	–	5
34	M-236	3 FYP	112	355	–	–	–	–	–	6

[1] Building started at Gorkii, transferred to Molotovsk but laid up during the war, transferred for completion to Leningrad.
[2] Building started at Gorkii, transferred to Molotovsk but laid up during the war. On transfer to Leningrad destroyed by accident.
[3] Planned to be built at Gorkii, but never laid down and cancelled.
[4] Planned to be built at Kolomna, but never laid down
[5] Building started at Gorkii, but laid up during the war. Transferred to Leningrad for completion.
[6] Planned to be built at Gorkii, but never laid down. A new *M-236* built after the war.

Table A3 (contd.): Submarines of the *RKKF/VMF*, laid down or ordered, 1926–45

No.	Name	Order	Yard	Yard No.	Laid down	Launched	Commiss.	22.06.41	Fleet	Notes
\multicolumn{11}{l}{**Submarines (*Series XVI*, 838t normal, Project 97)**}
1	*S-47*	3 FYP	196	154	20.02.41	–	–	–	–	1
2	*S-48*	3 FYP	196	155	20.02.41	–	–	–	–	1
3	*S-49*	3 FYP	196	156	20.02.41	–	–	–	–	1
4	*S-50*	3 FYP	196	157	–	–	–	–	–	2
5	*S-57*	3 FYP	196	158	–	–	–	–	–	2
6	*S-58*	3 FYP	198	371	22.04.41	–	–	–	–	3
7	*S-59*	3 FYP	198	372	22.04.41	–	–	–	–	3
8	*S-60*	3 FYP	198	373	22.04.41	–	–	–	–	3
9	*S-61*	3 FYP	198	374	–	–	–	–	–	4
10	*S-62*	3 FYP	198	375	–	–	–	–	–	4
11	–	–	–	–	–	–	–	–	–	5
12	–	–	–	–	–	–	–	–	–	5
13	–	–	–	–	–	–	–	–	–	5
14	–	–	–	–	–	–	–	–	–	5

[1] Laid down at Leningrad, but building stopped aftr the start of the war and not taken up again.
[2] Planned to be laid down at Leningrad, but cancelled after the start of the war.
[3] Laid down at Nikolaev, building stopped after the war started. In August 1941 destroyed on the slips to avoid capture by the Germans.
[4] Planned to be laid down at Nikolaev, but cancelled after the war started.
[5] Planned but not ordered and laid down.

Experimental Submarine (no *Projekt* number)

No.	Name	Order	Yard	Yard No.	Laid down	Launched	Commiss.	22.06.41	Fleet	Notes
1	*M-400*	–	112	551	39	–	–	–	–	1

[1] Building not completed.

Experimental Submarine (*Projekt 95*, 102t normal)

No.	Name	Order	Yard	Yard No.	Laid down	Launched	Commiss.	22.06.41	Fleet	Notes
1	*M-401*	–	196	135	16.11.39	31.05.41	23.11.42	–	KSFl	1

[1] Building started at Leningrad, transferred for completion to the Caspian Sea and used there for tests.

There were several projects studied and prepared during the war, but not ordered or laid down:

Projekt 98: Planned by yard 112, small submarine
Projekt 99: Minelaying submarine MZ, 1,230t normal for 60–80 mines. Two variants.
Projekt 101: Cruiser submarine KU of 1,550t normal.
Projekt 105: Two variants, small submarines of 250–300t normal and 100–110t normal.
Projekt 106: Medium submarine, 590t normal, follow on project for *SC*-classes.

Table A4: Lend-Lease vessels in the *VMF*, 1941–53

No.	Soviet Name	Nat.	ex-Name	Original Commission	Soviet Commission	Return to Former Nat.	Fleet, Decomm. § or Loss +	
Battleships (ex-British, 29,150t stdd.)								
1	Arkhangel'sk	Brit	Royal Sovereign	01.05.16	30.05.44	04.02.49	SF	
Cruisers (ex-US, 7,050t stdd.)								
1	Murmansk	US	Milwaukee	20.06.23	10.04.44	16.03.49	SF	
Destroyers (ex-British, ex-US, 1,190t stdd.)								
1	Derzkii	Brit US	Chelsea, ex-Crowninshield	06.08.19	16.07.44	27.06.49	SF	
2	Deyatel'nyi	Brit US	Churchill, ex-Herndon	17.04.20	16.07.44	–	SF 16.01.45+	
3	Doblestnyi	Brit US	Roxbourgh, ex-Foote	21.03.19	01.08.44	12.08.52	SF	
4	Dostojnyi	Brit US	St Albans, ex-Thomas	25.04.19	16.07.44	28.02.49	SF	
5	Druzhnyi	Brit US	Lincoln, ex-Yarnall	29.11.18	26.08.44	24.08.52	SF	
6	Zharkii	Brit US	Brighton, ex-Cowell	17.03.19	16.07.44	04.03.49	SF	
7	Zhguchii	Brit US	Leamington, ex-Twiggs	28.07.19	16.07.44	30.01.50	SF	
8	Zhestkii	Brit US	Georgetown, ex-Maddox	10.03.19	01.08.44	04.02.49	SF	
9	Zhivuchii	Brit US	Richmond, ex-Fairfax	06.04.18	16.07.44	24.06.49	SF	
Submarines (ex-British, *S*-class, 670t normal)								
1	V-1	Brit	Sunfish	13.03.37	30.05.44	–	SF 27.07.44+	
Submarines, (ex-British, *U*-class, 540t normal)								
1	V-2	Brit	Unbroken	29.01.42	30.05.44	10.02.49	SF	
2	V-3	Brit	Unison	19.02.42	30.05.44	10.02.49	SF	
3	V-4	Brit	Ursula	22.12.38	30.05.44	10.02.49	SF	
Patrol Ships (ex-US, 1,509t normal, Frigates, Storozhevoj korabl')								
1	EK-1	US	Charlottesville	10.04.44	12.07.45	17.02.50	TOF	[1]
2	EK-2	US	Long Beach	08.09.43	12.07.45	17.02.50	TOF	[2]
3	EK-3	US	Belfast	24.11.43	12.07.45	–	29.04.60§*	
4	EK-4	US	Machias	23.12.43	12.07.45	17.02.50	TOF	[2]
5	EK-5	US	San Pedro	23.10.43	12.07.45	17.02.50	TOF	[2]
6	EK-6	US	Glendyle	01.10.43	12.07.45	17.02.50	TOF	[3]
7	EK-7	US	Sandusky	18.04.44	12.07.45	17.02.50	TOF	[2]
8	EK-8	US	Coronado	17.11.43	12.07.45	17.02.50	TOF	[2]
9	EK-9	US	Allentown	24.03.44	12.07.45	17.02.50	TOF	[2]
10	EK-10	US	Ogden	20.12.43	12.07.45	17.02.50	TOF	[2]
11	EK-11	US	Tacoma	06.11.43	16.08.45	17.02.50	TOF	[4]

[1] 1952 transferred to Columbia.
[2] 1953 transferred to Japan.
[3] 1951 transferred to Thailand.
[4] 1951 transferred to South Korea.
* On 18.12.48 damaged in a storm, put into reserve, later used as base hulk.

Table A4 (contd.): Lend-Lease Vessels in the *VMF*, 1941–53

No.	Soviet Name	Nat.	ex-Name	Original Commiss.ion	Soviet Commission	Return to Former Nat.	Fleet, Decomm. § or Loss +	
Patrol Ships (ex-US, 1,509t stdd., Frigates, *Storozhevoj korabl'*)
12	*EK-12*	US	*Pasco*	15.04.44	16.08.45	17.02.50	TOF	1
13	*EK-13*	US	*Hoquiam*	06.05.44	16.08.45	17.02.50	TOF	2
14	*EK-14*	US	*Albuquerque*	20.12.43	16.08.45	17.02.50	TOF	1
15	*EK-15*	US	*Everett*	22.01.44	16.08.45	17.02.50	TOF	1
16	*EK-16*	US	*Sausalito*	04.03.44	16.08.45	17.02.50	TOF	2
17	*EK-17*	US	*Bisbee*	15.02.44	26.08.45	17.02.50	TOF	3
18	*EK-18*	US	*Rockford*	06.03.44	28.08.45	17.02.50	TOF	4
19	*EK-19*	US	*Muskogee*	16.03.44	26.08.45	17.02.50	TOF	4
20	*EK-20*	US	*Carson City*	24.03.44	28.08.45	17.02.50	TOF	1
21	*EK-21*	US	*Burlington*	03.04.44	28.08.45	17.02.50	TOF	3
22	*EK-22*	US	*Gallup*	19.02.44	28.08.45	17.02.50	TOF	5
23	*EK-25*	US	*Bayonne*	14.02.44	04.09.45	17.02.50	TOF	1
24	*EK-26*	US	*Gloucester*	44	09.09.45	17.02.50	TOF	1
25	*EK-27*	US	*Poughkeepsie*	08.09.44	09.09.45	17.02.50	TOF	1
26	*EK-28*	US	*Newport*	08.09.44	09.09.45	17.02.50	TOF	1
27	*EK-29*	US	*Bath*	08.09.44	09.09.45	17.02.50	TOF	1
28	*EK-30*	US	*Evansville*	01.11.44	09.09.45	17.02.50	TOF	1

[1] 1953 to Japan
[2] 1951 to South Korea
[3] 1952 to Colombia
[4] 1950 to South Korea
[5] 1951 to Thailand

No.	Soviet Name	Nat.	ex-Name	Original Commiss.ion	Soviet Commission	Return to Former Nat.	Fleet, Decomm. § or Loss +	
Minesweepers (ex-US *Admirable* class, 850t stdd.)
1	*T-111*	US	*Advocate*	06.43	25.06.43	11.07.56	SF	1
2	*T-112*	US	*Agent*	07.43	07.07.43	15.10.55	SF	2
3	*T-113*	US	*Alarm*	08.43	05.08.43	07.04.56	SF	
4	*T-114*	US	*Alchemy*	08.43	11.08.43	–	SF 13.08.44+	
5	*T-115*	US	*Apex*	08.43	17.08.43	01.09.55	SF	
6	*T-116*	US	*Arcade*	08.43	26.09.43	11.07.56	SF	3
7	*T-117*	US	*Arch*	06.09.43	09.09.43	15.10.55	SF	2
8	*T-118*	US	*Armada*	09.43	16.09.43	–	SF 13.08.44+	
9	*T-119*	US	*Aspire*	09.43	29.09.43	11.07.56	SF	2
10	*T-120*	US	*Assail*	10.43	05.10.43	–	SF 24.09.44+	
11	*T-271*	US	*Disdain*	26.12.44	21.05.45	07.08.48	TOF	4
12	*T-272*	US	*Fancy*	13.12.44	20.05.45	07.08.48	TOF	4
13	*T-273*	US	*Indicative*	26.05.44	20.05.45	07.08.48	TOF	4
14	*T-274*	US	*Marvel*	06.09.44	20.05.45	07.08.48	TOF	4
15	*T-275*	US	*Measure*	03.05.44	21.05.45	07.08.44	TOF	4
16	*T-276*	US	*Method*	10.07.44	20.05.45	07.08.48	TOF	4
17	*T-277*	US	*Mirth*	12.08.44	21.05.45	07.08.48	TOF	4
18	*T-278*	US	*Nucleus*	19.01.44	21.05.45	07.08.48	TOF	4

[1] 13.04.44 renamed *Starshii lejtenant Lekarev*, 1963 accommodation vessel, 1969 stricken.
[2] *T-112* 13.04.44 renamed *Starshii lejtenant Vladimirov*. 1966 transport vessels.
[3] 1963 used for rocket tests.
[4] 1948 transferred to 'Glavpromorrybprom', later stricken.

Table A4 (contd.): Lend-Lease Vessels in the *VMF*, 1941–53

No.	Soviet Name	Nat.	ex-Name	Original Commiss.ion	Soviet Commission	Return to Former Nat.	Fleet, Decomm. § or Loss +	
Minesweepers (ex-US *Admirable* class, 850t stdd.) *(continued)*								
19	T-279	US	Palisade	09.03.44	20.05.45	21.09.51	TOF	1
20	T-280	US	Penetrate	31.03.44	21.05.45	07.08.48	TOF	2
21	T-281	US	Peril	20.04.44	21.05.45	03.12.56	TOF	3
22	T-282	US	Rampart	18.11.44	20.05.45	07.08.48	TOF	2
23	T-283	US	Candid	31.10.43	16.08.45	28.06.47	TOF	4
24	T-284	US	Caution	10.02.44	16.08.45	11.07.56	TOF	3
25	T-285	US	Bond	30.08.43	16.08.45	03.12.56	TOF	3
26	T-331	US	Admirable	20.04.43	17.05.45	28.06.47	TOF	4
27	T-332	US	Adopt	31.05.43	17.05.45	27.02.56	TOF	3
28	T-333	US	Astute	17.01.43	17.05.45	27.03.56	TOF	3
29	T-334	US	Augury	17.03.44	17.05.45	27.03.56	TOF	3
30	T-335	US	Barrier	10.05.44	17.05.45	01.09.55	TOF	5
31	T-336	US	Bombard	31.05.44	17.05.45	04.03.53	TOF	6
32	T-337	US	Caravan	21.01.44	17.08.45	03.12.56	TOF	3
33	T-338	US	Captivate	30.12.43	16.08.45	03.12.56	TOF	3
34	T-339	US	Capable	05.12.43	16.08.45	03.12.56	TOF	3

[1] 1951 put into reserve, 1957 stricken
[2] 1948 transferred to *Glavpromorrybprom*, later stricken.
[3] 1956 Firewatcher vessel, 1960 stricken.
[4] 1947 put into reserve and used as hydrographic vessel, 1958 stricken.
[5] 1955 put into reserve, Firewatcher vessel.
[6] 1953 put into reserve, 1963 stricken.

Table A5: Soviet warships and submarines lost, 1939–45

NORTHERN FLEET

Destroyers

1	20.07.41	*Stremitel'nyi*	Off Ekaterinskii gavan' near Polyarnoe sunk by German Ju-87 A/C of 12/L.G.1.
2	20.11.42	*Sokrushitel'nyi*	In 73 30 N/43 00 E by a broken back in heavy seas, wreck sunk on 22.11.42.
3	16.01.45	*Deyatel'nyi*	In 69 04 N/36 40 E by torpedo of the German submarine *U 956*.

Submarines

1	20.10.39	*Shch-424*	In Kola-Bay by collision with trawler *RT-43*. April 1970, raised and scrapped.
2	13.11.40	*D-1*	In 70 52 N/48 45 E Motovskij-Bay by diving accident.
3	10.01.42	*M-175*	In 70 09 N/32 50 E Varanger Fjord by torpedo of German submarine *U 584*.
4	08.04.42	*Shch-421*	In 71 06.8 N/26 53 E damaged by German flanking mine barrage *Hannelore*, laid on 18.03.42 by minelayer *Ulm*, sunk next day by Soviet submarine *K-22* after taking off the crew.
5	24.04.42	*Shch-401*	Off the Varanger Peninsula lost due to an unknown reason, possibly on a mine of a German flanking barrage or in a diving accident. The assumed loss by an erroneous attack by the Soviet TKA 13 is not true; this attack was directed against the German U-boat *U 454* which was slightly damaged.
6	12.05.42	*K-23*	After a missing attack against a German convoy *K 23* surfaced some distance from the German A/S vessels *UJ 1101*, *UJ 1109* and *UJ 1110* and tried to escape in a gun battle until it was forced to dive by arriving German airplanes. The A/S vessels closed again and in 71 52 N/27 35 E started D/C attacks. In a D/C carpet from *UJ 1109* there appeared oil and wreckage and *UJ 1110* dropped additional D/Cs until the sinking of the submarine was clear by surfacing papers and books. The sinking took place about 63 miles N of Nordkyn.
7	10.06.42	*D-3*	Departed on 11.06 for a patrol off the Tanafjord and sank between this date and 15.06. Very probably on a German mine of the flanking barrage *III*, laid on 24.05 by the minelayer *Ulm*.
8	04.07.42	*M-176*	Departed on 20.06 for a patrol in the Varangerfjord and sank between this date and 04.07 on a German mine of the flanking barrage *V*, laid on 10.06 by the minelayers *Ostmark* and *Ulm*, or by *M16* on 03.07 or *M23* on 04.07 with D/Cs.
9	07.08.42	*M-173*	Departed on 06.08 for a patrol off Vardö and sank probably between 07 and 14.08 off Vardo by a German mine of the flanking barrage *V*, laid on 10.06 by the minelayers *Ostmark* and *Ulm*. Or else there was a last signal by *M-173* on 16.8.42 and the boat was lost after this date, possibly by D/Cs of the German minesweeper *M11*.
10	01?09.42	*K-2*	Departed on 25.08 for a patrol off the Tanafjord and sank probably between 01 and 07.09 off the Tanafjord on a German mine, probably of the flanking barrage *III* laid on 24.05 by the minelayer *Ulm*.
11	08?11.42	*M-121*	Departed on 08.11 for a patrol in the Varangerfjord. Sunk between 08.11 and 14.11 in Varanger Fjord probably by a German mine of a flanking barrage laid by the minelayers *Ostmark* amd *Ulm*.
12	08?02.43	*K-22*	Departed with *K-3* on 04.02 for a group operation between Vardö and Nordkyn. Sunk probably between 08.02 and 14.02 on a German mine of the flanking barrage *NW 10* laid on 25.01.43 by the minelayer *Skagerrak*.
13	21.03.43	*K-3*	Departed on 13.03 and sunk between North Cape and Nordkyn by D/C attack of the German A/S vessels *UJ 1102*, *UJ 1106*, and *UJ 1111*, which delivered the fatal attack.
14	14.05.43	*M-122*	In 69 56 N/32 57 E10, off Cape Zyp Navolok by an attack of two German FW-190 fighter bombers of 14/J.G.5.
15	05.07.43	*M-106*	In 70.30.8 N/30.58 E located by a German A/S group and sunk by three D/C attacks from *UJ 1206* and *UJ 1217* and by ramming by *UJ1217*.
16	14?07.43	*Shch-422*	Departed on 30.06 for a patrol between Vardö and Makkaur. Sunk probably between 02 and 14.07 on a German mine of a flanking barrage laid by the minelayer *Skagerrak*.

Table A5 (contd.): Soviet warships and submarines lost, 1939–45

NORTHERN FLEET *continued*

17	09?09.43	*K-1*	Departed on 05.09 for a patrol off Cape Zhelaniya against German U-boats. Sunk between 09 and 21.09 N of Cape Zhelaniya by a mine (from German minefield *Zarin*, laid by cruiser *Admiral Hipper* and destroyers *Z 23*, *Z 28*, *Z 29*, *Z 30* and *Richard Beitzen* on 29.06.42??) or a diving accident.
18	02?10.43	*M-172*	Departed 01.10 for a patrol in the Varangerfjord. Sunk probably between 02 and 11.10 on a German mine of a flanking barrage *Schlußakkord*, laid on 07.09 by the minelayer *Roland*.
19	03?10.43	*Shch-403*	Departed 01.10. for a patrol between Tana- and Kongsfjord. Sunk between 04 and 17.10 probably off Tanafjord by a German mine of one of the flanking barrages laid on 03 or 19.08 by the minelayer *Roland*.
20	18?10.43	*M-174*	Departed on 14.10 for a patrol in the Varangerfjord. Sunk between 18 and 24.10 probably on a German mine of one of the flanking barrages *NW 32* or *NW 33*, laid on 23.07 or 11.08 by the minelayers *Kaiser* and *Ostmark*.
21	06?12.43	*S-55*	Departed 04.12 for a patrol off Nordkyn and Tanafjord. Sunk between 06 and 23.12 off Cape Nordkyn and Tanafjord by a German mine of a flanking barrage *Koffer gepackt*, laid on 28.06 by the minelayer *Roland*.
22	28.02.44	*M-108*	Departed on 21.02 for a patrol off the Kongsfjord. Sunk on 28.02 off Kongsfjord by a mine of a German flanking barrage, probably laid by the minelayer *Roland* in autumn 1943.
23	10.03.44	*S-54*	Departed on 03.03. Sunk on or after 10.03 (last signal) probably off Bosfjord or Cape Berlevaag on a German mine, laid probably in autumn 1943 by the minelayer *Roland*.
24	27.07.44	*V-1*	Sunk on transfer to the Northern Fleet in 64 34 N/61 16 E by the British *Liberator* A/C 'V' of the RAF squadron 86 in error.
25	21.09.44	*Shch-402*	Sunk in 71 05 N/26 19 E off Gamvik in error by torpedo of one of three Soviet A/C of Mine-Corp Regt.

Patrol Ships

1	11.08.41	*SKR 27/Zhemchug*	Between Mys Svyatoj Nos and Mys Kanin Nos by submarine torpedo of the German *U 451*.
(2)	12.05.42	*SKR-29/Brilliant*	In Iokanka by bombs of German aircraft. Salvaged on 12.09.42, repaired and recommissioned 1944.
(3)	08.12.42	*SKR-15/Smerch*	Sunk by attack of German aircraft at Vaenga, later raised and restored to service in 1943.
4	23.09.44	*SKR-29/Brilliant*	In 76 10 N/87 45 E by torpedo of the German submarine *U 957*.

Minesweepers

1	12.08.44	*T-118*/ex-USS *Armada*	In 73 22 N/66 35 E by torpedo from the German submarine *U 365*.
2	12.08.44	*T-114*/ex-USS *Alchemy*	In 73 22 N/66 35 E by torpedo from the German submarine *U 365*.
3	24.09.44	*T-120*/ex-USS *Assail*	In 75 15 N/81 30 E by torpedo from the German submarine *U 739*.
4	22.11.44	*T-109*/ex-HMS *MMS-203*	Lost in a storm off Sangeiskij Island.

Table A5 (contd.): Soviet warships and submarines lost, 1939–45

BALTIC FLEET

Battleships
1	23.09.41	*Marat*	Off Kronstadt by bombs of German Ju-87 dive bomber of III/St.G.2. Partially repaired and used as stationery gunfire battery *Petropavlovsk*.

Cruisers
1	18.09.41	*Petropavlovsk* ex-Germ *Lützow*	Was not commissioned. In Leningrad by German Army gunfire. 1943 salvaged but not repaired, used as accommodation hulk *Tallinn*.

Leaders
(1)	23.09.41	*Minsk*	In Kronstadt by bombs of German aircraft of 'Luftflotte 1'. Salvaged in November 1942 and recommissioned.

Destroyers
1	23.06.41	*Gnevnyi*	In 59 26 N/22 20 E on a mine of the German barrage *Apolda*, laid by the German minelayers *Tannenberg*, *Brummer* and *Hansestadt Danzig*.
2	23.06.41	*Lenin*	In Libau scuttled to avoid capture by the Germans.
3	19.07.41	*Serdityi*	In 58.50.9 N/23.13 E by German aircraft with bombs.
4	27.07.41	*Smelyi*	Near Cape Kolkasrags, Riga Bay, by torpedo of German MTB *S 54*.
5	08.08.41	*Karl Marks*	In Karalakht Bay near Loksa by bombs of German Ju-88 bomber of K.Fl.Gr.806.
6	18.08.41	*Statnyi*	In 58.53.5 N/23.11.1 E by a mine laid by the German 2nd MTB Flotilla.
7	24.08.41	*Engel's*	In 59.48.8 N/25.31 E by a mine of the *Juminda/Valkjärvi* barrages, laid by the German minelayers *Cobra*, *Kaiser* and *Konigin Luise*, and the Finnish minelayers *Riilahti* and *Ruotsinsalmi*.
8	28.08.41	*Yakov Sverdlov*	Near Mokhni by a mine of the *Juminda/Valkjärvi* barrages
9	28.08.41	*Skoryi*	Mokhni – Cape Juminda by a mine of the *Juminda/Valkjärvi* barrages.
10	28.08.41	*Kalinin*	Mokhni – Cape Juminda by a mine of the *Juminda/Valkjärvi* barrages.
11	28.08.41	*Volodarskii*	Mokhni – Cape Juminda by a mine of the *Juminda/Valkjärvi* barrages.
12	28.08.41	*Artem*	Mokhni – Cape Juminda by a mine of the *Juminda/Valkjärvi* barrages.
(13)	21.09.41	*Steregushchii*	In Kronstadt by bombs of German aircraft of Ju 87 Stukas of St.G.2. Salvaged in 1944 and recommissioned.
13	05.11.41	*Smetlivyi*	In 59.41.6 N/24.10 E by a mine of the *Corbetha*-barrage, laid by the German minelayers *Cobra*, *Kaiser* and *Konigin Luise*.
14	14.11.41	*Surovyi*	Near Keri by a mine of the new *Juminda* barrages, laid by the German minelayers *Cobra* and *Kaiser*.
15	14.11.41	*Gordyi*	In 59.47 N/25.09 E by a mine of the *Corbetha* barrage.

Submarines
1	02.01.40	*S-2*	In Södra Kvarken on a Finnish mine laid by minelayer *Lovkii*.
2	23.06.41	*M-78*	In 57 28 N/21 17 E by torpedo of the German submarine *U 144*.
3	23.06.41	*S-1*	In Libau scuttled to avoid capture by the Germans.
4	23.06.41	*Ronis*	In Libau scuttled to avoid capture by the Germans. 27.10.41 raised and scrapped.
5	23.06.41	*Spidola*	In Libau scuttled to avoid capture by the Germans.
6	23.06.41	*M-71*	In Libau scuttled to avoid capture by the Germans.
7	23.06.41	*M-80*	In Libau scuttled to avoid capture by the Germans.
8	24.06.41	*S-3*	Off Cape Uzhava by D/Cs and hand grenades of German MTBs *S35* and *S60*.
9	26.06.41	*M-83*	Off Libau scuttled. From 05.08 to 27.10.1941 raised by Germans and scrapped.
10	28?06.41	*S-10*	Departed 23.06 for a patrol in the Danzig Bay. Sunk on 28/29.06 by unknown cause. (Not by *S 59* and *S 60*, which operated off the Irben Strait).
11	28.06.41	*M-99*	In 59 20 N/21 12 E, off Dagö Island by torpedo of the German submarine *U 149*.

Table A5 (contd.): Soviet warships and submarines lost, 1939–45

BALTIC FLEET *continued*

12	01.07.41	*M-81*	In 59.08.6 N/22.58.1 E by mine, laid by the German minelayer *Brummer*.
13	21.07.41	*M-94*	In 58.51 N/22.02 E by torpedo of German submarine *U 140*.
14	02.08.41	*S-11*	In 58 41 N/22 25 E, in the Soelo-Sund by a mine laid by the German 2nd S-Flotilla.
15	28.08.41	*S-5*	Departed Tallinn on 28.08. Sunk in 59 49 N/25 32 E between Mokhni and Cape Juminda by a mine (see above).
16	28.08.41	*Shch-301*	Departed on 11.08 for a patrol off Landsort. On the return voyage between 28/29.08 sunk, in 56 10 N/16 38 E on a mine of the *Juminda* barrage during the evacuation of Tallinn.
17	30?08.41	*S-6*	Departed on 22.08 for a patrol off Karlskrona. Sunk probably between 28 and 30.08 on the return voyage on a mine 10 miles east off the southern tip of Öland, wreck found in 1999.
18	25.08.41	*M-103*	Departed on 13.08 for the western part of the Finnish Gulf. Sunk between 25.08 and 28.08 on a mine in 59 13 N/23 09 E. Wreck located in 1999.
19	09.09.41	*P-1*	Departed on 10.09 for a transport mission. Sunk probably between 10 and 17.09.41 in Finnish Gulf by a mine.
20	21 ?09.41	*Shch-319*	Departed on 20.09 from Lavansaari for a patrol off Libau, but sunk on the way out probably on 22/23.09 on a mine in the Finnish Gulf.
21	23.09.41	*M-74*	In Kronshtadt in general repair. Sunk by bombs of German aircraft of 'Luftflotte 1', salvaged 1942, but not repaired and decommissioned.
22	12.10.41	*S-8*	Departed 11.10 for a patrol. Sunk probably on the way out between 12 and 14.10 by a mine W of Keri.
23	12.10.41	*Shch-322*	Departed on 10.10. Probably sunk on 11.10 after a collision with the patrol vessel *MO-310* or on the way out on a mine in Finnish Gulf.
24	30.10.41	*KALEV*	Departed on 16.10 for a mine operation off Tallinn. Sunk probably on 30.10/01.11 near Naissaari by a mine of the *Corbetha* barrage (see above).
25	08.11.41	*L-1*	In Leningrad by German Army gunfire, salvaged 1944 but not repaired. 1949 scrapped.
26	05?11.41	*Shch-324*	Departed on 02.11 for a patrol in the area of Utö. Sunk probably between 05 and 07.11 in the western part of the Finnish Gulf by a mine, possibly on the *Apolda* barrage (see above).
27	14.11.41	*L-2*	Departed on 10.11 on a minelaying mission in the Danzig Bay. Sunk near Keri by a mine of the newly laid *Juminda* barrage (see above).
28	14.11.41	*M-98*	Departed on 10.11 for a patrol off Tallinn. Sunk in 59.47 N/25.09 E by a mine of the new laid *Juminda* barrage.
29	13.06.42	*Shch-405*	Near Seiskaari by accident or a mine.
30	15.06.42	*M-95*	In 60.05 N/27.02 E by a mine, or Finnish A/C 5B-1 of 1/6 Group.
31	15.07.42	*Shch-317*	Returning from a successful patrol off southern Sweden damaged on 12.07 by a mine in the western part of the Finnish Gulf, sunk on 15.07 by the Finnish minelayer *Ruotsinsalmi* and the patrol boat *VMV 16*, supported by aircraft with DCs. But may also have been sunk by D/Cs of the Swedish destroyer *Stockholm* at 57.52 N/16.55 E.
32	02.09.42	*M-97*	Departed on 25.08. Sunk probably on 02/03.09 in 59 50 N/24 30 E Suursaari on a mine of the *Seeigel* barrage. 1997/98 wreck located.
33	03.10.42	*Shch-320*	Departed on 04.10 for a patrol in the area of Bornholm. But probably sunk between 04 and 06.10 on a mine between Suursaari and Kallbadagrund.
34	14?10.42	*Shch-302*	Departed on 10.10 for a patrol in the area of Cape Ristna. But sunk probably on a mine between 11 and 14.10 in the area of Pakri, or possibly also by a Finnish SB-2 aircraft.
35	15.10.42	*Shch-311*	Departed on 13.10 for a special operation. Sunk off Porkkala by D/Cs of the Finnish patrol boat *VMV 15*.
36	27.10.42	*Shch-308*	After announcing her return from a patrol off Cape Ristna on 27.10 attacked, rammed and sunk by the Finnish submarine *Iku Turso*.
37	21.10.42	*S-7*	In 59.50.1 N/19.32 E by torpedo of the Finnish submarine *Vesihiisi*.
38	14?11.42	*Shch-304*	Departed on 06.11 for an operation off Cape Ristna. Sunk probably between 14 and 21.11 in the Finnish Gulf on a mine.

Table A5 (contd.): Soviet warships and submarines lost, 1939–45

BALTIC FLEET *continued*

39	05.11.42	*Shch-305*	In 60 09 N/19 11 E, in the Aalands Sea, by torpedo of the Finnish submarine *Vetehinen*.
40	12.11.42	*Shch-306*	After an operation between Cape Ristna and Danzig Bay sunk between 12 and 14.11 probably on the return voyage in the Finnish Gulf near Nargon on a mine.
41	12.42	*M-72*	In Kronshtadt during repairs by German gunfire. 1943 salvaged, but not re-commissioned.
42	01.05.43	*Shch-323*	In the Morskoi Canal by a mine of the German operation *Brutmaschine*. 1944 salvaged, but not repaired.
43	24.05.43	*Shch-408*	On 22.05 near Vaindlo heavily damaged by D/Cs of the Finnish minelayer *Rülahti* and 6 VMV patrol boats. On 23/24.05 again depthcharged by the minelayer *Ruotsinsalmi*. The wreck again depthcharged by KFKs of the German 31.M/S Flotilla.
44	01.06.43	*Shch-406*	Near Porkkala-Udd by D/Cs of German landing vessels of the 24 F-Flotilla, supported by Ar-196 aircraft and finally by the Finnish minelayer *Rülahti*.
45	15?08.43	*S-12*	Departed on 28.07. Sunk between 01 and 15.08, probably on a mine near Porkkala Udd.
46	13.08.43	*S-9*	Departed on 30.07 and sunk between 13.08 and 05.09, probably near Tytärsaari by a mine or off Neugrund by D/Cs of the German 24 L Flotilla and the 31 M/S Flotilla.
47	07.09.44	*M-96*	On 7 or 8.09 in Narva Bay by a mine.
48	04.01.45	*S-4*	In 54 55 N/19 39 E in Danzig Bay by accidental ramming of the German torpedoboat *T 3*.

Patrol Ships

1	28.08.41	*Sneg*	Off Cape Juminda by a mine of the *Juminda-Valkjärvi* barrages.
2	28.08.41	*Tsiklon*	Off Cape Juminda by a mine of the *Juminda-Valkjärvi* barrages.
(3)	22.09.41	*Vikhr*	In Kronshtadt by bombs of German aircraft of 'Luftflotte 1'. Salvaged in 1942 and repaired with machinery of *Purga*.
3	03.12.41	*T-297/Virsaitis*	In 59.54.5 N/25.29 E by a mine. of the *Corbetha* barrage
4	24.08.42	*Burya*	In 59.49 N/27.30 E by a mine.
5	01.09.42	*Purga*	In the Ladoga Sea sunk. Raised and machinery transferred to repair *Vikhr*. Not repaired.

Minesweepers

1	24.06.41	*T-208/Shkiv*	In 59 06 N/ 23 01 E by torpedo of the German MTBs *S 35* and *S 60*.
2	01.07.41	*T-298/Imanta*	Sunk on a mine in the Tagalakht Bay.
3	06.07.41	*T-216*	In 59.09.5 N/22.37.5 E by a German mine.
4	30.07.41	*T-201/Zaryad*	In 59.06 N/22.00 E by German mine.
5	03.08.41	*T-212/Shtag*	In 58.39 N/22.23.5 E by a German mine, probably laid by the 2nd S Flotilla.
6	11.08.41	*T-213/Krambol*	In 59.49.4 N/25.36 E by a mine of the *Juminda-Valkjärvi* barrages.
7	14.08.41	*T-202/Buj*	Near Cape Juminda by a mine of the *Juminda-Valkjärvi* barrages.
8	18.08.41	*T-51/Pirmunas*	Off Moonsund by torpedo of the German MTB *S 58*.
9	24.08.41	*T-209/Knekht*	In 59.47.3 N/25.16.9 E by a mine of the *Juminda-Valkjärvi* barrages.
10	24.08.41	*T-214/Bugel'*	In 59.46.8 N/25.17.2 E by a mine of the *Juminda-Valkjärvi* barrages.
11	25.10.41	*T-203/Patron*	Near Keri by a mine, probably of the new *Juminda* barrage.
12	14.11.41	*T-206/Verp*	Near Keri by a mine, probably of the new *Juminda* barrage.
13	25.11.41	*T-56/Klyuz*	Sunk on a mine east of Hanko.
14	24.08.42	*T-204/Fugas*	In 59.47 N/27.28 E by a mine.
15	02.10.42	*T-57/Udarnik*	Sunk on a mine off Seiskari.
16	11.01.45	*T-33/Korall* (ex-*T-76*)	Near Aegna by torpedo of German submarine *U 745*(?).

Gunboats

(1)	27.09.41	*Pioner*	Sunk at Kronshtadt by air attack, raised on 29.10.43 and recommissioned 30.12.45.
(2)	16.11.42	*Krasnoe Znamya*	In Lavansaari by torpedoes of Finnish MTBs *Syoksy*, *Vinuri* and *Vinha*, salvaged in 1943, repaired and modernized, 1944 recommissioned.

Table A5 (contd.): Soviet warships and submarines lost, 1939–45

BLACK SEA FLEET

Cruisers
1	12.11.41	*Chervona Ukraina*	In Sevastopol by bombs of German Ju-97 dive bombers of II/St.G.77 aircraft.

Leaders
1	26.06.41	*Moskva*	Off Konstanza by gunfire from German railway battery 'Tirpitz' or by torpedo of Soviet submarine *Shch-206* in error.
2	02.07.42	*Tashkent*	Off Novorossijsk by bombs of German aircraft of I/K.G.76 damaged, towed by *Bditel'nyj* into Novorossijsk and sunk there at the pier.
3	06.10.43	*Kharkov*	W of Tuapse by bombs of German Ju-87 dive bombers of III/St.G.3.

Destroyers
1	01.07.41	*Bystryi*	Off Sevastopol by a ground mine laid by a German aircraft of II/K.G.64. Salvaged but dismantled.
2	21.09.41	*Frunze*	In 46.10.3 N/31.29.7 E by bombs of German Ju-87 dive bombers of St.G.77.
3	06.03.42	*Smyshlennyi*	In 45.01.5 N/36.46 E by a mine.
4	03.04.42	*Shaumyan*	In 44.33.9 N/37.59.1 E ran aground in a snowstorm after its crew had become intoxicated during shore leave in Novorossijsk.
5	14.05.42	*Dzerzhinskii*	In 44.27 N/33.19 E by a mine.
6	08.06.42	*Sovershennyi*	In Sevastopol by bombs of a German Ju 87 dive bomber of II/St.G.77 (damaged before on 30.09 and 12.11.41 by bombs of German aircraft and in repair).
7	10.06.42	*Svobodnyi*	At Sevastopol by bombs of a German Ju 88 bombers.
8	26.06.42	*Bezuprechnyi*	40 miles S of Cape Aju-Dag by bombs of a German Ju 88 aircraft of Air Commander South.
9	02.07.42	*Bditel'nyi*	In Novorossijsk by bombs of German bombers of I/K.G.76.
10	06.10.43	*Besposhchadnyi*	W of Tuapse by bombs of German Ju-87 dive bombers of III/St.G.3.
11	06.10.43	*Sposobnyi*	W of Tuapse by bombs of German Ju-87 dive bombers of III/St.G.3

Submarines
1	26.06.41	*Shch-206*	Off Konstanza possibly in error sunk by D/Cs of the Soviet destroyer *Soobrazitel'nyj*, or sunk on 03.07.41 on a mine of a flanking barrage off Konstanza.
2	18.10.41	*M-58*	Departed 16.10. Sunk between 18 and 21.10 off Konstanza by a mine of a flanking barrage, laid by the Romanian minelayers *Amiral Murgescu*, *Regele Carol I* and *Dacia*, or on 18.10.10 by Bulgar A/C 10.5 miles off Cape Shabla.
3	28.10.41	*M-59*	Departed 26.10. Sunk between 28.10 and 01.11 off Sulina by a mine of a flanking barrage laid by the three mentioned minelayers.
4	30.10.41	*M-34*	Departed 28.10. Sunk between 30.10 and 03.11 off Konstanza by a mine of a flanking barrage laid by the three mentioned minelayers.
5	12.11.41	*S-34*	Departed 08.11. Sunk on 12 or 13.11 off Cape Emine by a mine of a flanking barrage, laid by the minelayers *Amiral Murgescu* and *Dacia*.
6	16.11.41	*Shch-211*	Departed 14.11. Sunk between 16 and 30.11 off Varna by a mine of a flanking barrage, laid by the minelayers *Amiral Murgescu* and *Dacia*.
7	06.12.41	*Shch-204*	Departed 25.11. Sunk probably on 06.12.41 in 42 53,7 N/28 03,6 E by Ar-196 A/C of Bulgarian Sq. 161. Wreck located on 04.06.83.
8	15.03.42	*Shch-210*	Departed 12.03. Sunk probably on 13.03 in 43.03 N/35.25 E by an attack of an He-111 airplane of KG.100. There is also a report of a sinking between 15 and 28.03 off Cape Shabla by D/Cs of the Bulgarian patrol boats *Belomorets* and *Chernomorets* or on a mine of a flanking barrage, laid by the Romanian minelayers.
9	20.06.42	*Shch-214*	Off Cape Aitodor by torpedo of the Italian *MAS 571*.

Table A5 (contd.): Soviet warships and submarines lost, 1939–45

BLACK SEA FLEET continued

10	26.06.42	S-32	In 44 12 N/33 48 sunk by attack of an He-111 A/C of 2/KG 100 S of Aju Dag (see destroyer *Bezuprechnyj*).
11	26.06.42	D-6	At Sevastopol during general repair scuttled to avoid capture.
12	26.06.42	A-1	At Sevastopol during general repair scuttled to avoid capture.
13	24.08.42	M-33	Departed 19.08. Sunk at 46.20.3 N/30.54.3 by a mine of the field S.33, laid by *Amiral Murgescu* and *Dacia*. 07.51 raised and scrapped.
14	26.08.42	Shch-208	Departed 21.08. Sunk between 26.08 and 08.09 between Konstanza and Portitskoe Girlo by a mine of a flanking barrage, probably laid by *Amiral Murgescu* and *Dacia*. 1980 wreck located.
15	26.09.42	M-60	Departed 15.09. Sunk at 46.20.3 N/30.54.3 E by a mine of the field S.33 (see above). 07.51 raised and scrapped.
16	01.10.42	M-118	In 45 46 N/29 34,8 E off Cape Burnas by D/Cs of the Romanian gunboats *Stihi* and *Ghiculescu* or by a mine of *Sperre 32*.
17	14.10.4	Shch-213	5.5 miles east of Portitskii Girlo between Konstanza and Olinka by D/Cs of the German A/S vessel *Xanten*.
18	15.12.42	L-24	Departed 10.12. Sunk between 15 and 29.12 off Cape Shabla by a mine of a flanking barrage *S.15*. 1988 wreck located.
19	17.12.42	M-31	In the Gibriani Bay by D/Cs of the German A/S vessel *Xanten*.
20	19.12.42	Shch-212	Departed 01.12. Sunk between 11 and 19.12, probably by a mine of *Sperre 44* S of Fidonisi Island, laid on 29.10.42.
21	28.08.43	Shch-203	Departed 20.08. Sunk probably on 26.08 by torpedo of the Italian midget submarine *CB-4* in 45.18.7 N/32.46.6 E.
(22)	22.09.43	M-51	At Ochemchiri by an accident, salvaged on 25.09 and repaired.
23	04.11.43	A-3	At Kalamitskij Bay by D/Cs of German A/S vessel *Schiff 9* or on a mine.
24	04.12.43	D-4	At Kalamitskij Bay by D/Cs of German A/S vessels *UJ 103* and *UJ 102*.
25	04.01.44	M-36	At Kobuleti in 41.58.8 N/41.40 E by accident.
26	30.01.44	L-23	Probably sunk on the return voyage from Karkilitskii Bay by bombs of a German BV-138 reconnaissance plane of AG 125 80 miles S W of Tuapse.
27	16.02.44	Shch-216	In 44 36,5 N/32 04 4 E West of Cape Tarkhankut by D/Cs of German A/S vessel *UJ 104*.
28	18.04.44	L-6	Possibly at 43.25 N/31.32 E by D/Cs of German A/S vessel *UJ 103*.
29	20.02.45	TS-2 (ex-Rom. *Rechinul*)	Sunk at Poti by an accidental explosion of its own torpedo. Raised 28.02.45 and returned to service.

Minesweepers

1	12.09.41	T-402/*Minrep*	Off Feodosiya by a German magnetic mine.
2	05.01.42	T-405/*Vrzyvatel'*	Near Yevpatoriya by German gunfire of an Army battery and beached.
3	13.06.42	T-413	Off Cape Feolent by bombs of a German Ju-88 bomber.
4	27.02.43	T-403/*Gruz*	In 44.39.3 N/37.47.3 E by torpedo of German MTBs *S 51*, *S 26* and *S 47*.
5	15.06.43	T-411/*Zashchitnik*	20 miles W of Sukchumi by torpedo of the German submarine *U 24*.
6	02.09.44	T-410/*Vrzyv*	At 43.51 N/29.12 E by torpedo of the German submarine *U 19*.

River Monitors and Gunboats

1	19.09.41	*Udarnyi*	Off Kinburn by bombs of German aircraft.
2	21.09.41	*Krasnaya Armeniya*	In 46.10.3 N/31.29.7 E by bombs of German Ju-87 dive bombers of St.G.77.
3	27.02.43	*Krasnaya Gruziya*	In 44.39.58 N/37.47.14 E by torpedo of a German MTBs *S 51*, *S 26* and *S 47*.
4	10.01.45	*Araks* (ex-Rom. *Capitan Dumitrescu*)	Sunk at Odessa by a mine left over from the war. Raised but not repaired because of extensive damage.

Table A5 (contd.): Soviet warships and submarines lost, 1939–45

PACIFIC

Submarines

(1)	39	*Shch-128*	Sunk by accident, raised and restored to service.
1	08.41	*M-49*	Between 10 and 16.10 in 42 08 N/131 38 E area by a Soviet mine.
2	08.41	*M-63*	Between 10 and 17.10 in 42 10 N/132 27 E area by a Soviet mine.
3	18.07.42	*Shch-138*	At Nikolaevsk/Amur by a torpedo explosion. Raised but sunk under tow in the Amur estuary. Raised again and taken to Sovetskaya Gavan, not restored due to extensive damage. 11.07.43 decommissioned.
4	11.10.42	*L-16*	During transfer from Vladivostok – Dutch Harbor – San Francisco in the area of San Francisco sunk in 95 41 N/138 56 W by torpedo of the Japanese submarine *I-25*, which thought to have attacked a US submarine.
(5)	31.08.43	*Shch-130*	Sunk in America Bay by collision with *Shch-128*, raised on 02.09.43 and restored to service.
(6)	25.04.45	*Shch-139*	Sunk in North Vladimir Bay by an accidental explosion of its own torpedo, but on 07.05.45 raised and restored to service.
7	23.08.45	*L-19*	Departed 19.08 for a patrol off Sakhalin. Sunk probably on 23/24.08 on a mine in the Laperouse Strait.

Table A6: Warships and submarines taken as war booty into the *VMF*, 1944–53

No.	Soviet Name	Nat.	Former Name	Original Commission	Soviet Commission	Stricken	Fleet	Notes	
Battleship (ex-Italian *Conte di Cavour*-class, 24,410t stdd.)
1	*Novorossijsk*	Ital	*Giulio Cesare*	14.05.14	24.01.49	30.10.55	ChF	Sunk	1
Old Battleship (ex-German *Schleswig-Holstein*-class, 12,983t stdd.)
1	–	Germ	*Schleswig-Holstein*	06.07.08	–	25.06.47		Sunk	2
Coastal Defence Battleship (ex-Finnish *Väinämöinen*-class, 3,900t stdd.)
1	*Vyborg*	Finn	*Väinämöinen*	30.12.32	22.04.47	25.09.66	KBF	Scrapped	3
Aircraft Carrier (ex-German *Graf Zeppelin*-class, 24,700t stdd.)
1	*PB-101*	Germ	*Graf Zeppelin*	–	19.09.45	18.08.47		Sunk	4
Heavy Cruiser (ex-German *Deutschland*-class, 11,700t stdd.)
1	–	Germ	*Lützow* (ex-*Deutschland*)	01.04.33	–	22.07.47		Sunk	5
Heavy Cruiser (ex-German *Seydlitz*-class, 16,974t stdd.)
1	–	Germ	*Seydlitz*	–	–	10.03.47		Scrapped	6
Light Cruiser (ex-German *Nürnberg*-class, 6,520t stdd.)
1	*Admiral Makarov*	Germ	*Nürnberg*	02.11.35	13.02.46	20.02.59	KBF	Scrapped	7
Light Cruiser (ex-Italian *Duca d'Aosta*-class, 8,317t stdd.)
1	*Kerch'*	Ital	*Emanuele Filiberto Duca d'Aosta*	13.07.35	30.03.49	20.02.59	ChF	Scrapped	8
Destroyers (ex-Romanian *Regina Maria*-class, 1,400t stdd.)
1	*Letuchii*	Rom	*Regina Maria*	07.09.30	20.10.44	03.07.51	ChF	Returned	9
2	*Likhoi*	Rom	*Regele Ferdinand I*	07.09.30	20.10.44	03.07.51	ChF	Returned	9
Destroyers (ex-Romanian *Marasesti*-class, 1,391t stdd.)
1	*Legkii*	Rom	*Marasesti*	15.05.18	20.10.44	12.10.45	ChF	Returned	10
2	*Lovkii*	Rom	*Marasti*	15.07.17	20.10.44	12.10.45	ChF	Returned	10

[1] 06.02.49 taken over by a Soviet crew in Albania and brought to Sevastopol, service with the ChF. Sunk on 30.11.55 probably on a mine from the WWII in the bight of Sevastopol.
[2] 1946 salvaged at Gdynia, on 26.09.46 taken to Tallinn and included in the ships list of the VMF, but not repaired, scuttled on 25.06.47 near the Neugrund bank in the Finnish Gulf.
[3] 05.06.47 with Soviet crew taken to Kronshtadt fortress, 12.01.49 classified as monitor, scrapped.
[4] 1945 raised at Stettin, taken to Leningrad for tests with the Krylov institute, discussions about repairing the ship as a carrier, but not realized, sunk on 18.08.47 by TK and destroyer torpedoes during tests in the Central Baltic.
[5] 1946 raised at the 'Kaiserfahrt' and taken to Kronshtadt, but no repair possible, sunk on 22.07.47 during tests in the Central Baltic.
[6] 1946 salvaged at Gdynia and taken to Leningrad, completion as light carrier discussed, but not realized, scrapped.
[7] 05.01.46 transferred to Liepaya, served in the KBF, from 21.02.57 as training cruiser, scrapped.
[8] 02.03.49 taken over by Soviet crew and brought to Odessa, served in the ChF, from 17.02.56 as training cruiser, scrapped.
[9] Taken over n 29.08.44 at Konstanza, returned to Romania on 03.07.51 to become *D.22* and *21*, later *D.10* and *D.9*
[10] Taken over on 29.08.44 at Konstanza, returned to Romania to become *D.10* and *D.12*.

Table A6 (contd.): Warships and submarines taken as war booty into the *VMF*, 1944–53

No.	Soviet Name	Nat.	Former Name	Original Commission	Soviet Commission	Stricken	Fleet	Notes	
Destroyers (ex-German *Leberecht Maas*-class, 2,239t stdd.)								
1	*Prytkii*	Germ	*Friedrich Ihn*	09.04.38	13.02.46	22.03.52	KBF	Scrapped	1
2.	*Pylkii*	Germ	*Erich Steinbrinck*	30.05.38	13.02.46	19.02.58	KBF	Scrapped	1
Destroyer (ex-German *Karl Galster*-class, 2,411t stdd.)								
1	*Prochnyi*	Germ	*Karl Galster*	21.03.39	13.02.46	25.06.56	KBF	Scrapped	2
Destroyer (ex-German *Z-31*-class, 2,657t stdd.)								
1	*Provornyi*	Germ	*Z-33*	06.02.43	13.02.46	03.04.58	KBF	Scrapped	3
Destroyer (ex-Japanese *Akatsuki*-class, 1,680t stdd.)								
1	*Vernyi*	Japan	*Hibiki*	31.03.33	22.07.47	20.02.53	TOF	Scrapped	4
Destroyer (ex-Japanese *Terutsuki*-class, 2,701t stdd.)								
1	*Vnezapnyi*	Japan	*Harutsuki*	29.12.44	25.09.47	04.06.69	TOF	Scrapped	5
Destroyer (ex-Italian Soldati-class, 1,690t stdd.)								
1	*Legkii*	Ital	*Fuciliere*	15.01.39	13.03.50	21.01.60	ChF	Scrapped	6
2	*Lovkii*	Ital	*Artigliere*	30.06.38	24.02.49	27.03.60	ChF	Scrapped	6
Light Destroyer (ex-German 'Flottentorpedoboot 39', 1,294t stdd.)								
1	*Primernyi*	Germ	*T-33*	16.06.44	13.02.46	09.11.56	KBF	Scrapped	7
Light Destroyer (ex-German 'Torpedoboot 35', 839t stdd.)								
1	*Podvizhnyi*	Germ	*T-12*	03.07.40	13.02.46	13.03.59	KBF	Scrapped	8
Light Destroyer (ex-German 'Torpedoboot 37', 853t stdd.)								
1	*Poryvistyi*	Germ	*T-17*	28.08.41	13.02.46	30.12.59	KBF	Sunk	9
Light Destroyer (ex-Japanese *Matsu*-class, 1,262t or 1,289t stdd.)								
1	*Vetrennyi*	Japan	*Hatsuzakura*	28.05.45	22.07.47	19.02.59	TOF	Scrapped	10
2	*Vozrozhdennyi*	Japan	*Kiri*	14.08.44	22.07.47	20.12.69	TOF	Scrapped	11
3	*Volevoi*	Japan	*Kaya*	30.09.44	22.07.47	01.08.59	TOF	Scrapped	12
4	*Volnyi*	Japan	*Shii*	13.03.45	22.07.47	08.08.60	TOF	Scrapped	13

[1] *Prytkii* serving from 15.02.46 to 22.03.52 in the KBF, *Pylkii* from 15.02.46 to 30.04.49, then in reserve, both scrapped.
[2] Served from 15.02.46 to 30.11.54 in the KBF, then reserve until scrapped.
[3] Served from 15.02.46 to 30.11.54 in the KBF, then training vessel until transferred to the Leningrad naval base; from 1958 used as an accommodation hulk, scrapped in 1961.
[4] Served until 05.07.48 in the 5.VMF of the TOF, then in reserve until stricken and scrapped.
[5] Not in active service, on 14.02.49 put into reserve and used for tests; 31.01.55 accommodation hulk, 1969 scrapped.
[6] *Legkii* served in the ChF, 30.11.54 became test vessel *TsL-57*, scrapped in 1960. *Lovkii* was until 25.07.43 the *Camicia Nera*, served in the ChF, on 30.12.54 became test vessel *TsL-58*, on 17.10.55 *KVN-11*. Scrapped in 1960.
[7] Served in the KBF, from 28.12.54 test vessel *PKZ-63*, 1957–58 scrapped.
[8] Served in the KBF 08.04.53 put into reserve, early 1959 transferred to the Ladoga Lake, up to 1991. Used as training unit at the Leningrad naval base. Finally sunk. 30.12.54 renamed *Kit*.
[9] Served in the KBF, 25.06.49 reserve, 07.09.49 renamed *Uts-6* as test vessel, up to 24.12.55.
[10] 02.10.47 renamed *Vyrazitel'nyi*, 17.06.49 test vessel *TsL-26*.
[11] 17.06.49 renamed test vessel *TsL-25*, 03.10.57 *PM-65*.
[12] 17.06.49 renamed test vessel *TsL-23*, 10.06.58 *OT-61*.
[13] 17.06.49 renamed test vessel *TsL-24*, 18.11.59 *OT-5*.

Table A6 (contd.): Warships and submarines taken as war booty into the *VMF*, 1944–53

No.	Soviet Name	Nat.	Former Name	Original Commission	Soviet Commission	Stricken	Fleet	Notes	
Light Destroyer (ex-Japanese *Otori*-class, 840t stdd.)
1	*Vnimatel'nyi*	Japan	*Kiji*	31.07.37	21.10.47	31.10.57	TOF	Scrapped	[1]
Light Destroyers (ex-Italian *Ciclone*-class, 910t stdd.)
1	*Ladnyi*	Ital	*Animoso*	14.08.42	30.03.49	31.01.58	ChF	Scrapped	[2]
2	*Letnyi*	Ital	*Fortunale*	16.08.42	30.03.49	20.10.58	ChF	Sunk	[3]
3	*Lyutyi*	Ital	*Ardimentoso*	14.12.42	23.11.49	04.12.59	ChF	Scrapped	[4]
Old Light Destroyers (ex-German 'Torpedoboote', 670 or 766t stdd.)
1	*Porazhayshchii*	Germ	*T-107*	30.04.12	13.02.46	12.03.57	KBF	Scrapped	[5]
2	*Prozorlivyi*	Germ	*T-158*	18.10.08	13.02.46	31.05.61	KBF	Scrapped	[6]
3	*Pronzitel'nyi*	Germ	*T-190*	02.10.11	13.02.46	30.04.49	KBF	Scrapped	[7]
Patrol Ships (ex-Romanian *Smeul*-class, 260t stdd.)
1	*Musson*	Rom	*Sborul*	Late 1914	20.10.44	06.11.45	ChF	Returned	[8]
2	*Toros*	Rom	*Smeul*	1915	20.10.44	06.11.45	ChF	Returned	[8]
Patrol Ships (ex-Manchurian *Haifen*-class, 184t stdd.)
1	*Veter*	Man	*Haifen*	1935	13.09.45	28.02.48	TOF	To Merch. Fl	[9]
2	*Shtil'*	Man	*Hailun*	1935	13.09.45	28.02.48	TOF	To Merch. Fl	[9]
Patrol Ship (ex-German 'Flottenbegleiter', 840t stdd.)
1	*Buran*	Germ	*F-7*	15.02.37	25.02.46	30.09.56	KBF	Scrapped	[10]
Patrol Ship (ex-Japanese *Shimushu*-class, 869t stdd.)
1	*EK-31*	Jap	*Shimushu*	30.06.40	22.07.47	16.05.59	TOF	Scrapped	[11]
Patrol Ships (ex-Japanese *Ukuru.*-class, 940t stdd.)
1	*EK-41*	Jap	*Ikino*	08.45	26.08.47	01.06.61	TOF	Scrapped	[12]
2	*EK-47*	Jap	*Kozu*	03.05.45	25.09.47	25.01.69	TOF	Scrapped	[13]

[1] 17.06.49 renamed test vessel *TsL-27*, 20.09.54 *PKZ-96*.
[2] Served in the Black Sea Fleet, 30.12.54 renamed test vessel *TsL-61*.
[3] Served in the Black Sea Fleet, 30.12.54 renamed test vessel *TsL-59*.
[4] Served in the Black Sea Fleet, 30.12.54 renamed test vessel *TsL-60*, 29.04.58 *PKZ-150*.
[5] 22.12.50 renamed *Kazanka*, served with the Northern Baltic Fleet, 28.11.50 in reserve.
[6] 22.12.50 renamed *Araks*, 25.02.57 test vessel *UTS-67*. Served in the Northern Baltic Fleet. Since 28.11.50 in reserve.
[7] Served with the Northern Baltic Fleet.
[8] 27.08.44 captured at Konstanza. 12.10.45 returned to Romania, 06.11.45 stricken.
[9] 22.08.45 captured at Port Arthur. Served in the TOF. 28.02.48 transferred to the Merchant Marine.
[10] Served in the Northern Baltic Fleet. 07.05.51 floating base, 1957–58 scrapped at Ventspils.
[11] Served in the 7th VMF, 22.07.47 in reserve, 16.09.57 floating base, scrapped in 1959.
[12] Served in the 5th VMF, 17.06.49 hydrographic vessel. Scrapped in 1961.
[13] Served in the 7th VMF, 05.07.48 in reserve, 31.01.51 floating base, 1969 scrapped.

Table A6 (contd.): Warships and submarines taken as war booty into the *VMF*, 1944–53

No.	Soviet Name	Nat.	Former Name	Original Commission	Soviet Commission	Stricken	Fleet	Notes	
Patrol Ships (ex-Japanese *Type C*-class, 745t stdd.)
1	*EK-34*	Japan	*No. 105*	04.46	22.07.47	03.12.60	TOF	Scrapped	1
2	*EK-35*	Japan	*No. 227*	08.45	22.07.47	11.03.58	TOF	Scrapped	2
3	*EK-39*	Japan	*No. 79*	16.07.45	26.08.47	30.08.60	TOF	Scrapped	3
4	*EK-40*	Japan	*No. 221*	08.45	26.08.47	11.03.58	TOF	Scrapped	4
5	*EK-43*	Japan	*No. 71*	20.05.45	25.09.47	31.01.64	TOF	Scrapped	5
6	*EK-45*	Japan	*No. 77*	08.45	25.09.47	25.01.69	TOF	Scrapped	6
Patrol Ships (ex-Japanese *Type D*-class, 740t stdd.)
1	*EK-32*	Japan	*No. 34*	04.11.44	22.07.47	23.07.58	TOF	Scrapped	7
2	*EK-33*	Japan	*No. 196*	31.03.45	22.07.47	11.03.58	TOF	Scrapped	8
3	*EK-36*	Japan	*No. 52*	01.11.44	26.08.47	11.03.58	TOF	Scrapped	8
4	*EK-37*	Japan	*No. 78*	04.04.46	16.08.47	11.03.58	TOF	Scrapped	8
5	*EK-38*	Japan	*No. 142*	46	22.07.47	11.02.55	TOF	Sold	9
6	*EK-42*	Japan	*No. 48*	45	26.08.47	02.06.59	TOF	Scrapped	10
7	*EK-44*	Japan	*No. 76*	20.02.45	25.09.47	25.05.55	TOF	Sold	11
8	*EK-46*	Japan	*No. 102*	03.03.45	25.09.47	21.01.60	TOF	Scrapped	12
Minelayer (ex-Romanian *Amiral Murgescu*-class, 812t stdd.)
1	*Don*	Rom	*Amiral Murgescu*	40	20.10.44	27.05.88	ChF	Scrapped	13
Minelayer (ex-Japanese *Kamishima*-class, 800t stdd.)
1	*Katun'*	Japan	*Kamishima*	30.07.45	15.09.47	09.11.56	TOF	Scrapped	14
Minesweepers (ex-German *Type 35*, 682–685t stdd.)
1	*T-912*	Germ	*M 7*	31.10.38	13.05.46	26.11.57	ChF	Sunk	15
2	*T-913*	Germ	*M 29*	04.09.40	13.05.46	30.09.56	ChF	Scrapped	16
3	*T-914*	Germ	*M 30*	31.10.40	13.05.46	22.10.58	ChF	Scrapped	17
4	*T-915*	Germ	*M 151*	05.05.41	13.05.46	12.08.64	ChF	Scrapped	18
5	*T-916*	Germ	*M 204*	24.08.41	13.05.46	07.07.56	ChF	Scrapped	19

[1] Served in the 7th VMF, 05.07.48 in reserve, 1961 scrapped.
[2] Served in the 7th VMF, 05.07.48 in reserve, 1958 scrapped.
[3] Served as rescue vessel, 1953–60 in TOF, 1960 scrapped.
[4] 05.07.48 in reserve, 17.06.49 rescue vessel, 23.04.53 to 11.03.58 TOF, 1958 scrapped.
[5] Served in the 5th VMF, 05.07.48 in reserve, and reclassified as hydrographic vessel, 1953–1960 TOF.
[6] Served in the 7th VMF, 05.07.48 in reserve, 31.01.55 floating base. 1969 scrapped.
[7] Served in the 5 VMF, 30.11.54 in reserve, 30.12.54 *TsL-63*, 1959 scrapped.
[8] Served in the 5 VMF, 30.11.54 in reserve, 30.12.54 all renamed *Turgaj, Naryn, Mugrab*. Scrapped.
[9] 05.07.48 in reserve, *TsL-38*. 11.02.55 to China.
[10] Served in 7 VMF, 05.07.48 *TsL-42*, 17.06.49 *Abakan*, as reporting ship. 1959 scrapped.
[11] Served in 5 VMF, 05.07.48 in reserve, *TsL-44*, 17.11.54 *SKR-49*. 25.06.55 to China.
[12] Served in 7 VMF, 05.07.48 in reserve, *TsL-46*, as target vessel. 1960 scrapped.
[13] Captured on 29.08.44 at Konstanza. Served as training vessel, 18.01.47 floating base. Staff vessel. 1988 scrapped at Sevastopol.
[14] Served in the 7 VMF, 05.07.48 in reserve, 21.12.54 *OT-15*. Scrapped.
[15] 27.07.46 arrived at Sevastopol. 17.10.55 staff vessel *Bel'bek*, 07.05.57 target *TsL-5*. 1958 sunk near Feodosiya.
[16] As *T-912*. 11.11.47 hydrographic vessel *Tuman*, 1956 scrapped.
[17] As *T-912*. 18.12.54 reserve, 1958 scrapped.
[18] As *T-912*. 09.01.53 rescue vessel *Skalistyi*.
[19] 02.08.46 arrived at Sevastopol, 19.09.52 reclassified as hydroacoustic vessel *Barograf*.

Table A6 (contd.): Warships and submarines taken as war booty into the VMF, 1944–53

No.	Soviet Name	Nat.	Former Name	Original Commission	Soviet Commission	Stricken	Fleet	Notes	
Minesweepers (ex-German *Type 35*, 682–685t stdd.) *continued*									
6	T-917	Germ	M 254	16.06.41	13.05.46	26.10.57	ChF	Scrapped	[1]
7	T-918	Germ	M 3	10.12.38	13.05.46	17.11.59	ChF	Scrapped	[2]
8	T-919	Germ	M 203	03.06.41	13.05.46	01.06.61	ChF	Scrapped	[3]
9	T-920	Germ	M 34	26.06.43	13.05.46	21.02.57	ChF	Scrapped	[4]
10	T-921	Germ	M 17	17.01.40	13.05.46	20.10.58	ChF	Scrapped	[5]
11	T-922	Germ	M 255	11.10.41	13.05.46	31.01.58	ChF	Scrapped	[6]
12	T-923	Germ	M 256	11.10.41	13.05.46	19.10.59	ChF	Scrapped	[7]
13	T-924	Germ	M 155	27.01.42	13.05.46	27.03.80	ChF	Scrapped	[8]
Minesweepers (ex-German *Type 40*, 543t stdd.)									
1	T-701	Germ	M 267	08.03.45	27.12.45	20.10.60	KBF	Scrapped	[9]
2	T-702	Germ	M 279	21.10.44	27.12.45	27.08.65	KBF	Scrapped	[10]
3	T-703	Germ	M 324	29.11.42	27.12.45	21.01.60	KBF	Scrapped	[11]
4	T-704	Germ	M 342	07.06.42	27.12.45	20.01.60	KBF	Scrapped	[11]
5	T-705	Germ	M 377	27.10.44	27.12.45	20.01.60	KBF	Scrapped	[11]
6	T-706	Germ	M 401	30.11.42	27.12.45	10.02.59	KBF	Scrapped	[12]
7	T-707	Germ	M 406	02.06.43	27.12.45	21.01.60	KBF	Scrapped	[11]
8	T-708	Germ	M 411	29.10.42	27.12.45	21.08.59	KBF	Scrapped	[13]
9	T-709	Germ	M 423	29.11.42	27.12.45	10.02.59	KBF	Scrapped	[14]
10	T-710	Germ	M 431	29.09.42	27.12.45	12.09.59	KBF	Scrapped	[15]
11	T-711	Germ	M 291	05.08.43	27.12.45	07.10.69	KBF	Scrapped	[16]
12	T-712	Germ	M 330	21.10.44	27.12.45	12.09.59	KBF	Scrapped	[15]
13	T-713	Germ	M 348	19.09.43	27.12.45	12.08.64	KBF	Scrapped	[17]
14	T-714	Germ	M 386	09.10.43	27.12.45	04.05.63	KBF	Scrapped	[18]
15	T-715	Germ	M 405	29.04.43	27.12.45	28.01.58	KBF	Scrapped	[19]
16	T-716	Germ	M 425	31.01.43	27.12.45	12.09.59	KBF	Scrapped	[15]
17	T-717	Germ	M 446	08.06.43	27.12.45	30.06.60	KBF	Scrapped	[20]
18	T-718	Germ	M 461	25.03.43	27.12.45	12.09.59	KBF	Scrapped	[15]
19	T-719	Germ	M 467	31.10.42	27.12.45	12.08.64	KBF	Scrapped	[21]
20	T-720	Germ	M 470	27.02.43	27.11.45	04.11.66	KBF	Scrapped	[22]

[1] As *T-916*. 18.12.54 reserve, 12.01.55 special vessel *Nerpa*, 26.11.57 *OT-44*. Glavtorchermeta.
[2] As *T-916*. 01.04.47 special vessel *Issledovvatel*. 1959 scrapped.
[3] As *T-916*. 25.02.53 reserve, rescue vessel *Lajla*. 1961 scrapped.
[4] As *T-916*. 23.08.52 to Caspian Flotilla, 16.03.53 rescue vessel *Aragats*. Scrapped.
[5] As *T-916*. 17.10.55 staff vessel *Kacha*. 1958 scrapped.
[6] As *T-916*. 14.08.46 reserve. Test vessel, 07.10.46 *Ispytatel*. 1958 scrapped.
[7] As *T-916*. 18.11.54 reserve, 12.01.55 rescue vessel *Beshtau*, 18.03.58 *PKZ-143*. 1959 scrapped.
[8] As *T-916*. 01.09.55 reserve, 17.10.55 *TsL-66*, 04.12.56 firefighting ship *BRN-31*, 1980 scrapped.
[9] 15.02.46–24.12.55 Southern KBF, 20.10.60 reserve, Glavtorchermeta. Scrapped.
[10] As *T-701*, 26.05.56 *DG-33*, 19.02.59 *TsL-16*. 1960 scrapped.
[11] As *T-701*. 12.02.60 *OT-9* or 25.05.56 *DG-34*. 19.02.59 *TsL-17*. 1960 scrapped.
[12] As *T-701*. 10.02.59 reserve, scrapped.
[13] 15.02.46 southern KBF, 04.09.53 transferred to SF, 18.12.54 reserve, 12.01.55 rescue vessel *Yrma*. 06.01.59 storm damage off Mogilevskii Irl., 02.06.59 to Glavtorchermeta at Murmansk base.
[14] As *T-701*. 10.02.59 stricken and scrapped.
[15] As *T-701*. 10.02.59 stricken, 1959–60 Glavtorchermeta at Tallinn. *T-716*, 56: *DG-35*, 59: *TsL-18*.
[16] 15.02.46–24.12.55 Northern KBF, 24.10.51 renamed *Meridian'N* as rescue vessel, 1969 scrapped.
[17] 01.05.46 to 01.09.55 Northern KBF, 17.10.55 renamed *Vint* as hydrographic vessel. 1964 scrapped.
[18] 17.03.46–18.12.54 Southern KBF, 12.01.55 rescue vessel *Pulkovo*. 1963 scrapped.
[19] As *T-711*. 04.09.53 transferred to SF. 12.01.55 rescue vessel *Kengur*. 1958 scrapped.
[20] As *T-711*, 24.10.51 hydrographic vessel *Buj*. 1960 scrapped.
[21] As *T-711*, 06.10.51 rescue vessel *Alagez*. 1964 scrapped.
[22] 17.03.46 at Pillau to Northern KBF, 12.01.55 hydrographic vessel *Briz*. 1966 scrapped.

Table A6 (contd.): Warships and submarines taken as war booty into the *VMF*, 1944–53

No.	Soviet Name	Nat.	Former Name	Original Commission	Soviet Commission	Stricken	Fleet	Notes
Minesweepers (ex-German *Type 40*, 543t stdd.) *continued*								
21	*T-721*	Germ	*M 265*	15.01.44	25.02.46	31.01.64	KBF	Scrapped [1]
22	*T-722*	Germ	*M 341*	19.04.42	25.02.46	30.06.60	KBF	Scrapped [2]
23	*T-723*	Germ	*M 369*	21.09.43	25.02.46	31.01.64	KBF	Scrapped [3]
24	*T-724*	Germ	*M 407*	19.06.43	25.02.46	31.01.64	KBF	Scrapped [3]
25	*T-725*	Germ	*M 415*	15.03.43	25.02.46	01.06.61	KBF	Scrapped [4]
26	*T-726*	Germ	*M 437*	28.04.43	25.02.46	01.06.61	KBF	Scrapped [5]
27	*T-727*	Germ	*M 443*	01.02.43	25.02.46	20.04.64	KBF	Scrapped [6]
28	*T-728*	Germ	*M 456*	21.07.43	25.02.46	21.04.60	KBF	Scrapped [7]
29	*T-729*	Germ	*M 484*	20.01.43	25.02.46	21.01.60	KBF	Scrapped [8]
30	*T-730*	Germ	*M 496*	07.06.43	25.02.46	05.06.70	KBF	Scrapped [9]
Minesweeper (ex-Japanese *W-19*-class, 648t stdd.)								
1	*T-28*	Jap	*W-23*	31.03.43	15.09.47	07.03.86	TOF	Scrapped [10]
River Monitors (ex-Romanian *Bratianu*-class, 680t normal)								
1	*Azov*	Rom	*Ion C. Bratianu*	07	30.10.44	03.07.51	ChF	Returned [11]
2	*Mariupol'*	Rom	*Alexandru Lahovari*	07	30.10.44	03.07.51	ChF	Returned [11]
River Monitor (ex-Romanian *Ardeal*, 450t normal)								
1	*Berdyansk*	Rom	*Ardeal*	04	30.10.44	03.07.51	ChF	Returned [11]
River Monitors (ex-Romanian *Bucovina*, 550t normal)								
1	*Izmail'*	Rom	*Bucovina*	15.09.15	30.10.44	03.07.51	ChF	Returned [11]
2	*Kerch'*	Rom	*Basarabia*	11.04.15	30.10.44	03.07.51	ChF	Returned [11]
Gunboats (ex-Romanian *Dumitrescu*-class 375t normal)								
1	*Angara*	Rom	*Ghigulescu*	1	20.10.44	14.10.45	ChF	Returned [12]
2	*Araks*	Rom	*Dumitrescu*	1	20.10.44	19.01.45	ChF	Scrapped [13]
3	*Akhtuba*	Rom	*Stihi Eugen*	1	20.10.44	14.10.45	ChF	Returned [12]
Gunboats (ex-Manchurian *Shun Tien*-class, 270–290t normal)								
1	*KL-55*	Man	*Shun Tien*	20.09.34	24.09.45	06.06.56	Amur Fl	River Fl [14]
2	*KL-57*	Man	*Yang Min*	20.09.34	24.09.45	06.06.56	Amur Fl	River Fl [14]
3	*KL-56*	Man	*Chin Jen*	35	24.09.45	25.08.54	Amur Fl	River Fl [14]
4	*KL-58*	Man	*Ting Pien*	35	24.09.45	06.06.56	Amur Fl	River Fl [14]

[1] As *T-701*. 12.11.47 hydrographic vessel *Kurs*. 1964 scrapped.
[2] As *T-701*. 06.10.51 reclassified as rescue vessel *Chugush*. 1960 scrapped.
[3] As *T-701*, 15.08.51 and 01.09.55 reserve, 06.10.55 and 17.10.55 hydrographic vessels *Volnomer* and *Taran*. 1964 scrapped.
[4] As *T-701*. 01.09.55 reserve, 17.10.55 hydrographic vessel *Reostat*, 1961 scrapped.
[5] As *T-701*. 24.10.52 reserve, hydrographic vessel *Gigrograf*. 1961 scrapped.
[6] As *T-701*. 08.01.53 reserve, 25.02.53 rescue vessel *Dzhinal*. 1964 scrapped.
[7] As *T-701*. 01.09.55 reserve. 17.10.55 decontamination vessel *DG-36*. 1960 scrapped.
[8] As *T-701*. 07.04.56 reserve. 25.05.56 decontamination vessel *DG-11*. 1960 scrapped.
[9] As *T-701*. 01.09.55 reserve, 17.10.55 decontamination vessel *DG-12*. 1960 scrapped.
[10] Served in the 5 VMF. 05.07.48 reclassified target vessel *TsL-28*, 12.03.55 *PM-61*. 1986 scrapped.
[11] Served in the Danube Flotilla. 03.07.51 returned to Romania, became *M-202*, *M-201*, *M-207*, *M-205* and *Basarabia*.
[12] Returned to Romania, getting the old names again.
[13] After being damaged, stricken and scrapped.
[14] Former Manchurian river gunboats, built in Japan. Served in the Amur Flotilla. 04.06.49 renamed *Bashkiriya*, *Yakutiya*, *Buryat-Mongoliya*, *Chuvashiya* again on 02.04.51 into *Anadyr'*, *Ayat*, *Bureya*, *Atrek*. 1954/56 transferred to the Ministry for River Transport.

Table A6 (contd.): Warships and submarines taken as war booty into the *VMF*, 1944–53

No.	Soviet Name	Nat.	Former Name	Original Commission	Soviet Commission	Stricken	Fleet	Notes	
Big Submarine (ex-German *Type IXC/40*, 1,144t normal)									
1	*N-26-B26*	Germ	*U 1231*	09.02.44	13.02.46	13.01.68	KBF	Scrapped	1
Big Submarines (ex-German *Type XXI*, 1,621t normal, later Soviet *projekt 614*)									
1	*N-27-B27*	Germ	*U 3515*	14.12.44	13.02.46	01.09.72	KBF	Scrapped	2
2	*N-28-B28*	Germ	*U 2529*	31.01.45	13.02.46	25.03.58	KBF	Scrapped	3
3	*N-29-B29*	Germ	*U 3035*	12.03.45	13.02.46	25.03.58	KBF	Scrapped	4
4	*TS-5 (R-1)*	Germ	*U 3538*	–	–	08.08.47	–	Sunk	5
5	*TS-6 (R-2)*	Germ	*U 3539*	–	–	08.08.47	–	Sunk	5
6	*TS-7 (R-3)*	Grm	*U 3540*	–	–	08.08.47	–	Sunk	5
7	*TS-8 (R-4)*	Germ	*U 3541*	–	–	28.02.48	–	Scrapped	6
8	*TS-9 (R-5)*	Germ	*U 3542*	–	–	28.02.48	–	Scrapped	6
9	*TS-10 (R-6)*	Germ	*U 3543*	–	–	28.02.48	–	Scrapped	6
10	*TS-11 (R-7)*	Germ	*U 3544*	–	–	28.02.48	–	Scrapped	6
11	*TS-12 (R-8)*	Germ	*U 3545*	–	–	28.02.48	–	Scrapped	6
12	*TS-13*	Germ	*U 3546*	–	–	09.04.47	–	Scrapped	7
13	*TS-15*	Germ	*U 3547*	–	–	09.04.47	–	Scrapped	7
14	*TS-17*	Germ	*U 3548*	–	–	09.04.47	–	Scrapped	7
15	*TS-18*	Germ	*U 3549*	–	–	09.04.47	–	Scrapped	7
16	*TS-19*	Germ	*U 3550*	–	–	09.04.47	–	Scrapped	7
17	*TS-32*	Germ	*U 3551*	–	–	09.04.47	–	Scrapped	8
18	*TS-33*	Germ	*U 3552*	–	–	09.04.47	–	Scrapped	8
19	*TS-34*	Germ	*U 3553*	–	–	09.04.47	–	Scrapped	8
20	*TS-35*	Germ	*U 3554*	–	–	09.04.47	–	Scrapped	8
21	*TS-36*	Germ	*U 3555*	–	–	09.04.47	–	Scrapped	8
22	*TS-37*	Germ	*U 3556*	–	–	09.04.47	–	Scrapped	8
23	*TS-38*	Germ	*U 3557*	–	–	09.04.47	–	Scrapped	8
Medium Submarines (ex-Romanian *Requinul*-class, 636t normal)									
1	*TS-1*	Rom	*Requinul*	08.43	20.10.44	03.07.51	ChF	Returned	9
2	*TS-2*	Rom	*Marsouinul*	09.43	20.10.44	20.02.45	ChF	Wrecked	10
Medium Submarine (ex-Romanian *Delfinul*-class, 650t normal)									
1	*TS-3*	Rom	*Delfinul*	31	20.10.44	12.10.45	ChF	Returned	11

[1] 06.12.45 at Liepaya, served in the South Baltic Fleet, 09.06.49 renamed *B-26*, 7.08.53 reserve, 15.09.53 combat training hulk *KBP-33*, 27.12.56 training hulk *UTS-33*, scrapped at Riga.
[2] As *U 1231*. On 09.06.49 renamed *B-27*. 10.06.55 reserve, 19.09.55 block ship *Bsh-28*. 09.01.57 training hulk *UTS-3*, scrapped.
[3] 16.12.45 at Liepaya. Served in the South Baltic Fleet. 09.06.49 renamed *B-28*. 29.12.55 in reserve. 18.01.56 floating torpedo firing station *PZS-34*. Scrapped.
[4] As *TS-28*. 09.06.49 renamed *B-29*. 29.12.55 reserve. 18.01.56 floating torpedo firing station *PZS-31*. Scrapped.
[5] Captured on the slip at Danzig, launched on 15.07.45, 08.03.47 renamed *R-1*, *R-2*, *R-3*. 08.08.47 sunk 20sm NW Cape Ristna.
[6] Captured incomplete on the slips at Danzig. 08.03.47 renamed *R-4*, *R-5*, *R-6*, *R-7*, *R-8*. 28.02.48 scrapped.
[7] Captured incomplete on the slips at Danzig. 08.03.47.
[8] No keel laid, prefabricated sections captured, 09.04.47 scrapped.
[9] 04.08.47 renamed *N-39*, 16.06.49 *S-39*.
[10] 04.08.47 renamed *N-40*, 16.06.47 *S-40*, 20.02.45 wrecked by torpedo explosion at Poti, 28.11.50 wreck stricken and scrapped.
[11] 12.10.45 returned to Romania, took old name again.

Table A6 (contd.): Warships and submarines taken as war booty into the *VMF*, 1944–53

No.	Soviet Name	Nat.	Former Name	Original Commission	Soviet Commission	Stricken	Fleet	Notes	
Medium Submarines (ex-German *Type VII, VIIC/41*, 769t normal)								
1	TS-14	Germ	U 250	12.12.43	–	20.08.45	–	Scrapped	1
2	N-22-581	Germ	U 1057	20.05.44	13.02.46	16.10.57	KBF	Scrapped	2
3	N-23-582	Germ	U 1058	10.06.44	13.02.46	25.03.58	KBF	Scrapped	3
4	N-24-583	Germ	U 1064	29.07.44	13.02.46	12.03.74	KBF	Scrapped	4
5	N-25-584	Germ	U 1305	13.09.44	13.02.46	01.03.58	KBF	Sunk	5
Medium Submarine (ex-Italian *Flutto*-class, 930t normal)								
1	N-41-571	Ital	*Marea*	07.05.43	24.02.49	27.12.56	ChF	Scrapped	6
Medium Submarine (ex-Italian *Acciaio*-class, 697t normal)								
1	N-42-542	Ital	*Nichelio*	30.07.42	24.02.49	12.03.58	ChF	Scrapped	7
Small Submarines (ex-German *Type IIB*, 279t normal)								
1	TS-16	Germ	U 9	21.08.35	–	12.12.46	–	Scrapped	8
2	–	Germ	U 18	04.01.36	–	26.05.47	–	Sunk	9
3	–	Germ	U 24	10.10.36	–	26.05.47	–	Sunk	9
Small Submarine (ex-German *Type XXIII*, 234t normal)								
1	M-31	Germ	U 2353	09.01.45	04.12.45	63	–	Scrapped	
Midget Submarines (ex-Italian *CB*-class, 36t normal)								
1	TM-4	Ital	CB 1	27.01.41	20.10.44	16.02.45	–	Scrapped	10
2	TM-5	Ital	CB 2	27.01.41	20.10.44	16.02.45	–	Scrapped	10
3	TM-6	Ital	CB 3	10.05.41	20.10.44	16.02.45	–	Scrapped	10
4	TM-7	Ital	CB 4	10.05.41	20.10.44	16.02.45	–	Scrapped	10

[1] Sunk on 30.07.44, raised and taken into dry dock at Kronshtadt, 12.04.45 repair planned, 20.08.45 wreck stricken and scrapped.
[2] Served in the South Baltic Fleet, 09.06.49 renamed *S-81*. 30.12.55 in reserve, transferred to SF, after use in atomic tests in 1957 scrapped.
[3] Served in North Baltic Fleet, 09.06.49 renamed *S-82*. 18.01.56 renamed *PZS-32*. Scrapped.
[4] Served in North Baltic Fleet, 09.06.49 renamed *S-83*, 18.01.56 *PZS-33*, 01.06.57 *UTS-49*. 1974 scrapped.
[5] Served in the North Baltic Fleet, 09.06.49 renamed *S-84*. 30.12.55 in reserve, transferred to SF, 01.03.58 sunk during atomic tests off Novaya Zemlya.
[6] Served with the ChF, 16.06.49 renamed *S-41*. Scrapped at Novorossijsk.
[7] Served with the ChF, 16.06.49 renamed *S-42*. Scrapped.
[8] 20.08.44 sunk at Konstanza, raised and 19.04.45 taken to Nikolaev, repair not possible, scrapped.
[9] 20.08.44 damaged at Konstanza, 14.02.45 and 07.06.45 raised but repair not possible, sunk on 26.05.44 in the area of Sevastopol by the Soviet submarine *M-120*.
[10] 08.09.43 taken over by Romania. 29.08.44 captured at Konstanza. 20.10.44 ChF, 16.02.45 decommissioned and scrapped.

Table A7: Warships of the *VMF*, laid down or ordered, 1945–53

No.	Name	Order	Yard	Yard No.	Laid down	Launched	Commiss.	Fleet	Notes
Aircraft Carriers (*Projekt 72*, 23,700t stdd.)									
1	–	–	–	–	–	–	–	–	1
2	–	–	–	–	–	–	–	–	1
Battleship (*Projekt 23NU*, 59,650t stdd.)									
1	Sovetskaya Rossiya	21.01.38	402	102	20.07.40	–	–	–	2
Battleships (*Projekt 24*, 72,950t stdd.)									
1	–	–	–	–	–	–	–	–	3
2	–	–	–	–	–	–	–	–	3
Battlecruisers (*Projekt 82*, 36,500t stdd.)									
1	Stalingrad	31.08.51	444	400	05.12.51	54	–	–	4
2	Moskva	31.04.51	189	406	09.52	–	–	–	5
3	Kronshtadt	?	402	–	(05.55)	–	–	–	6
4	–	–	–	–	–	–	–	–	7
5	–	–	–	–	–	–	–	–	7
6	–	–	–	–	–	–	–	–	7
7	–	–	–	–	–	–	–	–	7
Heavy Cruisers (*Projekt 66*, 26,230t stdd.)									
1	–	08.52	194	–	–	–	–	–	8
		–	189	–	(53)	–	–	–	8
2	–	–	444	–	(54)	–	–	–	8
3	–	–	372	–	(56)	–	–	–	8
4	–	–	402	–	(56)	–	–	–	8
Light Cruisers (*Projekt 65*, 14,500t stdd.)									
–	–	–	–	–	–	–	–	–	9
Light Cruisers (*Projekt 68-bis*, 13,230t stdd.)									
1	Sverdlov	03.12.47	189	408	15.10.49	05.07.50	15.05.52	KBF	
2	Dzerzhinskii	03.12.47	444	374	21.12.48	31.08.50	18.08.52	ChF	10
3	Ordzhonikidze	03.12.47	194	600	19.10.49	17.09.50	30.06.52	KBF	11
4	Zhdanov	01.12.48	189	419	11.02.50	27.12.50	31.12.52	KBF/ChF	12

[1] During WWII several versions of *projekts 71* and *72* carriers were studied, the smaller *projekt 71* was cancelled in 1950/52, the *projekt 72* finally in 1955. There was also a *projekt 85* of 23–24,000t stdd. studied.
[2] The ship was put into conservation in July 1941, in September 1945 planned to a revised *projekt 23NU* but the plan was cancelled probably in 1953 and the materials in the building dock broken up.
[3] The ships were planned in September 1945, but never ordered or laid down.
[4] On 26.06.53 cancelled, launched to be used as test target for missiles.
[5] On 11.04.53 cancelled, broken down on the slip.
[6] Laid down to *projekt 82R* with cruise missile armament, but cancelled in October 1955.
[7] Several versions studied with different armaments, but never ordered or laid down.
[8] Planned to be laid down during 1953–56 at the yards 194 (changed to 189), 444, 402 and 372, to be completed from 1957 to 1959. Finally cancelled in 1954 before laying down.
[9] Several versions studied with different displacements and armaments, but plan cancelled in 1947.
[10] Rebuilt 1960–62 to *projekt 70E* with A/A missile armament.
[11] 05.04.62 sold to Indonesia, 05.08.62 at Surabaja commissioned as *Irian*, served up to 1972.
[12] 1972 commissioned after rebuilding to *projekt 68-U-1* as command cruiser.

Table A7 (contd.): Warships of the *VMF*, laid down or ordered, 1945–53

No.	Name	Order	Yard	Yard No.	Laid down	Launched	Commiss.	Fleet	Notes
Light Cruisers (*Projekt 68-bis*, 13,230t stdd.) *continued*									
5	*Aleksandr Nevskii*	01.12.48	194	625	30.05.50	07.06.51	31.12.52	KBF/SF	
6	*Admiral Nakhimov*	01.12.48	444	375	27.06.50	29.06.51	27.03.53	ChF	1
7	*Admiral Ushakov*	09.11.50	189	420	31.08.50	29.09.51	08.09.53	KBF/ChF	2
8	*Admiral Lazarev*	09.11.50	194	626	06.02.51	26.06.52	30.12.53	KBF/TOF	
9	*Mikhail Kutuzov*	09.11.50	444	385	23.02.51	29.11.51	30.12.54	ChF	2
10	*Aleksandr Suvorov*	26.02.51	189	436	26.02.51	15.05.52	31.12.53	KBF/TOF	2
11	*Admiral Senyavin*	31.08.51	189	437	31.10.51	21.12.52	30.11.54	KBF/TOF	3
12	*Dmitrii Pozharskii*	31.08.51	189	445	31.03.52	25.06.53	31.12.54	KBF/TOF	
13	*Shcherbakov*	31.08.51	194	627	06.51	24.04.53	–	KBF	4
14	*Admiral Kornilov*	31.08.51	444	395	06.11.51	17.03.54	–	ChF	4
15	*Koz'ma Minin*	31.08.51	194	628	06.52				
			402	303	28.01.53	53	–	SF	5
16	*Dmitrii Donskoi*	31.08.51	194	629	04.53				
			402	304	53	–	–	SF	5
17	*Molotovsk*	25.09.53	402	301	15.07.52	25.05.54	30.11.54	SF/KBF	6
18	*Murmansk*	25.09.53	402	302	28.01.53	24.04.55	22.09.55	SF	
19	*Kronshtadt*	25.09.53	189	453	04.53	11.09.54	–	KBF?	7
20	*Tallinn*	25.09.53	189	454	28.09.53	28.05.55	–	KBF?	7
21	*Varyag*	–	189	460	05.02.54	05.06.56	–	KBF?	7
22	–	–	194	631	–	–	–	KBF?	8
23	–	–	444	396	–	–	–	ChF?	8
24	–	–	189	470	–	–	–	KBF?	8
25	–	–	402	305	–	–	–	SF?	8
Destroyer leaders (*Projekt 47*, design of 1941)									
–	–	–	–	–	–	–	–		9
Destroyers (*Projekts 37* and *39*, small destroyers)									
–	–	–	–	–	–	–	–		9
Destroyers (*Projekt 40*, Big Fleet destroyer of 1944, 3,296t stdd.)									
–	–	–	–	–	–	–	–		9
Destroyers (*Projekt 30-bis*, 2,316t stdd.)									
1	*Smelyi*	03.12.47	190	601	16.05.48	29.09.49	21.12.49	KBF	
2	*Stojkii*	03.12.47	190	602	16.11.48	01.02.49	19.04.50	KBF	
3	*Ognennyi*	03.12.47	402	178	14.08.48	17.08.49	28.12.49	SF	10
4	*Otchetlivyi*	03.12.47	402	179	29.10.48	14.09.49	28.12.49	SF	
5	*Ostryi*	03.12.47	402	180	21.12.48	16.04.50	25.08.50	SF	
6	*Otvestvennyi*	03.12.47	402	181	11.06.49	12.04.50	31.08.50	SF	
7	*Otmennyi*	03.12.47	402	182	08.10.49	17.06.50	06.11.50	SF	
8	*Otryvistyi*	03.12.47	402	183	03.12.49	25.08.50	10.12.50	SF	

[1] 1955–57 rebuilt to *projekt 67EP* as cruise missile test ship, stricken 1961.
[2] Modernized to *projekt 68A*.
[3] 1972 commissioned after rebuilding to *projekt 68-U-2* as command cruiser.
[4] Planned to be completed to *projekt 68-bis ZIF* with amended dual-purpose armament, laid up after launching, cancelled 02.09.59.
[5] Transferred for building to Molotovsk, renamed on 25.09.53 to *Arkhangel'sk* and *Vladivostok*, cancelled on 02.09.53, broken up in the building docks.
[6] On 03.08.57 renamed to *Oktyabrskaya revolyutsiya*. 1976–77 modernized to *projekt 68A*.
[7] Laid up after launching, cancelled on 02.09.53, scrapped in 1961.
[8] Cancelled in August 1952 before being ordered and laid down.
[9] *Projekts* studied during WWII and cancelled in September 1945.
[10] 1957–62 modernized to *projekt 31*.

Table A7 (contd.): Warships of the *VMF*, laid down or ordered, 1945–53

No.	Name	Order	Yard	Yard No.	Laid down	Launched	Commiss.	Fleet	Notes
Destroyers (*Projekt 30-bis*, 2,316t stdd.) *continued*								
9	*Otrazhayushchii*	03.12.47	402	184	03.03.50	01.10.50	17.12.50	SF	
10	*Bditel'nyi*	03.12.47	445	1101	10.06.48	30.12.48	25.10.49	ChF	
11	*Bezuderzhnyi*	03.12.47	445	1102	20.07.48	31.03.49	30.12.49	ChF	
12	*Bujnyi*	03.12.47	445	1103	15.04.49	23.09.49	29.08.50	ChF	
13	*Bezuprechnyi*	03.12.47	445	1104	15.07.49	31.12.49	09.09.50	ChF	
14	*Besstrashnyi*	03.12.47	445	1105	29.09.49	31.03.50	31.10.50	ChF	
15	*Boevoi*	03.12.47	445	1106	21.12.49	29.04.50	19.12.50	ChF	1
16	*Vstrechnyi*	03.12.47	199	6	29.04.48	20.05.49	07.12.49	TOF	
17	*Vedushchii*	03.12.47	199	9	31.07.48	21.08.49	26.12.49	TOF	
18	*Vazhnyi*	03.12.47	199	12	30.10.48	04.09.49	29.12.49	TOF	
19	*Vspyl'chivyi*	03.12.07	199	13	15.02.49	14.05.50	30.09.50	TOF	
20	*Velichavyi*	03.12.47	199	14	04.08.49	14.05.50	31.10.50	TOF	
21	*Skoryi*	07.10.48	190	603	15.02.48	14.08.49	26.09.50	KBF	2
22	*Surovyi*	07.10.48	190	604	15.08.49	01.10.49	31.10.50	KBF	
23	*Serdityi*	07.10.48	190	605	22.12.49	15.04.50	20.12.50	KBF	
24	*Sposobnyi*	07.10.48	190	606	01.03.50	20.12.50	28.01.51	KBF	3
25	*Stremitel'nyi*	07.10.48	190	607	15.05.50	15.04.51	04.07.51	KBF	4
26	*Sokrushitel'nyi*	07.10.48	190	608	15.09.50	30.06.51	28.11.51	KBF	
27	*Otradnyi*	01.12.48	402	188	10.05.50	30.12.50	20.07.51	SF	
28	*Ozarennyi*	01.12.48	402	189	06.07.50	07.03.51	28.07.51	SF	
29	*Bystryi*	01.12.48	445	1107	20.02.50	28.06.50	19.12.50	ChF	
30	*Burnyi*	01.12.48	445	1108	18.05.50	29.08.50	04.06.51	ChF	5
31	*Vertkii*	01.12.48	199	15	05.11.49	22.07.50	14.12.50	TOF	
32	*Vechnyi*	01.12.48	199	16	12.01.50	30.08.50	15.12.50	TOF	
33	*Vikhrevoi*	01.12.48	199	17	28.02.50	15.09.50	18.03.51	TOF	
34	*Svobodnyi*	15.04.49	190	609	27.11.50	20.08.51	23.06.52	KBF	
35	*Statnyi*	15.04.49	190	610	01.03.51	28.10.51	04.08.52	KBF	
36	*Oberegayushchii*	15.04.49	402	190	23.09.50	11.05.51	20.10.51	SF	
37	*Okhrayayushchii*	15.04.49	402	191	25.11.50	26.07.51	28.11.51	SF	6
38	*Ostorozhnyi*	15.04.49	402	192	25.01.51	25.09.51	20.12.51	SF	
39	*Okrylennyi*	15.04.49	402	193	24.03.51	17.10.51	31.12.51	SF	
40	*Besposhchadnyi*	15.04.49	445	1109	28.05.50	30.09.50	27.06.51	ChF	7
41	*Bezshalostnyi*	15.04.49	445	1110	12.07.50	30.12.50	06.07.51	ChF	8
42	*Vidnyi*	15.04.49	199	18	27.05.50	17.05.51	21.12.51	TOF	
43	*Vernyi*	15.04.49	199	19	15.07.50	17.05.51	26.12.51	SF	6
44	*Smetlivyi*	15.03.50	190	611	24.05.51	17.11.51	05.08.52	KBF	9
45	*Smotryashchii*	15.03.50	190	612	21.06.51	19.02.52	04.11.52	KBF	
46	*Sovershennyi*	15.03.50	190	613	16.07.51	24.04.52	24.12.52	KBF	
47	*Otzhyvchivyi*	15.03.50	402	194	30.05.51	29.12.51	20.12.52	SF	
48	*Otchayannyi*	15.03.50	402	195	25.08.51	29.12.51	25.11.52	SF	10
49	*Opasnyi*	15.03.50	196	196	20.10.51	01.06.52	09.12.52	SF	6
50	*Bezzavetnyi*	15.03.50	445	1111	28.09.50	30.03.51	11.11.51	ChF	11
51	*Besshumnyi*	15.03.50	445	1112	31.10.50	31.05.51	30.11.51	ChF	6

[1] 25.11.64 to Indonesia as *Darmuda*, served up to 1973.
[2] 29.06.58 to Poland as *Wicher*, served to 1975.
[3] 15.12.57 to Poland as *Grom*, served to the 1970s.
[4] 1957–62 modernized to *projekt 31*.
[5] 30.06.59 to Egypt, 01.62 as *Suez*, served up to 1985.
[6] 1957–62 modernized to *projekt 31*.
[7] 30.06.59 to Egypt, 01.62 as *Damietta*, 15.07.68 returned, again old name.
[8] 28.02.64 to Indonesia as *Brawidjaja*. up to 1973 in service.
[9] 14.11.55 to Egypt, 11.06.56 renamed *Al Zaffer* up to 30.07.87 in service.
[10] In June 1968 to Egypt as replacement for *Al Nasser*, from 1973 as *6 October* up to 30.07.87 in service
[11] 30.06.59 to Indonesia as *Sultan Iskandar Muda*, 1969 in reserve, 9 1971 scrapped.

Table A7 (contd.): Warships of the *VMF*, laid down or ordered, 1945–53

No.	Name	Order	Yard	Yard No.	Laid down	Launched	Commiss.	Fleet	Notes
Destroyers (*Project 30-bis*, 2,316t stdd.) *continued*									
52	*Bespokojnyi*	15.03.50	445	1113	16.01.51	30.06.51	21.12.51	ChF	1
53	*Vnezapnyi*	15.03.50	199	20	23.09.50	14.06.51	28.12.51	TOF	2
54	*Vnimatel'nyi*	15.03.50	199	21	31.10.50	02.08.51	26.12.51	TOF	
55	*Vyrazitel'nyi*	15.03.50	199	22	14.12.50	26.08.51	29.12.51	TOF	3
56	*Volevoj*	15.03.50	199	23	01.03.51	11.09.51	29.12.51	TOF	4
57	*Vol'nyi*	15.03.50	199	24	12.06.51	13.07.52	31.12.52	TOF	
58	*Vkradchivyi*	15.03.50	199	25	14.07.51	04.06.52	31.12.52	TOF	
59	*Ser'eznyi*	22.06.51	190	616	25.10.51	13.07.52	04.12.52	KBF	
60	*Solidnyi*	22.06.51	190	617	04.01.52	17.08.52	31.12.52	KBF	5
61	*Stepennyi*	22.06.51	190	618	11.02.52	22.09.52	11.02.53	KBF	
62	*Pyl'kii*	22.06.51	190	619	20.04.52				
			445		–	31.07.52	31.12.52	ChF	6
63	*Ozhivlennyi*	22.06.51	402	197	12.01.52	04.08.52	24.01.53	SF	
64	*Ozhestochennyi*	22.06.51	402	198	03.04.52	26.09.52	14.03.53	SF	
65	*Bezboyaznennyi*	22.06.51	445	1114	26.03.51	31.08.51	11.01.52	ChF	7
66	*Bezotkaznyi*	22.06.51	445	1115	22.06.51	31.10.51	04.10.52	ChF	
67	*Bezukoriznennyi*	22.06.51	445	1116	29.07.51	31.01.52	30.09.52	ChF	
68	*Bessmennyi*	22.06.51	445	1117	12.09.51	31.03.52	10.12.52	ChF	8
69	*Vdumchivii*	22.06.51	199	26	05.11.51	31.07.52	31.12.52	TOF	
70	*Vrazumitel'nyi*	22.06.51	199	27	15.12.51	03.09.52	10.01.53	TOF	
71–90	–	–	–	–	–	–	–	–	9
Destroyers (*Projekt 41*, 3,010t stdd.)									
1	*Neustrashimyi*	15.03.50	190	614	05.07.50	29.01.51	31.01.55	KBF	
2	–	12.50	190	?	?	–	–	–	10
3	–	12.50	402	?	?	–	–	–	10
4	–	12.50	402	?	?	–	–	–	10
5–110	–	–	–	–	–	–	–	–	11
Destroyers (*Projekt 56*, 2,667t stdd.)									
1	*Spokojnyi*	19.08.52	190	701	04.03.53	28.11.53	27.06.56	KBF	
2	*Svetlyi*	19.08.52	190	702	04.03.53	27.10.53	17.09.55	KBF	
3	*Speshnyi*	19.08.52	190	703	30.05.53	07.08.54	30.09.55	KBF	
4	*Skromnyi*	19.08.52	190	704	27.07.53	26.10.54	30.12.55	KBF/SF	12
5	*Svedushchii*	03.09.52	190	705	07.12.53	12.02.55	31.01.56	KBF/SF	13
6	*Smyshlenyi*	03.09.52	190	706	23.02.54	24.05.55	28.06.56	SF	13,14
7	*Blestyashchii*	03.09.52	445	1201	20.02.53	27.11.53	30.09.55	ChF	13
8	*Byvalyi*	03.09.52	445	1202	06.05.53	31.03.54	21.12.55	ChF	13
9	*Bravyi*	03.09.52	445	1203	25.07.53	28.02.55	09.01.56	ChF	15

[1] 30.06.59 to Indonesia as *Sandjaja*, up to 1971 in service.
[2] 17.02.59 to Indonesia as *Sawunggaling*, up to 1971 in service.
[3] 22.11.62 to Indonesia as *Singamangaradja*, up to 1971 in service.
[4] 17.02.59 to Indonesia as *Siliwangi*, up to 1973 in service.
[5] 14.11.55 to Egypt, 11.06.56 renamed *Al Nasser*, 15.07.68 returned, again old name.
[6] Transferred for completion from Leningrad to Nikolaev. 28.02.64 to Indonesia as *Diponegoro*, up to 1973 in service.
[7] Modernized to *projekt 31*.
[8] In June 1968 to Egypt as replacement for *Damietta* under this name in service up to 1986.
[9] About 20 more planned, some possibly started, but never completed.
[10] Three more vessels ordered, and probably started, but not completed and cancelled.
[11] Of the 110 vessels first planned, the project was at first reduced to 100, but on 02.06.51 cancelled.
[12] Rebuilt to *projekt 56-A*.
[13] Rebuilt to *projekt 56-PLO* with A/A missile armament.
[14] On 29.10.58 renamed *Moskovskii komsomolets*.
[15] On the slipway reconstructed to *projekt 56-K*.

Table A7 (contd.): Warships of the *VMF*, laid down or ordered, 1945–53

No.	Name	Order	Yard	Yard No.	Laid down	Launched	Commiss.	Fleet	Notes
\multicolumn{10}{l}{**Destroyers (*Projekt 56*, 2,667t stdd.)** *continued*}
10	*Vyzyvayushchii*	03.09.52	199	81	25.07.53	20.05.55	09.01.56	TOF	1
11	*Veskii*	03.09.52	199	82	30.01.54	31.07.55	30.03.58	TOF	
12	*Vdokhnovennyi*	03.09.52	199	83	31.08.54	07.05.56	31.10.56	TOF	1
13	*Vozmushchennyi*	03.09.52	199	84	30.12.54	08.07.56	31.12.56	TOF	1
14	*Skrytnyi*	15.09.53	190	707	25.07.54	27.09.55	30.09.56	KBF	2
15	*Soznatel'nyi*	15.09.53	190	708	25.09.54	15.01.56	31.10.56	KBF	2
16	*Spravedlivyi*	15.09.53	190	709	25.12.54	12.04.56	20.12.56	KBF	2,3
17	*Besslednyi*	15.09.53	445	1205	01.04.54	05.11.55	31.10.56	ChF/TOF	1
18	*Burlivyi*	15.09.53	445	1206	05.05.54	28.01.56	28.12.56	ChF/TOF	1
19	*Blagorodnyi*	15.09.53	445	1207	05.03.55	30.08.56	18.07.57	ChF	1
20	*Vozbuzhdennyi*	15.09.53	199	85	29.07.55	10.05.57	31.10.57	TOF	4
21	*Vliyatel'nyi*	15.09.53	199	86	29.10.55	10.05.57	06.11.57	TOF	
22	*Vyderzhannyi*	15.09.53	199	87	30.06.56	24.06.57	10.12.57	TOF	5
23	*Nesokrushimyi*	29.04.54	190	710	15.06.55	20.07.56	30.06.57	SF	4
24	*Nachodchivyi*	29.04.54	190	741	19.10.55	30.10.56	18.09.57	SF	4
25	*Nastojchivyi*	29.04.54	190	742	03.03.56	23.04.57	30.11.57	KBF/SF	4
26	*Plamennyi*	29.04.54	445	1208	03.09.55	26.10.56	31.08.57	ChF	6
27	*Naporistyi*	19.01.55	445	1209	17.08.55	30.12.56	31.10.57	ChF	6
\multicolumn{10}{l}{**Missile Destroyers (*Projekt 56* and *56M*, 22,890t stdd. or 2,767t stdd.)**}
1	*Bedovyi*	03.09.52	445	1204	01.12.53	31.07.55	30.06.58	ChF	7
2	*Neulovimyi*	29.04.54	190	743	23.02.57	27.02.58	30.12.58	KBF	8
3	*Neuderzimyi*	19.01.55	199	88	23.02.57	24.05.58	30.12.58	TOF	8
4	*Prozorlivyi*	17.10.55	445	1210	23.02.57	24.05.58	30.12.58	ChF	8
5	*Neukrotimyi*	17.10.55	199	89	57	–	–	TOF	9
\multicolumn{10}{l}{**Patrol Ships (*Projekt 42*, 1,339t stdd.)**}
1	*Berkut*	08.12.48	820	101	25.04.50	08.04.51	10.05.52	SF/TOF	
2	*Kondor*	08.12.48	820	102	28.06.50	17.05.51	10.05.52	SF/TOF	
3	*Grif*	08.12.48	820	103	18.09.50	03.09.51	25.10.52	SF/Kfl	10
4	*Krechet*	08.12.48	820	104	15.12.50	27.11.51	18.12.52	SF/Kfl	11
5	*Orlan*	08.12.48	820	105	30.04.51	09.05.52	17.03.53	SF/Kfl	12
6	*Sokol'*	26.03.49	820	100	17.08.49	11.09.50	04.12.52	SF/Kfl	12
7	*Lev*	13.01.50	820	106	30.04.51	24.05.52	17.03.53	SF/ChF	
8	*Tigr*	13.01.50	820	107	01.07.52	29.09.52	25.04.53	SF/ChF	

[1] Rebuilt to projekt 56-PLO with A/A missile armament.
[2] Rebuilt to *projekt 56-A*.
[3] 25.06.70 to Poland as *Warszawa*, on 01.01.86 deleted.
[4] Rebuilt to *projekt 56-A*.
[5] 20.02.67 renamed *Dal'nevostochnyi komsomolets*.
[6] Rebuilt to *projekt 56-PLO*.
[7] On the slipway reconstructed to *projekt 56-EM*.
[8] On the slipway reconstructed to *projekt 56-M*.
[9] Probably only material collected, but not laid down. Cancelled.
[10] 1965 transferred to Kaspian Flotilla, renamed *Sovetskii Azerbajdzhan*.
[11] 1968 transferred to Kaspian Flotilla, renamed *Sovetskii Dagestan*.
[12] 1976 transferred to Kaspian Flotilla, renamed *Sovetskii Turkmenistan* and *Komsomolets Azerbajdzhana*.

Table A7 (contd.): Warships of the *VMF*, laid down or ordered, 1945–53

No.	Name	Order	Yard	Yard No.	Laid down	Launched	Commiss.	Fleet	Notes
\multicolumn{10}{l}{**Patrol Ships (*Projekt 50*, 1,068t stdd.)**}
1	*Leopard*	13.11.51	820	108	21.12.51	30.04.53	30.06.54	SF	
2	*Gornostaj*	07.12.51	445	1120	20.12.51	30.06.52	12.01.53	ChF	
3	*Pantera*	07.12.51	445	1121	21.02.52	20.08.52	21.05.54	ChF	1
4	*Rys'*	07.12.51	445	1122	22.04.52	31.12.52	21.05.54	ChF	
5	*Yaguar*	07.12.51	445	1123	23.07.52	14.02.53	24.04.54	ChF	2
6	*Bars*	07.12.51	820	109	25.04.52	25.07.53	30.06.54	SF	
7	*Rosomakha*	01.02.52	820	110	19.06.52	16.08.53	30.04.54	SF	
8	*Sobol'*	01.02.52	820	111	27.09.52	05.11.53	13.10.54	KBF	3
9	*Sarych*	09.02.52	445	1124	24.09.52	31.03.53	31.08.54	ChF	4
10	*Zubr*	13.05.52	199	41	29.08.52	09.02.53	31.05.54	TOF	4
11	*Bizon*	13.05.52	199	42	04.10.52	09.07.53	30.06.54	TOF	4
12	*Puma*	19.05.52	445	1125	25.11.52	29.04.53	31.08.54	ChF	4
13	*Volk*	19.05.52	445	1126	26.02.53	23.07.53	31.10.54	ChF	
14	*Kunitsa*	19.05.52	445	1127	27.05.53	30.11.53	23.12.54	ChF	
15	*Barsuk*	19.05.52	820	112	02.12.52	27.02.54	15.09.54	KBF	
16	*Korsak*	05.07.52	445	1128	01.08.53	29.04.54	30.04.55	ChF	4
17	*Kuguar*	05.07.52	820	113	27.03.53	31.12.53	31.08.54	KBF	
18	*Enot*	05.07.52	820	114	17.10.53	09.04.54	30.10.54	KBF	3
19	*Filin*	05.07.52	820	115	27.08.53	06.06.54	09.12.54	KBF	6
20	*Lun'*	05.07.52	820	116	20.10.53	05.08.54	27.12.54	TOF	
21	*Aist*	05.07.52	199	43	25.12.52	25.08.53	27.08.54	TOF	4
22	*Laska* (ex *Giena*)	05.07.52	199	44	05.03.53	18.05.54	25.10.54	TOF	
23	*Norka*	14.03.53	445	1129	12.01.54	29.04.54	30.04.55	ChF	4
24	*Kobchik*	14.03.53	829	117	26.12.53	02.11.54	31.05.55	KBF	10
25	*Tur*	14.03.53	802	118	24.03.54	16.12.54	31.05.55	KBF	5
26	*Pelikan*	14.03.53	199	45	01.08.53	18.04.54	25.10.54	TOF	4
27	*Pingvin*	14.03.53	199	46	10.09.53	13.08.54	31.12.54	TOF	
28	*Gepard*	01.06.53	199	47	21.12.53	13.08.54	31.12.54	TOF	
29	*Voron*	07.10.53	445	1130	12.03.54	11.11.54	18.06.55	ChF	
30	*Los'*	07.10.53	820	119	26.05.54	29.03.55	31.07.55	TOF	
31	*Grifon*	17.10.53	445	1131	15.04.54	11.11.54	18.06.55	ChF	4
32	*Olen'*	07.11.53	120	120	02.08.54	29.04.55	27.08.55	SF	5
33	*SKR-51*	20.02.54	445	1132	25.06.54	26.02.55	28.09.55	ChF	
34	*SKR-52*	04.05.54	445	1133	01.09.54	15.04.55	28.11.55	ChF	7
35	*SKR-50*	04.05.54	820	194	12.10.54	16.08.55	03.01.56	TOF	
36	*SKR-53*	03.06.54	445	1134	20.11.54	15.04.55	31.12.55	ChF	8
37	*SKR-54*	01.07.54	820	131	20.12.54	31.08.55	31.12.55	TOF	
38	*SKR-55*	01.07.54	820	160	18.02.55	30.09.55	31.12.55	TOF	
39	*SKR-56*	16.07.54	820	173	16.04.55	06.01.56	21.05.56	SF	9

[1] 1977 renamed *Sovetskii Turkmenistan*.
[2] 1968 renamed *Komsomolets Gruzii*.
[3] 10.10.59 ceded to the GDR as *Karl Liebknecht* and *Friedrich Engels*, after modernisation.
[4] 1964-66 to Indonesia
[5] 15.12.56 sold to the GDR as *Karl Marx* and *Ernst Thälmann*.
[6] 1957 to Finland as *Filin*.
[7] 1957 to Bulgaria as *Derzki*.
[8] 1967 renamed *Tuman*.
[9] 1977 renamed *Sovetskii Azerbaidzhan*.
[10] 1986 to Bulgaria, as *Bodry*.

Table A7 (contd.): Warships of the *VMF*, laid down or ordered, 1945–53

No.	Submarine	Order	Yard	Yard No.	Laid down	Launched	Commiss.	Fleet	Notes
\multicolumn{10}{l}{**Patrol Ships** (*Projekt 50*, 1,068t stdd.) *continued*}
40	*SKR-57*	06.10.54	445	1135	23.12.54	21.07.55	28.02.56	ChF	
41	*SKR-58*	06.10.54	445	1136	15.03.55	21.07.55	07.05.56	ChF	
42	*SKR-59*	15.04.55	820	147	21.06.55	02.02.56	25.05.56	TOF	
43	*SKR-63*	17.10.55	445	1137	05.05.55	28.10.56	30.05.57	ChF	
44	*SKR-60*	17.10.55	820	149	08.12.55	13.04.56	29.06.56	SF	
45	*SKR-61*	17.10.55	820	151	17.10.55	24.05.56	23.08.56	TOF	
46	*SKR-62*	20.12.55	820	155	21.12.55	27.06.56	25.09.56	TOF	1
47	*SKR-64*	20.12.55	820	156	08.02.56	01.08.56	31.10.56	KBF	2
48	*SKR-66*	09.02.56	445	1138	10.02.56	30.05.56	29.09.56	ChF	3
49	*SKR-67*	09.02.56	446	1139	01.03.56	10.07.56	22.12.56	ChF	
50	*SKR-65*	09.02.56	820	161	28.03.56	04.09.56	27.12.56	KBF	
51	*SKR-68*	01.03.56	820	167	17.05.56	27.10.56	23.03.57	KBF	
52	*SKR-69*	25.04.56	820	125	29.07.56	28.12.56	30.05.57	KBF	4
53	*SKR-70*	09.06.56	820	126	13.08.56	19.02.57	20.06.57	SF	
54	*SKR-71*	18.07.56	820	127	21.09.56	03.04.57	13.07.57	SF	
55	*SKR-72*	30.07.56	820	128	26.01.57	16.05.57	26.09.57	SF	
56	*SKR-73*	12.11.56	820	129	24.12.56	21.06.57	30.09.57	SF	
57	*SKR-74*	07.02.57	820	130	04.02.57	27.07.57	26.11.57	TOF	
58	*SKR-75*	07.02.57	820	132	14.03.57	03.09.57	30.12.57	TOF	
59	*SKR-76*	12.04.57	820	133	29.04.57	16.12.57	15.06.58	SF	5
60	*SKR-77*	12.04.57	820	134	17.06.57	20.01.58	29.06.58	SF	6
61	*SKR-80*	31.07.57	820	136	17.09.57	13.03.58	31.07.58	SF	
62	*SKR-81*	09.08.57	820	138	17.10.57	15.04.58	31.08.58	SF	
63	*SKR-10*	26.10.57	820	139	27.11.57	30.05.58	21.10.58	TOF	
64	*SKR-4*	24.12.57	820	140	28.01.58	30.07.58	13.12.58	KBF	
65	*SKR-5*	24.12.57	820	141	20.03.58	01.09.58	31.12.58	KBF	
66	*SKR-8*	24.12.57	820	142	24.04.58	18.10.58	31.12.58	KBF	
67	*SKR-14*	03.07.58	820	143	29.05.58	09.01.59	09.59	KBF	
68	*SKR-15*	03.07.58	820	144	10.07.58	27.02.59	01.10.59	KBF	

[1] 1969 renamed *Irkutskii komsomolets*.
[2] 1962 renamed *Komsomolets Litvii*.
[3] 15.10.58 to Bulgaria as *Smeli*.
[4] 1957 to Finland.
[5] 1968 renamed *Arkhangel'skii komsomolets*.
[6] 1979 renamed *Sovetskii Dagestan*.

Table A8: Submarines of the *VMF*, laid down or ordered, 1945–53

No.	Name	Order	Yard	Yard No.	Laid down	Launched	Commiss.	Fleet	Notes
	Submarines (*Project 96*, and *96bis*, 280t normal)								1
1	M-236	29.03.48	112						2
			196	355	19.02.47	19.06.48	19.10.48	KBF	
2	M-237	29.03.48	112						
			196	373	15.03.47	27.07.48	29.11.48	KBF/ChF	
3	M-238	29.03.48	112						
			196	374	25.04.47	21.08.48	07.12.48	KBF/ChF	
4	M-239	29.03.48	196	375	07.06.47	02.10.48	14.07.49	KBF/ChF	
5	M-240	29.03.48	196	376	27.08.48	22.11.48	30.07.48	KBF/ChF	
6	M-241	29.03.48	196	377	31.08.48	30.12.48	30.07.49	KBF/ChF	
7	M-242	29.03.48	196	378	30.09.48	30.03.49	30.07.49	KBF/ChF	
8	M-243	29.03.48	196	379	31.10.48	30.04.49	31.08.49	KBF/ChF	
9	M-244	29.03.48	196	380	24.11.48	01.06.49	01.10.49	KBF/ChF	
10	M-245	29.03.48	196	381	30.11.48	30.06.49	31.10.49	KBF	2
11	M-246	29.03.48	196	382	25.01.49	24.07.49	16.11.49	KBF	2
12	M-247	29.03.48	196	383	14.02.49	31.08.49	22.11.49	KBF/ChF	
13	M-248	08.12.48	196	384	24.02.49	26.09.49	23.11.49	KBF/TOF	
14	M-249	08.12.48	196	385	25.04.49	30.10.49	31.12.49	KBF/TOF	
15	M-250	08.12.48	196	386	28.06.49	28.11.49	02.06.50	KBF/TOF	
16	M-251	08.12.48	196	387	02.10.49	26.03.50	10.07.50	KBF/TOF	
17	M-252	08.12.48	196	388	22.10.49	26.03.50	10.07.50	KBF/TOF	
18	M-253	08.12.48	196	389	09.11.49	30.03.50	29.07.50	KBF/TOF	
19	M-270	26.11.49	196	500	23.12.49	24.04.50	29.07.50	KBF	2
20	M-271	26.11.49	196	501	31.01.50	30.04.50	28.08.50	KBF	3
21	M-272	26.11.49	196	502	25.02.50	13.06.50	11.09.50	KBF	
22	M-273	26.11.49	196	503	18.03.50	20.07.50	28.09.50	KBF/TOF	
23	M-274	26.11.49	196	504	25.04.50	18.09.50	31.10.50	KBF	2
24	M-275	26.11.49	196	505	25.05.50	23.09.50	18.11.50	KBF/TOF	
25	M-276	26.11.49	196	506	28.06.50	17.10.50	25.12.50	KBF/TOF	4
26	M-277	26.11.49	196	507	31.07.50	12.50	24.05.51	KBF/TOF	4
27	M-278	08.04.50	196	508	31.08.50	19.01.51	28.05.51	KBF/TOF	4
28	M-279	08.04.50	196	509	12.10.50	10.02.51	09.06.51	KBF/TOF	4
29	M-280	06.10.50	196	510	20.12.50	14.04.51	21.07.51	KBF/TOF	
30	M-281	06.10.50	196	619	04.02.51	29.04.51	23.08.51	KBF/TOF	
31	M-282	11.12.50	196	620	11.03.51	12.06.51	14.09.51	KBF/TOF	
32	M-283	11.12.50	196	621	02.04.51	03.07.51	30.09.51	KBF/TOF	
33	M-284	11.12.50	196	622	03.05.51	11.08.51	31.10.51	KBF/TOF	
34	M-285	11.12.50	196	623	31.05.51	14.09.51	12.02.52	KBF/TOF	
35	M-286	11.12.50	196	624	29.06.51	15.10.51	25.06.52	KBF/TOF	
36	M-287	08.02.51	196	625	25.06.51	15.11.51	25.06.52	KBF/TOF	
37	M-288	08.02.51	196	626	24.08.51	24.01.52	24.07.52	KBF/TOF	
38	M-289	08.02.51	196	627	27.09.51	28.04.52	27.08.52	KBF/TOF	
39	M-290	08.02.51	196	628	10.11.51	27.05.52	30.09.52	KBF	5
40	M-291	06.04.51	196	629	28.12.51	01.07.52	25.11.52	KBF/TOF	
41	M-292	26.02.52	196	644	15.04.52	30.09.52	12.01.53	KBF/TOF	
42	M-293	26.02.52	196	645	10.02.52	02.10.52	12.01.53	KBF/TOF	
43	M-294	26.02.52	196	646	29.05.52	22.10.52	26.02.53	KBF/TOF	

[1] M-200-203 were ordered, built and commissioned up to the end of WWII. M-204-206, M-214-218, M-233-234 were ordered and started to be built before the end of WWII but commissioned only after the war. M-219 was lost before commissioning (see Table A3). M-210-213, M-220-236 were ordered before WWII, but never begun. M-236 was reordered 1947/48. Three submarines *projekt 96* were transferred to Bulgaria. On 18.06, 25.09, 18.10.54 and 27.05.55 one, one, three, and one submarines were transferred to Poland. 1954-55 four submarines were transferred to China. 1954-57 Four submarines were transferred to Romania.

[2] These submarines were transferred to Poland.

[3] This submarine was transferred to Egypt.

[4] Transferred to China.

[5] Transferred to Poland.

Table A8 (contd.): Submarines of the *VMF*, laid down or ordered, 1945–53

No. Submarine   Order   Yard   Yard No.   Laid down   Launched   Commiss.   Fleet   Notes

Submarines (*Projekt 97*, see Table 3, Submarines *Series XVI*, 841t normal)
The plan was then to build five at 196, five at 198 and four at 112.

Submarines (*Projekt 98*, Big Transport Submarine)
The plan was to build the submarines at 112. But no submarine started, cancelled

Submarines (*Projekt 99*, Big Minelayer Submarine *MZ*, 1230t normal)
No submarine laid down.

Submarines (*Projekt 101*, Big Cruiser Submarine *KU*, 1550t normal)
No submarine laid down.

Submarines (*Projekt 105*, Small Submarine, ca.300t normal),
No submarine laid down

Submarines (*Projekt 106*, Medium Submarines, follow on for *Series X-bis*, 590t normal)
No submarine laid down.

Submarines (*Projekt 601*, former *Projekt 97* or *Series XVI*)
No new submarine laid down.

Submarines (*Projekt 602*, Small Submarine, follow on for *M*-class)
No submarine laid down.

Submarine (*Projekt 604*, Small Minelayer Submarine, 235t normal)
Was the rebuilt *Series XII-bis* submarine *M-171*, see Table 3.

Submarines (*Projekt 605*, Small Transport Submarines, 2–300t, or 5–600t normal)
No submarine laid down.

Submarines (*Projekt 606*, Midget Submarine, 34t normal, *Projekt 606-bis*, 36.5t normal)
No submarine laid down.

Submarines (*Projekt 607*, Medium Transport Submarine, 740t normal)
No submarine laid down.

Submarines (*Projekt 609*, Follow on for *L*-class, *Series XIII-bis*)
No submarine laid down.

Submarines (*Projekt 610*, Midget Submarine, 40t normal)
No submarine laid down.

Submarines (*Projekt 612*, Medium Submarine, later incorporated into *Projekt 615*)
No submarine laid down.

Submarines (*Projekt 614*, former German war booty, *Type XXI*, see Table 6)

Submarines (*Projekt 616*, follow on building of the German *Type XXVI* Walter-Submarine)
No submarine laid down.

Submarine (*Projekt 618*, Closed-cycle submarine of medium size)
No submarine laid down.

Submarines (*Projekt 621*, Big Amphibious submarine, 5845t normal, 10 tanks *T-34*)
No submarine laid down.

Submarines (*Projekt 626*, Transport Submarine, 3400t normal)
No submarine laid down.

Submarines (*Projekt 632*, Transport Submarine, 2500t normal)
No submarine laid down.

Submarines (*Projekt 637*, Closed-cycle Walter submarine)

Table A8 (contd.): Submarines of the *VMF*, laid down or ordered, 1945–53

No.	Submarine	Order	Yard	Yard No.	Laid down	Launched	Commiss.	Fleet	Notes
\multicolumn{10}{l}{**Submarines (*Projekt 611*, 1831t normal)**}										1
1	*B-61*	13.11.50	196	580	10.01.51	26.07.51	31.12.53	KBF	
2	*B-62*	08.01.51	196	631	06.09.51	29.04.52	31.12.53	KBF/TOF	2
3	*B-63*	15.10.51	196	632	06.02.52	18.07.52	30.06.54	TOF	
4	*B-64*	15.10.51	196	633	15.05.52	29.11.52	31.12.54	SF	3
5	*B-65*	13.11.51	196	634	24.07.52	21.03.53	06.12.54	KBF/SF	
6	*B-66*	01.02.52	196	635	15.12.52	30.06.53	29.12.54	SF/TOF	
7	*B-67*	10.05.52	196	636	26.03.53	05.09.53	30.06.56	SF	4
8	*B-68*	10.05.52	196	637	04.06.53	31.10.53	27.11.55	TOF	
9	*B-69*	05.07.52	196	638	14.09.53	18.06.54	31.12.55	SF	5
10	*B-70*	06.12.54	402	351	14.05.54	18.09.55	29.06.56	SF	
11	*B-71*	06.12.54	402	402	07.06.54	19.05.56	30.09.56	SF/TOF	
12	*B-72*	06.12.54	402	403	16.11.53	18.09.55	30.06.56	SF/TOF	
13	*B-73*	30.11.54	402	404	16.08.54	16.01.57	30.11.57	SF	2
14	*B-74*	28.01.55	402	305	27.09.54	05.06.56	31.10.56	SF	
15	*B-75*	23.01.56	402	306	11.11.54	08.07.56	06.11.56	SF	
16	*B-76*	22.03.56	402	307	24.01.55	25.08.56	28.11.56	SF	
17	*B-77*	05.04.56	402	208	07.05.55	20.09.56	30.11.56	SF	
18	*B-78*	12.11.56	402	209	16.07.55	13.06.57	30.11.57	SF	2,6
19	*B-79*	22.12.56	402	210	19.12.55	16.07.57	03.12.57	SF	2
20	*B-80*	30.07.56	402	111	01.02.56	16.01.57	13.07.57	SF	
21	*B-81*	03.11.56	402	112	10.04.56	12.05.57	13.07.57	SF	
22	*B-82*	12.11.56	402	113	15.06.56	12.05.57	17.08.57	SF	
23	*B-88*	27.12.56	402	514	17.08.56	04.07.57	25.09.57	SF	
24	*B-89*	09.01.57	402	515	05.02.57	21.09.57	13.12.57	SF	2
25	*B-90*	09.01.57	402	516	25.10.56	17.08.57	30.10.57	SF	
26	*B-91*	09.01.57	402	517	25.01.57	26.11.57	15.07.58	SF	

[1] The plan was to build 40 units of this project, but the plan was reduced.
[2] Rebuilt to *projekt 611AV* with two ballistic missiles RM-11 FM.
[3] 1956/57 rebuilt to *projekt 611-P* with ballistic missile P-10.
[4] Rebuilt to *projekt B-611*.
[5] Rebuilt to *projekt P-611*.
[6] 09.10.62 renamed *Murmanskii komsomolets*

Medium Submarines (*Projekt 613*, 1080t normal)

No.	Submarine	Order	Yard	Yard No.	Laid down	Launched	Commiss.	Fleet	Notes
1	*S-61*	01.12.48	198	376	11.04.50	22.07.50	18.11.52	ChF	1,2
2	*S-62*	01.12.48	198	377	22.07.50	17.09.50	18.11.52	ChF	3
3	*S-63*	01.12.48	198	378	18.09.50	05.11.50	06.11.52	ChF	4
4	*S-64*	01.12.48	198	379	15.11.50	07.02.51	04.11.52	ChF	5
5	*S-65*	01.12.48	198	380	11.02.51	28.04.51	30.12.52	ChF	6
6	*S-66*	01.12.48	198	381	15.05.51	06.11.51	03.01.53	ChF	7
7	*S-67*	01.12.48	198	382	19.11.51	01.11.52	07.02.53	ChF	7

[1] 25.02.50 renamed *Komsomolets*
[2] 09.58–12.62 rebuilt to *projekt 665* with four cruise missiles.
[3] Rebuilt to *projekt 640* as radar early warning vessel.
[4] Rebuilt to *projekt 666* as rescue vessel.
[5] Rebuilt to *projekt 644* with two cruise missiles.
[6] Rebuilt to *projekt 613RV* with new torpedoes R-11.
[7] Modernized to *projekt 613V*.

Table A8 (contd.): Submarines of the *VMF*, laid down or ordered, 1945–53

No.	Submarine	Order	Yard	Yard No.	Laid down	Launched	Commiss.	Fleet	Notes
Medium Submarines (*Projekt 613*, 1080t.normal) *(continued)*									
8	S-80	08.12.48	112	801	13.03.50	21.10.50	02.12.51	Kfl/SF	1,2
9	S-43	26.11.49	112	802	27.06.50	31.12.50	29.12.52	SF	3
10	S-44	26.11.49	112	803	21.10.50	10.05.51	31.12.52	SF	
11	S-45	26.11.49	112	804	30.12.50	16.06.51	31.12.52	Kfl/SF	
12	S-46	26.11.49	112	805	27.03.51	09.08.51	31.12.52	SF	4
13	S-140	20.03.51	112	201	05.06.51	09.12.51	18.03.53	KF/SF/TOF	5
14	S-141	20.03.51	112	202	27.07.51	30.12.51	11.04.53	KF/SF/TOF	5
15	S-142	20.03.51	112	203	20.09.51	16.02.52	19.05.53	KF/SF	6
16	S-143	20.03.51	112	204	06.11.51	06.04.52	08.04.53	KF/SF/TOF	7
17	S-144	20.03.51	112	205	11.12.51	27.04.52	24.04.53	KF/SF	
18	S-68	11.06.51	198	406	15.12.51	01.11.52	20.04.53	ChF	
19	S-69	11.06.51	198	407	15.01.52	16.11.52	10.04.53	ChF	4
20	S-145	07.07.51	112	301	25.01.52	16.06.52	30.06.53	KF/SF/TOF	5
21	S-146	07.07.51	112	302	09.02.52	07.08.52	30.06.53	KF/SF/	8
22	S-147	07.07.51	112	303	05.03.52	15.09.52	21.12.53	SF	
23	S-148	07.07.51	112	304	15.04.52	05.10.52	30.12.53	KF/SF	9
24	S-149	07.07.51	112	305	17.05.52	25.10.52	30.09.53	KF/ChF	10
25	S-70	13.11.51	198	408	12.07.52	26.12.52	12.07.53	ChF	4
26	S-71	13.11.51	198	409	25.10.52	06.53	06.10.53	ChF	
27	S-72	13.11.51	198	410	18.11.52	24.05.53	20.09.53	ChF	
28	S-73	13.11.51	198	411	31.01.53	15.03.53	05.10.53	ChF	10,11
29	S-150	13.11.51	112	401	16.06.52	05.11.52	25.09.53	KF/SF/TOF	5
30	S-151	13.11.51	112	402	14.07.52	22.11.52	30.09.53	KF/ChF	10
31	S-152	13.11.51	112	403	31.08.52	21.12.52	28.09.53	SF	6
32	S-153	13.11.51	112/198	404	09.08.52	30.01.53	31.12.53	KBF	
33	S-154	13.11.51	112/198	405	06.09.52	18.02.53	31.12.53	KBF	5
34	S-74	19.05.52	198	412	26.02.53	31.07.53	24.11.53	ChF	5
35	S-75	19.05.52	198	413	31.01.53	08.08.53	12.12.53	ChF	12
36	S-76	19.05.52	198	414	20.04.53	30.05.53	31.12.53	ChF	5
37	S-77	19.05.52	198	415	27.05.53	30.10.53	28.02.54	ChF/SF/TOF	13
38	S-78	19.05.52	198	416	25.06.53	30.10.53	29.05.54	ChF/SF/TOF	
39	S-79	19.05.52	198	417	18.07.53	31.12.53	30.05.54	ChF/SF/TOF	14

[1] Rebuilt to *projekt 644* with two cruise missiles.
[2] Sunk on 27.01.61, raised and re-commissioned.
[3] Modernized to *projekt 613S*.
[4] Rebuilt to *projekt 644* with two cruise missiles.
[5] Modernized to *projekt 613V*.
[6] 09.58–12.62 rebuilt to *projekt 665* with four cruise missiles.
[7] 27.10.69 renamed *Ulyanovskii komsomolets*.
[8] 1957 rebuilt to *projekt P613* with one P-5 missile.
[9] 14.12.58 rebuilt to research vessel *Severyanka*.
[10] Rebuilt to *projekt 640* as radar early warning vessel.
[11] Modernized to *projekt 613* R&S.
[12] Transferred to North Korea
[13] 12.10.72 renamed *Tyumenskii komsomolets*
[14] Transferred to Indonesia, renamed *Tjakra*.

Table A8 (contd.): Submarines of the *VMF*, laid down or ordered, 1945–53

No.	Submarine	Order	Yard	Yard No.	Laid down	Launched	Commiss.	Fleet	Notes
Medium Submarines (*Projekt 613*, 1080t normal) *(continued)*									
40	S-86	19.05.52	198	418	17.07.53	31.08.53	03.06.54	ChF/SF/TOF	1
41	S-87	19.05.52	198	419	04.09.53	11.12.53	18.06.54	ChF/SF/TOF	
42	S-88	19.05.52	198	420	22.10.53	31.12.53	30.09.54	ChF/SF/TOF	
43	S-155	19.05.52	112	501	30.09.52	16.03.53	18.12.53	SF	2
44	S-156	19.05.52	112	502	25.10.52	01.04.53			
			198				31.12.53	KBF	3
45	S-157	19.05.52	112	503	25.11.52	07.04.53	30.11.53	Kfl/SF	
46	S-158	19.05.52	112	504	23.12.52	16.05.53	31.12.53	Kfl/SF	4
47	S-159	19.05.52	112	505	15.01.53	23.05.53	05.11.53	Kfl/SF	
48	S-160	19.05.52	112	601	10.02.53	01.07.53	10.03.54	Kfl/SF	1
49	S-161	19.05.52	112	602	09.03.53	27.06.53	26.03.54	Kfl/SF	1
50	S-162	19.05.52	112	603	25.03.53	08.07.53	28.04.54	KBF	5
51	S-163	19.05.52	112	604	15.04.53	11.07.53	29.03.54	Kfl/KBF	
52	S-164	19.05.52	112	605	25.04.53	09.10.53	12.04.54	Kfl/SF	6
53	S-165	05.07.52	112	701	15.05.53	10.10.53	10.05.54	Kfl/SF	
54	S-166	05.07.52	112	702	28.05.53	27.10.53	15.07.54	KBF	
55	S-167	05.07.52	112	703	13.06.53	05.11.53	30.07.54	KBF	7
56	S-168	14.03.53	112	704	30.06.53	14.11.53	23.07.54	SF	1
57	S-169	14.03.53	112	705	13.07.53	27.11.53	29.07.54	Kfl/KBF	
58	S-170	14.03.53	112	901	27.08.53	19.12.53	26.07.54	KBF	
59	S-171	14.03.53	112	902	08.09.53	30.12.53	10.08.54	KBF	7
60	S-172	14.03.53	112	903	21.09.53	11.02.54	30.08.54	KBF	1
61	S-173	14.03.53	112	904	30.09.53	16.02.54	18.09.54	Kfl/SF/TOF	
62	S-174	14.03.53	112	905	22.10.53	27.02.54	23.09.54	KBF	
63	S-175	14.03.53	112	111	31.10.53	16.03.54	10.10.54	KBF	8
64	S-176	21.08.53	112	112	17.11.53	28.03.54	10.10.54	SF/TOF	1
65	S-177	21.08.53	112	113	27.11.53	14.04.54	26.09.54	KBF	
66	S-178	21.08.54	112	114	12.12.53	10.04.54	20.10.54	SF/TOF	1
67	S-179	21.08.53	112	115	26.10.53	22.04.54	05.11.54	SFrTOF	
68	S-89	21.08.53	198	421	15.10.53	27.03.54	30.08.54	ChF	1
69	S-180	12.10.53	112	211	31.12.53	15.05.54	09.12.54	KBF	8
70	S-181	12.10.53	112	212	22.01.54	22.05.54	23.11.54	SF	
71	S-182	12.10.53	112	213	30.01.54	29.05.54	08.12.54	Kfl/KBF	
72	S-187	12.10.53	189	455	28.01.54	23.08.54	28.02.55	KBF	
73	S-90	14.11.53	198	422	12.11.53	31.12.53	22.09.54	ChF	
74	S-91	14.11.53	198	423	27.10.53	23.12.53	28.08.54	SF/TOF	
75	S-95	24.11.53	198	424	23.11.53	29.05.54	29.09.54	ChF	
76	S-96	24.11.53	198	425	04.12.53	27.06.54	31.10.54	ChF	
77	S-97	24.11.53	198	426	24.12.53	28.03.54	17.11.54	ChF	

[1] Modernized to *projekt 613V*.
[2] 09.58–12.62 rebuilt to *projekt 665* with four cruise missiles.
[3] Renamed *Komsomolets Kazakhstana*.
[4] 1959 rebuilt to *projekt 644* with two cruise missiles. 1962–1964 rebuilt to *projekt 644.7* with two P-7 missiles.
[5] 1959 rebuilt to *projekt 644* with two P-5D missiles.
[6] Rebuilt to *projekt 665* with four cruise missiles.
[7] Transferred to Syria.
[8] Transferred to Egypt, renamed *S.1. S.2*.

Table A8 (contd.): Submarines of the *VMF*, laid down or ordered, 1945–53

No.	Submarine	Order	Yard	Yard No.	Laid down	Launched	Commiss.	Fleet	Notes
\multicolumn{10}{l}{**Medium Submarines (*Projekt 613*, 1080t normal)** *(continued)*}								
78	S-98	04.12.53	198	427	03.01.54	30.03.54	31.08.54	ChF	
79	S-100	04.12.53	198	428	22.02.54	24.05.54	30.12.54	ChF	
80	S-183	04.12.54	112	214	15.02.54	09.06.54	14.12.54	Kfl/KBF	1
81	S-188	24.12.54	189	456	31.03.54	30.08.54	28.02.55	KBF	
82	S-217	24.12.54	198	429	28.02.54	24.05.54	31.12.54	ChF	
83	S-184	03.01.54	112	215	23.02.54	19.06.54	18.12.54	Kfl/KBF	2
84	S-185	01.02.54	112	311	28.02.54	29.06.54	20.12.54	Kfl/SF	3
85	S-189	01.02.54	189	457	31.03.54	04.09.54	09.03.55	KBF	
86	S-218	01.02.54	198	430	28.02.54	24.05.54	17.03.55	ChF	4
87	S-331	01.02.54	199	51	30.03.54	19.09.54	31.12.54	TOF	3
88	S-186	11.03.54	112	312	13.03.54	10.07.54	30.12.54	KBF	
89	S-192	11.03.54	112	313	24.03.54	20.07.54	22.12.54	SF	
90	S-193	20.03.54	112	314	31.03.54	14.08.54	28.04.55	KBF	2
91	S-194	04.05.54	112	315	10.04.54	31.07.54	17.08.55	SF	3
92	S-190	03.06.54	189	458	01.06.54	21.05.55	29.10.55	KBF/SF	
93	S-191	03.06.54	189	459	01.06.54	09.06.55	31.10.55	KBF	
94	S-195	03.06.54	112	411	20.04.54	04.09.54	17.08.55	SF	3
95	S-196	03.06.54	112	412	30.04.54	28.08.54	25.05.55	KBF	5
96	S-197	03.06.54	112	413	15.05.54	17.09.54	01.04.55	Kfl/SF	3
97	S-198	03.06.54	112	414	22.05.54	26.09.54	24.03.55	Kfl/SF/TOF	
98	S-199	03.06.54	112	415	31.05.54	30.09.54	28.02.55	Kfl/SF	
99	S-219	03.06.54	198	431	25.03.54	10.12.54	30.04.55	ChF/SF/TOF	4
100	S-220	03.06.54	198	432	31.03.54	21.12.54	28.04.55	ChF/SF/TOF	
101	S-221	03.06.54	198	433	31.03.54	08.06.54	31.05.55	ChF/SF/TOF	3,6
102	S-200	14.06.54	112	511	09.06.54	13.09.54	29.03.55	Kfl/SF	
103	S-222	14.06.54	198	434	03.05.54	19.02.55	31.05.55	ChF/KBF/SF/TOF	3
104	S-261	14.06.54	112	512	19.06.54	20.10.54	02.04.55	Kfl/SF/TOF	
105	S-223	16.07.54	198	435	10.06.54	04.08.54	30.06.55	ChF/KBF/SF/TOF	4
106	S-224	16.07.54	198	436	20.05.54	20.08.54	30.06.55	ChF/KBF/SF/TOF	3
107	S-225	16.07.54	198	437	29.05.54	16.03.55	16.07.55	ChF/KBF/SF/TOF	4
108	S-226	16.07.54	198	438	04.06.54	16.03.55	30.07.55	ChF/KBF	3,2
109	S-227	16.07.54	198	439	05.08.54	08.10.54	31.08.55	ChF/KBF	2
110	S-228	16.07.54	198	440	20.09.54	25.06.55	16.09.55	ChF/KBF	2
111	S-262	16.07.54	112	513	30.07.54	24.10.54	30.06.55	SF/TOF	
112	S-263	16.07.54	112	514	09.07.54	30.10.54	30.06.55	SF/TOF	
113	S-264	16.07.54	112	515	17.07.54	16.11.54	31.07.55	KBF	
114	S-265	16.07.54	112	611	27.07.54	30.11.54	30.07.55	KBF	7
115	S-266	16.07.54	112	612	05.08.54	10.12.54	02.08.55	SF	3
116	S-267	16.07.54	112	613	16.08.54	29.12.54	09.07.55	SF	
117	S-268	16.07.54	112	614	24.08.54	12.01.55	31.07.55	SF	
118	S-269	16.07.54	112	615	01.09.54	25.01.55	29.07.55	SF	

[1] Transferred to Syria.
[2] Transferred to Egypt, renamed *S.5, S.4, S.7, S.8, S.6*.
[3] Modernized to *projekt 613V*.
[4] Transferred to Indonesia. Renamed *Kagabanda, Kagagangsang, Khendvadjala, Alugoro*.
[5] 03.06.66 renamed *Psovskii komsomolets*.
[6] 26.08.80 renamed *Komsomolets Tadzhikistana*.
[7] Transferred to Poland.

Table A8 (contd.): Submarines of the *VMF*, laid down or ordered, 1945–53

No.	Submarine	Order	Yard	Yard No.	Laid down	Launched	Commiss.	Fleet	Notes
Medium Submarines (*Projekt 613*, 1080t normal)									
119	*S-270*	16.07.54	112	711	14.09.54	09.02.55	27.08.55	SF	
120	*S-271*	16.07.54	112	712	27.09.54	15.02.55	31.08.55	KBF	
121	*S-272*	16.07.54	112	713	02.10.54	24.02.55	30.09.55	SF	
122	*S-355*	16.07.54	189	461	28.07.54	30.06.55	12.11.55	KBF	1
123	*S-332*	21.07.54	199	52	22.10.54	11.06.55	27.11.55	TOF	
124	*S-333*	21.07.54	199	53	04.12.54	11.06.55	20.11.55	TOF	
125	*S-356*	21.07.54	189	462	08.10.54	19.08.55	28.12.55	KBF	
126	*S-357*	21.07.54	189	151	25.08.54	26.07.55	26.12.55	KBF	2
127	*S-273*	17.09.54	112	714	13.10.54	01.03.55	31.08.55	SF	
128	*S-276*	30.11.54	112	912	20.11.54	30.03.55	21.10.55	SF	
129	*S-277*	30.11.54	112	913	27.11.54	12.04.55	30.09.55	SF/KBF	
130	*S-278*	30.11.54	112	914	09.12.54	19.04.55	12.11.55	KBF	1
131	*S-274*	06.12.54	112	715	22.10.54	12.03.55	20.08.55	SF	
132	*S-275*	06.12.54	112	911	01.11.54	22.03.55	25.10.55	SF	
133	*S-279*	28.01.55	112	915	20.12.54	23.04.55	20.10.55	KBF	1
134	*S-280*	28.01.55	112	121	30.12.54	02.06.55	22.09.55	KBF	3
135	*S-281*	28.01.54	112	122	15.01.55	07.06.55	07.10.55	Kfl/SF	
136	*S-282*	28.01.55	112	123	25.01.55	11.06.55	25.10.55	Kfl/SF	
137	*S-284*	28.01.55	112	125	14.02.55	23.06.55	12.11.55	Kfl/SF	
138	*S-283*	18.03.55	112	124	31.01.55	17.06.55	31.10.55	Kfl/SF	4
139	*S-285*	18.03.55	112	131	22.02.55	08.07.55	31.12.55	SF	
140	*S-286*	18.03.55	112	132	05.03.55	23.07.55	31.12.55	KBF/SF	
141	*S-229*	06.04.55	198	201	25.06.54	25.06.55	25.09.55	ChF	5
142	*S-230*	06.04.55	198	202	20.12.54	25.07.55	29.09.55	ChF	
143	*S-231*	06.04.55	198	203	29.12.54	25.07.55	19.10.55	ChF	
144	*S-232*	06.04.55	198	204	22.02.55	19.09.55	30.11.55	ChF	
145	*S-233*	06.04.55	198	205	04.02.55	30.03.55	26.12.55	ChF	
146	*S-287*	06.04.55	112	133	05.03.55	23.07.55	31.12.55	KBF/SF	
147	*S-288*	06.04.55	112	134	25.03.55	16.08.55	31.12.55	KBF/SF/TOF	
148	*S-289*	06.04.55	112	135	05.04.55	30.08.55	29.12.55	Kfl/SF	
149	*S-291*	06.04.55	112	142	26.04.55	21.09.55	02.02.56	KBF/SF	
150	*S-234*	15.04.55	198	206	09.03.55	18.08.55	16.12.55	ChF	
151	*S-235*	15.04.55	198	207	31.03.55	04.06.55	08.02.56	ChF/SF/TOF	6
152	*S-290*	15.04.55	112	141	15.04.55	13.09.55	03.02.56	Kfl/SF/TOF	6
153	*S-293*	15.04.55	112	144	23.05.55	10.10.55	29.02.56	Kfl/SF/TOF	6
154	*S-294*	15.04.55	112	145	03.06.55	20.10.55	11.04.56	Kfl/SF	7
155	*S-297*	15.04.55	112	153	09.07.55	19.11.55	31.08.56	SF	
156	*S-334*	15.04.55	199	54	10.03.55	02.09.55	09.12.55	TOF	
157	*S-358*	15.04.55	189	152	03.01.55	01.10.55	24.05.56	KBF	8
158	*S-359*	15.04.55	189	153	24.01.55	26.04.56	30.09.56	KBF/SF/TOF	
159	*S-360*	15.04.55	189	154	17.03.55	29.04.56	30.09.56	KBF	

[1] Transferred to Poland, renamed *Bielik, Sobol, Kondor*.
[2] 17.09.76 renamed *Ul'yanovskii komsomolets*.
[3] Transferred to Egypt.
[4] 23.09.67 renamed *Vladimirskii komsomolets*.
[5] Rebuilt to *projekt 613-D4* as test submarine for ballistic missile R-21.
[6] Transferred to Indonesia, renamed *Trisula*.
[7] Modernized to *projekt 613V*.
[8] Taken over by Albania.

Table A8 (contd.): Submarines of the *VMF*, laid down or ordered, 1945–53

No.	Submarine	Order	Yard	Yard No.	Laid down	Launched	Commiss.	Fleet	Notes
\multicolumn{10}{l}{**Medium Submarines (*Projekt 613*, 1080t normal)**}
160	S-292	07.05.55	112	143	10.05.55	29.09.55	31.03.56	Kfl/SF/TOF	1
161	S-295	31.05.55	112	151	11.06.55	02.11.55	25.07.56	Kfl/SF	
162	S-296	31.05.55	112	152	06.06.55	05.11.55	30.06.56	Kfl/SF	
163	S-300	01.06.55	112	153	09.07.55	19.11.55	31.08.56	SF	
164	S-335	13.06.55	199	55	25.03.55	02.09.55	28.12.55	TOF	
165	S-236	25.06.55	198	208	15.04.55	30.09.55	08.02.56	ChF/SF/TOF	1
166	S-237	25.06.55	198	209	27.04.55	31.10.55	14.02.56	ChF/SF/TOF	
167	S-240	03.08.55	198	452	20.08.55	23.01.56	29.05.56	ChF/KBFF	2
168	S-241	03.08.55	198	453	30.08.55	29.03.56	30.06.56	ChF/KBFF	2
169	S-326	03.08.55	112	155	31.07.55	24.12.55	19.07.56	Kfl/SFrT(OF	3
170	S-327	03.08.55	112	161	18.08.55	10.01.56	17.07.56	Kfl/SFrT(OF	3
171	S-328	03.08.55	112	162	30.08.55	20.01.56	24.08.56	Kfl/SFrrOF	
172	S-238	27.08.55	198	210	26.06.55	19.11.55	28.04.56	ChF/SFrTOF	
173	S-239	27.08.55	198	451	29.06.55	14.12.55	24.05.56	ChF/SF	1
174	S-325	27.08.55	112	154	23.07.55	29.11.55	17.08.56	Kfl/SF/TOF	3
175	S-242	01.09.55	198	454	28.09.55	29.03.56	30.06.56	ChF/KBFF	2
176	S-243	01.09.55	198	211	19.11.55	12.04.56	25.08.56	ChF	
177	S-244	01.09.55	198	212	14.12.55	12.04.56	31.08.56	ChF	4
178	S-250	01.09.55	198	455	20.10.55	29.03.56	24.07.56	ChF	
179	S-329	01.09.55	112	163	12.09.55	14.01.56	28.07.56	Kfl/SF	
180	S-339	01.09.55	112	171	15.10.55	10.02.56	31.07.56	Kfl/SF	
181	S-340	01.09.55	112	172	27.10.55	27.02.56	10.08.56	Kfl/SF	
182	S-341	01.09.55	112	173	04.11.55	06.03.56	08.09.56	KBF/SF	
183	S-338	08.09.55	112	165	08.10.55	20.02.56	24.08.56	Kfl/SF	
184	S-245	29.10.55	198	213	24.12.55	20.04.56	14.09.56	ChF	4
185	S-246	29.10.55	198	455	21.10.55	29.03.56	24.07.56	ChF	
186	S-342	29.10.55	112	174	18.11.55	13.03.56	18.09.56	KBF/SF	
187	S-343	29.10.55	112	175	26.11.55	27.03.56	25.09.56	Kfl/SF	
188	S-344	29.10.55	112	181	10.12.55	03.05.56	24.09.56	Kfl/S F	
189	S-336	14.12.55	199	56	15.06.55	02.05.56	03.09.56	TOF	
190	S-337	02.01.56	199	57	30.08.55	02.05.56	31.08.56	TOF	
191	S-345	02.01.56	112	182	27.12.55	18.05.56	11.10.56	KBF/SF	
192	S-346	02.01.56	112	183	31.12.55	29.05.56	22.10.56	KBF/SF	
193	S-361	02.01.56	189	155	23.03.55	10.05.56	30.11.56	KBF	
194	S-374	02.01.56	198	215	16.02.56	09.06.56	31.10.56	ChF	
195	S-375	02.01.56	198	216	29.02.56	21.09.56	23.01.57	ChF/SF	
196	S-347	23.01.56	112	184	11.01.56	09.06.56	26.11.56	KBF/SF	
197	S-376	23.01.56	198	217	31.03.56	21.09.56	31.12.56	ChF/SF	
198	S-377	23.01.56	198	218	17.04.56	30.10.56	23.02.57	ChF/SF	
199	S-390	23.01.56	199	58	28.10.55	02.05.56	31.10.56	TOF	
200	S-348	09.02.56	112	185	23.01.56	29.06.56	30.11.56	KBF/SF	
201	S-349	09.02.56	112	191	10.02.56	04.07.56	31.12.56	KBF/SF	
202	S-391	01.03.56	199	59	28.12.55	30.06.56	30.11.56	TOF	1

[1] Transferred to Indonesia.
[2] Taken over by Albania.
[3] Transferred to North Korea.
[4] Transferred to Bulgaria, renamed *Slava, Pobeda*.

Table A8 (contd.): Submarines of the *VMF*, laid down or ordered, 1945–53

No.	Submarine	Order	Yard	Yard No.	Laid down	Launched	Commiss.	Fleet	Notes
Medium Submarines (*Projekt 613*, 1080t normal)									
203	*S-365*	03.04.56	189	254	29.02.56	21.02.58	30.06.58	SF	
204	*S-392*	05.04.56	199	60	18.02.56	18.09.56	23.07.57	TOF	
205	*S-393*	05.04.56	199	61	29.03.56	18.09.56	24.07.57	TOF	
206	*S-362*	15.04.56	189	251	31.05.56	13.10.56	31.05.57	SF	
207	*S-363*	15.04.56	189	252	12.01.56	16.11.56	17.09.57	SF	1
208	*S-364*	09.06.56	189	253	31.01.56	09.04.57	31.12.57	KBF	
209	*S-378*	03.07.56	198	456	17.04.56	30.10.56	24.03.57	ChF/SF	
210	*S-379*	03.07.56	198	457	09.06.56	29.12.56	29.04.57	ChF/SF	
211	*S-380*	30.07.56	198	458	19.06.56	29.12.56	30.06.57	ChF/SF	
212	*S-381*	30.07.56	198	459	21.07.56	27.02.57	24.05.57	ChF/SF	
213	*S-382*	30.07.56	198	460	06.08.56	28.02.57	29.06.57	ChF/SF	
214	*S-383*	12.11.56	198	461	25.09.56	25.02.57	28.08.57	ChF/SF	
215	*S-384*	12.11.56	198	462	29.09.56	15.04.57	02.61	ChF	2

[1] 27.10.81 stranded near Karlskrona as 'Whiskey on the rocks', repaired.
[2] Planned to be completed on 15.04.57, but rebuilt to *projekt 613C*.

Medium Submarines (*Projekt 616*, German *Type XXVI*)
Project only studied, no orders placed, only *projekt A615* submarine *M-361* built as *projekt 637* to the Walter concept.

Medium Submarine (*Projekt 617*, 950t normal)

1	*S-99*	26.03.49	196	617	05.02.51	05.02.52	20.03.56	KBF	1

[1] 17.05.59 damaged by accident, irreparable, decommissioned.

Small Submarines (*Projekt 615*, 392t normal)

1	*M-254*	26.03.49	196	579	17.03.50	31.08.50	31.07.53	KBF	

Small Submarines (*Projekt A615*, 411t normal)

1	*M-255*	01.08.53	196	664	08.09.53	16.09.54	10.12.55	KBF	
2	*M-256*	21.08.53	196	665	23.09.53	15.09.54	21.12.55	KBF	1
3	*M-257*	12.10.53	196	666	10.11.53	30.09.54	10.12.55	KBF	
4	*M-258*	12.10.53	196	667	18.11.53	04.11.54	21.12.55	KBF	
5	*M-259*	22.04.54	196	668	12.01.54	05.11.54	13.12.55	KBF	
6	*M-351*	03.06.54	194	801	24.03.54	04.07.55	03.08.56	ChF	2
7	*M-260*	26.07.54	196	669	14.02.54	21.05.55	31.07.56	ChF	
8	*M-261*	26.07.54	444	1070	23.02.54	12.07.55	31.07.56	ChF	
9	*M-352*	26.07.54	194	802	10.04.54	07.10.55	30.09.56	KBF	
10	*M-262*	25.08.54	444	1071	20.03.54	12.07.55	31.07.56	ChF	
11	*M-263*	25.08.54	444	1072	08.04.54	02.08.55	02.11.56	KBF	
12	*M-354*	30.11.54	194	804	23.06.55	06.06.56	25.11.56	KBF	
13	*M-265*	06.12.54	444	1074	15.07.54	09.09.55	30.09.56	KBF	
14	*M-353*	06.12.54	194	803	15.05.55	26.04.56	30.09.56	ChF	
15	*M-266*	30.12.54	444	1075	30.08.54	30.10.55	30.09.56	KBF	
16	*M-267*	30.12.54	444	1078	15.10.54	14.01.56	30.09.56	KBF	
17	*M-264*	10.08.55	444	1073	04.06.54	14.09.55	30.09.56	KBF	
18	*M-268*	02.01.56	444	1079	20.11.54	13.01.56	29.12.56	KBF[1] 27.10.81 stranded	

[1] Sank on 26.09.57, raised and re-commissioned.
[2] Sank on 22.08.57, raised and re-commissioned.

Table A8 (contd.): Submarines of the *VMF*, laid down or ordered, 1945–53

No.	Submarine	Order	Yard	Yard No.	Laid down	Launched	Commiss.	Fleet	Notes
\multicolumn{10}{l}{**Small Submarines (*Projekt A615*, 411t normal)** *continued*}
19	*M-269*	03.05.56	444	1080	30.11.54	17.03.56	27.08.57	ChF	
20	*M-295*	03.05.56	196	701	10.01.55	03.04.56	16.08.57	ChF	
21	*M-355*	18.05.56	194	806	08.07.55	17.04.57	01.08.57	KBF	
22	*M-296*	25.05.56	196	702	01.02.55	04.04.56	23.12.58	KBF	
23	*M-297*	09.06.56	196	703	05.08.55	29.07.56	23.12.58	ChF	
24	*M-298*	09.06.56	196	704	02.08.55	31.06.56	31.08.57	ChF	
25	*M-356*	18.07.56	194	816	05.04.56	27.04.57	20.08.57	KBF	
26	*M-299*	30.07.56	196	705	19.09.55	04.10.56	30.11.57	ChF	
27	*M-361*	30.07.56	194	817	05.55	03.57	24.08.62	KBF	1
28	*M-300*	09.01.57	196	711	27.09.55	12.10.56	30.11.57	ChF	
29	*M-301*	09.01.57	196	713	07.01.56	23.02.57	27.12.58	KBF	
30	*M-302*	09.01.57	196	715	24.12.55	25.02.57	23.12.58	KBF	

[1] Built to the revised *projekt 637* as test vessel for Walter Turbines.

Note on Soviet and Russian Sources

Domestic and foreign scholars faced serious difficulties in studying Soviet naval policy during almost all the seven decades of Soviet rule because of a strict ban on public discussion. There were no open sources providing the detailed information concerning Soviet naval programmes, or the Soviet Navy's strategic plans, operations schedules, locations, size, armaments, training, reserves, etc. The Soviet secrecy law covered not only detailed information but general information too. Thus, the official data on Soviet naval policy and the Soviet Navy have not been available for most of the past 80 years, except for general information, such as numbers of ships, aircraft, and their general location.

Therefore the authors of open studies, including the well-informed Soviet naval historians V.I. Achkasov, N.B. Pavlovich and A.V. Basov, could not provide complete information about Soviet naval programmes, naval strategy and naval conduct during the pre-war period. Apparently, Soviet authors were forbidden from using the official data when recording the Soviet Navy's development after World War II.

Nevertheless, there are some high-quality open sources, necessary for every historian, which deal with Stalin's ocean-going fleet. For example, hundreds of 'former Old Fleet officers' served in the Naval Forces of the Workers' and Peasants' Red Army, and the Soviets were short of good, experienced 'red commanders'.

A number of people, including N.L. Klado, V.M. Altfater, A.V. Nemits, B.B. Zherve, M.A. Petrov, V.A. Belli, V.A. Alekin, I.S. Isakov, P.D. Bykov, N.V. Novikov and A.V. Shtal', managed to distinguish themselves as brilliant naval theorists and historians. Their works, published from the end of the 1910s to the beginning of the 1940s, mainly in *Morskoi Sbornik (Naval Magazine)*, provide a broad view on Soviet naval strategy, operational art and tactics during the pre-World War II period. In addition, there were several 'young red commanders' such as A.P. Aleksandrov, K.I. Dushenov, I.K. Kozhanov, A.M. Yakimychev and N.V. Alyakrinskii, who suggested a 'more appropriate' Red Fleet strategy, known as the 'small war at sea' strategy. Their works were published from the mid-1920s up to the beginning of the 1930s in *Morskoi Sbornik* and other Soviet military periodicals.

Unfortunately, almost all of these 'red commanders' died or were purged by *NKVD* before the outbreak of World War II. Up to the end of the 1950s the works of former Tsarist officers had, in general, been strictly prohibited because Soviet officials described their point of view as part of the 'Mahanian reactionary-bourgeois theory of the possession of the sea'. Meanwhile the theory of planning for a 'small war at sea' was presented as a more 'progressive' and appropriate Red Fleet strategy during the first 'Five Year-Plan' period. But, for most scholars, the works of the prominent spokesmen of the Red Fleet's 'young school' were not available either.

Between the late 1950s and the early 1960s, the *Izbrannye Proizvedeniya (The Essential Works)* of the famous Red Army leaders and theorists M.V. Frunze and M.N. Tukhachevskii were published. Both placed a great emphasis on mighty ground forces as well as a strong air force, but with only a 'small fleet'. Stalin's successor, Nikita Khrushchev, at least during the first half of the decade of his rule over the Communist Party and the Soviet Union, held the same point of view. He criticized Stalin's 'personality cult' as well as his pre-war naval policy and ambitious naval planning. The first post-war Soviet shipbuilding programme was therefore stopped. Admiral of the Fleet of the Soviet Union N.G. Kuznetsov, promoted to Commander-in-Chief of the Navy during Stalin's rule, was replaced by Admiral S.G. Gorshkov. All uncompleted heavy units of Stalin's ocean-going fleet were scrapped as well as several just commissioned light cruisers of the 68-bis project. Those events in combination led to the shortage of open works about Stalin's ocean-going fleet between the mid-1950s and the beginning of the 1960s.

At the same time, several very important formerly classified works were published, including *Poteri boevykh korablei i sudov Voenno-morskogo flota, transportnykh, rybolovnykh i drugikh sudov SSSR v Velikuyu Otechestvennuyu vojnu 1941–1945gg. (The Losses of Combat, Transport, Fishery and Other Ships of USSR during the Great Patriotic War, 1941–1945)* and the three-volume *Boevaya deyatel'nost' podvodnykh lodok Voenno-morskogo flota SSSR v Velikuyu Otechestvenuyu vojnu 1941–1945 gg. (The Submarine Operations of the USSR Navy during the Great Patriotic War, 1941–1945)*. Some of these books have proved quite useful in order to understand the basic principles of Soviet naval strategy. They were declassified at the end of the 1980s.

In the mid-1960s Soviet scholars paid attention to the works of Red Army theorists written before World War II. In 1965, the anthology *Voprosy strategii i operativnogo iskusstva v sovetskikh voennykh trudakh (1917–1940) (The Soviet Theorists' Point of View on Problems of Strategy and Operational Art (1917–1940))* was published. Some essential essays by B.B. Zherve, A.P. Aleksandrov, V.A. Belli and other Soviet naval theorists were included in that book.

Boevoi put' Sovetskogo Voenno-morskogo flota (The History of the Soviet Navy), which was published at the same time, became the first complete history of the Soviet Navy. Unfortunately, the authors, headed by N.A. Piterskii, did not provide an accurate explanation of Stalin's naval policy.

In 1967, the classified document *Bulleten 'Glavnogo Shtaba i Boevoj podgotovki Voenno-Morskogo Flota No. 16 (The Bulletin of the Main Staff and Combat Training Department of the Soviet Navy, Number 16)* was issued by the Main Staff of the Soviet Navy, which contained the brilliant work of K.A. Stal'bo, the prominent Soviet military theorist and naval historian.

Stalbo's study was titled *Sostoyanie Sovetskogo flota i voenno-morskogo iskusstva v 1941 godu i osnovnyie itogi ikh razvitiya v khode Vtoroj mirovoj i Velikoj Otechestvennoj vojn (The Soviet Navy and Art of Sea Warfare in 1941: The General Results of Soviet*

Navy and Art of Sea Warfare Developments during World War II and the Great Patriotic War). This became an openly available work at the end of 1980s.

Stal'bo did not provide detailed information covering the Soviet Navy's development during the pre-World War II period. Mainly, he paid attention to the influences of alternative naval strategies on the operational art and tactics of the Soviet Navy from the beginning of the 1920s up to the end of the Great Patriotic War. This point of view was more realistic than those provided in previous historical works published in the USSR. Specifically, Stal'bo criticized Soviet naval planning just before the war broke out, and highlighted the disparity between the actual Soviet Navy missions run during the Great Patriotic War and the essence of Soviet naval doctrine on the eve of war. Stal'bo advocated the 'old school' theorists. He stated that B.B. Zherve had only propagated the use of capital ships, but had not spread 'bourgeois naval theories'. Besides, Stal'bo wrote, by the mid-1930s the Soviet Navy had had to abandon 'a small war at sea theory' as a naval concept.

This point of view was accepted by the Soviet Navy's leadership as correct. By the end of 1960s, Admiral of the Fleet of the Soviet Union S.G. Gorshkov prepared the first version of his well-known essay *Morskaya moshch' gosudarstva (The Seapower of the State).* The Commander-in-Chief of the Soviet Navy confirmed Stal'bo's appreciation of those who had distinguished themselves during the initial period of Soviet Navy history. Gorshkov followed the official course, and criticized Stalin's naval programme. At the same time, he also advocated the basic idea of Stalin's naval policy; that is, that the Soviet Union was in need of a balanced ocean-going fleet.

Gorshkov's point of view strongly influenced almost all Soviet naval historians working in the field from the beginning of 1970s to the end of the 1980s. The most striking example is a study made in 1973 by V.I. Achkasov and N.B. Pavlovich entitled, *Sovetskoe Voenno-morskoe Iskusstvo v Velikoj Otechestvennoj vojne* (US edition – *Soviet Naval Operations in the Great Patriotic War, 1941–1945).* Having followed their Commander-in-Chief, the authors of this book stated that the pre-war Soviet shipbuilding programme had been unbalanced. Specifically, they pointed to the shortage of mine-sweepers, anti-submarine ships, and of modern aircraft, as well as the lack of landing ships. However, they did not advocate the idea of a 'big ocean-going and seagoing fleet', but avoided dealing with this theme.

In contrast to this point of view, the authors of the official study *Istoriya vtoroi mirovoi vojny 1939–1945 v dvenadtsati tomakh (The History of World War II in Twelve Volumes)* offered severe criticism of pre-war Soviet naval policy. They characterized Stalin's naval programme as inadequate, and indicated some factual errors in the Soviet Navy's pre-war combat manuals. Overall, they offered an explanation of the Soviet Navy's role during the Great Patriotic War that was more suited to high-ranking officers in the Soviet Army. This revealed the hidden competition among the main branches of the Soviet Armed Forces.

At the beginning of the 1980s, the next official report was begun. It was entitled *Boevaya letopis' voenno-morskogo flota 1941–1942 (The Soviet Navy Combat Chronology, 1941–1942).* This work would become the first open source to be generally based on classified archive documents.

In 1988, the Military Publishing House of the Soviet Ministry of Defence offered for sale a reference book by S.S. Berezhnoi entitled *Korabli i suda VMF SSSR 1928–1945 (Combat Ships and Auxiliaries of the USSR Navy, 1928–1945)*. In this book the author provided accurate data for the Soviet Navy's development during the 1930s and the Great Patriotic War, but did not describe the fate of every commissioned ship. Neither did S.S. Berezhnoi include in his book any detailed information about the numerous uncompleted ships. The book was also illustrated very badly because of a lack of funds and low-quality printing.

At the end of the 1980s, Gorbachev's new policies of 'perestroika' and 'glasnost' shocked the KGB and the other Soviet secret services. In 1991, with the collapse of the Soviet Union, the official dam was breached, and hundreds of publications explaining the Stalin's naval policy were offered to domestic and foreign readers. Generally, these were low-quality, amateur works, providing so-called 'hot facts', and contained numerous mistakes.

Meanwhile, some very important and high-quality studies were being published, including *Tri veka Rossijskogo flota (Three Centuries of the Russian Navy)*, by B.I. Rodionov and some other well-informed Russian naval historians; *50 let Velikoi pobedy. Opyt primeneniya sovetskogo voenno-morskogo flota vo vtoroj mirovoi vojne i ego znachenie v sovremennykh usioviyakh (50th Anniversary of the Great Victory: The Experience of Soviet Naval Operations during World War II, its Importance under Contemporary Conditions)*, edited by N.D. Zakorin; *Boevaya letopis' Voenno-Morskogo Flota (The Soviet Navy Combat Chronology 1917–1941); Boevaya letopis' Voenno-Morskogo Flota 1941–1942* (2nd edition); V.N. Burov's *Otechestvenhoe voennoe korablestroenie v tret'em stoletii svoej istorii (Domestic Shipbuilding During the Third Century of its History)* and *Rabotche-Krestianskii Voenno-Morskoi Flot v predvoennye gody 1936–1941 (The Workers' and Peasants' Red Fleet on the Eve of the War 1936–1941)*, by V.Yu. Gribovskii.

In 1996, V.P. Kuzin, and V.I. Nikol'skii, published their excellent book *Voenno-Morskoj Flot SSSR 1945–1991 (The USSR Navy 1945–1991)*. This provided a broader view of Soviet naval policy and naval strategy, but mainly of Soviet naval programmes. Unfortunately, only a small number of copies of this book were printed. At the same time, A.B. Morin published several very interesting studies providing detailed data on Soviet shipbuilding activities and the features of Soviet combat ships. In addition, A.M. Petrov, D.A. Aseev and A.P. Nikolaev, and others presented a well-researched study, *Oruzhie Rossijskogo flota (The Weapons of the Russian Fleet)*, E.A. Shitikov, V.N. Krasnov and V.V. Balabin, published *Korablestroenie v SSSR v gody Velikoi Otechestvennoi vojny (USSR Shipbuilding during the Great Patriotic War)*.

There is also the great five-volume series, prepared by a team of well-known shipbuilding historians under the leadership of I.D. Spasskii, *Istoriya Otechestvennoj Sudostroenija (History of National Shipbuilding)*, of which volume IV covers the period 1925–45, and volume V the years 1946–91. V.I. Dmitriev published his *Sovetskoe Podvodnoe Korable-stroenie (Soviet Submarine Shipbuilding)*, covering the period up to 1945, while A.S. Pavlov completed the story with his *Voennye Korabli SSSR i Rossii 1945–1995 (Warships of the USSR and Russia, 1945–1995)*.

Since the beginning of 1990s very interesting articles have been published in the Russian magazines and newspapers. They have been very useful for scholars, seeking a comprehensive explanation of the Soviet Navy developments during the twentieth century.

The authors of these articles are S.A. Balabin, S.S. Berezhnoi, A.A. Chernyshev, V.Yu. Gribovskii, A.V. Karpenko, V.N. Krasnov, L.A. Kuznetsov, A.B. Morin, V.N. Nikol'skii, A.V. Platonov, V.P. Semenov, E.A. Shitikov, B.P. Tyurin, V.Yu. Usov, A.M. Vasil'ev, V.V. Yarovoi and I.G. Zakharov.

At the same time several very important classified studies, written between the mid-1950s and the end of the 1960s, had become open sources. So the main archive documents covered the period of Stalin's ocean-going fleet creation had been declassified.

Nevertheless, the authors of the above-mentioned works were not able to discover the true reasons that forced Stalin to alter his naval policy in the mid-1930s. We believe that it is the essence of our mission.

Bibliography

BOOKS

50 let Velikoi pobedy. Opyt primeneniya sovetskogo voenno-morskogo flota vo vtorov mirovoi vojne i ego znachenie v sovremennykh usioviyakh, ed. I.V. Kasatonov. St Petersburg, Tsentral'naya Kartugrafitcheskaya Fabrika VMF, 1997.

Achkasov, V.I., Pavlovich, N.B., *Sovetskoe Voenno-morskoe Iskusstvo v Velikoi Otechestvennoi vojne*. Moscow, Voenizdat, 1973. (*Soviet Naval Operations in the Great Patriotic War 1941–1945*, Annapolis, MD, US Naval Institute Press, 1981.)

Aleksandrov, A.P., *Kritika teorii vladeniya morem*. Leningrad, Voenno-Morskaya akademia RKKA, 1932.

Aleksandrov, A.P. Isakov, I.S. and V.A. Belli, *Operatsii podvodnykh lodok*, Vol. 1. Leningrad, Voenno-Morskaya akademiya RKKA, 1933.

Aleksandrov, A.P., *Operatsii na morskikh soobshcheniyakh. Operativnyi Ocherk.* Leningrad, Voenno-Morskaya akademia RKKA, 1934.

Barbarossa: The Axis and the Allies, ed. John Erickson and David Dilks. Edinburgh, Edinburgh University Press, 1994.

Bargoni, Franco, *L'impegno navale Italiana durante la guerra civile Spagnola 1936–1939*. Rome, Ufficio Storico della Marina Militare, 1992.

Beitter, Gerda, *Die Rote Armee im 2.Weltkrieg: Eine Bibliographie*. Schriften der Bibliothek für Zeitgeschichte No. 24, Koblenz, Bernard & Graefe, 1984.

Belli, V.A., *Konspekt-tesizy. Tema: Morskie teatry SSSR v sostave obshchego fronta borby. Zadachi flotov SSSR.* Leningrad, Voenno-Morskaya akademia RKKA, 1938. *Tema: Operatsii po unitozheniyu nepriyatel'skogo flota v more*. Leningrad, Voenno-Morskaya akademia RKKA, 1938. *Tema: Operativnie raschety, napriazhenie, normirovanie*. Leningrad, Voenno-Morskaya akademia RKKA, 1938.

Berezhnoi, S.S., *Korabli i vspomogatel'nye suda Sovetskogo Voenno-morskogo flota (1917–1927)*. Moscow, Voenizdat, 1981.

Berezhnoi, S.S., *Korabli i suda VMF SSSR 1928–1945*. Spravochnik. Moscow, Voenizdat, 1988.

Berezhnoi, S.S., *Flot SSSR Korabli i suda lendlisa*. Spravochnik. St Petersburg, Velen, 1994.

Berezhnoi, S.S., *Trofei i reparatsii VMF SSSR*. Spravochnik. Yakutsk, 1994.

Berezovskii N.Yu., Berezhnoi, S.S., Nikolaeva, Z.V., *Boevaya letopis' Voenno-morskogo flota 1917–1941*. Moscow, Voenizdat, 1992.

Berlinskaya (Potsdamskaya) Konferentsiya rukovoditelei trekh soyuznikh derzhav – SSSR, SshA i Velikobritanniya (17 iyulya–2 avgusta 1945 g.). Sbornik Dokumentov. Moscow, 1984.

Boevaya letopis Voenno-morskogy flota 1941–1942, ed. G.A. Ammon. Moscow, Voenizdat, 1983.

Boevoi put' Sovetskogo Voenno-morskogo flota, ed. N.A. Piterskij. Moscow, Voenizdat, 1964, 3rd edn, ed. V.I. Achkasov *et al.* Moscow, Voenizdat, 1974.

Bogatyrev, S.V., *Poteri boevykh korablei i katerov VMF SSSR v period Velikoi Otechestvennoi vojny 1941–1945 gg.* Spravochnik. L'vov, IPG 'Marine-Polejdon', 1994.

Bogatyrev, S.V., Strel'bitskij, K.B., *Poteri flotov protivnika na morskikh TVD v Velikoj Otechestvennoi vojne 1941–1945*. Lvov, TriO, 1992.

Breyer, Siegfried, *Enzyklopädie des sowjetischen Kriegsschiffbaus*. Vol. I: *Oktoberrevolution und maritimes Erbe*. Vol. II: *Konsolidierung und erste Neubauten*. Vol. III: *Flottenbau und Plansoll*. Herford, Koehler, 1987, 1989, 1991.

Burov, V.N., *Otechestvennoe voennoe korablestroenie v tret'em stoletii svoej istorii*. St Petersburg, Sudostroenie, 1995.

Conquest, Robert, *Am Anfang starb Genosse Kirow*. Düsseldorf, Droste, 1970.

Conquest, Robert, *Ernte des Todes*. Munich, Langen-Müller, 1988.

Conquest, Robert, *Stalin: Breaker of Nations*. London, Weidenfeld & Nicolson, 1991.

Conway's All the World's Fighting Ships 1922–1946. London, Conway's, 1980.

Conway's All the World's Fighting Ships 1947–1995. London, Conway's, 1995.

Coox, Alwin D., *Nomonhan. Japan against Russia 1939*, Vols 1, 2. Stanford, CA, Stanford University Press, 1985.

Coutau-Bégarie, *La puissance maritime soviétique*. Paris, Economica, 1983.

Das deutsche Bild der russischen und sowjetischen Marine. Supplement 7/8 to *Marine-Rundschau*, September, 1962.

Das Deutsche Reich und der Zweite Weltkrieg, ed. Militärgeschichtliches Forschungsamt. Stuttgart, Deutsche Verlagsanstalt 1979ff. (10 volumes planned, vols 1–6 published up to 1999).

Deutscher, I., *Stalin, A Political Biography*. London, Oxford University Press, 1967.

Djilas, M., *Conversations with Stalin*. London, Hart-Davis, 1962.

Dmitriev, V.I., *Atakuyut podvodniki*. Moscow, Voenizdat, 1964.

Dmitriev, V.I., *Sovetskoe podvodnoe korable-stroenie*. Moscow, Voenizdat, 1990.

Dotsenko, V.D., *Morskoi biograficheskii slovar'*. St Petersburg, Logos, 1995.

Dotsenko, V.D., *Bitvy Rossiskogo flota XVII–XX vv*. St Petersburg, Petro-Rif, 1997.

Egorov, A.I., *Razgrom Denikina*. Moscow, Gosizdat, 1936.

Fairhall, David, *Russia Looks to the Sea: A Study of the Expansion of Soviet Maritime Power*. London, Deutsch, 1971.

Fock, Harald: *Vom Zarenadler zum Roten Stern*. Herford, Mittler, 1985.

Frunze, M.V., *Reorganizatsiya RKKA. Materiali X S'ezdu RKP*. Moscow, Voennaya tipografiya Shtabe RKKA, 1921.

Frunze, M.V., *Sobranie Sochinenii*, 3 vols. Moscow/Leningrad, Gosizdat, 1926–29.

Frunze, M.V., *Izbrannye Proizvedeniya*, 2 vols. Moscow, Voenizdat (2nd edn, 1965) 1957.

Garzke, W.G. and R.O. Dulin, *Battleships*. Vol. 2: *Allied Battleships in World War II*. Annapolis, MD, US Naval Institute, 1980.

Gel'fond, G.M., *Sovetskii Flot v vojne s Japonei*. Moscow, Voenizdat, 1958.

Generaloberst Halder. Kriegstagebuch. 3 vols, ed. Hans-Adolf Jacobsen. Stuttgart, Kohlhammer, 1962–64.

Glavnyi Shtab Voenno-morskikh sil SSSR, *Sbornik materialov po opytu boevoi deyatel'nosti Voenno-morskikh sil SSSR*. Vol. 35, *Opyt perevoda korablej VMS po vnytrennym vodnym putyam SSSR*. Moscow, Voenizdat, 1948. Vol. 39, *Opyt perevozok podvodnykh lodok i malykh korablei po zheleznym dorogam v Velikoi Otechestvennoi vojne*. Moscow, Voenizdat, 1951.

Glavnyi Shtab Voenno-morskogo flota, *Poteri boevykh korablei i sudov Voenno-morskogo flota, Transportnykh, Rybolovnykh i drugikh sudov SSSR v Velikoi Otechestvennoi vojne 1941–1945 gg*. Moscow, Voenizdat, 1959.

Glavnyi Shtab Voenno-morskogo flota, *Boevaya Deyatel'nost' Podvodnykh lodok Voenno-morskogo flota SSSR v Velikoi Otechestvennoi vojne 1941–1945 gg*. Vol. I, *Podvodnye lodki Severnogo flota v Velikoi Otechestvennoi vojne*. Vol. II, *Padvodnye lodki Krasnoznamennogo Baltijskogo flota v Velikoi Otechestvennoi vojne*. Vol. III, *Podvodnye lodki Chernomorskogo i Tikhookeanskogo flotov v Velikoi Otechestvennoi vojne*, ed. G.I. Shchedrin *et al.*, Moscow, Voenizdat, 1968–70.

Godlevskii, G.F., Grechanyuk, N.M., Kononenko, V.M., *Pokhody boevye. Eskadra Chernomorskogo flota v Velikoi Otechestvennoi vojne*. Moscow, Voenizdat, 1966.

Golovko, A., *Vineste s Flotom* (English: *With the Fleet*). Moscow, Progress, 1979.

Gomm, Bernhard, *Die russischen und sowjetischen Kriegsschiffe 1856–1945*. Selbstverlag o.J.

Gorshkov, Sergei G., *Morskaya moshch' gosudarstva*. Moscow, Voenizdat, 1970, 2nd edn, 1976, 3rd edn, 1979.

Granovskij, E., Morotov, M., *Poteri korablei osnovnykh boevykh klassov vo vtoroi mirovoi vojne 1939–1945 gg*. Chast vtoraya, *Poteri voenno-morskikh flotov stran'osi' ikh satellitov*. Moscow, Izdat 'CheRo' (Retrospektiva vojny na more, vypusk 6, 1995).

Greger, René, *Die russische Flotte im Ersten Weltkrieg 1914–1917*. Munich, Lehmanns, 1970. English edn, *The Russian Fleet 1914–1917*. London, Ian Allan, 1972.

Gribovskii, V.Yu., *Raboche-Krestiansky Voenno-morskoi flot v predvoennye gody 1936–1941*. St Petersburg, Vyschee Voenno-Morskoe uchilische imeni M.V. Frunze, 1996.

Groehler, Olaf, *Selbstmörderishe Allianz. Deutsch–Russische Militärbeziehungen 1920–1941*. Berlin, Vision Verlag, 1992.

Gröner, Erich, *Die deutschen Kriegsschiffe 1815–1945*. Fortgeführt von Dieter Jung and Martin Maass. Koblenz, Bernard & Graefe, 1982–94, 8 vols.

Herrick, Robert W., *Soviet Naval Strategy: Fifty Years of Theory and Practice*. Annapolis, MD, US Naval Institute Press, 1968.

Hildermeier, Manfred, *Geschichte der Sowjetunion 1917–1991*, Munich, Beck, 1998.

Hillgruber, Andreas, *Hitler, König Carol und Marschall Antonescu. Die deutsch–rumänischen Beziehungen 1938–1944*. Wiesbaden, Steiner, 1965.

Hillgruber, Andreas, *Hitlers Strategie. Politik und Kriegführung 1940–1941*. Frankfurt/M., Bernard & Graefe, 1963.

Hillgruber, Andreas and Gerhard Hümmelchen, *Chronik des Zweiten Weltkrieges*. Düsseldorf, Droste, 1978.

Hingley, Ronald, *Joseph Stalin: Man and Legend*. New York, McGraw-Hill, 1974.

Hitlers Weisungen für die Kriegführung 1939–1945, ed. Walther Hubatsch. Frankfurt/M., Bernard & Graefe, 1962.

Huan, Claude et Jürgen Rohwer, *La Marine Soviétique*. Notes et Études

Documentaires No. 4479–80. Paris, October 1978.
Hümmelchen, Gerhard, *Handelsstörer. Handelskrieg deutscher Überwasserstreitkräfte im Zweiten Weltkrieg*, 2nd edn, Munich, Lehmanns, 1967.
Hussini, Mahroz Mahmud el-, *Soviet–Egyptian Relations, 1945–1985*. London, Macmillan, 1987.
Isakov, I.S., *Desantnaya operatsiya*. Moscow, Voenmorizdat, 1934.
Isakov, I.S., *Kharakter sovremennoi vojny i operatsii na more*. Moscow, Voemorizdat, 1940.
Isakov, I.S., *Okeanologiya, geografiya i voennaya istoria Izbrannye trudy*. Moscow, Nauka, 1984.
Istoriya Otechestvennogo Sudostroeniya v pyati tomakh, ed. I.D. Spasskii. St Petersburg, Sudostroenie. Vol. 4, *Sudostroenie v period pervykh pyatiletok i velikoi Otechestvennoi vojny 1925–1945 gg.* 1996. – Vol. 5, *Sudostroenie v poslevoennyj period 1945–1991 gg.*, 1996.
Istoriya voenno-morskogo iskusstva, ed. S.E. Zakharov. Moscow, Voenizdat, 1969.
Istoriya Vtoroi Mirovoi Vojny 1939–1945, Vols I–XII. Moscow, Voenizdat, 1973–82. German edn, *Geschichte des Zweiten Weltkrieges*. Berlin (Ost), Militärverlag, 1975–82.
Ivanov, L., Smirnov, P., *Anglo-amerikanskoe morskoe sopernichestvo*. Moscow, Institute of World Economics and Politics, 1933.
Jane's Fighting Ships 1949/50 to 1956/57, 8 vols, ed. Raymond V.B. Blackman. London, Sampson Low, Marston & Co. 1957–59.
Jonge, Alex de, *Stalin and the Shaping of the Soviet Union*, London, Collins, 1986.
Jordan, John, *Soviet Submarines 1945 to the Present*. London, Arms & Armour Press, 1989.
Jordan, John, *Soviet Warships 1945 to the Present*. Revised and expanded edition. London, Arms and Armour Press, 1992.
Karschawin, B.A., *Das deutsche Unterseeboot U 250*. Neue Dokumente und Fakten. St Petersburg, Jena, 1994.
Kasatonov, I., *Flot vykhodit v okean*. St Petersburg, Astra-Lyuks, 1995.
Kharlamov, N., *Difficult Mission. War Memoirs. Soviet Admiral in Great Britain during the Second World War*. Moscow, Progress, 1983.
Khor'kov, A.G., *Grozovoi iyun'*. Moscow, Voenizdat, 1991.
Kirshin, Yu., *The Soviet Military Doctrine of the Pre-War Years*. Moscow, Voenizdat, 1990.
Koval'chuk, V.M., *Stroitel'stvo VMF SSSR v period mezhdu Grazhdanskoi i Velikoi Otechestvennoi vojnoi. Razvitie operativnikh i takticheskikh vzgliadov v Sovetskom Voenno-morskom flote*. Leningrad, 1958.
Kozlov, I.A., Shlomin, V.S., *Severnyi flot*. Moscow, Voenizdat, 1966.
Krasnoznamenyi Baltijskii flot v bitve za Leningrad 1941–1944 gg., ed. V.I. Achkasov, Moscow, Nauka, 1973.
Krasnoznamenyi Baltijskii flot v zavershayushchii period Velikoi Otechestvennoi vojny 1944–1945 gg., ed. V.I. Achkasov, Moscow, Nauka, 1975.
Krasnoznamenyi Baltijskii flot v Velikoi Otechestvennoi voine 1941–1945. Stat'i i Ocherki, ed. A.M. Samsonov, Moscow, Nauka, 1984.
Kriegstagebuch des Oberkommandos der Wehrmacht (Wehrmachtführungsstab) 1939–1945, ed. Percy Ernst Schramm, Walther Hubatsch, Andreas Hillgruber und Hans-Adolf Jacobsen. Frankfurt/M., Bernard & Graefe, 4 vols, 1961–65.

Kriegstagebuch der Seekriegsleitung 1939–1945. Part A, 68 vols, ed. Werner Rahn, Gerhard Schreiber and Hansjoseph Maierhöfer. Herford, Mittler, 1988–97.
Krivosheev, G.F. (ed.), *Soviet Casualties and Combat Losses in the Twentieth Century*. London, Greenhill Books, 1997.
Kuzin, V.P., Nikol'skij, V.I., *Voenno-Morskoi flot SSSR 1945–1991*. St Petersburg, Istoricheskoe Morskoe Obshchestvo, 1996.
Kuznetsov, N.G., *Nakanune*. Moscow, Voenizdat, 1966.
Lagevorträge der Oberbefehlshaber der Kriegsmarine vor Hitler 1939–1945, ed. Gerhard Wagner. Munich, Lehmanns, 1972.
Laqueur, Walter, *Stalin. Abrechnung im Zeichen von Glasnost*. Munich, 1990.
Les Flottes de Combat 1950–1957, ed. Henri and J. Le Masson. Paris, Société d'Éditions Géographiques, Maritimes et Coloniales, 1950–57, 8 vols.
Liddell Hart, Basil, *The Soviet Army*. London, Weidenfeld & Nicolson, 1956.
Ludri, I.M., *O taktike malogo flota*. Moscow, 1928.
Majster, Yu., *Vojna v Vostochnoevropejskikh vodakh 1941–1945. Baltika 1941–1945*, ed. M. Morozov. Moscow, Izdat 'CheRo', 1995 (Antologiya vojny na more, Vypusk 5).
Maurer, E.A. and M. Reichman, *Global War: An Atlas of World Strategy*. New York, William Morrow, 1943.
Meister, Jürg, *Der Seekrieg in den osteuropäischen Gewässern 1941–1945*. Munich, Lehmanns, 1958.
Meister, Jürg, *Soviet Warships of the Second World War*. London, Macdonald & Jane's, 1977.
Meretskov, K.A., *Na Sluzhbe Narodu*. Moscow, Voenizdat, 1970.
Mitchell, Donald W., *A History of Russian and Soviet Sea Power*. London, Deutsch, 1974.
Molotov, V., *Stalin and Stalin's Leadership*. Moscow, Progress, 1950.
Moore, John E., *The Soviet Navy Today*. London, Macdonald & Jane's, 1975.
Morin, Arkadi und Nikolai Walujew, *Sowjetische Flugzeugträger, Geheim 1910–1995*. Berlin, Brandenburgisches Verlagshaus, 1996.
Morin, A.B., *Legkie krejsera tipa 'Chapaev' i tipa 'Sverdlov'*. St Petersburg, Tsitadel', 1997.
Müller, Rolf-Dieter and Gerd Ueberschär, *Hitler's War in the East 1941–1945. A Critical Assessment*. Oxford, Berghahn Books, 1997.
Neue Forschungen zum Zweiten Weltkrieg, ed. Jürgen Rohwer and Hildegard Müller. Schriften der Bibliothek für Zeitgeschichte No. 28. Koblenz, Bernard & Graefe, 1990.
Nikol'skii, V.I., Litinskii, D.Yu., *Eskadrennye minonostsy tipa 'Smelyi', proekt 30-bis*. St Petersburg, Istoricheskoe Morskoe Obshchestvo, 1994.
Niestlé, Axel, *German U-boat Losses during World War Two. Details of Destruction*. Annapolis, MD, US Naval Institute Press, 1998.
Oberkommando der Kriegsmarine/Kriegswissenschaftliche Abteilung, *Der Ostseekrieg gegen Rußland im Jahre 1941*. Operationen und Taktik, Heft 12, Berlin, January 1944.
Oberkommando der Kriegsmarine/3. Abteilung Seekriegsleitung, *Nachtrag zum Handbuch für Admiralstabsoffiziere, Sowjetrußland, Kriegsschiffsliste (abgeschlossen 31.3.1941)*. Berlin, OKM, 1941.
Oruzhie Rossijskogo flota. St Petersburg: Sudostroenie, 1996.

Panteleev, Yu.A., *Polveka na flote*. Moscow, Voenizdat, 1974.
Pavlov, A.S., *Voenno-morskoj flot Rossii 1996 g.*, Spravochnik, Vypusk 4. Yakutsk, 1996. English language edn, *Warships of the USSR and Russia 1945–1995*. Annapolis, MD, US Naval Institute Press, 1997.
Perepiska Predsedatelya Soveta Ministrov SSSR s prezidentami SshA i prem'er ministrami Velikobritannii vo vremya Velikoi Otechestvennoi vojny 1941–1945 gg. Moscow, 1976. Vols 1–2.
Petrov, M.A., *Morskaya taktika. Boevaya deyatel'nost' flota*. Leningrad, Redaktsionno-izdat, Otdel morskogo vedostva, 1924.
Petrov, M.A., *Podgotovka Rossii k mirovoi vojenna na more*. Moscow/Leningrad, Gosvoenizdat, 1926.
Petrov, M.A., *Morskaya oborona beregov v opyte poslednikh vojn Rossii*. Leningrad, Voennaya tipografiya Upravleniya delami Narkomvoenmor i RVS SSSR, Voenno-Morskaya akademia VMF, 1940.
Petrovskii, V.A., *Vedenie morskikh operatii*. Leningrad, Voenno-Morskaya akademia VMF, 1940.
Philbin, Tobias R., *The Lure of Neptune. German–Soviet Naval Collaboration and Ambitions 1919–1941*. Columbia, University of South Carolina Press, 1994.
Piterskij, N.A., *Die Sowjetflotte im Zweiten Weltkrieg*, trans. Erich Pruck and ed. Jürgen Rohwer. Oldenburg, Stalling, 1966.
Platonov, A.V., *Sovietskie boevye korabli 1941–1945 gg.*, Vol. III. *Podvodnye lodki*. St Petersburg, Al'manakh Tsitadel', 1996.
Polmar, Norman, *Chronology of the Cold War at Sea 1945–1991*. Annapolis, MD, US Naval Institute Press, 1998.
Polmar, Norman and Thomas B. Allen, *Spy Book: The Encyclopedia of Espionage*. London, Greenhill Books, 1997.
Post, Walter, *Operation Barbarossa. Deutsche und sowjetische Angriffspläne 1940/41*. Hamburg, Mittler, 1995.
Rodionov, B., Dotsenko, V., Kostev, G. et al., *Tri veka Rossijskogo flota*, 3 vols, St Petersburg, 1996.
Rohwer, Jürgen, *Die Versenkung der jüdischen Flüchtlingstransporter Struma und Mefkure im Schwarzen Meer (Februar 1942 und August 1944)*. Schriften der Bibliothek für Zeitgeschichte, No. 4 Frankfurt/M., Bernard & Graefe, 1965.
Rohwer, Jürgen, *66 Tage unter Wasser. Atom-U-Schiffe und Raketen*. Oldenburg, Stalling, 1965.
Rohwer, Jürgen, *Superpower Confrontation on the Seas*. The Washington Papers No. 26. Beverly Hills, CA, Sage, 1975.
Rohwer, Jürgen, *Der Krieg zur See 1939–1945*. Gräfelfing, Urbes, 1992.
Rohwer, Jürgen und Gerhard Hümmelchen, *Chronology of the War at Sea 1939–1945. The Naval History of World War Two*. London, Greenhill Books, 1992.
Roskill, Stephen W., *The War at Sea 1939–1945*. Vols I–III. London, HMSO, 1954–61.
Ruegg, Bob and Arnold Hague, *Convoys to Russia 1941–1945: Allied Convoys and Naval Surface Operations in Arctic Waters 1941–1945*. Kendal (UK), World Ship Society, 1992.
Russell, Richard A., *Project Hula: Secret Soviet–American Cooperation in the War against Japan*. Washington Naval Historical Center, The US Navy in the Modern World Series, No. 4, 1997.

Rüstungswettlauf zur See 1930–1941. Von der Abrüstung zum Wettrüsten, ed. Jürgen Rohwer. Bonn, Bernard & Graefe, 1991.

Salewski, Michael, *Die deutsche Seekriegsleitung 1935–1945*, 3 vols. Frankfurt/M., Bernard & Graefe, 1970–73.

Samsonov, A.M., *Krakh fashistskoi agressii*. Moscow, Nauka, 1980.

Seaton, Albert, *The Russo-German War 1941–45*. London, Barker, 1971. German edn, *Der russische–deutsche Krieg 1941–1945*. Frankfurt/M., Bernard & Graefe, 1973.

Seaton, Albert, *Stalin as Military Commander*. New York, Praeger, 1976.

Semirjaga, M.I., *The Winter War. Looking Back after Fifty Years*. Moscow, Novosti, 1990.

Shaposhnikov, B.M.G., *Mozg armii*, 3 vols, Moscow/Leningrad, Gosizdat, 1927–29.

Shaposhnikov, B.M.G., *Japono-kitajskaya vojna: kolonial'naya politika Japonia v Kitae 1937–1941*. Moscow, Nauka, 1970.

Shaposhnikov, B.M.G., *Vospominaniya. Voen.-Nauch*, 2nd edn, Moscow, Voenizdat, 1982.

Shitikov, E.A., Krasnov, V.N., Balabin, V.V., *Korable-stroenie v SSSR v gody Velikoi Otechestvennoi vojny*. Moscow, Nauka, 1995.

Shtemenko, S.M., *General'nyi Shtab v gody vojny*, 2 vols, Moscow, Voenizdat, 1968–73.

Sokolovskii, V.D., *Voennaya Strategiya*. Moscow, Voenizdat, 1963. German edn, *Militär-Strategie*, ed. Uwe Nerlich. Cologne, Markus Verlag, 1965.

Souvarine, Boris, *Staline, Aperçu historique du Bolchévisme*. Paris, Champ Libre, 1977. German edn, *Stalin Anmerkungen zur Geschichte des Bolschewismus*. Munich, Bernard & Graefe, 1980.

Soviet Naval Developments, ed. Norman Polmar. Annapolis, MD, The Nautical and Aviation Publishing Co. of America, 1979.

SSSR v Velikoi Otechestvennoi vojne 1941–1945 gg. Kratkaya Khronika, ed. Akademiya Nauka SSSR, Institut Istorii, Moscow, Voenizdat, 1964.

Staatsmänner und Diplomaten bei Hitler. Vertrauliche Aufzeichnungen über Unterredungen mit Vertretern des Auslandes 1939–1941, ed. Andreas Hillgruber. Frankfurt/M., Bernard & Graefe, 1967.

Strel'bitskii, K.B., *Poteri protivnikov Sovetskogo Voenno-morskogo flota 1918–1940*. Lvov, Mezhdunarodnyj Tsentr istorii flota, 1995.

Strel'bitskii, K.B., *Avgust 1945. Sovetsko-japonskaya vojna na more. Tsena Pobedy*. Lvov, Mezhdunarodni Tsentr istorii flota, 1996.

Sudoplatov, Pawel A. and Anatolij Sudoplatov, *Der Handlanger der Macht. Enthüllungen eines KGB-Generals*. Düsseldorf, Econ, 1994.

Svechin, A.A., *Strategiya*. Moscow, Gosvoenizdat, 1926, 2nd edn, Moscow, Voennyi vestnik, 1927.

Telpuchovskii, V.S., *Velikaya Otechestvennaya vojna Sovetskogo Soyuza 1941–1945*. Moscow, Voenizdat, 1959. German edn, *Die sowjetische Geschichte des Großen Vaterländischen Krieges 1941–1945*, ed. Andreas Hillgruber and Hans-Adolf Jacobsen. Frankfurt/M., Bernard & Graefe, 1961.

The Sources of Soviet Naval Conduct, ed. Philip S. Gillette and Willard C. Frank Jr. Lexington, MA, Lexington Books, 1990.

The Soviet Navy, ed. M.G. Saunders. London, Weidenfeld & Nicolson, 1958.

German edn, *Die Rote Flotte. Ihre Geschichte, ihr Einsatz im Kriege und ihre heutige Stärke*. Oldenburg, Stalling, 1959.

Tomashevich, A.V., *Taktika protivolodochnoi borby*. Moscow/Leningrad, Voenmorizdat, 1940.

Triandafillov, V.K., *Kharakter operatsii sovremennykh armii*, 4th edn. Moscow, Gosvoenizdat, 1937.

Triandafillov, V.K., *The Nature of the Operations of Modern Armies*, trans. William A. Burhans, ed. Jacob W. Kipp. Ilford, Frank Cass, 1994.

Trotskii, Lev D., *My Life*. London, Butterworth, 1930. German edn, *Mein Leben. Versuch einer Autobiographie*. Frankfurt/M., 1961.

Trotskii, L.D., *Stalin*. London, Harper, 1946.

Trusov, G.M., *Podvodnye lodki v Russkom i Sovetskom flote*. Leningrad, Gossoyuzizdat, 1963.

Tucker, Robert C., *Stalin as a Revolutionary 1879–1929*. New York, Norton, 1974.

Tucker, Robert C., *Stalin in Power: 1929–1941*. New York, 1990.

Tukhachevskii, M.N., *Budushchaya vojna*. 6 vols., Moscow, IV Upravlenie Shtabe RKKA, 1928.

Tukhachevskii, M.N., *Nashi uchebno-takticheskie zadachi*. Moscow/Leningrad, Gosizdat, 1929.

Tukhachevskii, M.N., *Izbrannye i proizvedeniya*, Vol. 1, *1918–1927gg*, Vol. 2, *1928–1937gg*. Moscow, Voenizdat, 1964.

Ulam, Adam, *Stalin: The Man and his Era*. New York, Viking, 1973.

Voenno-morskoi flot. Tsentral'naya Voenno-morskaya Biblioteka, *Voenno-morskaya Literatura. Ukazatel' knig i statei*, 1946–53 (3 vols), 1954–55, 1956, 1957, 1958, 1959, 1960, 1961, 1962, 1963–65, 1966–70 (2 vols), 1971–73, 1974–76, 1977–80 (2 vols), 1981–84, 1985–90. Leningrad, Tsentralnaya Voenno-morskaya Biblioteka, 1955–89.

Voenno-morskoi slovar, ed. V.N. Chernyavin. Moscow, Voenizdat, 1990.

Volkogonov, Dmitrii A., *Triumf i tragediya: Politicheskii portret I.V. Stalina*. Moscow, Novosti, 1989. German edn, *Stalin, Triumph und Tragödie*. Düsseldorf, Claasen, 1989.

Volkogonov, Dmitrii A., *Lev Trotskii. Politicheskii portret*. Moscow, Novosti, 1992.

Vtoraya Mirovaya vojna. Kratkaya istoriya, ed. P.A. Zhilin. Moscow, Nauka, 1984.

Weinberg, Gerhard, *A World at Arms. A Global History of World War II*. New York, Cambridge University Press, 1994.

Westwood, J.N., *Russian Naval Construction, 1905–1941*. London, Macmillan, 1994.

Weyers Flotten-Taschenbuch, ed. Alexander Bredt. Munich, J.F. Lehmanns, vols 1953, 1954/55, 1956/57, 1958.

Whitley, M.J., *The German Cruisers of World War II*. London, Arms & Armour Press, 1985.

Wolfe, Thomas, *Soviet Strategy at the Crossroads*. Cambridge, MA, Harvard University Press, 1964. German edn, *Sowjetische Militärstrategie*. Cologne, Opladen, Westdeutscher Verlag, 1967.

Woodward, David, *The Russians at Sea*. London, Kimber, 1965.

Zakharov, S.E. *et al.*, *Krasnoznamennyi Tikhookeanskii flot*, 2nd edn Moscow, Voenizdat, 1973.

Zeidler, Manfred, *Reichswehr und Rote Armee 1920–1933. Wege und Stationen einer ungewöhnlichen Zusammenarbeit*. Munich, Oldenburg, 1993.

Zherve, B.B., *Strategiya – Lektsii, tchitannyie slushateliam Kursov Kommissarov Flota*. Petrograd, 1919–21.

Zherve, B.B., *Osnovy voenno-morskoi strategii*. Moscow, 1919–21.

Zherve, B.B., *Znachenie voenno-morskoi sily dya gosudarstva*. Moscow, 1923.

Zherve, B.B., *Desantnaya operatsiya*. Leningrad, Voenno-Morskaya akademia RKKA, 1931.

Zhilin, P.A., Yakushevskii, A.S., Kul'kov, E.N., *Kritika osnovnykh kontseptsii burzhyaznoi istoriografii vtoroi mirovoi vojny*. Moscow, Nauka, 1984.

Zhukov, G.K., *Vospominaniya i razmyshleniya*, Vols 1, 2. Moscow, Novosti, 1974. Engl. edn, *Reminiscences and Reflections*. Moscow, Progress, 1985, 2 vols.

Zonin, S., *Admiral L.M. Galler: Zhizn' i flotovodcheskaya deyatel'nost*. Moscow, Voenizdat, 1991.

Zonin, S., *Flagman Povest ob admirala L.M. Gallere*. St Petersburg, Äastra-Lyuks', 1995.

ARTICLES

Achkasov, V.I., 'Die sowjetische Kriegsflotte im Verlauf des "Großen Vaterländischen Krieges"', *Marine-Rundschau*, 62 (1965), pp. 268–77.

Achkasov, V.I., 'Die Durchbruchsoperation der Baltischen Rotbanner-Flotte von Reval auf Kronstadt', *Marine-Rundschau*, 64 (1967), pp. 26–44.

Afonin, N.N., 'Lideri eskadrennykh minonostsev tipa "Leningrad"', *Sudostroenie*, No. 3 (1985), pp. 66–9.

Afonin, N.N., 'Lider eskadrennykh minonostsev "Tashkent"', *Sudostroenie*, No. 7 (1985), pp. 49–51.

Afonin, N.N., 'Uchebnoe sudno "Komsomolets"', *Sudostroenie*, No. 10 (1988), pp. 42–3.

Afonin, N.N., 'Pis'ma tchitatelei po voprosam istorii', *Sudostroenie*, No. 11–12 (1994), pp. 57–62.

Ajsenberg, B.A., '"Krejser bandit" ne vyshedshii na svoyu "bol'shuyu" dorogy', *Ocherki voenno-morskoi istorii*, Kharkov o.J., Soderzhanie No. 2, pp. 22–6.

Ajsenberg, B.A., 'Podvodnye lodki proekta 651', *Ocherki voenno-morskoi istorii*, Kharkov o.J., Soderzhanie No. 2, pp. 54–7.

Aleksandrov, A.P., 'A Critical Analysis of the Theory of Naval Supremacy', *Morskoi sbornik*, No. 10 (1929).

Aleksandrovskii, A.F., '"Kirov", Pervenets Sovetskogo kreiserstroeniya', *Sudostroenie*, No. 11 (1986), pp. 31ff.

Antonov, A., 'Raketnye PLA proektov P-627A, 653 i 639', *Morskoi sbornik*, No. 11 (1986), pp. 72–6.

Antonov G.I., 'The March into Poland', in B. Liddell Hart, *The Soviet Army*, London, Weidenfeld & Nicolson, 1956, pp. 73–8.

Balabin, S.A., 'Gremyashchii i drugie. Eskadrennye minonostsy proekta 7', *Modelist-Konstruktor*, No. 2, 8 (1996).

Baltzer, Uwe, 'Die Entwicklung der sowjetischen Marine 1945–1968', *Marine-Rundschau*, 65 (1968), pp. 256–81.

Basov, A.V., 'Der Bau der Seekriegsflotte der UdSSR vor dem Zweiten Weltkrieg 1921–1941', in *The Naval Arms Race 1930–1941*, ed. Jürgen Rohwer, *Revue Internationale d'Histoire Militaire, No. 73*, Bonn, Bernard & Graefe, 1991.

Berezhnoi, S.S., 'Sovietskii VMF 1945–1995. Kreisera, bol'sh'ie protivolodochnie korabli, esmitsy', *Modelist-Konstruktor*, No. 1 (1995), pp. 1–32.

Besymenskii, Lew, 'Die Rede Stalins am 5.Mai 1941. Dokumentiert und interpretiert', *Osteuropa*, 1992, pp. 242–64.

Bil'din, V.F., 'Tyazhelye kreisera tipa "Stalingrad"', *Sudostroenie*, No. 7 (1994), pp. 63–7.

Bil'din, V.F., 'Opytnaya torpednaya PLA proekta 645', *Morskoi sbornik*, No. 8 (1993), pp. 59–62.

Breyer, Siegfried, 'Die Kreuzer "K" und "L" der deutschen Kriegsmarine ("Seydlitz" und "Lützow")', *Marine-Rundschau*, 63 (1966), pp. 20–28.

Breyer, Siegfried, 'Ehemalige deutsche Kriegsschiffe unter sowjetischer Flagge', *Marine-Rundschau*, 69 (1972), pp. 731–6.

Breyer, Siegfried, 'Zwanzig Jahre "Sverdlov"-Klasse', *Marine-Rundschau*, 71 (1974), pp. 32–40.

Breyer, Siegfried, 'Sowjetischer Schlachtschiffbau', *Marine-Rundschau*, 72 (1975), pp. 141–63.

Breyer, Siegfried, 'Der sowjetische Kriegsschiffbau von 1945 bis zur Gegenwart', *Marine-Rundschau*, 74 (1977), pp. 486–91.

Breyer, Siegfried, 'Großkampfschiffbau in der Sowjetunion', in S. Breyer, *Großkampfschiffe*, Vol. III. Munich, Bernard & Graefe, 1979, pp. 139–69.

Breyer, Siegfried, 'Vor 50 Jahren: Sowjetische Schlachtkreuzer mit Krupp Kanonen', *Marine-Forum*, 9 (1991), pp. 301–3.

Chernyshev, A.A., '"Parizhskaya kommuna" v okeane', *Gangut*, No. 15, St Petersburg, (1998), pp. 9–14.

Chernyshev, V., 'Morskaya taktika za dva desiatiletia', *Morskoi sbornik*, No. 12 (1937), pp. 17–29.

Christopher, C., 'The Fate of the "Tashkent"', *Warship International*, No. 4 (1994), pp. 249–60.

Dabakov, G.M., 'Vtoraya kupel', ili nalet na bukhtu Norkapel'lakht', *Gangut*, No. 9, St Petersburg (1995), pp. 74–83.

Erikson, Rolf, 'Soviet Battleships', *Warship International*, No. 2 (1974).

Evgrafov, B., 'Dvaventsa a admirala Levchenko', *Morskoi sbornik*, No. 11 (1990), pp. 82–97.

Fischer, Alexander, 'Kollektive Sicherheit und imperialistischer Krieg', *Saeculum*, XXVIII (1977), pp. 432ff.

Förster, Jürgen, 'Die deutsche Kriegspolitik und die Sowjetunion 1940/41', in H. Boog *et al.* (eds), *Das Deutsche Reich und der Zweite Weltkrieg*, Bd. 4. Stuttgart, Deutsche Verlagsanstalt, 1983, pp. 3–37.

Forstmeier, Friedrich, 'Die sowjetische Landung im Hafen von Noworossijsk und der Kampf um Stadt und Hafen vom 10–15.9, 1943', *Marine-Rundschau*, 57 (1960), pp. 321–44.

Forstmeier, Friedrich, 'Die Räumung von Odessa im Oktober 1941', *Marine-Rundschau*, 62 (1965), pp. 8–33.

Forstmeier, Friedrich, 'Die Versenkung des sowjetischen Flottillenführers "Charkov" und der Zerstörer "Sposobnyi" und "Besposhchadnyi" vor der

Südküste der Krim am 6 Oktober 1943', *Marine-Rundschau*, 63 (1966), pp. 325–36.

Frank, Willard C., 'Naval Operations in the Spanish Civil War 1936–1939', *Naval War College Review*, XXXVII (1984), pp. 24–55.

Frank, Willard C., 'Politico-Military Deception at Sea in the Spanish Civil War, 1936–1939', *Intelligence and National Security*, V, No. 3 (1990), pp. 84–112.

Frank, Willard C., 'Misperceptions and Incidents at Sea: the "Deutschland" and "Leipzig" Crises, 1937', *Naval War College Review*, XLIII, No. 2 (1990), pp. 31–46.

Frank, Willard C., 'German Clandestine Submarine Warfare in the Spanish Civil War, 1936', *New Interpretations in Naval History*, IXth Naval History Symposium, Annapolis, 18–20 October 1989, ed. W.M. Roberts and J. Sweetman. Annapolis, MD, US Naval Institute, 1991, pp. 107–23.

Gobarev, Victor, 'Khrushchev and the Military: Historical and Psychological Analyses', *Journal of Slavic Military Studies*, Vol. 1, No. 3 (September 1998), pp. 128–44.

Greger, René, 'Sowjetischer Schlachtschiffbau', *Marine-Rundschau*, 71 (1974), pp. 461–79.

Greger, René, 'Russische Schlachtschiff-Projekte von 1914–1917', *Marine-Rundschau*, 73 (1976), pp. 165–1269.

Greger, René, '"Imperator Nikolai I", das letzte in Rußland gebaute Schlachtschiff', *Marine-Rundschau*, 71 (1976), pp. 582–90.

Greger, René, 'Neue Bilder zum Schicksal des Kreuzers "Petropavlovsk"', *Marine-Rundschau*, 75 (1978), pp. 786–7.

Greger, René, 'Geschichte des russischen und sowjetischen Bordflugwesens', *Marine-Rundschau*, 76 (1979), pp. 761–70.

Greger, René, 'K.u.K. Monitore unter sowjetischer Flagge', *Marine-Rundschau*, 77 (1980), pp. 400–5.

Greger, René, 'Anfänge des sowjetischen Kreuzerbaus', *Marine-Rundschau*, 86 (1989), pp. 228ff.

Gribovskii, V.Yu., 'Podvodnye lodki tipa "Pravda"', *Sudostroenie*, No. 7 (1989), pp. 34–6.

Gribovskii, V.Yu., 'Linejniye korabli tipa "Sovetskii Soyuz"', *Sudostroenie*, No. 7 (1990), pp. 55–9.

Gribovskii, V.Yu., 'The "Sovietskii Soyuz" Class Battleships', *Warship International*, No. 2 (1993), pp. 164ff.

Gribovskii, V.Yu., 'Na puti k "bol'shomu morskomu floty": korablestroitel'nye programmy Voenno-morskogo flota SSSR v predvoennye gody', *Gangut*, No. 9, St Petersburg, 1995, pp. 3–21.

Gribovskii, V.Yu., 'K istorii sozdaniya storozhevykh korablei tipa "Yastreb"', *Sudostroenie*, No. 4 (1997), pp. 87–90.

Howard, Michael, 'The Russian Ally', in *History of the Second World War, Grand Strategy, Vol. IV*. London, HMSO, 1970, pp. 31–47.

Huan, Claude, 'Die sowjetischen U-Boote 1960', *Marine-Rundschau*, 58 (1961), pp. 197–203.

Huan, Claude, 'Die sowjetischen Landungsoperationen auf der Krim 1941–1942', *Marine-Rundschau*, 59 (1962), pp. 337–55.

Hümmelchen, Gerhard, 'Unternehmen "Eisstoß". Der Angriff der Luftflotte

1 gegen die russische Ostseeflotte im April 1942', *Marine-Rundschau*, 56 (1959), pp. 226–32.

Ivanov, L., 'Morskie vooruzheniya kapitalisticheskikh gosudarstv i ugroza vojny', *Morskoi sbornik*, No. 1 (1937), pp. 109–25.

Jablonski, Walter, 'Sowjetische U-Bootrüstung 1949–1978', *Marine-Rundschau*, 77 (1980), pp. 547–56.

Karpenko, A.V., 'U istokov sozdaniya raketnykh korably', *Gangut*, No. 16, St Petersburg (1998), pp. 67–82.

Kasatonov, V., 'Vitse-admiral N.G. Kuznetsov', *Voenno-istoricheskii zhurnal*, No. 7 (1982), pp. 93–5.

Klink, E., 'Deutsche-finnische Waffenbrüderschaft 1941–1944', *Wehrwissenschaftliche Rundschau*, 5 (1958), pp. 389–412.

Komarov, A., 'Konets Krigsmarine. Reshenie voprosa o razdele germanskogo flota', *Morskoi sbornik*, No. 5 (1999), pp. 76–82.

Kostev, G., 'Morskie strategicheskie', *Morskoi sbornik*, No. 12 (1999), pp. 65–71.

Kostrichenko, V.V., 'Gibel' esmintsa "Svobodnyi"', *Ocherki voenno-morskoj istorii*, Kharkov o.J., Soderzhanie No. 2, pp. 2–3.

Kostrichenko, V.V., 'Sekrety stalinskogo korablestroeniya', *Ocherki voenno-morskoj istorii*, Kharkov, o.J., Soderzhanie No. 2, pp. 33–5.

Kostrichenko, V.V., 'Nabeg na Konstantsu', *Ocherki voenno-morskoj istorii*, Kharkov 1998, Soderzhanie No. 2, pp. 46–52.

Krasnikov, B.Ya., 'Boevye povrezhdeniya, borba za zhivuchest' i remont legkogo krejsera proekta 26-bis "Molotov"', *Ocherki Voenno-morskoi istorii*, No. 2, pp. 36–45.

Krasnov, V.N., 'Linkory tipa "Sovetskii Soyuz"', *Morskoi sbornik*, No. 6 (1990), pp. 60ff.

Krasnov, V.N., 'Stalinshina v VMF i korabliestroenie', *Sudostroenie*, No. 7 (1990), pp. 64–9.

Krasnov, V.N., 'Kreisera tipa "Kronshtadt"', *Morskoi sbornik*, No. 8 (1990), pp. 53–6.

Krasnov, V.N., 'Sudostroenie i sudoremont na Chernom more v 1941–1944 godakh', *Gangut*, No. 9, 1995, pp. 22–36.

Krueger, V.A., Manuilov, Yu.V., Semenov, V.P., 'Podvodnye lodki proekta 613', *Sudostroenie*, No. 5–6 (1994), pp. 59–65.

Kuznetsov, L.A., 'Ne isklyuchalas' i postroika avianostsa', *Gangut*, No. 3 (1992), pp. 63–70.

Kuznetsov, N.G., 'Ispanskii Flot v Borbe za respubliky', *Voenno-istoricheskii zhurnal*, No. 4 (1962), pp. 53–72.

Lemachko, Boris, 'Die "Taschen"-Schlachtschiffe des Amur', *Marine-Rundschau*, 77 (1980), No. 6, pp. 356–8.

Litvinenko, Dmitrii, 'Plany vozhdya. Pervaya poslevoennaya programma stroitel'stva flota', *Morskoi sbornik*, No. 2 (1997), pp. 100–4.

Main, Steven J., 'The Arrest and "Testimony" of Marshal of the Soviet Union M.N. Tukhachevskii', *Journal of Slavic Military Studies*, Vol. 10, No. 1 (1997), pp. 151–95.

Maslennikov, V.N., 'Podvodnye lodki tipa "Malyutka"', *Sudostroenie*, No. 5 (1989), pp. 62–4.

McGwire, Michael, 'Der Hintergrund der sowjetischen Marine-Politik', *Marine-Rundschau*, 66 (1969), pp. 307–24.

Meister, Jürg, 'Unternehmen "Wunderland"', *Marine-Rundschau*, 52 (1955), pp. 1–8.

Meister, Jürg, 'Die sowjetischen amphibischen Operationen 1939–1945', *Marine-Rundschau*, 52 (1955), pp. 124–36.

Meister, Jürg, 'Det tysk-sovietiska marina samarbetet aren 1920–1941', *Tidskrift i Sjövesendet*, September (1955), pp. 491–513.

Meister, Jürg, 'Der Einsatz der sowjetischen Schiffsartillerie gegen Landziele 1939/45', *Marine-Rundschau*, 53 (1956), pp. 215–22.

Meister, Jürg, 'Der Seekrieg im finnisch–russischen Winterkrieg 1939/1940', *Marine-Rundschau*, 55 (1958), pp. 66–73.

Meister, Jürg, 'Der sowjetisch-japanische Seekrieg', *Marine-Rundschau*, 57 (1960), pp. 3–18.

Mikoyan, Stepan A., 'Barbarossa and the Soviet Leadership: A Recollection', in *Barbarossa: The Axis and the Allies*, ed. John Erickson and David Dilks. Edinburgh University Press, 1994, pp. 123–33.

Monakov, M.S., 'Sud'by doktrin i teorii', *Morskoi sbornik*, No. 11, 12 (1990), 3, 4 (1991), 3 (1992), 3, 5 (1994).

Monakov, M.S., 'Strategicheskiye zadachi VMF v posledniye 100 let', *Morskoi sbornik*, No. 10 (1996).

Monakov, M.S., 'Dolgoye echo vojny', *Morskoi sbornik*, No. 8 (1997).

Monakov, M.S., 'Zachem Stalin stroil okeanskii flot?', *Morskoi sbornik*, No. 12 (1998), pp. 74–9.

Morin, A.B., 'Eskadrennye minonostsy tipa "Gnevni"', *Gangut*, No. 2, St Petersburg, 1994.

Morin, A.B., 'Eskadrennyi minonostsev "Ognevoi"', *Sudostroenie*, No. 5–6 (1995), pp. 42–52.

Morin, A.B. and Petrov, N.P., 'Bystrohodnye (Bazovye) Tral'shchiki tipy "Fugas"', *Sudostroenie*, No. 10 (1994), pp. 62–9.

Müller, Klaus-Jürgen, Jürgen Rohwer and J.R. Fredland, 'Abrüstung (1918–1934), Wiederaufrüstung (1935–1939)', in *Seemacht. Von der Antike bis zur Gegenwart*, ed. E.B. Potter, C.W. Nimitz and J. Rohwer. Herrsching, Pawlak, 1982, pp. 445–85.

Nevezhin, V.A., 'The Pact with Germany and the Idea of an "Offensive War" (1939–1941)', *Journal of Slavic Military Studies*, Vol. 8, No. 4 (December 1995), pp. 809–43.

Nikol'skii, V.N., 'Storozhevye korabli proekta 42', *Sudostroenie*, No. 11–12 (1994), pp. 63–6.

Nikol'skii, V.N., 'Storozhevye korabli proekta 50', *Sudostroenie*, No. 1 (1995), pp. 66–9.

Nikol'skii, V.N., Tyurin, B., Prorozhetskii, V., 'Eskadrennye minonostsy proekta 30-bis', *Morskoi sbornik*, No. 10 (1992), pp. 51–6.

Petrov, M.S., 'Zametki o taktike malogo flota', *Morskoi sbornik*, No. 9 (1925), pp. 45–61.

Platonov, A.V., 'Iz letopisi sozdaniya Sovetskikh avianostsev', *Sudostroenie*, No. 5 (1992), pp. 42–5.

Platonov, A.V., 'Eskadrennyi minonosets "Storozhevoi"', *Gangut*, No. 9, St Petersburg (1995), pp. 36–49.

Rabinerzon, Yu.A., 'Perevooruzhenie krejsera "Admiral Nakhimov" udarnym raketnym oruzhiem po proektu 67EP', *Gangut*, No. 15, St Petersburg, 1998, pp. 45–54.

Rahn, Werner, 'Ibiza und Almeria. Eine Dokumentation der Ereignisse vom 29. bis 31. Mai 1937', *Marine-Rundschau*, 68 (1971), pp. 389–406.

Rohwer, Jürgen, 'Die sowjetische U-Bootwaffe in der Ostsee 1939–1945', *Wehrwissenschaftliche Rundschau*, 6 (1956), pp. 547–68.

Rohwer, Jürgen, 'Die sowjetische Flotte im Zweiten Weltkrieg', *Jahresbibliographie der Bibliothek für Zeitgeschichte*, 32 (1960), pp. 383–410.

Rohwer, Jürgen, 'Wider die Fälscher der Geschichte des Zweiten Weltkrieges. Eine 'Battle of the Pips' im Eismeer', *Marine-Rundschau*, 58 (1961), pp. 266–74.

Rohwer, Jürgen, 'Der Minenkrieg im Finnischen Meerbusen (I), Juni–August 1941 (II), September–November 1941', *Marine-Rundschau*, 64 (1967), pp. 16–25, 94–102.

Rohwer, Jürgen, 'Esperienze tecniche e tattiche dell'arma subaquea Sovietica nel secondo conflitto mondiale', *Rivista Marittimo*, 7–8 (1967), pp. 39–83.

Rohwer, Jürgen, 'Strategische Konzepte und Schiffbauprogramme der Vereinigten Staaten und der Sowjetunion seit 1945 unter Berücksichtigung Großbritanniens und Frankreichs', in *Seemacht und Außenpolitik*, ed. Dieter Mahncke and Hans-Peter Schwarz. Frankfurt/M., A. Metzner, 1974, pp. 191–259.

Rohwer, Jürgen, 'Admiral Gorshkov and the Influence of History upon Seapower', *US Naval Institute Proceedings*, May 1981, pp. 150–74.

Rohwer, Jürgen, 'Die Sowjetunion wird eine Seemacht', in *Seemacht. Von der Antike bis zur Gegenwart*, ed. E.B. Potter, C.W. Nimitz, J. Rohwer. Herrsching, Pawlak, 1982, pp. 1016–43.

Rohwer, Jürgen, 'Russian and Soviet Naval Strategy', in *Soviet Seapower in Northern Waters. Facts, Motivation, Impact and Responses*, ed. John Kristen Skogan and Arne Olav Brundtland. London, Pinter Publishers, 1990, pp. 3–17.

Rohwer, Jürgen, 'Alternating Russian and Soviet Naval Strategies', in *Sources of Soviet Naval Conduct*, ed. P.S. Gillette and W.C. Frank, Jr. Lexington, MA, Lexington Books, 1990, pp. 90–120.

Rohwer, Jürgen, 'Les stratégies navales soviétiques et les programmes de construction navale (1921–1941)', *Dossier 47. L'évolution de la pensée navale III*. Paris, 1993, pp. 171–208.

Rohwer, Jürgen, 'Soviet Naval Strategies and Building Programs, 1922–1941', *Acta No. 19, XIXth International Colloquium of Military History*, Ankara, 1994, pp. 421–50.

Rohwer, Jürgen, 'Il programma navale di Stalin', *Storia Militare*, No. 20-III (May 1995), pp. 4–13.

Rohwer, Jürgen, 'Weltmacht als Ziel? Parallelen in Stalins und Hitlers Flottenbau-Programmen', in *Politischer Wandel, organisierte Gewalt und nationale Sicherheit*. Munich, Oldenburg, 1995, pp. 161–80.

Rohwer, Jürgen, 'Stalin's Battleships and Battlecruisers', *The Northern Mariner*, VII, No. 3 (July 1997), pp. 1–11.

Rohwer, Jürgen and Mikhail Monakov, 'The Soviet Union's Ocean-Going Fleet 1935–1953', *The International History Review*, 18, IV (1996), pp. 837–68.

Rössler, Eberhard, 'Vom UG-Typ der Kaiserlichen Marine zur russischen

S-Klasse', in *Die deutschen U-Boote und ihre Werften*. Munich, Bernard & Graefe, 1979, pp. 25–31.

Rzheshevskii, O.A., 'Between the Two Fires'. Paper at the International Conference on 'Barbarossa' at the University of Leeds, 21–23 June 1991.

Savel'ev, E.V., 'Ot Skapa-Flou do Vaengi na likore "Arkangel'sk"', *Gangut*, No. 9, St Petersburg (1995), pp. 84–95.

Semenov, V.P., 'Bol'shie torpednye dizel-elektricheskie PL proekta 611', *Morskoi sbornik*, No. 11 (1994), pp. 61–5.

Sergeev, N., 'Admiral Flota Sovetskogo Soyuza I.S. Isakov', *Voenno-istoricheskii zhurnal*, No. 8 (1984), pp. 85–8.

Shchedrolosev, V.V., 'Konvojnye operatsii eskadrennykh minonostsev Severnogo flota v Velikoj Otechestvennoj vojne', *Gangut*, No. 9, St Petersburg (1995), pp. 59–67.

Shitikov, E.A., 'Stalin i voennoe korabliestroenie', *Morskoi sbornik*, No. 12 (1993), pp. 58ff.

Shitikov, E.A., 'Ispytaniya korablei na Novoi Zemle', *Morskoi sbornik*, No. 5 (1994), pp. 71–7.

Shmakov, P., 'Pervye Sovetskie PLA proekta 627', *Morskoi sbornik*, No. 1 (1995).

Stepakov, V.N., 'Na bortu "BT-521" (Iosif Stalin)', *Gangut*, No. 9, St Petersburg (1995), pp. 68–73.

'Tajny podvodnoj vojny. Maloizvestnye stranitsy Vtoroi mirovoi vojny na more 1939–1945', *Moskovskii klub istorii flota*, No. 1 (1995), No. 2 (1996), No. 3 (1998), No. 4 (1996).

Tributs, V.F., 'Podvodniki Krasnoznamennogo Baltijskogo Flota v 1942 g.', *Voenno-istoricheskii zhurnal*, No. 11 (1960), pp. 20–6. German, 'Die U-Boot-offensive der Baltischen Rotbannerflotte in der Ostsee 1942', *Marine-Rundschau*, 60 (1963), pp. 80–107.

Tributs, V.F., 'Die Räumung der Garnison von Hangö', *Marine-Rundschau*, 64 (1967), pp. 103–10, 158–74.

Twardowski, Marek and Boris Lemachko, 'Soviet Union', in *Conway's all the World's Fighting Ships 1922–1946*. London, Conway's, 1980, pp. 318–46.

Tyurin, B.P., 'Kreiseri tipa 68', *Gangut*, No. 6 (1993), pp. 10–25.

Tyurin, B., Balabin, V., 'Podvodnyi minnyi zagraditel' "Leninets"', *Morskoi sbornik*, No. 1 (1993), pp. 71–3.

Ueberschär, Gerd, 'Die "Volksregierung" Kuusinen in der "Demokratischen Republik Finnland" im Kalkül Stalins und Hitlers 1939/1940', in *Finnland Studien*, Wiesbaden, Steiner, 1990, pp. 227–47.

Uitli, M., 'Germanskie esmintsy na Baltike 1944–1945 gody', *Gangut*, No. 15, St Petersburg (1998), pp. 127–32.

Usov, V.Yu., 'Tyazhel'nye kreiseri tipa "Kronshtadt"', *Sudostroenie*, No. 11 (1989), pp. 57ff.

Usov, V.Yu., 'Krasnoznamennyi kreiser "Maksim Gorkii"', *Sudostroenie*, No. 12 (1990), pp. 59–61.

Usov, V.Yu., 'Krejser "Maksim Gorkii"', *Gangut*, No. 1, St Petersburg (1993).

Uspenskij, M.N., 'Kamuflyazh korablej na severnom flote v gody Velikoi Otechestvennoi vojny', *Gangut*, No. 9, St Petersburg (1995), pp. 96–106.

Vasetskii, N., 'Kronshtadt skimyatezh vzglyad skvoz' gody', *Morskoi sbornik*, No. 3 (1991), pp. 79–6.

Vasil'ev, A.M., 'Linejny korabl' proekta 24', *Gangut*, No. 15, St Petersburg (1998), pp. 32–44.

Vasil'ev, A.M., 'Linejnye korabl VMF SSSR predvoennykh proektov', *Gangut*, No. 16, St Petersburg (1998), pp. 53–66.

Vasil'ev, A.M., 'Pervyi boevoi pokhod Otryada legkikh sil', *Gangut*, No. 9, St Petersburg (1995), pp. 50–59.

Vasil'ev, A.M., 'Krupnye nadvodnye korabli v programmakh Sovetskogo voennogo sudostroeniya (1936–1966gg.)', *Sudostroenie*, No. 6 (1997), pp. 82–91.

'Velikaya Otechestvennaya Dem' za Den'. Khroniki Iyunya 1941 v May 1945', monthly in *Morskoi sbornik*, No. 6 (1991), to No. 5 (1995).

Volkogonov, Dmitri A., 'The German Attack, the Soviet Response', in *Barbarossa: The Axis and the Allies*, ed. John Erickson and David Dilks. Edinburgh University Press, 1994, pp. 76–96.

Vorob'ev, V.F., 'Krugosvetka rejdera "Komet"', *Gangut*, No. 16, St Petersburg (1998), pp. 83–97.

Yarovoi, V.V., 'Kreiseri tipa "Kirov" i "Maksim Gorkii"', *Sudostroenie*, No. 7 (1985), pp. 46–8.

Zakharov, I.G., 'Naval Shipbuilding in Russia', *Sudostroenie*, No. 10 (1996), pp. 64ff.

Zani, Luciano, 'La Marine Italiana e l'Unione Sovietica tra la due guerre. Parte Prima, 1929–1933', *Bolletino d'Archivo dell'Ufficio Storico della Marina Militare*, Anno VIII (June 1994), pp. 99–151.

Zherve, B.B., 'Flot segodnyashnego dnia. Boevye sredstva', *Krasnyi flot* (February 1922).

Zonin, S.A., 'Nepravi sud', *Morskoi sbornik*, No. 2 (1991), pp. 78–84.

Zubov, E.N., Narushev, A.A., 'Sudostroenie y gody Velikoi Otechestvennoi vojny', *Ekonomika sudostroit., prom-sti.*, No. 1 (1969).

Index

INDEX OF NAMES

Abankin, P.S., 191
Achkasov, V.I., 1, 293, 295
Alafuzov, V.A., 8, 166, 190
Alekin, V.A, 294
Aleksandrov, A.P., 6, 7, 23, 24, 27, 54, 66, 102, 104, 293, 294
Alferov, V.I., 150
Al'tfater, V.M., 293
Alyakrinskii, B.E., 74
Alyakrinskii, N.V., 74, 78, 293
Amel'ko, N.N., 1
Amosov, I.A., 1, 2, 4
Andreyev, N.N., 135
Andreyev, V.A., 190
Antipin. A.A., 205
Antonescu, Ion, 115, 127
Antonov, A.I., 188
Apukhtin, P.A., 150
Asafov, A.N., 37, 38, 48
Aseev, D.A., 296
Ashik, V.V., 152, 211

Bajkov, I.I., 190. 191
Balabin, V.V., 296, 297
Basistyi, N.E., 191
Basov, A.V., 293
Bazilevskii, S.A., 31, 193
Behncke, P., 32
Bekauri, V.I., 49, 161
Belli, V.A., 122, 123, 125, 191, 293, 294
Benesch, Edouard, 69
Berakso, G.M., 203
Berens, E.A., 7, 15, 17n
Berezhnoi, S.S., 2, 296, 297

Berezhnyak, A.Ya., 211, 214
Berg, A.I., 35
Beriev, G.M., 211
Beriya, L.P., 78, 186, 188, 209
Bespolov, F.E., 95, 194
Blinov, S.P., 15, 16
Blyukher, V.K., 60, 70, 80
Boris III, 127
Brauchitsch, W. von, 115
Breyer, Siegfried, 4
Budyennyi, S.M., 25, 60, 133
Bukharin, N.I., 19, 30, 59, 60, 77
Bul'ganin, N.A., 145, 186, 216
Burov, V.N., 4, 297
Bykov, P.P., 293
Bzhezinskii, V.I., 16, 35, 45, 51, 62, 63, 74, 78, 95, 161

Carol II, 115
Cavagnari, D., 34
Chelomey, V.N., 210, 211, 214
Chernyshev, V.K., 126
Chicherin, G.V., 32
Chilikin, B.G., 74
Churchill, W.S., 115, 166, 174, 179, 189
Cook, S., 180
Cunningham, Andrew, 180

Deane, John R., 166
Deribin, E.A., 47, 158, 161, 206
Dikovich, L.V., 196
Dmitriev, V., 4, 297
Dmitrievskii, V.S., 161
Dombrovskii, A.V., 7, 17n
Drozd, V.P., 65, 80
Dubinin, N.P., 74, 150

Dushenov, K.I., 7, 23, 27, 34, 46, 54, 78, 102, 223, 293
Dybenko, P.Ye., 25

Egoriev, V.E., 104
Ejdeman, P.P., 69
Erikson, Rolf, 4
Evgrafov, Ya.E., 162

Fel'dman, B.M., 69
Filoff, Bogdan, 115
Fisher, A.L., 153, 201
Flerov, N.G., 210
Franco, F., 64, 116
Frank, Willard C., 5
Frinovskii, M.P., 78, 79, 223
Frolov, A.S., 190
Frunze, M.V., 7, 16, 19, 20, 21, 22, 294

Galler, L.M., 7, 30, 60, 70, 76, 79, 87, 97, 150, 155, 162, 185, 186, 190
Gamarnik, Y.B., 70
Garsoev, A.N., 54
Gigurtu, Ion, 115
Golikov, F.I., 133
Golovko, A.G., 65, 80, 145, 191, 200
Gorbachev, M. 296
Gorkii, Maksim, 34
Gorshkov, S.G., 1, 224, 293, 295
Grauerman, L.S., 74
Greger, René, 5
Gribovskii, V.Yu., 297
Gusev, S.I., 12

Halder, Franz, 115, 127
Heinrichs, Erik, 127
Hitler, Adolf, 41, 59, 65, 96, 102, 110, 111, 112, 113, 114, 115, 116, 117, 118, 127, 128, 131, 132, 133, 135, 144
Huan, Claude, 5
Hull, Cordell, 165

Ignat'ev, N.I., 25, 27, 30
Ilyushin, S.V., 212
Isachenkov, N.V., 150, 186, 199
Isakov, I.S., 7, 31, 70, 79, 87, 89, 97, 122, 123, 124, 125, 151, 152, 157, 158, 191, 217, 293
Isanin, N.N., 215

Ivanov, L. 42, 102
Izmailov, M.F., 7, 17n

Junkers, H., 32

Kadatskii-Rudnev, I.N., 78
Kaganovich, L.M., 69, 145
Kaganovich, M.M., 69
Kahn, David, 135
Kamenev, L.B., 19, 58, 60
Kamenev, S.S., 12
Karakhan, L.B., 19, 30
Karpenko, A.V., 297
Kassatsier, A.S., 74, 78, 208
Kaverin, F.A., 212
Keitel, Wilhelm, 113
Kharitonov, I.V., 97, 152
Kharlamov, N.M., 191
Khrushchev, N.S., 196, 216, 234, 297
Kimbar, Yu.Yu., 54
King, Ernest J., 166, 180
Kire'ev, G.P., 25, 26, 70, 78
Kirov, S.M., 31, 36, 59, 60
Kiselev, N.A., 197
Klado, N.L., 7, 294
Kopershinskii, Ya.A., 100, 154, 192
Kopp, L.B., 32
Kork, A.I., 25, 70
Korolev, S.P. 211, 214
Kozhanov, I.K., 7, 17n, 23, 60, 64, 70, 102, 223, 293
Kovalev, S.N., 215
Krasin, L.B., 32
Krasnov, V.N., 296, 297
Krestinskii, N.N., 35, 85
Krylov, A.N., 15
Kryuger, E.E., 331, 37,
Kukel', V.A., 7, 17n
Kurchatov, I.V., 210
Kulakov, V, 191
Kuzin, V.P., 296
Kuznetsov, N.G., 8, 65, 79, 87, 90, 106, 114, 118, 119, 120, 125, 135, 144, 145, 152, 153, 159, 160, 162, 166, 178, 179, 180, 185, 186, 187, 188, 189, 190, 191, 192, 195, 200, 201, 205, 211, 216, 217, 224, 293
Kuznetsov, L.A., 297
Kvitskii, S.A., 17n

Leahy, W.D., 88
Lenin, V.I., 19
Leskov; P.N., 14
Levchenko, G.I., 7, 70, 79, 165, 190, 191, 192
Libel', E.P., 74
Lie, Trygve, 179
Lieth-Thomsen, H. von der, 33
Litvinov, M.M., 32, 41, 54, 59, 111, 165, 222
Liventsev, F.P., 193
Loewenfeld, W. von, 32
Lohmann, W., 32
Loshchinskii,N,G., 155, 193
Lubimov, P., 34
Ludri, I.M., 7, 17n, 23, 24, 45, 48, 54, 64, 70, 102, 221, 223

Mahan, A.T., 7
Maiskii, M.M., 65
Maksimov, A.S. 7, 17n
Malenkov, G.M., 145, 186, 211
Malinin, B,M., 31, 35, 36, 37, 48, 49, 158
Maltsev, N., 199
Malyashkin, I.G:, 160
Mannerheim, C.G., 112
Manukhov, V.V., 158
Marks, E., 115
Maslov, A.I., 49, 50, 74, 192
Matskii, Ya.M., 150
Matsuoka, Yosuke, 127, 134
Maurer, E.A., 117
Maxwell, William S., 166
McCarthy, E., 180
Meister, Jurg, 5
Mekhlis, L.S., 80, 133
Meretskov, K.A, 78, 116, 131
Mezhenninov, S.A., 25
Michael (King), 115
Mikoyan, A.I., 148
Milgram, N., 191
Mola, E., 64
Molotov, V.M., 41, 77, 87, 89, 111, 116, 118, 127, 128, 132, 145, 179, 221
Monakov, M.S., 1
Morin, A.B., 296, 297
Muklevich, R.A., 11, 23, 24, 25, 26, 27, 28, 31 33, 34, 62, 69, 70, 74, 102, 223
Mussolini, Benito, 65, 111, 116, 127

Narykov, K.P., 192
Neganov, V.I., 192, 203
Nemits, A.V., 7, 12, 13, 17n, 293
Nikitin, V.A., 36, 45, 51, 52
Nikolaev, A.P., 296
Nikol'skii, V.I., 296, 297
Nogid, L.M., 155
Nosenko, I.I., 162, 186, 188
Novikov, N.V., 214

Oktyabrskii, F.S., 80, 145
Olsen, Clarence E., 166
Oras, P.Yu., 32, 33, 35
Ordzhonikidze, G.K., 47, 70, 221
Orlov, M., 211
Orlov, V.M., 31, 37, 42, 45, 48, 58, 60, 62, 63, 64, 65, 69, 70, 74, 75, 78, 97, 221, 223

Panteleev, Yu., 152
Pantserzhanskii, E.S., 7, 14, 70
Papkovich, P.F., 37, 48
Paul, Prince Regent, 127
Pavlov, A.S., 296
Pavlov, D.G., 132
Pavlovich, N.B., 293, 295
Pell', G.N., 25, 26, 54
Penzin, K., 191
Peregudov, V.N., 210
Petlyakov, V.,M., 78
Pétain, H.Ph., 116
Petrov, A.M., 296
Petrov, M.A., 7, 14, 23, 25, 27, 30, 54, 102, 293
Petrovskii, V.A., 122, 123
Pilsudski, Josef, 59
Piterskij, N.A., 294
Platonov, A.V., 297
Platonov, V.I., 191
Polyushkin, F.F., 161, 193
Popov, B.D., 166,
Potapov, Yu.P., 150
Preobrashenskii, Y.
Primakov, V.M., 69,
Pugashev, S.A., 25
Putna, V.K., 70
Pyatakov, G.I., 60

Radek, K.B., 32
Raeder, Erich, 113, 128
Rall', Yu.F., 35, 123, 155, 199
Ramzin, L.K., 51
Raskol'nikov, F.K., 7, 17n
Rechister, D., 191
Red'kin, A.M., 150, 186, 188
Reichman, M., 117
Ribbentrop, Joachim von, 116
Rimski-Korsakov, V.P., 30, 62, 63, 74, 78, 95
Rodionov, B.I., 296
Rokossovskii, K.K., 78
Rohwer, Jürgen, 1, 2,
Roosevelt, F.D., 88, 164, 165, 166, 179, 222
Rudnitskii, M.A., 49, 150, 158
Rutkovskii, V.I.; 122, 123
Rychagov, P.V., 132
Rykov, A.I., 16, 19, 30, 60, 77

Sakharov, A.D., 210
Savichev, A.S., 198
Schleicher, K. von, 32
Schulenburg, F.W. Graf von der, 116, 127
Seeckt, Hans von, 32
Seldyuk, P.I., 48
Semenov, V.P., 4, 297
Sergeev, N.D., 191
Sergeev, P.A., 150
Shaposhnikov, B.M., 25, 26, 76, 116
Shershov, A.P. 62
Shimanskii, Yu.A., 36, 37, 48, 53
Shitikov, E.A., 296, 297
Shtal', A.V., 125, 293
Sirianni, G., 34
Sivkov, A.K., 34, 70, 78
Smirnov, A.K., 132
Smirnov, P., 42
Smirnov, P.A., 78, 79, 223
Smirnov, P.I., 76
Smirnov-Svetlovskii, E.S., 70, 78
Sobelev, A. 180
Sokolov, A.G., 204
Sorge, Richard, 135
Spasskii, I. D., 4, 296
Speranskii, A.V., 78
Spindler, A., 32, 33
Stakhanov, A., 60
Stal'bo, K.A., 294, 295

Stalin, I.V., 19, 20, 23, 28, 30, 31, 34, 41, 42, 43, 52, 58, 59, 60, 64, 65, 66, 67, 69, 70, 71, 75, 76, 77, 78, 79, 80, 87, 89, 95, 96, 97, 102, 110, 111, 113, 116, 118, 125, 131, 132, 133, 134, 135, 139, 144, 145, 166, 179, 185, 186, 187, 188, 189, 190, 191, 192, 193, 194, 106, 197, 198, 199, 200, 201, 202, 205, 210, 215, 216, 221, 222, 223, 224, 294, 295
Starkov, O., 2, 4
Stasevich, P.G., 62, 71, 105
Stavitskii, S.P., 75, 95, 104, 105, 122, 124, 151, 186, 191
Stepanov, G.A., 190
Stepanov, S.F., 74
Stol'yarskii, G.M., 124
Strel'bnitskii, K.B., 4
Strel'tsov, B.Ya., 74, 78

Taptygin, I.F., 153
Tevosyan, I.T., 87, 113, 119, 186, 188
Timoshenko, S.K., 112, 116, 131, 132, 133, 134, 144, 145
Tolotskii, E.S., 204
Tolstoi, Sergei, 135
Tomashevich, A.V., 123
Tomskii, M.P., 19, 30, 60, 77
Toshakov, A.A., 15, 16, 25, 26, 30
Trakhtenberg, P.O., 36, 52, 78
Triandafillov, V.K., 20, 23, 25, 26, 222
Tributs, V.F., 1, 8, 80, 145, 155, 190
Trotskii, L.D., 6, 7, 12, 19, 20, 58, 69, 70, 77
Troyanovskii, A.A., 88
Truman, Harry S., 179, 216
Tsushkevich, A.E., 78
Tukhachevskii, M.V., 4, 20, 21, 22, 23, 24, 25, 26, 27, 32, 48, 60, 67, 70, 222, 293
Tupolev, A.N., 31, 35, 53, 78, 152, 201
Tyulenev, I.V., 132
Tyurin, B.P., 297

Uborevich, I.P., 34, 70
Ul'rikh, V.V., 69, 78
Umanskii, K.A, 133
Unshlikht, J.A., 25, 32, 33
Usov, V.Yu., 297
Ustinov, D.A., 188, 211

Vasilev, A.M., 297
Vasilevskii, S.A., 131, 161

Vekman, A.K., 17n5, 50
Venkov, I., 2, 4
Viktorov, M.V., 7, 17n, 25, 26, 60, 64, 70, 72, 75, 78, 97, 223
Vinogradov, N.I., 191
Vladimirskii, L., 199
Vlas'ev, N.I., 25, 26, 27, 31, 54
Vlasov, V.G., 150
Volkogonov, D., 1, 4, 223
Vorontsov, M..A., 145
Voroshilov, K.E., 22, 24, 25, 26, 31, 43, 47, 58, 60, 69, 71, 75, 80, 87, 104, 111, 116, 145, 221
Vosnessenskii, N.A., 145, 188
Vyshinskii, A.Yu., 60, 133

Welles, Sumner, 133
Wilson, W., 64

Yagoda, G.G., 60, 77
Yakir, J.E., 25, 26, 69
Yakob; O.F., 52
Yakovlev, A.A., 150, 152, 201
Yakymichev, A.M., 24, 27, 54, 293
Yarovoi, V.V., 297
Yegorov, A.I., 25, 58, 60, 63, 70, 72, 76, 97, 221, 223
Yegorov, S.A., 205, 206
Yeliseev, I., 191
Yermash, L.L., 193
Yeshov, N.I., 60, 69, 78
Yevgrafov, Ya.E., 206
Yukhnin Ye.I., 214,
Yumashev, I.S., 65, 80, 190, 191, 192, 216
Yunovidov, Yu.M., 192,

Zakharov, I.G., 297
Zakharov, S.E., 191
Zakhorin, N.D., 296
Zakupnev, Z.A., 78
Zelenoi, A.P., 7, 17n
Zenker, A., 33
Zhdanov, A.A., 60, 79
Zherve, B-B.,7, 14, 21, 23, 27, 30, 54, 214, 215, 216
Zhilin, P.A., 1
Zhukov, A.A., 150
Zhukov, G.K., 111, 130, 131, 132, 134, 144, 145, 217, 224
Zhukovskii, D.D., 203

Zinov'ev, G.E., 19, 58, 60, 70
Zof, V.I., 7, 11, 12, 15, 16, 17n, 21, 22, 23, 33, 70
Zonin, S., 4, 190
Zotov, K., 190, 191
Zozulya, F.V. 190

INDEX OF SHIPS

A, Deutsches Panzerschiffe, 61
A-1, Soviet submarine, 175n
A-1–A-5, Soviet submarines, 137
A-3, Soviet submarine, 169
Admirable, American minesweeper, 164, 167, 173, 184
Admiral Butakov, Russian cruiser, 16, 24, 35
Admiral Hipper, German heavy cruiser, 82
Admiral Kornilov, Soviet cruiser (*projekt 68-bis*), 198
Admiral Lazarev, Russian cruiser (old), 16, 24, 28
Admiral Lazarev, Soviet cruiser (*projekt 68-bis*), 198
Admiral Makarov, Russian armoured cruiser, 8, 17n
Admiral Makarov, Soviet cruiser (ex German), 181
Admiral Nakhimov, Russian cruiser (old), 17n, 28
Admiral Nakhimov, Soviet cruiser (*projekt 68-bis*), 198, 211, 212
Admiral Scheer, German pocket battleship, 66
Admiral Senyavin, Soviet cruiser, 198
Admiral Ushakov, Soviet cruiser, 198
Adopt, American minesweeper, 173
Advocate, American minesweeper, 172
Agent, American minesweeper, 172
AKA-105/No.106, Soviet MTB, 156
Akhtuba, Soviet net layer, 183
Aktivnyi, Soviet river monitor, 157
Alarm, American minesweeper, 172
Albatros, German torpedoboat, 66
Albatros, Soviet patrol ship, 173, 192
Aleksandr Nevskii, Soviet cruiser, 198
Aleksandr Suvorov, Soviet cruiser, 198
Alfredo Oriani, Italian destroyer, 51
Allentown, American frigate, 173
Ametist, Soviet patrol ship, 136, 171
Amiral Murgescu, Romanian minelayer, 171
Andrej Pervosvannyi, Russian battleship, 14, 17n, 79
Angara, Soviet staff vessel, 183
Animoso, Italian destroyer, 184
Apex, American minesweeper, 172
Arcade, American minesweeper, 172

Arch, American minesweeper, 172
Archimede, Italian submarine, 66
Ardimentoso, Italian destroyer, 184
Arkhangel'sk, Soviet battleship (ex British), 165, 178, 184, 188
Arkhangel'sk, Soviet battlecruiser (*projekt 82*), 196
Arkhangel'sk, Soviet cruiser (*projekt 68-bis*), 198
Arseni Rasskin, Soviet minesweeper, 171
Artem, Soviet destroyer, 136, 175n
Artigliere, Italian destroyer, 184
Artillerist, Soviet subchaser, 156
Askold, Russian cruiser, 8
Asov, Soviet river monitor, 167
Aspire, American minesweeper, 172
Astute, American minesweeper, 173
Augury, American minesweeper, 173
Avrora, Russian/Soviet cruiser, 14, 136
Azard, Soviet destroyer, 35

B-2, Sopvioet submarine, 136
B-26–B-30, Soviet submarines, 182
B-61–B-82, Soviet submarines, 205
B-64, Soviet missile submarine, 212
B-67, Soviet missile submarine, 214
B-88–B-91, Soviet submarines, 205
Baku, Soviet destroyer leader (*projekt 20*), 46
Baku, Soviet destroyer leader (*projekt 38*), 51, 138, 170, 172, 175n
Baleno, Italian destroyer, 46
Ballila, Italian submarine, 35, 46
Bandiera, Italian submarine, 35
Barletta, Italian auxiliary cruiser, 66
Barrier, American minesweeper, 173
Bars, Russian submarine, 24
Batrak, Soviet submarine, 33
Bayan, Russian armoured cruiser, 8, 17n,
Bditel'nyi, Soviet destroyer, 137, 175n
Bedovyi, Soviet missile destroyer, 211
Belfast, American frigate, 173
Berdyansk, Soviet river monitor, 167
Besposhchadnyi, Soviet destroyer, 137, 169
Bezuprechnyi, Soviet destroyer, 137, 175n
Bismarck, German battleship, 61, 82, 84, 85, 113
Blago'ev, Soviet freighter, 66
Blokha, Soviet midget submarine, 63
BO-101–BO-103, Soviet subchasers, 156
BO-108–BO-110, Soviet subchasers, 156
BO-122, Soviet subchaser, 156

BO-131–BO-142, Soviet subchasers, 156
BO-201–BO-212, Soviet subchasers, 164
BO-213–BO-232, Soviet subchasers, 165
BO-233–BO-246, Soviet subchasers, 165
BO-301–BO-329, Soviet subchasers, 167
BO-303–BO-304, Soviet subchasers, 184
BO-331–BO-332, Soviet subchasers, 167
BO-335, Soviet subchaser, 167
Bodryi, Soviet destroyer, 137, 171
Bogatyr, Russian cruiser, 17n
Bojkii, Soviet destroyer, 137, 171
Bombard, American minesweeper, 173
Bond, American minesweeper, 173
Boresza Svobody, Soviet battleship, 17n,
Borodino, Russian battlecruiser, 8,
Botsman, Soviet subchaser, 149
Bravyi, Soviet missile destroyer, 214
Bremen, German passenger liner, 112
Brighton, British destroyer, 172
Brilliant, Soviet patrol ship, 137, 175n
Bugel', Soviet minesweeper, 136
Buj, Soviet minesweeper, 136
Buran, Soviet patrol ship, 181
Burevestnik, Soviet patrol ship, 192
Burun, Soviet patrol ship, 138, 173
Burya, Soviet patrol ship, 136, 168
Bystryi, Soviet destroyer, 137, 174n

C-3, Spanish submarine, 66
Canarias, Spanish heavy cruiser, 66
Candid, American minesweeper, 173
Capable, American minesweeper, 173
Captivate, American minesweeper, 173
Caravan, American minesweeper, 173
Caution, American minesweeper, 173
Chajka, Soviet patrol ship 192
Chapaev, Soviet cruiser, 98, 99, 121, 151, 192
Charlottesville, American frigate, 172
Cheka, Soviet minesweeper, 138, 173
Chelsea, British destroyer, 172
Chervona Ukraina, Soviet cruiser, 28, 30, 79, 90, 136, 175n
Chesme, Russian battleship, 8,
Chkalov, Soviet cruiser, 98, 99, 114, 121, 151, 192
Churchill, British destroyer, 170
Coronado, American frigate, 173
Cowell, American destroyer, 172
Crowninshield, American destroyer, 172

INDEX

D-1, Soviet submarine, 137
D-2, Soviet submarine, 136, 171
D-3, Soviet submarine, 137, 175n
D-4, Soviet submarine, 169
D-4–D-6, Soviet submarines, 137
D-6, Soviet submarine, 175n
Dal'nomershchik, Soviet subchaser, 149
Dardo, Italian destroyer, 46,
Dekabrist, Soviet submarine, 24, 28, 31, 34, 36
Delfino, Italian submarine, 35
Delfinul, Romanian submarine, 172
Derzkii, Soviet destroyer, 165, 172
Des Geneys, Italian submarine, 35
Des Moines, American heavy cruiser, 187, 196
Desna, Soviet depot ship, 183
Deutschland, German pocket battleship, 31, 61, 66, 82, 85, 181
Deyatel'nyi, Soviet destroyer, 165, 170
Diana, Russian cruiser, 17n
Diligente, French minesweeping aviso, 53
Disdain, American minesweeper, 173
Dmitrii Lysov, Soviet minesweeper, 192
Dmitrii Pozharskii, Soviet cruiser, 198
Dnestr, Soviet A/S vessel, 167
Doblestnyi, Soviet destroyer, 165, 172, 184
Don, Soviet minelayer, 167, 171
Donets, Soviet depot ship, 183
Dostojnyi, Soviet destroyer, 165, 172
Dreadnought, British battleship, 14, 61, 79
Druzhnyi, Soviet destroyer, 165, 172, 184
DS-2–DS-10, Soviet landing vessels, 167
DS-5, Soviet landing vessel, 166
DS-9, Soviet landing vessel, 166
DS-31–DS-45, Soviet landing vessels, 167
DS-43, Soviet landing vessel, 166
DS-47–DS-50, Soviet landing vessels, 167
Dunkerque, French battleship, 31, 61, 75
Dzershinskii, Soviet destroyer (old), 137, 175n
Dzerzhinskii, Soviet patrol ship, 45, 138, 173
Dzershinskii, Soviet cruiser (*projekt 68-bis*), 198, 214

E-1, German U-Boat design, 45
EK-1–EK-2, Soviet patrol ship, 172
EK-1–EK-.30, Soviet patrol ships, 167
EK-3, Soviet patrol ship, 184
EK-3–EK-30, Soviet patrol ships, 173
EK-11–EK-30, Soviet patrol ships, 184
EK-31–EK-47, Soviet patrol ships, 183

Elsaß, German battleship, 33
Emanuele Filiberto Duca d'Aosta, Italian cruiser, 184
Emden, German cruiser, 33,
Engels, Soviet destroyer, 33, 136, 174n
Erevan, Soviet destroyer leader, 121, 174n, 192, 200, 210
Erich Steinbrinck, German destroyer, 181
Ersatz Preulßen, German pocket battleship, 61
Eugenio di Savoia, Italian cruiser, 50, 98

F 7, German patrol ship, 181
Fairfax, American destroyer, 172
Fancy, American minesweeper, 173
Fencer, British escort carrier, 165
Ferraris, Italian submarine, 66
Fiume, Italian heavy-cruiser, 35
Foote, American destroyer, 172
Fortunale, Italian destroyer, 184
Francesco Nullo, Italian destroyer, 34
Friedrich Ihn, German destroyer, 181
Frunze, Soviet cruiser (old), 24
Frunze, Soviet battleship (old), 16, 27, 28, 35
Frunze, Soviet destroyer (old), 34, 137, 169
Frunze, Soviet cruiser (*projekt 68*), 98, 121, 151, 174n, 192
Fuciliere, Italian destroyer, 184
Fugas, Soviet minesweeper, 53, 92, 101, 136

G-5, Soviet MTB-type, 53, 54
Gafel', Soviet minesweeper, 136, 171
Gak, Soviet minesweeper, 136
Gallant, British destroyer, 66
Gangut, Russian battleship, 14, 24
Garpun, Soviet minesweeper, 137, 171
Gearing, American destroyer, 153
General Alekseev, Russian battleship, 8,
General Mola, Spanish submarine, 66
General Sanjurjo, Spanish submarine, 66
Georgetown, British destroyer, 172
George Washington, American nuclear missile submarine, 215
Giovanni Bausan, Italian submarine, 36
Giulio Cesare, Italian battleship, 184, 217
Glendyle, American frigate, 173
Gneisenau, German battleship, 113
Gnevnyi, Soviet destroyer, 46, 52, 92, 136, 174n
Goeben, German battlecruiser, 30
Gordyi, Soviet destroyer, 136, 174n, 175n

Gornostoi, Soviet patrol ship, 203
Graf Zeppelin, German aircraft carrier, 113, 181, 199
Grazhdanin, Soviet battleship, 17n
Gremyashchii, Soviet destroyer, 137, 172
Grom, Soviet patrol ship, 138, 173
Gromoboi, Russian armoured cruiser, 8, 17n
Gromkii, Soviet destroyer, 137, 172
Groza, Soviet patrol ship; 137, 172
Grozyashchii, Soviet destroyer, 136, 170
Groznyi, Soviet destroyer, 137, 172
Gruz, Soviet minesweeper, 137
Gür, Turkish submarine, 45

H-N, German battleships, 113
Harutsuki, Japanese destroyer, 183
Hatsuzaukra, Japanese destroyer, 183
Hav, British auxiliary minesweeper, 172
Hibiki, Japanese destroyer, 183
Hunter, British destroyer, 52

Ikino, Japanese frigate, 183
Ilmarinan, Finnish coast defence ship, 31, 73
Imperator Aleksandr II, Russian battleship, 17n
Imperator Pavel I, Russian battleship, 17n
Indicative, American minesweeper, 173
Ioann Slatoust, Russian battleship, 17n
Iosif Stalin, Soviet icebreaker, 51, 112
Iskatel', Soviet minesweeper, 137, 171
Izmail', Russian battlecruiser, 14, 16, 21, 35, 97, 98
Izmail', Soviet river monitor, 167
Izyaslav, Russian destroyer, 79

Jan Wellem, German whale factory, 112

K-1, Soviet submarine, 170
K-1–K-2, Soviet submarines, 137
K-2, Soviet submarine, 161
K-3, Soviet submarine (series XIV), 136, 147, 169, 175n
K-3, Soviet nuclear submarine, 210
K-21, Soviet submarine, 171
K-21–K-23, Soviet submarines, 136, 147, 172, 175n
K-22, Soviet submarine, 169
K-23, Soviet submarine, 175n
K-27, Soviet nuclear submarine, 210
K-51, Soviet submarine, 149, 171

K-52, Soviet submarine, 149, 171
K-53, Soviet submarine, 149, 171
K-54, Soviet submarine, 158
K-55, Soviet submarine, 149, 171
K-56, Soviet submarine, 149, 171
K-96, Soviet missile submarine, 213
Kaganovich, Soviet cruiser, 98, 121, 149, 172
Kako, Japanese cruiser, 81
Kalev, Soviet submarine (ex Estonian), 136, 175n
Kalinin, Soviet destroyer (old), 135, 175n
Kalinin, Soviet cruiser (*projekt 26-bis*), 198, 99, 121, 149, 172
Kamishima, Japanese minelayer, 183
Kapsyul', Soviet minesweeper, 138, 173
Karl Galster, German destroyer, 181
Karl Liebknecht, Soviet destroyer, 137, 171
Karl Marx, Soviet destroyer, 136, 174n
Katashima Maru, Japanese minelayer, 183
Katun', Soviet minelayer, 183
Kaya, Japanese destroyer, 183
Kem, Soviet mirie counter measures ship, 183
Kerch, Soviet river monitor, 167
Kerch, Soviet cruiser (ex Italian), 184
Kharkov, Soviet destroyer leader, 137, 169, 174n
Khasan, Sovietmonitor, 149, 157, 158
Kiev, Soviet destroyer leader (*projekt 38*), 51
Kiev, Soviet destroyer leader (*projekt 48*), 99, 100, 121, 174n, 192, 200
Kinburn, Russian battlecruiser, 8,
King George V, British battleship, 61
Kinugasa, Japanese cruiser, 81
Kiri, Japanese destroyer, 183
Kirov, Soviet patrol ship, 45, 92, 138, 173
Kirov, Soviet cruiser, 46, 50, 63, 64, 83, 84, 92, 98, 136, 170
Knekht, Soviet minesweeper, 136
Komet, German auxiliary cruiser, 112
Komintern, Soviet cruiser, 14, 24, 136, 169
Komsomol', Soviet freighter, 66
Komsomolets, Soviet training ship, 21, 35, 97, 98
Komsomolets, Soviet torpedo cutter, 157, 193
Kontradmiral Choroshkhin, Soviet minesweeper, 149, 171
Korall, Soviet minesweeper/and patrol ship, 136, 168
Korshun, Soviet patrol ship, 192
Kozma Minim, Soviet cruiser,198
Kozu, Japanese frigate, 183

INDEX

Krambol', Soviet minesweeper, 136
Krasnaya Gruziya, Soviet gunboat, 169
Krasnyi Kavkaz, Soviet cruiser, 28, 33, 35, 45, 91, 137, 171
Krasnyi Krym, Soviet cruiser, 91, 137, 171
Kronshtadt, Soviet battlecruiser (*projekt 69*), 96, 114, 121, 195, 199
Kronshtadt, Soviet battlecruiser (*projekt 82*), 196
Kronshtadt, Soviet cruiser (*projekt 68-bis*), 198
Kuban, Soviet A/S vessel, 167
Kuban, Soviet depot ship 183
Kuloi, Soviet mine counter measures ship, 183
Kujbyshev, Soviet destroyer (old), 137
Kujbyshev, Soviet cruiser (*projekt 68*), 108, 121, 151, 174n, 192
Kushka, Soviet mine counter measures ship, 183

L-1, Soviet submarine, 175n
L-1–L-3, Soviet submarines, 136
L-2, Soviet submarine, 175n
L-3, Soviet submarine, 171
L-4-L-5, Soviet submarines, 171
L-4–L-6, Soviet submarines, 137
L-6, Soviet submarine, 169
L-7–L-14, Soviet submarines, 173
L-7–L-19, Soviet submarines, 138
L-15, Soviet submarine, 172
L-15–L-16, Soviet submarines, 170, 175n
L-17–L-18, Soviet submarines, 173
L-19, Soviet submarine, 170
L-20, Soviet submarine, 147, 149, 172
L-21, Soviet submarine, 149, 171
L-22, Soviet submarine, 147, 149, 172
L-23, Soviet submarine, 147
L-24, Soviet submarine, 149
L-23–L-24, Soviet submarines, 169
L-23–L-25, Soviet submarines, 174n
L-55, British/Soviet submarine, 35, 37, 136
Ladnyi, Soviet destroyer, 184
L'Audacieux, French destroyer leader, 45
Lazar Kaganovich, Soviet icebreaker, 117
Lazar Kaganovich, Soviet cruiser (*projekt 26-bis*), 149, 172
Lazo, Soviet monitor, 158
Leamington, British destroyer, 172
Legkii, Soviet destroyer (ex Romanian), 167, 171
Legkii, Soviet destroyer, (ex Italian), 184
Lembit, Soviet submarine (ex Estonian), 136, 171, 204,

Lena, Soviet net layer, 183
Lenin, Soviet icebreaker, 112
Lenin, Soviet destroyer, 136, 173n
Leningrad, Soviet destroyer leader, 35, 36, 51, 54, 92, 136, 170
Leninets, Soviet submarine, 37
Leone, Italian destroyer, 34
Letnyi, Soviet destroyer, 184
Letuchii, Soviet destroyer, 167, 171
Likhoi, Soviet destroyer, 167, 171
Lincoln, British destroyer, 172
Littorio, Italian battleship, 61, 62, 85
Long Beach, American frigate, 172
Lovkii, Soviet destroyer (ex Romanian), 167, 171
Lovkii, Soviet destroyer, (ex Italian), 184
Lugan, Soviet depot ship 183
Lützow, German heavy cruiser, 96, 113, 175n, 181, 195, 199
Lützow, German pocket battleship (heavy cruiser), 181
Lyutyi, Soviet destroyer, 184

M-1–M-22, Soviet submarines, 173
M-1–M-28, Soviet submarines, 137
M-3, German minesweeper, 182
M-7, German minesweeper, 182
M-17, German minesweeper, 182
M-23–M-28, Soviet submarines, 172
M-29–M-30, German minesweepers, 182
M-30, Soviet submarine, 137, 172
M-31, Soviet submarine, 169
M-31–M-36, Soviet submarines, 137, 169
M-32, Soviet submarine, 172
M-33, Soviet submarine, 169
M-34, Soviet submarine, 175n
M-34, German minesweeper, 182
M-35, Soviet submarines, 172
M-36, Soviet submarine, 169
M-43–M-48, Soviet submarines, 173
M-43–M-49, Soviet submarines, 138
M-51, Soviet submarine (Series VI), 169
M-51, Soviet submarine (ex German type XXIII), 181
M-51–M-52, Soviet submarines, 137, 172
M-54–M-55, Soviet submarines, 137, 172
M-58–M-59, Soviet submarines, 137, 175n
M-58–M-60, Soviet submarines, 137
M-60, Soviet submarine, 137, 169

M-62, Soviet submarines, 137, 172
M-63, Soviet submarine, 138
M-71, Soviet submarine, 174
M-71–M-81, Soviet submarines, 136
M-74, Soviet submarine, 175n
M-77, Soviet submarine, 171
M-78, Soviet submarine, 174n
M-79, Soviet submarine, 171
M-81, Soviet submarine, 174n
M-80–M-81, Soviet submarines, 174n
M-83, Soviet submarine, 136, 174n
M-90, Soviet submaruine, 136, 171
M-94, Soviet submarine, 174n
M-94–M-99, Soviet submarines, 136
M-95, Soviet submarine, 168
M-96, Soviet submarine, 168
M-97, Soviet submarine, 168
M-98, Soviet submarine, 175n
M-99, Soviet submarine, 173n
M-102, Soviet submarine, 171
M-102–M-103, Soviet submarines, 136
M-103, Soviet submarine, 175n
M-104–M-105, Soviet submarines, 172
M-104–M-108, Soviet submarines, 149, 175n
M-106, Soviet submarine, 169
M-107, Soviet submarine, 172
M-108, Soviet submarine, 169
M-111–M-113, Soviet submarines, 147, 172
M-111–M-122, Soviet submarines, 175n
M-114–M-116, Soviet submarines, 147, 172
M-117, Soviet submarine, 172
M-117–M-118, Soviet submarines, 147
M-118, Soviet submarine, 169
M-119, Soviet submarine, 149, 172
M-120, Soviet submarine, 147, 172
M-121–M-122, Soviet submarines, 149, 169
M-151, German minesweeper, 182
M-155, German minesweeper, 182
M-171, Soviet submarine, 159, 171
M-171–M-176, Soviet submarines, 138, 160
M-172–M-174, Soviet submarines, 169
M-175–M-176, Soviet submarines, 175n
M-200–M-201, Soviet submarines, 149, 171
M-200–M-203, Soviet submarines, 175n
M-202–M-203, Soviet submarines, 149, 172
M-203–M-204, German minesweepers, 182
M-204–M-206, Soviet submarines, 193
M-214–M-219, Soviet submarines, 193

M-234–M-253, Soviet submarines, 193
M-254, Soviet submarine, 208
M-254–M-256, German minesweepers, 182,
M 265, German minesweeper, 182
M-267, German minesweeper, 182
M-270–M-294, Soviet submarines, 193
M-291, German minesweeper, 182
M-324, German minesweeper, 182
M-330, German minesweeper, 182
M-341–M-342, German minesweepers, 182
M-348, German minesweeper, 182
M-361, Soviet submarine, 208
M-369, German minesweeper, 182
M-386, German minesweeper, 182
M-400, Soviet experimental submarine, 162
M-401, Soviet experimental submarine, 94, 148, 161 162, 2O8
M-401, German minesweeper, 195,
M-405–M-407, German minesweepers, 182
M-411, German minesweeper, 182
M-415, German minesweeper, 182
M-423, German minesweeper, 182
M-425, German minesweeper, 182
M-431, German minesweeper, 182
M-437, German minesweeper, 182
M-443, German minesweeper, 182
M-446, German minesweeper, 182
M-461, German minesweeper, 182
M-467, German minesweeper, 182
M-470, German minesweeper, 182
M-484, German minesweeper, 182
M-496, German minesweeper, 182
Machias, American frigate, 173
Maddox, American destroyer, 172
Maksim Gorkii, Soviet cruiser, 51, 98, 99, 136, 170, 174n
Malygin, Soviet icebreaker, 112
Manara, Italian submarine, 34, 35
Marasesti, Romanian destroyer, 171
Marasti, Romanian destroyer, 171
Marat, Soviet battleship, 9, 24, 33, 35, 82, 84, 85, 91, 136, 170, 175n
Marea, Italian submarine, 184
Mariupol', Soviet river monitor, 167
Marsovoi, Soviet submarine chaser, 149
Marti, Soviet minelayer, 44, 53, 136
Marvel, A190,merican minesweeper, 173
Mashinist, Soviet subchaser, 149

Measure, American minesweeper, 173
Mekhanik, Soviet subchaser, 149
Metel', Soviet patrol ship, 138, 173
Method, American minesweeper, 173
Miguel Cervantes, Spanish cruiser, 66
Mikhail Kutusov, Soviet cruiser, 198
Mikoyan, Soviet icebreaker, 174n
Milwaukee, American cruiser, 164, 172
Mina, Soviet minesweeper, 137, 171
Miner, Soviet subchaser, 156
Minrep, Soviet minesweeper, 137
Minsk, Soviet destroyer leader, 51, 92, 136, 170, 175n
Mirth, American minesweeper, 173,
MMS-90, British minesweeper 172
MMS-203, British minesweeper, 172
MMS-212, British minesweeper, 172
MMS-1005, British minesweeper, 172
MMS-10123, British minesweeper, 172
MO-103, Soviet subchaser, 160
MO-435–MO-458, Soviet subchasers, 164
Molniya, Soviet patrol ship, 138, 173
Molotov, Soviet cruiser, 51, 98, 99, 137, 151, 169, 171
Molotovsk, Soviet cruiser, 198
Moskva, Soviet destroyer leader (*projekt 38*), 137, 174n
Moskva, Soviet battlecruiser (*projekt 82*), 196
Murmansk, Soviet cruiser (ex American), 164, 172, 184, 188
Murmansk, Soviet cruiser, (*projekt 68-bis*), 198
Musson, Soviet patrol ship, 167, 171
Myoko, Japanese heavy cruiser, 80

N-22–N-25, Soviet submarines, 182
N-26–N-30, Soviet submarines, 182
N-41–N-42, Soviet submarines, 184
Narvalo, Italian submarine, 35
Nastoichivyi, Soviet destroxer, 1, 2
Navarin, Russian battlecruiser, 8,
Navdochik, Soviet subchaser, 149
Nelson, British battleship, 62, 74
Neustrashimyi, Soviet destroyer, 201
Nezamozhnik, Soviet destroyer, 34, 137, 171
Nichelio, Italian submarine, 184
No. 34, No. 48, No. 52, No. 76, No. 78, No. 102, No. 142, No. 196, Japanese corvettes, 183
No. 71, No. 77, No. 79, No. 105, No. 221. No. 227, Japanese corvettes, 183

North Carolina, American battleship, 61
Novik, Russian destroyer, 8, 14, 24, 31, 44, 51, 52, 91
Novorossijsk, Soviet battleship, 184, 217
Nucleus, American minesweeper, 173
Nürnberg, German Light Cruiser, 181

O, German battlecruiser, 113
Obchayannyi, Soviet destroyer, 174n
Obraztsovyi, Soviet destroyer, 192
Obshitel'nyi, Soviet destroyer, 174n
Obuchennyi, Soviet destroyer, 174n
Odarennyi, Soviet destroyer, 192
Ogden, American frigate, 173
Ognevoi, Sovietdestroyer, 1100, 149, 153, 154, 171, 192
Okhotnik, Soviet destroyer, 192
Oktyabrskaya revolyutsiya, Soviet battleship (old), 24, 33, 44, 91, 136, 170
Oktyarbskaya revolyutsiya, Soviet cruiser (*projekt 68-bis*), 198
Opytnyi, Soviet destroyer, 51, 147, 170
Ordzhonikidze, Soviet destroyer leader (*projekt 38*), 51
Ordzhonikidze, Soviet cruiser (*projekt 68*), 121, 174n
Ordzhonikidze, Soviet cruiser (*projekt 68-bis*), 198
Orel', Soviet patrol ship, 192
Osmotritel'nyi, Soviet destroyer, 192
Otlichnyi, Soviet destroyer, 192
Otmennyi, Soviet destroyer, 174n
Otvashnyi, Soviet destroyer, 192
Ozornoi, Soviet destroyer, 153, 154, 174n, 192

P, German battlecruiser, 113
P-1, Soviet submarine, 175n
P-1–P-3, Soviet submarines, 136
P-1–P-12, German pocket battleships, 113
Palisade, American minesweeper, 173
Pamyat Merkuriya, Russian cruiser, 14, 24
Pantelejmon, Russian battleship, 17n
Pantera, Italian destroyer, 34
Paravan, Soviet minesweeper, 101, 138, 173
Parizhskaya kommuna, Soviet battleship, 24, 30, 34, 44, 90, 91, 137, 171
Patron, Soviet minesweeper, 136
Pechora, Soviet depot ship, 183
Penetrate, American minesweeper, 173
Perekop, Soviet monitor, 149, 158
Peril, American minesweeper, 173

Pervenets, Soviet motor torpedo boat, 35
Petropavlovsk, Russian battleship (old), 9, 24, 170, 175n
Petropavlovsk, Soviet heavy cruiser (ex German, *projekt 83*), 113, 121, 175n, 181, 195
Petrovski, Soviet destroyer, 34
Pigmei, Soviet midget submarine, 49, 161
Pinega, Soviet depot ship, 182
Podsekatel', Soviet minesweeper, 138, 173
Podvishnyi, Soviet torpedo boat, 181
Poltava, Russian battleship, 16, 24, 45
Polyarnaya Svezda, Soviet training vessel, 44
Ponoy, Soviet netlayer, 183
Porayayushchii, Soviet torpedo boat, 181
Poryvistyi, Soviet torpedo boat, 181
Pravda, Soviet cruiser, 24
Pravda, Soviet submarine, 37, 123
Presidente Smetona, Latvian minesweeper, 136
Primernyi, Soviet destroyer, 181
Prinz Eugen, German heavy cruiser, 113
Prochnyi, Soviet destroyer, 181
Profintem, Soviet cruiser, 28, 30, 34
Pronzitel'nyi, Soviet torpedo boat, 181
Provodnik, Soviet minesweeper, 138, 173
Provornyi, Soviet destroyer, 181
Prozhektorist, Soviet subchaser, 149
Prozorlivyi, Soviet torpedo boat, 181
Prytkii, Soviet destroyer, 181
PSK-301–PSK-304, Soviet patrol ships, 137
Purga, Soviet patrol ship (*projekt 2*), 136,
Purga, Soviet icebreaker patrol ship (*projekt 52*), 101, 154, 192
Pyl'kii, Soviet destroyer, 181

Q, German battlecruiser, 113

R-1, Soviet experimental submarine, 161, 208
R-1–R-8, Soviet submarines, 205
R 25, R 28, R 53, R 58, R 63, R 65, R 87, R 90, German motor minesweepers, 182
R 103, R 105, R 107, R 113, R 121, R 122, German motor minesweepers, 182
R 124, R 149, R 233, R 237, R 245, R 254, German motor minesweepers, 182
R 257, R 258, R 262, R 265, R 269, R 270, German motor minesweepers, 182,
R 288, R 289, R 302, R 303, R 305, R 307, German motor minesweepers, 182
R 308, R 310, R 311, R 312, German motor minesweepers, 182
R 409–R 423, German motor minesweepers, 182
RA 102, RA 104, RA111, RA 112, RA 204, German river minesweepers, 182
Raimondo Montecuccoli, Italian cruiser, 45, 46, 49
Rampart, American minesweeper, 173
Ranger, American aircraft carrier, 97
Rastoropnyi, Soviet destroyer, 138, 192
Razumnyi, Soviet destroyer, 147, 170, 172, 175n
Raz'yarennyi, Soviet destroyer, 147, 170, 172, 175n
Raz'yashchii, Soviet destroyer, 138, 172
Redkii, Soviet destroyer, 149, 153, 172
Redo, Soviet experimental submarine, 208
Regele Ferdinand, Romanian destroyer, 171
Regina Maria, Romanian destroyer, 171
Rekordnyi, Soviet destroyer, 138, 172
Requinul, Romanian submarine, 172
Reshitel'nyi (I), Soviet destroyer, 52, 79
Reshitel'nyi (II), Soviet destroyer, 15, 47, 172
Respublika, Soviet battleship, 17n
Retivyi, Soviet destroyer, 147, 172
Revnostnyi, Soviet destroyer, 147, 172, 175n
Revolutsiya, Soviet battleship, 17n
Rezkii, Soviet destroyer, 149, 172
Rezvyi, Soviet destroyer, 138, 172
Richelieu, French battleship, 61
Richmond, British destroyer, 172
Ronis, Soviet submarine (ex Latvian), 137, 174n
Rossiya, Russian armoured cruiser, 17n
Rostislav, Russian battleship, 17n
Roxborough, British destroyer, 172
Royal Sovereign, British battleship, 165, 172
Rubin, Soviet patrol ship, 137, 172
Rulevoi, Soviet subchaser, 149
Ryanyi, Soviet destroyer, 138, 172
Rym, Soviet minesweeper, 136, 171
Ryujo, Japanese aircraft carrier, 97
Ryurik, Russian armoured cruiser, 17n

S 11, S 16, S 24, German motor torpedo boats, 182
S 50, S 65, S 81, S 82, S 86, German motor torpedo boats, 183
S 99, S 101, S 109, S 110, S 113, S 118, S 123, German motor torpedo boats, 183
S 132, S 135, S 175, S204, S209, S211, S214, German motor torpedo boats, 183

INDEX   327

S 219, S 222, S 227, S 704, S 707, S 708, S 709,
   German motor torpedo boats, 183
S-1, Soviet submarine, 136, 174n
S-2, Soviet submarine, 112
S-3–S-11, Soviet submarines, 136, 174n
S-4, Soviet submarine, 168
S-5, Soviet submarine, 175n
S-6, Soviet submarine, 175n
S-7, Soviet submarine, 168
S-8, Soviet submarine, 175n
S-9, Soviet submarine, 168
S-10, Soviet submarine, 174n
S-11, Soviet submarine, 174n
S-11–S-13, Soviet submarines, 147
S-12, Soviet submarine, 168
S-13, Soviet submarine, 171
S-14–S-15, Soviet submarines, 149
S-14–S-17, Soviet submarines, 172
S-14–S-21, Soviet submarines, 175n
S-16, Soviet submarine, 149
S-17, Soviet submarine, 149
S-18, Soviet submarine, 171
S-19, Soviet submarine, 171
S-19–S-20, Soviet submarines, 149
S-20, Soviet submarine, 149, 171
S-21–S-26, Soviet submarines, 193
S-31, Soviet submarine, 171
S-31–S-34, Soviet submarines, 137
S-32, Soviet submarine, 175n
S-33, Soviet submarine, 171
S-34, Soviet submarine, 175n
S-35, Soviet submarine, 174n, 193
S-36–S-38, Soviet submarines, 174n
S-41–S-42, Soviet submarines, 184
S-43–S-46, Soviet submarines, 206
S-51, Soviet submarine, 147, 170, 172, 175n
S-52–S-53, Soviet submarines, 149, 173
S-54, Soviet submarine, 138, 169
S-54–S-56, Soviet submarines, 170, 175n
S-55, Soviet submarine, 169
S-55–S-56, Soviet submarine, 147
S-56, Soviet submarine, 172
S-61–S-79, Soviet submarines, 206
S-80, Soviet submarine, 206
S-81–S-84, Soviet submarines, 182
S-86–S-91, Soviet submarines, 206
S-92, Soviet experimental submarine, 161
S-95–S-98, Soviet submarines, 206

S-99, Soviet submarine 206
S-100, Soviet submarine, 206
S-101–S-102, Soviet submarines, 136, 144, 172, 175n
S-103–S-104, Soviet submarines, 149, 172
S-140–S-200, Soviet submarines, 206
S-146, Soviet missile submarine, 213
S-217–S-246, Soviet submarines, 206
S-250, Soviet submarine, 206
S-261–S-297, Soviet submarines, 206
S-300, Soviet submarine, 206
S-325–S-329, Soviet submarines, 206
S-331–S-349, Soviet submarines, 206
S-355–S-365, Soviet submarines, 206
S-375–S-384, Soviet submarines, 206
S-390–S-393, Soviet submarines, 206
Sandusky, American frigate, 173
San Pedro, American frigate, 173
Sapfir, Soviet patrol ship, 137, 172
Sborul, Romanian torpedo boat, 171
Scharnhorst, German battleship, 61, 62, 75, 77, 82, 95, 113
Schleswig-Holstein, German battleship, 181
Sealion, British submarine, 175n
Seawolf, British submarine, 175n
Seawolf, American nuclear submarine, 210
Serdityi, Soviet destroyer, 135
Sergo Ordzhonikidze, Soviet destroyer leader, 51
Sergo Ordzhonikidze, Soviet destroyer, 51
Seryshev, Soviet monitor, 158
Settembrini, Italian submarine, 35
Sevastopol', Russian battleship (old), 24, 171
Sevastopol', Soviet battlecruiser (*projekt 69*), 96, 114, 121, 151 174n, 195
Seydlitz, German heavy cruiser, 113, 151, 199
Sh-4, Soviet motor torpedo boat, 28, 53
Shaumyan, Soviet destroyer, 35, 137, 175n
Shch-101, Soviet submarine, 160
Shch-101–Shch-102, Soviet submarines, 138, 173
Shch-103, Soviet submarine, 92,
Shch-104–Shch-125, Soviet submarines, 112, 138, 173
Shch-104–Shch-134, Soviet submarines, 138
Shch-126, Soviet submarine, 173
Shch-127, Soviet submarine, 173
Shch-128–Shch-137, Soviet submarines, 173
Shch-135–Shch-138, Soviet submarines, 147
Shch-138, Soviet submarine, 170
Shch-139, Soviet submarine, 137, 173

Shch-201–Shch-202, Soviet submarines, 171
Shch-201–Shch-215, Soviet submarines, 137
Shch-203, Soviet submarine, 169
Shch-204, Soviet submarine, 175n,
Shch-205, Soviet submarine, 171
Shch-206, Soviet submarine, 174n,
Shch-208, Soviet submarine, 169
Shch-209, Soviet submarine, 172
Shch-210–Shch-211, Soviet submarine, 175n,
Shch-212, Soviet submarine, 169
Shch-213, Soviet submarine, 169
Shch-214, Soviet submarine, 175n,
Shch-215, Soviet submarine, 172
Shch-216, Soviet submarine, 147, 169
Shch-301, Soviet submarine, 175n
Shch-301–Shch-304, Soviet submarines, 136
Shch-302, Soviet submarine, 168
Shch-303, Soviet submarine, 171
Shch-304–Shch-306, Soviet submarines, 136, 168
Shch-304–Shch-311, Soviet submarines, 136
Shch-307, Soviet submarine, 171
Shch-308, Soviet submarine, 136, 168
Shch-309–Shch-310, Soviet submarine, 136, 171
Shch-311, Soviet submarine, 1136, 168
Shch-317, Soviet submarine, 168
Shch-317–Shch-320, Soviet submarines, 136
Shch-318, Soviet submarine, 171
Shch-319, Soviet submarine, 175n,
Shch-320, Soviet submarine, 168
Shch-322, Soviet submarine, 175n
Shch-322–Shch-324, Soviet submarines, 136
Shch-323, Soviet submarine, 168
Shch-324, Soviet submarine, 175n,
Shch-401, Soviet submarine, 175n,
Shch-401–Shch-404, Soviet submarines, 137
Shch-402–Shch-403, Soviet submarines, 169
Shch-404, Soviet submarine, 172
Shch-405, Soviet submarine, 168
Shch-405–Shch-406, Soviet submarines, 136
Shch-406, Soviet submarine, 168
Shch-407, Soviet submarine, 171
Shch-407–Shch-408, Soviet submarines, 147
Shch-408, Soviet submarine, 168
Shch-411–Shch-412, Soviet submarines, 193
Shch-421, Soviet submarine, 175n
Shch-421–Shch-422, Soviet submarines, 137
Shch-422, Soviet submarine, 169
Shcherbakov, Soviet cruiser, 198

Shchit, Soviet minesweeper, 137, 171
Shika, British auxiliary minesweeper, 172
Shilka, Soviet river monitor, 157
Shkiv, Soviet minesweeper, 136
Shkval, Soviet patrol ship, 137, 171
Shii, Japanese destroyer, 183
Shimushu, Japanese frigate, 183
Shpil', Soviet minesweeper, 136
Shtag, Soviet minesweeper, 136
Shtorm, Soviet patrol ship, 137, 171
Shtandart, Russian yacht, 53
Shturman, Soviet subchaser, 149
Sil'nyi, Soviet destroyer, 135, 147, 170
Simbirtsev, Soviet monitor, 158
Sinop, Russian battleship, 17n
Sivash, Soviet monitor, 158, 193
SK-521–SK-527, Soviet patrol boats, 165
SKR-28, Soviet patrol ship, 172
SKR-30, Soviet patrol ship, 172
Skoryi, Soviet destroyer, 147, 175n
Slavnyi, Soviet destroyer, 136, 170, 199
Smelyi, Soviet destroyer (*projekt 7-u*), 136, 174n, 175n
Smelyi, Soviet destroyer, (*projekt 30-bis*), 201
Smerch, Sovietpatrol ship, 137, 172
Smetlivyi, Soviet destroyer, 136, 175n
Smeul, Romanian torpedo boat, 171
Smyshlennyi, Soviet destroyer, 137, 175n
Sneg, Soviet patrol ship, 136, 175n
Sokrushitel'nyi, Soviet destroyer, 152, 187
Soobrazitel'nyi, Soviet destroyer, 137, 170
Sovershennyi, Soviet destroyer, 137, 171, 174n
Sovetskaya Belorossiya, Soviet battleship, 95, 120
Sovetskaya Rossiya, Soviet battleship, 95, 120, 187, 194
Sovetskaya Ukraina, Soviet battleship, 95, 120, 174n, 194
Sovestkii Soyuz, Soviet battleship, 95, 120, 194
Spidola, Soviet submarine (ex Latvian), 137, 173n
Sposobnyi, Soviet destroyer, 147, 169
St Albans, American destroyer, 172
Stalin, Soviet icebreaker, 112
Stalin, Soviet destroyer (old), 138, 172
Stalin, Soviet destroyer, (*projekt 30K*), 192
Stalinabad, Soviet destroyer leader, 121
Stalingrad, Soviet battlecruiser (*projekt 69*), 96
Stalingrad, Soviet battlecruiser (*projekt 82*), 196, 210
Statnyi, Soviet destroyer, 147, 174n

INDEX

Stefa, British auxiliary minesweeper, 172
Steregushchii, Soviet destroyer, 136, 170, 174n, 175n
Stojkii, Soviet destroyer, 136, 170
Storozhevoi, Soviet destroyer, 52, 100, 136, 149, 153, 170, 174n
Strashnyi, Soviet destroyer, 170, 173n, 174n
Strela, Soviet minesweeper, 138, 173
Stremitel'nyi, Soviet destroyer, 137, 175n
Strogyi, Soviet destroyer, 147, 170
Strojnyi, Soviet destroyer, 147, 170
Sulev, Estonian torpedo boat, 136
Sunba, British auxiliary minesweeper, 172
Superb, British cruiser, 198
Surovyi, Soviet destroyer, 136, 175n
Svetlana, Russian cruiser, 14, 28
Sverdlov, Soviet cruiser (*projekt 68*), 121, 174n
Sverdlov, Soviet cruiser (*projekt 68-bis*), 198, 216
Svirepyi, Soviet destroyer, 147, 170
Svobodnyi, Soviet destroyer, 149, 174n, 175n
Svyatoi Evstafi, Russian battleship, 17n

T-1–T-8, Soviet minesweepers, 138, 173
T-12, T-17 German torpedo boats, 181
T-25, Soviet minesweeper, 183
T-33, German torpedo boat, 181
T-76, Soviet minesweeper, 168
T-101–T-104, Soviet auxiliary minesweepers, 172
T-101–T-107, Soviet auxiliary minesweepers, 163
T-103, Soviet auxiliary minesweeper, 170
T-105, Soviet auxiliary minesweeper, 184
T-106, Soviet auxiliary minesweeper, 172
T-107, German torpedo boat, 181
T-108–T-110, Soviet minesweepers, 164, 172
T-109, Soviet auxiliary minesweeper, 170
T-111–T-113, Soviet minesweepers, 172
T-111–T-120, Soviet minesweepers, 164
T-114, Soviet minesweeper, 170
T-115–T-117, Soviet minesweepers, 172
T-118, Soviet minesweeper, 170
T-119, Soviet minesweeper, 172
T-120, Soviet minesweeper, 170
T-121–T-122, Soviet minesweepers, 172
T-158, German torpedoboat, 181
T-181–T-186, Soviet minesweepers, 165, 171
T-181–T-202, Soviet minesweepers, 164
T-187–T-192, Soviet minesweepers, 165, 171
T-193–T 202, Soviet minesweepers, 165
T-196, German torpedo boat, 181

T-201–T-202, Soviet minesweepers, 174n
T-201–T-216, Soviet minesweepers, 136
T-204, Soviet minesweeper, 168
T-205, Soviet minesweeper, 171
T-206, Soviet minesweeper, 174n, 175n
T-209, Soviet minesweeper, 174n
T-210, Soviet minesweeper, 168
T-211, Soviet minesweeper, 171
T-212–T-214, Soviet minesweepers, 174n
T-215, Soviet minesweeper, 171
T-216, Soviet minesweeper, 174n
T-217, Soviet minesweeper, 147, 154
T-218, Soviet minesweeper, 136
T-219, Soviet minesweeper, 149, 154, 171
T-220–T-221, Soviet minesweepers, 192
T-222–T-225, Soviet minesweepers, 171
T-222–T-249, Soviet minesweepers, 155
T-250, Soviet minesweeper, 155, 170, 192
T-254, Soviet minesweeper, 155, 170, 192
T-271–T-285, Soviet minesweepers, 167, 173
T-285, Soviet minesweeper, 170, 184
T-299, Soviet minesweeper, 174n
T-331–T-339, Soviet minesweepers, 167, 173
T-351–T 391, Soviet minesweepers, 155
T-351–T-352, Soviet minesweepers, 171
T-353, Soviet minesweeper, 168
T-354–T-376, Soviet minesweepers, 171
T-377, Soviet minesweeper, 168
T-378, Soviet minesweeper, 171
T-379, Soviet minesweeper, 168
T-380–T-386, Soviet minesweepers, 171
T-387, Soviet minesweeper, 168
T-388–T-391, Soviet minesweepers, 171
T-401, Soviet minesweeper, 171
T-401–T-413, Soviet minesweepers, 137
T-403, Soviet minesweeper, 169
T-404, Soviet minesweeper, 171
T-405, Soviet minesweeper, 175n,
T-406–T-409, Soviet minesweepers, 171
T-410–T-411, Soviet minesweepers, 169
T-412, Soviet minesweeper, 171
T-413, Soviet minesweper, 175n,
T-414, Soviet minesweeper, 154
T-434–T-435, Soviet minesweepers, 155
T-439–T-441, Soviet minesweepers, 156
T-440–T-441, Soviet minesweeper, 171
T-459–T-464, Soviet minesweepers, 171
T-459–T-479, Soviet minesweepers, 156

T-451, Soviet minesweeper, 155
T-453, Soviet minesweeper, 155
T-521–T-527, Soviet minesweepers, 167, 173
T-523, Soviet minesweeper, 184
T-588–T-611, Soviet minesweepers, 167, 173
T-610, Soviet minesweeper, 170
T-651–T-655, Soviet minesweepers, 167
T-666–T-669, Soviet- minesweepers, 167
T-671–T-680, Soviet minesweepers, 167
T-685–T 694, Soviet minesweepers, 167
T-701–T-730, Soviet minesweepers, 182
T-804–T 805, Soviet trawler minesweeper, 183
T-807–T-808, Soviet trawler minesweeper, 183
T-810, Soviet trawler minesweeper, 183
T-912–T-924, Soviet minesweepers, 182
T-925–T-928, Soviet trawler minesweepers, 183
Tacoma, American frigate, 167
Taifun, Soviet patrol ship, 136, 149, 171
Takao, Japanese heavy cruiser, 80, 85
Tallinn, Soviet heavy cruiser (*projekt 83*), 175n, 181, 199, 211
Tallinn, Soviet cruiser, (*projekt 68-bis*), 198
Tashkent, Soviet destroyer leader, 46, 51, 52, 99, 100, 136, 175n
Tbilisi, Soviet destroyer leader, 51, 138, 172
Terek, Soviet A/S vessel, 167
Terek, Soviet hydrographic vessel 183
Thomas, American destroyer, 172
Tigre, Italian destroyer, 34
Tigris, British submarine, 175n,
Timiryazev, Soviet freighter, 66
Tirpitz, German battleship, 185
TK-21–TK-22, Soviet torpedo cutters, 164
TK-202–TK-243, Soviet torpedo cutters, 164
TK-244–TK-272, Soviet torpedo cutters, 165
TK-503, Soviet torpedo cutter, 199
TK-517–TK-518, Soviet torpedo cutters, 166
TK-527–TK-528, Soviet torpedo cutters, 166
TK-537–TK 540, Soviet torpedo cutters, 166
TK-547–TK-550, Soviet torpedo cutters, 166
TK-559–TK-570, Soviet torpedo cutters, 166
TK-578–TK-580, Soviet torpedo cutters, 166
TK-587–TK-590, Soviet torpedo cutters, 166
TK-597, Soviet torpedo cutter, 166
TK-1002–TK-1004, Soviet torpedo cutters, 182
TK-1005–TK 1030, Soviet torpedo cutters, 183.
Toros, Soviet patrol ship, 137, 167, 171
Torpedist, Soviet subchaser, 149, 156

Torricelli, Italian submarine, 66
Tral', Soviet minesweeper, 137, 171
Trento, Italian heavy cruiser, 35
Tricheco, Italian submarine, 35
Trident, British submarine, 175n
Tri Svyatitel'ya, Russian battleship, 17n
Triumph, British aircraft carrier, 200
Toros, Soviet minesweeper, 138, 173
Tryumnyi, Soviet subchaser, 149
TS-1, Soviet submarine, 172
TS-1–TS-3, Soviet submarines, 167
TS-3, Soviet submarine, 172
TS-5–TS-9, Soviet submarines, 205
TS-5–TS-13, Soviet submarines, 183
TS-10–TS-12, Soviet submarines, 205
TS-13, Soviet submarine, 205
TS-15, Soviet submarine, 183, 205
TS-17–TS-19, Soviet submarine, 183, 205
TS-32–TS-38, Soviet submarines, 183, 205
Tsesarevich, Russian battleship, 17n
Tsiklon, Soviet patrol ship, 136, 175n
Tucha, Soviet patrol ship, 136, 179
Tuloma, Soviet depot ship, 183
Turbine, Italian destroyer, 66
Turbinist, Soviet subchaser, 149
Twiggs, American destroyer, 172
Tyumen-Ula, Soviet netlayer, 183

U-25, German submarine, 45
U-34, German submarine, 66
U-250, German submarine, 160, 190, 205
U-1057–U-1058, German submarines, 182
U-1064, German submarine, 182
U-1231, German submarine, 182
U-1305, German submarine, 182
U-2353, German submarine, 182
U-2529, German submarine, 182
U-3035, German submarine, 182
U-3041, German submarine, 182
U-3515, German submarine, 182
U-3535–U 3554, German submarines, 205
Udarnyi, Soviet river monitor, 157
Unbroken, British submarine, 172
Unison, British submarine, 172
Uragan, Soviet patrol ship, 24, 28, 31, 35, 36, 92, 108, 137, 172
Uritskii, Soviet destroyer, 137, 172
Ursula, British submarine, 172

V-1, Soviet submarine, 169
V-1–V-4, Soviet submarines, 165
V-2–V-4, Soviet submarines, 172
Väinämöinen, Finnish coastal defence ship, 183
Valerian Kujbyshev, Soviet destroyer, 172
Varyag, Russian cruiser (old), 8,
Varyag, Soviet cruiser (*projekt 68-bis*), 198
Vasilii Gromov, Soviet minesweeper, 149, 155, 171, 192
Vega, Norwegian A/S trawler, 172
Vekha, Soviet minesweeper, 138, 173
Vernyi, Soviet destroyer, 83
Verp", Soviet minesweeper, 101, 136
Vetrepnyi, Soviet destroyer, 183
Viborg, Soviet coastal defence ship, 183
Vidlitsa, Soviet river monitor, 157
Vikhr, Soviet patrol ship, 135, 171, 175n
Vilyui, Soviet minelyaer, 183
Virsaitis, Soviet minesweeper (ex Lithuanian), 136
Vitse Admiral Drozd, Soviet destroyer, 170
Vladimir Polukhin, Soviet minesweeper, 101, 149, 158, 171, 192
Vladivostok, Soviet cruiser, 198
Vlastnyi, Soviet destroyer, 192
Vnezapnyi, Soviet destroyer, 183
Vnimatel'nyi, Soviet destroyer, 183
Vnushitel'nyi, Soviet destroyer, 191
Vojkov, Soviet destroyer, 138, 172
Volevoj, Soviet destroyer, 183
Vol'nyi, Soviet destroyer, 183
Volodarskii, Soviet destroyer, 136, 175n
Vologda, Soviet mine counter-measures ship, 183
Voron, Soviet patrol ship, 192
Voroshilov, Soviet cruiser (ex *Admiral Butakov*), 24, 28, 35, 44
Voroshilov, Soviet cruiser (*projekt 26*), 50, 98, 137, 171, 174n
Vozrozhdennyi, Soviet destroyer, 183
Vrzyv, Soviet minesweeper, 137
Vrzyvatel', Soviet minesweeper, 137
Vynoslivyi, Soviet destroyer, 191
V'yuga, Soviet patrol ship, 136, 138, 173

W 23, Japanese minesweeper, 183
Wade Hampton, American freighter, 164
Worcester, American cruiser, 198

Yakor, Soviet minesweepers, 137, 171
Yakov Sverdlov, Soviet destroyer, 136, 175n

Yamato, Japanese battleship, 61
Yarnall, American destroyer, 172
Yastreb, Soviet patrol ship, 101, 149, 154, 171, 192

Zarnitsa, Soviet patrol ship, 138, 173
Zarya, Soviet minelayer, 169
Zaryad, Soviet minesweeper, 136
Zarya Svobody, Soviet battleship, 17n
Zashchitnik, Soviet minesweeper, 137
Zhdanov, Soviet cruiser, 198
Zenitchik, Soviet subchaser, 149
Zharkii, Soviet destroyer, 165, 172
Zheleznyakov, Soviet destroyer (old), 137, 171
Zheleznyakov, Soviet cruiser (*projekt 68*), 98, 121, 151, 192
Zhemchug, Soviet patrol ship, 101 137, 175n
Zhestkii, Soviet destroyer, 165, 172
Zhguchii, Soviet destroyer, 165, 172, 184
Zhivuchii, Soviet destroyer, 165, 172
Zorkii, Soviet patrol ship, 192

INDEX OF PROJECTS

Projekt number/type of ships

1	destroyer leader, 35, 36, 57, 91, 103, 136, 137, 170
2	patrol ship, 35, 36, 91, 103, 136, 137, 138, 171, 172, 173
3	minesweeper, 53, 91, 103, 136, 171
4	patrol ship, 35, 36, 91, 103, 138, 171, 173
7	destroyer, 46, 51, 52, 78, 90, 91, 103, 120, 121, 136, 137, 138, 146, 147, 153, 170, 171, 172
7-U	destroyer, 52, 91, 100, 103, 120, 121, 136, 137, 146, 147, 153, 170, 171
20-I	destroyer leader, 46, 91, 99, 100, 103, 137
21	battleship, 62, 95
22	heavy cruiser, 75, 76, 95, 96
23	battleship, 74, 75, 76, 81, 82, 84, 85, 91, 95, 103, 119, 120, 146, 150, 194, 195
23-bis	battleship, 150, 195
23-NU	battleship, 150, 187, 194, 195
24	battleship,. 151, 187, 194, 195, 216
25	battleship, 74, 75, 95, 96

26	cruiser, 76, 91, 98, 103, 120, 136, 137, 170, 171	63	nuclear missile cruiser, 214, 215
26-bis	cruiser, 98, 99, 170, 171, 172	64	battleship, 75, 76, 95, 96
26-bis2	cruiser 98, 99, 121, 146, 172	64	missile cruiser, 213, 214
29	patrol ship, 85, 91,100, 101, 103, 120, 121, 146, 154, 171, 173, 178, 192	65	cruiser, 187, 198, 199
		66	heavy cruiser, 187, 196, 197, 216
29-bis	patrol ship, 154, 188, 202, 203	67	missile cruiser, 211
29-K	patrol ship, 154, 172, 202, 203, 208	67EP	missile cruiser, 211
30	destroyer, 75, 81, 84, 91, 100, 103, 120, 121, 146, 153, 154, 171, 178, 192, 201	67SI	missile cruiser, 211
		68	cruiser, 75, 76, 81, 83, 84, 91, 97, 98, 99, 103, 119, 120, 121, 146, 151, 152, 178, 192, 199
30-bis	destroyer, 187, 192, 201, 202, 208, 216	68-bis	cruiser, 187, 192, 196, 198, 199, 208, 211, 212, 214, 216
30-A	destroyer, 154		
30-K	destroyer, 153, 154, 201, 202, 208	68-bis	ZIF cruiser, 198, 199
35	destroyer, 100, 153, 187	68-I	cruiser, 99, 114, 151
36	destroyer, 154	68-K	cruiser, 151, 197, 198, 199, 208
37	small destroyer, 154, 188, 202	69	battlecruiser, 76, 77; 81, 82, 84, 85, 91, 96, 103, 113, 119m 120, 146, 151, 187, 195
38	destroyer leader, 51, 91, 103, 136, 138, 170,		
39	patrol ship, 36, 91, 103, 136, 154, 171	69-I	battlecruiser, 96, 114
40	destroyer, 153, 187, 201, 202	70E	missile cruiser, 214
40	big submarine, 158	71	aircraft carrier, 75, 76, 97, 98, 103, 119, 152, 189
40-H	destroyer, 153		
41	destroyer, 187, 201, 202, 203, 208	71-A	aircraft carrier, 97, 98, 200
42	patrol ship, 203, 208	71-B	aircraft carrier, 97, 152, 200
43	patrol ship, 101, 103, 172	72	aircraftcarrier, 152, 187, 189
45	destroyer, 51, 91, 103, 106, 147, 170	72-IIB	aircraft carrier, 200
48	destroyer leader, 75, 91, 99, 100, 103, 120, 121, 146, 153	72-III-M	aircraft carrier, 200
		73	minesweeper, 155
48-K	destroyer leader, 153, 192, 201, 202	73-K	minesweeper, 155, 192
50	patrol ship, 203, 208	75	cruiser, 198
52	icebreaker patrol ship, 101, 103, 146, 154, 192	80	experimental submarine, 161
		81	missile cruiser, 214
53	minesweeper, 53, 91, 101, 103, 120, 121, 171, 173	82	battlecruiser 151, 187, 195, 196, 197, 211, 216
53-U	minesweeper, 101, 103, 136, 137, 138, 146, 147, 154, 171, 192	82-R	battle cruiser, 196
		83	heavy cruiser, 96, 113, 195, 197, 211
56	destroyer, 201, 202, 208, 211, 214	84	lightcruiser, 198, 199
56-E	missile destroyer, 211	85	aircraft carrier, 200, 201, 216
56-M	missile destroyer, 211	95	experimental submarine, 159, 161, 162, 209
57	missile destroyer, 211		
58	missile cruiser, 214	96	small submarine, 159, 207, 208, 209
58	minesweeper, 101, 103, 146, 154, 171, 173	96-bis	small submarine, 161, 188, 193
		97	medium submarine, 159
59	minesweeper, 91, 101, 103, 120, 121, 146, 155, 171, 192	99	minelaying submarine, 158, 159
		101	big submarine, 158
59-K	minesweeper, 155	105	small submarine, 161, 208
60	minesweeper, 101, 103	106	medium submarine, 161, 208

INDEX

122	submarinechaser, 149, 156
122a	submarine chaser, 156, 193
122b	submarine chaser, 156, 193
123	motor torpedo boat, 198, 204
123-bis	motor torpedo boat, 157
138	armoured cutter, 157
145	landing vessel, 204
151	minesweeper, 203, 204
152	submarine chaser 156
160	armouredcutter, 157
161	armoured cutter, 157
163	motor torpedo boat, 157
164	patrol boat, 156
183	motor torpedo boat, 204
183-R	missile motor boat, 214
185	landing vessel, 204
186	armoured cutter, 157, 193
194	patrol boat, 156, 157
200	motor torpedo boat, 204
205	missile motor boat, 204
253	minesweeper, 101, 155, 204
253-K	minesweeper, 193
253-L	minesweeper, 155, 171
253-LP	minesweeper,193
254	minesweeper, 156, 203
254-K	minesweeper, 204
254-M	minesweeper, 204
255	minesweeper, 203, 204
255-K	minesweeper, 204
259	minesweeper, 203
263	minesweeper, 155
264	minesweeper, 203
265	minesweeper, 203
322	minesweeper, 203
450	landing vessel, 204
601	submarine, 159
602	small submarine, 161
604	small submarine, 160
605	transport submarine, 162
606	experimental midget submarine, 161
606-bis	midget submarine, 161
607	transport submarine, 162, 163
608	medium submarine, 159, 160, 205
608-I	medium submarine, 160
610	midget submarine, 161
611	big submarine, 159, 188, 205, 207, 209, 212, 215
611AV	missile submarine, 213, 214, 215
612	small submarine, 161, 207, 208
613	medium submarine, 160, 188, 206, 207, 209, 214, 215
614	big submarine, 183, 188, 205, 207
615	small submarine, 188, 208, 209
A615	small submarine, 207, 208, 209
616	medium submarine, 206, 207
617	medium submarine, 206, 207, 209
624	missile submarine, 212
627	nuclear submarine, 210
P627-A	nuclear submarine, 210, 212
629	missile submarine, 213, 215
633	missile submarine, 215
637	small submarine, 208
640	missile submarine, 215
641	missile submarine, 215
644	missile submarine, 213
645	nuclear submarine, 210
651	nuclear missile submarine, 214
659	nuclear missile submarine, 214, 215
665	nuclear submarine, 214
675	missile submarine, 214
1124	armoured cutter, 157
1125	armoured cutter, 157, 193
1190	monitor, 102, 103, 149, 157, 193
A	battleship, 63, 64, 74, 75
APPS	experimental midget submarine, 48, 161
B	battleship, 63, 64, 74, 75
BO	submarine chaser, 156
D-3	motor torpedo boat, 159
F-25	missile battlecruiser, 211
F-25A	missile battlecruiser, 211, 212
F-25B	missile battle cruiser, 213
G-5	motor torpedo boat, 52, 101, 156
Gibbs & Cox	battleship 89, 95
KE	big submarine, 158, 159, 205
KU	big submarine, 158, 205
MK	light cruiser, 99, 151, 152
MO-2	patrol boat/submarine chaser, 52
MO-4	patrol boat/submarine chaser, 52, 156
MO-6	patrol boat, 156
MT-1	minesweeper, 155
MT-2	minesweeper, 155
MZ	minelaying submarine, 158
OD-200	patrol boat, 156, 193
OD-200-bis	patrol boat, 193

P-2	big missile submarine, 212, 214
P-10	patrol boat, 156
P-19/03	torpedo cutter, 157
PP-19-OK	patrol boat, 156
SB-12	river monitor, 157
SB-30	river monitor, 157
SB-57	river monitor, 157
Sh-4	motor torpedo boat, 52
TD-200	motor torpedo boat, 193
TM-200	motor torpedo boat, 157
TM-200-bis	motor torpedo boat, 193
UP-41	battleship, 62, 63, 74, 95
X	cruiser, 63, 95, 96
ZN-II-45	battleship, 195

Submarine series number/type

I	big submarine, 24, 35, 36, 49, 50, 55, 92, 93, 103, 171
II	minelaying submarine, 35, 48, 49, 50, 55, 92, 93, 103, 171
III	medium submarine, 37, 49, 50, 55, 92, 93, 94, 103, 171
IV	big submarine, 37, 49, 50, 55, 92, 93, 103, 123, 162
V	medium submarine, 37, 46, 49, 50, 55, 92, 93, 94, 103, 160, 171, 173
V-bis	medium submarine, 46, 49, 59, 55, 92, 93, 94, 171, 173
V-bis2	medium submarine, 47, 49, 50, 55, 92, 93, 94, 171, 173
VI	small submarine, 37, 49, 50, 55, 92, 93, 94, 103, 173
VI-bis	small submarine, 48, 49, 50, 55, 92, 93, 94, 103, 160, 172, 173
IX	medium submarine, 45, 47, 49, 50, 55, 92, 93, 94, 103
IX-bis	medium submarine, 47, 49, 50, 93, 94, 146, 147, 159, 171, 173, 193, 209
X	medium submarine, 47, 49, 50, 55, 92, 93, 94, 103, 171, 172, 173
X-bis	medium submarine, 49, 50, 93, 94, 121, 146, 147, 171, 173, 193, 209
XI	minelaying submarine, 48, 49, 50, 55, 92, 93, 103, 159, 173
XII	small submarine, 48, 49, 50, 55, 92, 93, 94, 103, 121, 146, 147, 160, 161
XIII	minelaying submarine, 49, 50, 92, 172, 173
XIII-bis	minelaying submarine, 49, 50, 93, 103, 121, 146, 147, 158, 171, 172
XIV	big submarine, 49, 50, 75, 93, 1039 121, 148, 158, 171, 172
XV	small submarine, 93, 94, 103, 121, 146, 147, 160, 171, 193, 206
XVI	medium submarine, 93, 103, 121, 146, 159, 193
APSS	midget submarine, 56

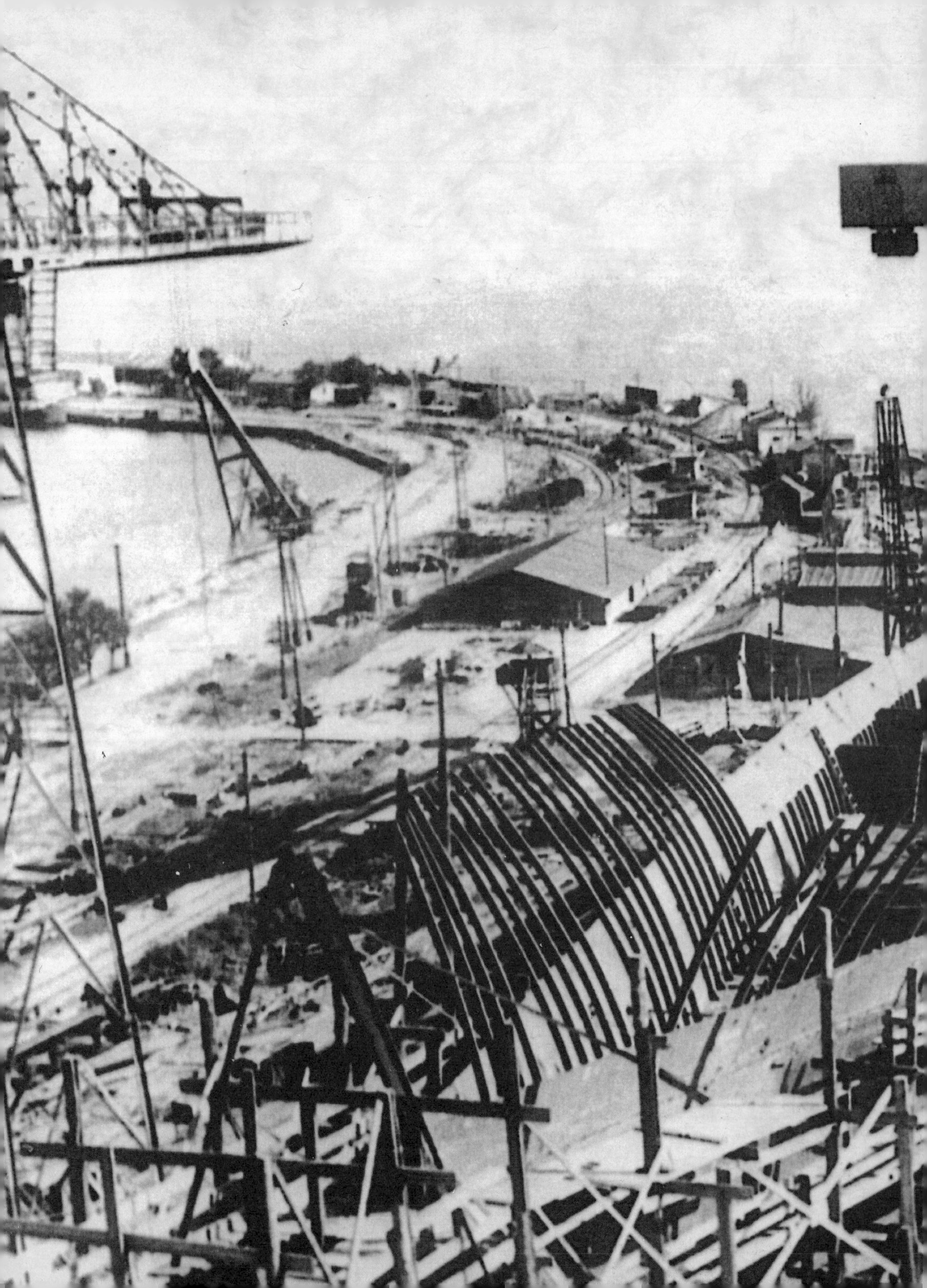